W9-BZV-401

To the
Golden
Shore

To the Golden Shore

America goes to California —1849

Compiled
and edited by

Peter Browning

GREAT WEST BOOKS   LAFAYETTE, CALIFORNIA

Cover design by Larry Van Dyke

Manufactured in the United States of America

Great West Books
PO Box 1028
Lafayette, CA 94549

Library of Congress Cataloging-in-Publication Data

To the golden shore : America goes to California—1849 / compiled
   and edited by Peter Browning.
      p.   cm.
   Includes index.
   ISBN 0–944220–07–X (alk. paper)
     1. California—Gold discoveries—Sources.
   2. California—History—1846–1850—Sources.
   I. Browning, Peter, 1928–
   F865.T6 1995
   979.4'04—dc20   95–35819

Contents

Acknowledgments

I owe thanks to Malcolm E. Barker, publisher of Londonborn Publications and author of *Book Design & Production for the Small Publisher,* for his many valuable suggestions about *how* this book should look, and *why.*

Thanks are also due to Carlo G. Carlucci, a friend of Malcolm's, who provided the Latin and French translations and citations that appear as footnotes toward the end of the chapter, "The Overland Routes."

The staff of the California Room at the San Francisco Public Library were most helpful in rounding up a number of midnineteenth century books and permitting me to photograph some of the illustrations therein.

I also greatly appreciate the unknown people who preserved the old newspapers for posterity. The fact that newspapers of those days were printed on rag paper meant that they lasted more than 100 years, in good condition—until the development of microfilm.

And that's how I acquired the material for this book: hundreds of hours spent looking at microfilm and taking notes; more hours copying the hundreds of items I wanted; *many* more hours typing the items into my computer, and formatting the pages on the screen.

Now the words are back on paper again—acid-free paper, like the paper on which they were originally printed.

PETER BROWNING

Sources of Illustrations

Soulé, Frank; Gihon, John H.; and Nisbet, James. *The Annals of San Francisco,* 1855.
Pages 1, 21, 33.
Hutchings' California Magazine. Page 9.
Letts, John. *A Pictorial View of California,* 1853.
Pages 39, 64, 85, 128, 178, 197, 232, 234, 252, 360.
X.O.X. *Outline History of an Expedition to California,* 1849.
Pages 54, 56, 98, 108, 116, 127, 324, 404.
Ryan, William R. *Personal Adventures in Upper and Lower California in 1848–49,* 1850.
Pages 59, 264, 316.
Century Magazine, April 1891. Pages 143, 174, 248, 274, 329, 344, 400.
Upham, Samuel. *Notes of a Voyage to California,* 1878. Pages 206, 223, 228, 272, 381, 394.
McIlvaine, William, Jr. *Sketches of Scenery and Notes of Personal Adventure in California and Mexico,* 1849. Page 397.
Bartlett, John Russell. *Personal Narrative of Explorations . . . during the Years 1850, '51, '52, and '53,* 1854. Pages 280, 295, 363, 389.
Emory, William H. *Notes of a Military Reconnoissance . . . Made in 1846–47,* 1848.
Pages 286, 379.
Pim, Bedford. *The Gate of the Pacific,* 1863. Page 303. (Courtesy, the Bancroft Library.)
Courtesy, the Bancroft Library. Pages 266, 369.
Irena Narell. Page 219.

Introduction

"Know ye that at the right hand of the Indies there is an island named California, very close to that part of the Terrestrial Paradise, which was inhabited by black women, without a single man among them, and that they lived in the manner of Amazons. They were robust of body, with strong and passionate hearts and great virtues. The island itself is one of the wildest in the world on account of the bold and craggy rocks. Their weapons were all made of gold; and also the trappings of their wild animals with which they make their forays after being domesticated.

"The island everywhere abounds with gold and precious stones, and upon it no other metal was found. . . In this island, named California, there are many griffins on account of the great ruggedness of the country which was infested with wild animals. . . .

"Whenever a man came to the island he was promptly killed and eaten. . . There ruled over that island of California a queen [Calafia] of majestic proportions, more beautiful than all others, and in the very vigor of her womanhood. She was desirous of accomplishing great deeds. She was valiant, and courageous, and ardent, with a brave heart, and she had visions to execute nobler actions than had been performed by any other ruler." (From *Las Sergas de Esplandián*, by the Spanish writer Montalvo, published in about 1500, as a continuation of the Portuguese novel, *Amadis de Gaula*.)

Gold was discovered in California by James W. Marshall in the South Fork of the American River on January 24, 1848. Most Americans of that time knew nothing about California other than that it was on the Pacific coast—if they even knew that. California was distant, difficult to get to, and was only lightly inhabited. It might as well have been the mysterious, exotic, and dangerous land created by Montalvo in *Las Sergas de Esplandián*.

In 1841 the Bartleson-Bidwell Party was the first group of emigrants to reach California via the overland route. The travail of the Donner Party, trapped in the snow in the Sierra Nevada during the winter of 1846–47, with the resulting suffering, starvation, cannibalism, and death, was well known. It was not a tale that would encourage many to follow the same route. Before 1848 there was actually more emigration to Oregon than to California.

The news of the gold discovery trickled out to San Francisco and Monterey. Once the citizenry realized that the gold stories were true, the towns and farms were emptied of their population—everyone went to the gold 'diggings.' It took months for the news to reach the settled parts of the United States; the report of gold in California was first published in an Eastern newspaper on August 19 of 1848. Many of the early stories were disbelieved; many people were skeptical, feeling certain that it was another hoax or 'bubble.' Confirmation of the amazing discovery was not made official until President Polk's annual message, in early December.

The urge, the desire, the excitement, the fever, the mania to go to California engulfed the country within days. What was known about California and the miraculous discovery of wealth within 'easy' grasp was reported at great length in the only significant medium in the middle of the nineteenth century—the newspapers.

With the exception of footnotes and a small number of editorial notes, everything in this book is taken from newspapers of the time. The source of each item is identified by three letters and the date, in parentheses, at the end of the item. The letter designations are: CPD, *Cleveland Plain Dealer*; ISJ, *Illinois State Journal* (Springfield); NYH, *New York Herald*; PPL, *Philadelphia Public Ledger and Daily Transcript*; and WNI, *Washington National Intelligencer.* These papers used material from all the rest of the country: Boston, St. Louis, New Orleans, etc.

There are articles, reportage, editorials, sermons, poetry, songs, advertisements, and a multitude of letters from those who were striving toward California via all the routes: the Isthmus of Panama, around Cape Horn and through the Strait of Magellan, the Overland Route across the plains, the Gila River route, several routes through Mexico, and across Nicaragua.

Here is the California Gold Rush—upheaval, adventure, suffering, death, great success, and tragic failure—as it was presented to and understood by people in the United States. This is what captivated them, uprooted their lives, and sent them off into the great unknown.

Peter Browning
Lafayette, California
August 1995

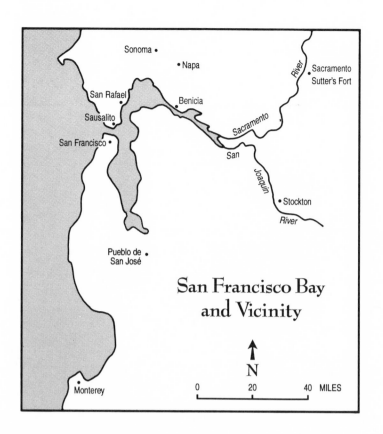

Sonoma

Napa

San Rafael

Benicia

Sausalito

San Francisco

Sacramento
Sutter's Fort

River

Sacramento

San

Joaquin

Stockton

River

Pueblo de
San José

San Francisco Bay
and Vicinity

N

0   20   40   MILES

Monterey

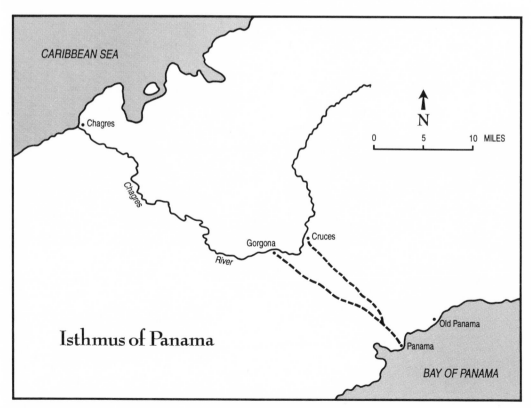

CARIBBEAN SEA

Chagres

Chagres

River

Gorgona

Cruces

N

0   5   10   MILES

Old Panama

Panama

Isthmus of Panama

BAY OF PANAMA

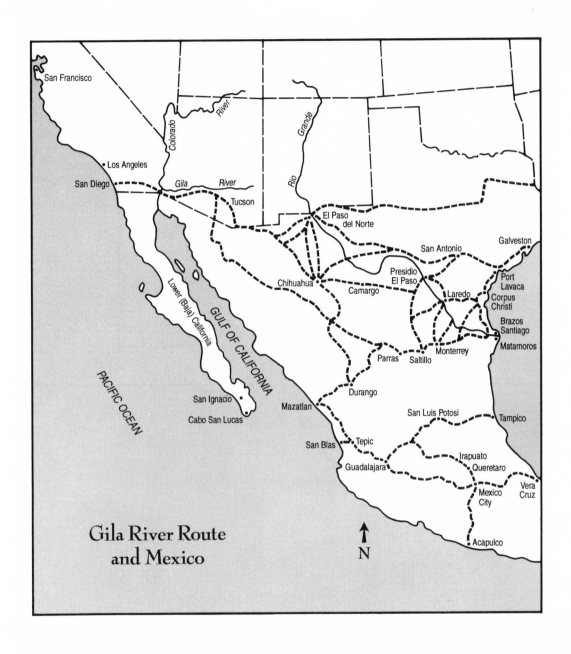

Gila River Route
and Mexico

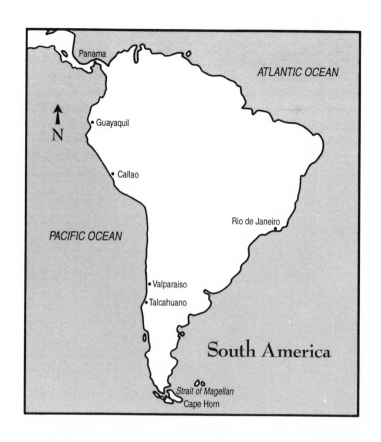

Panama

ATLANTIC OCEAN

N

• Guayaquil

• Callao

Rio de Janeiro

PACIFIC OCEAN

• Valparaiso

• Talcahuano

South America

Strait of Magellan
Cape Horn

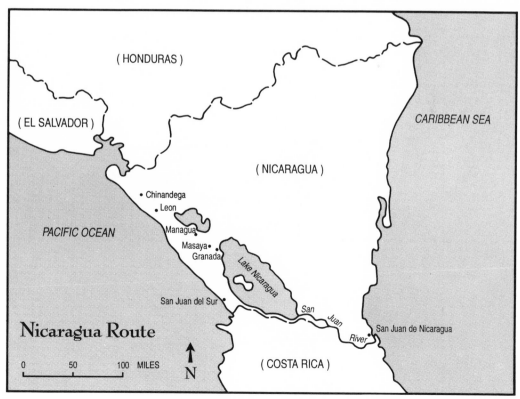

(HONDURAS)

(EL SALVADOR)

CARIBBEAN SEA

(NICARAGUA)

• Chinandega

• Leon

Managua

PACIFIC OCEAN

Masaya •
Granada •

Lake Nicaragua

San Juan del Sur •

San Juan de Nicaragua

San Juan River

Nicaragua Route

0   50   100 MILES

N

(COSTA RICA)

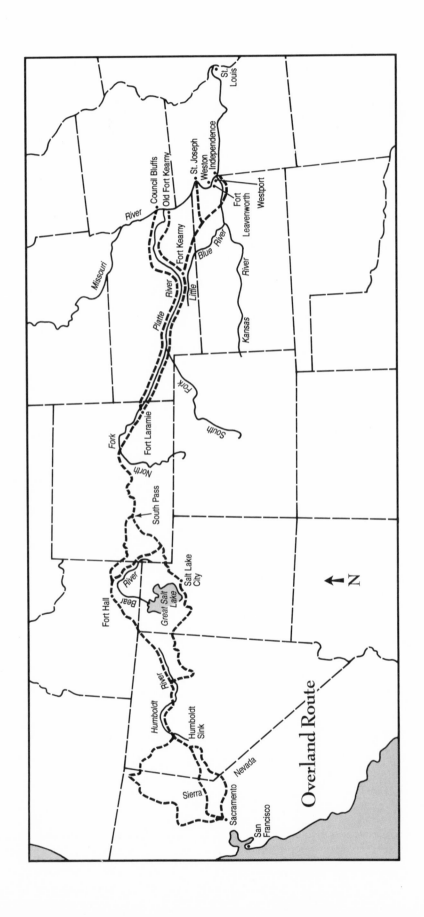

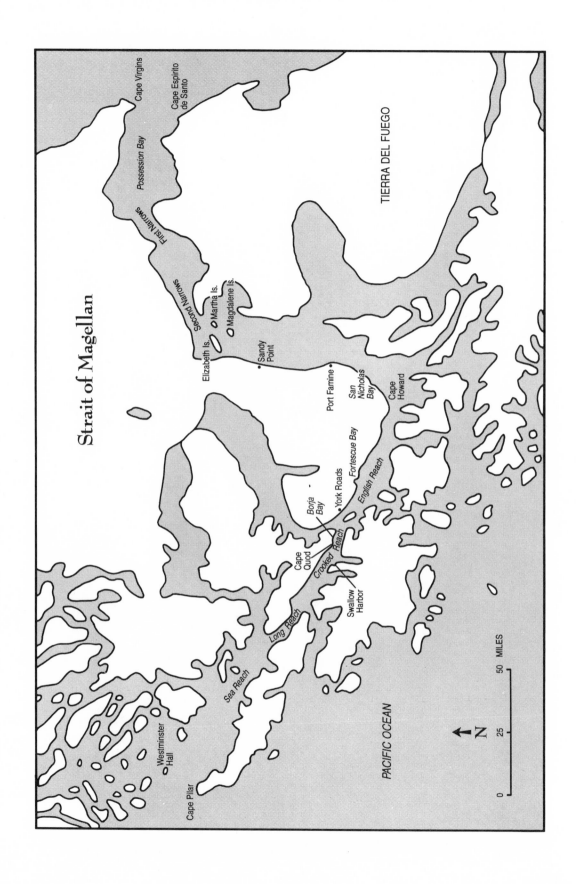

Before the Gold

The Proclamation of Commodore Stockton, Governor of California

I, Robert F. Stockton, Commander-in-Chief of the United States forces in the Pacific Ocean, and Governor of the Territory of California, and Commander-in-Chief of the army of the same, do hereby make known to all men that, having by right of conquest taken possession of that territory known by the name of Upper and Lower California, I do now declare it to be a Territory of the United States, under the name of the Territory of California.

(WNI, Dec. 8, 1846.)

From California

The Boston Daily Advertiser publishes the following extract from a letter dated Yerba Buena,[1] California, November 18, 1846, received by a mercantile house in that city:

My last was dated 25th August, when I informed you that the country was entirely in possession of the Americans. Since then the natives have revolted. More than two months now the leeward country has been under the Mexican flag. The Commodore left but small forces there, and came to the north with most of his men; the Californians immediately commenced an insur-

Island and Cove of Yerba Buena.

---

1. Yerba Buena (Spanish for 'good herb'), was the original name for the city of San Francisco, taken from a sweet-smelling herb that grew in profusion in Yerba Buena Cove—a cove whose shore originally reached the intersection of Montgomery and Jackson streets.

rection, and had but little trouble in driving the few Americans from the country, or taking them prisoners. From St. Louis Obispo to St. Juan Capustan, the country is in possession of the Californians. One hundred and fifty Americans, under Gillespie, have possession of St. Diego. Col. Fremont, with five hundred men and four pieces of artillery, left Monterey on the 16th instant for the south, where the U. S. ship Congress awaits his movements. Two months must elapse before peace is restored. The windward coast has remained comparatively quiet. Over five hundred men have emigrated here this season, many of whom are now engaged with Col. Fremont, and the others are forming a busy settlement about St. Francisco. This is the central point, and we have already something of a town; next year two hundred houses will be built, being double the number now existing. As Americans can now hold property here, they have taken advantage of the times to secure building lots; speculation is active; large tracts of land are daily changing hands, and we see the bustle of American industry in all the north of California.

(WNI, April 6, 1847.)

California—Bah!

The Detroit Daily Advertiser has been permitted to publish a private letter from a gentleman of that city, who went out to California in Col. Stevenson's New York regiment. The writer says, among other things:

I have been in California since April 18, 1847; have seen but little of the country myself, but have conversed much with various persons, some of whom have visited every part of it, and can confidently assert, and do assert, that California, taken altogether, is a most miserable God-forsaken country, the jumping-off place, fit only for Mormons, Millerites, and monomaniacs. It has been most flagrantly misrepresented—most villainously belied. The climate, if healthy, which is unquestion-

able, is excessively disagreeable about here, on account of the violent winds and fogs. The fog is often so heavy that water drips from the roofs as if it had been raining, and when coming over the hill it looks more like a snowstorm than any thing else. Overcoats and flannels are worn the year round; summer clothes are useless. From sunrise to 10 A. M. it is usually quite pleasant; then comes the wind and the fog, either of which is more disagreeable than any weather I ever saw in the States. So much for what country I have seen about San Francisco, the 'American Italy,' as some foolish people have called it.

The Bay of San Francisco, as regards commercial purposes, merits all the most enthusiastic have said of it. It is, probably, the finest bay in the world, and it alone may save California from utter condemnation. Other parts of the country are more objectionable even than this; some for the total absence of moisture, and all of it generally for the want of tillable land. Oh, how the emigrants who come here will be disappointed! I wish they all knew what I know. It would save many a one from much misery and suffering; the which will surely follow any *attempt* to settle here for agricultural purposes. Speaking of game here, I have been out twice; the first time I shot a rattlesnake of the most venomous kind, and the last time I was chased home by a cougar or puma, a species of tiger, a *leetle* too thick for comfort around here. One of them was killed here last week which measured seven feet ten inches from tip of nose to tip of tail. They are found eleven feet long about here, and are more ferocious than the grisley bear. The natives call them lions. (WNI, Dec. 25, 1847.)

The Donner Party

We gave an account, some time since, of the dreadful sufferings of a company of emigrants from Illinois, Missouri, &c. on their journey to California last Winter. The Illinois Journal of Dec. 16 contains a long and really interesting letter, addressed to

Miss Mary Keys of Springfield, Ill. by Miss Virginia Reed, the step-daughter of one of the sufferers. It is dated from California, the 16th of May last [1847], and we have made the following selections:

MY DEAR COUSIN: * * * * We went on in that way three or four days, until we came to the big mountain, or the California Mountain. The snow was then about three feet deep. There were some wagons there. The owners said that they had attempted to cross, but could not. Well, we thought we would try it; so we started, and they in company with us, with their wagons. The snow was then up to the mules sides. The farther we went up, the deeper the snow got—so that the wagons could not go on. They then packed their oxen, and went on with us, carrying a child apiece, and driving the oxen in the snow up to their waists. The mule that Martha and the Indian was on was the best one, as they went and broke the road; and that Indian was the pilot. We went on that way two or three miles, and the mules kept falling down in the snow, heads foremost, and the Indian said he could not find the road.

Caught in the Snow

We stopped and let the Indian and Mr. Stanton go on and hunt the road. They went on and found it to the top of the mountain, and came back and said they thought we could get over if it did not snow any more. But the people were all so tired by carrying their children that they could not go over that night. So we made a fire and got something to eat, and mother spread down a buffalo robe, and we all laid down upon it, and spread something over us, and mother sat up by the fire, and it snowed one foot deep on the top of the bed that night. When we got up in the morning, the snow was so deep we could not go over the mountain, and we had to go back to the cabins that were built by the emigrants three years ago, and built more cabins, *and stay there all Winter, as late as the 20th Feb. and without father.*

Nothing to Eat

We had not the first thing to eat. Mother made an arrangement for some cattle, giving two for one in California. The cattle were so poor that they could hardly get up when they laid down. We stopped there the 4th of November and stayed till the 20th of Feb. and what we had to eat I can hardly tell you, and we had Mr. Stanton and the Indian to feed. But they soon left to go over the mountains on foot, and had to come back. They then made snow shoes and started again, and a storm came, and they had again to return. It would sometimes snow ten days before it would stop. They waited till it stopped snowing, and then started again. I was going with them, but took sick and could not go. There were fifteen persons left in this company, and but seven got through—five women and two men. A storm came on, and they lost the road and got out of provisions, and those that got through had to eat those who died.

Not long after they left we had eaten all our provisions, and we had to put Martha at one cabin, James at another, Thomas at another, and mother and Eliza and Milt and I dried up what little meat we could get, and waited to see if we could cross over the mountain—and we had to leave the children. O, Mary! you will think that hard—to leave them with strangers, and not to know whether we ever would see them again. We told them we would bring them back bread, and then they were willing to stay. We went and were out five days in the mountains. Eliza gave out and had to go back. We went on that day, and the next day we had to lay by and make snow shoes. We went on another day, and could not find the road and had to go back. I could get along very well while I thought we were going ahead, but as soon as we had to turn back I could hardly walk. We reached the cabins, and that night there was the worst snow-storm that we had the whole Winter, and if we had not come back we could not have lived through it. We had now nothing to eat but hides. *O! Mary, I would sit and wish I had what you all wasted.* We stayed at Mr. Breen's. They had meat all the time. We had to kill little Cash (the dog) and eat him. We ate his entrails, and feet, and hide, and everything about him. My dear cousin, you often say you can't do this and you can't do that; but never say you can't do anything—you don't know what you can do until you try.

Starvation

There were fifteen in the cabin that we were in, and one-half of us had to lay in bed all the time. There were ten died while we were at the cabins. We lived on little Cash a week; and after Mrs. Breen would cook her meat and boil the bones two or three times, we would take them and boil them three and four days at a time. Mother went down to the other cabin and got half a hide, bringing it in snow up to her waist. It kept on snowing and would cover the cabins, do all we could to prevent it, so that we could not get out for two or three days at a time. We would have to cut pieces of the logs on the inside to make a fire with. The snow was five feet deep on the top of the cabin. Father, as we afterwards learnt, started out for us with provisions, but could not reach us, for the dreadful storms and deep snow, and after he had come into the mountains eighty miles, had to cache his provisions and go back on the other side to get a company of men to assist him. Hearing this they made up a company at Suter's Fort, and sent out to our relief. We had not eaten anything for three days; we were out on the top of the cabin, and saw a party coming. Oh! my dear cousin, you don't know how glad we were. One of the men we knew. They stayed with us three days to recruit us a little, so that we could go back with them. There were twenty-one of us who left with them, but after going a piece, Martha and Thomas gave out, and the men had to take them back. Mother and Eliza and I came on. One of the party said he was a Mason, and pledged his

honor that if he did not meet father he would go back and save his children.

Leaving the Children

O! Mary, that was the hardest thing yet—to leave the children in those cabins— not knowing but they would starve to death. Martha said, well mother, if you never see me again, do the best you can. The men said they could hardly stand it; it made them cry—they said it was best for us to go and the children to be taken back. The men did so, and left for them at the cabin a little meat and flour. We went on over a high mountain as steep as stair steps in snow which was up to our waists. Little James walked all the way. He said every step he took he was getting nearer father and nearer something to eat. When we had traveled five days we met father with thirteen men on their way to the cabins. O, Mary! you don't know how glad we were to see him again. He heard we were coming and he made some sweet-cakes the night before at his camp to give us and the other children. The men left the cabins with seventeen persons. Father brought Martha and Thomas into where we were. None of the men he had with him were able to get back to the cabins, their feet was frozen so bad. No other company went out and brought all the persons in from there. They are all in now from the mountains but four, who are at a place called the Starved Camp, and a company has gone to their relief. There were but two families, of the whole number in the mountains, that got out safe. Our family was one of them. Thank God we have all got in with our lives, and we are the only family that did not have to eat human flesh.

We are all very well pleased with the country, particularly with the climate. Let it be ever so hot a day, the night is always cold. It is a beautiful country. It is mostly in valleys and mountains. It is the greatest country for cattle and horses you ever saw. The people here ride from eighty to one hundred miles a day on horseback. This country just suits father and I for riding. Some of the Spaniards have from 6 to 7,000 head of horses, and from 15 to 16,000 head of cattle. Tell the girls that this is the greatest place for marrying they ever saw, and they must come to California if they want to marry.—Father is now down at San Francisco. He is going to write when he comes back. Give my love to all. So no more at present, my dear cousin.

VIRGINIA E. B. REED
(CPD, Jan. 14, 1848.)

"Seeing the Elephant"[2]

The origin of this now common and expressive phrase is thus described:

Some years since, at one of the Philadelphia theatres, a pageant was in rehearsal in which it was necessary to have an elephant. No elephant was to be had. The "wild beasts" were all travelling, and the property-man, stage director, and manager almost had fits when they thought of it. Days passed in the hopeless task of endeavoring to secure one; but at last Yankee ingenuity triumphed, as it always does, and an elephant was duly made to order of wood, skins, paint, and varnish. Thus far the matter was all well, but as yet they had found no means to make the said combination travel. Here again the genius of the manager, stage director, and property-man "stuck out," and two of the "supes" were duly installed as legs. Ned C——, one of the true and genuine "b'hoys," held the responsible station of *fore-legs*, and for several nights he played that heavy part to the entire satisfaction of the manager and the delight of the audience. The part, however, was a very tedious one, as the elephant was obliged to be on the stage for about an hour, and Ned was too fond of the bottle to remain so long without "wetting his whistle," so he sets his wits to work to find a way to carry a "wee drop" with him. The eyes of the elephant being made of two porter bottles, the necks in, Ned conceived the brilliant idea of filling them with "good stuff." This he fully carried out, and, elated with his success, willingly undertook to play the *fore-legs* again.

Night came, the theatre was crowded with the denizens of the Quaker city; the music played its sweetest strains, the whistle sounded, the curtain rose, and the play began. Ned and the *hind-legs* marched upon the stage. The elephant was greeted with round upon round of applause. The decorations, the trappings, were gorgeous, the Prince seated upon his back, the elephant, all were loudly cheered. The play proceeded; the elephant was marched around the stage. The *fore-legs* got dry, and withdrew one of the corks, *treated the hind-legs,* and drank the health of the audience in a bumper of genuine *elephant eye* whiskey—a brand, by the way, till then unknown. On went the play, and on went Ned drinking. The concluding march was to be made—the signal was given and the *fore-legs* staggered towards the front of the stage. The foot-lights obstructed his way; he raised his feet and stepped—plump into the orchestra. Down went the *fore-legs* on the leader's fiddle; over of course turned the elephant, sending the Prince, closely followed by *hind-legs,* into the middle of the pit. The manager stood horror-struck, the Prince and *hind-legs* lay confounded, the boxes in convulsions, the actors choking with laughter. And poor Ned, casting one look, a strange blending of drunkenness, grief, and laughter, at the scene, fled hastily out of the theatre, closely followed

---

2. At the time of the California gold rush, "seeing the elephant" meant to go to California, see the sights, and dig for gold. One who had "seen the elephant" had seen everything, and was, therefore, experienced and sophisticated. The phrase later acquired the meanings of "to celebrate" and "to be seduced"—both of which were quite appropriate.

by the leader, with the wreck of his fiddle, performing various cut and thrust motions in the air.

The curtain dropped on a *"scene* behind *scenes."* No more pageant, no more *fore-legs*, but every body holding their sides—music, actors, pit, gallery, and boxes—rushed from the theatre, shrieking between every breath—"HAVE YOU SEEN THE ELEPHANT?"

(WNI, April 6, 1848.)

Vernal Land

MONTEREY, California, Feb. 4th, 1848.

Our community has been thrown into spasms lately by the discovery of several quicksilver mines. They are said to be rich beyond all the dreams that ever shook mining rods before. You have only to knock a rock to pieces, kindle a fire under it, catch the vapor, and it rolls off a liquid stream of quicksilver. Every conceivable vessel is now in requisition for collecting this precious vapor; some take pots from their kitchen and some take warming pans from their beds—all for catching and condensing vapor. Quicksilver will soon be so plenty here that we can fix out our pumps for thermometers, our lakes for mirrors, and the doctors will be ready to salivate a continent.

We are now in the depth of winter—if winter it may be called, where the young flowers are springing out of the ground, the trees covered with living foliage, and the birds singing on the boughs. I have been in the four great quarters of the globe, but of all climates in the winter give me this. It is a perpetual May, and only wants a pole—as for the dancing, the people dance the year round. They continue it all night, and last Sunday—no unusual thing—the ladies went directly from the ball-room to the church, where they squatted down on the pavement and fell fast asleep, till the priest thundered at them an invective about their waltzing so late into the Sabbath morning; when the word waltz reached their dreaming ear, up they

jumped ready to take another whirl, supposing it was their leader's voice. What a pity for them that the whirling faith of the Dervish is not the true one.

But there is one thing in which the women here out do those of any other country. If a mother with you has half a dozen children, she feels as proud as a peacock. But here she thinks nothing of having twenty, and considers herself a tolerably good mother in having twenty-five, and even thirty. She begins to have them while she is only a child, and continues to have them till she is so old she has to put specks on to see them. She makes no more ado about it than a hen dropping an egg, when she goes quietly off the nest without even a cackle. They come so thick and fast, you will often see five or six generations stretched along the same table. And what is equally remarkable, the birth of each child, instead of breaking down the constitution of the mother, only seems to impart fresh force to the salient energies. So much for babies and the hopes for those who come here for progeny more than plunder.

The U. S. Squadron for the Pacific, excepting the Warren, is now at Mazatlan, Guaymas, and La Paz. There was a little fighting in taking Guaymas, and Commander Selfridge, of the Dale, lost a leg.

> But now in parties just as gay,
>   As in the battle brave,
> Goes to the font, review and play,
>   With one foot in the grave.

Give my love to all our Philadelphia friends and tell them their city is very good where it stands, but it would be much better located in California, on the shores of the broad Pacific.—Here Nature piles her mountains, stretches her plains, and rolls her rivers on a grand scale.—You feel like one let out into the boundless universe— like a butterfly into the eternal space. But I must close this, which has been written as much to warp my mind from thoughts of home as for the edification of your readers.

Ever faithfully yours,   W. C. [Walter Colton].[3] (CPD, June 3, 1848.)

Treaty of Peace

The President's Message

To the Senate and House of Representatives of the United States.

I lay before Congress copies of a treaty of peace, friendship, limits and settlement between the United States and the Mexican republic, the ratifications of which were duly exchanged at the city of Queretaro, in Mexico, on the 30th day of May, 1848.

The war in which our country was reluctantly involved, in the necessary vindication of the national rights and honor, has been thus terminated; and I congratulate Congress and our common constituents, upon the restoration of an honorable peace.

The extensive and valuable territories ceded by Mexico to the United States constitute indemnity for the past, and the brilliant achievements and signal successes of our arms will be a guaranty of security for the future, by convincing all nations that our rights must be respected. The results of the war with Mexico have given to the United States a national character abroad which our country never before enjoyed. Our power and our resources have become known, and are respected throughout the world; and we shall probably be saved from the necessity in engaging in another foreign war for a long series of years. It is a subject of congratulation that we have passed through a war of two years' duration, with the business of the country uninterrupted, with our resources unexhausted, and the public credit unimpaired.

New Mexico and Upper California have been ceded by Mexico to the United States, and now constitute a part of our country. Embracing nearly ten degrees of latitude, lying adjacent to the Oregon Territory, and extending from the Pacific ocean to the Rio Grande, a mean distance of nearly a thousand miles, it would be difficult to estimate the value of these possessions to the United States. They constitute of themselves a country large enough for a great empire, and their acquisition is second only in importance to that of Louisiana in 1803. Rich in mineral and agricultural resources, with a climate of great salubrity, they embrace the most important ports on the whole Pacific coast of the continent of North America. The possession of the ports of San Diego, Monterey, and the bay of San Francisco, will enable the United States to command the already valuable and rapidly increasing commerce of the Pacific. The number of our whaleships alone, now employed in that sea, exceeds seven hundred, requiring more than twenty thousand seamen to navigate them; while the capital invested in this particular branch of commerce is estimated at not less than forty millions of dollars. The excellent harbors of Upper California will, under our flag, afford security and repose to our commercial marine; and American mechanics will soon furnish ready means of ship-building and repair which are now so much wanted in that distant sea.

In this vast region, whose rich resources are soon to be developed by American energy and enterprise, great must be the augmentation of our commerce; and with it new and profitable demands for

---

3. Walter Colton (1797–1851) arrived in California in 1846 as the chaplain of the USS *Congress.* He was appointed *alcalde* (an alcalde was an all-purpose municipal officer—a combination of mayor, justice of the peace, and policeman) of Monterey by Commodore Stockton. Colton and Robert Semple founded *The Californian,* the first newspaper in California, beginning publication on August 15, 1846. Colton was a frequent correspondent of eastern newspapers; his recollections appeared as *Three Years in California,* published in 1850.

mechanic labor in all its branches, and new and valuable markets for our manufactures and agricultural products.

While the war has been conducted with great humanity and forbearance, and with complete success on our part, the peace has been concluded on terms the most liberal and magnanimous to Mexico. In her hands, the territories now ceded had remained, and, it is believed, would have remained almost unoccupied, and of little value to her or any other nation; whilst as a part of our Union, they will be productive of vast benefits to the United States, to the commercial world, and the general interests of mankind. (CPD, July 11, 1848.)

From Upper California

CORRESPONDENCE OF THE
JOURNAL OF COMMERCE
MONTEREY, ALTA CALIFORNIA
April 19, 1848.

All Upper California is very tranquil; the people have resumed their old habits, and seem as contented as if the present flag had ever waved over them. Col. Mason makes a good governor; he is discreet and efficient. All his measures are characterized for their good sense.[4]

The squadron is at Mazatlan, and will be obliged to stay there or in that vicinity, unless troops can be found to garrison the place. Col. Mason has sent to the great Mormon settlement on the Salt Lake and to Oregon to enlist men for the purpose. He may get some Mormons, but the Oregonians have about as much as they can do in taking care of their wild Indians.

The rains, which are now over, have been abundant, and we shall have a plentiful harvest. The large emigration which is expected will find provisions cheap. We have here almost as many emigrants from Oregon as from the States. They go there first, but bring up here. This is a much finer climate. I doubt if there is a climate in the world than can rival it in equability, softness, and salubrity. All we want is a few showers during the summer months, and it would then be an Eden; but whither can you fly from the effects of the fall?

It is Holy Week here, and I have ordered all the grogshops and places of amusement closed till Saturday. This is an old custom and not a bad one, especially so far as the liquor is concerned. It were better in this particular if Holy Week continued the year round. Whatever the whites may do, no one here is permitted to sell liquor to an Indian. The penalty is one hundred dollars and six months' imprisonment. It is a salutary law, and productive of immense good to the aborigines. I enforce it without any regard to the standing of the person who may violate it; but have in some cases remitted the sentence after ninety days or so of imprisonment.

I like many traits in the Californians; they are the most respectful and polite people in the world. No Californian ever thinks of entering my office with his spurs on. They are but little read, but are now sending their children to our schools. The rising generation will have more intelligence but not more true amiability than their parents. They have ten times as much respect for law as our emigrants, and are quite as honest in their dealings. The women in habits of industry surpass the men. A California woman would live and flourish where one of our females would despond and starve. W. C. [Walter Colton, Alcalde of Monterey.]

(WNI, Aug. 5, 1848.)

---

4. Col. Richard Barnes Mason (1797–1850) was the military governor of California from May 1847 to February 1849. Fort Mason and Mason Street in San Francisco are named for him.

From the Pacific

Prospects of California— Riches of the Country

Extract of a letter from an officer of rank to a friend in Washington, dated
MONTEREY, CALIFORNIA, April 19, 1848.

California cannot support a dense population; there is too much open country, only fit for grazing purposes, extensive ridges of mountains, with large level plains between them, most of which are destitute of timber, and, with small exceptions, cannot be cultivated for want of moisture; no rains from March to the latter part of November, or some time in December. Some of the valleys might be irrigated and made to produce the most abundant crops. The country I have no doubt is rich, very rich, in minerals—quicksilver, silver, gold, and copper.

There is not a single navigable river in California, except those entering into the bay of San Francisco. How far they are navigable, and for what sized boats (must be small ones) I know not. San Francisco bay will be the great commercial point on this coast—it *cannot* be any other place. Monterey is a handsome site for a large town, has a population perhaps a little rising of 1,200, but no back country; harbor easy of access, and altogether an open roadstead, is perfectly safe, as the northerly winds never blow home, (as the sailors say,) and it is protected from the southeasters. Climate most delightful; the ground never freezes, and seldom any frost; woollen clothing comfortable the whole year round. This is along the coast. A short distance (say 15 or 20 miles) in the interior, the weather is very warm in the summer; vegetation commences with the first rain in November or December, and by July the grass is all parched up by the sun. *Washington Union.*

(PPL, August 16, 1848.)

Native Californians Throwing the Lasso.

[Editor's note: The following letter, which appeared in the *New York Herald* on August 19, 1848, contains the first announcement of the California gold discovery to be published in an eastern newspaper. No doubt the greater part of the letter was indeed written by a "New York Volunteer," but a number of passages are worded almost identically to passages in the Special Edition of the *California Star* that was published in San Francisco on the same date—April 1, 1848. This edition was printed at the instigation of the newspaper's publisher, Samuel Brannan, as the best method of publicizing and promoting the gold discovery. Brannan had stores at Sutter's Fort and at the Mormon Diggings (site of one of the early gold discoveries), and stood to benefit greatly from a 'rush' to the 'diggings.' The letter has been reprinted here in its entirety, with my added subheadings and some additional paragraph breaks.]

Affairs In Our New Territory

SAN FRANCISCO, Alto California, April 1, 1848

Interesting Narrative of the Voyage to California, by a New York Volunteer—Commodore Stockton, General Kearny, Colonel Fremont—San Francisco—Customs—Religion—Cattle—Produce—Press—Inhabitants, &c., &c.

Being a subscriber to and constant reader of your invaluable paper in New York, and from its vast circulation, its love of truth, its political independence, and generally the first to give publicity to foreign and important news, I take the liberty of addressing you these lines, which, if not important to you, will be satisfactory to numbers of your subscribers, who have friends in this far-distant clime.

We sailed from New York in October, 1846, in the Thomas H. Perkins, as one of the 1st regiment of New York volunteers;

and on the 6th March, 1847, came to anchor in San Francisco bay, or, what was called the Bay of Sir Francis Drake, in the Pacific, in north latitude 37° 47'. On our arrival here the regiment was divided up and down the coast—two companies remaining here, one about 60 miles north, at a town called Sonoma, three to Monterey, distant 120 miles from here, two to Santa Barbara, further south, and the residue further south still, to Puebla de los Angelos, I being attached to one of the companies stationed here as hospital steward, under Asst. Surgeon R. C. Parker, with whom I had lived in Centre Street, New York, for some time previous to our departure.

No War to Fight

On making inquiry after landing, we learned to our regret that the fighting in the two Californias was over—that there had been some well-contested skirmishes and battles fought only a few weeks previous to our landing, between the Mexicans (or Californians, rather) and Commodore Stockton and his men, he having commanded personally in the field, and reinforced by detachments under General Kearny and Fremont; and from the united bravery and skill of the officers, together with the hardiness and intrepidity of the volunteers and marines, the enemy was completely defeated; and since that time the Californians remained tranquil, until about a month since, when some of our men had a few skirmishes at La Paz and Puebla de Los Angelos, one of our men, belonging to company B, being killed, and two wounded—the enemy not daring to encounter them in fair field fighting, but kept up a continual firing at the little gallant band in the town for two days and upwards; however, they were dispersed and scattered from their hiding places, their flag captured, and many of them killed and wounded, and now we are again in tranquillity. To give you an account of the war and movements of the army is useless, as the greater part of our information is derived from United States papers, as the communication by Mazatlan is uncertain and difficult, and by Panama tedious; however, we learned last night by private information, that a proposal has been made by the Mexican government to Gen. Scott, to surrender to the Americans the Californias, New Mexico, and some other places of value, on condition that he would protect the tottering government for a few years, till the intestine wars and sanguinary parties would be extirpated; which, we understand, is likely to meet the approbation of our government in Washington, as their object is not to annihilate the government of Mexico, but conquer a peace.

This portion of the globe may in a future time become valuable in mercantile affairs, as well as the immense wealth which commerce, industry, and speculation may reap from the mines of gold, silver, quicksilver, saltpetre, coal, &c., &c., which abound in these districts. If the roads were in such state as to afford emigrants the means of travelling with facility, and with more despatch, so as to avoid the hardships some encounter in travelling over snow—as has been experienced by the unfortunate sufferers last year, when some of them subsisted for a number of days on hides and venison flesh—then would this country be worth contending for.

The bay of San Francisco is one of the best harbors in America, or perhaps in the world; the entrance is good and safe, and inside a deep, wide bay, extending upwards of 100 miles, sheltered from all winds, an excellent anchorage, and as healthy as any port of the Union.

The town of San Francisco (formerly "Yerba Buena") had only a few shantees or camp-like cabins when we arrived, with the exception of half a dozen houses built of adobes or sun baked brick, now exhibits a pleasing prospect—upwards of 150 houses, some of which vie with our American cities for elegance and accommodation. Town lots which cost only $16, are now selling for $100 to $200, and some at $600. Wharves are building, streets formed clear over the hills, and great taste evinced in the improvements. We have an excellent barrack, and adjoining is the custom house, under the skilful direction of Captain Fulsom [sic], Quartermaster.[1] There are two excellent hotels, billiard rooms, and an extensive lumber yard.

High Prices

Lumber is very dear, $50 per M. for boards, &c., on account of the distance they are brought; but now we receive a supply from Oregon of lumber, as well as wheat and dry goods, which tend to lower the prices.

All kind of merchandise were exceedingly dear when we first landed, and until lately; but now the place is well supplied, and instead of 300 per cent profit, they are now content to sell at cent per cent[2] over New York prices current. The brig Sabine, of Boston, Capt. Vincent, is now discharging a valuable cargo from Boston, and we have many arrivals from the Sandwich Islands, China, and southern ports, as well as from the United States. We are accumulating a revenue; goods of all kinds, lumber excepted, pays a duty of 20 per cent on the valuation here. Liquor sells dear. Brandy, gin, rum, and aguadente are sold at $150 per bottle, and retailed at one rial per glass. Wine the same; they have some Californian

---

1. Joseph L. Folsom (1817–1855) came to California as a captain and quartermaster of Stevenson's Regiment of New York Volunteers. He became one of the wealthiest landowners in the state. The town of Folsom, and Folsom Street in San Francisco, are named for him.
2. One hundred percent markup.

wines that they sell cheaper, but it is of rather inferior quality. Boots are $8 to $10 per pair; shoes $3. Black and blue cloths very dear, as well as ready made clothing—tailors' work being very high. Tea from $1 to $2 per lb., that is, good souchong, or green; but the inferior kind is cheap. Butter is four rials or half a dollar per lb., notwithstanding the vast number of cows; but the Californians, who own the principal part, are too indolent to milk or churn.

Cows are large, and good milchers, and sell from $12 to $16 each. Horses are very numerous, but not very large, a few exceptions only, and sell from $8 to $50 each. You can get a serviceable mare for $8, and a horse for $15, but they are very skittish, and till broken down, difficult for Americans to catch. The Mexicans, however, have no difficulty, it being their chief employment, lassoing and taming wild horses. Most of our men have purchased horses; their saddle, bridle and spurs are all different from ours, strong and heavy; their enormous long spurs rattle like chains, and some have little bells attached. The natives never ride without the riata, or raw hide rope or lasso, and at which they are very expert; they will throw the noose on a horse's head or neck, at the distance of twenty yards, at full speed, and the pummel of their saddles are so fashioned as to take a turn of the riata round it and bring up a wild horse, cow or ox.

Traits of the Mexicans

The men are generally lazy, fond of riding, dancing and gambling. Their chief game is called monte; it is a mere game of chance, and it is not unusual to see $200 staked on the turn of a single card. The women will gamble as well as the men.

The men are mostly addicted to liquor. The women are, or may be generally considered handsome, with dark, fascinating eyes and good features; the better kind very courteous, but, in general, indolent; they dress rich and costly, are addicted to fandangoing and gallantry, but not much coquetry; sociable, kind, and good-natured, beautiful and extravagant, and chiefly overkind; but of this I am no judge.

Both males and females are not so religious as the French. They are fond of ceremony, but the dreadful intestine feuds, and tyranny exercised by the military commanders and despotic rulers over the lower class, render them generally revengeful and irreligious. The missions owned by the clergy in former times were mostly ransacked previous to the present war, and clerical influence is on the decline. They will in no wise, nor on any account, embrace any other religion, although they do not strictly adhere to any of the rules of their own. There is only one Catholic priest in all these upper districts, half Indian, but a very zealous preacher, and, they say, a good Christian.

The lands in California are mostly used for grazing, and are varied, in large tracts, from three leagues square to fifty leagues. Some men own 20,000 head of cattle, but the mountains and hills are not fit for agriculture, on account of the want of rain—we have scarcely any from April to December—but the valleys and low grounds, particularly where they can be irrigated, produce abundantly. M. Luther Van Helvetia,[3] on the river Sacramento, raises annually twelve to twenty thousand bushels of wheat, which he gets entirely reaped by the Indians. General Vallyo [sic], and his brother, in Sonoma, own most all

---

3. A peculiar way of referring to John Augustus Sutter (1803–1880), who was born in Germany but was raised partly in Switzerland. He came to California in 1839, became a Mexican citizen, and was given a large land grant. He called his vast holdings Nueva Helvetia; the headquarters of his rancho was Sutter's Fort.

the good lands northward from here, and we expect, as soon as this country is under American law, that taxation will cause them to sell their lands in farms or quantities to suit emigrants, which will be the first step towards improving this country. Almost all the luxuries of nature, as respects the vegetable kingdom, thrive here. Potatoes are raised only by a few; as yet they sell for six rials the arobe of 25 lbs.; nor can they boast of much fruit as yet in Lower California. At the mission they raise apples, pears, &c.—they cost us here a dollar the hundred. Beef is the only or principal sustenance of man; it is sold at 2½ to 3 cents per lb., but it is cheaper to purchase the creature. The hide will sell for one and a half dollars, and then the meat will cost no more than one cent per lb.; it is seldom better. Flour is sold at $12 per barrel, but it will be in the decline.

We have got a first outline of American law here. Each district has an Alcalde or chief magistrate, or two together, with a town council—but like every new colony, for want of better, we are obliged to have some men whose first object is self-protection. We have two weekly newspapers here, who print the conduct of public officers in their true colors, but without much effect. One paper, edited by Mr. Bucklew, is called the *Californian;* the other is under Mormon influence, called the *Star,* but it is not supposed to sparkle very brightly, particularly in summer weather. We have, as yet, no higher court for the trial of criminal offences, than the court martial; and this, like every new colony, populated by people of a roving, headstrong disposition, renders murders frequent. Mostly all carry pistols and dirk knives. Horse stealing is quite common, also, on the mountains.

Wild Indians

The Indians are not very hostile here. A few of them are located on each ranch or farm, living in huts, and work for their food and a little clothing. The wild Indians frequent the mountains, go almost naked, use bows and arrows, and sometimes are brought in by their governor to work for the season, and return in the winter. They are not over fastidious in respect to dress, a small patch of skin in front only, and sometimes a little patch between the shoulders. The Digger tribe being next us here, are the most abject, loathsome creatures in the world. They are revengeful and lazy, and are kept in a kind of slavery and bondage by the rancheros, and often flogged and punished. Their performing all the drudgery and heavy labor, leaves but little demand for laborers of white complexion; and, besides, there are numbers of Conyackers [Kanakas] or Sandwich Islanders, here, who work reasonably.

Mechanics here, however, get good wages; three dollars per day. Board here is pretty dear; $16 per month in the taverns, and four times that much in the hotels. Young women are very scarce here—very few Americans. There are a few Mormons. Some of our countrymen, however, get married to Californians or Mexicans.

Having given you a hasty outline of the army, the geography, &c., of California, I overlooked a few facts which may be interesting to you, respecting the imports and exports of this country, together with the mineral kingdom and shipping. Several mines have been discovered in this country; one at Santa Clara, on this bay, belonging to Messrs. Forbes, with the labor of fifteen hands, in three weeks, yielded 11,200 lbs. of quicksilver, worth in Mexico two dollars per pound. Two silver mines have been discovered, also, one about three miles from Sonoma, on the lands of Mr. Illig, and another on the lands of J. F. Reed, Esq., about four miles from the Puebla de San Jose, which is supposed to be very rich, and the enterprising proprietor has already commenced operations.

A Rumor of Gold

I am credibly informed that a quantity of gold, worth in value, $30, was picked up lately in the bed of a stream of the Sacramento. There are also numerous mines of coal, and some of copper discovered in this neighborhood, to the Southward and Northward. Two immense caves are known to exist in the vicinity of Clear Lake, North of this bay, and about 112 miles from Sonoma; one containing inexhaustible quantities of saltpetre, the other abounding in sulphur, and both said to be of the purest quality.—There are immense beds of copper ore, lately discovered, in the vicinity of said lake. Little, however, is known in relation to coal, in California, as yet; however there are different reports of its having been discovered in various places—Santa Cruz mountains, San Luis Obisbo, San Diego, and Todos los Santos.

There is another discovery, of a copious fountain of semi-fluid asphaltum, near Santa Barbara, running into the sea, and impregnating the atmosphere for several miles. This substance becomes hard, so as to break like rosin, when exposed to the cold air, and is highly combustible. It has been already exported, to be used in the arts, in Peru, and has been used as fuel in steamboats in Chili. Near the lower Pueblo los Angelos, there are extensive fields where it is continually boiling up from the earth. This is believed to be the asphaltum petroleum, or "mineral tar" of commerce. At present it is used in covering the flat earthen roofs of California houses, to render them impervious to rain. Perhaps this may be the asphaltum of the ancients, so much spoken of by Josephus in his "Wars of the Jews." Limestone has been found in abundance, and already all the lime necessary to be mixed with the quicksilver ore, in the extensive mine near Santa Clara, can be procured in the vicinity. Several soda springs are interspersed in all parts of this country, particularly in the mountains. There is one near Sonoma, and another near the above described quicksilver mines, which are considered by judges to be equal to Saratoga or Balston waters, and similar to the Congress water. We have received information lately, that a large emigration from China may be soon expected. We have already two or three "Celestials" among us, who have found ready employment. We were yesterday shown a specimen of salt, taken from a large bowl spring, twelve miles west of the Sacramento, which is of fine quality.

Golden Hopes

The gold mine discovered in December last, on the south branch of the American fork, in a range of low hills forming the base of the Sierra Nevada, distant thirty miles from New Helvetia, is only three feet below the surface, in a strata of soft sand rock. From explorations south twelve miles, and north five miles, the continuance of this strata is reported, and the mineral said to be equally abundant, and from twelve to eighteen feet in thickness; so that, without allowing any golden hopes to puzzle my prophetic vision of the future, I would predict for California a Peruvian harvest of the precious metals, as soon as a sufficiency of miners, &c., can be obtained.

Number of Vessels arrived at this Port, from April 1st, 1847, to April 1st, 1848.— From New York, 2; Sandwich Islands, 14; Oregon, 8; San Pedro, 4; Monterey, 16; Bodega, 3; Santa Cruz, 5; San Pedro, 4; Chili, 3; North-West Coast, 4; Southern Coast, 2; New Bedford, 6; New London, 3; San Diego, 2; Sitka, 1; Callao, 2; Canton, 1; Boston, 1; United States, 2. Men-of-War— U. S. ships Preble, Congress, Columbus, and sloop Dale.

Of the above, sixteen were whalers; so that you will perceive this is destined to be a place of great trade before long.

I will give you an abridged sketch of the imports and exports, obtained through the politeness of Capt. Fulsom, U. S. Army, and collector of this port, for the three months ending December 31st, 1847:—Total value of exports for the quarter, $49,597.53. Of this amount, $30,353.85 were of the produce of California, and shipped as follows:—$320 to the Sandwich Islands, $21,448.35 to Peru, $560 to Mazatlan, (Mexico,) $7,285.50 to Russian America, (Sitka,) $700 to Tahiti; $19,343.68 were of the produce of foreign countries, and shipped as follows:—$2,060 to the United States, $12,442.18 to the Sandwich Islands, (of which $11,340 were coined gold and silver,) and $4,840.50 to Mazatlan, Mexico.

The total value of imports for the same period was $53,589.73. Of this amount $6,790.54 came from the United States, $7,701.59 from Oregon, $3,676.44 from Chili, $31,740.73 from the Sandwich Islands, $2,471.59 from Sitka, Russian America, $492.57 from Bremen, and $550.54 and $160 from Mexico. This shows a large balance against us as yet, and has occasioned a heavy drain of cash to meet the balance. The principal exports, as yet, are hides and tallow; but when our mines and forests come into operation, we expect to turn the scale. At present the duty on American merchandise is 20 per cent, which must be borne by the inhabitants. This is shameful.

The climate is delightful and healthy. In San Francisco the wind blows mostly from the west. We expect to be disbanded next fall, many of the regiment not relishing the country. I have not space to give you the market prices, but hope ere long to be able to forward them.

(NYH, August 19, 1848.)

Life in California

We have received, says the St. Louis Reveille, several interesting letters from Lewis Dent, Esq., who is at present engaged in the practice of law in Monterey, California.

MONTEREY, CALIFORNIA, April, 1848.

Dear Reveille:—It is now Sabbath afternoon. The hills around me are all green, and the air is warm as a June day at home. I have on the table before me a large bouquet of beautiful *floras del bompo*, (wild flowers) gathered this morning from the neighboring hills. My office is in the dwelling house of Gen. Alvarado, former Governor of the Territory under the Mexican supremacy. It opens into the most public thoroughfare of Monterey, the capital of California. It is, as I said before, Sabbath afternoon. I have not seen a preacher since I came to California, and consequently have not heard a sermon; but before me, instead of a meeting-house, with "tapering spire," I see some forty Californians, all in gay-colored robes, and most nondescript pants, glittering at all points with silver cords and buttons. This dress is very picturesque. Every one of these Californians, to a man, is on horseback, where they may, with propriety, be said to live. Their horses are superb, and their saddles and bridles literally shine with silver.

Californian Centaurs

A Californian will go half his time without the actual necessaries of life, to decorate himself and horse on fast-days, with spangles of the precious metal. This is a Californian's weakness. These fellows are the children of generals, governers, colonels, &c., of the fallen republic, and were, many of them, concerned in the affair at San Pasqual, which resulted in their own repulse, but at a cost of exactly one-third of Gen. Kearney's command. They present a fine appearance on horseback, darting and dashing about, and performing feats of remarkable agility, and anon sweeping away with the fleetness of the wind to the neighboring hills. Thus performing, they look like the Centaurs of the heathen mythology, to be half-horse, and, in that respect, only less wonderful than some of our Kentuckians, who claim their other moiety to be of alligator extraction, with a "small sprinkling" of the snapping-turtle.

We possess here but indifferent materials for the constitution of good government, and I fear, under present circumstances, the political acumen of our statesmen at home will be thoroughly tested in the effort to furnish an adequate polity. The people have a great predilection for revolution, as their history abundantly proves. During the Mexican supremacy, and even at later dates, under the administration of Com. Stockton, they have exhibited their uneasy character under the restraint of wholesome law. It will be impossible to reconcile them to our utilitarian institutions (at least so far as to secure them against disaffection,) until their natures become radically changed. They do not resemble us in a single particular; their history, language, and laws are different, and their interests will clash with ours. They are, in short, our opposites in every respect; and so long as these facts exist, so long will they be dissatisfied with the political system under which we are contented to live, and consequently disposed to change it. Our laws must be carefully introduced among them. We must endeavor to assimilate ourselves to them, and imperceptibly lead them to appreciate our most enlightened code, and adopt our better customs. Yet will they prove stubborn pupils, and more likely appeal to the lance to resist, than to the rectitude of our intentions to justify innovation.

A Barbarous People

These descendants of the first settlers have sunk to the level of the Indians, while the good philanthropists themselves were endeavoring to elevate the character of their savage brethren to their own; and as the latter are impossible to be reclaimed by human laws from their barbarous state, so I think it will be found a difficult task to reconcile the Californians to a system of government fitted for an enlightened people, which they have long ceased to be. Without a government, and without laws, they have made a retrograde movement to a state of nature, and in that condition we should meet them, not with a refined and polished system, but with such simple laws as our Saxon ancestors had among

the woods of Germany, or along the northern shore of the Caspian sea, applying such laws to their primitive condition, and increase in refinement as they increase in civilization.

At present the country is quiet, but I do not imagine it will long continue so. Already I can see much jealousy abroad! Although the Californians are so utterly devoid of every principle of patriotism as to be indifferent to the disasters of their country, they will still persist in adhering to old associations, and regard with an evil eye every effort made at innovation. The change is already perceptible, and they begin to feel it. This is the occasion of their hostility. Taking into consideration their past history, and the genius of the race, I should believe a military despotism to be the form of government most suited to their condition. They will never be able to appreciate a more liberal policy. To extend the right of suffrage and free representation to them, under present circumstances, would be like throwing jewels before swine.

They are physically and morally superior to the New Mexicans, or even the inhabitants of Sonora; but this, indeed, if nothing more can be said in their favor, is no very great compliment; for every one is aware, who is at all acquainted with those provinces, that a more worthless and depraved set of wretches never blotted the face of creation. I speak dispassionately. I cannot believe that I am influenced in my remarks by any feeling of prejudice. And every man will be forced to the same conclusion who has ever had an opportunity to know and judge of these people.

Lewis Dent.[4]

(PPL, August 24, 1848.)

---

4. Lewis Dent (1823–1874), a native of Missouri, came to California in 1847 and was a lawyer in Monterey. He was a member of the California constitutional convention in 1849, and was later a judge of the superior and circuit courts.

Our New Territory

The New Territories—The Slavery Question

The treaty of Mr. Trist, done at Guadaloupe Hidalgo, in February last, secures to the United States, in addition to the boundary of the Rio Grande for Texas, the territories of New Mexico and Alta California.

The issue of this Presidential contest depends entirely upon questions growing out of these acquisitions.

The slavery question is paramount—indeed, it is the only question of the campaign—it is a question absolutely contingent to our recent annexations, and a question which, *per se,* is to settle the cast and policy of the next administration.

Practically, the question of admitting into, or excluding slavery from, New Mexico and California, amounts to nothing. New Mexico, excepting the narrow margin of the Rio Grande, is a desert of barren sand plains and mountains. The margin of the river is occupied and cultivated, by means of irrigation, to its capacity, barely producing sufficient for a population which requires two-thirds less to support it than the same proportion of negro slaves. Nine-tenths of California are an irreclaimable desert region of sands, chasms, rocks and bald mountains. The slip lying along the Pacific, and flanked in its whole extent on the east by the Sierra Nevada, embracing the valley whose waters are emptied into the magnificent inland bay of San Francisco, is the only portion of California that will pay for the exploration. This region produces the staples of the North and the South, and may be made highly productive of olive oil, wine, cotton, sugar, and tobacco. Slave labor, then, would here be profitable, in opposition to free white labor. But the Indians who swarm along the defiles and valleys of the Sierra Nevada, living mostly upon acorns, and the nuts of the pine trees which grow among the eternal snows, can be hired by the cattle raisers and farmers for just enough of the coarsest offal and garbage to satisfy their hunger. Captain Sutter employs large numbers of these Indians upon such terms. They are nearly all naked, and such as occasionally flourish at the rancho in a cotton shirt have acquired it in the way of extra compensation. With an aggregate of some twenty thousand of such Indians, at all times ready to work for the smallest allowance of the coarsest food, it would be impossible by act of Congress to establish negro slavery in California. A Southern negro would starve upon the quantity and quality of subsistence which would fatten three or four California Indians. A bounty of one hundred dollars upon every negro slave taken out to California, would not insure the establishment of negro slavery there. The fact is, it can never be established there while the thousands of wild and Christian Indians that infest the borders of the Sierra Nevada continue to exist. For all practical purposes, therefore, we see that the question of "free soil," as regards New Mexico and California, is sheer humbug. The soil can never be anything else than "free," and, by far the most of it so entirely free as to be totally uninhabited, until the day of the prophet shall come when the desert of the Great Basin shall blossom like the rose.[1]

(NYH, Sept. 8, 1848.)

---

1. "The desert shall rejoice, and blossom as the rose." (*Isaiah 35:1.*)

Mexico and California

Major Emory, in his account of his tour from the Missouri frontier to Santa Fe, thence down the Rio Grande to near El Paso del Norte, thence westward to the river Gila, and down that river to where it empties into the Colorado, and thence to the Pacific ocean, (a distance of 1,200 miles,) says that with the exception of the narrow valley of the Rio Grande, and some fertile patches along the Gila, which last, however, can only be cultivated by irrigation, all is barrenness and desolation.[2] The Journal of Commerce, summing up the results of his observations, says:—

The fact unquestionably is, that as a whole, the portion of California and New Mexico lying south of lat. 36° 30′ is about the most worthless territory upon which the sun ever shone; while the portion north of that latitude, along with much poor land, comprises extensive tracts of most excellent soil, together with the best harbor in the world, that of San Francisco, and mines of quicksilver, gold, and other valuables, and withal an abundance of live oak and other timber suitable for ships and all the wants of a large and prosperous community. The largest of these fertile tracts is the Sacramento valley, which Col. Fremont describes as 50 or 60 miles wide by about 500 long, embracing an area of 25,000 or 30,000 miles, equal to two-thirds of the State of New York. The Sacramento empties into the bay of Francisco, and so all this fine country is immediately connected with that wonderful harbor. Here are the principal American settlements in California, and here too must inevitably be the seat of enterprise, commerce, and wealth of Northwestern America. Monterey, the capital of California, which lies to the southward of San Francisco, is also north of lat. 36° 30′; and in short, so far as is yet known, the portion of California lying south of that latitude is worthless compared with the northern portion. Slaves would starve to death on a great part of it, and their masters with them.

(PPL, September 18, 1848.)

Our New Territory

CALIFORNIA, June 1, 1848.

We still live and have our being in this "Farest West," with only one serious apprehension, that we are in danger of having more gold than food, for he that can wield a spade, and shake a dish, can fill his pockets, *a su gusto*.[3] Oh! this California climate certainly influences dispositions. A Californian never dreams of work. Some on horseback have to exert themselves in taming wild horses and cattle, and in the after management of them, but *"válgame dios,"*[4] those who obtained a stay in this world by headwork, when in office, or obtained credit on the hopes of one, (a Californian will pay his debts, but takes his own time in doing this or any other good thing,) had to get up a *pronunciamento*, occasionally, as funds or credit ran low; the natives having, by the change of flags, been brought to a stand still, must get ahead as they best can by the ownership of a few leagues of land and a few thousand head of cattle.

---

2. William Hemsley Emory (1811–1887), a topographical engineer, explorer, and cavalry officer. This account was published as: Thirtieth Congress, First Session, Sen. Ex. Doc. No. 41. *Notes of a Military Reconnoissance from Fort Leavenworth, in Missouri, to San Diego, California . . . . Made in 1846–7 with the advanced guard of the Army of the West.* The account was richly illustrated, with precise details of the route of travel and of conditions encountered. It was printed in February 1848 in an edition of 10,000 copies.
3. At his pleasure.
4. God help me!

'Tis now the Yankee turn, beginning in October, 1846, under Lieut. Washington Bartlett, alcalde of the town of Yerba Buena. Hundreds of our countrymen obtained in that town, at $15 each, house lots of 50 varas square, (136 English feet).[5] This they continued under Judge Bryant and Judge Hyde, one an editor, the other a lawyer of your city. Houses costing $100 to $1,000 sprung up like the story of Aladdin's times. Fifty varas lots, without any improvements, sold from 100 to 1,000 Mexican dollars. Merchants, lawyers, blacksmiths, carpenters, etc., became owners of snug little houses. Many sent home for their families; all was doing well. Mechanics obtained four to eight dollars per day; even some of the volunteers came in for a large share by the well-timed and prudent permission of their officers, while they performed their duty to government. Lawyers, $50 a fee; the merchant made 100 per cent; clerks and schoolmasters, $500 to $1,000 per annum. Every one appeared happy and contented, making money without trouble, like a Californian, imagining Providence had taken them under special protection. When all this was in the full blast of successful operation, and no probability of its being brought to a close—*presto!* some one proclaimed that there was, on the branches of the Sacramento, "gold for the gathering." This cry, I believe, began from the Mormons; immediately the most thoughtless, the most sanguine, took horse or launch for the rivers of wealth. In less than one month they returned to Yerba Buena, now San Francisco, with a few hundred dollars of gold dust, worth in the States, $17 per ounce.

Pans, Cups, Picks, and Spades

The whole mass of foreign population struck, not for higher wages, but for none at all—spades and shovels rose from $2 to $10; tin pans and cups, to unheard of prices; a few considerate turners and blacksmiths remained to make spades and picks, and turn wooden dishes to wash out the sand. These few are now making $20 to $40 per day; cooks and boatmen demand $30 per month. The result, in a few words, is that more than half, I think three fourths, of the houses, in some towns, are vacated. A passage in the launch rose from nothing to $4 to $8 to $16. Every one brought more astonishing news of this El Dorado of rivers whose bottoms were gold, only requiring to step in, scoop up a handful of black sand, move the hand a few minutes in the water, and there remained the pure thing itself. Rivers, whose banks glittered with the fine black sand, impregnated with quantities of gold that glistened still more until the "eyes ached." Pans and shovels sold for $30 on the spot; $20 a day was demanded by one to spend a day to go to the nearest rancho for a quarter of meat, or $20 a day to cook for a mess of ten men, $2 a man. This, they say, was submitted to for a few days. Whether these golden stories of rivers of gold were true or false, could not immediately be known. This much was seen. No one from the gold regions had any time to talk or spin street yarns; but with more tools, tea, coffee, flour and crackers, paid for in gold dust itself at $14 per ounce, they were off again. There was no waiting for what the Germans call a stand point. No hesitation—no more misbelief—by the most skeptical; all must go; and, truly, in some towns, all have gone.

---

5. A vara is thirty-three inches, and thus 50 varas equal 137.5 feet. The blocks were laid out three lots east-west and two lots north-south. When the area south of Market Street was surveyed, blocks had the same number of lots. But the lots were 100 varas square, which is why those blocks to this day have twice the area of the ones north of Market.

Near two hundred houses in the town of San Francisco are closed by the owners.

Benicia, a small town of a year's growth, situated forty miles from the entrance of San Francisco Bay, had but two men left, who were earning $30 a day by the ferry. Monterey is now showing strong symptoms of the gold fever, its inhabitants, in general, thinking they are sufficiently rich, can afford for a few days longer to let well enough alone; but onward goes this fever, raging strongly in the brains of all, depopulating towns, carrying off men, women, and children. A six-year-old child can gather $2 or $3 a day; a man $10 to $30; old and young ladies in proportion; according to how they admire to stand two feet deep in the water, or can dig with shovels, or roll round a wooden dish or basket.

Should these reports continue the year out, and prove to be true, and I continue a monthly report, the mighty *Herald* for three nations, paying its owner (so he says, or the printer does the saying for him) $30,000 per year, would stop, for want of hands, like the newspapers of California. Who would print *Heralds* at $3 or $4 a day, when in the Far West he could gather a cup of gold a day? I had better stop as I am, or your men will quit as it is.

Astonishing Tales

The Indian wars are depopulating the Oregon. Peace will soon disband the volunteers on the Pacific. The astonishing tales from this country, of rivers with bottoms and banks of gold—of quicksilver—pent up for thousands of years in leagues of mountains—only waiting the rush to the Pacific of that ever-restless, never-contented Yankee race, to loose it from its con-

finement—to make gold and mercury as plenty as all can desire. This news, spreading over the Atlantic States, these three continuing causes, will soon fill California from all parts of our country.

No more. You will not believe a quarter of what I have told you, and your readers not a half; the writer is bound to believe much of it—all of it. How long the banks of our rivers will produce gold dust is our affair. Those who have travelled these splendid regions say there is no end to their riches, although there must be to
  SU AMIGO Y PAISANO.[6]
  (NYH, Sept. 18, 1848.)

Interesting from California—The Discovery of Gold Mines

CALIFORNIA, July 1, 1848.

My last to you was one month since. In that I gave you facts stronger than fiction, with the intimation that you and your thousands of *Herald* readers would not believe the statement. Were I a New Yorker, instead of a Californian, I would throw aside your paper and exclaim, Bennett[7] had better fill his paper with, at least, probable tales and stories, and not such outrageous fictions of rivers flowing with gold. However, for my own satisfaction, I will fall back upon the fact that the writer knows all he writes to be very near the truth, and the many who know his signature, in particular the officers of the navy, will not doubt his statements of California.

A Revolution in Society

Oh! this California, to what will it come at last? Revolution after revolution, for years, have vacated your houses, and caused your fields to be deserted; and now, when we supposed that both houses and

---

6. "YOUR FRIEND AND COUNTRYMAN." Thomas Oliver Larkin (1802–1858), born in Massachusetts, settled in California in 1832. He became the foremost merchant in Monterey, and in 1844 was appointed U.S. Consul in Mexican California. In later communications to the *Herald* he simply signs himself PAISANO.
7. James Gordon Bennett (1795–1872), founder and editor of the *New York Herald*.

fields were occupied by another class of men, men whom nothing could remove—*presto*, a gold fever arises—strikes every one, and drives every one from his home. This writer has visited the golden country, this *"Placer,"* in comparison to which the famous El Dorado[8] is but a sand bank. The Arabian Nights tales of simplicity, are fit only for children; the walks of Irving's gold hunters are now brought into existence, and facts brought to light which our great writer could never have dreamt of. Our territory is turned up-side down—people are leaving their wives and children, and laughing at an offer of ten dollars per day to finish a contract. A

Thomas O. Larkin

mechanic says politely to his employer: "Sir, your wages were high, your conduct just and correct; but I am doing myself an injustice in remaining any longer hammering leather or jointing boards, at four or five dollars a day, when a week's ride brings me to the *"Placer,"* where an ounce and more of gold awaits each day's digging."

The Country in Ferment

The forge stops, the boards remain unplaned, houses are closed, dinners uncooked, the sick recover, the plaintiff leaves his case untried, the defendant is gone, the Alcalde going, stores and hotels are closed—our newspapers stop, editors, clerks, lawyers, devils, clergymen, brickmakers, alcaldes, constables, soldiers, and sailors, some with a spade or pickaxe, others with a tin pan or wooden bowl, paid for at a thousand per cent on the former price, are forming partnerships, all bound to the American Fork and Feather River, branches of the Sacramento. Rivers whose banks and bottoms are filled with pure gold—where a Hingham bucket of dirt,[9] with a half hour's washing in running water, produces a spoonful of black sand, containing from seven to ten dollars worth of gold. At this minute, I can see in front of our hotel, the boarders on their last blow, (the house closes to-morrow,) playing in the open street with imaginary cups, bowls, pans, picks, crowbars, and spades—digging gold with the highest glee; their

8. A legendary city or country of fabulous wealth, sought for by the Spanish in South America but never found.

9. Hingham buckets were widely known and used—an ordinary bucket but considered to be of high quality. They were produced by a firm in Hingham, Massachusetts that also produced "dumb bettys, tubs, keelers, firkins, nest boxes, and piggins." (*Hingham Old and New,* Mason A. Foley.) That is: chamber pots, tubs, shallow tubs or vessels for cooling liquids, small wooden vessels for butter or lard, a series of boxes of graduated sizes, and cream pails.

hands and legs, heels and heads, moving in every known mode of a gold digger. This writer has seen, the past month, at these "diggins," fifty dollars demanded by a carpenter to leave his spade and take his plane and chisel, per day, and over a hundred dollars refused for a rough-made machine to wash gold in that was made by the man in a day. A spade or shovel sells for ten dollars; tin pans for the same, and flour at the rate of thirty-six dollars a barrel. A common day's work of a man turns out from five to thirty dollars; one hundred dollars has been obtained in one day. A machine put together of a hundred feet of boards, and worked by a company of five men, some days yielded one pound of gold dust—the size of the grains differing from the point of a pin to a piece worth six dollars. I have seen a piece worth sixteen dollars. A beer bottle will contain from fifteen to eighteen pounds, the filling of which, small as its compass is, occupied several weeks of the labor of one man. Where one pound is saved, many go down stream from the imperfect mode of washing.

Tools, among the workmen, will soon be of less price. Clothing and provisions will continue high. Ten dollars is demanded for a horse to go to the nearest store, twenty-five miles; fifty dollars for a wagon, and this on a remarkably good road. The whole country is on a rush—in a ferment. At the gold regions, a man has hardly time to speak or eat. While some have washed out only three or four dollars in a day, there are cases of over a hundred dollars being obtained in a day from the work of one man. It requires no skill. The workman takes any spot of ground or bank he fancies; sticks in his pick or shovel at random; fills his basin; makes for the water, and soon sees the glittering results of his labor. Where, and how, all this is to end, is beyond my comprehension. Sufficient for me is the knowledge of the day. That the "*Placer*" of California will bring into the country thousands and thousands of emigrants, is clear. Many believe the

peace was only requisite to do this, not the gold fever. Many believe the digging for gold, on the branches of the Sacramento, will continue for an age; how it can, by any possibility, and in a few years, I do not know. We are already aware of its being found over a space of one hundred miles in length, and but little of the Sacramento Valley has been explored for anything but elk and deer. The gold limits cannot this year be defined. That the space is immense, the quality of the root of all evil beyond all calculation, is certain. I would, by-the-by, advise all debtors having money in gold, to pay it off before the article is under par. Our country pays Mexico a certain sum for the newly acquired territory. The men under arms this year, and sent to Mexico, could all have found room for a spade and pick-axe on our golden banks. Thirty thousand of this army would have required but a few months to pay this sum, and all the expenses of the war, had they had the opportunity to have been placed in the gold diggings of California.

Gone to the "Placer"

As it is, the "*Placer*," pronounced *placera* is fast having its thousands of laborers. House-keepers and farmers have shut up and left their businesses, re-filled their wagons, made tents, laid in provisions, and gone with their families. Almost every clerk, mechanic, or laborer is gone, or preparing to go. Ships are losing their crews and volunteer companies their men—all are for the "*Placer*." Grass will soon grow in the streets. Those who lived by house rents must now seek another occupation. The Californians have not yet, as a people, caught the gold fever, and should they wish to revolt again, their task would be easy; they would encounter not only empty houses but empty towns. All that these towns experience in California, the towns in Oregon soon will. Who will remain there to fight the Indians, or at best, raise wheat that he cannot sell, when on the borders of the Sacramento river he can obtain a pound of gold a month, and pay his expenses besides! Hoping this fever will not affect your affairs as much as it does mine, I remain

PAISANO. (NYH, Sept. 17, 1848.)

The New El Dorado

WASHINGTON, Sept. 19, 1848.

The Gold Beds of California—Great Sensation in Washington.

All Washington is in a ferment with the news of the immense bed of gold, which, it is said, has been discovered in California. Nothing else is talked about. Democrats, whigs, free soil men, hunkers, barn-burners, abolitionists—all, all, are engrossed by the wonderful intelligence.[10] The real El Dorado has at length been discovered, and hereafter let not cynics doubt that such a place exists. The *Union*, ever ready to make political capital, triumphantly says, "there Messrs. Webster, Bell, and Co., there is the country you sneeringly declared was not worth having! Why, it is a solid mass of gold, which, if worked properly, would pay all the expenses of the late war in a fortnight! The great difficulty is, that there is no way of keeping the gold,

as every vessel, or box, which might answer to stow it away, is of more value than even the gold itself. This certainly is a drawback, but Yankee ingenuity will doubtless get over it. What a pity Congress is not now in session. If it was, and Whitney[11] was to press his railroad scheme, it would be sure to pass, and, once built, what loads of passengers would be sure to be booked for the "great West," which now means California.[12]

A Golden Humbug?

Now, for our part, we do not know what to think of this gold story. It looks marvellously like a speculation to induce a rapid emigration; but then again, it is certified by the American Alcalde, at Monterey, and the American Alcalde is a very proper man, having once been a Presbyterian preacher, and, of course, a Presbyterian preacher would not tell a falsehood. It must be true. Gold, hereafter, will not be worth half as much as paper. Here is an end at once to "old Bullion's"[13] triumph in the currency. We can already see the old United States Bank, Phenix-like, rising from its ashes and disseminating its "paper rags" throughout the country, at a pre-

---

10. "Hunkers" and "barnburners" were two opposing factions of the New York State Democratic Party; the terms were in use from 1845 to about 1852. Both words were derogatory. Hunkers were ultra-conservatives who were accused of being professional office-holders, wanting only to 'hunker down' in their comfortable positions and never make a move. The name seems to have derived from the Dutch word *hunkeren*, meaning to hanker after something, to be hungry for something—in this case, for political office. Those who did so naturally became known as 'hunkerers'—soon shortened to "hunkers." Barnburners were ultra-liberal activists who were accused of being so radical that they would burn down a barn in order to get rid of the rats.

11. Asa Whitney (1797–1872), an early railroad promoter. In 1844 he urged Congress to charter a railroad to the Pacific via the South Pass—the route eventually followed by the Union Pacific in 1869. He spent seven years pushing the project, but encountered only indifference.

12. "The best business you can go into you will find on your father's farm or in his workshop. If you have no family or friends to aid you, and no prospect opened to you there, turn your face to the great West, and there build up a home and fortune."
(Horace Greeley, *To Aspiring Young Men*.)

13. "Old Bullion" was a nickname for Thomas Hart Benton (1782–1858), father-in-law of John C. Frémont, one of the first Senators from Missouri, a strong supporter of western expansion, and an advocate of hard money.

mium. It is said that one of the proprietors of the *Union*, who has lately invested a considerable sum in a Virginia gold mine, has already sold out, and is preparing to start for California, where the precious metal can be got by buckets full, instead of—as in the Virginia mine—merely by a spade full at a time. It may all be true, or it may turn out to be a second diamond mine story; we should be sorry, at this enlightened age, to declare our disbelief in anything—except, indeed, the disinterested motives of politicians, or that the barnburners in the New York Custom House feel particularly at ease just now.

(NYH, Sept. 21, 1848.)

From California

Mr. Edward F. Beale,[14] Passed Midshipman, arrived in this city [Washington] on Saturday, from Commodore Jones's squadron in the Pacific, and is said to have performed the most rapid journey from the Pacific to Washington. He left Commodore Jones at La Paz on the 1st of August, came by Mazatlan, and arrived at the port of San Blas on the 10th, and pushed his way by horses and mules across the country to the city of Mexico, where he arrived on the 17th. He was detained by Mr. Clifford three days for despatches, and in forty-eight hours passed from Mexico to Vera Cruz, about 275 miles, sleeping not more than ten minutes at a time. From Vera Cruz he sailed to Mobile, and arrived here on Saturday evening. Mr. Beale crossed from the Pacific at San Blas to the Gulf at Vera Cruz in the unexampled journey of ten days on the road, and was detained at Mexico three days.

The most extraordinary intelligence which Mr. Beale brings is about the real El Dorado, the Gold region in California. His accounts of the extraordinary richness of the gold surface, and the excitement it had produced among all classes of people, inhabitants of the country and of the towns, among seamen and soldiers, are confirmed by letters from Com. Jones and from Mr. Larkin, the United States Navy Agent at Monterey, California. Mr. Beale states that the whalers had suspended their operations—the captains permitting their seamen to go to the gold region, upon condition that every ounce of gold the seamen obtained should be given to the captain for $10, making six or seven dollars by the bargain. The towns were being evacuated, mechanics, &c. going to the attractive spot. The two newspapers had been suspended, the compositors going off to gather gold for themselves.

The "Union" publishes the following letter from Mr. Larkin to the Secretary of the Navy:

U. S. NAVY AGENCY,
Monterey, California, July 1, 1848.

SIR: Since my last letter to you, written in San Francisco, I have visited the "Placer," or gold region of California, and found it all it had been represented to me. My anticipations were fully realized. The part I visited was the south fork of the river American, which joins the Sacramento at Sutter's Fort, or two miles from it. This river has its north and south forks, branching more than twenty miles from Fort Sutter. On these two forks there are over 1,000 people digging and washing for gold. On Bear creek and Hulo creek,

---

14. Edward Fitzgerald Beale (1822–1893). On December 8, 1846, Beale distinguished himself at the battle of San Pascual, east of San Diego. He, Kit Carson, and an Indian scout crawled through Mexican lines surrounding General Kearny's beleaguered dragoons, reached San Diego, and brought help from the naval forces there to relieve Kearny. In 1853 Beale led an independent (unofficial) survey for a railroad to the Pacific. In 1857 he was the instigator of the U.S. Army's experiment with the use of camels in the Southwest.

branches of Feather river, many are now beginning to work. It is supposed that the banks and bottoms of these small streams contain vast quantities of gold, and that the valleys between them are rich with the same metal. The people are now working at many places; some are eighty miles from others.

Gold Machines

The place I visited was about a league in extent; on this were about fifty tents; many have not even this covering. At one tent, belonging to eight single men, I remained two or three days. These men had two machines made in a day, from eighty to one hundred feet, inch boards, and very roughly put together. Their form was something like a child's cradle, without the ends; at one end there was a moveable sieve or rack to wash down the dirt and shake off the stones. Holes were made in the bottom of the machine to catch the gold this wash stopped, and this was scraped out hourly. These two machines gathered each day I was present three-fourths to one pound each, being three to four ounces of gold per man. These men had worked one week with tin pans; the last week with the machine. I saw the result of the first day's work of two brothers, (Americans,) one had seven dollars, the other eighty-two; they worked on the same five yards of land; one, however, worked less than the whole day. Their plan, like hundreds of others, was first with a pick and shovel, clear off two feet of the top earth, then put in a tin pan or wooden bowl a shovel of dirt, go into running water, with the hand stir up the dirt and heave out the stones, until they have remaining a spoonful of emery or black sand, containing one to five dollars. This can be done once or twice a day.

Hundreds at Work

Each day is causing some saving of labor by the improvements in the rough machines now in use. The day I left, some small companies of from five to eight men had machines from which they anticipate five or six hundred dollars a day. There certainly must this day be at work on the different Placers several hundreds of Americans and others, who are cleaning one ounce of gold a day. I have this week seen in Monterey a Californian who shows four hundred dollars of gold from the labor of one week; much of it was the size of wheat. I myself weighed one piece from his bag, and found the weight an even ounce. He, like many others, only went up to the gold regions to see the place, borrowed tools, worked a few days, and came home to show his labor, and take up brothers and cousins and provisions. Flour at the "Placer" is scarce at $16 per 100 lbs. At almost this price it must continue, as people are forsaking their fields. I do not think I am exaggerating in estimating the amount of gold obtained on the rivers I have mentioned at ten thousand dollars a day for the last few days. There is every reason to believe the amount will not this season (unless the washers are driven from their work by sickness) be any less. In this case the addition of workmen now joining the first ones, and the emigrants from the Atlantic States we shall have in October and December, will soon swell the value of California gold that will be washed out to an unheard-of value.

Exodus to the Mines

Many who have seen the "Placer" think it will last thirty or forty years. I should think that it would afford work two or three years to many thousands of people, and may for very many years, as I cannot calculate the extent of country having gold. The working of quicksilver mines, like everything else, is stopped; three-fourths of the houses in the town of San Francisco are shut up. Houses in Monterey are being closed this week; the volunteer companies of Sonoma and San Francisco have lost several men by desertion. Under the present excitement, a ship-of-war or any other vessel lying at anchor in San

Francisco would lose many men. In that town there is hardly a mechanic remaining. I expect the same in Monterey in two weeks. Both newspapers have stopped. All or nearly all the hotels are shut up. One of my clerks who received $500 and board [annually] now receives in his store near New Helvetia (Sutter's Fort) $100 per month; my others are fast closing their books to leave me. In fact, I find myself, or shall this month, without a clerk, carpenter, or servant, and all my houses, formerly rented, given up to me. In two weeks Monterey will be nearly without inhabitants.

I am, with much respect,

THOMAS O. LARKIN.[15]

(WNI, Sept. 21, 1848.)

California

Everything coming from this newly acquired country, the great Pacific slope, is of interest to every America reader. The following is from Walter Colton, the author and prettiest writer in America, and the present Alcalde of Monterey.

Correspondence of the
Philadelphia North American

MONTEREY, UPPER CALIFORNIA,

July 2, 1848.

MESSRS. EDITORS: The mineral wealth of California is being rapidly developed. Mines of silver, quicksilver, copper, zinc and lead have been found in our mountains.

But a recent discovery has thrown all others into the shade. The sands which border Feather River and the American Fork abound in particles of gold—resembling in shape snow-flakes. These are separated from the sand by stirring them in water in a basin or bowl. A person will collect by this simple process from one to two ounces of gold a day—some have gone as high as six and eight ounces. I have just been conversing with a man who in six days gathered $500 worth. He has one piece which weighs an ounce. There are probably now not less than 5,000 persons, whites and Indians, gathering this gold. San Francisco, Sonoma, Santa Cruz, and San Jose are literally deserted by their inhabitants; all have gone to the gold regions.—The farmers have thrown aside their plows, the lawyers their briefs, the doctors their pills, the priests their prayer books, and all are now digging gold. The diamond-brooched gentleman and the clouted Indian work side by side, lovingly as if they had been rocked in the same cradle. Tin pans to wash the sparkling sand in have sold as high as $8 a piece, shovels for $10, and wooden bowls for $5! A trough scooped from a hollow tree, ten feet long, and with a willow sieve attached, sells for $125. Boards are $500 for 1,000 feet.

A very large company left Monterey to-day for the gold scene—some on horses, some in wagons, some in carts, some on foot, and some on crutches. The tract of land where the gold is found covers a hundred miles in one direction and fifty in another. It is said that ten thousand men in ten years could not exhaust it. As soon as the news reaches Oregon we shall have a large emigration from that quarter. Nobody thinks of fighting here any longer—the natives have gone for gold, the sailors have run from the ships, and the soldiers from their camps for the same purpose. . . .

We want, in California, some good school books, a few good teachers, and a few good off-hand preachers. All these would find persons to read and to listen. We are gathering the elements of a great and influential community—if we are not ruined by this gold excitement.—There never was yet a people strong in wealth

---

15. This letter is similar to an official letter, dated June 28, that Larkin sent to Secretary of State James Buchanan in Washington. (*The Larkin Papers*, v. 7, 301–5.)

and sound in morals in the midst of gold and silver mines.

You talk of farmers! Why, I saw a farmer here brand, last week, a thousand calves, all of one year's growth, and he is considered here rather a small farmer. You reckon by acres, and we here by miles and leagues. Your sheep produce one lamb in a year—ours always two, and often four. Your streams have a few minnows in them, and ours are paved with gold!

Very truly yours,   W. C.
(CPD, Sept. 23, 1848.)

A Case of Asiatic Cholera

appeared at St. Louis, Missouri, on the 11th inst. Dr. Thomas Barbour, of that city, publishes in the St. Louis Republican of the 14th instant, a full description of the case. The patient was Mr. H. Palmer, an organ builder. He died within forty-eight hours. Dr. Barbour was called to see him on Monday, when the patient remarked that he had the Asiatic Cholera, being familiar with it, having had the disease before, in London, his native city.

The Doctor adds that the epidemic, to be treated successfully, should be met at the very earliest moment possible after the appearance of the first symptoms. He therefore recommends persons experiencing the first symptoms to resort at once to the following remedy, which every one can prepare, and use with safety. Take gum camphor, gum opium, African cayenne, and oil of cloves, each one ounce, and Hoffman's anodyne liquor, one pint. Shake up the ingredients frequently, in a bottle,

and in ten to twenty days, filter through paper. Dose for adults, 30 to 60 drops every second, third, or fourth hour, until the stomach and bowels are relieved. It should be taken in a wine glass full of water. This the Doctor used extensively during the prevalence of the Cholera in 1833, and he found it an excellent preventive of the disease.   (PPL, September 23, 1848.)

Letter from New York

[Correspondence of the Public Ledger]
NEW YORK, Sept. 21, 1848.

The news from California has caused a tremendous excitement in this city. Official letters have reached here that the late account about the gold mines discovered in the neighborhood of St. Francisco is not only correct, but in all probability falls below the mark. The crews of the whaling ships in the harbor have all turned to gold washing; but whether the gold will hold for thirty or forty years as anticipated no one can tell. . . .

To-day and yesterday a perfect emigration fever has sprung up, and the new line mail steamers for California and Oregon will no sooner begin to run than even Texas will be forgotten in the brighter prospects of California. If the whole population of California turns out to wash gold, they must of course get their provisions from New York or Philadelphia; so that, in the end, the farmers and the merchants and the mechanics of the old States will be made to share the prosperity of the new.

(PPL, September 23, 1848.)

CALIFORNIA.—Life, Manners and Customs of the Inhabitants; its History, Climate, Soils, Mines, and Productions. Published for gratuitous distribution; can be obtained at the Canchalagua Depot, 36 Broadway.

Excitement

Intelligence from California

LA PAZ, LOWER CALIFORNIA, July 28, 1848.

Skirmishes with the Mexicans—The Gold Region—Crime—Naval News

Although you may have heard of the fights which we had with the Mexicans since December last, I think it as well to mention them, leaving it discretionary with you to publish them or not. The first occurred at San Antonio, in rescuing two midshipmen, Messrs. Duncan, son of the Hon. M. Duncan, late M. C. of Ohio, and Willey, Sergeant Scallan, three marines, one sailor, and some others, in the whole about twenty, comprised our force, and we beat the greasers handsomely; killing three, wounding others, and putting the remainder to flight. The number of Mexicans engaged was forty, or more. I must mention an incident that occurred.

Routing the Mexicans

One of our officers, Captain Steele, when reconnoitering, was very near being killed; a shot was fired at him from a cuartel[1] close by, and the ball penetrated his saddle, and lodged in the shoulder of it, doing no other damage. This annoyed him exceedingly, and he directed his men to dismount and rally under cover of a church close by. While rallying, Lieutenant Halleck, of the Marine Corps, came up, and he was requested to step out and ascertain the best plan of assaulting and taking the cuartel. The balls flew so thick around him that he was unable to do so. "Come boys, then," said Capt. S., "come on!" and we went straight into the cuartel. We routed them.

In an ambuscade on our return, our force dismounted and put a party of Mexicans to flight, and captured their captain, who was severely wounded. We then returned to our quarters—leaving behind us but one man, Sergeant Thomas M. Hipwood, of Company B, who was instantly killed in charging the cuartel—having ridden 120 to 140 miles, in twenty-eight hours.

Desertions

We have received very exciting news from Upper California—gold has been discovered there in great quantities, and it is said that one man got $1,500 worth in ten days. The place in which it was found is three hundred miles east of San Francisco, and is thirty miles square. Every one is going there—even Uncle Sam's troops. Some forty men of Company C, stationed at Sonoma, went in, and laying down their arms, saying they had no further use for them, marched off to the gold region. Twenty-five deserted from San Francisco barracks, and the Southampton was obliged to sail, as the crew would have deserted likewise. There are twenty-five hundred persons there now, and the number will be increased one thousand more when this regiment is disbanded.

The Mormons have the police establishment of the place, and defy Col. Mason and his whole force, to drive them off. Crime is very prevalent; and murders are allowed, if they are not very atrocious or cruel. (NYH, Oct. 2, 1848.)

---

1. Barracks or quarters.

FOR UPPER CALIFORNIA.—The well-known New York and Havre packet ship Silvie de Grasse, Capt. Rich, will be despatched from New York on the 1st of November for San Francisco, Monterey, &c. She has elegantly-furnished cabin accommodations and fine and lofty between decks. The price of passage in the cabin is two hundred and fifty dollars, and in the steerage, with provisions, one hundred and fifty dollars. For further particulars apply to
CORCORAN & RIGGS. (WNI, Oct. 18, 1848.)

From the St. Louis Republican

The accounts which have reached the United States concerning the auriferous region of country on the Sacramento and its branches has, as was to be expected, induced hundreds, we might say thousands, of our citizens to turn their eyes in that direction. The air of official authority which the publications were made to bear, having come from some officer of the army or navy, the description of the ease with which the gold is obtained, and the high prices of all commodities for sale and labor, have aroused a spirit of speculation and a desire to visit that country among all classes of the community. Old men, as well as the middle-aged and young, have golden visions of wealth before them, and are preparing to try their *luck* in this far-distant land.

Golden Exaggerations

A short time ago we were favored with a sample of the gold found on the Sacramento, and forwarded to this place by Col. Mason, now Governor of California. The possession of this little specimen has enabled us to see something of the workings of the fever. If it be not epidemic, it is at least widely diffused. The first symptom is an application to examine our specimen— following which, comes the inquiry as to the quickest and most practicable means of getting there, and what is best to be done when there—whether to take merchandise and exchange it for gold, or to go and dig for it—winding up invariably with the inquiries, What do you think of the reports?

Are the mines as rich as they are represented? Is the project a favorable one? &c.

Now, we do not know any thing more about this matter than others who have had an opportunity of obtaining such information. If our opinion is worth any thing, we can say that the mines must be extremely rich, if half of all those who now intend going there realize their hopes. It may be that a large auriferous region has been discovered, and we are bound to believe so from the representations which have been published; but that it is the El Dorado described, we very much doubt.

The True Reasons?

Such discoveries are usually greatly magnified and embellished by those who undertake to describe them, and the prospect held out always exceeds the reality— at least this is the case to the operators. Emigrants and settlers are wanted in California, and what so captivating as these gold visions? There are many town lots and broad acres for sale there, and what so conducive to the profit of the landholder as a flood of emigrants? There are some circumstances attending the publications in reference to this matter that make us doubtful of the extent of the representations, and lead us to suspect the motives which have prompted them. Of these we may speak hereafter; but this strikes us as undeniable, that the possessor of a gold mine is not very apt, voluntarily, to ask other men to come in and share it with him. But *we shall see what we shall see.*

We were yesterday visited by a gentleman who has been for many years a conductor of gold mines in Mexico. He examined our specimen, and then informed us that he had travelled over a large portion of the Sacramento region in search of gold mines, described the evidence he found, and concluded by assuring us that after spending five thousand dollars in experiments and attempts at discoveries, he came out *minus* the investment. This is one side; our readers may compare it with the other. (WNI, Oct. 14, 1848.)

The New American Territory

[From the London Times, Sept. 16]

There is really a great deal of interest to be acquired in the seizing of California, just taken by the United States. We mean that there is something very amusing in the spectacle of the most inquisitive and tenacious people in the world turned loose into a huge, mysterious, unexplored region. . . . It is certain that, at this moment, no human being of Caucasian extraction has any conception of what may be discoverable on the ten degrees of the globe's surface between the Rio del Norte and the North Pacific Ocean; and it is almost as certain that in two years' time there will be a railroad right across the province, and boarding houses at every station. It is something in these dull times to have a real true *terra incognita* in store, with Americans for adventurers. The truth is, that the Colorado beats the Oxus hollow; for there was a time when Bactriana was a civilized and accessible region enough, whereas there is no certainty that the spot of ground indicated by lat. 36, long. 112, was ever trodden by any foot but that of an Indian horse-stealer. We say no certainty, because there is mystery, in the highest degree, attached to this country. A blue book, stamped with all the authority of a Parliament warrant, positively states that "independent nations, living in large towns, and known only by report," are presumed to exist within the old domains of Mexico, and, as none such turned up the other day, during the forays between Santa Fe and Vera Cruz, we must conclude they lie somewhere hereabouts, if anywhere. The existence of the cities in question is not exactly so well ascertained as was that of paradise by Sir John Mandeville,[2] who "had not, indeed, reached the spot, but had seen the walls thereof;" it bears rather a stronger analogy to that of El Dorado, of which some Indians told Raleigh's sailors that they had once seen the reflection in a lake. Seriously, though, there is actually an enormous indefinite area to be explored and fifty thousand adventurers ready to rout and ransack every corner of it, like the undertakers at the drawers and cupboards in Hogarth's picture of the Dead Miser.

A Primitive Province

Perhaps our readers would like to learn something of the known state of California, as a *point de depart* from which to venture into those interesting details which will, no doubt, reach us by every American mail. Under the old Spanish monarchy, Upper or New California was one of the three provinces composing the Viceroyalty of New Spain. Its settlement, however, was limited to the establishment of some eighteen or twenty "missions" located along the coast, which were dedicated to the various saints whose titles still survive between Francisco and Diego, and which were calculated with a precision and a certainty attainable by none but Spaniards, to render the colonization of the country altogether an impossibility. San Diego, the southernmost of these, and the point where the new American frontier will debouch upon the Pacific, was

---

2. The pen name of a Liége physician who compiled a fanciful and mainly fictional book of travels, written in French and published between 1357 and 1371. It was translated into many languages, and achieved remarkable popularity.

founded in 1769, before which year there was no European settlement upon the coast. Between this period and 1800 were founded the others, all on the same model, and all running the same course. The aspect of the *presidios* was not materially varied under the rule of the emancipated republic.

The Metropolis of San Francisco

When Captain Wilkes landed at San Francisco, he found, at the chief anchorage of this noble port, a "town," of which the constituent elements are thus enumerated:—"A large frame house, occupied by an agent of the Hudson's Bay Company; a store kept by an American; a billiard-room and bar; a poop-cabin of a ship, occupied as a dwelling by an Anglo-American captain; a blacksmith's shop, and some outbuildings." As this is decidedly the most famous colony on the coast, it would be rather perverting the proverb to say "Ex pede Herculem,"[3] but we probably may save ourselves the trouble of describing San Carlos, or Santa Barbara, or La Purissima Concepcion. In these delightful settlements resides the present white population of the province, numbering, perhaps, about 3,000 souls; and some 9,000 or 10,000 Indians, it is calculated, roam abroad in the mysterious wilds of the interior. The whites are true sons of Old Spain, with every thing of a Castilian but his bravery. But for the presence of certain English and Americans, the Indians would infallibly drive them into the sea. After calm observation and mature reflection, Captain Wilkes is compelled to pronounce that "they may be termed cruel to their wives, in a greater degree still to their slaves and cattle, and exceedingly ignorant of every thing but extortion, riding horses, and catching bullocks."

A true Yankee graft upon this valuable stock must yield a wonderful result, and we shall not be long before we see it. We described, lately, the precautions which have been so promptly taken to bring the new territory safely under hand, and it appears that the work of discovery has already commenced.

From the Bowels of the Earth

At present, the great attraction seems rather in the bowels of the earth than on its surface, and hundreds of independent citizens are at work with their pickaxes, like treasure seekers in the Hartz mountains. Quicksilver is the main object of search, and we are told, in a semi-official and perfectly serious report, of one mine, about 13 miles from San Francisco, "so rich, that the gentleman who surveyed it under the directions of the government was so much affected by salivation, that his mouth was sore for a period of ten days after he had concluded the survey." It is anticipated that quicksilver will thus be an article of as regular exportation from the western, as breadstuffs from the eastern coasts of the States; several mining companies are already established, and California is even now spoken of by Transatlantic journalists in that phrase which so attracted Mr. Martin Chuzzlewit, as "one of our most remarkable provinces of our country, sir."

We should rather conceive doubts, from the configuration of this part of the continent, whether the mineral wealth, so characteristic of the great spinal plateau of Anahuac[4] did, in reality, extend so far beyond its termination as to be met with in North California. But, like the young farmers in the fable, who dug for a treasure and discovered it in the enrichment of their farm, which had followed upon the labor bestowed, the Americans will, no doubt,

---

3. From a part we may judge the whole.
4. A geographical (not political) district of Mexico: the great plateau, about 200 miles long and 75 miles wide between 18° 40′ and 20° 30′, in which Mexico City is located.

find their account in the improvement and civilization of this hitherto unproductive country. With territory, at least in places, highly fruitful, a climate free from the noxiousness of the opposite coast, and a temperature not otherwise than equable, they can hardly fail of a return for their labor, and, if they do not discover any New Peru, or any fresh variety of the human race, they will, at least, make a vast tract of the earth's surface subservient to the increasing wants of man.

(NYH, Oct. 17, 1848.)

Gold-Hunting

The Gold Mines in California

From the various accounts that have been received from California, we think there is little room to doubt that that newly acquired territory of the United States is rich, to an extraordinary and almost unparalleled degree, in mineral resources. We were not disposed to place much reliance on the first statements which we got from there, because the finding of gold among the sands of rivers, in such large quantities as were represented, is altogether unprecedented, and we expected the population of San Francisco, who deserted that town and rushed to the auriferous region, would soon return to their usual pursuits, disappointed. This has not occurred. The people of San Francisco are still scattered along the banks of the Sacramento and its tributary rivers, and are as busy as they were at first, in the work of gathering the precious metals.

The Devil Take the Hindmost

Instead of the accounts first received from there being exaggerations, they were, if the intelligence recently received from that country is to be credited, rather within the truth. The excitement in that territory on the subject is increasing, too; old and young, male and female, the lame, the halt, and we verily believe the blind, too, are on their way to the land of promise and gold, cup and tin kettle in hand, to avail themselves of the riches so unexpectedly developed. The men of the sea vie with those of the land in pursuit of the treasure—the occupant of the bench is capsized in endeavoring to outrun the sheriff—the lawyer jostles against his client—the farmer and mechanic throw aside their implements, and there is nothing but a busy, exciting race, each on his own account, and the devil take the hindmost, to reach the gold region first, and to be the first in reaching the rivers, among the sands of which they find the object of their pursuits.

This picture is not too highly colored. It is beyond all question that gold, in immense quantities, is being found daily in this part of our territory, and that every pursuit or trade or business is abandoned. If the product is as great as it is represented to be, and the trouble of gathering it so slight, it will effect great changes in the value of the precious metals all over the world. As yet, we have received no importations of the gold thus gathered; but this is accounted for by the fact that every vessel which anchors in the neighborhood of California is immediately deserted by her crew, sailors being as much affected with the mania as landsmen, and as desirous of gathering the rich material. The value of gold and silver will, of course, fall in proportion to the quantity which may be added to the stock now in the world; and if things remain unaltered in California, they will be within the reach of the poorest before many years. (NYH, Nov. 28, 1848.)

Gold-Hunting in California

The mania for gold-hunting, which seems to have taken complete possession of the Californians, had not in the least abated at the date of the latest advices. The following letter appears in the New York papers:

MONTEREY, SEPTEMBER 15, 1848.

Messrs. Grinnell, Minturn & Co.:

SIRS: I embrace this opportunity to inform you of my situation, which is bad enough. All hands have left me but two; they will stay till the cargo is landed and ballast in, then they will go. Both mates will leave in a few days, and then I will have only the two boys, and I am fearful that they will run. I have got all landed but nine hundred barrels; on Monday I shall get off ballast if the weather is good. There's no help to be got at any price. The store ship that sailed from here ten days ago took three of my men at $100 per month; there is nothing that anchors here but what loses their men. I have had a hard time in landing the cargo; I go in the boat every load. If I get it on shore I shall save the freight. As for the ship, she will lay here for a long time, for there's not the least chance of getting a crew. The coasters are giving $100 per month. All the ships at San Francisco have stripped and laid up. The Flora, of New London, is at San Francisco; all left. You probably have heard of the situation of things here. A sailor will be up at the mines for two months, work on his account, and come down with from two to three thousand dollars, and those who go in parties do much better. I have been offered twenty dollars per day to go, by one of the first men here, and work one year. It is impossible for me to give you any idea of the gold that is got here.

Yours respectfully,

CHRISTOPHER ALLYN.

Captain of the ship Isaak Walton.[5]

(WNI, Nov. 29, 1848.)

San Francisco, winter of 1848–49.

5. A ship of 800 tons that arrived at San Francisco in August 1848 with naval stores from New York.

Gold Fever

California

M. EDITOR: Any person strolling along our docks cannot but be struck with the quantity of merchandise of all kinds, which is marked and being shipped to the new El Dorado—California. I find that nearly a million of dollars worth of supplies have been shipped from this port alone, of which not less than $400,000 have been sent within the last thirty days. In addition to this, we hear daily of outfits from almost every port of any note on the Atlantic coast, as well as from Liverpool and Havre.

(NYH, Dec. 2, 1848.)

WASHINGTON, Dec. 1, 1848.

The Gold Mania—Letter to the Secretary of the Navy from California—Reflections Thereon

The California gold mania is again in the ascendant, and bids fair to depopulate this side of the continent altogether. The accounts of the immense riches to be acquired in this new El Dorado, instead of abating, are every day arriving in a more authentic shape, till even the most incredulous are compelled to believe. . . . The Secretary of the Navy has very kindly permitted us to make some extracts from a private letter just received by him from California . . . written by a gentleman occupying an official position in Monterey, the Alcalde of the place. . . .

MONTEREY, Sept. 16, 1848.

The citizens of California are very anxious for the establishment of a branch mint in this territory. There is very little coined money in the country, and the consequence is they are obliged to sell their grain and wheat at a ruinous sacrifice. . . . The people are obliged to carry their grain gold in their fobs, corners of their pocket handkerchiefs, and in goose quills, for change.

It is calculated that over two millions of dollars are taken out of the mines in grain gold per month—and this sum will be more than quadrupled another season.

The head of the emigrant column for the year has already reached California. They will throw themselves *en masse* into the mines. There will also be a large emigration from Oregon, and also from the Sandwich Islands; and there will be a heavy tide over the Isthmus as soon as the steamers are on their destined track.

Incredible Truth

When the wealth in these gold mines is really known and believed, there will not be wagons and steamers enough that can be spared to bring the emigrants here. You are now all incredulous—you regard our statements as the dreams of an excited imagination—but what seems to you mere fiction, is a stern reality. It is not gold in the clouds or in the sea, or in the centre of a rock-ribbed mountain, but in the soil of California, sparkling in the sun and glittering in its streams. It lies on the open plain, in the shadows of the deep ravines, and glows on the summits of the mountains, which have lifted for ages their golden coronets to heaven.

As an evidence of the facility with which it is procured, let one or two facts suffice. Every sailor that now ships from a port in California gets his $50 per month, and but very few can be procured at those wages. An offer of $100 a month would be rejected by nine-tenths of those now engaged in the mines. They consider their labor there good for $30 a day, and it often realizes them even more. Even the poor Indian, when you talk of hiring him, shakes his bag of gold in your eyes. The consequence is, we have no hired laborers, no servants; every man must black his own boots. This is practical democracy; no theory, no talking about equality. We are all on a level by that great law of circumstances which none can surmount. The rounds of your ladder, it is true, are of gold—but your neighbor's ladder runs just as high. (NYH, Dec. 3, 1848.)

An Englishman upon the California Discoveries

[FROM THE LONDON NEWS OF OCTOBER 12]

We always thought that, if the Spanish race was good for any thing, it was for discovering gold mines and working them. In Mexico especially, from the time of the invasion of Cortez to the expulsion of Rodil, gold-finding seemed the only branch of industry to which the hidalgo race would condescend or would apply; and yet here have the Spaniards been some hundred years in possession of a country where gold is found to be like "flakes of snow," and they saw it not. Jonathan[1] coveted North California simply for its hides and for its harbor of San Francisco; but no sooner does he get possession of it than his keen scent soon discovers the great object of human pursuit—gold.

There appears to be little doubt that considerable quantities of the precious metal have been found on the Rio Sacramento, which empties itself into the Bay of Francisco; and, as may be supposed, the discovery has had a magical effect on the population. The habits of this population and their trade are no where better described than in the graphic pages of "Two Years Before the Mast." It would require

Dana's pen to depict the present metamorphosis.

The coast and its town are deserted of their population. Hide-curers and beef jerkers, padre and hidalgo, the lazy Indian and active Sandwich Islander—men, women, and children have all set off for the Sacramento, with every house utensil that could hold water, to serve to wash earth, for the finding of the precious metallic sediment. Never did pots and pans reach a price: earthenware is worth its weight in silver—a wooden bowl is quite a fortune. A revolution similar to that which has affected the human race in so many European capitals, notably in Paris, Berlin, and Vienna, has befallen California crockery; and whilst printers' devils have become statesmen, and taken to represent in the one, mugs, jugs and porringers have sold and been prized as costly plate in the other.

True Democracy

Indeed, the resemblance might be carried further, the Californian revolution not having been confined to crockery. The discovery of gold in the Sacramento, like that of communism on the Seine, has produced a confusion of rank and a startling degree of equality.[2] The Governor and the mendicant, the Indian and the Don, the conquering Yankee and the subject lepero, stand side by side, up to their knees in the sands of the river, poking, scraping, washing, all intent on the one great object. Meals are neglected, and when had, paid for at a price that distances the Clarendon—vestments forgotten, dignity thrown aside, the

---

1. Often "Brother Jonathan," a generic name for Americans—the equivalent of the term "John Bull," meaning the English. Both "Jonathan" and "Yankee" were originally derogatory terms applied by the English to New Englanders, but both came to mean Americans in general, and "Yankee" was adopted by Americans as a name implying energy and ability.
2. Eighteen forty-eight was a revolutionary year in most of Europe. In France, King Louis Philippe was dethroned and the Second Republic was formed. This was also the year in which Karl Marx and Friedrich Engels published the *Communist Manifesto*—a statement of the principles of modern communism.

comforts and the decencies of life alike lost in the American Pactolus.[3] Even politics have disappeared, and republicanism ceased to be preached for the moment; for two newspaper editors have declared themselves without readers, and have deserted pen and scissor for spade and bowl.

We must hear more of this El Dorado before we bestow upon it serious attention. There are some textures which will not bear many weeks' washing, and the gold mines of the Sacramento may be one of them. It may even happen that this discovery of gold may in the end produce poverty, not wealth. The vessels which are weekly crowding in great number the harbor of San Francisco will get too numerous to export the gold, while they may no longer get the provisions, the hides, the produce which they sought. Old Spain knows well what it is to have a population abandon the cultivation of the soil, in order to wander forth in search of gold, the peninsula having not yet recovered from the effects of that mania. Population, however, will not fail in the Sacramento, for the American press is so busy working the mine of wonder, that we should not be surprised to find the population of whole States migrating over the Rocky Mountains into the fabulous regions of North California. (WNI, Dec. 4, 1848.)

President Polk's Message

[The following excerpts from the president's annual message (the equivalent of our present State of the Union address, given in January) in effect put the government's seal of legitimacy on the California gold discovery; it was now official. There would always be sceptics and naysayers, but the great majority of the citizenry became true believers.]

It was known that mines of the precious metals existed to a considerable extent in California at the time of its acquisition. Recent discoveries render it probable that these mines are more extensive and valuable than was anticipated. The accounts of the abundance of gold in that territory are of such an extraordinary character as would scarcely command belief were they not corroborated by the authentic reports of officers in the public service, who have visited the mineral district, and derived the facts which they detail from personal observation. Reluctant to credit the reports in general circulation as to the quantity of gold, the officer commanding our forces in California visited the mineral districts in July last, for the purpose of obtaining accurate information on the subject. His report to the War Department of the result of his examination, and the facts obtained on the spot, is herewith laid before Congress. When he visited the country, there were about four thousand persons engaged in collecting gold. There is every reason to believe that the number of persons so employed has since been augmented. The explorations already made warrant the belief that the supply is very large, and that gold is found at various places in an extensive district of country.

Information received from officers of the navy and other sources, though not so full and minute, confirm the accounts of the commander of our military force in California. It appears, also, from these reports, that mines of quicksilver are found in the vicinity of the gold region. One of

---

3.   A river in ancient Lydia, in Asia Minor, famous for its golden sands.

them is now being worked, and is believed to be among the most productive in the world.

The effects produced by the discovery of these rich mineral deposits, and the success which has attended the labors of those who have resorted to them, have produced a surprising change in the state of affairs in California. Labor commands a most exorbitant price, and all other pursuits but that of searching for the precious metals are abandoned. Nearly the whole of the male population of the country have gone to the gold district. Ships arriving on the coast are deserted by their crews, and their voyages suspended for want of sailors. Our commanding officer there entertains apprehensions that soldiers cannot be kept in the public service without a large increase of pay. Desertions in his command have become frequent, and he recommends that those who shall withstand the strong temptation, and remain faithful, should be rewarded.

This abundance of gold, and the all-engrossing pursuit of it, have already caused in California an unprecedented rise in the price of the necessaries of life.

The vast importance and commercial advantages of California have heretofore remained undeveloped by the government of the country of which it constituted a part. Now that this fine province is a part of our country, all the States of the Union, some more immediately and directly than others, are deeply interested in the speedy development of its wealth and resources. No section of our country is more interested, or will be more benefited, than the commercial, navigating, and manufacturing interests of the eastern States. Our planting and farming interests in every part of the Union will be greatly benefited by it. As our commerce and navigation are enlarged and extended, our exports of agricultural products and of manufactures will be increased; and in the new markets thus opened, they cannot fail to command remunerating and profitable prices.

The acquisition of California and New Mexico, the settlement of the Oregon boundary, and the annexation of Texas, extending to the Rio Grande, are results which, combined, are of greater consequence, and will add more to the strength and wealth of the nation than any which have preceded them since the adoption of the Constitution. (NYH, Dec. 6, 1848.)

WASHINGTON, Dec. 5, 1848.
The President's Message and California.

The President's message will tax nine tenths of the country newspapers to their very utmost, to print it all in one number. It took up some three hours in the reading to-day, in the Senate, and there were several Senators who sat out the entire reading. What fortitude—what patriotism—what generosity were thus exhibited! . . .

The bill of Mr. Douglass,[4] providing for the admission of California as a State into the Union, does not intend to appropriate the limits of that territory as the boundary of the new State, but to run the eastern boundary along the top of the Sierra Nevada mountains, from which, to the Pacific, there is a breadth of about one hundred miles, more or less, to about four hundred miles long, with the bay of San Francisco in the middle—the Sacramento flowing down into it from the north, the San Joaquin from the south, and between the long valley of these two rivers, thus meeting from exactly opposite directions, between this valley and the sea there is a low range of mountains called the Coast Range, sloping down in sand hills to the sea shore. The basin, therefore, of the bay of San Francisco, comprehending the long and narrow valley of the Sacramento and

---

4. Senator Stephen A. Douglas (1813–1861) of Illinois.

San Joaquin, with the lofty and stupendous Sierra Nevada range on the east, and the low coast range between the valley and the Pacific, comprehends Mr. Douglass's proposed State of California. It also comprehends the water power, the great bay, the fisheries, the timber region, the agricultural alluvion, and the gold deposits of California—all that is worth having, or inhabitable of the territory. The Great Basin, which lies east of the Sierra Nevada, is a blank desert of two thousand five hundred miles in circumference, of mountains, of bald rocks, deep chasms, and burning sand plains; a region which, unless sprinkled over with gold dust, will be uninhabited by white men till the day of judgment. Mr. Douglass can, therefore, afford to throw nine tenths of the territory of California out of his bill for future appropriations.

Meantime, we should like to have some of this gold dust from California assayed and analyzed, to ascertain whether it is mica, or iron pyrites, or gold.

(NYH, Dec. 7, 1848.)

Interesting Despatch from California

Among the documents received by the Secretary of War, and communicated with the president's message, is the following letter from Col. Mason, the military commandant of California, who presents the fullest description we have seen of the gold "placers" of that distant region.

HEADQUARTERS, 10th MILITARY DEP'T,
Monterey, California, Aug. 17, 1848.

Sir: I have the honor to inform you that, accompanied by Lieut. W. T. Sherman,[5] 3rd artillery, A. A. A. General, I started on the 12th of June last, to make a tour through the northern part of Califor-

nia. . . . We reached San Francisco on the 20th and found that all, or nearly all, its male inhabitants had gone to the mines. The town, which a few months before was so busy and thriving, was then almost deserted. On the evening of the 24th the horses of the escort were crossed to Sousoleto [Sausalito] in a launch, and on the following day we resumed the journey by way of Bodega and Sonoma to Sutter's Fort, where we arrived on the morning of the 2d July. Along the whole route, mills were lying idle, fields of wheat were open to cattle and horses, houses vacant, and farms going to waste. At Sutter's there was more life and business. Launches were discharging their cargoes at the river, and carts were hauling goods to the fort, where already were established several stores, a hotel, &c. Captain Sutter had only two mechanics in his employ (a wagon maker and a blacksmith) whom he was then paying ten dollars a day. Merchants pay him a monthly rent of $100 per room, and whilst I was there, a two story house in the fort was rented as a hotel for $500 a month.

Mormon Diggings

At the urgent solicitation of many gentlemen, I delayed there to participate in the first public celebration of our national anniversary at that fort, but on the 5th resumed the journey, and proceeded twenty-five miles up the American fork to a point on it now known as the Lower Mines, or Mormon Diggings.[6] The hillsides were thickly strewn with canvass tents and bush arbors; a store was erected, and several boarding shanties in operation. The day was intensely hot, yet about two hundred men were at work in the full glare of the sun, washing for gold—some with tin pans, some with close woven Indian

---

5. William Tecumseh Sherman (1820–1891), of Civil War fame.
6. The first name(s) for what was soon called Mormon Island. Gold was discovered here on March 2, 1848. It was not actually an island, but rather a sand bar separated from the river bank by an overflow channel. The location is now under the waters of Folsom Lake.

Mormon Island, South Fork of the American River.

baskets, but the greater part had a rude machine, known as the cradle. This is on rockers, six or eight feet long, open at the foot, and at its head has a coarse grate, or sieve; the bottom is rounded, with small cleets nailed across. Four men are required to work this machine; one digs the ground in the bank close by the stream; another carries it to the cradle, and empties it on the grate; a third gives a violent rocking motion to the machine, whilst a fourth dashes on water from the stream itself. The sieve keeps the coarse stones from entering the cradle, the current of water washes off the earthy matter, and the gravel is gradually carried out at the foot of the machine, leaving the gold mixed with a heavy fine black sand above the first cleets. The sand and gold mixed together are then drawn off through augur holes into a pan below; are dried in the sun, and afterwards sepa-rated by blowing off the sand. A party of four men, thus employed at the lower mines, averaged $100 a day. The Indians, and those who have nothing but pans or willow baskets, gradually wash out the earth, and separate the gravel by hand, leaving nothing but the gold mixed with sand, which is separated in the manner before described. The gold in the lower mines is in fine bright scales, of which I send several specimens.

On the 7th of July I left the mill, and crossed to a small stream emptying into the American fork, three or four miles below the saw mill. I struck the stream (now known as Weber's creek) at the washings of Sunol[7] & Co. They had about thirty Indians employed, whom they pay in merchandise. They were getting gold of a character similar to that found in the main fork, and doubtless in sufficient quantities to

---

7. Antonio María Suñol, a native of Spain, who deserted from the French ship *Bordelais* in 1818; the namesake of the town of Sunol.

satisfy them. I send you a small specimen, presented by this company, of their gold. From this point, we proceeded up the stream about eight miles, where we found a great many people and Indians—some engaged in the bed of the stream, and others in the small side valleys that put into it. These latter are exceedingly rich, and two ounces were considered an ordinary yield for a day's work. A small gutter, not more than a hundred yards long, by four feet wide, and two or three feet deep, was pointed out to me as the one where two men—William Daly and Perry McCoen—had, a short time before, obtained $17,000 worth of gold. Capt. Weber informed me that he knew that these two men had employed four white men and about a hundred Indians, and that, at the end of one week's work, they paid off their party, and had left $10,000 worth of this gold.[8] Another small ravine was shown me, from which had been taken upwards of $12,000 worth of gold. Hundreds of similar ravines, to all appearances, are as yet untouched.

Gold in Every Pocket

I could not have credited these reports had I not seen, in the abundance of the precious metal, evidences of their truth. Mr. Neligh, an agent of Commodore Stockton, had been at work about three weeks in the neighborhood, and showed me in bags and bottles over $2,000 worth of gold; and Mr. Lyman, a gentleman of education, and worthy of every credit, said he had been engaged with four others, with a machine, on the American fork, just below Sutter's mill; that they worked eight days, and that his share was at the rate of $50 a day; but hearing that others were doing better at Weber's place, they had removed there, and were then on the point of resuming operations. I might tell of hundreds of similar instances; but, to illustrate how plentiful the gold was in the pockets of common laborers, I will mention a simple occurrence which took place in my presence when I was at Weber's store. This store was nothing but an arbor of bushes, under which he had exposed for sale goods and groceries suited to his customers. A man came in, picked up a box of Seidlitz powders,[9] and asked its price. Capt. Weber told him it was not for sale. The man offered an ounce of gold, but Capt. Weber told him it only cost 50 cents, and he did not wish to sell it. The man then offered an ounce and a half, when Capt. Weber had to take it. The prices of all things are high, and yet Indians, who before hardly knew what a breech cloth was, can now afford to buy the most gaudy dresses. . . .

Gold in Every Stream

Before leaving Sutter's, I satisfied myself that gold existed in the bed of the Feather river, in the Yubah and Bear, and in many of the small streams that lie between the latter and the American fork; also, that it had been found in the Cosumnes to the south of the American fork. In each of these streams the gold is found in small scales, whereas in the intervening mountains it occurs in coarser lumps.

Mr. Sinclair, whose rancho is three miles above Sutter's on the north side of the American, employs about 50 Indians

---

8. Charles M. Weber, a native of Germany, came to California in 1841 with the Bartleson-Bidwell party, the first emigrant party to reach California overland. He founded the town of Tuleburg, which he renamed Stockton in honor of Commodore Robert F. Stockton, who had taken possession of California for the United States.

9. A mild laxative, arbitrarily named for a village in Bohemia where there is a spring impregnated with magnesium sulphate and carbonic acid. One dissolved two powders separately, mixed them, and drank the mixture when it effervesced.

on the north fork, not far from its junction with the main stream. He had been engaged about five weeks when I saw him, and up to that time his Indians had used simply closely woven willow baskets. His net proceeds (which I saw) were about $16,000 worth of gold. He showed me the proceeds of his last week's work—fourteen pounds avoirdupois of clean-washed gold.

The Indians Prosper

The principal store at Sutter's fort, that of Brannan & Co., had received in payment for goods $36,000 (worth of this gold) from the 1st of May to the 10th of July. Other merchants had also made extensive sales. Large quantities of goods were daily sent to the mines, as the Indians, heretofore so poor and degraded, have suddenly become consumers of the luxuries of life.

The most moderate estimate I could obtain from men acquainted with the subject, was, that upwards of four thousand men were working in the gold district, of whom more than one-half were Indians; and that from $30,000 to $50,000 worth of gold, if not more, was daily obtained. The entire gold district, with very few exceptions of grants made some years ago by the Mexican authorities, is on land belonging to the United States. It was a matter of serious reflection with me, how I could secure to the government certain rents or fees for the privilege of procuring this gold; but upon considering the large extent of country, the character of the people engaged, and the small scattered force at my command, I resolved not to interfere but to permit all to work freely, unless broils and crime should call for interference.

Absence of Crime

I was surprised to learn that crime of any kind was very unfrequent, and that no thefts or robberies had been committed in the gold district. All live in tents, in bush arbors, or in the open air; and men have frequently about their persons thousands of dollars worth of this gold, and it was to me a matter of surprise that so peaceful and quiet a state of things should continue to exist. Conflicting claims to particular spots of ground may cause collisions, but they will be rare, as the extent of country is so great, and the gold so abundant, that for the present there is room and enough for all. Still, the government is entitled to rents for this land, and immediate steps should be devised to collect them, for the longer it is delayed the more difficult it will become. One plan I would suggest is, to send out, from the United States, surveyors, with high salaries, bound to serve specified periods.

A superintendent to be appointed at Sutter's fort, with power to grant licenses to work a spot of ground, say 100 yards square, for one year, at a rent of from 100 to 1,000 dollars, at his discretion; the surveyors to measure the ground, and place the rentor in possession.

A better plan will be to have the district surveyed and sold at public auction to the highest bidder, in small parcels, say from 20 to 40 acres. In either case, there will be many intruders, whom for years it will be almost impossible to exclude.

Desertion is Rampant

The discovery of these vast deposits of gold has entirely changed the character of Upper California. Its people, before engaged in cultivating their small patches of ground, and guarding their herds of cattle and horses, have all gone to the mines, or are on their way thither. Laborers of every trade have left their work benches, and tradesmen their shops. Sailors desert their ships as fast as they arrive on the coast, and several vessels have gone to sea with hardly enough hands to spread a sail. Two or three are now at anchor in San Francisco with no crew on board. Many desertions, too, have taken place from the garrisons within the influence of these mines; twenty-six soldiers have deserted from the post of Sonoma, twenty-four from that of San Francisco, and twenty-four from Monterey. For a few days the evil appeared so threatening, that great danger existed that the garrisons would leave in a body; and I refer you to my order of the 25th of July, to show the steps adopted to meet this contingency. I shall spare no exertions to apprehend and punish deserters, but I believe no time in the history of our country has presented such temptations to desert as now exist in California. The danger of apprehension is small, and the prospect of high wages certain; pay and bounties are trifles, as laboring men at the mines can now earn in one day more than double a soldier's pay and allowances for a month; and even the pay of a lieutenant or captain cannot hire a servant.

Astonishing Wages

A carpenter or mechanic would not listen to an offer of less than fifteen or twenty dollars a day. Could any combination of affairs try a man's fidelity more than this? and I really think some extraordinary mark of favor should be given to those soldiers who remain faithful to their flag throughout this tempting crisis. No officer can now live in California on his pay, money has so little value; the prices of necessary articles of clothing and subsistence are so exorbitant and labor so high, that to hire a cook or servant has become an impossibility, save to those who are earning from thirty to fifty dollars a day. This state of things cannot last forever. Yet from the geographical position of California, and the new character it has assumed as a mining country, prices of labor will always be high, and will hold out temptations to desert. I therefore have to report, if the government wish to prevent desertions here on the part of men, and to secure zeal on the part of officers, their pay must be increased very materially. Soldiers, both of the volunteer and regular service, discharged in this country, should be permitted at once to locate their land warrants in the gold district. Many private letters have gone to the United States giving accounts of the vast quantity of gold recently discovered, and it may be a matter of surprise why I have made no report on this subject at an earlier date. The reason is, that I could not bring myself to believe the reports that I heard of the wealth of the gold district until I visited it myself. I have no hesitation now in saying that there is more gold in the country drained by the Sacramento and San Joaquin rivers than will pay the cost of the present war with Mexico a hundred times over. No capital is required to obtain this gold, as the laboring man wants nothing but his pick and shovel and tin pan, with which to dig and wash the gravel; and many frequently pick gold out of the crevices of rocks with their butcher knives, in pieces from one to six ounces.

Incredible Profits

Mr. Dye, a gentleman residing in Monterey, and worthy of every credit, has just returned from Feather river. He tells me that the company to which he belonged, worked seven weeks and two days, with an average of fifty Indians (washers), and that their gross product was two hundred and seventy-three pounds of gold. His share (one-seventh), after paying all expenses, is about thirty-seven pounds, which he brought with him, and exhibited in Monterey. I see no laboring man from the mines who does not show his two, three, or four pounds of gold. A soldier of the artillery company returned here a few days ago, from the mines, having been absent, on furlough, twenty days. He made, by trading and working during that time, $1,600. During these twenty days, he was travelling ten or eleven days, leaving but a week in which he made a sum of money greater than he receives in pay, clothes, and rations, during a whole enlistment of five years.—These statements appear incredible, but they are true.

(NYH, Dec. 8, 1848.)

California and Its Gold

[From the Boston Courier]

If we were disposed to believe half the tales now current respecting the adventures of those of our countrymen who have lately visited the territory of Northern California, we might easily come to the persuasion that another Peru had been discovered. The new region just annexed to the American Union, we are assured, abounds with gold beyond any other territory now known to exist. The soil may be coined into ingots by the acre; you have only to scratch the dirt under your feet, and you are dusted with clouds of the precious metal. Sailors run away from ships on the coast, and ballast their pockets with pigs of the genuine yellow stuff, twenty-four carats fine! No body gets less than some thousands of dollars in an excursion of a week or two to the mines—though indeed we are not told of mines in particular, but are led, by these magnificent accounts, rather to the inference that the country is all gold, and may be chopped up into bars with a broad axe and sent to the mint. The arithmetic of the story is rising rapidly, and has already reached a respectable figure. Fifteen millions of dollars, safely collected, bagged, and tied up, form a part of yesterday's accounts. Tomorrow we expect something that will rise far above this, and make Atahualpa's ransom, or the city of Manoa, a mere eight-penny matter in the comparison.

A Fool's Paradise

We do not wonder that these tales have begun to turn people's heads. Adventurers are starting off for California by the dozen, the score, and the hundred, hardly allowing themselves time to pull on their boots, and put bread and cheese in their pockets. Now, as there is something approaching to a possibility that these enterprising individuals may find themselves in a fool's paradise at the end of their journey, they would do well to ask one another, before they set out, what they expect, and what reasons they have for expecting it. We suggest this to them as an act of common prudence—if prudence can be expected of any body going a gold-hunting.

That there may be gold in California is not at all improbable, but let prudent people be upon their guard. The "golden legend" is as old as the time of the Conquistadores. There have been stories of this description current in California and on the northwestern border of Mexico for two centuries and more. The Indians, it was said, kept the custody of the mines with the most jealous care, and would never allow the whites to approach them. The red men played the part of the red dragon in the fairy tale that guarded the enchanted treasure. The Spaniards, however, were not able to light upon the particular tribe that kept watch over the gold, though they made many expeditions in search of them.

By what magical art or extraordinary good luck our countrymen have been able to discover, in the course of a month, what escaped the avaricious eye of the Spaniards for more than two centuries, we are unable to conjecture, especially when we call to mind the fact that the latter have long been familiar with gold mining, while the American adventurers are deficient in that knowledge, and apply the name of gold to every thing that looks yellow. The barber's basin is easily transformed to Mambrino's helmet by eyes in an ecstasy, always looking out for enchantments.

The Folly of Gold

We observe in some newspapers a great exultation at this supposed discovery of riches in California, as if the value of the territory were immensely enhanced by it. *The last thing that we should desire for the prosperity and permanent welfare of a country would be the discovery of a gold mine in it. Hardly any thing can be more certain to repress industry, productive labor, thrifty habits, and social improvement in general.* The richest mining soils under the sun *are peopled by the poorest communities.* The owners of Potosi and Real del Monte *cannot pay their debts.* Spain and Portugal, after gorging themselves with the gold and silver and diamonds of the Western World, *became the most impoverished, weak, and despised of all the European kingdoms.* The same spectacle is exhibited on a small scale as on a large one. All travellers inform us that the approach to a mining district in South America *is uniformly indicated by marks of poverty and wretchedness—ragged people, ruinous dwellings, neglected agriculture, sloth, ignorance, squalor, dirt, and dissipation.* Lieut. Hardy, who explored a part of California and that portion of northern Mexico bordering on our newly-acquired empire of El Dorado, states that he *never knew a gold-hunter who became rich;* and that even a productive mine was good for nothing except to a rich man, who could furnish capital to work it. California and Mexico have already swallowed so many thousands of pounds sterling, which fine stories, like those of the present day, drew from the pockets of the London speculators. These persons, we trow, will be among the very last to believe the tale of the fifteen millions.

All is not gold that glistens. The first settlers of Virginia sent home to England a shipload of shining earth, in the firm belief that guineas were to be made from it. Of those sanguine adventurers, who are at this moment setting out for California to seek their fortunes among the rocks of the Cordilleras and the wormwood wastes of the Great Salt Desert, probably not one in five hundred could distinguish gold ore from iron pyrites. These explorers will be well qualified to send home stories of Aladdin's lamp!

A Siren Song

How much of this alluring tale consists of plain fact, how much of exaggeration, and how much of pure invention, we shall be better able to judge when some of our eager adventurers now on the start for the land of promise get back again. At present we counsel them to *think twice before they shoulder their packs.* One thing is pretty certain, and it is the only fact that wears the appearance of certainty. These extravagant relations have already produced their effect on the spot, in a manner very little acceptable to the inhabitants. The mania of gold-hunting has swallowed up every other thought and desire. One letter says, "All other business is neglected, wheat is left standing in the fields, houses and farms are deserted," &c. Another person writes, "Flour is worth sixty-four dollars a barrel, and all the necessaries of life command the most exorbitant prices; unless large quantities of breadstuffs reach the country, much suffering must ensue." A fine prospect for new settlers!

If California is to thrive, it must be *by possessing a population of industrious men, who will devote themselves to agriculture and the useful arts.* Let no one go thither with his head full of golden dreams, expecting to find the land one entire and perfect chrysolite. The romance of *El Dorado* cost the Spaniards more blood, treasure, fatigue, and suffering than all their real conquests and acquisitions in the Western world. It is to be hoped that our own times will not witness a copy of that delusion. (WNI, Dec. 9, 1848.)

Comments on the Message

That portion of the President's Message which treats of the Golden Region will be read with thrilling interest. It will set on fire the young men of the country. The Yankee spirit will be aroused, and a rush will be made to this newly discovered Eldorado. If 40,000 young men, lured by the fancied wealth of Mexico, would climb, amid shot and shell, the hills of Monterey, storm the castle of San Juan, brave the pass of Cerro Gordo, with how much more alacrity will they fly to a country all our own, where no peril attends the enterprize, and whose boundless harvests of gold are certified to by the President of the Nation?

What a god-send to that country and to this are these native gold deposits. They are better than all the Wilmot Provisos[10] and newspaper thunder forged by all the political vulcans of the land, to *prevent the extension of Slavery. The slave-holder cannot lease his slaves, thank God, to go there himself, and he dare not take them with him.* His large plantation and niggers is all the property he has, and no body wants to buy either *about these days.* But the Yankee—the free-men of the North, are not encumbered with any such "peculiar" property. They want but a day's notice to dispose of their goods and chattels, shake hands with their friends, and be off. They will appropriate that country to themselves, and in less than two years will claim pre-emption rights to every rood of it.[11] Good. This is right. The *workies,* the men who are not ashamed to earn their bread by the sweat of their brows, are the very ones to own this country. The silk-stockinged, slave-holding gentleman, who never did a day's work in his life, will stand a poor chance in California if he ever gets there.

(CPD, Dec. 8, 1848.)

The Gold Region in California— Startling Discoveries

The Eldorado of the old Spaniards is discovered at last. We have now the highest official authority for believing in the discovery of vast gold mines in California, and that the discovery is the greatest and most startling, not to say miraculous, that the history of the last five centuries can produce.

In every direction vessels are being prepared to carry out passengers and merchandise to California. The steam lines between this city and Chagres, and from Panama to Monterey, will be crowded with passengers of all descriptions, for years to come. The mania for emigrating to California is spreading in every direction, and almost puts down and suppresses the dread of the cholera. Adventurers from every street in the city are concerting measures and collecting funds to pay their passages to California, where they intend to make their fortunes. . . . This mania or madness is only in its commencement.

(NYH, December 9, 1848.)

JIM GRANT GOING TO CALIFORNIA.—Jim Grant, the popular hair-dresser of Ann street, and well known throughout this country, sails to-day for California, and the "gold diggings" in that region. For many years past he has occupied a place in Ann street, where he shaved with much skill, and talked on politics with equal wit and sense. He has resisted all sorts of temptations hitherto, but the California gold fever has carried him off, as one of its first victims. He goes from this city to Chagres, thence crosses the isthmus to Panama, from which port he will proceed to Monterey and San Francisco. Jim has saved a little money during the last few years, which he has laid out in merchandise, suitable for California, and we should not be at all surprised, judging from his energy, skill, and adroitness, to see him return in a few years a *millionaire*, and perhaps a mandarin. Success to him. He is one of the most

---

10. In early August 1846, about twelve weeks after the Mexican War began, President Polk asked Congress to appropriate $2 million to be used to bribe General Santa Anna into ceding California to the United States. David Wilmot, a Democratic congressman from Pennsylvania, proposed an amendment to the bill stating that in any territory acquired in this manner "Neither slavery nor involuntary servitude shall ever exist," a phrase taken from the Northwest Ordinance of 1787. The bill passed the House but was rejected by the Senate, and thus for the time being the question of slavery in California went unresolved.
11. Rood: a unit of land measure; approximately one-fourth of an acre.

honest, trust-worthy, well-doing, and good principled young men, that can go out in any expedition. He is bound to succeed.

(NYH, Dec. 9, 1848.)

WASHINGTON, Dec. 8, 1848.

Ho! For California—Gold! Gold!

When the incredulous apostle saw the prints of the nails in the hands and feet of his master, he believed in his identity—so the skeptic, with regard to the gold stories that come teeming in from Alta California, will have his doubts extinguished in a visit to the library of the War Department. He will there find upon a table a number of glass phials, containing the California gold, and gold washings and pickings in their several varieties, as taken from the earth. Some of the washings are in the form of small yellow scales; some of them have the appearance of black sand, impregnated with shining particles; another variety is of the general color of small pieces of lead ore, with yellow spots over its surfaces; and there are several phials containing lumps of from ten to twenty pennyweights each of pure gold, as picked out of the soil, but looking as if it had passed through the furnace, so free does it appear to be of all dross.

A number of persons have been up to examine the specimens in the War Office to-day, and the gold fever is spreading its contagion even in the city of Washington.

We should not be surprised if, six months hence, there were three hundred thousand able-bodied white men in the valley of the Sacramento.

(NYH, December 10, 1848.)

FOR CALIFORNIA.—HARNDEN & CO. HAVE MADE arrangements to place companies in California. Persons desirous of emigrating, and having a cash capital of over $200, can join an association upon the most favorable terms. Also, those of larger means can avail of an arrangement that will secure them the most important advantages. These joint associations embrace to those disposed to emigrate, not only the most economical, comfortable, and speedy mode, but will probably result in a large profit to each of the members over and above the cost of passage. The association will exclude all who are not temperate men. Apply to HARNDEN & CO., 6 Wall street, New York, and 8 Court street, Boston.

(NYH, December 9, 1848.)

The California Gold Mines

The value of gold, as everyone knows, chiefly depends upon its scarcity. It would be highly interesting to speculate, at length, upon the consequences likely to result from such an influx of gold.

The nominal rise of all commodities, the unprecedented fluctuation in prices, will produce human misery enough to slake even "Satan's own innate thirst of evil."

Governments now on the brink of ruin will be able to pay up their enormous national debts, taking up their stock at par, and strictly redeeming the plighted faith of the State, but reducing the holders of government securities from affluence to poverty.

At the first tidings of the probable depreciation of gold, all the minions of fortune, all the rich whose wealth consists of gold, or in securities which represent gold—such as bank stock, state stock, insurance, canal, railroad, or turnpike stock, or in mortgages or notes, or anything which has a stated value in dollars stamped upon it—will take the alarm and begin looking about for investments which cannot be affected by the appreciation of gold; and then such a scramble for real estate will take place as will make the United States forget 1836.

Those wealthy religious corporations, which heretofore have warily persevered in leasing their real estate for long terms, with covenants of renewal, will find their ground rents, though nominally still the same, inadequate to the support of clerical pomp. This circumstance will recoil upon the salaries of the expounders of the gospel; and then, alas! green turtle and woodcock must disappear from their tables; the lawn of their surplices must give way to plain muslin; the silks and furs of their stylish wives to simple dimity, for the stated yearly salary of a bishop of New York will not procure the amount of commodities which a single donation party now affords to the humble curate of a country parish.

Behold, then, the power of Mammon once exerted for a worthy object, in reducing the ministers of religion to the simplicity of the primitive church.

(NYH, December 10, 1848.)

Money Market

Saturday, Dec. 9—5 P.M.

The California gold fever rages in Wall street to an enormous extent, and fancy stocks[12] have taken an upward start upon the strength of it. Every one is talking about going to California, and all kinds of opinions are expressed relative to the effect upon the present value of property, in the event of the supply of gold from that region proving as large as anticipated. Dozens of ships are fitting out at each port, for the transportation of goods of all kinds to San Francisco; and it is impossible to tell what the existing excitement will lead to. It is likely to increase, rather than diminish, as every account from the gold region will be believed, no matter how much exaggerated. (NYH, December 10, 1848.)

---

12. Blue-chip stocks.

Gold Mania

The California Gold Mania— Its Probable Effects

The gold mania rages with intense vigor, and is carrying off its victims hourly and daily. Preparations for emigration to the land of promise and gold, on the most extended scale, are being made, and ships, freighted with all the necessary articles of life, are being got in readiness at all our ports, and will sail with all expedition for Monterey and San Francisco. The cholera is entirely overlooked in this new excitement, and the gold fever is carrying off more victims than that dread disease. Vessels are about to sail from all the Atlantic ports, and our young men—including mechanics, doctors, lawyers, and we may add, clergymen—are taking leave of old associations, and embarking for the land of wealth, where the only capital required for making a fortune is a spade, a sieve, or tin colander, and a small stock of patience and industry.

Those of our country who rush madly and wildly into the speculation, may be unfortunate in their golden anticipations; but the prosperity of the country at large will be promoted by these discoveries. Commerce, with all its abundant blessings, will be extended to a region comparatively unknown previous to this period. The aboriginal inhabitants of this hitherto wild and uncultivated part of the continent, will become consumers of manufactures; and in return for what they consume, they will give the wealth which they gather from the soil and streams of their country. This addition to the wealth of the world will stimulate commerce and manufactures, here and elsewhere, and especially in this country. The effect of this will be to raise California from a state of nature to a point of industry never dreamt of.

These will be the immediate effects of these grand discoveries in California. But what will be its ultimate effects? That this country will be ruined by these discoveries, provided they are as wonderful as they are represented to be, as old Spain was from a similar state of things, three centuries ago, we do not think. The merchandise which will be required in exchange for this wealth can be furnished by ourselves, on account of our geographical position, on much better terms than any other country could produce them. In this way, therefore, we would be gainers by the discovery; and the settlement of California with an enterprising and active population, together with the facilities offered by the commodious harbors in that part of our territory, and its being incorporated into our Union, would in a short time open a market to us in Asia and China, which has hitherto, to a very great extent, been unoccupied by us, and monopolized by other nations. Let that great mart be brought to our own doors, as it would be by the settlement of California, the building of cities, &c., on our Western coast, and the establishment of steamships on the Pacific, and the trade of those densely populated countries will as naturally fall under our control as that water will find its level. The mediate effects, therefore, of these discoveries, will be to enrich this country in a remarkable degree, and to give full vent to that spirit of enterprise so characteristic of our people. The country will accordingly prosper, in an unprecedented degree, for many years to come; but ultimately there must be a revulsion—a most terrible revulsion—one that will affect countries which are covered with debt, much more than it will this. Property will increase in price, but not in value. The intrinsic worth of a house or a farm will remain the same, because they contribute to man's wants. So with every thing else of the kind. Gold and silver will, however, depreciate, because their only value consists in their scarcity.

(NYH, Dec. 11, 1848.)

[From the NYH, Dec. 11, 1848.]

WANTED—GOLD FROM THE CALIFORNIA GOLD REGION in exchange for Ready Made Clothing, which the subscribers offer for sale at the lowest market prices, from their large and well assorted Stock, at their wholesale warehouse, No. 37 William street, (the largest in the city.) This is a rare opportunity, as one of the firm has a thorough knowledge of what suits the California Gold Region Trade. BIRNHEIMERS, NEWHOUSE & CO.

CALIFORNIA.—A GENTLEMAN, A SCIENTIFIC GOLD AND SILVER Refiner, by profession, with all the implements of his business, and who has been located on a gold mine in Virginia, is open to treat with any persons of capital and respectability, to accompany them to California and the gold regions. Reference as to his ability can be furnished. None need apply to him unless they have the above requisites. May be seen daily at No. 29 Ann street, from 8 A.M. to 4 P.M. N.B.—Gold Dust, Ore, and Sweeps, refined, melted and assayed, and the true value given.

EXPRESS FOR CALIFORNIA—WILL LEAVE ON OR ABOUT THE 16TH instant, via Chagres, Panama, San Francisco, Monterey; also, the Gold Regions and Military Posts in Upper California. Small parcels and packages received up to 10 o'clock on the day of sailing. Two messengers who go out in the steamer will superintend the forwarding of packages to the above named ports. Time through, seventy days. All packages and parcels to be left at S. Woodworth's, 29 Park Row.
    J. W. SULLIVAN & CO.

FOR CALIFORNIA AND OREGON.—THE SUBSTANTIAL AND ELEGANT Steamship Isthmus will leave this port for Chagres and Havana, on Monday, 25th of December, at 12 o'clock. No berth secured until paid for. After cabin in state rooms. Passage to Havana, in saloons, $60; to Chagres in do., $150. Forward cabin—Passage to Havana, forward, $50; to Chagres, do., $100. This ship has good accommodations for 16 deck passengers, and will berth them below and mess them with the crew to Chagres for $65. The passengers by this vessel will connect with the Panama line. For passage, &c., apply to   M. O. ROBERTS, 188 West street.

FOR CALIFORNIA.—THE ADVERTISER, WHO HAS A PERFECT knowledge of the Spanish, speaking both Spanish and English fluently, and who is a good accountant, would like to engage as a clerk, or assistant, with some person about to establish business in California. Address "L. V.," Herald office.

FOR CALIFORNIA—*A Venture*—A gentleman, who will leave Washington on the 1st of January, 1849, for the Gold Regions, makes the following proposition to any person having $500 or $800. He has a life insurance policy for $2,000, (all paid,) permitting him to travel to any place in the world, which policy will be placed in the hands of the person advancing $500 or $800, and in case of death, the proceeds will accrue to the holder. The subscriber will return to Washington in twelve months, and whatever may be realized within the time he may be absent, the holder of the policy will receive one fourth of the amount, and the policy taken up by paying the amount loaned.

Further information can be obtained by addressing X. X., through the Post Office, Washington, within ten days.

P. S. The gentleman is a married man, and will leave his family. He is acquainted with mercantile business and a mechanic, in good health, and can refer to the best citizens for sobriety, industry, perseverance, &c. All that is wanting is the money, and he fully believes that a good speculation is here offered to any person who has the money to invest, independent of the advantage of having a person in the gold region who will communicate with him, and give correct information as to what is represented about that El Dorado of the West.

The Gold Mines of California— Railroad to the Pacific

If the accounts which we are daily receiving from California, concerning the gigantic mineral discoveries in that region, are to be relied upon, the western portion of our territory will, in a few years, rival the Atlantic coast in opulence, in population, the extent of its commerce, and in all the advantages which, to a great extent, are confined to the eastern division of the continent at present.

A great revolution—a wonderful change in the commerce of the world, and especially in that of the United States—will be the immediate result. But we must expedite communication between that distant part of our territory and the Atlantic coast. The trade of Asia and China is, and has been for a long series of years, monopolized by England, and that trade is, to a great extent, an exchange of the precious metals for the teas and silks of that portion of the world. It is carried on with disadvantages which we, from our geographical position, would be exempt from, provided

we availed ourselves of the facilities which the God of nature has bestowed upon us so liberally. We have the gold and silver on the spot, as is proved by the recent discoveries in California. In this respect we enjoy an advantage over England of no common kind; and in another, an advantage of still greater importance—that is, in the facilities which we possess of uniting the eastern and western shores of our territory by railroad.

As matters now stand, we are distant from San Francisco nineteen thousand miles; to all intents and purposes we, in New York, are no nearer to that part of our territory than Liverpool is, for vessels from both ports must double the Cape, thereby encountering the well-known perils of that dangerous navigation, in addition to making the voyage of the duration of from four to five months. By the proposed union, therefore, fully sixteen thousand miles in the distance between New York and San Francisco would be saved; for a railroad from the Mississippi to California, through the Rocky Mountains, by the Great South Pass—which, by-the-way, seems to have been excavated by nature for the express purpose of a railroad from the eastern to the western shore of the American continent—would not be longer than twenty-five hundred miles. It is clear and evident that if this communication were formed, and these mines of gold and silver in California are as prolific as they are represented to be, we would have the means within ourselves of controlling the commerce of the whole civilized world.

We would assume the position which we are geographically entitled to, that of the *entrepot* of exchange and commerce between Asia and Europe, and virtually become the dispensers of the blessings which attend upon commerce to the whole civilized world. The proposed communication would become the great highway of the nations of the earth, all of which would be tributary to us. The United States would then, indeed, fulfill its destiny, and work changes the like of which the world has never dreamt of. Let that communication be made, and the vista of the future would be so stupendously and overcomingly magnificent, that at the bare attempt to penetrate it, the human mind would be paralyzed. Cities, villages, towns, manufactories, ships, steamers, and every other evidence of industry, would start into existence as if by the wand of the magician; the busy land of labor and trade would triumph over the solitude of the desert; the inhabitants of the great East would be as familiar to us as those of Europe are; the wealth of the most extensive markets in the world would be thrown open to us; in a word, as we have before stated, we would become the *entrepot* of the commerce of the whole world; and become the greatest nation of ancient or modern times, to which all others would render homage and pay tribute. (NYH, Dec. 12, 1848.)

FOR SAN FRANCISCO, CALIFORNIA.—THE SPLENDID FAST sailing New York built ship Christoval Colon, Francis C. Coffin, master, will meet with immediate dispatch. For freight or passage, having superior accommodations, apply to: SPOFFORD, TILESTON & CO., 48 South street.
N. B.—Capt. Coffin having had great experience in this trade, will take charge of consignments, and as this ship is one of the fastest sailing vessels on the ocean, an admirable opportunity is now offered to those who wish to visit the gold regions of California. (NYH, Dec. 11, 1848.)

Ho! for California!

The Discovery of El Dorado—Its Position, and its Advantages to the Commerce of the United States— The Way to get there

Already the active and the enterprising, in which our country happily abounds, are in full chase to obtain the earliest advantages the new field offers. From all directions they are pouring in, with vigor and spirit; and the only check which reaches the universal desire to dig for gold, is the want of knowledge and of means to lead them to the spot wherein is concentrated their hopes of future greatness.

For the information of many who purpose going to California, we will state that there are but two routes by which it may be reached with any degree of comfort or economy. Persons desirous of saving time should take what is called the land route, or, more properly, the Chagres or Isthmus route. The Chagres steamer leaves this port monthly, as also do the British West India mail steamers, one of which is now in port, and reaches the mouth of the river in about ten days. Canoes are here employed, and passengers carried thirty miles up, when they are transferred to the backs of mules, and in this way reach Panama in two days, where they will take either a steamer or sailing vessel for San Francisco.—The distance by this conveyance from New York to San Francisco is about 5,500 miles—thus set down:—From New York to Chagres, 2,000, Chagres to Panama, 50, Panama to San Francisco, on the arc of a great circle, 3,440. The whole distance will occupy from 25 to 30 days. The cost of crossing in this way the Isthmus, from the best sources of information, will not exceed $20, being performed, as we have already stated, by canoes and mule carriage. The former will soon give way to the steamer Orus, which has been purchased to run on the Chagres river. Passengers are in the habit of crossing the Isthmus, who take the British line of steamers down the west coast of South America, which seems to establish the feasibility of its being crossed without difficulty. Passengers should provide themselves with the means to guard against contingencies, as they may arrive, from the non-arrival of the steamers at Panama. The greatest difficulty in going by this route will consist in a large amount of baggage; nothing over 150 pounds weight can be carried with safety. The price of passage on our steamers from New York to California, by the above route, first class, is $420. There is a medium class of passengers taken for considerably less, or sailing vessels leaving here for Chagres will take passengers for much less.

The other route we speak of doubles Cape Horn. This is the most acceptable, as far as cost and facilities are concerned, but the loss of time balances the difference in price of passage. Ships are loading in this city for the Pacific, that will take passengers to their destination at from $300 down to $100—the price, in fact, depends upon circumstances and on the accommodations offered.

The distance from New York to California, via Cape Horn, is about 17,000 miles, and will occupy about 150 days. Vessels generally, bound to the northwest coast, touch in at Valparaiso, Callao, or Panama. The only chance to forward or carry goods to California is by ships bound direct; and now that there are so many up, freights are not very expensive. Another new route will be opened in a few weeks, through the Isthmus of Tehuantepec in Mexico. The connection is expected to be made by uniting the navigable waters of the Guasacualce [Coatzacoalcos] to those of the Chimalapa, the former running in the Gulf of Mexico, the latter in the Pacific. The dividing ridge to be cut through is in height 1,375 feet; but the greatest difficulty here will be in securing a conveyance on the Pacific. The terminus of this road is not known by vessels trading on the west coast. The communication with this new route on the Atlantic side will be with New Orleans, principally, and, when completed, opportunities from that city will be frequent. (NYH, Dec. 13, 1848.)

The California Transport

BY MAJOR G. W. PATTEN, U. S. A.
[WNI, Dec. 13, 1848.]

Thy rising steamers kiss the coaxing breeze,
      And day is breaking
Where the cloud hung dark,
      For many a moon thy home is on the seas—
            Fill—and away, thou bark!

Within thy thick-ribbed sides
      Are stores of weight;
The gay robed soldier and the trader plain
      Together crowd thy deck—a motley freight
            Of gallantry and gain.

Some have embark'd full buoyant
      With the dream of wealth
Amass'd by toil of diver bold—rich jewels
      Glist'ning far 'neath crystal stream,
            Hallow'd by legends old.

Tempted are some by
      Tale of shining ore
Hid in the cave of far Francisco's land,
      Or brighter spots on Sacramento's shore
            Sprinkled with golden sand.

Some have gone forth
    Whose roving bosoms burn
To feel the freshness of a foreign sky—
    Of these—of all shall some at length return—
        Some have gone forth to die.

And they are with thee—
    Thou shalt rock their head—
Whose smile is placid and whose voice is mild:
    Deal gently with them on their heaving bed,
        Thou bark of Ocean wild!

Thy wings shall waft thee swiftly
    o'er the stream
Whose constant current moves by
    mystic sway;
Bright isles shall greet thee
    With their dangerous gleam
        Upon thy flashing way.

High on the coast where swift Magellan's tide
    Unites two oceans—mightiest of the sphere—
Strange tawny bands shall
    Pause to see thee glide
        Along thy proud career.

Thy frame shall quiver where the
    mountain surge
Replies in thunder to the monsoon's roar,
And the wild sea-fowl screams the
    sailor's dirge by Patagonia's shore.

And thou shalt sleep, becalm'd,
    till heart shall tire,
Where the Earth's axle shows its least incline,
    While glows the tropic sun with equal fire
        Along the burning line.

Yea! waves shall lift thee,
    wild winds shall sweep,
And Ocean's monsters flash athwart thy way:
    Yet thou shalt cope undaunted with the deep,
        A wrestler stern at play.

Then onward! o'er the far majestic seas!
    Day is breaking where the cloud hung dark,
Columbia's banner flutters on the breeze,
    Fill—and away, thou bark!

HO! FOR CALIFORNIA.—But before you go be sure and call at TENNENT'S Washington Gallery, N. W. corner of SECOND and CALLOWHILL Streets, and get one of their beautiful Daguerreotypes to leave with your friends. Only one dollar, and executed in the highest style of the art.   (PPL, Dec. 20, 1848.)

Gold Mines

Major Noah's Sunday Times says that argument is useless, the people are intoxicated, and he gives it up, leaving them to take experience if they will not take warning. . . . When these golden dreams were first proclaimed, we said a few words about *exaggeration;* and our opinion has not been shaken by subsequent accounts. We doubt not that gold is found in California, and in quantities sufficient to enrich a few and impoverish multitudes. But we do not yet believe that this newly discovered gold region will yield enough in a few years to pay off our national debt, reimburse all the expenses of the Mexican war, change the relative value of the "precious metals" throughout the world, and *Chrœsusize* every one of the multitudes that will now blindly rush to California. This is the hot stage of the fever, producing delirium. Wait, Messrs. Gold Hunters, Messrs. *Midases*, till the cold supervenes, and *then* note well what the patient says. If you do not *then* have some instinctive whisperings about your own auricular longitude, call us no prophet.

The world has witnessed gold humbugs. As Jonathan would say, "*I've hearn folk talk afore neow, and middlin glib tew; but they must talk a little 'cuter to make a fool o' me.*" The discovery of America was a great gold humbug. The Spaniards had the first picking, and got enough to ruin them. But they did not find what they asserted, and the assertion of which half depopulated Spain, big lumps of gold on every foot of American soil. Thousands of thousands rushed to Hispaniola, after that gold of which returning adventurers talked so

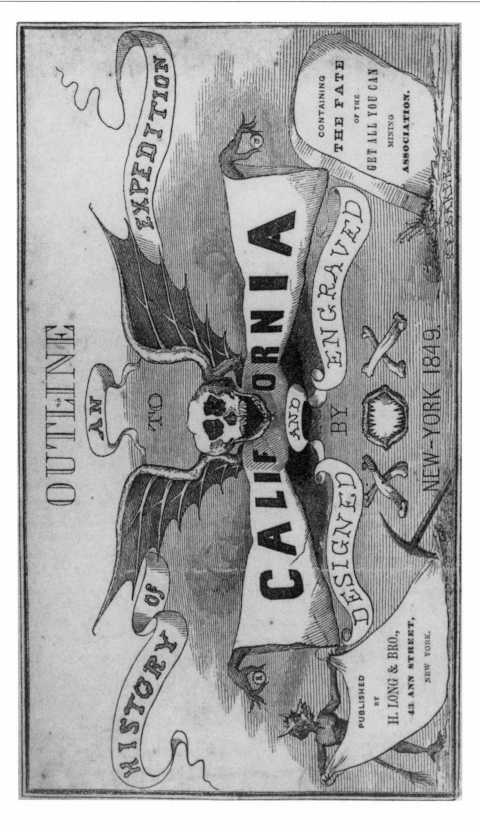

largely; but they never found it. The Portugese followed, and said that all Brazil was gold. But it was not. The first gang of English adventurers to Virginia were lured by reports of gold, but found none. The more sagacious and prudent Dutch went after sugar, coffee, and nutmegs, and grew rich upon them. The Dutch have always been wise enough to steer clear of mines, knowing that the most profitable way of getting gold was buying it with something to supply human wants.

In our days came the gold humbug of North Carolina. Every acre of "pine barren" was a deposit of gold, and some said that it grew there as an annual crop. At least some speculators sowed their land with it, and then sold the "growing crops" at enormous prices. But the crops never grew, for the seed never *came up.* Next followed the gold humbug of South Carolina, a continuation of the last, which raged for a time. Then Georgia entered the field, and bragged and blustered for a time. But Georgia has become cool, and its gold-hunting has ceased to be anything more than a secondary and ordinarily profitable business—when judiciously and economically conducted. Without statistics at hand, we are near the truth in estimating the annual produce from all of our Southern gold mines at $500,000.

But how can we doubt in the face of all this testimony? We do not doubt. We admit that California affords gold. But for all these glittering accounts, we make sundry allowances. The Spaniards, the keenest gold-hunters in the world, have occupied the Californias during three centuries, and yet have never discovered these magnificent treasures lying upon the surface! "Appella, the Jew, may believe it!"[1] This gold was first discovered in digging for a mill-race, near the grounds of Captain Suter [sic] the Swiss settler, on Feather River, a small branch of the river Sacramento. At once the whole population of San Francisco, Monterey, and other settlements rush to this region, and discover that the whole region of the second *lift,* quite up to the Sierra Nevada, or Snowy Ridge, is filled with gold, and that it is all washed from this ridge, which is one vast gold mine. If the whole country, between the plain on the coast and the Sierra Nevada be a diluvial deposit of gold, why has it not been discovered before? Was a spade or shovel never put into the ground till Captain Suter dug for that mill-race? The rude agriculture of the Spaniards and Indians would necessarily have revealed some of this gold. And if it has been found all over the surface, why was not some of it discovered before this digging?

The Sacramento rises in the Sierra Nevada, in about N. Lat. 42, the San Joaquim in the same ridge in about Lat. 36. Both unite near the bay of San Francisco, and fall into it as one. Through this whole distance of six degrees, about four hundred miles, many rivers fall into these two from the Western ridge, the first elevation above the coast plain, and a multitude fall into them from the Sierra Nevada. Now if the whole Sierra contains gold, the metal would have been washed by the union of the Sacramento and San Joaquim, breaking through the first ridge before they reach the bay of San Francisco, along the banks of this union, and along the shores of this bay. But the Spaniards found none of it in the course of three centuries. What then is the conclusion? A gold mine exists somewhere at the head of Feather River, which has furnished these diluvial deposits; they cannot be extensive, and will soon be exhausted. They probably come from some part of the Sierra, and it may contain other mines. But when the diluvial deposits, probably not extending beyond the banks

---

1. *Credat Judæus Apella non ego.* "The Jew Apella may believe this, not I." (Horace, *Satires.*)

Death and the Devil laying a snare to catch subjects. The Devil encircles California with his tail, and from his magic pipe sends forth his emissaries to fill the place with bait.

and meadows of Feather River, are exhausted, mining among the granite ridges of the Sierra Nevada will be like mining in the gold regions of Old Mexico and Peru, not abundantly profitable. The Spaniards, who have been the best, the most scientific miners in the world, leave a proverb. It says, "whoever works a gold mine will be impoverished; whoever works a silver mine *may* make a fortune, though the chances are a against him; whoever works an iron mine will surely grow rich."

We shall next analyze the accounts of Messrs. Mason, Larkin, Colton, and others. (PPL, Dec. 15, 1848.)

The Golden Age

Gold! and gold! and gold without end!
He hath gold to lay by, and gold to spend,
Gold to give, and gold to lend,
    And reversions of gold in future.
In wealth the family revell'd and roll'd,
Himself and wife and sons so bold;—
And his daughters sang to their harps of gold
"O bella eta del' oro!"

Gold and gold! and nothing but gold!
The same auriferous shrine behold
    Wherever the eye could settle!
On the wall—the sideboard—the ceiling sky—
On the gorgeous footmen passing by,
In coats to delight a miner's eye
    With seams of the precious metal.

Gold! and gold! the new and the old!
The company ate and drank from gold,
    They revell'd, they sang, and were merry,
And one of the Gold Sticks rose from his chair,
And toasted "the lass with the golden hair,"
    In a bumper of golden sherry.

Gold! still gold! It rain'd on the nurse,
Who unlike Danae, was none the worse;

There was nothing but guineas glistening!
Fifty were given to Doctor James,
For calling the little baby names,
And for saying, Amen!
The clerk had ten,
And that was the end of the christening.[2]
    (CPD, Dec. 16, 1848.)

Walter Colton's Report

Poor Hood's golden legend of Miss Kilmansegg and her Precious Leg will be recalled, says the Buffalo Commercial, to the minds of many as they read the extracts from Col. Mason's report in relation to the Gold Mines in California. The incredulity with which the first accounts of the extraordinary wealth of that region were received must now give way. . . . These accounts will in all likelihood turn the heads of many who believe that gold is the chief good of life, and induce a great emigration to the El Dorado that the chivalrous Raleigh dreamed of and vainly sought, but which now seems to be found.

To help on the matter we give the following from a letter by the Rev. Walter Colton, late Chaplain in the Navy, and now Alcalde of Monterey. He writes from that town under date of Aug. 29.

"The gold discoveries still continue—every day brings some new deposits to light. It has been found in large quantities on the Sacramento, Feather river, Yerba [Yuba] river, the American Fork—north and south branches—the Cosamer [Cosumnes], and in many dry ravines, and indeed on the tops of high hills. . . .

"At present the people are running over the country and picking it out of the earth here and there, just as a thousand

2. These stanzas are excerpted from Thomas Hood's *Miss Kilmansegg and Her Precious Leg,* referred to in the following story. The poem, subtitled "A Golden Legend," begins: "To trace the Kilmansegg pedigree / To the very root of the family tree / Were a task as rash as ridiculous." And ends: "Gold! Gold! Gold! Gold! / Good or bad a thousand-fold! / How widely its agencies vary— / To save—to ruin—to curse—to bless— / As even its minted coins express, / Now stamp'd with the image of Good Queen Bess, / And now of a Bloody Mary."

hogs, let loose in a forest, would root up ground nuts. Some get eight or ten ounces a day, and the least active one or two. They make the most who employ the wild Indians to hunt it for them. There is one man who has sixty Indians in his employ:—his profits are a dollar a minute. The wild Indians know nothing of its value, and wonder what the pale faces want to do with it; they will give an ounce of it for the same weight of coined silver, or a thimble full of glass beads, or a glass of grog. And while white men themselves often give an ounce of it, which is worth at our mint eighteen dollars or more, for a bottle of brandy, a bottle of soda powders, or a plug of tobacco.

"As to the quantity which the diggers get, take a few facts as evidence. I know seven men who worked seven weeks and two days, Sundays excepted—on Feather river, they employed on an average fifty Indians, and got out in these seven weeks and two days two hundred and seventy-five pounds of pure gold. I know the men and have seen the gold, and know what they state to be a fact—so stick a pin in there. I know ten other men who worked ten days in company, employed no Indians, and averaged in those ten days fifteen hundred dollars each; so stick another pin there. I know another man who got out of a basin a rock, not larger than a wash bowl, two pounds and a half of gold in fifteen minutes; so stick another pin there. Not one of these statements would I believe, did I not know the men personally, and know them to be plain matter of fact men—men who open a vein of gold just as coolly as you would a potato hill.

"A larger party, well-mounted, are following up the channel of the Sacramento, to discover where this gold, found in its banks, comes from; and imagine that near the river's fount they will find the yellow mass itself. But they might as well hunt the fleeting rainbow. The gold was thrown up from the bed of the ocean with the rocks and sands in which it was found, and still bears, where it has escaped the action of the elements, vivid traces of volcanic fire. It often encases a crystal of quartz, in which the pebble lies as if it had slumbered there from eternity; its beautiful repose sets human artifice at defiance. How strange that this ore should have lain here, scattered about in all directions, peeping every where out of the earth, and sparkling in the sun, and been trod upon for ages by white men and savages, and by the emissaries of every scientific association in the world, and never till now have been discovered. What an ass man is with all his learning! He stupidly stumbles over hills of gold to reach a rare pepper pod, or rifle a bird's nest.

". . . A stranger coming here would suppose he had arrived among a race of women, who, by some anomalous provision of nature, multiplied their images without the presence of the other sex. But not a few of the women have gone too, especially those who had got out of tea—for what is woman without her tea-pot—a pythoness without her shaking tripod—an angel that has lost his lyre. Every bowl, tray, warming pan, and piggin[3] have gone to the mines. Every thing, in short, that has a scoop in it that will hold sand and water. All the iron has been worked up into crowbars, pick-axes, and spades. And all these roll back upon us in the shape of gold. We have therefore a plenty of gold, but little to eat, and still less to wear. . . ."

(CPD, Dec. 16, 1848.)

---

3.   A pail or other cylindrical container, having one stave longer than the rest as a handle.

The Disorder of Society

[From the Boston Journal, Dec. 12.]

We publish below a letter from a highly respectable gentleman in Monterey, California, in relation to the gold fever in that place. The writer of the letter [Thomas O. Larkin] has long been a resident of California, and has filled an official station under the United States government.

MONTEREY, California, Aug. 1, 1848.

Dear Friend:—It will be almost impossible for you to comprehend the disorder that now prevails here in regard to every thing except gold digging. Unsaleable goods on hand in the year 1846, now sell with astonishing rapidity, and there is nothing but what finds a ready and quick market. If I had sent home ten months ago $20,000 for goods, I should have soon been able to remit the like sum; but, instead of that, I laid out all my ready cash and more in the purchasing of lands, building of houses, &c., until I now own 20 leagues of land, 100 house lots, and a dozen houses; when, to my utter astonishment, in a few short weeks my property was not worth a cent. Though rich in one sense, I am miserably poor, as my houses nearly all stand empty, and are the source of no income. The cause of this I will briefly relate.

In January or February last, some Mormons digging a mill race for Captain Sutter ... found a small quantity of yellow metal which proved to be gold. This discovery led to others. The news soon reached the town of San Francisco; but for a short time little or no attention was paid to it, even when some of it was brought there for sale. In the month of April the great quantities of this precious metal which came into market commenced to attract the attention of the people in Northern California, and a gradual diminishment of the inhabitants was soon perceptible. On 1st June I was in San Francisco. Mellus and Howard, and some of the largest merchants, had then but about $15,000 worth of this gold; but before I left, Mr. Brannan, a resident of that place, who had been trading at the Placero handed, in my presence, to Mellus and Howard, three bottles containing twenty pounds of gold. From that time onward it has been arriving in large quantities in bottles, phials, &c. About the middle of June I passed over a portion of the Placero, which is supposed to be in extent about 100 by 80 miles; but in my opinion it is far greater, for there is not a direction in which you can go, but what there is gold. It seems almost inexhaustible. At that time there were about 1,600 people, all foreigners,

Monterey in 1848.

working the Placero, which then yielded about $15,000 per day. At the present time it yields about $30,000. As the number of workers has increased, it is not now exclusively confined to foreigners, as a great number of the natives have commenced working, and now may be seen the representatives of almost every country on the globe—even the wild Indian tribes. I think at the lowest estimate the month of July yielded half a million of dollars, reckoning the gold at $16 per ounce.

The valleys of the Sacramento, which but a short time since were hardly known, are now wide and dusty roads. Half of the houses in Monterey are empty, and at least two thirds of those in San Francisco. The hotels and stores have all been closed, and many farms have no occupants whatever. The hotel in San Francisco, however, again opened, under the direction of Robert Parker of New York; but the expenses must be enormous, as he pays his head steward, a black man, $1,700 per year, the second $1,300, and the cook $900. In Monterey, at the present time, there is no place of entertainment, and strangers arriving, and officers stationed here, some days hardly know where to get anything to eat, even without the necessary comforts.

It would have afforded me great pleasure to have had you dine with me on the memorable 4th of July, as we fared sumptuously on bread and coffee, with an Indian in attendance. Many families are without a single servant, and I find it very difficult sometimes to get anything done whatever. There are no mechanics now left in town except one, a blacksmith; and I assure you his forge proves to him a real "Placero," as crowbars and pickaxes are in great demand. There are at San Francisco two or three vessels with only a man on board of each, as the crews have all deserted for the purpose of digging gold. The garrisons here have also lost a great many men, and in all probability will lose many more. I think the towns in the lower part of Upper California must share soon the fate of San Francisco and Monterey, as the whole population are going crazy—old as well as young, are daily falling victims to the gold fever.

From my corridor I can gaze upon the deserted streets of the town, and behold nothing therein but occasionally the fair sex. Every woman who chooses can now find ready employment in making up clothing for the gold diggers, and at a great price. The market now contains nothing whatever, and it is with great difficulty that we can get anything, even the common necessaries of life. Horses command any price, and saddles cannot be bought for love or money, so great is the demand for these articles. I have but two houses occupied at the present time; the rest are as useless as so many piles of stones.

I have a company of three or four Americans fitted out with four or five carts and oxen, and $5,000 worth of goods, provisions and clothing, which are now at the Placero. I fitted out another at my Sacramento Rancho, under the head man and his two brothers. I was to have one third. They started with ten Indians, but at that time I was only able to obtain ten shirts and pants for them, (which, however, they only required on the part of decency, as their bodies had never before made the acquaintance of clothing,) but unfortunately they did not remain but a few days.

There is one party of six foreigners who, since the 15th of June, have worked over 100 wild Indians; they take from 6 to 12 pounds of gold per day. The head man, Chs. W. Weber, told me that his sixth part amounted to over $1,000 per week, which is certainly bright prospects considering that they commenced without capital. . . .

A large portion of the diggers, in the months of May and June, washed from $75 to $100 a day, at $16 per ounce. I have seen many Californians bring to town $500 and $600 in gold, having dug and washed for it less than two weeks. Some persons who commenced working at the time of discovery, by the employment of Indians, now have from $5,000 to $20,000 each. Mr. Dye, a resident of this place, returned a few days since; he was a member of a company who, in the short space of seven or eight weeks, obtained 240 lbs. of gold, clear of all expenses. This company consisted, I believe, of seven or eight men.

No doubt after reading the foregoing you will ask, is this possible?—Is not the writer under a delusion, or been most grossly imposed upon? or is the order of nature in California about changing—all to be rich—none poor? Yet do not doubt, for it is but true, however exaggerated it may now appear. But a little time will elapse before you will be convinced of the truth of what I now write to you in regard to this extensive placer. (NYH, Dec. 14, 1848.)

Song of the Gold Digger

[NYH, Dec. 17, 1848.]
Dig—dig—dig—
To pierce for the golden ore;
Dig—dig—dig—
Till you sweat at every pore.
Dig—dig—dig—
To root in the deep black sand,
And this is to be a citizen
Of a free and a Christian land!

And it's oh! to be a slave
To the Heathen and the Turk,
To rid the hands of a Christian man
From such dirty and toilsome work!

Wash—wash—wash—
Till the back is almost broke;
Wash—wash—wash—
With your legs and your thighs in soak;
Wash—wash—wash—
Revolving an old tin pan,
And wobbling about with a shake and a
   splash,
Till you doubt you're a Christian man!
Soul and body and mind,
Mind and body and soul,
Oh! can it be right when they're all confined
To the basin and the bowl?

Pile—pile—pile—
When it's only a little heap—
Pile—pile—pile—
Till it "graderly" grows more deep—
Pile—pile—pile—
And stow it away in a bag,
Till you gaze with eyes of wild surprise
On the contents of that rag!
Oh! can it be here I stand?
And can it be gold I see?
Ho! ho! I am off for a Christian land
To spend it so merrily!

The Gold Region

After a careful examination of the accounts from the "Gold Region," by Col. Mason, Mr. Larkin, Mr. Colton and others, we ascribe three-fourths to exaggeration, produced by excitement. Each of the narrators seems to have been dazzled, and in no condition to consider sober realities. Col. Mason, who travelled up the American Fork, a branch of the Sacramento, saw gold on its banks, and on those of the tributaries. But all his statements of quantities rest upon the authority of others. *This person told me this, and that person told me that.* Now as all these persons were occupied *digging,* and highly excited, they gave themselves no time for inspecting the operations of each other; and hence neither of them was the best authority for the success of his neighbors. And under such excitement, we must take for granted that great stories would readily start up from trifles, and grow rapidly in travelling. But taking the whole of Col. Mason's estimate, founded upon what he was told, we find an aggregate not very astonishing. Four thousand men are engaged in digging, and obtained $30,000 or $50,000 daily. Assuming $40,000 as the daily average, we find only $10 daily for each man. If then 4,000 men dig incessantly during the 312 working days of the year, the aggregate produce will be only $1,248,000. If the diggers be 40,000, the annual produce will be only $12,500,000. If then 400,000 men dig gold annually for ten years, at this ratio of produce the quantity obtained will be $1,250,000,000. And considering that the present circulating coin of the world is $5,000,000,000, and that the consumption of gold in the arts, since the process of magnetic gilding was discovered, has annually increased, we do not apprehend any monetary disturbance, or enormous augmentation of prices, or depreciation of the precious metals, even should 400,000 men dig gold in California every working day of the next ten years, at a produce of $10 by each. But nobody can dig gold during the rainy season of three months; and 400,000 men will not be employed there; and the diluvial deposits on these branches of the Sacramento will not endure for ten years. If the gold endures for five years, and 40,000 men dig during 210 days of each year, each gathering $10 daily, the whole produce will be only $96,000,000 annually, or $480,000,000 in five years. The coin now in the United States amounts to $96,000,000, and the paper to twice as much. If then the whole of this paper be extinguished, and its place be supplied by gold, the amount of "circulating medium" among us would be precisely equal to the present. And if the remainder of this gold, $288,000,000, should go abroad, as it would, we see nothing very alarming to our own country or the world.

The account of Mr. Colton, formerly a chaplain in the Navy, now *alcalde,* or *mayor* of Monterey, a town of a dozen mud huts, is amusing. At all times a pleasing and fanciful writer, he has become more fanciful than ever through his inoculation with the "yellow fever." After describing the gold region, like Col. Mason, in glowing terms, he says that one man employs fifty "wild Indians" to dig gold, who are astonished at the avidity of the "pale faces" for this "yellow dirt," of which the "wild Indians" aforesaid cannot comprehend the value!! That is enough, Mr. Colton! It stamps all the rest! "Wild" Indians in California! And ignorant of gold! California has been governed by the Spaniards for three hundred years, who have partially civilized the Indians in all of their colonies. For two centuries at least, these "wild" Indians of California have lived by pasturage and agriculture, and not by hunting; and ever since the region has been known in American trade, *hides,* from cattle raised and owned by men under Spanish laws have been its staple commodity. And if Mr. Colton will stray beyond California, and find an Indian on the whole North American continent, *wild or tame,* ignorant of gold, and astonished at the avidity of the "pale faces" for "yellow dirt," he will find something that does not exist. This is a little too strong. Make your humbugs credible, Messrs. Californians! Do not tax credulity too heavily.

Another account tells us that as a party were travelling up the valley of the Sacramento, and stopped a stream to kindle a fire to cook their breakfast, one of them dipped a tin cup full of sand from the stream, washed it, and found at the bottom several lumps of gold, of considerable size. And this is in a region which these keen gold hunters, the Spaniards, have occupied for three hundred years, without discovering these riches!

Then what means all this exaggeration? First, it means that the discovery of diluvial gold, confined to a small region, has intoxicated the whole population of California, as a similar discovery intoxicated the North Carolinians about twenty years ago. Secondly, it means that extensive grantees of land in California want settlers, and know that a gold fever will bring them there by tens of thousands. And when they arrive, they will find that digging for gold, while paying ten dollars for a shirt, and fifty dollars for a barrel of flour, is unprofitable. Having crowded into the gold region, and finding enough for all, they will quarrel and fight; and we shall soon receive deplorable accounts. The last accounts tell us that some of the squatters already begin to talk of *cheating* the Mormons, those standing objects of lawless and cruel aggression, out of the gold which they have already gathered. But the climate and soil are good, the country has the elements of prosperity, and will flourish after the "yellow fever" subsides.
(PPL, Dec. 19,1848.)

HO! FOR CALIFORNIA—GREAT CHANCE FOR SPECULATION!—THE subscriber has on hand 400 pairs well made BOOTS, just finished, within a month, strong and fashionable, the right kind precisely to ship for California, and the kind, too, that are described as selling them at from $10 to $15 per pair, which he will sell at retail for $2.50, or by the dozen at the very low price of $2.15 per pair, thus affording a tremendous profit to the adventurer. They are warranted well made, as we not only manufacture the boots, but also *dress the leather* to make thereof, at my Southwark factory. For sale at the Store, No. 78 N. SECOND ST., between Arch and Race. JOHN T. HOLLOWAY. (PPL, Dec. 20, 1848.)

HO! HO! HO! FOR CALIFORNIA! HO! LAST NOT LEAST!!—PERSONS going out to the gold regions are seriously advised to take, among other necessaries, a good lot of Tombstones. A great saving can be effected by having their inscriptions cut in New York beforehand. These articles can be had in all variety to suit the gold country, at short notice, at the marble yard of
M. R. TAUNITZ, 536 Broadway. (NYH, Dec. 18, 1848.)

Isthmus of Panama

California Gold Region, The Isthmus of Panama

J. G. BENNETT, Esq.:

SIR:—In accordance with your request, I will endeavor to give you such information as I possess on the subject of travelling across the Isthmus of Panama; and I trust that it may prove somewhat useful to such of our fellow citizens as are about to try this route. Let us suppose the traveller once safely arrived at

THE TOWN OF CHAGRES.

This town, as it is usually called, but in reality village or collection of huts, is situated at the mouth of the river Chagres, where it empties into the Atlantic ocean.

It is but a small village, and the harbor is likewise small, though secure. It is formed by the jutting out of a narrow neck of land, and is defended by the castle, which is built on a high bluff on the other side. The village is merely a collection of huts, and is situated in the midst of a swamp—the ground is low, and the continual rains which prevail at Chagres keep it in a swampy condition; so much so, that logs of wood are laid along the centre of the streets, to enable passengers to avoid the deep mud which is always to be found there. Chagres is inhabited by colored people, entirely, with the exception of some few officials at the castle and in the custom-house. Its population, (I speak of it previous to the present influx,) was probably not more than 500 in all, if so much.

ITS CLIMATE

is without doubt, the most pestiferous for whites in the whole world. The coast of Africa, which enjoys a dreaded reputation in this way, is not so deadly in its climate as is Chagres. The thermometer ranges from 78° to 85° all the year, and it rains every day. Many a traveller, who has incautiously remained there for a few days and nights, has had cause to remember Chagres; and many a gallant crew, who have entered the harbor in full health, have, ere many days, found their final resting place on the dank and malarious banks of the river. Bilious, remittent, and congestive fever, in their most malignant forms, seem to hover over Chagres, every ready

Chagres from the Anchorage.

to pounce down on the stranger. Even the acclimated resident of the tropics runs a great risk in staying any time in Chagres; but the stranger, fresh from the North and its invigorating breezes, runs a most fearful one.

ACCOMMODATIONS FOR TRAVELLERS

are scanty and inferior indeed, unless the place has altered very much of late. There are no accommodations, as it has always been the rule for passengers to hurry up the river without even stopping an hour among the huts; and this brings us to the

RIVER JOURNEY,

which is performed in canoes, propelled up the stream by means of poles. There are two points at which one may land, viz: the villages of Gorgona and Cruces. The distance from Chagres to the first named is about 45 or 50 miles—to the latter, some 50 or 55 miles. The traveller, who for the first time in his life embarks on a South American river like the Chagres, cannot fail to experience a singular depression of spirits at the dark and sombre aspect of the scene. In the first place, he finds himself in a small canoe, so small that he is forced to lay quietly in the very centre of the stern portion, in order to prevent it upsetting. The palm leaf thatch (or *toldo*, as it is termed on the river) over his portion of the boat, shuts out much of the view, while his baggage, piled carefully amidships, and covered with oiled cloths, *encerrados* as they are termed, is under the charge of his active boat man, who, stripped to the buff, with long pole in hand, expertly propels the boat up stream, with many a cry and strange exclamation. The river itself is a dark, muddy, and rapid stream; in some parts quite narrow, and again at other points it is from 300 to 500 yards wide. Let no one fancy that it resembles the bright and cheerful rivers which are met with here at the North. No pleasant villages adorn its banks—no signs of civilization are seen on them; nothing but the sombre primeval forest, which grows with all the luxury of the tropics down to the very mar-

gin of its swampy banks; and the mangrove, and all the tribe of low bushes, which love to luxuriate in marshy grounds, fringe the sides of the river, affording a most convenient place of resort for the alligators, with which the marshy country swarms. The sensible traveller, however, who remains quiet in his boat and makes no adventurous visits on shore, is perfectly safe from any harm from these animals, or the small panthers, monkeys, and deadly snakes with which the country on each bank of the river abounds. But those adventurous spirits who, here in New York, talk of landing on the banks and shooting game enough for their provisions, will find the thing to be impossible; as, even if they were to succeed in crossing the marshy banks onto firm ground without suffering from the alligators, they would find the forest so thick and tangled as to forbid further passage, and lucky indeed would they be if they got back to their boat unharmed by snakes or other poisonous reptiles.

The journey to Cruces or Gorgona is not a long one. Of course its length depends on the heaviness of the boat, and the number of hands poling it up. A light canoe, with two active boatmen and but one passenger in it, will reach Cruces in ten or twelve hours, whilst a heavier one might require thirty-six hours to accomplish the passage. The passenger must take his provisions with him, as none are to be had on the river, and a good water filter will be found a great convenience, as the river water is so muddy that it is apt to derange the bowels, unless filtered in some way before drinking it. In view of the great and sudden influx of passengers to Chagres at the present time, it is impossible to say how they will all be accommodated with canoes, and what the river journey will cost. In former times the supply of canoes was quite limited, and the charge depended on the celerity with which the journey was performed. A doubloon ($16) was the lowest charge for a single passenger, and from that up to two, three, and even four doubloons. As for taking out boats from here, and rowing them up the river, I should think it would be a hopeless attempt. Hardy boatmen from our southwestern States, who are accustomed to a much similar mode of travel on their rivers, would probably be able to accomplish it; but in that burning and unhealthy climate, for young men fresh from the North, unacquainted with the dangers of such navigation, and all unacclimated, to attempt such a feat would be madness indeed. Let us, however, suppose the journey completed, and our adventurers safely arrived at

CRUCES.

He may now congratulate himself on his having achieved the most toilsome part of his journey, and but twenty-one miles of land route intervenes between him and the glorious Pacific Ocean. Cruces is a small village situated on a plain, immediately on the banks of the river, which here are high and sandy. Gorgona, the other landing place, is a few miles below Cruces, and is likewise a small village, very similar to Cruces—in fact, all South American villages resemble one another very much. From these two points, both about the same distance from Panama, there are roads to that city, which roads unite about nine miles from it. Starting from either point he commences his

JOURNEY ACROSS THE ISTHMUS.

The usual method of performing it is on horse or on mule-back, with another mule to carry the baggage and a muleteer who acts as guide. The road is a mere bridle path, and as the rains on the Isthmus are very heavy, and there is more or less of them all the year round, the mud-holes and swampy places to be crossed are very numerous. Those who here in New York talk gaily of a walk across the Isthmus, as if the road were as plain and easy as some of our macadamized turnpikes, would alter their tone a little, could they see the road as

it is. As for shooting game on the route, the same difficulties present themselves as on the river, viz: the wild beasts and reptiles with which the bush, or *monte*, as it is there termed, abounds, besides the great risk of losing oneself in the woods. Certainly wild pheasants, guinea-hens, parrots, macaws, and a variety of splendid birds, unknown in these latitudes, do abound in the wilds there; but the difficulties in hunting them are such as to make it impossible for any save the native Indians to follow it with any success. The most rational, and, indeed, the only safe plan for the stranger to pursue, is to carry his provisions with him. That is the plan universally adopted by the natives, who would look on any one as insane were he to propose to depend on chance game for his meals on the journey. Ham, biscuit, sausages, preserved meats, and such kinds of portable provisions, are the best to carry. As for walking from Cruces to Panama, in case mules are scarce, the feat is by no means impossible, provided the traveller arrives in Cruces in good health, and has but little baggage. It might easily be done with the assistance of a guide; but let no stranger, unacquainted with the language and new to such countries, attempt it without a guide. Having then started from Cruces, either on horse or on foot, after a toilsome journey of some eight to ten hours, the savannah of Panama is at last reached, and the sight of the broad and glittering Pacific ocean, and the white towers of the Cathedral of Panama, which are seen at the distance of about four miles from the city, give the now weary traveller assurance that his journey will shortly end; and another hour's toil brings him to the suburbs of the famed

CITY OF PANAMA.

He will find, however, that with this, as with most other South American cities,

"'Tis distance lends enchantment
   to the view,
And clothes the mountain
   with an azure hue."[1]

The city of Panama is situated on the shores of the bay of that name, and a most beautiful bay it is, too.

THE HEALTHINESS OF PANAMA

is far greater than that of Chagres. With due care, avoiding all excesses and the night air, a person can preserve his health; still, the heavy rains and continual damp atmosphere render it necessary to take every precaution.

And now, having taken the traveller for California across the Isthmus, let me conclude by giving a word of advice.

If he has a passage engaged through to San Francisco, the Isthmus route is decidedly the quickest, and, all things considered, the least weary.

But—and I speak now more particularly to those who have but a limited amount of funds—just sufficient to carry them through to San Francisco without any stoppages—let these travellers beware how they try the Isthmus, if they have only engaged passage as far as Chagres. After their toilsome journey to Panama—if they escape delay and fever at Chagres—they may have to wait weeks for a passage to San Francisco, and when the long wished for opportunity occurs, they will find themselves unable to take it, as their expenses in Panama will have exhausted their means. Thus, situated in a strange, unhealthy country, moneyless and friendless, their spirits depressed by their situation, it requires no prophet to predict a heartrending termination to their golden schemes. Trusting that many of this class of passengers will pause and reflect ere they place themselves in such an unfortunate position, I am, sir, your most obedient servant. New York, Dec. 17, 1848.

VIATOR   (NYH, Dec. 18, 1848.)

The Boys Leaving from the East

The golden calf was never more devoutly worshipped by the Israelites under Moses than it is now in New York, Philadelphia, Baltimore, and other places. A letter written in New York says:

"No pen can describe the excitement that pervades all classes of citizens on the subject of California mines. The literary men have taken the fever in its most virulent form. No less than three writers for the press have informed me to-day that they will leave for San Francisco within two weeks. Clerks are throwing up their situations, lawyers abandoning the courts, doctors giving up their practice, merchants winding up their affairs, preparatory to leaving for the gold 'diggins.' Ships are fitting out rapidly for the land of promise. Eleven are advertised in this morning's papers to sail 'with despatch.' There will be no lack of provisions in California six months hence. George Law, Esq., the great steamboat proprietor, has issued proposals, offering to take out emigrants for $100 each, under certain conditions.

(CPD, Dec. 20, 1848.)

SPANISH LANGUAGE—SPANISH LANGUAGE SO NECESSARY TO persons going to California, taught by a lady, who will devote her whole attention to persons desirous of acquiring this language in a short space of time. Address, by letter, Panama, Herald Office.

---

1. Correctly, the last two lines are: "And robes the mountain / in its azure hue."
   (Thomas Campbell, *Pleasures of Hope.*)

HO! FOR THE GOLD REGIONS! GREAT BARGAINS IN DRY GOODS AND shoes! The subscriber, having some idea of emigrating to the gold regions, will commence from this day to run off his stock of Dry Goods at uncommonly low prices, for cash only. I have a good stock of Domestic Goods, among which are—
Brown cottons, yard wide, for 5 cents
Bleached ditto from ¼ cents up
5,000 yards Prints, from ¼ cents up
Tickings 6 cents, red, yellow, and white Flannels, 12 cents
Linsey 10 cents, Cassinets[2] from 25 cents up
Together with an endless variety of cheap Goods, to which I invite the attention of purchasers who wish to save 25 per cent. Call early, as I wish to be off in the first boat.   T. B. BROWN, 7th street, near Northern Market. (WNI, Dec. 21, 1848.)

CALIFORNIA GOLD—PFEIFFER AND FRANCKE, MANUFACTURERS OF jewelry and watches, No. 35 Courtlandt street, would inform the trade and public in general, that they have made up a large assortment of fine and fashionable jewelry, out of California gold, for the present holidays, which they offer to the trade and their friends at the lowest wholesale prices. N. B.—C. F. Pfeiffer, watchmaker, formerly 168 Broadway.

[From the New London Star, Dec. 16.]

We are permitted to make the following extracts from a letter received by a gentleman in this city, last evening, from his friend, a young man of respectability at California:—

San Francisco, August 17, 1848.

I take the first opportunity to inform you of my safe arrival here, last Sunday, the 13th inst., after a passage of 29 days from the Sandwich Islands. Instead of finding San Francisco a warm, pleasant climate, as I expected to, I find it a bleak, cold, and barren soil. The whole appearance of the place, at first, is unfavorable; but it is very healthy, and I never enjoyed better health in my life than since my arrival in this section of country.

There are about 1,000 buildings in the town of San Francisco, which are mostly small. There is but little work doing here now, as almost every body has left and gone to the gold mines, where they are making their fortunes. . . . I intend to stop here a short time only, but proceed to the gold mines, where I shall remain until I line my pockets with the precious metal. When I left New London you had some idea of coming to California during the next season. You can do well if you come— if you conclude to, start in the spring and come by land, bringing with you money enough to pay your necessary expenses, together with some good substantial clothes, your gun, &c. The news of peace was declared here last Friday, and the inhabitants had a regular blow-out. The country is in a very unsettled condition, and club-law seems to be the law of the land at present. Every one deems it necessary for his personal safety to furnish himself with a good brace of pistols. I am at

---

2. An invented word, borrowed from 'cassimere,' which is itself a variation on 'Cashmere.'
    A cassinet is a garment made from a combination of cotton and wool, or of wool and silk.

present stopping with a young gentleman, in the house (or what you would call a shanty), the door of which has been pierced with a ball, which, a short time since, sent a man to his long home. But do not be frightened—there are many good and respectable people living here, and I find no difficulty.

[From the Albany Argus, Dec. 16.]

We have been favored with an extract of a letter from Mr. Beattie, one of the Albanians in the California regiment, which we publish below:—

San Francisco, California, August 22, 1848.

We have just arrived this morning from Sonoma, and expect to be discharged from the service in about three days. . . . I have been offered the appointment of Sheriff for the district of Sonoma, and I think I shall accept it for a short time.

We are all making preparations to go to the gold region, where I expect to get at least $10,000 worth of gold before I return home. . . . I shall be in old Albany in eighteen months, if nothing happens.[3]

[From the Baltimore American, Dec. 16.]

The following extract from a letter, dated at San Francisco, 12th October, 1848, from John M. Finley, Esq., will prove interesting to his numerous friends.

I am selling off slowly the heavy part of my cargo, viz, brown shirting, ticks, kremlins, stripes, duck, Russia sheeting, hardware, &c.[4] All these articles are wanted. The attention of the whole population is entirely devoted to the gold region. They are going to and fro continually, taking up goods and bringing down gold dust in payment for their purchases. Much sickness prevails, and many die—as

much from want of medical attention and good nursing as from disease; but the truth is they are so entirely absorbed by the mania for gold that they care nothing for comfort, and submit to every privation.

[From the Albany Atlas, Dec. 16.]

Expeditions for California are organizing at Boston, Plymouth, Salem, Newburyport, Providence, Bristol, Hartford, Windsor, New Haven, Albany, Buffalo, Brooklyn, Troy, New York, Newark, Philadelphia, Pittsburgh, Baltimore, Washington, and New Orleans.

Every village in the north and west has its aspirants, who eagerly await the first chance of emigrating to the promised land. The emigration to the new territories is only limited by its present cost. It is perhaps fortunate that there is this regulator to the feverish uneasiness of the public.

The *Syracuse Journal* says that the "gold mania" is making considerable progress in that city. It will, doubtless, carry off many victims. (NYH, Dec. 18, 1848.)

The Consuming Fever

SENECA FALLS, Dec. 18, 1848.

The gold fever runs ahead of the cholera, by tens of thousands, in this district. A perfect diarrhœa of emigration threatens to bring down all Western New York upon the torrid zone, and thence transmit its excited inhabitants to California. The days of the crusades are revived; "the days of chivalry" are not gone; and hundreds of thousands of the "humble dwellers upon earth" will, in a short time, have quitted homes, wives, fathers, and children, to wander off over the snowy Cordilleras to El Dorados of Western America.

If the excitement in other portions of

---

3. Belden Beattie arrived in California in 1847 with Stevenson's Regiment of New York Volunteers. He died at San Francisco in 1849.
4. "Kremlins" is a borrowing from crinolines: a variety of strong linen. "Russia sheeting" is also a strong linen, unbleached, used in garments, towels, and embroidery.

the country only approximates to the intensity of feeling in this region, something must be done by Congress to protect the populating of these "old free States." Every individual in our village—and it is an enthusiastic vicinity—has been seized by this deep, consuming fever. The aged almost curse the feeble limbs which refuse to perform the duties of their physical calling. Youth cannot contain itself within the ordinary bounds of prudence and foresight. No thought of danger, or death to be met with in myriad shapes, far off in a distant land, by the shores of the Pacific, deters it from bright hopes and golden anticipations. Married men deprecate connubial bliss, and the fond relations incurred by the commission of matrimony. But the plague spot does not stop when it has wandered up to the boundaries of virility—the ladies, God bless 'em (as the fourth of July toast always says), participate in this all-absorbing, all-engrossing contemplated occupation. Woman smiles upon the undertaking; the inference is easy—it must consequently succeed.

A Region of Ferment

You know we have always been somewhat given to a diverted state of mind in this peculiar locality, giving birth to, or violently supporting, every new light, moral, political, religious or otherwise, that has made its appearance during the last twenty years. The mourners of the sainted Captain William Morgan were more melancholy here than in any other hot-bed of anti-masonry. Land speculation raged in our midst, from 1830 until 1838, to a fearful extent. In 1840, old Tip[5] rendered the whole village slightly inebriate, which transgression had to be atoned for by a regular temperance penance in 1841. The "original Mormons" first commenced their labors in this interesting neighborhood—whilst a respectable number of faithful Millerites continue to this day looking forward hourly to the desirable season of the millennium.[6]

But it was reserved for the summer of 1848 to complete the great moral triumph that we have always been gaining. Friend Lucretia Mott, of Philadelphia, that clever but saucy nigger, Frederick Douglass, the Hon. Ansel Bascom, and a highly talented lady of our village, called a convention, and struck boldly for the great cause of women's rights, as they are, in some particulars, understood and enunciated by

---

5. A reference to William Henry Harrison (1773–1841), ninth president of the United States. In 1811 Harrison, leading an army of approximately 1,100 men, defeated the Indians at the Battle of Tippecanoe, on the Wabash River in Indiana. His victory, twenty-nine years later, got him elected president. He was a great hero, known as "Old Tippecanoe," and was a victorious candidate running on the slogan of "Tippecanoe and Tyler too." He died one month after he was inaugurated.

6. This humorous editorial in the Syracuse newspaper is simply telling the plain truth. The people of central New York state were remarkably susceptible to every religious notion and 'ism' that came down the road. Joseph Smith, the founder of Mormonism, published the Book of Mormon in 1830 at Palmyra, New York. Millerites were the followers of William Miller, who predicted the Second Coming of Christ, and even had the exact date—October 22, 1843. His followers, by the thousands, sold their worldly goods, donned the appropriate robes and—in order to reduce their travel time to heaven—awaited the Second Coming on high places, such as hilltops, roofs, haystacks. Both the antimasonry movement and the temperance movement got their starts in the region, which was dubbed with the well-earned sobriquet of "The Burned-over District."

Fanny Wright, and the Hon. Philosopher Greeley, of bran bread memory.[7] But all the feeling upon the sundry subjects of anti-masonry, land speculation, Tippecanoe, temperance, Mormonism, Millerism, free soil, women's rights, was nothing to the tornado of excitement now caused by this new discovery of America. When matters all come to a focus, and our daring treasure hunters are ready to decamp for the field of their future labors, I shall give you a more minute account of the plans and arrangements of our bold *voyageurs.*

(NYH, Dec. 21, 1848.)

Gold

Admitting all that has been reported of the gold regions of California to be true to the utmost, all sober-minded men must nevertheless regard it, in a national view, as rather a misfortune than a source of congratulation. Visions of golden sands and precious masses are filling, and it may be said fevering the minds of thousands, and if the epidemic continues we expect to find them soon abandoning the plough and the work-bench, the fundamental sources of a nation's prosperity, for that wealth which "perishes in the using." As far as our experience of history runs, no nation which abounded in gold was ever distinguished for one solitary characteristic of true greatness, or of that which is more estimable, true happiness. There are some axioms connected with this subject, of which the following are worthy of consideration:

The desire for sudden wealth is always morally injurious, and operates as an effectual check to ordinary industry.

Great wealth, suddenly acquired, is seldom beneficial to the possessors or their children.

The plough and spade, employed in agriculture, are the surest and most effectual gold diggers.

All history, as well as gospel, informs us that the best form of human happiness is to be found in moderated desires, industrious and virtuous habits, in the fear of God, and in the disposition which induces us to lay up our treasures in heaven, and not on earth.[8]—*Norfolk Herald.*

(WNI, Dec. 21, 1848.)

CALIFORNIA—UNITED STATES RIFLES, WELL ADAPTED FOR USE in that country; also, Allen's patent six barreled Pistols, for sale singly or in quantities by H. F. COOPER, 178 Broadway.   (NYH, Dec. 27, 1848.)

---

7. Lucretia Mott and Elizabeth Cady Stanton (the "highly talented lady of our village") convened the first woman's rights convention in the United States, in Seneca Falls in July 1848. Frederick Douglass, the renowned orator, journalist, and prime figure in the anti-slavery movement was also at the convention. Ansel Bascom, of Seneca Falls, supported equal voting rights for blacks, but couldn't quite bring himself to support women's suffrage. Fanny (Frances) Wright, a native of Scotland, was a radical leader, a powerful lecturer, and an author in the long drive toward social justice: women's rights, abolition of slavery, educational reforms, etc. Horace Greeley, founder and publisher of *The New York Tribune,* was also a crusader for progress in social welfare. He had a tendency to enthusiastically support various radical causes, including those connected with food, drink, and diet. The "bran bread" was actually graham bread, developed by Dr. Sylvester Graham as a health food—still in existence as Graham crackers.
8. "Lay not up for yourselves treasures upon earth, where moth and rust doth corrupt, and where thieves break through and steal: / But lay up for yourselves treasures in heaven." (*Matthew 6:19–20.*)

CALIFORNIA—PERSONS FITTING OUT FOR CALIFORNIA, AND WHO are in want of Tobacco, either for speculation or private use, are respectfully invited to call at our store and examine a new description of tobacco, put up expressly for the Californian market. It is put up in half pound slabs, with tin envelopes to protect it from dampness, and packed in convenient sized packages. It is warranted to resist the decaying effects of a six months' voyage; and it is confidently believed to be the only kind of Chewing Tobacco, either Cavendish or fine cut, that will stand a voyage to California. The attention of shippers is invited to the above. JOHN ANDERSON & Co., 106 Broadway, corner Pine st.   (NYH, Dec. 21, 1848.)

$130 TO CALIFORNIA, AND FOUND.—THE CALIFORNIA MUTUAL Association, having purchased the splendid ship Panama, have resolved upon taking a few passengers at the above price. —The Panama is a first class ship of 200 tons burthen—an exceedingly fast sailer, and will positively leave between the 1st and 5th of January. Application for passage or freight (which will be taken extremely low) to be made to the President of the Association, 11 Spruce street, up stairs.
     (NYH, Dec. 21, 1848.)

THE EMIGRANT'S GUIDE TO THE GOLD MINES, PUBLISHED THIS morning, and for sale by all the booksellers in town and country, Three Weeks in the Gold Mines, or adventures with the Gold Diggers of California, in August, 1848, together with advice to emigrants, and full instructions upon the best method of going there, living expenses, &c., and a complete description of the country, with a Map and four illustrations. By Henry I. Simpson, of the New York Volunteers. This work gives a vivid and life-like description, not only of Gold Digging, but of entire California. There are four illustrations of the Digging of Gold, from drawings made on the spot, and a map which not only shows the entire country, but all of the routes which lead to it. In short, this work possesses every possible information relating to the Gold Regions and how to get to them. Price, with the map, 15 cents. Enclose this sum in a prepaid letter directed to JOYCE & CO., 40 Ann street, New York, and it will be sent you by mail. Price without the map. 12½ cts.   (NYH, Dec. 21, 1848.)

CALIFORNIA AND ITS MINERAL WEALTH.—MERCHANTS AND traders that are about starting to the above El Dorado, the subscriber would advise them to purchase a lot of shirts which he has manufactured expressly for that market; and they may rely upon the fact, that nothing would pay them a handsomer profit than the above article. Call and judge for yourselves. Cheap for cash.
     M. WILSON, 83 William street, cor. Maiden Lane.
N. B.—A large assortment of Canton Flannel shirts and under drawers, constantly on hand.   (NYH, Dec. 21, 1848.)

FOR CALIFORNIA.—THE SPLENDID COPPER FASTENED AND newly coppered Packet Ship Orpheus, will sail for San Francisco on the 15th of January, positively. The above ship is built of live oak and of immense strength, and is notorious as a very fast sailer; has made the passage to Liverpool in 13½ days, and to Cork in 11 days, and will no doubt make the passage to San Francisco from 30 to 60 days before vessels sailing at the same time. A limited number of passengers only will be taken. No passage secured till paid for. For passage and for 500 barrels of freight apply to
SAMUEL L. TRACY, 27 Old Slip, corner Front, up stairs. (NYH, Dec. 27, 1848.)

GOLD WASHERS AND TEST PANS.—THE UNDERSIGNED HAVING had considerable experience at the Dahonega mines, Georgia, having overseed 150 hands on the celebrated Calhoun mine, can furnish sample and practical means for collecting and washing gold; he can furnish the old plan of cradles, rockers, and the plan of using hides; but he offers some decided improvements in machines for companies of six, twelve or more, with an easy worked and most efficient hand water power. He offers for individuals alone, a beautiful, efficient, simple, and portable apparatus, combining a set of sieves, a washer, and means for collecting the flour gold dust by mercury; all of which weighs about 5 lbs., and can be packed in a knapsack. Please call and see the above at the office of the Diaphragm Filter, 349 Broadway, corner of Leonard street. WALTER M. GIBSON. (NYH, Dec. 27, 1848.)

GOOD LIVING ON THE WAY TO CALIFORNIA.—WELLS, MILLER & PROVOST, apprises emigrants and shippers to California and elsewhere that they have constantly on hand an extensive variety of preserved provisions, such as roasted meats, poultry, soup, vegetables, fish, lobsters, oysters, clams, &c. These provisions are put up in canisters holding one and two pounds each, and retain perfectly their natural flavor and nutritious qualities for twenty-one years in any climate. Canisters are constantly kept open in their office for the inspection of purchasers, and none sold except for those of their own manufacture, which are in all cases warranted to keep. Every variety of pickles, preserves, brandy fruits, jellies, jams, sauces, catsups, &c., put up in packages for exportation. Catalogues may be had at their warehouse, No. 217 Front street. (NYH, Dec. 27, 1848.)

CALIFORNIA.—A PROFESSOR OF LONG EXPERIENCE IN TEACHING the languages, wishes to open a course of Spanish for those persons who are desirous of departing for California. He can devote two hours of the morning and two in the evening, so as to render his pupils capable of understanding this beautiful language in a very short time, by the Oral Method. Terms moderate. Apply at No. 47 Bond st. DON PEDRO. (NYH, Dec. 21, 1848.)

California

We want words to convey an idea of the extent of the gold fever in New York. Knots of people cumber the pavement in Wall street, discussing the best possible mode of getting quickly to the land of promise. The seats on the Battery are occupied by persons, some with maps, others with paper and pencil, some inquiring anxiously, others confidently asserting and gesticulating, and not one in the crowded mass thinking or speaking of any thing short of the gold region. Unlucky is he who expresses a doubt, as for instance: "There have been humbugs where the assertions seemed as truthful as the gold reports; you remember the iron mountain in Missouri?" A general set is made at such a one. "You must be worse than an infidel if you call in question testimony so circumstantial and so unanimous, and here is the real gold pouring in to us! Is that a humbug?"

At church, in the theatre, at the table, in every hotel, the talk is of California.

The office of Howland & Aspinwall has been so besieged with applicants for information and for tickets of passage from Panama, that they have opened a separate office in their third story for the purpose. There stands an impatient young man, repeating through the day to the anxious crowd, "The berths are all taken for the steamers to March 1st, and we will not open the books for the steamers beyond that date, for we are not certain that they will be at Panama as early as expected; besides, so many desperate people wait there, that the vessels may be taken forcible possession of, and likely will be, to the exclusion of those who buy tickets here."

Via Chagres

Many vessels are going filled with passengers to Chagres, under the hope of being in time for the steamer of January 5th, at Panama, in spite of the cautions publicly given to them. A little ferry steamer, "The Isthmus," goes thither on Monday next with 114 passengers. If she catches a norther in the Gulf it will give her a hard trial. It is almost certain that thousands will be detained for months in that port on the Pacific, without house room, at high charges for food, and at great danger of sickness from exposure to unaccustomed heat during the rainy season, to say nothing of the awkwardness of being in a strange land, where their grumbling will be wasted on ears that hear and don't understand.

Around the Horn

It may be safely assumed that thirty vessels out of sixty advertised will go filled, this month, with emigrants and goods round the Horn, which is a voyage of from four to six months. One half of these are young gentlemen unused to labor, many young physicians, &c.; the other half are mechanics, generally associated in bodies of thirty or more. But every man goes out with a single eye to the gold. The goods sent are probably selected without much knowledge of the wants of the country, judging by the large shipments of salt beef to be sold in competition where cattle are killed chiefly for the hide and tallow; most of the meat being thrown away or sold for a trifle.

This long route is perhaps the shortest at this time, and certainly the only one to be depended upon. Panama is a dilapidated town on the Pacific, and it is not uncommon for vessels to be detained for months waiting for wind.

Via Mexico

The Mexicans who are established in New York, and the Consul, advise the route by way of Vera Cruz, City of Mexico, Guadalajara, San Blas, and Mazatlan. The latter is the largest seaport they have on that side—it carries on a trade with China, and many coasting vessels are owned there. It is said that a company of twenty might rely on being able to charter a vessel, at all times, for San Francisco. The public stageing is rapid and regular to within two hundred miles of the coast. The road is good and food plenty all the way, but the stage fare is high, $50 for the 280 miles between Vera Cruz and Mexico. Robberies are by no means so frequent as represented. Half a dozen armed men run very little risk, particularly if observed to be Americans. What is called the rainy season away from the coast, presents little impediment; the dry seasons being as three or four to one of wet.

After all that we have learned we conceive that we are qualified to give advice to many whose opportunities confine them to vague and unauthentic sources of information.

We have no doubt of the existence of grain gold in the soil, and of the profitable employment its search has given to labor, and while we have reason to take in the large allowance of the published reports of the extent of the gold lands and their inexhaustibility, we do not doubt that for a year to come a large amount of gold will be found, and profitable washings may be made for some few years, before adventurers are driven to the expensive and hazardous enterprise of delving into the granite-like rocks that yield a trace of metal to a block of stone.

But we cannot bring ourselves to understand how persons from this climate, and used to regularity of food and shelter, can hope to preserve their health and their lives, when they are at work up to their knees in water, with a broiling sun frying their brains by day, and the cool air and damp ground counteracting upon their exhausted bodies by night.

Doubtless the valley of the Sacramento is very fertile, and no one can question that a large commercial seaport town will be built up with unexampled rapidity—probably at San Francisco; and in so large a country many minor towns must arise. The Government, for reasons understood, will do every thing to favor the development of its resources and to secure its speedy population. It is by no means a wilderness now, and ten years will find society plenty there, and of the best kind.

They who go there early with an eye to those advantages, irrespective of gold, can scarcely be disappointed in the result. But they must count upon rough fare for a time, until they can gather about them the comforts of life. (PPL, Dec. 22, 1848.)

The Very Latest Intelligence

The following astounding intelligence is copied from the Boston Herald. The Herald declares that no other paper has the news.

Highly important from California!—Great Excitement among the People!!—Gold Region Inexhaustible!!!—A new People and Gold Forest!!!!

By the arrival of the barque Ariel, Capt. Tudacher, we are placed in possession of despatches from California to the very latest date, and a little later. The Ariel sailed from Province Town on a whaling voyage, but has returned with a cargo of gold dust, valued at $7,500,000, besides a quantity of hides and tallow.

When Capt. Tudacher left San Francisco, the people were returning from the gold washing.

The excitement was tremendous.

Not finding vacant storehouses in which to place the precious metal, the people were piling it up in the public streets, as tom-cods used to be of yore, in the streets of Watertown, Mass.—Barricades of solid ingots of gold actually impeded the travel.

Iron has become scarce, and nails and bolts manufactured out of pure gold were in common use.

Several whale ships, their bottoms having been scraped in crossing the bar of the harbor, had been refitted with golden sheathing, in the place of copper.

A railroad from San Francisco to the washings was already begun, the rails of which were fabricated out of the purest gold. (Some fears were entertained by

Gov. Mason that it would not prove of sufficient strength.)

A golden gridiron is among the most
common articles of domestic economy.

The Californian buffaloes are killed
with golden bullets, cast in golden moulds
(with a trifling alloy,) and California ducks
and pigeons are brought down with gold-
en ball shot. A foundry of golden cannon
balls is about to be established under the
direction of Col. Stevenson, the celebrated
pipe laying engineer.

The stories in circulation in the United
States respecting the extent of the gold region, are not a circumstance to the real estate of the case.—Capt. Tudacher informs
us (and his word is as good as any of the
Tudachers on Cape Cod,) that a *gold forest
and a new race of beings* had actually been
discovered. This marvellous forest lies due
east from Ciudad de los Angelos about
seven hundred miles, in a distant country
which has hitherto been considered impassable by travellers, and consequently
unexplored.

The golden forest has been ascertained
to comprise a region of two hundred and
forty miles square; the people are extraordinary specimens of humanity. The riches
of this district cannot be conceived by the
wildest imagination. They are really incredible. The Eldorado of Sir Walter
Raleigh was a fool to it. Diamond mines
whose depths have never been discovered
exist in abundance. They are said to under-
mine the golden forest, and to be far more
extensive than the coal mines of Pictou
[Nova Scotia], and are so brilliant that the

whole country is illuminated at night as if
by millions of Drummond lights.[9]

The buildings in this extraordinary
country are large and massive, (none less
in size than the Tremont House in Boston,)
of a conical shape, and built of solid gold,
cemented by diamonds, (paste, probably.)
The trees in this forest average about a
hundred feet in belt—all solid gold! Their
height is enormous. They are felled by
means of a sort of triangular saw, with diamond teeth, worn to a sharp edge. A single
tooth of this instrument would be considered a princely fortune in Europe or the
United States.

The people have a language of their
own; but all that could be comprehended
relative to their origin was that they were
"Children of Gas." In the vernacular of the
natives, their country is called "Aurifera."
The ladies are of an amorous complexion,
and extremely partial to red hair; an additional inducement to emigrate thither. The
boys play at taw with huge diamonds instead of marbles—one of which would pay
the whole expense of the introduction of
Cochituate water into Boston, and leave a
sufficient surplus to build a gold fence
around the Common.[10]

We could scarcely believe the above
accounts, were they not substantiated by
the crew of Captain Tudacher. And that
gentleman himself being one whose veracity we never yet heard questioned, contrib-
utes to strengthen us in the opinion that
his statements, astounding as they are, are
really true and correct.

P.S. Capt. Tudacher says that while in

---

9. Named for Captain T. Drummond, a British engineer; also called a calcium light. An
    oxyhydrogen flame is directed onto pure lime, heating it to incandescence and producing a
    brilliant white light. Originally used to illuminate the front of the stage in theaters; hence
    the expression 'in the limelight.'
10. Prior to 1848, the municipal water supply for Boston was pumped through hollow pine logs
    from Jamaica Pond. In that year a new pipeline—cast-iron pipe—was laid from Long Pond,
    about sixteen miles to the west-southwest of Boston. At the same time, the pond reacquired its
    original Indian name, Lake Cochituate, which it still retains.

Aurifera he saw a criminal executed for stealing a ten-penny nail, who was stuffed to death with diamonds, administered with a golden ladle as large as a kettle-drum. (CPD, Dec. 21, 1848.)

THE CALIFORNIA EMIGRANT
By "One of 'Em"
Tune—*Oh! Susannah!*

I come from Salem city,
    With my wash-bowl on my knee;
I'm going to California,
    The gold dust for to see.
It rained all night the day I left,
    The weather it was dry,
The sun so hot I froze to death—
    Oh! brothers! don't you cry!
    Oh! California!
    That's the land for me!
    I'm going to Sacramento,
    With my wash-bowl on my knee!

I jumped aboard the 'Liza ship,
    And travelled on the sea,
And every time I thought of home,
    I wished it wasn't me!
The vessel reared like any horse
    That had of oats a wealth;
It found it couldn't throw me, so
    I thought I'd throw myself!

I thought of all the pleasant times
    We've had together here;
I thought I ort to cry a bit,
    But couldn't find a tear.
The pilot bread was in my mouth,
    The gold dust in my eye,
And though I'm going far away,
    Dear brothers, don't you cry!

I soon shall be in Francisco,
    And then I'll look all 'round,
And when I see the gold lumps there,
    I'll pick them off the ground.
I'll scrape the mountains clean, my boys,
    I'll drain the rivers dry.
A "pocket full of rocks" bring home—
    So brothers, don't you cry!

    Oh! California!
    That's the land for me!
    I'm going to Sacramento,
    With my wash-bowl on my knee!
    [NYH, Dec. 28, 1848.]

Movements for California

The master of the steamer "Eudorus," of 145 tons register, offers twenty berths, with a chance to sling thirty hammocks; and vessels are advertised at other Maine ports for the land of promise.

The Hope On—Hope Ever Company, in Bridgeport, Connecticut, will start in January, and go over land by way of St. Louis and Santa Fe. The schooner "Miranda" is to sail from Fair Haven for California about the 10th of January; and we see that companies are forming in Hartford, New Haven, and several other places of "steady habits." The nutmeg men must look sharp, though, as some New Yorkers are buying a quantity of old copper, so intermixed with a certain composition, as to pass readily for pure gold, among the unsuspecting. This villainous material it is intended to ship off as soon as possible, and when it reaches San Francisco it is to be stored away, and offered for sale to the "green horns" from the States, who it is presumed, will eagerly buy up the spurious article, if offered cheap, instead of perilling life and limb at the "washing."

Newburyport is to have a finger in the placer, judging from the vessels advertised in the Herald. The brig "Forest" will take passengers for $125; and Mr. Charles H. Porter, who sends the brig "Charlotte," will go by the steamer of March 1, via Panama. The schooner "Queen of the West" will take passengers to Chagres for $40, and the owner thinks that this "low price, with good fare, and a prospect of accumulating a fortune in a short time, should be an inducement for any young man to take passage without delay."

Down East the fever is subsiding. Mr. Pike, of Calais, has offered to carry passengers to San Francisco for $400 each.

[From the New Orleans Picayune, Dec. 19.] A Missouri printer absquatulated[11] recently to the gold digging, leaving office, types, debts, creditors, and all, to look out for themselves.

[From the Baltimore Sun, Dec. 27.] A meeting of the "California Mining Company," composed of young men of Howard District, was held on Saturday at Endicott's Mills, to elect officers.

At Havre de Grace also, several young men will shortly leave for California, and at Elkton some purpose going out in the vessels which are to sail from Baltimore, and others purpose joining the Philadelphia company, under Gen. Cadwalader.

[From the Philadelphia Bulletin, Dec. 27.] An expedition to California by the Arkansas route is to start from Fort Smith by the 1st of April. . . . Rev. Isaac Owen and C. P. Hesler, of Bloomington, Indiana, also propose to raise a company to start for Oregon and California next spring. Mr. Owen was recently the agent of the Indiana Asbury University, and has been appointed missionary of the Indiana Conference to California. (NYH, Dec. 28, 1848.)

FIRE ARMS! FIRE ARMS!!—CALIFORNIA RIFLES, SIX BARREL Revolvers, and every other description of Pistols, Muskets, Blunderbusses, Bowie Knives, and a full assortment of Guns, double and single barrels, for sale low by B. JOSEPH, 74 Maiden lane. (NYH, Dec. 28, 1848.)

CALIFORNIA GOLD MINES.—PERSONS INTENDING TO EMBARK FOR that region, will do well to call at Jones', 14 Ann st., and supply themselves with French boots at from $3.50 to $4.50; double sole water proof boots from $4.50 to $6. (NYH, Dec. 27, 1848.)s

---

WHO GOES TO CALIFORNIA WITHOUT A TENT, WILL SLEEP IN THE open air.—This being true, miners and others should provide themselves with India Rubber Tents, Air Beds, Pillows, Rubber Camp Blankets, long Mining Boots, Gold Bags, Isthmus Bags (for pack mules), Portable Boats, and a variety of other indispensable articles made expressly for the purpose, and for sale at the
GOODYEAR RUBBER EMPORIUM,
159 Broadway, Rathbun's Hotel. (NYH, Dec. 28, 1848.)

CALIFORNIA—FOR SAN FRANCISCO DIRECT—A FIRST CLASS ocean Steamship, of 1,800 tons burthen, will be despatched for the above port early in the month of February, should a sufficient number of passengers offer to make it an object. This will be undoubtedly the best possible way of reaching the Gold mines in the shortest time—avoiding all contingencies which are feared may happen on other routes. The steamship has unsurpassed accommodations for passengers, both in cabin and steerage. Her machinery has been well tested, and can be relied upon; and as a sea craft, she has no superior. For passage apply to
J. HOWARD & SON, 73 South street. (NYH, Dec. 29, 1848.)

---

11. Departed hurriedly; skedaddled.

FOR SAN FRANCISCO, CALIFORNIA, AND THE GOLD REGIONS—The splendid fast sailing ship ROBERT BROWNE, commanded by Capt. F. G. Cameron, one of the ablest and most experienced Captains out of the port of New York, and late first in command of the U. S. frigate Macedonian under Com. De Kay, during her late mission of mercy to Ireland. The ship will sail on or about the 10th of January. Frederick Jerome, who distinguished himself in saving the lives in the Ocean Monarch, is engaged as mate. A skilful and experienced Physician and Surgeon accompanies the expedition, which is made up of none but respectable and steady persons. Advantages are here offered rarely to be met with, and cannot but be satisfactory to all desirous of joining the Association. The ship will have a cargo of 300 barrels of flour, 400 do. of beef, 300 do. pork, 500 do. bread, 50 do. meal, 50 do. rice, 20 do. sugar, 100 do. potatoes, 50 do. beans, 30 bags of coffee, 5 bbls. of vinegar, 10 hhds. molasses, 10 bbls. of mackerel, 10 do. of onions, 10 boxes of soap, 20 kegs of butter, 5 sheets of tea, 50 quintals of codfish. The ship and cargo will belong to the passengers, and each passenger will be entitled to 4 barrels of freight, besides his baggage. It is believed by competent men, that the balance of the provisions when the vessel arrives at San Francisco, will sell for more than the price of the passage, and it is supposed that the ship in that port, will be worth from 30 to $40,000. To those who wish to emigrate to the Gold Region, this offers superior advantages in many respects. P.S.—As the lists are fast filling up, the berths should be secured without delay.—For further particulars, apply to the Captain, on board, foot of Dover street. Freight taken on reasonable terms.—Passage, with a share of Cargo and vessel, $250. (NYH, Dec. 27, 1848.)

TIN ROOFING FOR CALIFORNIA.—THE SUBSCRIBERS ARE NOW prepared to execute all orders for roofing to be sent to the above place. They can be packed so that the freight will be a mere trifle. Instructions and a model will accompany each roof, so that an inexperienced hand can cover a building of 1,000 square feet in from one to two days. Orders to any considerable amount will be attended to in person, by one of the firm, who intends leaving in a few days for the above place. Some roofs already completed for that market may be seen at S. R. & G. W. Trembley's Manufactory, 136 Chrystie street, New York.

The Gold Fever

SAN FRANCISCO, Upper California
Sept. 7, 1848.

VERY DEAR FRIEND: Since I last wrote to you, while in Callao, many changes have taken place to cause much anxiety in my mind, which I will enumerate in the course of this letter. My passage to Honolulu was a very pleasant one of 32 days—a distance of 5,300 miles. I arrived there on the 18th, and sailed again on the 31st of July for this port, where I arrived on the 27th of August. The gold fever we heard of at the island, and thought it much exaggerated; but since my arrival here it has been fully substantiated, and is the cause of our selling the cargo at a profit from 100 to 500 per cent. This, you will say, is first-rate business, and so it is; but there are many charges to equal the sales; for instance, seamen's wages $40 per month. I have lost eight of my crew, and I am now the best off of any ship in port, for the most of them have lost all except the master and mates. My dear friend, if you or Caddy had only come out with me, you could have made your fortunes in one or two years, by going to the gold mines and attending professionally to the sick; nothing short of an ounce of gold dust for a visit, and the gold is 22 to 23 carats fine.

Sunday, 17th Sept.—O, my dear friend, if you had only come out with me, I feel sure we could soon make a fortune. I have conversed with several persons, just from the mines, within the last few days. One young man told me that he had got as much as $700 worth in a day, and never less than $50. Another one, a Frenchman, says he pitched his tent on a place, and remained and worked under it seven weeks without moving it, and got $27,000 worth of gold dust; one piece weighed three pounds and seven ounces, equal to $712. These stories you may think untrue, but they are nevertheless as true as I am now writing to you, and not in the least exaggerated. I cannot tell, under present circumstances, when we shall leave this port, for I much fear that we cannot get a crew to get to sea with in under two or three months. There is no end to the gold; it is over the whole of Upper California, say for 200 miles in length by from 60 to 100 in breadth.

BENJAMIN HILL, formerly Captain of the Ship Orpheus. (NYH, Dec. 29, 1848.)

The Pulpit on the Gold Fever

Rev. Dr. Putnam preached a sermon at Boston, Mass., on Sunday last, upon the California mania. The Transcript says:

That there is gold in abundance in California, the Reverend gentleman said there was no doubt. But among the adventurers, when the lottery was wound up, there would probably be some splendid prizes and many dismal blanks. Change of climate and habits, and privations, will be fatal to some. Then it is likely there will be a large gathering there of the desperate ruffians of all lands. The miners will multiply fast, and soon crowd and interfere, and deadly affrays will ensue. There will be a mania for robbing as well as for digging. And many will part with their gold, and leave their bodies to the vultures, some where in the wilderness on the road to San Francisco. Of those who return successful it is doubtful whether their gold would prove to them a blessing. Riches thus obtained, implied by a revolution and entire unsettling of mind, [subvert] the spirit and process of acquiring our own wealth. Mr. Putnam said had there been gold in these vallies there would have been no New England here for us but only another Mexico. The barren sands of Plymouth were more prolific in blessing than all the auriferous soil of California. More of that new found treasure will flow in upon Massachusetts if she stays at home, and keeps up the hum of her thousand-fold avocations, than if all her population should go forth in a mass to gather the hoards for herself.

(CPD, Dec. 29, 1848.)

A Good Hole

The following incident is related by a correspondent at Monteresy:

"Provisions are very scarce, and to obtain them many murders have been committed, or the purchase of them at exorbitant prices has indirectly but eventually led to murder. One story, relating to an affair of this kind, may deserve a place here. A man who had what is called a *good hole* had been digging incessantly for two days, when he was accosted by one carrying a bucket containing food of some kind. The whole of this the digger purchased for about one hundred dollars in virgin gold; and, while devouring it, the man who had sold the provisions took possession of the hole. After finishing his repast, the gold-hunter ordered the fellow out; but on his positively refusing to come, knocked his brains out with a pick-axe, took from the pockets the virgin gold that had purchased the meal, and then dragging the body out of the hole himself, continued the digging.

This, I believe, is really true, just as I have told it."

Jack Bunsby on California— Gold vs. Potatoes

The following bit is from the New York Sunday News

Being asked what he thought of the gold panic, BUNSBY crossed his boots, took a whiff, and said, "If so be as how gold can be got in California for digging, why, good; the only question would be, to dig or not to dig. And so, but then, do ye see, a man must do something else besides digging. He must eat, drink, sleep, and be clothed withal—and if all the people turn gold diggers, who shall perform all the other kind of work? Now, if so be, a man should dig gold, and fill his pockets, why, so. And, if so be, another man should dig praties, and fill a tin kettle, and put it over a fire, in unison with some wild kids and a few yarbs,[12] and a man who had been digging the gold should come and say, give me some of that 'ere mess, why, so, also. Now, what would the pratie-digger say? How much gold have you dug? Oh, says the gold digger, I have had great luck to-day, but I am very hungry. Good, says the pratie-digger; give me two-thirds of your gold, and you shall dine with me. Why, you inhospitable fellow, do you want to rob? No, says the pratie-digger, but go and eat your gold. I'll eat my dinner alone, and save what is left until to-morrow, and then I can go and dig gold, and you can dig praties for yourself. Now, says Bunsby, the pratie-digger would be the best off, for the other could not wait until the morrow for a dinner, and it's therefore my opinion that digging praties may be, under some circumstances, more profitable than digging gold, and my name's Jack Bunsby."

(WNI, Dec. 30, 1848.)

---

12. Praties, wild kids, and yarbs: Potatoes, wild pea- or bean-pods, and herbs.

The Panic to Go

Independent Way to California

WASHINGTON, DECEMBER 25, 1848.

The newspapers have already stated to the Public that the distance from New York to Francisco Bay, via Cape Horn, is about 17,000 miles; via Panama about 5,000; climate at the Isthmus unhealthy; board expensive; detention possibly a month; and when the passenger arrives at the "gold diggings" he will have no house until he builds one.

The independent route is for a man to fit up a wagon and pair of horses, and, taking his family, go the land route.

From New York to New Helvetia, Sutter's Fort, by the map is 2,530 miles; by the travelled route about 3,000 miles. From New York to St. Louis, 1,074; from St. Louis to Fort Leavenworth to Fort Laramie, 617; from Fort Laramie to South Pass, 315; from South Pass to Gold Diggings, Feather river, about 750; making the whole distance from New York 3,063 miles.

The half-way house or middle station on this route is at the intersection of the road with the Nebraska river, about 250 miles west of Fort Leavenworth, due west from New York. Here in some future time may be a great City of the Plains—it may be called Ne-obraska. From this place to Fort Laramie is a pleasant ride over the plains of 350 miles, where is destined to be another great city.

The settlers most wanted in California and on the land route are household and personal mechanics, blacksmiths, carpenters and builders, furniture-makers, tin-plate workers, hatters, tailors, shoemakers, female mechanics, milliners, mantua-makers, seamstresses—all these will be wanted as permanent settlers, because those who dig gold will spend it, and the industrious mechanics will finally obtain it.

A mechanic who wishes to go to California should take his wife and children with him. For his purpose he should prepare a wagon (on springs, with good India rubber cover) and pair of horses: this is a house on wheels; his family is with him; he is at home. His loading should consist of light articles of furniture and food, the light tools belonging to his trade, light articles of books—printed books for children and spelling books and New Testaments; these he can exchange on the way for food, thus giving food for the mind and receiving food for the body; an axe, a rifle and as many light articles of merchandise as he has room for will complete his load. With such equipment a man may travel through the settlements and make the journey over the plains an excursion of pleasure.

He should take a blank book with him and keep a journal. This, if well kept, might sell for enough to pay his expenses; at any rate, it would be perused with satisfaction by his children and grandchildren: the future historians and the antiquaries will look for these journals and treasure them up with great care.

By choosing this mode of travelling a man is commander of his own team, and all his cares are with him; he can stop where work is in plenty and prices high. He may find "El Dorado" before he reaches the gold mines. If he continues his journey he may reach Fort Leavenworth by the first of March. Here he joins the caravan and proceeds to Fort Laramie, which he may arrive at by the middle of April. Here will be a resting place; perhaps he may conclude to abide here for a season. Here the gold-diggers will concentrate on their return from California; here come the Indians with their buffalo meat and game and furs to exchange for clothing and ammunition; here mechanics will be wanted to supply the wants of all the multitude who congregate near Fort Laramie.

Let the mechanic, then, aim to arrive at Fort Laramie; from thence he can take his leisure to go into California.

C. F. L. (WNI, Jan. 1, 1849.)

More About Gold Hunting

The *mania* for Gold Hunting has not simply disturbed and unsettled the minds of those hitherto contentedly in steady and profitable avocations, and completely intoxicated the more speculative and adventurous, but it has filled the minds of the mercantile, mechanical, and commercial community with the most extravagant ideas as to the amount of goods and mechanical labor that will be required to satisfy the demand of the *gold hunters.* Because the temporary excitement in California has caused the abandonment of all productive labor, and a universal and simultaneous *rush* for the gold region, and thereby enhanced the price of every thing—prices corresponding with the reckless and extravagant habits which successful *gold gathering* invariably engenders—by reason of this, and obviously without considering that the causes which have produced these high prices must be temporary and the demand necessarily limited—our merchants and manufacturers have shipped and are shipping cargoes of goods to the gold region, and mechanics by the hundreds and thousands are anxious to emigrate to that golden country, vainly supposing that the present high prices and wages are to continue. Now the result of this will most certainly be great losses and disappointment.

Admitting that this "yellow fever" carries off to California as many as the most sanguine have estimated—even there has gone and are about going to the gold market (according to the Journal of Commerce) an immense amount of all kinds of goods and provisions—enough to enable the entire population of *El Dorado* to furnish themselves, by the beginning of next summer, cheaper than any other people on the earth's surface. One vessel took three thousand pieces of calico—enough to outwardly adorn the women of all sorts and complexions who will be in the territory for a year to come. Six thousand dozen Panama and chip hats, with numberless fur and cloth caps, have been shipped—enough to supply the demand for years to come, as the natives wear no such head gear; they can be used for ladles and strainers in mining, and thus may turn out a "speculation" as extraordinary as the warming pans which Timothy Dexter shipped to the West Indies.[1] Thirty thousand pairs of boots and shoes have already been sent forward, but the gold digger's costume is said to be "a shirt and pair of breeches"—toes are used in scratching the golden soil—where then is to be the market for these boots and shoes, and for as many more that will be sent?

Fifteen hundred bales of domestic cottons have already been shipped; enough to supply the people of that country with several hundred yards each, until Messrs. Aspinwall & Co. build their railroad across the Isthmus. There have also been sent to the party-colored senoritas of that auriferous region, immense quantities of silks, satins, lace veils, &c., which will be appropriate adornments for women-kind who smoke cigars and go barefoot.

---

1. Timothy Dexter (1747–1806), rose from poverty to wealthy eccentricity by means of speculation in depreciated Continental currency during and after the Revolution. According to his own accounts, he was adept at selling unlikely goods in unlikely markets. In the instance mentioned above, he sent 42,000 warming pans to Cuba, where they were sold as cooking utensils.

Shovels, spades, hoes, axes, and sieves enough have already been shipped, it is said, *to dig up and strain* the whole of California. Ships and vessels of all sorts and sizes have been freighted with every necessary and unnecessary article to "eat, drink, and wear," and to use in mining operations, and they are on their way to the "diggins;" and, if the ships now advertised for California take out similar loads of goods, then will the gold country be deluged with mining implements, groceries, wet and dry, dry goods, &c. Before the end of another year the Californians will be able to live, during the short period the market remains glutted, longer on a few shillings than any other people.

Facts like these, we should suppose, would deter men of the "business foresight" accorded to merchants from shipping any more goods, groceries, produce, or articles of any kind. But such is not the result; and while young men, under the influence of this mania, abandon their healthful and profitable daily avocations, and hazard health and life in a wild and reckless adventure, so also do the cool and "calculating" merchants, under the same influence, continue to send off their goods to a market sure to be glutted, and when a loss seems inevitable. (WNI, Jan. 4, 1849.)

Isthmus of Panama

We annex another account of this interesting Isthmus, compiled by a gentleman of the highest respectability of this city, which tallies in all respects with the description given by our previous correspondent, "Viator." After describing the bay and harbor of Chagres, he continues:

After being visited from the custom house, we were permitted to land with our baggage in a *cayuca* (as the canoes are called,) which took us to a mud flat, which extended from the town about 200 feet, nearly off to the channel of the river. Over this mud flat we were carried on negroes backs, who sank ankle deep at every step to the shore, where we picked our way

through the mud by stepping from stone to stone to the custom house, where our trunks were opened and underwent a very scrutinising examination. After which, we took them to the hotel; but such a hotel! A wicker work, jack straw house, plastered inside and out with clay or mud, with no flooring but mud, the roof thatched with palm leaves; and we had the privilege of paying two dollars a day for two ordinary meals, and a naked cot to sleep on, and extra charges for wheat bread and milk.

Chagres is a miserable looking place of some 150 or 200 mud huts, roofed with palm branches, with about 500 or 600 inhabitants, mostly negroes and mulattoes, and "cholas" or half breed Indians. I saw only one white man there, and he was a "rubio" from Curacao; he was the Collector of the port, and had a negro wife. The "rubios" are a mixed race of the white and negro blood, and generally have a reddish freckled face, curly red hair, and light eyes.

The town is built on swampy land, nearly surrounded by lagoons of muddy water, filled as far as the eye can penetrate with reeds and high cane grass, full of venomous reptiles and insects; poisonous serpents are said to often be seen about the streets and houses.—From the continual rains, the streets are knee deep in mud and only passable by stepping on logs and large stones placed at some distance apart; there might once have been paving, but it is now all gullied loose by the rains. In all parts of the world I have visited, I never saw more rainy weather and such heavy torrents of it as on this Isthmus, and all through the provinces of Choco, from the river of St. Juan of the Pacific, to the river Atrato, or Darien, which empties into the Atlantic, and I am informed it is so the whole year round, having no dry season except a short interval of scorching sunshine for a few hours on some days. The effluvia and miasma drawn up from the swamps, while the sun does shine, creates a nauseous steam or vapor, which is horrible to the smell, and is full of pestilence. *No traveller should land here if he can help it;* but if he can obtain a "cayuca," go direct from the vessel up the river, for a single week's residence here would almost insure sickness, and sometimes death to the stranger. Even the natives are a sickly, puny, miserable looking lot of beings always afflicted with agues, fevers, and other diseases.

JOURNEY UP THE RIVER CHAGRES

Passages can be had in the large cayucas, which carry cargoes, for four dollars, and in the small ones for twelve dollars. It is always preferable for single passengers to take the latter, which, when there is no freshet, will take one to Cruces in twenty-four hours, yet I was two days in getting there, stopping through the nights on the river, made fast to the limb of a tree, and it raining continually. The largest cayucas are often four and even six days on the passage. A small canoe has two negroes to pole and paddle, and sometimes wade, dragging the canoe after them round the points, the current being very rapid in some places where the river is narrow.

The canoes are long, low, and very narrow, with a small arched awning, about seven feet long, under which the passenger has to lie the whole time, with hardly room to sit up straight. They are made thus low to keep from being swept away by the branches and limbs of trees, stumps, and vines hanging over the banks of the river, and under which they are obliged to pass, to keep out of the strength of the current. In some places the river is so narrow that the branches of the trees hanging over its banks nearly intertwine together. . . . The scenery, after ascending a few miles, becomes beautiful—the trees and vines, festooned with flowers of rich variegated hues, overhang the banks of the river; while, here and there, as we turn a point, are seen, in the open vistas beyond, rich vallies, hills, and towering mountains, with the clouds wreathing along their sides—now and then obscuring their summits, then rolling away, in the distance exposing them for a few moments to the bright rays of the sun in all their magnificent verdure, with here and there a small "hacienda" and rude hut, surrounded with waving corn, sugar cane, and plantain trees; while there are continually crossing and recrossing, overhead, large flocks of noisy green parrots, paroquets, and wild pigeons, with many other small and large birds of beautiful plumage; and while a

Entrance to the River Chagres.

person is musing in wonder and admiration at the magnificent scenery of nature, down comes a sudden shower of rain, which obscures the whole behind a sombre curtain of thick mist, and obliges him to draw in his head beneath his small canopy of plantain leaves—reminding one of a tortoise drawing his head within his shell.

ROAD FROM CRUCES TO PANAMA

I remained in Cruces a fortnight and then went to Panama; the charge for a saddle mule was $5, and for a baggage mule and muleteer $3 more, making $8. I started after an early breakfast and arrived late in the afternoon, it rained nearly all the way; the road or mule path was in the worst of order. It was once paved in many places with huge round stones, but they were all washed loose by the rains, and the path gullied away in many places, so that the mules had at almost every step to pick their way between them, stepping in holes of mud and water up to their girths; and in many places the path is gullied away so deep and narrow that one is obliged to haul up his legs to keep them from being bruised by projecting rocks and crags, and in some places it is like ascending and descending flights of steps, with deep holes in them worn by the mules' feet, stepping single file after each other, with difficulty withdrawing their feet, as these holes are filled with wet clay almost of the consistency of putty. A person not accustomed would hardly be able to pick his way afoot without meeting with many falls. Even the sure-footed mule often makes a slip and throws his rider over his head, to the danger of life or limb, against the craggy rocks, or plump in the mud and water below. It is really surprising the poor animals can get along at all, with such heavy burthens; they do often fall under them, and here and there the road is strewed with their bones. Their backs, shoulders, and hips are often cruelly lacerated by chafes, and the skin torn from their legs by the rocks they have to step between. And yet with a little

trouble and expense, by widening, paving, and cutting drains, the roads might be kept in good order. Nothing appears to have been done to keep them in repair since the country became free from the dominion of old Spain. But mule owners command higher freight than they would get if it was kept in order.

At various places along the road are seen haciendas and open ranchos or huts, and women swinging listlessly in their hammocks, or sitting on mats, smoking cigarillos, while their little naked red skin half Indian children are playing about on the clay floors, and good looking cattle grazing in the fields. The soil is exceeding rich, being a deep loam, the color of Spanish brown, producing corn, sugar cane, rice, beans, peas, melons, and all the tropical fruits, if cultivated, in great abundance; but here they only cultivate enough for home consumption, and a little for the Panama market. A more indolent, lazy looking set no one ever saw, and yet they look fat and hearty; and the women, who are generally short in stature, with very remarkable small feet, and well turned ankles, have, some of them, very pretty features, with long glossy black hair, and large, full lustrous black eyes; indeed, many of the young "Cholas" (as the Indian women are called) are quite handsome, and all very kind and hospitable to strangers. (NYH, Jan. 7, 1849.)

To those who have the Gold Fever

CALIFORNIA, 17 Aug. 1848.

DEAR UNCLE—I write this to go hum to you by a vessel that sails when the folks on board are willin to go; but at present they are all gone gold diggin, and if they ain't no better off than I be in the way of keepin gold after it is dug out, I don't know when she will sail.

Every body quits work now and goes for gold. The whaleman drops the harpoon—the soldier drops the gun and bayonet, and the missionary drops the Bible, and as for tracts—the only tracks he makes or uses is right off to the gold region. I worked there myself about a month, and got as much gold as I thought would last me all my life, but it is nigh upon gone already. I wore out my shoes and trowsers and jacket, and when I come to buy new ones I found they were worth more than their weight in gold.—I wish Colonel Benton was here; I reckon he'd larn something new about gold; and other folks, too, who says that nothing is valuable but gold, say that I now know is an everlasting and eternal humbug. There ain't no prices now in all these diggins; the question is, when you ask the price of any thing, 'How much gold have you got?'—And then the measure is a handfull. I do raly believe, if things go on as they have begun and Californy gets to be a state of the Union and issues state bonds, no body will take any of them unless it is stipulated in bond that it never shall be paid off in gold no how and no way in the world. Tell aunt Nancy and cousin Betsey to sell off at once their gold beads and gold rings they set so much store by, for they ain't of no more valy than so much pewter. My notion is now that there is a great chance for trade by agreeing to buy any thing in creation (except gold,) and pay in gold so much per ounce, and the fellow who sells property for sich pay will be about as bad off as if he lent ice in August and agreed to take so much ice in January for pay.

I have heard much said about a 'golden age,'—well, I think we have got it now, and will find after all it ain't half so good as a corn and potatoe and pork age. I am considerably bewildered by this state of things, for I find the more gold one digs the more gold he has to pay for what he wants, and he ain't a bit better off in the end. I always thought we sot too much store by gold, and if a man had not gold he was nobody, no matter how much else he had; now a change is coming and gold has got to go down hill jest as it made other things go down hill. I began to think we have found here the head source of gold; and all the other gold diggins are but small streams and washings from this. There ain't no stock jobbing here and no companies chartered—every man does his own diggin. There are some speckelators here who try to make some folks think that the gold is what they call *'Mikey,'* but though you once told me not to believe that all was gold because it glittered, I guess I know the difference twixt gold and mikey as well as I know the difference twixt broad daylight and moonshine—so no more at present. Your loven nephew,

ESEKIEL BARNES, late Corporal, Company B, N. Y. Volunteers for California. (ISJ, Jan. 11, 1849.)

FOR CALIFORNIA.—$1,000 WANTED BY A PERSON GOING TO California, for which one half the entire proceeds of his labor for two years will be given, or the same for one year for one half the above amount. Reference and security given. Address T. C. E., Broadway Post Office. (NYH, Jan. 11, 1849.)

PISTOL BELTS AND HOLSTERS FOR CALIFORNIA.—All kinds of Pistol Belts and Holsters, Travelling Knapsacks, Knife Sheaths, Gun Slings, &c., made at the shortest notice by JOSEPH T. BELL, 186 Fulton street, opposite Church street, New York. (NYH, Jan. 11, 1849.)

GREAT BARGAINS.—J. VISSER, intending to start shortly for California, offers at cost, and only for cash, his whole stock of fancy goods, consisting of—
   Bonnets, Feathers, Flowers, Ribands, Capes
   Collars, Caps, Cuffs, Barbes, Berthes
   Real Malin and Valencienne Lace, Black Lace
   Blonde Scarfs, Coiffures, Wreaths, Fans
   Jewelry, and several other fancy Articles:
Together with an assortment of the cheapest Lace Dresses
ever offered for sale, from $5 to $12, double and single Skirts.
Fig'd Swiss Muslin, Tarletons, real India muslin lace Veila.
Fringes, Gimp, Buttons.
All persons owing me a bill will please settle.
      Penn. avenue, 5 doors above 9th street.   (WNI, Jan. 11, 1849.)

CALIFORNIA BAGS VS. TRUNKS—DAY, 23 CORTLANDT STREET, sells a Bag in which the traveller can put his clothing and enclose it perfectly water-tight. The same affair is so constructed that it can be transformed into a bed or pillow, life preserver, or float for crossing streams. This article is very cheap, and requires to be seen to be appreciated. Parties for California would profit by a visit to Day, whose long experience and skill ensures his customers peculiar advantages.

TO CALIFORNIA. FOR $160.—SAIL JANUARY 17TH.—IN GORDON'S California Association there are ten vacancies. This company has a splendid fast sailing Vessel, and takes out a small Steam boat for towing on the Sacramento. $4,000 worth of the best machinery for gold washing is supplied on shares. Part of the Association go overland, cost $190 (through Mexico) well armed and organized. Apply to George Gordon, President, 146 Market street, Philadelphia, or to W. O. Uhlhorn, 106 Front street, New York.

CAMP HAMPERS FOR CALIFORNIA—CONTAINING ALL THE POTS, camp kettles, frying pans, gridirons, plates, cups, knives and forks, spoons, &c. &c., necessary for the cooking and eating utensils, snugly put up in portable willow hampers, for messes of four, six, or a greater number of persons. Having had much experience in putting up hampers for old campaigners, we are enabled to select such as are indispensable, without encumbering with articles that could be dispensed with. Companies desiring Hampers put up, will please leave their orders as early as possible. SMITH & Co., 50 Maiden lane.

CALIFORNIA.—SINGER'S PATENT ROCK DRILLING MACHINE, for mining purposes; Houses and Stores of wood or iron, cheap Safes, Cooking Apparatus, &c., manufactured and for sale by   SHEPARD & CO., 242 Water street.

CALIFORNIA METALLIC BOATS—COPPER AND GALVANIZED IRON Boats, of all sizes, suitable for California in nests of 2, 3, and 4, stowing inside each other, occupying the room of one. A nest of 4 small boats, from 9 to 12½ feet long, will carry 18 persons. The weight of a metal boat is but half that of a wooden one. Heat and moisture have no effect; and they cannot leak or sink. Manufactured by STILLMAN, ALLEN & CO., Novelty Iron Works, foot of 12th street, E. R.

CALIFORNIA DAGUERREOTYPES — PERSONS ABOUT TO VISIT California, and desirous to leave their likenesses with their friends, would do well to call at BRADY'S, No. 205 and 207 Broadway, where by reason of new improvements and additions to the establishment, faithful and true likenesses may be obtained at the shortest notice. (NYH, Jan. 15, 1849.)

Increase of the Gold Excitement— Movements of the Migrants

The bark Josephine left yesterday morning for San Francisco, with thirty young men from the 7th ward. The vessel, as well as cargo, belongs to them. The Harriet Newell also left for the same place. The ship Tarolinta, Captain Cane, will be detained until Saturday morning. She takes out about 100 persons, and a large freight, owned principally by an association of young men, who go out in her.

[From the Boston Traveller, Jan. 9.] A number of enterprising young men, of Gloucester, masters of vessels employed in the Georges Bank Fisheries, having purchased the schooner Paragon, of Gloucester, are now fitting out for California. The Paragon will be commanded by Captain Haley, a man well acquainted on that coast, having recently returned from a three years' cruise in the Pacific. The Paragon is one of the old Grand Bank fishermen models, and is a good and substantial vessel, and is said to be an excellent sea boat and very fast sailer. The Boston clipper Edward Everett, schooner Boston, and others, must look out that they are not overhauled by the Paragon. The splendid schooner Loo Choo, of Gloucester, has been purchased by a company of young men, at the neighboring town of Rockport,

and will go out under the command of Captain Hale.

The ship Edward Everett cleared today for California, and will probably sail on Thursday. Her manifest of cargo is a very long one, consisting of 250 bbls. flour, 50,000 lbs. of bread, seed corn, frames of houses and boats, scales, and et ceteras innumerable, but not an item of spirituous liquors.

The Maria, which cleared yesterday, has, among other articles, a quantity of Mrs. Kidder's Cordial.

The ship Leonora, brigs Attila and Rodolph, have been purchased by different companies to proceed to California. The Attila belongs to a Plymouth company. The whaling ship Audley Clark has been purchased by a company in Newport for an expedition to California.

[From the Boston Journal, Jan. 9.] The bark Maria, Capt. Baker, cleared at this port yesterday for San Francisco, with a large assorted cargo and twenty-two passengers, among whom we notice the name of Mr. George Davis, of Worcester, Mass., son of Hon. John Davis. Mr. Davis is a young man of fine talents and a superior education, and we doubt not will assume a leading position in the affairs of the "new country," should he make it his residence.

The Maria has on board, among other articles, a house, painted, and in complete order for her immediate erection on her arrival out.

The brig Forest, of Newburyport, also cleared this forenoon for the same port. She has forty-five passengers, mostly sons of the old Bay State, and worthy representatives of her intelligence and industry—being mostly mechanics. The F. has a library on board, partly furnished by her owner, and the remainder by the American Home Missionary Society.

[From the Nantucket Inquirer.] The ship Aurora, Capt. Seth M. Swain, was cleared on Tuesday, for San Francisco direct, with passengers, and a cargo consisting principally of buildings framed ready to be put up, lumber, naval stores, provisions, and sperm candles. She takes out no intoxicating liquors; we were informed by one of her principal owners that it was resolved at the outset that nothing of the kind should form part of the cargo. The crew receive one dollar a month apiece, for the voyage out, with liberty to leave the ship on her arrival at San Francisco. They and the passengers are principally young men, and consist of some of our most intelligent, energetic, and respectable citizens. They are mostly mechanics, and go out to California in search of a less crowded field of industry, with the hope, too, at the same time, of being able to gather their share of the golden harvest that has been discovered in the valley of the Sacramento.

[From the New Orleans Times, Dec. 30.] Letters have been received in this city, from the capital of Mexico, containing later advices from California than any which have yet been published. One of these letters states that further discoveries have been made in the gold region, which yield even a more abundant supply of the article than the previous "diggings." The quantity gathered already amounted to at least $100,000 daily, and was constantly increasing, without apparently an exhaustion or any limit to the supply. There was a great deal of distress among all the diggers, for want of the common necessaries of life, and attended with very extensive sickness and mortality. Men loaded with gold appear like haggard vagabonds, clothed in filthy and tattered garments of the meanest kind. It is stated that one man, who had two barrels of brandy, sold them out at the mines, by the small wine glass, at rates which realized him fourteen thousand dollars in gold. Everything, and particularly articles of food and raiment, were at most unheard of prices, for gold was so plenty, and in the possession of every one, that it seemed to have lost its value.

Daily additions were made to the number employed in digging, though as yet no portion of the vast flood of emigration from the United States had arrived. The first arrivals of provisions, and other supplies, will no doubt realize larger profits than any previous instance that can be found in the annals of trade.

[From the Philadelphia Bulletin, Jan. 9.] The brig Oniota, Capt. Keene, sails from this port, on Wednesday morning next, direct for San Francisco. The Oniota is only 18 months old and is very strongly built. Her cargo, which is now on board, has been selected with the view of loading her in good ballast trim. The superior sailing qualities of the Oniota give the assurance that she will be among the very first vessels that will reach California from Philadelphia. The Oniota takes out the little steamer Islander, to run on some of the waters of the golden region.

The new clipper ship Greyhound, of 533 tons burthen, under the command of Capt. Claypool, cleared at the Baltimore Custom House on Tuesday for California. Her cargo consists of a great variety of articles, shipped by eighty-four different persons, and is valued at nearly $100,000. The manifests are thirty feet in length. The Greyhound also carries out thirty-nine passengers. (NYH, Jan. 11, 1849.)

Intelligence from Texas

[From the N. O. Delta, Jan. 2]

The cholera, we regret to state, had been prevailing with great fatality for some eight or ten days among the troops of the 8th Infantry, who were stationed at Port Lavaca. . . . The disease progressed with great mortality, 20 to 30 deaths occurring each day, and even as many as 40 on one day, out of 400, which was the original number of the troops.

The following letter, addressed to Major Tompkins, is considered official:—

Port Lavaca, Dec. 25, 1848.

MAJOR—The 8th Infantry arrived here on the 15th, and were all landed and encamped by the 20th. On the 21st, Major Gates, with five companies, left for Placedore Creek, ten miles off. The night of the 21st, about tattoo, a Norther commenced, and next morning several men were dead, with cramps and other symptoms of cholera. Since then, the mortality has been great. The encampment was abandoned on the 23d, and the troops furnished quarters in town. A large house was procured for an hospital, and as fast as they were taken, they were carried thither. On the 23d, twenty-two men were buried in a pit, and yesterday, twenty-eight men were interred near the same spot. Nine, this morning, were sent out for interment. These were, of course, without coffins, and at least fifteen have been buried with coffins. I am without any other data than my own observations, but not less than seventy or seventy-five have died since the 21st. . . . The cause of the disease may be ascribed to the severity of the Norther, which was accompanied by a cold rain and sleet, or snow. . . . Post mortem examinations exhibited empty, inflated stomachs, with coagulated blood about the heart and lungs.

(NYH, Jan. 11, 1849.)

Ho! For California! Increase of the Emigration: The Gold Excitement

The recent reports from the gold region have given another stir to emigration in this and other cities on the Atlantic. The owners and agents of the numerous vessels advertised for the coast are literally overwhelmed with applications for passage, and among those applying, two-thirds are known to be of that class of persons who are best calculated to give tone and character to trade and commerce. Associations of young men of talent and good standing in the world are still being formed here, and in other cities of the Union, combining wealth with all the other elements necessary to the speedy formation of a system of government which will, at no very distant period, place the new State on a level with many, if not with all, of the old ones.

The Tarolinta, which will sail this morning, takes out eighty-five cabin and about forty steerage passengers. Among them are Caleb Lyon,[2] of Lyonsdale, the well-known poet, and Frederick Jerome, the gallant sailor. The following lines are from the pen of Mr. Lyon:—

---

2. "Caleb Lyon of Lyonsdale enjoyed the reputation of designing the [California] state seal, although it was not justly his due. Major R. S. Garnet designed it, but being of a retiring disposition, gave his drawing to Lyon, who added some stars around the rim, and obtained the prize of $1,000. . . ." (Bancroft, *History of California*, vi, p. 285.)

Song

by Caleb Lyon, of Lyonsdale

Where the Sacramento's waters roll their
   golden tide along,
Which echoes through the mountains like
   a merry drinking song;
Where the Sierra Nevada lifts its crests
   unto the sky,
A home for freedom's eagles when the
   tempests sweeping by.
Where the bay of San Francisco—the
   Naples of the West—
Lies sleeping like an infant beside the
   ocean's breast;
There we go with dauntless spirits, and we
   go with hearts elate,
To build another empire—to found
   another State.

Ho! ye who love adventure, and ye who
   thirst for gold,
Remember ye the story of the Argonauts
   of old?
From the Pascagoula's valley to
   Kaataden's snowy land,
From beyond the Mississippi to our own
   Atlantic strand.
The Jasons are arousing, they who never
   dreamed of fears,
The sons of hardy Puritans and
   gallant Cavaliers,
Who go with dauntless spirits, and who go
   with hearts elate,
To build another empire—to found
   another State.

Then good bye to old Manhattan—our
   bark is on the tide,
Farewell to father, mother, to sister,
   wife, and bride,
And when her shores are fading we'll bless
   her through our tears,
She filled the cup of happiness through
   many pleasant years.
And the friends who dearly love us,
   within our hearts are set,
Whose tenderness and kindness we
   never can forget;
Yet we go with dauntless spirits, and go
   with hearts elate,
To build another empire—to found
   another State.

The good ship Tarolinta, with her gallant
   Captain Cave,

From our native shore will bear us
   in triumph o'er the wave;
By the isles of fair Bermuda—the
   emeralds of the West—
Where gales of ladened incense for ever
   love to rest,
And when the storm-wind rages, and
   thunders echo free,
We'll pass Terre del Fuego, the Charybdis
   of the sea;
By the land of Chimborazo we will sail
   with hearts elate,
To build another empire—to found
   another State.

There are now upwards of forty vessels advertised at this port, direct for San Francisco. The brig Orbit, Best, (180 tons,) will sail to-day. She has been purchased by a company of thirty-five young men belonging to Hudson, Columbia county, who have put into the fund $500 each—making a total of $15,000; of which $7,200 was paid for the vessel, and the residue laid out in stores for a two years voyage.

The schooner Anthem, Eldridge, left yesterday afternoon for San Francisco, via the Straits of Magellan. Captain E. intends sailing up the Sacramento river as far as Sutter's Fort.

This company go out under favorable circumstances; taking letters of introduction from our official dignitaries to those in command in California. They are provided with one year's provisions, a life boat, wagons, and the most approved machinery for mining; and last, though not least, Major General Winfield Scott has presented them with the tent which he used through the Mexican campaign.

The ship Brooklyn, Richardson, sailed yesterday morning. The B. is a large class vessel—has a full freight and a large number of passengers.

The ship Edward Everett, Smith, with its "California Mining and Trading Company," left Boston Thursday, having on board one hundred and fifty men; the crew consists of eighteen men, besides two cooks and three stewards, all of whom give their services for the passage out.

[From the Philadelphia Ledger, Jan. 12.]

The brig Osceola, for San Francisco, is expected to leave, with a full freight and crowded with passengers, on Sunday morning; and the Gray Eagle, for the same destination, will probably get off the next day.

At Utica one of the most extensive organizations has been formed, under the title of "The Utica Mining Company."—The capital stock $30,000, in shares of $100 each.

At Buffalo the "California Overland Association" sets out on the 20th inst., to embark at New York for Vera Cruz, and proceed thence by way of the city of Mexico to San Blas or Mazatlan.—The total cost for the three hundred composing the party is estimated at $27,675—or an individual cost of $92.25.

The brig Attila, (says the Boston Journal of last evening,) Capt. M. W. Baker, cleared at this port this forenoon for San Francisco, with 42 passengers. The Attila is owned by and has on board the "Plymouth California Trading Company," and is the eighth vessel which has cleared from this port for San Francisco. Her cargo is chiefly ship's stores, and does not embrace any spirituous liquor.

The clipper schooner Eclipse, (says the *Baltimore American* of yesterday,) Capt. Isaac H. Norris, cleared at the Custom House yesterday for San Francisco, and will sail to-day. The E. was formerly the celebrated pilot boat of that name, and is only 80 tons burthen. Capt. Norris intends avoiding the rough passage around Cape Horn by taking his little craft through the Straits of Magellan. Eight passengers go out in this vessel.

The directors of the State Mutual Life Insurance Company, in Worcester, Mass., have voted to decline all risks on the lives of persons going to California. It needs but an inspection of the accommodations of some of the passenger vessels now fitting out, to convince the directors of any company that such risks are not likely to be profitable. (NYH, Jan. 13, 1849.)

The Cholera in the West

There still seems considerable fatality among the passengers up the Mississippi. The *Louisville Journal* of the 4th instant says:—

The Western World passed here yesterday afternoon. She had a large number of deck passengers, mostly German emigrants. Nine of them and her pastry cook died of cholera. The Jewess, which also passed up yesterday, had three deaths. The steamer Aleck Scott, Capt. Swan, was at the mouth of the Ohio when the Connecticut left there, bound for St. Louis, with several hundred emigrants on board. Some fourteen or fifteen of them had died, and many were sick.

The following is from the St. Louis *Republican* of the 31st ult.:—

The steamers Grand Turk and Andrew Fulton arrived yesterday from New Orleans. The Grand Turk had eleven cases during the trip, of which number four died. The Andrew Fulton had seven cases on board at the time of her arrival. One of the deaths, Mr. Hoeher, a cabin passenger, occurred yesterday, when the boat was but a few miles below the city. At eleven o'clock he was apparently as healthy as any man on the boat, and at two a corpse. An eminent physician was on board, who rendered every possible assistance, but it was of no avail. He pronounced it a true case of Asiatic cholera.

(NYH, Jan. 13, 1849.)

President Polk's Message

[From the London Times of Dec. 23]

When scarce a day passes without bringing the inauguration of a constituent assembly, the address of a newly elected President, or the programme of a new constitution, the message of an American President reads like a thing of the past. By the rule of comparison the United States will soon be an ancient polity. The successor of Washington is an old friend. One feels therefore somewhat more patience than usual for the annual tax on our time, which a long series of Presidents have uniformly exacted. The Court style of the Union is so well known to the taste of this nation, that we need only say that it characterizes the Message. We can, however, add that Mr. Polk has given an account of American progress which will excite the interest and the admiration of the Old World. In the history of States there never was anything so rapid, and never did a preternatural growth appear to rest on so solid a foundation. All that one has ever read of families multiplied as the sands on the sea shore, of swarming tribes, of rising cities, and prosperous commonwealths, seems concentrated and magnified in this modern prodigy, whose Anglo-Saxon origins suggests in us so many regrets and not a little pride.

Mr. Polk hastens to the strong point of his Presidency—the enormous acquisition of territory effected within these four years by annexation, by treaty, or by war. Texas, Oregon, California, and New Mexico, are exultingly measured and almost weighed in the balance. They contain so many square miles and so many acres, and are equal to such and such countries; but as the English imagination will not revel with so much gusto on these various measurements, it may be sufficient to state that the United States now comprehend a territory almost as large as all Europe. The President expatiates with delight on the climate, the soil, and other natural advantages of the newly acquired regions. Their rivers, their harbors, their vicinities and bearings, are reviewed. But to one topic he returns again and again. The mines, or rather the fields of gold and quicksilver in California, are an inexhaustible fund of agreeable discussion and allusion. Paragraph after paragraph glitters with gold and groans with bullion. The four thousand gold hunters wildly scraping the sands, and filling their laps with solid wealth; the greedy haste with which whole crews desert their ships for this Lotus shore, and all the other circumstances of a real El Dorado are described with gloating ecstasy. A mint is forthwith to be established on the western coast, which is to deluge Asia and Polynesia with the glittering tokens of the fortunate Republic.

There was need of many mines to gild the Mexican war, and to pay its expenses. Those acquisitions have cost the Union twenty-five millions of our money. If in the course of twenty years the principal and the interest be repaid by the dust collected from the rivers of California, the Union may deem itself most fortunate. Mr. Polk, however, disdains to measure the war only by its results. He points to the energy, the military skill, the administrative capacity, the martial spirit, the indomitable perseverance, and the dexterous tact by which it has been so speedily brought to its desired consummation under circumstances of unparalleled difficulty. It is demonstrated that the Union, at a moment's warning, may undertake a war several thousand miles from home, with forces competent to any occasion, conduct that war with promptness and unity of purpose, and endure, without burden, all the necessary expense. A standing army, in the European sense of that word, is found to be unnecessary. Two million citizens, accustomed to arms, many of them practised in the rifle and hardened in the severities of the forest, ambitious for distinction, supply a never-failing fund of volunteers. The army of a republic consists not of privates, but of knights. Its very staple is heroic. What crowns, however, both the glory, the grace, and the ability of this conquest is, that all the States, all parties, and all professions, equally contributed their quota to the field, thus proving that Texas and New Mexico belong not more to this or that State than to all, and exhibiting also a pledge to the world of that terrible unanimity with which the Union will on future occasions prosecute its quarrels or its ends.

[From the London Spectator of Dec. 23d]

Beyond the Atlantic, James K. Polk has sent in his last message,—a huge volume, which combines the characteristics of the Parliamentary blue book, the historical essay, and the traveler's guide book. The most striking point in the document is its voucher for the wonderful and apocryphal stories of mineral riches in California. How alarmed Jefferson and Washington would be to see their republic grow as large as Europe, triumphant in wars of aggression and now poisoned by possessing mines like those of enervated Peru or despotic Russia!

[From the London Sun of Dec. 29th]

Whatever the Americans may think of the riches to be derived from the mines of gold and quicksilver discovered in California, they would act more wisely in observing the admirable results flowing from the approximation of their commercial system to the principles of free trade, than in pursuing the visionary speculations of a new and more seductive El Dorado. The recent explosion of the philosophic bubble of M. Cabet, should act as a timely warning to the dreamers of the United States. Icaria has melted away from the prairies of Texas as the *mirage* melts from the aridity of the wilderness.[3] According to M. Cabet, Icaria flowed with cream and honey, with the fruit of the olive and the juice of the grape, while, according to those who have adventured in search of this beautiful "land of promise," the whole account has proved to be in every particular the phantom of a gorgeous hallucination. The "rubies thick as gravel" are mere pebble, the diamonds mere flint, the harvest mere crops of poisonous weeds, the vintage stagnant pools reeking with stale exhalations. . . . With this revealed extravagance confronting them amidst the forests of Texas, will the people of the United States abandon themselves blindly to the fascinating allurements of the wealth said to be stored in the soil of California? . . .

With California it is impossible not to perceive that everything as yet is merely visionary. Even the most moderate estimates of the mineral riches buried in those newly acquired territories bear the stamp of the most preposterous exaggeration. Among these not the least remarkable is the official despatch forwarded to Washington by Colonel Mason, the officer in command at Monterey. . . .

He talks of the most precious products of the earth as abounding like dirt. His delineation of the two hundred men washing for gold in the American Fork, called the Mormon Digging, reminds one of the magnificent accounts furnished by Orme of the treasuries in the palace of Moorahedabad. Every circumstance in the process of purification is lingered over with the intensest relish—the men working in the broiling heat of the tropics—sifting the alluvial deposits of the stream in perforated tin pans, in the willow baskets woven by the hands of the Red Indians, or in crude rocking machines known among the initiated as cradles—straining off the mingled gold and dust through the augur holes into a receptacle below, and then blowing away the

---

3. Étienne Cabet (1788–1856), a French socialist who established Icaria, a utopian community that quickly failed.

sand as the husks are blown away by the breath of the winnow. As to the products of such strange labor, it is estimated by Col. Mason that a party of four men employed in this manner in the lower mines average one hundred dollars per diem. Even the gold mines in the interior of Russia pale in their splendor before the glittering earth of California.

Employing the undoubted productiveness of the country just forfeited by Mexico, and employing that productiveness rationally, the United States may ultimately derive extraordinary advantages from the acquisition. But plunging into wholesale speculation, like the dupes of the South Sea Delusion, they can only reach the miseries of beggary and embarrassment. We are the more disposed to insist upon this from a sense that the increasing enthusiasm which is already manifested throughout the United States in regard to the mines of California, is an augury of the expansion of a Bubble. Formerly the progress of such an expansion would have been watched with a kind of jealous satisfaction; but now that the interests of the different powers are becoming every day more blended together, it can only be observed with pain and anxiety.

(PPL, Jan. 15, 1849.)

POPPING THE QUESTION TO CALIFORNIANS.—"WELL, JOHN, WHERE will you get board in California?" Answer—"Well, I don't know, uncle Peter; I guess I can board at $1 per day in San Francisco." "Yes, but can you obtain board at the mines?" "Well, I don't know, uncle Peter." "Robert, how is it with you?" "O, uncle, I have made ample provision; I have on board vessel 4 barrels salt beef, 2 of pork, a lot of hard bread, pepper, salt, pots and kettles in abundance. I shall do my own cooking as well as digging." "Yes, Robert, but how will you get your barrels to the mines, without wagons or roads, from the head of navigation?" "Why, roll them there, uncle Peter." "You must store them in the sun, there being no buildings there. Will not the hoops shrink, loosen, the barrels leak and the contents spoil?" "Well, I don't know, uncle; I must think of that." "Richard, how have you arranged for your living at the mines?" "Well, uncle, I went down to Wells, Miller & Prevost's, No. 27 Front street, where they keep all kinds of Preserved Meats, Soups, Pickles, Preserves, Spiced Oysters, Sour Crout, &c., and purchased 400 lbs. of preserved roasted Meats, 200 pounds of preserved Vegetables, material for 400 pints Soup, one half barrel Sour Crout, (to keep off the scurvy,) for the sum of $155, which with the $20 I paid for 400 pounds bread, makes $175. So, you see, I have 1,400 lbs. food for a year, or quite 4 lbs. a day, for $3.50 per week. These provisions are put up in cannisters, and keep 21 years, retaining perfectly their natural flavor. I can, in bags, throw them on the backs of mules and go any where to the best diggings, over 200 miles distant, while poor John can't dig at all for want of food, and Robert must dig near by his barrel." "Well, Richard," says uncle Peter, "you can go to California with safety. You will get along in the world, my boy, sure."

Interesting Account of the Gold Region

[Correspondence of the New Orleans Crescent]
Monterey, California, Aug. 26, 1848.

At last, my dear brother, I can tell you of something wonderful in this hitherto uninteresting service. I listened an unbeliever to all the gold-diggers's stories of those who have been dropping in from the Placer, these last three or four months, until the Governor and Sherman returned; and even then, when the Colonel brought home handfuls of the pure metal, which had been given to him as specimens, and remarked to me, "Yes, it is all true, and the most remarkable part of it is that it is not exaggerated," I could not, or rather did not want to believe that an El Dorado had at last been found; and as Captain Smith, of the Dragoons, had just arrived from Los Angeles, to pay us a visit at my invitation, and to look at this upper country, I asked the Colonel to let me go with him to the mines, that we too might see. We left this on the 21st, and as the plains and mountains are rather dry and uninteresting now, we got over them as soon as convenient, passing, every few miles, carts, wagons, and families, foot and horsemen, all bound to the Placer. We found the farm-houses and villages almost deserted; and at the cabins where we stopped for meals, we heard only of the gold! The women would, after a little talk, go to their chests and bring out their bags, to show what fine large pieces the men had got for them. At San Jose, or the Pueblo, as they call it here, we found most of the houses shut up, and their owners gone too—one or two carts in the streets, and these were being got ready for the journey up.

I was agreeably surprised to find San Francisco a pretty little Yankee looking town, though we had to wade through two or three miles of sand hills, against a stiff nor'wester, just before reaching it. They have made the best of a bad site, on the side of a pretty steep hill, and hemmed in by high sand hills. They have stuck a board house under the lee of every sand bank or clump of bushes, and you cannot buy a sand hill there now for any money. They boast quite a good looking hotel, and talk of the mint, bank, market-house, and navy-yard, that will be, with quite a serious look, rather amusing to a stranger who has not seen the Placer; but if he happens in at some of the half dozen stores strung along the water-side, and sees some of the rough looking countrymen, who may have just arrived from the mines—(how very polite the store-keepers are to them now!)—the fellow takes out his buckskin purse, a foot long, and shakes half a dozen pounds or so of gold into the scales, to pay for his truck, with as much coolness as if it were sand. "Is it pretty rich up there?" "Oh, yes!" You wonder why the fellow came away; so, to find out if he was unlucky, you ask, "About how much did you get out?" "About two or three thousand dollars!" "And how long were you digging?" "About twelve days in all, but I didn't dig steady; I was on the river two or three days examining." "Why did you come away?" "Oh, I came down to buy goods, and I am going back to trade."

You next wonder why all you saw at dinner that day didn't go right off to the mines; but they were merchants and merchants' clerks, and the merchants have averaged sales of two or three thousand dollars daily, making about three hundred per cent on cost; and the merchants clerks get at least $300 per month. Why, the negro cook at the hotel gets $200 per month, and is going to leave next month for the mines! After seeing and hearing all this, one begins to think the place must grow.

After looking around thus and listening to some of the stories of gold or trade, we could hear of no launch going up that day, and so adjourned to dinner, where we sat down with some twenty well-dressed and happy-looking civilians; and before dinner was over every man had one or more bottles of champagne before him. They were all getting rich, and could af-

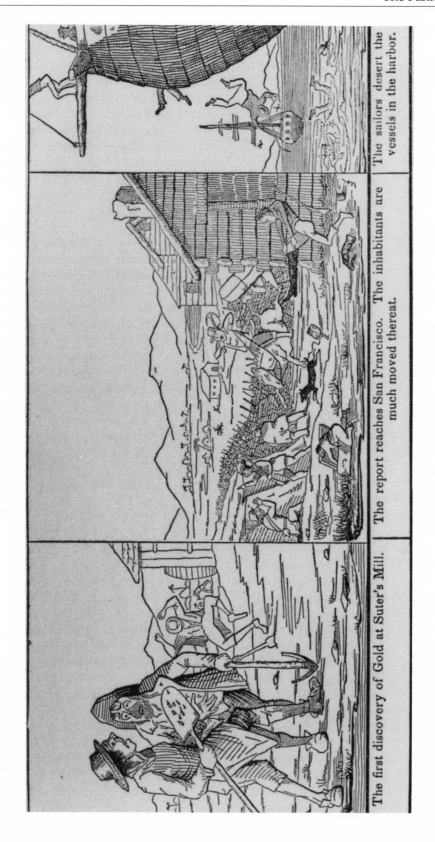

The first discovery of Gold at Suter's Mill. | The report reaches San Francisco. The inhabitants are much moved thereat. | The sailors desert the vessels in the harbor.

ford it; but it took three days of my pay. "Hurrah! hurrah!" cried out half a dozen, as one tall dry-looking genius, straightened about seven feet of his humanity, "a toast, a toast from the Judge!" "Do you know the Judge!" said one to me; "he is a trump, ain't he?" Of course, I knew him, and answered, "isn't he?" "Gentlemen," said the Judge, "I'm going to give a sentiment, can't make a speech, never could, but even Dr. Leatherbelly here," and he slapped another seven footer on the shoulder, who swallowed a large mouthful and the nick-name with rather a wry face, "even Dr. Leatherbelly, with all his preaching, must acknowledge the truth of my sentiment—that we are all here to make money!" A general roar acknowledged the tall chap a good judge of other men's intentions.

We rode to the Presidio, or remains of the old fort and barracks; but so bleak are the winds, and so exposed to their fury are the old adobe walls, that only two sides of the Presidio square remain standing, and they were in a miserable condition when the company of volunteers took up their quarters there. They are now roofed and ceiled inside. The fort shows the remains of a low walled demi-lune,[4] on what might be rendered an almost inaccessible little promontory. Not a gun is there now, and nothing done yet in the way of fortifying the bay; and I am afraid that now the gold at the Placer will attract all labor from public and other work in its vicinity for some years to come, except they pay in proportion. The volunteers had as much work as suited them, in putting their quarters in order; and those who did not desert, deserve great credit for remaining at their post at all, with such discomfort and bad pay. But they did not intend waiting more than a month longer for the peace.

On the third day the town had lost its novelty, for it was cold and no fire to be had. We began to criticise the cooking—want of ladies—the bleak wind and the sand—the wholesoul eagerness with which every man, woman and child on this place appeared to pursue gold. We were glad when the launch-owner could not find another bale to send up in his boat. So we were off . . . and evening found us in the mouth of the river—marshes and musketoes on either side—where we waited till day, and then found a broad, pretty and quiet stream, up which we sailed some sixty miles, to Sutter's landing. This is the only long, navigable and important river in the western acquisition of Uncle Sam's. Steamers will in a year be running many leagues above the mouth of Feather River, which is some distance above Sutter's. We found here half-a-dozen launches, a few wagons, and a motley set of vagabonds (whites, Indians, negroes, kanakas, Chinese and Chilenos). We walked with the late Mormon, now thriving merchant, over a dusty three miles to Sutter's Fort, which stands out from the bank of the river, on the open plain, and on ground so low that it is almost an island during the winter floods. . . . By sunset our horses were ready, and we were off for a night's ride to the lower, or Mormon diggings—so called from the Mormons, who discovered it. But it was cold, and we could not see the road—so we stopped and took some sleep, and the next morning rode down the hill to the bank of the American fork, which here makes a rapid between two rocky hills, and has deposited an island of an acre or so of sand and gravel among some rocks, which obstructed the way. It was like a camp meeting—plenty of booths and brush shanties lined the river bank; and, upon riding over the rough stones and gravel bank of the Island—which we did with difficulty, for it was full of newly-dug

---

4. A bastion having a crescent-shaped rear entrance.

pits and piles of stone—to reach the creek, now quite low and retired to the main channel, we saw, for the first time, the gold washers at work.

There were ranged along the edges of the stream at least a dozen washer machines, which are just like baby cradles, made of wood, only open at the foot, and with rounded or cylindrical bottoms, and a few brackets tacked across the bottom at intervals of a foot or so. They are set in or at the edge of the water on rockers, with a slope down stream; one man brings the earth or gravel, which is cleaned of the big stones, and throws it on the head or top of the cradle, which is formed of bars or a coarse sieve of sheet iron or copper, and another man stands at the head of the cradle in the water, which he dips up and dashes on the gravel or dirt as it is left on the grate—the earth, by this party, was taken from within a foot of the surface— while a third rocks the cradle, and thus keeping a stream of water passing through it in continual rolling from side to side, and very muddy, with the clayey and earthy matter washed out. The heavy sand and heavier gold all catches or lodges above the brackets. After the party has washed its morning's work of three or four hours, several pounds of this black iron, or magnetic sand, mingled with gold, are scraped from above the two or three upper brackets; most of the sand is then washed out by the hand in a tin pan, by holding the pan inclined just below the surface of the water, stirring the whole up, and stirring the water as it mingles with the sand, out at the lower edge of the basin, keeping one side below the stream all the while, to let in clean water, and take out more sand. The weight of the gold keeps it all the while at the lowest point of the basin, and it seems hard to wash or shake it out.

We looked on in wonder and astonishment for an hour, to see by what a simple process men were all around us getting rich. . . . We had satisfied our curiosity here, and wanted to reach the mill, or first discovery, that day. . . . A piece of ten acres or so has been penned off for Capt. Sutter, whose enterprising efforts to civilize this wilderness led to the discovery.

They tried to keep the matter secret, but too many knew it, and in three months from that time, that wilderness of hills— among which none but Sutter's men and Indians ever ventured alone for fear of the wild Indians—was now fast being settled; and the grisly bears, wolves and jackals, listened in astonishment to the frying pans hissing, babies crying, cow bells tinkling, and boys kicking up a shindy among the wagons—and there was no place left for them to go.

We left the saw-mill, and found by going up it, that the hill above it was a pretty high one, and following the windings of the road round the hills which were fast rising into mountains, we rode about noon into a ravine between two pretty high hills, which in winter holds quite a torrent. Parties of men were scattered along this canada like ants. It being late and very hot, but few were working. We passed on to another canada beyond, where the Californians had principally congregated, and it being Sunday, were lounging or gambling, and the Indians, their laborers, ditto— dressed *a la Adam*—and a miserable, brutish race they are, hardly know the use of fire to prepare their food, many of them living upon grass, seeds, and acorns—in the slightest little brush dens which it could be supposed would shelter a piece of mortality, and clothing themselves against the winter's snows and summer's heat, which are here severe, with nothing.

I rode from one end to the other of the main valley, in the dry diggings, and questioned almost every man there, and they all, without a single exception, were then making from two ounces to two hundred dollars per day, when they chose to work. Many had shanties with trinkets, blankets, and calicoes for the Indians, and comforts and necessaries for the whites. I think at least two thousand whites, including Californians, were on the dry diggings of the American Fork, and one thousand on the river, in different parts, washing. There cannot be less than two thousand on the Yuba, the north fork of the American, and on Feather river; on all of which the washings bring the finest gold, and in great abundance, at almost every deposit in the bed of the river; and it is a fact, which only the daily ocular proof I had convinced me of, that for many miles of wild and dreary space, watered by nearly all the eastern tributaries of the Sacramento, a traveller can get off his horse in the bed of any mountain stream, where the hills on either side are of gravelly red clay, and the slate creeps out of the bed of the gully, and there, in an hour's washing, he is sure to get some gold, sometimes a vial, sometimes two, three, or ten dollars worth. . . . Gold has been found abundant enough to attract the laziest sceptic in a large part of this district, and without any enthusiasm, which, by the way, has not formed part of my system since I came round Cape Horn to gain glory fighting Mexicans, I think the Californians—for gold is found in both— under the enterprising gold-loving Yankees, will export from six to ten millions of gold annually, in less than ten years.

It was estimated by the most intelligent, that over two hundred thousand dollars had been taken out when I was there, three months after it was made public, and by the small vagrant and vagabond population of California. Three-fourths of the men I saw working in the dry diggings were either runaway sailors or soldiers, or men who had left home suddenly, and might be called a drinking, fighting, but not a working population.

I intended to complete an account of our trip, which, towards the last, gave me an idea of the wild and rich plains of the Sacramento—when I saw the grisly bears within a few miles of a well travelled road, and hundreds of elk and antelopes, which, wild as they are, have not had time to get out of the way of the tide of gold-hunters rolling over the plains.

I expect to have a strange time of it here. Forts without soldiers—ordnance without men enough to guard them— towns without men—country without government, laws or legislators—and, what's more, no one disposed to stop to make them; and a sort of colonial territory of the United States, without even a communication with the home government for nearly two years, or with the navy for many months. The officers of the army here could have seized the large amount of funds in their hands, levied heavily on the country, and been living comfortably in New York for the last year, and not a soul in Washington be the wiser or worse for it. Indeed, such is the ease with which power can go unchecked and unpunished in this region, that it will be hard for the officers of government to resist temptation; for a salary here is certain poverty and debt, unless one makes up by the big hauls—the merest negro can make more than our present Governor, Colonel Mason, receives in toto. (NYH, Jan. 16, 1849.)

CALIFORNIA.—A YOUNG MAN OF LIMITED MEANS WOULD LIKE TO join some joint stock company, of undoubted character, about to proceed overland to California, for mutual protection and assistance, both on the route and after their arrival at the point of destination. Address, with names and references, stating estimated expenses and other particulars, H. W. B., at this office.

The Rush is On

"Jack Bung" off for California

[From Ned Buntline's Own][1]

DEAR NED:—I should have written you before, but I have been attacked with a glittering *yellow fever*; and my Esculapius affirms that nothing will cure me but a heavy dose of the "root of all evil"—say a thousand pounds troy weight—and likewise, in order to get it, I must proceed to California, and excavate it from beneath Dame Nature's hide, and apply it fresh *internally* to the breeches pocket.

I have a friend in California who was *carried off* by the same fever, and he writes me such encouraging news of his convalescence, that I have saddled up the "*old*

---

1. Ned Buntline (real name, Edward Zane Carroll Judson) was a teller of tall tales, writer of dime novels, and a notorious public nuisance. *Ned Buntline's Own* was a magazine he published for several years. Jack Bung was one of eight or ten pseudonyms he used. (Others were Jack Brace and Mad Jack.) The letter signed John Johnson Smith (another pseudonym) is, of course, also written by Buntline. Thus we have phony name number three writing to phony name number two who writes to the first phony name—who publishes both letters. All the names were changed to protect the guilty.

mare" and am gong to "cut across lots," as we Yankees term it, to the Gold region. I give you a copy of his letter for the benefit of your readers, for this epidemic is raging in all parts of the country. My friend is a person of undoubted veracity, as he studied for the ministry once, but gave up the vocation by reason of its not being a money making business. You may depend upon the truth of his statements:—

NEAR FEATHER RIVER, California
In the Gold Mines, July 27, 1848.

DEAR JACK:—I have been thinking for the last two weeks that I would write you; but I have been so busily employed in digging for the precious metal that I have had no time to do anything else. But I will spare you a few moments of my golden existence to tell you of my success. It is five weeks to-day since Sam Slygo and myself commenced digging gold. We had for our tools two small tin basins and a hand-basket, for which articles we paid the round sum of $2,800. In ten days we dug and washed out 3,680 pounds of pure virgin gold, or 44,162 ounces, which, at $16 per ounce, will amount to $706,592—a pretty fair sum for ten days' work! Every night, after getting through work, and sitting in the tent, we take off our boots to dry our feet, (for we stand in the river all day up to our knees in water,) and not a night passes but we empty from one to three pounds of fine gold dust or scales from each boot, which is the sediment of the river. I have no doubt but some of you New England coveys will think that that is getting rich fast enough; but I have found other places where I can get it in larger quantities than in the river, and not work so hard for it either.

Nearly a week since, Sam and myself concluded that we might find the gold in "dryer diggings" than those we had been to work in, so we started for the mountains to see what we could do there. After cruising around for six or eight hours, with poor luck, collecting only about twenty

pounds, I got tired and cross, and sat down at the foot of a hill; but Sam said he wasn't going to give it up so, and up the hill he started, while I took out my only remaining cigar, and began to smoke and doze. I had not been there over ten minutes, when I heard Sam shout to "stand from under!" and as I jumped up, I saw a mass of something come thundering down the hill at a tremendous rate; it brought up in a ravine at the foot of the hill. In a moment after, down came Sam about as fast as the preceding avalanche, screaming and yelling like a Camanche.

"What the deuce are you up to?" I cried. "Rolling rocks down just for the fun of seeing a fellow get out of the way!"

"Rock! rock and a half or two rocks! I don't care whether school keeps or not," cried Sam.—"Look at the rock, and see if it isn't one of the rocks we often read of, but seldom see."

And sure enough, come to look at it, it was one solid mass of gold! We have cut off about a third of it with cold chisels—something over a ton between us two; and we have discovered another nearly as large as this one, which we are going to work on soon.

Come out here by all means, if you wish to make your fortune. Bring out a box of Manuel Amore cigars, and I will give you a hundred weight of gold for them; for I'm half crazy for want of a cigar.

Yours in haste,
JOHN JOHNSON SMITH. (CPD, Jan. 16, 1849.)

The Character of the California Emigrants

The emigrants now leaving us for California appear to be remarkably orderly, respectable, and intelligent. They are men of energy and enterprise, and full of enthusiasm. It is a character of the emigration that we do not (as we willingly would) get rid of the worst part—the idle, the rowdies, the vagabonds—of our population; but we lose—with regret we say it—the finest portion of our youth, and in all cases such as possess some means—such as are not impelled to emigrate by want, but who rush forward in eager haste to the golden regions, from sheer ambition. The dissolute, idle, and necessitous, who with brawny arms and active limbs encumber our almshouses, and fill our streets with mendicants or burglars, are those who are left behind; not that the love of gold is less profoundly impressed upon their hearts, but that they want the means of conveying them away to the scene of the general scramble.

So much the better for California—so much the worse for us.

Our great city is a vast reservoir, into which streams of humanity are ever pouring from all parts of the world; and in these streams there come, sometimes, mixed up in the mass, some foul waters which stagnate among us. We want sewer, occasionally, to carry them off. Meantime, the stream flowing from us to California is a portion of our strength and pride. Well, be it so. Rather than regretting it, let us hope that our chivalrous and adventurous youth who are hurrying forward to the El Dorado, may in a year or two return home among us, having succeeded in obtaining the object of their pursuit—gold and happiness—a couple which, by the bye, we have never as yet in all our experience seen living happily and unitedly together. But what an emigration this is! How singular are the elements which compose it, when the gold contagion has seized even upon our poets, and they, too, are running off from us! Alas for the nymphs of Parnassus, when Plutus, the subterranean god, can thus entice away their devotees and admirers. But we think we have yet poetry and

poets enough left behind in New York; perhaps too much of the former, and not the very best of the latter.

(NYH, Jan. 17, 1849.)

ANOTHER LETTER FROM CALIFORNIA

A. G. Henderson has furnished the Boston Gazette with the following letter from Mr. B. P. Koozer,[2] now of California, but formerly a journeyman printer in that office.

Monterey, Upper California,
August 27, 1848.

Mr. Henderson—My object in writing to you is to inform you that I am in the U. S. service, and of the prospects and advantages to be gained in emigrating to California. . . . Our company has been reduced down to 20 from 172, by desertion. These men have made their fortunes, but have violated their oaths and dishonored their flag, by deserting in time of war.

We have just heard the news of peace, and I am on the fence as to whether I will desert or not, as I can easily make $150 per day at the mines.

One of our men, on a three months' furlough, brought back to Monterey with him twenty-seven pounds of virgin gold. This, at California prices ($10 per ounce) would be worth $3,240, or at the Boston prices, ($20 per ounce) $6,480. What do you think of that? I hate to desert—I hate to soldier for six dollars a month—I am almost crazy. Excuse this letter, as I have the gold fever shocking bad, and the "root of all evil" is in my mind night and day. . . . Do as you please, but I advise you to bundle up your traps and come to California. It is a good climate, and an agricultural country, which would warrant you to come independently of its mineral wealth.

---

2. Benjamin Park Koozer (spelled Kooser by Bancroft) arrived in California in 1847 with Company F of the 3rd U. S. Artillery regiment. His account of the company, *Pioneer Soldiers of California,* was published in the *Daily Alta California* in 1864. Koozer was editor and publisher of the *Santa Cruz Sentinel* for eleven years. He died in Santa Cruz in 1878 at the age of 56.

Bring your wife along, for a good wife is the scarcest article in California. Yours, in a bad fix, B. P. KOOZER.

(NYH, Jan. 19, 1849.)

Novel Adventures and Expeditions to California—Feminines— Progress of the Mania

A Mr. Koozer tells his friend in Boston to "bring his wife along with him, for a good wife is the scarcest article in California." Now, as most of the emigrants who have lately started for that region are young and enterprising men, and few of them married, we think the best shipment that could be sent hereafter to the gold diggings would be a consignment of young ladies, and as the demand, for some time, would be pretty brisk, there would be an excellent chance for clearing off the "upper shelves"—all those of a doubtful age, even verging to and perhaps including a large portion of the old maids.

The riches of the mines, and the scarcity of the ladies, persuade us that twenty or thirty cargoes of unmarried women, reaching the El Dorado of money and men, in six or eight months from this time, would be snapped up with more avidity than a similar shipment from England was, in our early history, by the settlers in Virginia. The rape of the Sabines would be nothing to it. The Rev. Mr. Colton, who is now wading up the shores of the Sacramento, and exploring the ravines of the Sierra Nevada, would make more by marriage fees, if the unruly Christians would only wait for the ceremony, than he could ever do by gathering the raw material.

Are there no Christian men or women in this vast metropolis, and in this benevolent country, to fit out such an expedition? Abby Folsom and Lucretia Mott, where are you?[3]

Should Lucretia and Abby, contrary to our expectation, turn a deaf ear to our appeal, we call upon the free soilers to take the matter up. This is a mode by which their favorite theories can be carried out more effectually than if they should go on blustering for centuries at their public meetings. An emigration of this kind to California would soon make it a territory, and the further agitation of the anti-slavery question would at once and for ever be put an end to. We call, then, upon all matrons and speculators, "rights of woman" women, and "rights of man" men, philanthropists, and free soilers, of all classes, creeds, and parties, to set on foot at once a movement of this kind. It would far transcend, in importance and effects, the expedition of the Puritans in the Mayflower, upwards of two hundred years ago; and when Plymouth rock, and all its associations, are forgotten, the female expedition to California would be handed down to the remotest posterity as the greatest event of modern civilization.

(NYH, Jan. 20, 1849.)

The Rush to California; Incidents on the Increase

SCENES IN NEW YORK

We will endeavor to give some idea of the revolution that is going on in our midst, caused by the thirst after gold. It is an epidemic, and now rages with a violence that threatens to depopulate New York.

In November last we were divided into three classes in the political world— the Cass men, the Van Buren men, and the

---

3. Lucretia Coffin Mott (1793–1880) and Elizabeth Cady Stanton launched the women's suffrage movement in 1848, at Seneca Falls, New York. Abby Folsom was born in England about 1792 and came to America in 1837. She was prominent in the anti-slavery movement, and was considered by some to be a harmless fanatic on the subject of free speech. She died in 1867.

Taylor men. In January, 1849, the city is divided into three great divisions: 1st, Those who are decided to go to California. 2d, Those who have not decided to go, but will leave as soon as they can raise the wind. 3d, Those who cannot leave under any circumstances.

The Cass men go to California. The Van Buren men are those who will go, if they can get a platform to go on.

The whigs and Taylor men are well enough as they are; they are content, for they have something to feed on here.[4]

The political community of Nov., 1848, is the California community of January, 1849. The hunkers, free soilers, and whigs, are the goers, the try-to-goers, and the stay-at-homers. In order to give a faithful and correct history of the events connected with this extraordinary state of things, and to impress the community with the magnitude and importance of the epoch, it will be necessary to preface it with an account of the great outpourings of a people from one land to another—from one section to another section of country. The first on record is related by Moses, who gave a very faithful account of the original sort of a California movement among the ancestors of our Chatham street people.[5] They made a move "from Egypt into a land—good land and large—unto a land flowing with milk and honey; unto the place of the Hittites, the Amonites, and the Perizites, and the Hivites, and the Jebusites." The first

exodus resembled in many respects the present California exodus. God commanded the original emigrators, "Ye shall not go empty; but every one shall borrow of his neighbor," &c. Judging from the proceedings in the courts of law here, to arrest absconding debtors, &c., our goers have been doing it without any command. They, too, have got tired of making bricks. They had to cross the Red Sea; our emigrants have to cross a blue one. But Providence raised up dry land, so that they did not have to boat it, and modern ingenuity has lessened the distance round the Horn, by providing mules to cross the Isthmus, and steamers at each end of the line.

The next great exodus was from Europe to America. The last was reserved to immortalize this century in general, and the administration of James K. Polk in particular. We shall make no comparison with the second exodus; it is altogether too voluminous. We shall imitate the great historian, Moses; be plain and simple in relating the great events of the present era. We shall not deal in generalities to a greater extent than he did. Moses tells the whole story, from the brick making and burning bush—what the bush said, and what all said, all did, until they got fairly off, and the sea tumbled in upon Pharaoh and the chariot wheels.

We shall follow his example by commencing with Jem Grant, the barber, and his party, who were the first to exodus

---

4. In the presidential election of 1848 the Whigs, recognizing that they had stumbled onto a good thing by running an old military hero (William Henry Harrison) in 1840, tried it again with Zachary "Old Rough and Ready" Taylor, the hero of Buena Vista. The Democrats nominated Lewis Cass of Michigan, another former general. In the North, a third party, the Free-Soil, was formed by a 'strange bedfellows' coalition of the abolitionist Liberty party, the Barnburners of New York state, and the antislavery Whig faction from New England. The Free-Soilers nominated Martin Van Buren, who had been president from 1837 to 1841. Van Buren didn't win any states, but he took enough votes away from Cass in New York that Taylor carried the state—and the election. The editorial writer was poking fun at the Free-Soilers for ostensibly needing "a platform to go on." The prime objective of the Free-Soilers was to pass the Wilmot Proviso; their platform slogan was "Free soil, free speech, free labor, and free men."

5. Immigrant Jews.

from sixpences and shaving among the whigs, as Moses and Aaron did from straw and brick making for the Egyptians. Moses gives a very graphic account of the trouble he and his party had before they got out of Egypt, and tells the whole story with great simplicity, and no doubt truthfulness, about the water, the frogs, the flies, the cattle, the biles, and every man borrowing of his neighbor—"the battened unleavened cakes," and victuals and provisions in general, which they took along with them, as also Joseph's bones, which they dug up, and the general confusion and mixed up mess before they all got off; or, to use the words of Moses, before the Lord "led the people about through the way of the wilderness and the Red Sea, and they went up harnessed out of the land Egypt." There are equally interesting details which can be minutely described in this modern exodus to California—the chartering of ships and brigs, the squads about the corners down in Wall street, at the Custom House; the financial arrangements, the renting of houses, sales of real estate, duping and victimizing, right and left, borrowing money, overcoats, pantaloons, old boots, cast off stockings, coal scuttles, sifters, and shovels, and iron utensils of all kinds. The burning bush, the serpent and rod, could not have astonished Moses and his friends more than the official documents of President Polk astonished this entire community. The hunkers had been crushed under foot; they were as bad off as the Israelites when they hankered after the flesh pots of Egypt. Pharaoh or General Taylor would prevent their getting any more of that kind of food. Offices and sinecures had been placed beyond their reach, and the announcement officially made by one of their leaders, that there was a "good land, and a large land, flowing with milk and honey," or what was better, gold dust and gold ore, created as much excitement in their minds as the official announcement of Moses in old Bible times.

Preparations were at once commenced to cross the sea, go to California, and upset and drive out the modern "Hittites, Amonites, and Hivites"—the Mexicans, Mormons, and Indians. There was a general ignorance in the community as to the whereabouts of this new region. Geography has never been a favorite study with the democracy. They know where the democratic headquarters are held in every ward, and there was a general rush to those places to compare notes and get information. Two or three days passed, when the discovery was made that there was a class in this community denominated (*par excellence*) shipping merchants, and they were supposed to know something about it.

Previous to this, large parties, amounting, it has been supposed, to several hundreds, from the number found suddenly missed, had started off of the sly, to be first in the gold field. Some put across Jersey, others followed the Harlem Railroad track; and letters have been received from various parts of the eastern and middle States, from individuals wandering about the country inquiring at every farm house on the road "the distance to California?" The counting rooms of all our shipping merchants were crowded with new faces, anxious to get a passage somewhere. They rushed down town from the upper wards, hopping and jumping over cotton bales and sugar boxes, worse than ever the frogs in Egypt did. Howland and Aspinwall had to engage new clerks to answer questions about the line of steamers between San Francisco and Panama. Rolls of bank bills poured into their cash-keepers hands like wisps of straw. One man has forced his way out onto the side walk in front of their store, holds up a paper, exclaiming—"I've got it;" "ha, ha—talk about your gold ore. Who's hunk now?" "How much?" "$150, and sure." "Can't get any more. Telegraph just come on from Mr. Aspinwall, who is in Washington, with his orders not to dispose of another ticket." Then there were sor-

The news reaches New York. | And creates an excitement. | Jonathan Swapwell, of Swapville, hears the news, and resolves to go to California. | Having taken leave of his mother, Deacon Twist advises him to remain, as the report is a snare of the devil.

rowful faces, and all eyes were turned towards sailing vessels.

We were among the crowd—one fellow says, "Damn the Panama boat—we can walk across the Isthmus." "Ha, ha—look at the chap. Patent leathers—walk across the Isthmus, eh?" says another.

Not a book was to be had in the book stores concerning California, at any price. The *Tribune* issued some stuff, and sold it like wildfire. Lecturers advertised "Lectures on California"—they were crowded. Theatres played "California" pieces, and took in hundreds. Not a brass filer in New York that did not make more than his wages by selling brass filings and dirt, picked up before new buildings, as genuine gold dust. Within a week, not a minister in New York that had not logged "California" into his sermons twice on a Sunday, and compared in his sermons pure religion to California gold. It was the rage everywhere.

The General Committee were called together at Tammany Hall. They met at 7, waited until 9; could not get up a quorum. The secretary and eight of their number were hooked for California, and busy packing up their traps for a start in the steamers Isthmus and Panama, to sail within a week. They said, "the General Committee be damned; they had other fish to fry than helping to pay up old political liabilities." One member has sold his place for $800, worth $2,000. Another is a grocer; he hurries up his collections, transfers his stock of butter and buckwheat flour for California traps and a ticket to the Isthmus; another is a teacher of elocution, and owns a patent bedstead—"to hell with the bedstead and elocution;" he sells out for $350 what he valued at $50,000; another is a dry goods dealer, salary $1,500—he has bought a brig, and advertises "for California direct." What a rush to get ready for the steamer! The driver of the new-style carriage for hotels, (the City Hotel one) owned both carriage and horses; he lets the steamboat passengers take care of them-selves; he is bound to be s steamer passenger; his horses and carriage are standing, at 10 o'clock, before Tatternall's, in Broadway; he says to the auctioneer, "Hough, I want you to sell my cattle and carriage." In half an hour, the late driver and owner walks down to pay his passage; he has $400 in bills in his pocket; he is ready to go.

It is Christmas morning, 12 o'clock, M. It rains, and the fog is so thick you can cut it. There are three hundred people on the dock to see the steamer off. "Captain! captain!" shout fifty voices. "Do ye go today?"

"Certainly; fog will rise—go in half an hour."

"Oh Lord! Here, Jim, for God's sake do go and get these damned bills changed at some exchange office—I forgot it;" and Malachi pulls out three or four hundred dollars in up country bills.

"Bill, here is a dollar; just run up Broadway and buy me that worth of paper—I forgot it, and they say it's worth fifty cents a sheet in California."

But who have we here? A man comes rushing down the pier, shouting at the top of his voice, "Capting, for C——'s sake, hold on; don't go yet; I'm a passenger;" and he forces his way through the crowd of laughing spectators, reaches the deck, throws down his linen sailor bag of dunnage, and the hoe in his hand, and sinks exhausted, saying, "Thank God; but I thought I was half an hour behind the time." Half an hour too late to go to California! as though it was merely the Brooklyn ferry boat. Scenes occurred at the starting of these boats which would make this community weep for a week at their ludicrousness. Old Moses himself couldn't begin to describe the ninety-ninth part of them.

New Year's arrived. It was not the New Year's of old times. It was a day that the great body of the male folks had devoted to call on their female friends to say farewell, and announce their immediate departure for California. California! every thing was California the first week of 1849. Every advertisement was headed California; and written posters were hung out from every store in town, from the large South street shipping merchant down to the penny trumpet and three cent gingerbread shop:—

California	soap to wash gold
"	blankets
"	coats
"	boots
"	hats
"	penknives
"	gold sifters
"	quack nostrums
"	anchors
"	toothpicks

All trades and professions are alive now. The entire community is aroused, and we shall see what we shall see, and continue to write down our record, and publish it for the benefit of posterity.

(NYH, Jan. 22, 1849.)

A Plea for the Red Man of California

Is there not something due to the aboriginal race of California, at this time? They are the original and rightful owners of the soil in which the discoveries of gold have been made. The principles of this ownership, as existing in other and elder parts of the Union, we have long acknowledged. Call it an inchoate possessory right—a usufruct in the soil—a right to hunt game in the forest, or fish in the streams; whatever title civilians are supposed to fix on, that right it is the policy of the Government to extinguish, before we proceed to occupy and parcel out the soil.

But there is a higher duty now pressing upon us. It is the duty we owe to our character for humanity in the protection of the race against the introduction of ardent spirits. Accounts which have appeared of the recent shipments for California show that ardent spirits have been sent in large quantities. It is by their use and sale to the natives that the highest expectations of gain in gold-hunting are based. It is well known that the Indians can best endure the vicissitudes of the season and the fatigues of search. They can subsist on less food and endure hunger better than the muscular men of European type. They are, at the same time, wretched judges of the cost and prices of articles of food and clothing required. They are ignorant of the standard value of gold. They are precisely the class of gold diggers who are likely to find most gold and realize least for it. But, small as their gains may be, it is the dictate of a sound public morality that they should not be poisoned with ardent spirits, and driven from the face of the country, without an effort to reclaim them to society and industry.

Another principle appears important to be tried with the California Indians. It is to fund, for their benefit, the entire amount of the consideration for their lands, and to pay the interest only in annuities. Every cent of these annuities should be devoted in aid of efforts to introduce agriculture, education, and christianity. The money paid to our Northern Indians, in coin, operates as a bonus on their destruction.

A Friend to the Red Race.
(WNI, Jan. 24, 1849.)

The Great Republic

It is only as a part of this great Republic that CALIFORNIA can enjoy the brilliant possibilities of her future destiny. If the commerce of Asia is to cross the Pacific and enter the Caribbean or Mexican seas, it is the United States which must command and protect the Isthmian gates; or if, as may be the case, that commerce should seek a still more advantageous highway by railroad across the Rocky Mountains, it is clear that such a highway never could, or would, be built except by the United States. It is, in fact, the United States which must do all political theorists suppose that California is to do.

It is the power, the wealth, and the energies of the American people only which can develop the natural resources and turn to profitable use the geographical advantages of the golden territory. It is only by and through them that California can revolutionize the Asiatic trade; which, without them, will continue to flow in its accustomed channels across the Indian Ocean and round the Cape of Good Hope. All the intelligent people who go to California know this—or they will there soon learn it; and there will be no thought or desire stronger in their hearts than that of remaining bone of the bone and flesh of the flesh of the republic. South Carolina is the only part of the United States which has enjoyed the privileges of the American Union that has ever had any desire to get out of it. Instead of nullification and secession, we shall hear, in California, of nothing but the one mighty cry of "the Union forever." The Union—yes, the Union! What to her were all the gold of the new mines, were the whole Snowy Sierra one solid ridge of the pure metal, compared with the blessings which the Union secures?—*North American.* (WNI, Jan. 22, 1849.)

Highly Important from the Gold Region

We have received intelligence from California, extending to as late as the 16th of November, being three weeks later information than what was previously received from that quarter.

Annexed will be found the long accounts given by our correspondent. This gentleman [Thomas O. Larkin] is well qualified to describe the gold movements in California. He has resided in that region since the year 1832, the most of the time in a public capacity, and has been at the gold region for weeks at a time. He was the first one who gave us, last summer, a statement of those vast discoveries. . . .

We have also received a private and confidential letter, which contains intelligence so extraordinary and so astounding, concerning the gold regions, that we forbear giving it to the public at this time, lest they would not credit it, and might only laugh at us for our pains, and accuse us of attempting to hoax and deceive the public.

According to those accounts, the extent of the gold region on the San Joaquin and Sacramento rivers extends a distance of eight hundred miles in length, by one hundred in width. It embraces not only gold, but quicksilver in almost equal abundance, particularly on the San Joaquin. It is estimated that a small population, actively engaged in mining operations in that region, could export one hundred millions of dollars in gold every year; and if this be so, an additional population might increase that amount to two or three hundred millions annually, and thereby, in a comparatively short time, completely upset the specie currency of the whole civilized world.

This is not fancy. Thousands and thousands of people from the islands in the Pacific, from Mexico, Peru, Oregon, and as far as China and the East Indies, as soon as they learn of these diggings, will crowd to California. . . . (NYH, Jan. 22, 1849.)

MONTEREY, CALIFORNIA, Nov. 16, 1848.
JAMES G. BENNETT, Esq.,
EDITOR NEW YORK HERALD—

We can now call ourselves citizens of the United States. We have now only to go by law, as we formerly went by custom—that is, when Congress gives us a government and code. The old foreign residents of California, having done very well for ten or twenty years without law, care but very little whether Congress pays early or late attention to the subject. Those who have emigrated from the Atlantic States within the last three or four years, deem the subject an important one; I only call it difficult. The carrying out a code of laws, under existing circumstances, is far from an easy task. The general government may appoint governors, secretaries, and other public functionaries; and judges, marshals, collectors, &c., may accept offices with salaries of $3,000 or $4,000 per annum; but how are they to obtain their petty officers, at half these sums, remains to be seen. The pay of a member of Congress will be accepted here by those alone who do not know enough to better themselves. Mechanics can now get $10 to $16 per diem; laborers on the wharfs or elsewhere, $5 to $10; clerks and storekeepers $1,000 to $3,000 per annum; some engage to keep store during their pleasure at $8 per day, or 1 to 1½ pounds of gold per month; cooks and stewards $60 to $100 per month. In fact, labor of every description commands exorbitant prices.

My previous information to you I merely forwarded to your office to open the way to the future belief of your many readers. I had not much expectation of being believed. The idea of mountains of quicksilver only waiting the ingenuity of man to make them pour forth as a stream—of rivers, whose bottoms and banks are of gold, is rather too much to play upon the credulity of New Yorkers or Yankees. I suppose my story passed as an enlarged edition of the Arabian Nights, improved and adapted to California.

Whether you or your readers took the tale for fiction or truth, I know not. Your last paper that has reached us is of April. This I know—the Sandwich Islands, Oregon, and Lower California are fast parting with their inhabitants, all bound for this coast, and thence to the great "placer" of the Sacramento Valley, where the digging and washing of one man that does not produce one hundred troy ounces of gold, 23 carats, from the size of a half spangle to one pound in one month, sets the digger to "prospecting," i.e., looking for better grounds. Your "Paisano" can point out many a man who has, for 15 to 20 days in succession, bagged up 5 to 10 ounces of gold a day.

Our placer, or gold region, now extends over 300 or 400 miles of country, embracing all the creeks and branches on the east side of the river Sacramento, and one side of the San Joaquin. In my travels I have, when resting under a tree and grazing my horse, seen a few pieces of pure gold picked up from the crevices of the rocks or slate where we were stopping. On one occasion, nooning or refreshing on the side of a stream entirely unknown to diggers or "prospectors," or rather, if known, not attended to, one of my companions, in lolling in the sand, said, "Give me a tin pan; why should we not be cooking in gold sands?" He took a pan, filled it with sand, washed it out, and produced in five minutes $2 or $3 worth of gold, merely saying, as he threw both pan and gold on the sand, "I thought so."

Perhaps it is fair that your readers should learn that however plenty the Sacramento Valley may afford gold, the obtaining of it has its disadvantages. From the 1st of July to the 1st of October, more or less, one half of the people will have fever and ague, or intermittent fever, which takes them from the first day of digging until they have been one hundred miles from the "Placer." In the winter, it is too cold to work in the water; but from next April to the following July, one million dollars of pure gold, per month, will be produced from the gold region, without digging more than three feet deep.

You may believe me when I say that for some time to come, California will export yearly, nearly or quite a half a million ounces of gold, twenty-two to twenty-four carats fine; some pieces of that will weigh sixteen pounds, very many one pound. Many men who began last June to dig gold with a capital of $50, can now show $5,000 to $15,000. I saw a man to-day, making purchases of dry goods, &c., for his family, lay on the counter a bag made of raw hide, well sewed up, containing one hundred ounces. I observed, that is a good way to pack gold dust. He very innocently replied—"*All the bags I brought down are that way; I like the size!*" *Five such bags in New York would bring near $10,000. This man left his family last August. Three months digging and washing, producing four or five bags of*

100 ounces each, is better than being mate of a vessel at $40 per month, as the man formerly was. His companion, a Mexican, who camped and worked with him, only had two or three cowhide bags of gold.

In this tough, but true, golden tale, you must not imagine that all men are equally successful. There are some who have done better; even to $1,000 for a month; many $1,000 during the summer. . . . Some left with only sufficient to purchase a horse and saddle, and pay the physician six ounces of gold for one ounce of quinine. An ounce of gold for advice given, six ounces a visit, brings the fever and ague to be rather an expensive companion. A well man has his proportionate heavy expenses, also, to reduce his piles or bags of gold. Dry beef in the settlements at 4 cents per lb., at the Placer, $1 to $2 per lb.; salt beef and pork, $50 to $100 per bbl.; flour, $30 to $75 per barrel; coffee, sugar, and rice, 50c. to $1 per lb. As washing is 50 cents to a dollar a garment, many prefer throwing away their used up clothes to paying the washerwoman; that is, if they intend returning to the settlements soon, where they can purchase more. As to shaving, I have never seen a man at the Placer who had time to perform that operation. They do not work on Sundays, only brush up the tent, blow out the emery or fine black sand from the week's work. . . .

I know a physician who, in San Francisco, purchased a common made gold washer at $20 or $30, made of 70 or 80 feet of boards. At a great expense he boated it up to the first landing on the Sacramento, and there met a wagoner bound to one of the diggings with an empty wagon, distant about fifty miles. The wagoner would not take up the machine under $100. The doctor had to consent, and bided his time. June passed over rich in gold; all on that creek did wonders, when the wagoner fell sick, called on his friend the doctor, whose tent was in sight; the doctor came, but would not administer the first dose under the old sum of $100, which was agreed to,

under a proviso that the following doses should be furnished more moderate. When a man's time is worth $100 a day to use a spade and tin pan, neither doctors nor wagoners can think much of a pound of gold, and you may suppose merchants, traders, and pedlars are not slow to make their fortunes in these golden times.

In San Francisco there is more merchandise sold now monthly than before in a year. Vessels after vessels arrive, land their cargoes, dispose of them, and bag up the dust and lay up the vessel, as the crew are soon among the missing. The cleanest clear out is where the captain followed the crew. There are many vessels in San Francisco that cannot weigh anchor, even with the assistance of three or four neighboring vessels. Supercargoes must land cargo on arriving, or have no crew to do it for them. Some vessels continue to go to sea with small crews, at $60 per month for green hands. Old hands are too wise for them, and prefer digging an ounce or two a day, and drinking hock and champagne at half an ounce a bottle, and eating bad sea bread at $1 per pound. I have seen a captain of a vessel, who by his old contract in the port from whence he sailed, was getting $60 per month, paying his cook $75, and offering $100 per month for a steward, his former crew, even to his mates, having gone a "prospecting."

Uncle Sam's ships suffer a little the same way, although they offer from $200 to $500 for the apprehension of a deserter. The Ohio, however, laid in the port of Monterey about a month, and lost only 20 or 30 men.

Col. Stevenson's regiment is disbanded; ninety-nine out of an hundred of whom have also gone "prospecting," including the Colonel, who arrived in Monterey last month from his last post, and was met by his men at the edge of the town to escort and cheer him into town. The captains, &c., have bought up country carts and oxen, turned drivers, and gone to the placer. Our worthy Governor, Colonel of

1st Dragoons, &c., having plenty of carts, wagons, horses, and mules, with a few regulars left, has also gone, but under better advantages, for the second or third time, to see the placer and the country, and have justice done to his countrymen or himself. Commodore Jones, lately arrived in Monterey, supposed it to be the capital, headquarters, &c., but found not even the Governor left! Where headquarters is, may be uncertain—whether in Monterey, Sutter's Fort, or in a four mule wagon trav-

elling over the gold region. Now, whether headquarters are freighted with munitions of war, &c., or whether the cargo consists of blankets, shirts, &c., to clothe the suffering Indians, for the paltry consideration of gold, no one cares or knows. But the principle should be, that if privates can or will be off making their thousands, those who are better able should not go goldless.

In these days all should have a chance. PAISANO. (NYH, Jan. 22, 1849.)

More of the Rush to the Gold Region; Scenes and Incidents

Those Who are Going to California, or the Propositionists

1st. The sailors and seafaring men. It is far easier for them to go than any other class. If vessels go they must go. But so many more are anxious to go out, than are required to man the vessels, that competition has reduced the wages; in fact, crews can be shipped in any quantity to man the vessels, and go the outward voyage to San Francisco, without wages. The situation of cook or steward commands a premium. In one instance, fifty dollars was paid by a reduced young man, who was anxious to go any how, and could raise this amount. He sailed from this port on the 10th inst., in the useful capacity of steward.

2d. Mechanics of all kinds are anxious to go; but this class of the community have, in most instances, families dependent upon them, who have heretofore derived their support from the weekly earnings of the father. Such men have a double difficulty in getting off; they are unable to raise the $250 to pay their passage and outfit, and have no means to provide for the support of their families while away. As a general rule, however, if they can raise the $250, they show their unbounded confidence in Providence by leaving their families to his care, with the prospect of remit-

tances from California, when they reach there, as collateral security. Tailors, hatters, cobblers, cabinet makers, house builders, masons, ship carpenters, caulkers, boat builders, coopers, gunsmiths, jewellers of all grades, blacksmiths and button makers—these rake and scrape together all the implements of their respective callings, so as to be independent when they get to the land of promise.

The third and most important class are the drones and loafers of a great city; the larger portion having been made so by circumstances over which they had no control. They are drones from necessity and habit. There was a time when they would have worked, if they could have got work to do—all these are determined to go; their ambition has been re-roused—there is an opening, and they are pushing into it. This class comprise broken down merchants, who see no prospect ahead of rising again in New York, ruined and disgraced brokers, blacklegs and gamblers, pickpockets and thieves, young men out of situations, newspaper editors, printers and reporters, ex-cashiers of banks, and last but not least of this third class are politicians, broken down office seekers, and ex-office holders in both parties, and a large and respectable body of custom house ducks, who at present hold office under the democratic party; but their tenure having been rendered very uncertain by the recent election of Gen. Taylor, "they stand not on the order of their going, but go at once."[6] The third class have various modes of raising money to get away with. A large portion have wealthy connexions, who are delighted to get them out of their sight, and don't hesitate to give them a liberal outfit. All the broken down, used up speculators, contractors, and builders are going. Street sweepers, under the present system, prefer a new climate.

The fourth class are the professional men, so called—doctors and lawyers—no clergymen have yet gone; the last have no idea of bearding the devil in his own den, and it is well known that one of Satan's favorite resorts is a gold region; he prefers the yellow atmosphere to his own torrid clime, and preachers of every grade are backward in going to California; their motives might be suspected; it might reasonably be supposed that they too had a squint for filthy lucre; besides, no women are going, and our clergymen don't understand Spanish, and heretic priests are not favorites with Mexican senoras or senoritas. Again, the prospect of raising up a paying congregation for some years is not favorable. Most of those going to California will never be translated to heaven for their early piety and matured Spiritual grace; they don't belong to that crowd. But the doctors and lawyers! The doctors can't compete with the lawyers. The lawyers (to be the embryo statesmen, governors, senators, judges, and members of Congress,) have an advantage; most of them possess small tin signs, that have cost fifty cents or a dollar; these are easily carried, and are coming down in all directions—sixty-eight were taken down in Nassau street in one

week, and the offices are to let. Most lawyers have managed, somehow or other, to get together a library. This they would want here; but Judge Lynch's court is probably the only one that will hold jurisdiction in Upper California until the gold is used up. These lawyers' libraries are worth $100 to $150. The booksellers Gould, Banks & Co.; Bangs, Richards & Platt, and Cooley, it is said, will realize large profits from the low prices at which they are enabled to purchase Blackstone, and Coke upon Lyttleton, from young lawyers who are going away; but even these sums are not quite sufficient; and this class are large borrowers in the market.

The fifth class comprises professors—daguerreotype painters, organists, boot blacks, chimney sweeps, geologists, patent medicine agents, sarsaparilla syrup venders, Hunter's red drop, and Mrs. Davis's cold candy, and all other classes unenumerated. Pawnbrokers are advancing liberally to aid the movement. Watches, diamond breastpins, gold shirt buttons, finger rings, are all turned into passage money. Ways and means have been adopted by those desirous of getting out that were never heard or dreamed of before; these must form the material for another sketch.

The California excitement has extended to every Northern State, New York being the fountain head, the great depot of the emigration; letters are pouring in here from all parts to every man of any note in the community. Harper, and other publishers, it is asserted, are obliged to employ an extra clerk to answer and read the numerous letters sent to them from persons well known in the literary world, asking for money to carry them out to California, and agreeing to furnish a portion of the gold they collect for such advance, or, in

---

6. "Stand not upon the order of your going, / But go at once." (Shakespeare, *Macbeth, III, iv, 119.*)

M. Crapo, a gentleman of fortune, resolves to go to California comfortably.

Their queer sensations the second day out.

The Cape Horn party embark.

nFrancisco. Passage $150 and found

case of disappointment, to furnish a work on California as collateral security.

The richest letters, however, that have been called forth by the California emigration and excitement have been those sent to various well known mercantile firms in this city, from a new set of correspondents in the country. These letters are prominent features of the movement; they exhibit the genius and resources of our countrymen in a new point of view. While we have nothing in the literary world, but the state stereotype writers of years past, to amuse and instruct the public, such letters are a relief, and will create quite a sensation. A mercantile firm of some celebrity, connected with navigation to California, has furnished us with a mass of letters, from which we select a few samples for publication. It seems this firm inserted in the daily papers the following advertisement:—

FOR CALIFORNIA DIRECT

The undersigned having purchased the ship Sample, a vessel of the first class, well fitted and found, capable of carrying 50 passengers, will sail on the 1st proximo. Persons desirous of emigrating to California immediately, will find it to their advantage to engage passage by the Sample. The passage will be $250—and the passenger will be furnished with a home and provisions for 18 months, from the day of departure. Such persons as can make satisfactory arrangements to go in the ship will please apply to

ENTERPRIZE & CO., Front street.

COLUMBUS, (Ohio) Jan. 7, 1849.
MESSRS. ENTERPRIZE & Co., New York.

GENTLEMEN:—Having noticed the advertisement concerning the ship Sample, of which you are the owners, I beg to say that I wish to engage passage in that ship. I wish to make a "satisfactory arrangement" with you to go in her. I am at this place, lecturing on the subject, as you will see by referring to the enclosed hand-bill, which I had struck off at an expense of $6 — for

250. I have mentioned the ship Sample and the name of your respectable firm, and asserted in the bill that I was your agent, should go out in the ship as such, and transact your business while the ship lay at the place. It would suit my purpose to do any business which you may have out there. As soon as I have made a sum sufficient to pay my expenses to New York I shall come on at once, and will then make a "satisfactory arrangement" to go out for your concern on reasonable terms. Of course my passage will be free. I will call on you as soon as I reach New York. In haste, yours &c.,

JAMES GIBSON.

PALMYRA, N. Y., Jan. 12, 1849.

GENTLEMEN:—The "satisfactory arrangement" for the passage I think I can give. I am teaching school here, and studying law with Mr. Cole—a man who has a very extensive law practice in this section. He says he has no doubt in his own mind that money can be made in California. I will hand you, on my arrival at New York, a draft drawn on Mr. ——, the Sergeant-at-arms of the House of Representatives, for $460, by the Hon. ——. This gentleman is elected to the next Congress, and the draft is good. He is entitled to more than that in——, but he has drawn for the exact amount Mr. Horace Greeley, of your city, said his predecessor was entitled to. As you are aware, this draft will fall due at any time after the 1st Monday in December, 1849.

We have had considerable snow up in these parts, but I do not think it will be a hard winter. I am, gentlemen, your obedient servant,   RICHARD WINGATE.

P. S.—I broke open this letter myself, in order to say that my outfit has cost me more than I expected, and being short of money, I have drawn a draft on you for $250, at sight, to pay my expenses as far as New York. I got it cashed at the bank in this place. The cashier knew you well, and did the draft with great pleasure. I will allow you to deduct this from the balance you will owe me.

WOODBURY, CONN., Jan. 13, 1849.

GENTS:—I am the pastor of the Presbyterian flock in this delightful village, and have been requested by a member of my congregation, (a most devout man by the name of Minor Galpin,) to address you a few lines in regard to his son, Job Galpin. The youth wishes to go to California in search of the root of evil, which has turned many righteous men from the paths of holiness. His father is a poor but deserving man, and attends the grist mill in Pomperamy Hollow, about a mile from the village centre. He will pay the expenses of his son as far as New York. Mr. Galpin has been a subscriber to the *Weekly Express*, for the past six months, and he thinks if you would call and see the editors of that paper, they would advance the necessary funds in order to get Galpin, junior, as a correspondent of that paper. He would write them from California, every week for twenty-five weeks, the time he purposes to stop. I can add, in behalf of young Galpin, that he has attended the North District School during the winter (in the summer he is in the mill with his father,) for the last three winters, and writes a neat, legible hand. Hoping you will be able to make a satisfactory arrangement with the editors of the *Express*, who I am given to understand are Eastern people, and trusting to hear from you ere a week has passed over our heads. I subscribe myself, in soberness and truth,   TIMOTHY GILLOT.

P. S.—If you will call at the office of the American Tract Society, in Nassau street, the agent will furnish you with a box of assorted tracts on the importance of religion. They are to be distributed to the gold diggers after your vessel arrives in the gold region. I have written to the agent, and enclosed $2.27 to pay for the same.

This amount was collected at a ladies' prayer meeting, held at the house of brother Galpin, on Monday evening last. Your ship was prayed for at that time.

EASTON, PENNSYLVANIA, Jan. 7, 1849.

Gentlemen:—Will your ship Sample sail positively on the 1st proximo? I wish to go out in her. I am a pedlar of India rubber suspenders and garters. I will tell you at once what I am willing to do. My brother drives on a line of stages, at $25 a month; he has consented to endorse my note for $250, payable in one year, with interest. His name is David. If you wish any more security, you can insure my life for $2,000, and if I die—then you may deduct the amount of $250, and pay the balance over to my brother. We have signed a writing to this effect before the justice of the peace. I enclose you the note. I will send the money from California the very first chance I find.

Please write me immediately the exact latest day I must be in New York, so as not to detain the ship. Put in your letter the name of any slap up hotel where I had better stop, and I will go right there when I reach York. Yours to command,
WM. NEIL.

These are but samples of thousands of similar letters that are sent from all parts of the country, from every class of the community, to persons whose names appear in print, or in any way connected with vessels going to California. Propositions to raise money to defray the cost of a passage, or to get out, are of such a ridiculous character that the only wonder is how any ideas so absurd could enter the brain of a human being.

Two respectable individuals belonging to the mechanic class called at the office of a merchant in Front street, who had advertised a vessel for California, and the following conversation actually occurred:—

Enter the Two California Propositionists.

"Is Mr. Enterprise in?"

Clerk—"He is. Do you wish to see him for anything particular? He is very busy just now."

"We do, very particular."

Clerk—"Walk in his private office—yonder."

Scene—The private office—Door carefully shut—Seats taken by the two Propositionists—Merchant lays down his pen, rubs his hands:—

"Well, gentlemen, what can I do for you to-day?"

"We wish to go to California. You have a ship going?"

"Yes; fine vessel—fast sailer—passage $250—how many?"

"Eight of us, all told."

"Eight. I must take a look at the passenger list—quite a number." (Looks at the list.) "We have room for only seven more; however, we will make no difference; I will engage for the whole eight."

"We have purchased a boat, this morning."

"Purchased a boat!—Ah, I see—you want to take a boat out with you—very good idea—you will find it useful in the rivers. The ship can take it on deck—we can make an arrangement, I have no doubt. Is that all?"

"No; how much would you pay us?"

"What did you say?—how much will I pay you?—What shall I pay you anything for?"

"There are calms at sea, isn't there? You are anxious to get the vessel out as quickly as possible, ain't you?"

"Certainly I am; but what——?"

"That's what we have come to see you about. We form a party of eight—we want to go to California, but we have no means. We have purchased an eight-oared boat—she was formerly the long boat of a brig that has been condemned as unseaworthy. We got her at a bargain. Three of our number are ship carpenters and caulkers—they are at work up in the 11th ward, fixing the old boat all ship shape. We can be ready in a week. Do you take?"

"Gentlemen, I really don't understand you; the ship Sample has very excellent boats. I do not want to buy any."

"Buy? That be damned!—we won't sell her. I'll tell you what we have made up our minds to do. We will put our boat aboard your ship. You shall give us a passage to California—that is to say, food and such things—for we will sleep under the boat on deck, make a sort of room of her at night, and whenever there comes a calm, (in the day time, mind), why, we will get out our boat, take a rope out with us, and pull away. We will tow the ship until it blows again. Will that be satisfactory?"

"What!—give eight persons a free passage to California on such an absurd promise? Nonsense!—you are not in your senses, men. My time is valuable—I cannot listen to such stuff."

"Stuff!—who do you call stuff, you bloody old thief? Calls itself a merchant, Bill—a stuck-up thing; yes, a thing you are—like that chap! a merchant!"

"Really, men, you must go; I will not sit here and listen to such language. This is my office. I will send for a policeman unless you go. Here, Richard, Thomas, book keeper, come here."

The two propositionists now began to make preparations for their departure; and when they had reached the outer door, the oldest sang out, at the top of his voice, "You are a sweet child, you are; you have it all your own way, now. Merchant!—bah! just let me catch you out some night—just let me see that ugly mug of yourn any where around the corners up in the old eleventh ward, and I'll give it fits. You be damned—you and your leaky old ship. She is a coffin, she is. We wouldn't a gone in her unless we had a boat of our own on board—would we, Bill?" And away the honest fellows started, to think of some other proposition.

(NYH, Jan. 24, 1849.)

Ho! For California!

The Emigration to El Dorado

MOVEMENTS IN NEW YORK

There are now up in this port, for California direct, and for Chagres and Vera Cruz, with emigrants for the gold regions, 69 vessels.

MASSACHUSETTS

The ship Capitol, of 687 tons, sailed yesterday for San Francisco from Boston. Her outward manifest is 13 feet long and has 465 articles of entry. It is the longest manifest ever produced at our Custom House. The Capitol also takes out the largest number of passengers of any one ship for a distant port.

RHODE ISLAND

The bark Naumkeag purchased for a California voyage—about $11,000. The bark Winthrop—$8,250—for California.

NEW JERSEY

At Perth Amboy—the schooner Roe—on the mutual plan. New Brunswick California Company, to sail on 1st February.

OHIO

Citizens giddy—golden prospects—pulled up stakes—the "promised land."

INDIANA

Two companies are forming—to the gold regions overland—to start from South Bend—1st of April—forty pounds baggage for each person.

LOUISIANA

The steamship Fanny left the levee—for Corpus Christi—California via Mazatlan—"land of gold."

MISCELLANEOUS

We hear of the formation of associations, or the departure of several citizens for California, in the following places, in Southern and Western States:—Cincinnati and Conneaut, Ohio; Platteville, Wisconsin; Dubuque, Iowa; Richmond, Va.; Columbia, S. C.; Tallahassee, Fla.; Port Hudson and Baton Rouge, La.; and Mobile, Ala.

Accounts from California

MONTEREY, CALIFORNIA, October 20, 1848.

At San Francisco, and in fact throughout all Upper California, gold, gold, gold is the cry. Fortunes are being made, squandered, recuperated. Everybody is going to the *placer*, is there, or has been there. Even the Governor could not resist making another visit to that region, and he has now removed his head-quarters thither. Desertions from the fort and the ship, of course, occur frequently, and the master of a merchantman now in port offers one hundred dollars a month for seamen to carry his ship to Callao, but has been unable to ship any, even at that price. Between twenty and thirty ships are lying at San Francisco, without the slightest prospect of obtaining crews.

But you can form no conception of the state of affairs here. I do believe, in my soul, everybody has run mad—stark, staring mad. Officers of the army have so far forgotten their dignity as to commence a system of speculation. Upon the road to the placer, wagons, with the brand U. S. upon them, may be seen, travelling at a brisk rate, and surrounded by parties of gentle men in high spirits, mounted on fine horses or strong mules, some of which are also branded as above, all taking a northward course. In these wagons are visible, saddle-bags, and pots, kettles, and other camp equipage; but if one could have a close examination, he would find, nicely stowed away underneath all these, goods for barter. What I tell you is the truth, and you need not be surprised at all at this, for, as I said before, everybody is mad. Talk of March hares—nonsense! the similitude must be changed to Yankees in California.

If I write harshly, I write truly. What I say of classes or individuals, they deserve. Let them, when away from here, and free from the excitement under which they are now laboring, calmly and dispassionately reflect upon what they did in California; let them searchingly examine their consciences, and they will be astonished at the numerous littlenesses of which they will stand charged by their own inward convictions. "But conscience doth not make cowards of them now;"[1] and they will have gold. But enough of this—perhaps I shall be mad myself in a day or two.

(NYH, Jan. 25, 1849.)

Mores Accounts from California

We are indebted to Mr. Israel Ketcham, of this city, for the use of the following letter from the gold region.

MONTEREY, UPPER CALIFORNIA,
October 29, 1848.

DEAR FATHER—When I last wrote to you from La Paz, I informed you that I was going to Monterey by land, but a few days before we were to start, the order was countermanded, and the troops were all ordered to the *Ohio.*

On the last day of August, Lower California was formally surrendered to the Mexican authorities; the next day we set sail for Monterey, stopping at San Jose to take on board Co. D; and after a long passage of 39 days, reached this place.

The gold fever continues to rage with unabated vigor, some persons finding $500 in one day; about three ounces is the general average. Goods of all descriptions are very dear; blankets selling as high as two ounces; revolving pistols have brought a pound of gold, and other articles in proportion.

I have made arrangements to visit the gold region, in company with Lieuts. Pendleton, Morehead, and Young.[2] We have bought two ox-carts, and shall take up five months' provisions with us. We expect to start in two or three days.

There is no law here; the strongest is the best fellow. The men have been stealing everything that they could lay their hands on, in the shape of provisions and horseflesh, for the purpose of getting up to the mines. Co. B was discharged from the service on the 23d inst., Cos. A and D on the 24th, and that ended the existence of the 1st regiment of New York volunteers.

Some of the men, led on by two or three chaps, have threatened to kill me for having court-martialed them at La Paz. I fancy they will have a good time in doing it. As I was standing talking to a friend, a few days ago, in the neighborhood of a house where about 36 of them are quartered, a fellow steps up to me and says— "You court-martialed me, and made it cost me money, didn't you?" I replied "Yes, in the line of my duty, I did; and under the same circumstances, would do so again." After a few more words he assaulted me, and I put a six-barreled pistol to his breast, and he then concluded it was not safe to be in such close contact. One of his friends called out, "Take the pistol away from

---

1. "Thus conscience does make cowards of us all." (Shakespeare, *Hamlet III, i, 56.*).
2. George A. Pendleton, Joseph C. Morehead, and Charles B. Young were lieutenants in Stevenson's First Regiment of New York Volunteers. Pendleton lived in Tuolumne County from 1849 to 1854. He died in 1871 in San Diego, where he had been county clerk for fourteen years. Morehead represented San Joaquin County in the first California Legislature, 1849–50. He died sometime before 1882. Young lived in San Francisco later in his life.

him;" but he thought it best not to try it. I do not apprehend any danger from them; therefore do not feel at all uneasy.

If I can make a good speculation at the mines, I intend to start for home in the spring—otherwise not.   T. E. K.[3]

[From the Washington Intelligencer, Jan. 24]

We are allowed to publish the following extract from a letter from an officer in the squadron of Commodore Jones, who gives a vivid and life-like picture of the state of things in California at the time of his writing.

UNITED STATES SHIP OHIO,
Monterey, California, Nov. 1, 1848.

It will be impossible for persons at a distance to realize the state of affairs here. Gold is the only subject discussed. It is bought and sold in grocer's scales. It is selling for $11 an ounce here, $10 at San Francisco, and $6 at the mines. It is worth over $18 in the United States. At the mines it is the only medium of exchange. The price of a glass of grog is a pinch of gold. The Indians had at first no idea, and have scarcely any now, of its relative value. They would offer all they had for anything that pleased them. A man from the mines told me that he had sold a blanket for $280 in gold, and the hat that he wore up there (an indifferent one) for $64. . . . Those who reap most in this golden harvest are the small traders; for, as a matter of course, the necessaries of life are scarce. One of these men informed me that he retailed flour at two dollars a pound, and said it had been four; he also sold sugar at $2 per pound, brandy $12 a bottle. Crowbars, pickaxes, &c., sold at first for an enormous price.

There are about ten thousand persons working. People are flocking all around. The mines are said to be inexhaustible. The present low price of gold cannot long last; for I suppose a mint will soon be established. Nor can the necessaries of life long remain as they are, though they will be high for some time. Nothing for consumption is made here, but cargoes are on their way from South America and the islands, and no doubt capitalists will soon have their agents, which alone would bring gold nearly to its proper value. I had a revolver, worth about $12 in the United States; as a special favor I parted with it for 3½ ounces of gold, equal to $65 in the United States. Persons are seen with gold valued at thousands of dollars, who, a few months since, would have considered themselves fortunate in having twenty dollars in their possession. Doctors are making fortunes fast. Their fee at the mines for feeling the pulse is an ounce of gold. It is said that some of them are making $100 per day. It is very sickly now at the mines.

(NYH, Jan. 26, 1849.)

Emigration to California

No one who has not the opportunity, as we have, of observing daily what is going on in the cities on the seaboard, can form any correct opinion of the extent of the emigration to the gold regions of California. We might fill several columns with the records of such movements. Take the following as a sample for to-day:

The New York Commercial Advertiser says: "Vessels continue to be bought up and put on the berth for the Pacific. To-day we have two Indiamen, the Samuel Russell and Helena, up for San Francisco. The ships South Carolina, Hamilton, Pacific, Panama, and Robert Browne, and barques Keoka and Eliza are nearly ready, and will be off in a day or two. Some of the vessels are only waiting for the bakers—the de-

---

3. Thomas E. Ketcham, a lieutenant in Company B of the New York Volunteers. He was a captain of California volunteers in the Civil War, and later a brigadier-general of militia. He lived in Stockton from 1871 to 1882.

mand for hard bread being such that it is with difficulty the contracts can be filled. Besides the above, *about sixty vessels are advertised from New York alone,* among them are some of the largest class."

The ship Pacific and barques Hersiles and Mazeppa, for Francisco, sailed from New York on Monday afternoon. The barque Templeton, for Chagres, was to sail on Tuesday. Each of these vessels takes out a number of passengers; the Pacific has more than one hundred.

A company is forming in Brooklyn, with a stock of $20,000, in shares of $1,000, with which it is proposed to purchase a first-class ship, and fit her out with two years' provisions. Even Jersey City sends out a number of her citizens. The schooner Acton, 316 tons, takes out a small joint-stock company, with a cargo consisting of provisions, merchandise, mechanics' and mining tools, blacksmiths' anvils, one steam-engine, sawmill, &c.

The schooner Montague was to sail on Tuesday from New Haven for California with 47 emigrants, most or all of them from Connecticut.

Barque Winthrop, of Augusta, (Me.) has been purchased by a company in Bristol, (R. I.) to be fitted for California.

The schooner Boston was to leave Boston on Tuesday and proceed through the Straits of Magellan. Also the ship Capitol, with about two hundred passengers; and the brig Josephine, with fifty passengers.

The Plymouth Memorial estimates that Plymouth will send a delegation of over seventy-five to California.

The California movements in New Bedford are thus stated in the Mercury:

"Eleven vessels are now posted at this port for San Francisco. The Magnolia has a full freight and about seventy-five passengers, and will sail about the 1st of February. Among the latter is a clergyman, a physician, several ladies, and a large number of enterprising young men, a portion of whom go out with the intention of becoming permanent settlers at California."

The Green Mountain Boys are on the move. A company of ten set out from Vergennes a little more than a week ago. They are to proceed by ship to Vera Cruz, and thence overland to the Pacific by way of the city of Mexico.

Mr. Audubon, Jr., the son of the distinguished naturalist of that name, is to head an overland expedition, getting ready in New York, to start for the mines. They are to go via St. Louis, and contemplate passing through Chihuahua to the region of the Gila.[4]

The Newport (R. I.) and California Company are making all possible haste to get off. Their ship, the Audley Clark, is being put in complete order, and a few days ago thirty oxen were slaughtered, and the beef salted for them. They number about seventy-five.

Pittsburg has also contributed to the long list of adventurers, an excellent company having left for Philadelphia, designing to take shipping around Cape Horn.

The ship Jane Parker will probably sail from Baltimore to-day, with seventy-five passengers.

A number of enterprising young gentlemen left Macon (Ga.) on the 26th of December for the Pacific. They go direct to New Orleans, whence they will take the regular steamer to Chagres.

---

4. The "distinguished naturalist" is, of course, John James Audubon. His son, John Woodhouse Audubon (1812–1862), published the record of his travels in 1852: *Illustrated Notes of an Expedition through Mexico and California.* (Reprinted in 1915.) *Audubon's Western Journal: 1849–1850,* was published in 1906; reprinted in 1984. *The Drawings of John Woodhouse Audubon, illustrating his adventures through Mexico and California, 1849–1850,* was published in 1957.

The pistol trade has been greatly improved by the California excitement, as will be seen by the following, from the Norwich Courier:

"We doubt whether there is any branch of business in New England which has received so sudden a stimulus from the California fever as the pistol making business. We were told the other day that our old friends, Messrs. Allen & Thurber, of Worcester, had on hand some $70,000 or $80,000 worth of their 'self-cocking revolvers' upon the breaking out of the gold mania; and they were on the eve of curtailing their operations, but such had been the demand for these weapons, on the part of the adventurers to California, that the old stock had been entirely sold off, and the orders for "a few more of the same sort" were coming in so thick and fast as to render it impossible to fill them. We see it stated also that the demand for Colt's pistols has suddenly increased in the same way, and that in order to meet it he has been obliged to enlarge his establishment and greatly add to the number of workmen employed. And with these increased facilities and means, he is unable to do more than partially supply the markets."

(WNI, Jan. 25, 1849.)

MASSACHUSETTS

Everybody seems to be on the point of going to California, judging from the preparations now making in this and other northern sea-ports. Vessels can hardly be purchased at the present time, and those which do change owners bring double their value two months since.

An impulse has been given to business of all kinds by these movements, and our merchants and mechanics are slowly but surely acquiring wealth indirectly from the "gold diggings." It is worthy of remark that the Southerners, notwithstanding their proverbially impulsive feelings, are much less excited by the gold stories than the more cold and calculating Northerners. The further south you go, the less is heard through the papers, at least, of the gold movements, and we know of no vessels which are fitting out for California in any port south of Norfolk.

The Worcester *Ægis* gives the following crumb of comfort to the gold diggers:—"A load of 300 stools, manufactured in Sterling, in this county, passed through our streets last week, boxed up for California. They are designed for seats for diggers. They are worth here about fifty cents, but may be considered as good for $10 to $25 each in El Dorado."

(NYH, Jan. 26, 1849.)

California Gold Movements

The record of the golden goings on, (and goings off, too,) all over the country, is now become a prominent and apparently a permanent peculiarity of the newspaper press, in every section of the Union—for now-a-days hardly a single exchange comes to us from city, town, or village, north or south, east or west, that does not record some sort of expedition on foot, in its immediate neighborhood, for the mines of California. The press, too, it may be remarked, for the last few weeks has been teeming with much good advice, and many timely warnings of the dangers and difficulties that unavoidably beset these adventurers—the great peril of the undertaking, both in a moral and in a physical point of view, has been thoroughly exposed from the pulpit; the wise ones in our halls of legislation, who in their day have seen and heard of manias before, have spent upon it a great deal of sarcasm and ridicule—but all, all in vain, seeing, as we do every day, ships leaving the wharves full of passengers for the "placers." The press may expostulate, the minister exhort, the senator remonstrate in vain. Gold diggers will be satisfied with nothing short of the dust, and to get at it, spade in hand, the appalling hardships weigh only as a feather in the scale of immigration. Ridicule is more important than anything else, perhaps, to counteract this "yellow fever," and some of the press, we observe, are making the most of it, none with happier effect than our neighbor of the *Globe,* who tells us thus—*New York Express.*

HOW TO FIND THE VALUE OF CALIFORNIA—Multiply Typee by Baron Munchausen—add the seven league boots of Jack the Giant Killer—carry the Moon Hoax, raised to its fiftieth power, with the amount of its unit figure in the columns of millions—cast out the nines, and subtract 17,000 miles on short rations. The remainder will be the square of the Arabian Night's Entertainments—to which add seventeen new voyages of Sinbad the Sailor—a topsail schooner load of Aladdin's lamps (latest patents) and the great carbuncle for Mount Jebungerbad—which gives light in two-thirds of Humbugstan—and divide the whole or your own jugular with a bowie knife. And the result will be astonishing. (CPD, Jan. 26, 1849.)

MISCELLANEOUS INCIDENTS

The following story was told yesterday by a New York clergyman:—He says that a widow lady of his congregation had a son who went to California in the Stevenson regiment. The lady was in rather straitened circumstances, and the wealthy members of the church were in the habit of collecting a purse to supply her with such necessaries as her limited means forbade her from purchasing. A short time ago, the usual supply was sent to her, which she refused to receive, and gave as a reason that she had just received a letter from her son in California, of the following gratifying purport:—"Dear Mother—Enclosed is a draft for $2,000; don't be sparing of it, for I have plenty of the same sort left." The minister said that a wish to authenticate the story led him to visit the widow, when he found the facts to be as above stated.—*Boston Traveller.* (NYH, Jan. 27, 1849.)

Additional Intelligence by the Steamship Crescent City

The Progress of the Emigrants Over the Isthmus

Chagres, New Granada, Jan. 2, 1849.
MR. BENNETT—

We left New York city on the 23d of December, at about 4 P.M., amid the loud huzzas of friends, hundreds of whom gathered on the wharf to bid us an affectionate adieu. We number some 130 passengers, from every section of the Union. There are men of talent and integrity among us. The emigrants, as a whole, have probably rarely been excelled, always excepting the pilgrim fathers. There is one gentleman, (Capt. Smith), who has been long engaged in mining operations in Georgia, and who has machinery for the mines weighing some 20 tons.

On leaving the wharf at New York, I noticed but two females, who waved their handkerchiefs most gracefully, and gave us their parting smiles. The stewardess is the only female we have on board, who is a legion in herself, and who has contributed very much to make us contented and happy. Extraordinary harmony has prevailed. All are armed to the teeth, which, I presume, warns all to respect each other. I have not heard one unkind word since I left New York, nor seen a wry face, only when off Cape Hatteras, and while crossing the Gulf stream diagonally, and in the trough of the sea, with the wind blowing tolerably hard.

Christmas, '48, was the sickest and saddest day I ever saw; the Crescent was a perfect hospital; all were sick, including some of the boat's officers, extending to even the crew. On the first day out, at table, the knives and forks rattled like hail; but on Christmas, hardly a man made his appearance at table. Such sighs, such groans, such anathemas of gold—such longing for friends and home, and safety, and such contortions, as on that unhappy Christmas I have never seen. One man (rather verdant) staggered up and down the cabin, solemnly vociferating that he had vomited a piece of his liver, and that he must soon die, bidding us all a most doleful adieu, asking us to kindly remember him to his wife and children, which proved, on analysis, to be a tremendous junk of beef he had swallowed the previous day without mastication. The stewardess, Mrs. Young, who has sailed with Capt. S. for some dozen years on the Havre route, gave us gruel for two days, for which we rewarded her subsequently with a purse of gold pieces amounting to considerable.

During the blow of Christmas, the stern was mutilated, the bulwarks stove, and the wheelhouse injured, washing Elias Pennel, of Portland, Me., overboard (when the sea was mountainous), who was most miraculously rescued by four men. . . . A more utterly reckless and daring attempt at rescue never occurred. True, a chair was thrown to the unfortunate man from the upper deck, at his own request, which showed his remarkable presence of mind, of which he made happy use, and which contributed much to his preservation. He was cool enough to take off his coat and boots in the water, and was perfectly composed when he was taken from the water. His rescue caused much joy on board, and those who saved him have been lions since. From the time we touched the Gulf Stream we have been in the trough of the sea, and in going and returning from Chagres, the trade winds will always place the vessel in the trough of the sea, which is a fact to be considered by all who are predisposed to sea sickness.

There are about 50 huts at Chagres, part with open roofs of one story, the population consisting of about 300 natives, men, women, and children. An alligator snapped at our boat going ashore yesterday, and the banks of the river, we learn, are literally covered with hideous reptiles. The castle at the mouth of the Chagres is about 200 years old, and has within its dismal walls about 80 beautiful brass pieces, with no soldiery in it—only a family of natives; and a large sample of all the abominable reptiles with which these poisonous and fatal latitudes abound are lurking within, around, about, and under it.

Stephen H. Branch.

Latoon, 12 miles from Chagres.
Jan. 3, 1849—6 P.M., in the doorway of a hut.
Mr. Bennett—

Four of us left Chagres at 12 M. to-day, in a canoe about twenty five feet long, three feet wide, and eighteen inches deep. Our average weight is 160 pounds; total 640 pounds. We have three boatmen, averaging 140 pound each—420 pounds. Our baggage weighs about 800 pounds—total 1,860 pounds. In high water, (as now,) in consequence of the recent heavy rains, the oarsmen paddle against a current of about three miles, or that of the East river. Our canoe has a thatch, or covering, composed of bamboo, leaves, and canvass. The thatch or roof is about two feet six inches from the bottom of the boat, and about eight feet long, under which four of us sit and lie in most uncomfortable position, with the air very close, and ants, white, green, and red spiders and gallinippers crawling all over us, with alligators snapping at us occasionally, (if we don't look out,) with now and then a hideous water snake leaping into the canoe. The rain has poured in torrents since we left, and we, after tea, (good heavens!) at the house or hog pen of one of our boatmen, at Latoon, embark for the night on our journey towards Gorgona, Chagres, and Panama.

Dr. Compound, having settled with his last patient, prepares to go.

Jack Sharp, alias Bogus Bill, prepares brass filings for the California market.

The Panama party leave in excellent spirits.

Preparing breakfast on the Chagres River.

The equator children are yelling and squawling in the contiguous huts; the pigs are squealing, the ducks cackling, and the reptiles on the banks are breathing the most frightful sounds. Before me is Jamaica rum, cocoanuts, oranges, lemons, sugar cane, and other poisonous substances, which my friends have eaten, and one of them has already had the gripes. Latoon has some twenty huts. From Chagres to this place I saw three or four residences, on rising ground, with cows, pigs, poultry, dogs, &c. One place, contrasted with the dismal scenery of Chagres, looked rather pretty, just emerging from the most sepulchral scenery that I ever gazed upon. But I must close, and now debark on my solemn journey for the night.

January 4, 1849.

Our supper last night at Latoon consisted of rice and a stew of bad meat, with a sprinkling of all the fruits I have yet seen in Granada. I smelt, but did not eat a particle. My comrades did, and they look blue this morning. On reaching the canoe last evening, to embark, we bailed it out, chopping up and casting overboard some dozen water snakes that had got into the boat while at tea. Last night was the hardest night I ever passed. It rained very hard. Our boatmen sang the most doleful songs, without cessation, all night. Bullfrogs rent the air with their unwelcome notes, the snakes hissed, and the alligators brought their jaws together so fiercely as to make the forest tremble. Amid this frightful scene, with the thermometer at 97, pent up in the veriest cubby hole you ever saw, where we could not move without endangering the lives of all, by upsetting the canoe—it was, altogether, a night of extreme suffering to us all. After witnessing the miserable sea-sick creatures on board the Crescent, and the tortures I experienced during my sea-sickness, I would not round Cape Horn for all California; yet I would double the Cape rather than to undergo a repetition of what I have already suffered on the river Chagres.

We stopped for the night at about 2 this morning, at a hut on the river, where two of us took lodgings for 3 hours—for which, with three cups of coffee which my comrades drank, we gave $1.60—and departed at about 5½ o'clock. Our bed was a piece of cloth spread on a bamboo floor, with a pillow about one foot long and six inches wide. It was the funniest pillow I ever saw. In the night, we heard some of the rascals whispering; but the glistening of our weapons, and a word between ourselves, and a slight movement towards arising amid the total darkness, scattered the cowardly assassins.

The males and females nearly all smoke; and men, women, and children especially, are very nearly in a state of nature. Their apparel costs them very little. (Here, before I forget it, let me tell all that the two greatest luxuries at sea are sponge-cake and apples. Never go to sea without apples. A man could have made a large sum of money on board the Crescent, with a few barrels of apples. They are excellent for sea-sickness.) Bring plenty of thick flannels—thank God for those flannels! Put them on about 3 days before you arrive at Chagres, or when you leave New York. Bring pen, ink, and paper, wafers, &c. Bring apples and sponge-cake as luxuries. Never lose sight of your baggage, if you can avoid it—especially money; avoid the night air; be cleanly; eat no fruit—remember this—not a speck. I have not tasted of fruit, and I am not sick as yet. STEPHEN H. BRANCH.

(NYH, Jan. 29, 1849.)

A Letter from one of the "Boys" in California

[From the Toledo Blade]
SAN FRANCISCO, Oct. 1, 1848.

DEAR TOM:—I have not received a single line from the States for more than three months, tho' lots of opportunities have occurred to transmit them I know. Oh! you lazy vagabond. I have unalloyed good news to write you. First, on the 15th of August my journal for the day ran thus:

Tuesday, Aug. 15, Presidio of San Francisco:—Disbanded! Discharged from U. S. service about 10½ o'clock A.M. Liberty!!! To the ear sweet sound to every volunteer. Immediately had my baggage upon an U. S. baggage wagon and turned my face toward town, where, upon my arrival, myself and two others hired a small house, and as citizens breathed the air of freedom. Perhaps we did but all get on a spree!

Second, on some day last June, a gold mine was discovered in the valley of the Sacramento, two days ride from Sonoma. It is universally conceded to be the richest mine in the world; men who are willing to work can average from one ounce to ten ounces per day, the average per day to an industrious man is from two to six, very few fall below it, and many a great way beyond it. I saw where one man took within six days, from a space of ground not bigger than the old distribution table in your Post Office, $65,000.—This man said he was satisfied, and let the place be known to a friend, who took out $5,000, and in turn gave it up to an acquaintance, from whom I have not heard.

I have been one week at the mines, and without any great effort brought away four pounds Troy, over $800. I left on account of the frequent occurrence of bilious fever, occasioned by the water getting low and bad to drink. This is the close of seven months perfectly dry, not one drop of rain until the day before yesterday, and a little yesterday. I have been since my return engaged in the Custom House at $8 per day; but within two or three days I shall be back to the mines again, there to remain until next June, when I shall take steamer from the bay to New Orleans, via Panama and Chagres, and if I don't have a pile of gold with me you may kick me, and if I do, I will kick you!

Tom, you can come out here and make as much money as you wish. Your best plan will be to get some one interested with you and buy a small vessel, say a topsail schooner of 250 or 300 tons, freight her with domestics, Jeans, ready-made clothing, boots, shoes, and whiskey; such a cargo will sell at any time, within the three coming years, at from 200 to 1,000 per cent advance. The lowest I ever knew a cargo of whiskey to sell in this market was $2.50 a gallon. Just the simple thing I have directed, you perform, and carry home with you from 30 to $75,000 clear profit, within 12 or 75 months from the time of your sailing. Your vessel will sell for 5 times her cost. All that I have told you is strictly and sacredly true, although it may appear strange to your ears.

I will be in Toledo by the 1st of August next, perhaps by the 4th of July. May be I will have a pile. I would not give an ounce to be warranted $50,000. No, not one dime. If you desire to make a fortune, now an opportunity offers that will not probably present itself again within the next two hundred years, and that is a greater length of time than things of earth and humanity will probably engage your attention.

The most unnatural state of things exists in this country at this time, owing entirely to the gold excitement. Common laborers receive $6 per day, and mechanics and clerks, book-keepers, &c., $8 to $10, and cannot be had at these rates for the very simple reason that they can go to the mines and get 20 ounces at least per day.

I must close this, Tom, adios, good night, and God bless you. Yours, ever,

A. W. RICHARDSON.[5]

(CPD, Jan. 29, 1849.)

Our Isthmus Correspondence

The California Gold Hunters—An English Ship of War taking away £20,000 sterling worth of the Gold Dust—The Quicksilver Mines—The Gulf Stream—The British Consul Prohibiting the use of Mules belonging to the English to any American for

transporting the Gold Dust—Sickness and Deaths on the Bark Anne and Julia, at Chagres—Scenery on the River Chagres—Deaths from Fatigue—The Thermometer at 99 degrees.

January 5—$6\frac{1}{2}$ A.M.

MR. BENNETT:—

Great God! I thank God we have arrived at this infernal place. We were the first boat up, having beaten every boat on the river. Grog and money made our men work for their lives. We are about to take breakfast, and to pass down to Cruces—and will, doubtless, be the first boat in; and then we will try our luck over the mountains. We have had a truly awful time. The current runs six miles in some places, and we came near being swamped and upset. The California, it is rumored, has arrived. If you come by way of the Isthmus, bring dimes and half dimes—they pass for shillings; and bring five-franc pieces—they pass for $1.25 each. My expenses up the river in a party of four cost to this place about $12; but I have been very lucky. Not more than half the passengers of the Crescent City will ever get to Gorgona, and certainly never to Panama. The roads are broken. There is good travelling on the waters. The thermometer is about 99 degrees this morning. I must close and run to the canoe. I will write at Panama, but doubt if you will get my letter, as every thing is uncertain. I have not eaten for twenty-two hours, and have been lying wet in the canoe since I left Chagres. I send you the truth, without exaggeration. My health is good, but irregularity of meals and fatigue, loss of sleep and regular meals, oppress me much; but I hope for the best.

Good bye. S. H. BRANCH.

Don't stop at Gorgona, nor Latoon, nor Chagres, and, above all, not at Cruces. Get a single canoe, with three oarsmen. Give them rum—not too much. Pay them some

---

5. Artemas W. Richardson, Company C of the First New York Volunteers. Apparently he never returned to Toledo; he was county surveyor in Tuolumne County, and died at Sonora in 1854.

money to put you through, while on the river, beyond the price you pay them when you start. Do anything to put you through, not stopping. Go to Cruces by a sure footed mule, at any price. Don't stop there, if you can help it. Give anything from Chagres to Panama to get through. You will see curiosities and peculiarities, and an atmosphere as sweet as any on the globe. I have acquired more knowledge of the wonders and beauties of creation since I left you than I had ever obtained in all my travels; but I have paid dearly for my information.

S. H. B. (NYH, Jan. 30, 1849.)

Panama, New Granada
Sunday, Jan. 7, 1849—7 P.M.

Two cases of Cholera are reported in the hotel where I am. I think communication between Panama and Cruces will be prohibited to-morrow, by the Alcaldes. And then what scenes of horror will befall the unfortunate passengers of the "Crescent City," at Cruces, where, and in the mountains, and on the river, most of them must be, as very few have arrived in Panama, and many of those who have arrived are sick and almost in a dying condition! I again beseech the good citizens of New York not to permit a vessel to leave for Chagres. Let the hardened wretch who attempts such a thing be lynched. Let the government mail come; but for God's sake, don't permit a solitary human being to leave his happy home and dear, free, native land, to participate in these miserable and melancholy scenes, that would elicit sighs and tears from a demon. Poor Taylor—George W. Taylor, I think, of Rhode Island—was found alone, by the native muleteers, in the mountains, who buried him, only one American being present, who happened to come up just as he was being launched into his grave.

My servant has just informed me that a gentleman who came in to-night, by the name of Thorne, is down with the cholera.

I can hear his dreadful cries—being in the very next room. (NYH, Jan. 30, 1849.)

The Effect of the California Gold News in Europe—Organization of Mining Associations in England

[From the London Times, January 5]

We know but little of the "gold district" of California; but we know enough of the great, unalterable laws of commerce, and enough of the history of all the El Dorados from the beginning of the world, to predict that cruel disappointment and misery await those whose haste to be rich leaves them no leisure to count costs. There is nothing really new in this California affair. We have had it all before, over and over again; and we know just as well what an El Dorado ends in, as we know at what o'clock the sun will rise to-morrow morning. We have had two of them already, in our own time, in the shape of Mexican mines, and "provisionally registered" railway bubbles; and he that runs may read. As regards this particular Californian El Dorado, any man with an atom of commercial shrewdness and sagacity may see at a glance, that it is about the most perilous venture in which the dupes of their own greed ever risked life and squandered money. A country without government, without magistracy, without law, except that of the bowie-knife and revolving pistol; a country to which all the buccaneering adventurers of two hemispheres are rushing, in armed swarms, each fearing to be behind the other; a country in which all the necessaries of life are run up, by the combined influences of scarcity and social insecurity, to an exorbitant and fabulous price—such a country will not only be a perfect pandemonium of all the passions, but (what is more germane to our present purpose) it will be a singularly difficult and dangerous place for making money. Of course a day will come when the rightful owners of the Californian gold district will assert their proprietary title, and send a sufficient military and police force to stop the scramble; but, let it be remembered, whenever that day comes, there is an end of the El Dorado. In the meanwhile, Californian emigration is simply gambling—with the chance of being wrecked, starved, robbed, or murdered. Why go so far, when dice are to be had at home?

On the whole, although we have never happened to see and handle any of that Californian gold, and although it is most favorably spoken of by the assayers, we unhesitatingly tell our readers that it is not, by many degrees, so free from alloy as the New York *savants* would have us think. And we earnestly entreat such of our countrymen as feel the remotest inclination to take a voyage of 20,000 miles, with the view of trying their luck in a scramble—which may be all over, by the way, before they reach their journey's end—to ask themselves two questions before starting. First, may not even gold be bought too dear? And, secondly, is it quite certain that there are not very good gold mines at home, that will handsomely pay the working?"

[From the Liverpool Mercury]

To those who are not old enough to recollect the mining mania of 1824 and 1825, and who may be allured by the very "promising" prospectuses which California mining companies have already begun to circulate, we should recommend the perusal of the article, "Mining Companies," in M'Culloch's Commercial Dictionary. They will there find a full and detailed exposition of the dire results of "an infatuation hardly second to that which led to the South Sea and Mississippi schemes." It is to be hoped that Englishmen, warned by the lessons of a bitter experience, will not, on any large scale, repeat the madness of an epoch so disgraceful in our commercial history. The blindness of the gambling spirit will now, as then, doubtless cause the ruin of a race of gulls. But we may, at least, indulge the expectation that the evil on the present occasion may be mitigated, and that the hastening to be rich may not make so very many poor as did the Real del Monte, Anglo Mexican, United Mexican, and other companies, which illustrated the former period.

Even were the gold region in California all that fancy paints it, the expense of distant management, the semi-barbarous condition of the inhabitants, the absence of settled government, and the high price of labor, would render the investment of capital in any mine or mines to be there worked, the most hazardous of experiments. It is related by Chevaller that the Real del Monte company required armed forces for the transportation of the ore from the mines to its place of destination, and that the miners were exposed to the murderous attacks of banditti. A share in this company's stock, which formerly brought 1,350 lbs., may now be purchased for the very moderate sum of five shillings.

The capitalist classes, however, are not the only parties who need to be warned against the risks of California. It is fearful to contemplate the sufferings that are in store for the private adventurers who can just scrape together £100 to carry them to the Valley of the Sacramento. The bones of thousands of these deluded creatures are doomed to mix with the gold dust of the plains. Already there are more deaths than burials among the gold finders, and murder and rapine diversify the process of acquirement. The gold fever in California may this year number as many victims as the cholera. To all, we say—Beware!

(NYH, Jan. 31, 1849.)

A New Gold Song

[From the London Sunday Times, Jan. 6]
AIR—"YANKEE DOODLE"

Now's the time to change your clime,
  Give up work and tasking;
All who choose be rich as Jews,
  Even without asking.
California's precious earth
  Turns the new world frantic;
Sell your traps, and take a berth,
  Across the wild Atlantic.
    Every one who digs and delves,
    All whose arms are brawny,
    Take a pick and help yourselves—
    Off to Californy.

Shakspeare, of undying fame,
  Whom they're going to play so,
Gave to gold a naughty name,
  Or made Timon say so.
And the mob their true lands leave,
  Corn and canes and 'taters,'
To appear, lest it deceive,
  As Californicators.
    Every one who digs and delves,
    Wear your hands quite horny,
    Take a pick and help yourselves,
    Off to Californy.

Gold is got in pan and pot,
  Soup-tureen or ladle,
Basket, birdcage, and what not,
  Even to a cradle!
El Dorado's found at last,
  Turba sed vivorum,
Loose their dazzled heads as fast,
  As Raleigh did before 'em.
    Choose your able-bodied men,
    Navvies bold and brawny;
    Give them picks and spades, and then
    Off to Californy.

How this flush of gold will end,
  We have statements ample;
Perhaps a few sacks they will send,
  Only for a sample.
But we hope this golden move
  Really is all true, sirs,
Else will Yankee Doodle prove
  A Yankee Doodle doo, sirs.
    Every one who digs or delves,
    Stout, and tough, and brawny,
    Buy a pick and help yourselves—
    Off to Californy.
(NYH, Jan. 31, 1849.)

Our Isthmus Correspondence

PANAMA, NEW GRANADA, Jan. 7, 1849.

I stopped one hour at Latoon and Gorgona, and at Cruces about twenty hours. While there, Captain Elliott, of the army, a Mr. Birch, of New Orleans, a Mr. Luckett, of do., and three natives died (it is said) of Asiatic cholera, which was raging with great violence at New Orleans when the Falcon left. . . .

Captain Elliott's grave was dug with a few little sticks and an earthen bowl, which is the custom at Cruces. Luckett and Birch died some two hours after their attack; and one of the natives who went out to sugar cane, went to his bed, and died in half an hour, in the most horrible convulsions, having had, as Mr. Birch did not, the ordinary symptoms of the cholera.

I have seen gentlemen who have been awaiting the arrival of the California some four months, and who are about to return to the States, the California not having been heard of. . . .

Several who attempted to walk, for want of means, from Cruces to Panama, became sick in the mountains. God have mercy on many between this place and Chagres, sick, disconsolate, and without money, in a strange land, far from their homes and friends.

From Chagres to Cruces is about three days' journey. I performed it in less time; but it cost me considerable money. When the natives lingered I gave them money. From Cruces to Panama is a day's journey; and immediately upon your arrival at Panama you should certainly bathe your entire body in brandy. No man was ever born, nor ever will be, with descriptive powers potent enough to describe the horrors of the ravine between Cruces and Panama. Chagres, Latoon, Gorgona, and Cruces are mud puddles, and abodes of death to the unacclimated, where five shakes of the fever and ague sometimes kill. The fatigue is dreadful in the canoes from Chagres to Cruces; but you can survive it if abstemious. Eat no fruit whatever; avoid the night air, &c.; but when you pass the great highway of nations for centuries, from Cruces to Panama, you will encounter dangers and fatigues that will try the stoutest heart.

The road or path is barely wide enough in many places for the mule to pass, and you are in constant danger of crushing both legs. You often descend a flight of cavities (formed by the feet of the mules for 200 years) some six feet, and if the mule slips you generally get a severe fall to the bottom of the precipice. Sometimes, in descending, the mule steps into a mire, and down you both go together, amid stones, prickly bush, and mud. The mule, and indeed the rider, often stand trembling some seconds on the brink of a precipice, ere either dare advance. At some points, with the embankment of rocks towering high above, it seems utterly impossible for even a man to pass; but you manage to get through by being condensed into a mighty small compass. But why attempt to describe it? It can't be done. In a word, from Cruces to Panama are naught but rocks, mire, gullies, ravines, precipices, and stones weighing from one to a hundred pounds, and every conceivable impediment of nature to harass you. It is horrible, most horrible; and with this apparently exaggerated description before you, you cannot form any conception of the dangers and fatigues of a journey from Cruces to Panama.

Panama is a walled city, with dilapidated walls, castles, and churches, of centuries old. Eight out of ten are probably blacks, who seem very happy. Yesterday was a festival, and they were out last evening in the brilliant moonlight in the public squares, singing and dancing merrily, all clad in white, with excellent instrumental music, &c. The river Chagres, with all its serpents, has much beautiful scenery. The rich products of the earth grow in luxurious wildness on its banks. The air

rings with the sweet notes of beautiful birds. From Chagres to Cruces the embankment gradually rises, and many a noble bluff towers high above the general elevation. As you enter Panama the scenery is truly sublime—on the left is the tranquil Pacific; on your right are majestic mountains, clad with perpetual snow; and before you is Panama, with its spires and ruins on every side. The road for some two miles has been paved for two hundred years, by the old buccaneers. The streets are about as wide as Greenwich and are paved like ours; the buildings, three stories, with balconies, and stores, generally superintended by the native women. The priests are about the streets this morning (Sunday) with their black gowns, black hats, and segars, seeming very happy. The population is about 10,000, all Catholics. The country is in a dreadful plight. The value of coin changes every hour. I would like to impart some intelligence to your readers respecting the state of the country; but it is so improbable that I might, perhaps, mislead your readers, which I am careful not to do.

Jan. 7—3 P.M.

O God! O God! Two of the Crescent passengers have just come into my apartment, just from Cruces, and wept like little children, from fatigue, having walked some four miles, giving $20 cash each for two mules which they met in the mountains, where they buried two men—one whose name was Taylor, who came out in the Falcon. An old gentleman, named Rogers, 65 years old, with three sons, has just come into my room, bowed down with sorrow.

The gold in California is plentiful according to the latest reports from there; but what is gold, compared with competency, contentment, surrounded by dear friends? STEPHEN H. BRANCH

(NYH, Jan. 31, 1849.)

By Land, Sea,— and Air?

California Intelligence

THE DEPARTURE OF THE STEAMSHIP FALCON

The departure of the steamship Falcon, from this port, to Chagres, yesterday, presented as interesting a scene as we ever witnessed. For a long time previous to the hour at which she was announced to sail, carriages, cabs, carts, and other vehicles poured down, in a continuous stream, to the dock at which she was moored, and emptied their contents of human beings, male and female, carpet bags, trunks, valises, guns, sacks, pistols, bowie knives, packing boxes, gold sifters, cradles, spades, shovels, picks, buckets of rubber and wood—in fact, every conceivable article that could be of benefit in the way of gold digging, or that would tend to the benefit of the gold diggers for their sustenance, luxury, or comfort, was strewed along the dock from which the Falcon was to leave. When we consider that the number of adventurers which sailed in the Falcon was two hundred, our readers can form an idea of the amount of baggage, of the various kinds we have mentioned, that was deposited on the dock.

But this was not all; for at least three thousand people, of all sexes, ages, classes, and conditions—fathers, mothers, sisters, cousins, brothers, nephews, nieces, aunts, grandmothers, grandfathers, &c., &c.— were congregated at the dock and around its vicinity, to bid adieu to their relatives, who were about to embark for the new El Dorado, with the hope of returning laden with the precious dust, that we are informed abounds so plentifully in the far-famed valley of the Sacramento. It was an interesting scene, and yet a melancholy one. It was interesting to see the adventurous spirit leaving family, home, friends, associations—everything, and embarking, buoyed up with hope, for the land of promise; but the silent tear that forced its way from the eye of age as well as from that of youth, notwithstanding all its buoyancy, imparted a solemnity to the scene which we shall ever remember. It was evident that the hour of trial had arrived—that the old to the young, the young to the old; the boy of sixteen to the mother of sixty and to the sister of fifteen, the brother to the brother and to the father, the betrothed to the betrothed, had to say that expressive and painful word—farewell, (perhaps forever,) and that, perhaps, it was the last interview on earth which was taking place between friends, relatives, and sweethearts. While this was transpiring an accident occurred, well calculated to throw a mantle of gloom over all. Death was exhibited in its reality. A block fell from aloft and fractured the skull of one of the firemen of the steamship. The corpse was taken ashore; also the man through whose agency the accident occurred. There, indeed, the uncertainty of life was manifestly and sadly realized to the two hundred who were taking their departure, and to the three thousand who assembled to bid them God-speed. (NYH, Feb. 2, 1849.)

Overland Route to California— Advice Gratis to Gold Seekers

Now that gold and California are all the rage, and when every body is itching to "get off," it may help a little to counteract the fever to show such as intend reaching El Dorado, by the overland route, a few of the inconveniences they must encounter before they reach the Sierra Nevada, or the golden waters of the Sacramento. We have been much amused as well as instructed by reading over a cleverly written communication in a late number of the St. Louis Republican, from one who has evidently "seen the elephant," detailing the pains and penalties in so racy and humorous a vein, that we cannot refrain from giving

our California friends a choice extract; in the hope that it may exercise a cooling influence upon their imaginations, overheated and distempered by the last news from the "placers." Listen:—

"You that start across the plains, by the time you reach Santa Fe, N. M., a distance of not less than 1,200 miles from St. Louis, will find your ambition and courage fail; and yet through to Santa Fe is a paradise to what you will see afterward. By the time you have been fifty days out, which will be the time you will be in going there, (or kill all your oxen and mules) you will wish yourselves back again at your work in St. Louis—mark my words. You must cook your own meals, which will be fun and sport for a few days, where good wood, water, and grass are plenty, but after you get 100 miles beyond Council Grove, you will hunt in vain for wood, and often for water and grass.

"Two men will use a barrel of flour before getting to Santa Fe, and 200 lbs. good bacon, about 30 lbs. coffee, and if you drink whiskey (a very necessary article by the way,) two men cannot miss using 10 gallons."

Temperance men will please make a note of this. Necessary to use ten gallons, mind! They who have been indiscreet enough to sign the pledge, will therefore see the necessity of recanting before going to the mines.

It is necessary to take a hardware shop with you—and it would appear that a victualling cellar on stilts might do well to follow in the rear:—

"You want a good ax, hatchet, pickaxe, crow-bar, spade, and shovel; an auger, inch chisel or two. You will want tin or pewter plates, tin cups, a good knife or two, spoon or two, coffee boiler, tea kettle, frying pan, spider, bake oven, and canteen; a little salt, pepper, saleratus, mustard, red pepper, plenty of pickles, and a good supply of vinegar; molasses tastes quite well on the plains—get plenty of matches, both lucifer and wax; get two blankets as your bedding; a cap is better than a hat."

There is a cruel complacency about the next extract, however, which cannot but have a salutary effect upon the most inveterate victim to the gold fever, that intends to travel over the mountains:—

Take some No. 6, for sure

"It matters not about the sun, you'll get used to it; your hat is blown by the wind into a 'cocked hat,' and then the sun has all advantages; wear shoes instead of boots for walking (unless you are afraid of snakes, of which you will see plenty of the largest kind of rattlesnakes.) You can kill dogs enough for fresh meat, as you arrive in their cities and towns; they always sit at the doors of their houses, and are either shot or caught. They are very palatable, and in eating them, at first, one is apt to get too easily down at a meal (especially at supper time,) which causes considerable noise in the lower regions, about the time one wants to sleep, but cannot for the constant barking of the dogs. To prevent this, take along some No. 6; a few drops put all to rest again.

"A good file would be useful when you arrive in the Buffalo Range, for you can't help killing an old bull, and while the boys are skinning, you can be filing your teeth, to be ready to enter on duty. As wild meat is of a running breed, and you of a tame one, you needn't be surprised to find yourself running the day after eating it. In case your run is more than you are used to, take a few drops of No. 6, and all is quiet. Be careful not to chase the wolves on foot—they are many, and are a sort of hyena; when they turn upon you they destroy both soul and body, and then run off with the bones. Some of them are old, with beards like Aaron's, that hang down to the ground—his only went to the skirt of his garment."

Bad enough, but what follows is worse:—

A Sweet Climate

"The wind blows all the time on the plains, and very hard; so much so as to cause you to complain; but you will get used to it after 3 or 4 months' blowing, and can't well live without it, for smothering down in the hollows. You can see a great way ahead; in some places a week's march in advance—mounds and the like. You will be apt to have rain and water plenty if you start early, and, consequently, get your jackets and blankets wet through, day and night; then come the trying times with the buffalo chips. They will neither burn nor blaze—so make up your mind to eat a raw dog, or any other raw meat, without hot coffee or warm stuff—except No. 6. If the weather continues rainy, so that you become tired of eating raw dogs or buffalo bull, just turn up one of your wagons, and cook enough under it to last several days, and pack your load on your mules or oxen, or your own back. Don't back out; gold is ahead, and you are in—'go it boots'—'live or die'—'a faint heart never won a fair lady.' If you get sick on the road, or your wagon burned up, don't give out as long as you can toddle along, and when you cannot proceed any farther, just lay down and rest, then up and travel by the moon till you overtake your companions. Then, if you lay several days, an Indian may come along and examine your head; if bald, he will respect your age and not scalp you, but hand you to the squaws for a plaything. If you have a good head of hair, he will only cut a little piece out, just about the crown, as a token of remembrance, which will either cure you or make the wolves come to prayers.

"You may have to swim some creeks, as Uncle Sam has not bridged the road yet, and there are a great many creeks. You will be very apt to pass ten or twelve of these a day, so that before your clothes get dry from one, you will be in another. This frequent cold bath causes cold chills on a fellow without any heat, and often death; when a little hole is dug, three or four feet deep, and the dead fellow rolled in, clothes and all, the dirt thrown over him; the wolves hold a council over his cold home, and soon tear him up and have a feast. It will be all the same a thousand years hence. The Psalm tunes these wolves keep up for days and nights is quite interesting to a tired, sleeping traveler; but their scratching and whispering in your ears soon become familiar, especially if a fellow gets one of his toes bit so hard as to make him cry out. Yet great care should be taken not to give false alarms in the night, or the stock become frightened and run off for miles, causing delays in marching."

We trust, however, our friends who have made up their minds to go to California—to go at all hazards—will not be discouraged at 'awful disclosures' of this kind. On the contrary, it can not but have the effect to make you think more of the gold region when you get there.—Away, then, overland, and put down the people who are talking of Indians, and wolves, and buffaloes, and rattlesnakes, as so many ignorant mortals, who do not believe that all is gold that glitters. But,—

"By the time you reach the gold region in California, you have expended some two hundred dollars, worn out all your clothes, become weary from the long march, eat up all you carried with you, had all your tools stolen from you—weak, sick, and unable to work, without friends to administer to your wants; without a comfortable house or home—thrown in among thousands of idle, dissipated, unfeeling brutes, intent on gain; penniless, poor, and without strength or means, or friends to assist you; surrounded by vulgar, rough, and uncouth rowdies, all engrossed in searching after gold—tattered, ragged, and cross—without law, discipline, or control—every one his own master—stealing here and lying there—inventing schemes to deprive the unsuspecting of their prospects and gains—laying hands on every thing palatable, wearable, or useful; where might and strength determine right, tho' wrong, and 'coward guilt to sheltering caverns fly,' until sickness, disease, and death close the scene. Then you may easily imagine worse than this picture, human vultures preying upon your carcass like cannibals gormandizing, in their hoarse laugh over fallen victims! It is, nevertheless, truer than fiction—the pure and certain results of rash and premature enterprise."

(CPD, Feb. 3, 1849.)

Raffling for a Woman

[From the N. Y. Sun]

A young girl residing in the upper part of the city was not long since desperately attacked with gold fever. The Sacramento and its precious sands were ever before her mind, but though handsome and of unblemished reputation, she was entirely without the means of accomplishing her wishes. Days passed, and yet she seemed no nearer securing a passage to California than at first. Fortunately at last she became acquainted with a party of young men who were going out on board one of the vessels bound for San Francisco. They wished a cook, and at once agreed to raffle for her. The amount paid for chances was to be given to her, and the fortunate fellow who won, was to marry her before leaving the city. If she did not fancy the person on whom the lot fell, then she was to pay her own passage out, and under protection of the whole party, was to cook and wash for them. The money was accordingly paid, and the girl raffled.—There was one person whom she hoped would win, but the fates were against her choice. A little shoemaker won her. The girl would not marry him, but true to her promise, she wrote a farewell letter to her friends in Connecticut, and she took passage with her comrade adventurers. (ISJ, Feb. 3, 1849.)

Sailing of the Steamship Crescent City—Great Excitement

The fine steamship Crescent City, Captain Stoddard, took her departure for Chagres, yesterday afternoon, at a few minutes before two o'clock, amidst the firing of cannon, and vociferous cheers from an immense multitude. She had been announced to sail at 1 o'clock; but owing to the great number of her passengers, and the confusion prevailing, it was found impossible to start at the hour appointed. About noon, crowds began to assemble on the pier; some through curiosity, others to bid farewell to friends and relatives. Among the number present, we observed many ladies come to take what seemed a last farewell of those most dear to them. The excitement on the boat and pier was very high, and a general feeling of hilarity pervaded the assemblage. "Is any man on the dock dead broke?" cried one of the passengers, at the top of his voice. A darkey, standing near by, replied "I am." He had scarcely answered, when a half dollar struck his cocoa-nut, and nearly brought him down, which he instantly resented by pocketing the insult. The individual who threw the money thought, no doubt, it was worse than useless for a man to take silver into a gold region.

The scene was extremely picturesque, and it was amusing to behold the various dresses of the passengers, attired as they were, some in India rubber, some in differently colored oil cloth—white, black, green, yellow—and some of no color at all. Here was one with an India rubber tent;

another with a life preserver as large as a balloon, and a pair of waterproof boots large enough to cover half his carcass. Every fashion of hat and cap was put in requisition—Dutch, French, Italian, Chinese, Spanish, down to the latest California slouch. Rifles, muskets, shot guns, and revolvers were to be seen strapped on the backs and sides of the adventurers, in a profusion that seemed to indicate an invasion of a different character to that of a gold region. The steamship Hermann, lying on the other side of the pier, was filled with spectators. Her decks being covered with snow, which had been falling fast all the fore part of the day, some persons commenced snow balling those on the dock. The compliment was returned in good earnest, and in a few moments hundreds were engaged in the animating sport, which continued for about half an hour. The balls flew thicker and faster than at Buena Vista, and reminded one of the storming of Chapultepec. The scene wound up by those on board the Hermann running up a white flag on the top of an umbrella, although they did not surrender till every man in the shrouds had been shot down. (NYH, Feb. 6, 1849.)

A Sick Gold Digger

We recommend the following extract from a letter from a young man formerly a compositor in this office. He went with the New York regiment of volunteers, and went to the regions of gold dust, and dug, and washed, and collected the yellow stuff:—N. Y. Paper.

CALIFORNIA, Region of gold dust,
Out-of doors, Nov. 20, 1848.

DEAR LEES:—Here I am in the gold region, digging like a nailer, when I am able. I had at one time about five pounds which I sewed up in bags, and tied to a belt which I had around my body. I thought I had enough, and started for San Francisco; but I found ere I had got half the way, my excessive shaking from the fever and ague had shook out all the dust I had left, and shook myself back to the gold dust ground again.

You have seen the Shaking Quakers, at Lebanon at their worship. Put a shovel in their hands and make them lean and thin, hungry and ragged; and you may guess what the diggers are in California. When you are too weak to shake, you can lie down, and when you are too sick to lie or stand, why you can die; nobody cares. The more there is sick, the better the prospects for the well.

Give me digging at the case, and a steak at the Franklin House, at dinner time, and you may dig for the "dust" with a hungry stomach and back as bare as a beggar.

The way they wash the dirt in this vicinity is to select the one that has the ague the worst—the bowl in hands is shaken beautifully.

Your old clothes and broken victuals would be a godsend. Can't you ask the hands in the office to make a collection to make up a package of cast off duds, and send them on; and I promise you all the dust I can gather in a month. I have got the dust, but unfortunately have got teeth, a stomach, and a back, which the dust cannot help.

If I can only get to work at the case again before I get to be a *case,* give me joy. Men's faces grow longer than their lives very shortly here. The good book tells us man's life is but a span, and there's not a face in a mile of me but is twice that length. My respects to the hands. Yours, &c. J. P.
(CPD, Feb. 7, 1849.)

"A few days in the Diggins"

BY A FREE AND INDEPENDENT

Landed at San Francisco, after a 'tarnll tossin of five months. This is comin thro' the small end of the Horn, I reckon, and there ought to be pretty considerably some on the other side to make up for leavin' my dry goods store and family fixins in Broadway.

Traded with a Down-Easter, who is makin' tracks for the settlement with 30,000 dollars in his carpet bag, for a spade, pick, scoop, and washin' trough—givin' 800 dollars for the plunder, and glad to get it, as Increase Niles Flint, of Salem, Mass., went 750, and he is a 'tarnal old hoss at a deal.

Swopped my traps and blankets, a quarter cask of pickled pork, and a demi-John of peach brandy which I had laid in, for six pounds of ginooine gold. Pretty considerable smart tradin.

Toted my tools to Hiram K. Dough-boy's boarding shanty and settled with him for blankets and board, at thirty dollars per diem. Catawampus prices here, that's a fact; but every body's got more dust than he knows what to do with.

Off to the diggins with a party; mighty small potatoes most of 'em; all sorts and colors, and everlastin ragged—Bay-states-men, Back-woodsmen, Buckeyes from Ohio, Hosses from Kentuck, Cape Cod Whalers, St. Francisco Indians, Lepers from Santa Cruz, Texan Volunteers, Philadelphia Quakers, a Latter-day Saint, six Irish Sympathizers, twelve Yankees, as many Britishers, a squad of Deserters, a Blackfoot Guide, a Methodist parson, and a Mormon Elder. A 'tarnal nigger tried to join us, but got cowhided.

Struck diggins, and got to serious washin'; parson began to ask a blessin', but seein' Silas T. Forks, of Orangeburg, N. Ca. helpin' plunder that those 'tarnal *Ingines* had absquatulated with blanket, pork, and brandy. Luckily I've got my tools.

Spent the night under a cotton tree; mighty sharp set in the morning, having eat nothin' since yesterday at twelve. Struck the trail of Zerubbabel W. Peabody, and traded with him for some bread and pork doins, for which the everlastin' old skin flint made me come down cruel, cleanin' me out of all I'd raised yesterday.

Zerubbabel says he ain't diggin, but goin' about with a provision and liquor store. It's amazin' how long headed men like Zerubbabel can be such darned idiots.

I've got out of the track of the settlement, and into a prime diggin'—all to myself—where the lumps of gold run as big as pigeon's eggs, himself, parson cut it short off, and we went to work, like niggers at cane hoin' agreein' to dig in company and share the profits. Cotched the Quaker sunnin' himself, and takin' kink out of his back with a Havannah. Convened a meetin', cow-hided Quaker, and at it again. Gold lyin' about like earth nuts, and riddlin' through the water like a hailstorm in a sherry cobbler.

Sounded the conch for grub, and found nobody got anything but that cute old coon, Zerubbabel W. Peabody of Staten Island, who had brought a bag of biscuit and some meat fixins.—The varmint wouldn't sell a notion under an ounce of dust, and sacked the whole bilin.

To work again; totted up at sun-down, and found we'd averaged 28 dollars per man. Got back to shanty; but before that darned Hiram K. Doughboy would let me inside the door, forced to pay down 30 dollars for day's board and lodgin'. So wound up 2 dollars worse than in the morning. Calculated to camp out in future, cut Hiram, and work on my own hook, havin' realized that Socialism ain't no go in gold diggin'.—Asked Hiram why he didn't go out with his bowie-knife and washing-pail. Hiram sniggered and said he warnt greedy, and preferred helpin' folks in his shanty. Hiram usent to be such a consarned fool.

Started alone—having swopped the gold I got from a Down Easter yesterday, for one blanket, half quarter cask of pork, and half demijon of brandy. Must convene that I've lost 60 percent by bargains; but a cargo of new diggers having just come in from Panama; great demand for such fixins, and forced to give what the old flint

of a Down-Easter chose to ask. He's made considerable some by his trade, that's a fact, and I doubt if he could have done better at the diggins.

Two days without seein food—gold gets more abundant than ever.

(CPD, Feb. 13, 1849.)

Hints for Emigrants to California

Remember.—That the earth is not very deep in those parts, and it may be very dangerous to dig too deep.

That many a man who has strictly minded his business, has found as good gold as there is in California.

That all who do not find gold there *who dig for gold only.*

That all the gold is not in California— and if all California were gold, it wouldn't be worth as much as Coney Island.

That if men will desert their country's flag for gold, it is an evil temptation.

That if it can be dug out of the rocks with a jack knife, it is not worth digging for, for any respectable jack knife is worth its weight a hundred times in gold.

That to a hungry man, a good sized *potatoe* is worth all the California *"carets."*

That all the gold in the country, if it cannot purchase happiness, is of no value.

That there are men who, if they owned all California, were it all gold, would not be satisfied.

That it is better to dwell with humble livers in content, than wear golden sorrow.

That "poor and content" is rich, and rich enough[1]—but riches without content is poor, as winter to him who never fears he shall be poor, although he were as rich as the mines of California.—*Journal of Commerce.* (CPD, Feb. 14, 1849.)

---

1. Shakespeare, *Othello III, iii, 172.*

Later Intelligence from California

These letters are from an officer of the U. S. ship St. Mary, and are, therefore, perfectly reliable.

U. S. Ship St. Mary,
Harbor of San Francisco, Dec. 19, 1848.

Here we are in California; the land so much talked of in the United States. We arrived here about five days ago, after a long and disagreeable passage of sixty-nine days from Valparaiso, stopping at Monterey, where we remained five days.

You have no doubt heard in the United States of the great excitement produced in this country by the discovery of immense gold mines. Well, you may believe everything you hear and see about them, no matter how exaggerated the reports may be, for 'tis all as true as the Gospel. Nothing is talked of here but gold ! gold! gold! We see it all around us—I do not mean where we can pick it up, but in the possession of every man about this country. The mines are about 250 miles from here, and men who go up there can pick up, on an average, from $1 to $2,000 worth of gold a day; but the provisions and clothing bring enormous prices—$30 for a pair of boots, $10 for a pair of shoes, $3 per pound for flour, and everything in proportion. Nobody does any work; nobody will work, except for gold. People go up there, pick up a quantity, come down, gamble it away or frolic, and then go back again for more. Another thing—almost all who go to the mines get sick, and a sickness from which they seldom recover—that is, if they are not well provided with food and clothing.

[The same writer, in a letter dated
24th of Dec., says:]

This San Francisco is all sorts of a town, I can tell you. Such a mixture of people I never saw in all my life—all nations and colors. The place is well filled now, as they cannot work at the mines, it is so very cold; but in the spring they will commence operations again. The diggers at the mines pick up about $700 worth of gold per day.

(PPL, Feb. 15, 1849.)

Our New York Correspondent

New York, February 10, 1849.

The first Balloon from New York for California and a market—has not sailed yet, but will shortly after dispatch—accommodations for passengers all taken up—letter bag still open. "I had a dream which was not all a dream;"[2] nor is the above announcement all a joke, however much it may have that appearance. There is a company here seriously at work constructing a balloon to carry passengers to California. The achievements of the human intellect are generally in some degree proportionate to the stimulus or strength of motive with which the object is pursued; and if ever so grand an achievement in aerostation is to be accomplished, perhaps the eager desire of people to get to the land of gold may be the very stimulus or motive necessary to produce so wonderful a result. "Hunger will break through a stone wall;"[3] who then shall say that the love of gold may not enable a man to sail round the earth in an air-balloon?

The company to which I have referred have their model balloon and apparatus just completed, and intend to make a public exhibition of it in the Broadway Tabernacle in the course of the coming week. The model balloon is twenty-four feet in length, and two feet in diameter at the centre, running to a point at each end. It is to move horizontally, point foremost, like a fish in the water. The motive power is a

---

2. Byron, *Darkness.*
3. "They say hunger breaks through stone walls; but I am as gaunt as lean-ribbed famine, yet I can burst through no stone walls." (John Marston, *Antonio's Revenge*, 1602.)

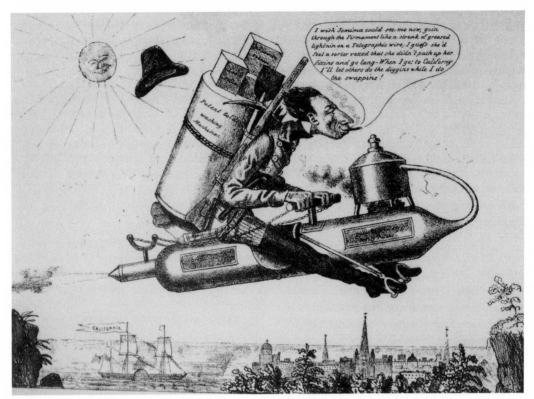

Mr. Golightly bound for California. On his back he carries a Patent Gold Washing Machine and packages of pills and tobacco. He's smoking a cigar, feeling mighty slick, and saying: "I wish Jemima could see me now, goin through the Firmament like a streak of greased lightnin on a Telegraphic wire. I guess she'd feel sorter vexed that she didn't pack up her fixins and go long. When I get to Californy I'll let others do the diggins while I do the swappins!

small steam engine, connected with a sort of screw propeller at the stern, which acts upon the air something like the wings of a wind mill. The inventor promises that it shall sail round the interior of the Tabernacle like a trout in a mill-pond, or perhaps more like a gold fish in a glass globe.

If the performance of the model proves satisfactory, he will immediately construct his passenger balloon for California, which he proposes shall be five hundred feet in length, and forty feet in diameter at the centre, running to a point at each end, like a parabolic spindle in geometry. A long cabin or saloon is to be suspended below the balloon for passengers, machinery, &c. The engine is to be about four-horse power. There are to be two screw propellers, the fans of each to be twenty feet in diameter. The rudder is so arranged as to vary the direction of the balloon to the right or left, or up or down, as circumstances may require. By calculation it is estimated that the balloon, of the size mentioned, filled with hydrogen gas, will carry about five tons besides its own weight and necessary machinery. This would enable it to carry perhaps fifty passengers with a reasonable amount of baggage.

The inventor says he can build his grand balloon in three or four weeks. He will make one or two trial trips, perhaps to Washington or Boston, before starting on his voyage across the Rocky mountains. It is hardly probable he will get to Washington in time for the inauguration, though it is possible he may be in time to help the out-going administration along by an overland passage to the head of a certain river, and thus save them the difficulties of its navigation.[4] The time estimated for a voyage to California is some four or five days, sailing only by daylight, and anchoring during the night. Upwards of two hundred names are already booked to secure the right of precedence in passages if the experiment is successful.

Now, this will appear to most people to be a ridiculous visionary project, and I have no idea of asking any one to put the least faith in it, or expect any thing to come of it. But, after all, does its success look more improbable than a description of the present achievements of steam on land and water would have appeared half a century ago? Or an account of the present telegraphic communications ten years ago? I am not prepared to say that something great and stupendous will not yet be accomplished in aerostation. It is not quite seventy years since all Paris turned out with wonderment to see a balloon, filled with heated atmospheric air, ascend a few hundred feet above their dwellings. This suggested to philosophers the idea of using hydrogen gas for like purposes, the extreme lightness of which enabled it to sustain great weight in the atmosphere. The subject was pursued for a while in France and England with great zeal, and in some cases with grand results. People began to ascend with balloons and make voyages of greater or less distance, till in one case they reached three hundred miles, and sometimes moved with a speed of seventy or eighty miles an hour. If a sufficient propelling power and a mode of steering can be successfully attached to the balloon, the grand problem would of course be solved.

(WNI, Feb. 15, 1849.)

From California

The New York papers contain a number of letters of the same tenor, of which we select the following from one of the discharged New York volunteers, which is so natural as to carry on its face evidence of its truth:

CORRESPONDENCE OF THE EXPRESS
SAN FRANCISCO, CALIFORNIA, Dec. 7, 1848.

The last letter I despatched to New York was in August last, just after our regiment (Colonel Stevenson's) was disbanded. My health since that time, thank Heaven, has been uninterruptedly good, albeit I have been at the washings, or in them rather, for several days at a time—often up to the very eyes in mud and water!

Most of our company (F) have formed a "copartnership" in the digging business. We work on the mutual plan, and live all together, pretty much after the system of that worthy philosopher, Charles Fourier. The tents which our regiment brought from New York are all worn out now, so that we are obliged to make a kind of mud hut on the mountainside to sleep in at night. These mud huts are grouped together grotesquely enough, and present, at a distance, very much the appearance of so many mole hills.

I have been at the diggings something like three months, and though I have scraped up enough of the dust to make me comfortable for life—if I can only get it shipped to New York—I would not go through the same suffering and privations again for ten times the quantity. There was, however, no alternative left but to go to the mines. Provisions, clothing, board, house rent—every thing, in fact, became all of a sudden so exorbitantly high, that to stay in San Francisco was but to starve. Many of

---

4. The river Styx. The reporter obviously believed that the outgoing Polk administration, deservedly, was on its way to hell.

our regiment had deserted, even before the news arrived; and desertions were taking place every day, and the Colonel himself was itching to get off.

There are several of my companions, who left New York with me, who have got more gold than they know rightly what to do with. But you may look for them all home some time next summer.

The United States storeship "Lexington" has been here for several weeks past. She is to sail for New York in a few days, and I am assured that she carries out an immense quantity of gold dust, consigned to several leading houses in New York. My errand here, just at this time, had for one of its objects the shipment of my gold home in this vessel, but I could effect no arrangement on any terms, as the ship has more now than she can well carry.

Of course, we have no law here, and are not likely to have any. Every man is his own legislator, his own judge and jury, and in some instances I could mention the administration of justice is dispensed summarily enough. Society, however, is not so bad as it might be; but, as I have already intimated, there is every reason to fear for the future.

Among the gold diggers are a great many printers, who are making a vastly more profitable speculation in picking up scales and lumps than they did in New York picking up the types. Indeed, every art and profession is well represented at the washings.

The whole amount of gold collected at the washings since the excitement first broke out is variously estimated; some put it down as high as four millions of dollars, but this I think is a little too high.

Mr. James Fitzgerald, whose family live in the Eighth avenue in New York, a few weeks since started on a tour of exploration into the interior, and has come back with equally astonishing news. He says silver in the back country is as plenty as the gold along the Sacramento. He has some specimens.

Who of you at home, seeing what a crowd of vagabonds we were on Governor's Island, would have ever imagined so great a change in our affairs. Many of us are nabobs now, instead of vagrants, as we were then. Capt. B. is rich, private S——mp——n is richer, and Colonel—— richest; but we have all made out pretty well, considering. (WNI, Feb. 16, 1849.)

Emigration to California—New Feature

The settlement of California, which is now going on so rapidly, resembles, in many of its features, the colonizing of the old Atlantic States, in gone-by times. The emigrants consist of the most enterprising and active men, who are willing to stake their little patrimonies, or the hard-gathered earnings of years—to leave their friends, relatives, and associations, and hazard all, even life itself, in the pursuit of fortune and independence.

One of the most extraordinary features of this emigration is the formation of companies of females, several of which are going on in different parts of the country. We believe New York will be the first in the field, and will take the lead in feminine emigration. Mrs. Farnham, formerly the matron of the female department of the State prison at Sing Sing, proposes to gather a company of respectable young women, and take them to the shores of California for the sum of two hundred and fifty dollars each. This is an excellent movement. There are thousands of young men in California, who will settle there after they have accumulated enough of gold to live upon in comfort for the rest of their lives. When they have done so, they will turn their attention to matrimony, and seek for partners. Indeed, it is not improbable that the ships containing the feminine cargo will be boarded at a distance from land, and every young woman engaged before the vessels reach the harbor of San Francisco, just as the emigrant vessels bound to the Atlantic coast from Europe, in former times, were hailed by the colonists, and their women passengers secured as wives before they set feet on the soil.

The presence of a number of respectable women in California would exercise a most happy influence on the morality of that country. It would prevent the male population from degenerating into a state of semi-barbarism, which they would oth-

erwise be liable to do. We therefore say to the young women of the Atlantic cities, go to California. You will not be there long without getting husbands, with their pockets filled with gold dust; whereas, if you remain where you are, you stand a chance of wasting your sweetness on the desert air, and pining away a life of single blessedness. (NYH, Feb. 19, 1849.)

CALIFORNIA.—Will be published in a few days a book containing the best routes and distances to California, with a description of watering-places, crossings, dangerous Indians, &c.; also the necessary outfit, equipment, and cost. This is an invaluable book for those who are bound to the sundown diggings of California. Price, single copies, 25 cents; wholesale price $15 per hundred. Address, postpaid, M. J. SLAMON, Greer's Printing-office, Washington. (WNI, Feb. 22, 1849.)

Accounts from California

[From the Brooklyn Eagle, Feb. 19]
We are indebted to Mrs. Lozier, of this city, for the following extract of a letter received from her husband, Mr. George T. Lozier, dated Flag-Ship Ohio, at sea; having sailed from San Francisco, 26th of December last, and containing intelligence as late as any received from that golden centre of the world's attention, and towards which the thoughts, desires, and persons of thousands upon thousands are rapidly converging.

"I have brought to bear all the means that I could muster, walked into the gold market, and have ——of the precious metal, for which I paid about $——the oz.; it goes by apothecaries weight, 12 ounces to the pound. At Mazatlan, their gold weight is 14 ounces to a pound, and it is said that we will get $14 per ounce, which makes it equivalent to $16 per ounce; we buy at $12 and sell at $14, and so, perhaps, I may make a trifle, and then, perhaps, a little on return trade, &c. &c. An overcoat, which cost only $7.50, brings $25 readily. No officer has been exempt from trafficking; none let the golden opportunity slip.

"There are many sickly and cadaverous-looking persons in San Francisco; some have irretrievably ruined their health. They have to work so much in the water, that all suffer more or less with fever and ague. That which is called the "dry diggings" is an upland marsh. The "wet diggings" is standing in the river up to your waist, and every time you stoop to get a pan or spade full of earth from the bottom, you dip your face in the water.

"Not a Mexican face is to be seen in San Francisco, and nothing but English spoken. All Yankees, and one-third New Yorkers. There is a Broadway, a Fulton, and a Washington market; a New York store and all that. Grog shops, a few—drinking and gambling is the order. The greater part of the gold has fallen into unworthy hands; but will soon be gathered into the coffers of the industrious, provident, and wise. Nothing short of a millionaire can be a rich man in California after next year. A man will be poor with only $10,000. Crime is rife, murders are frequent; the perpetrators of some have been taken and hung.
(NYH, Feb. 20, 1849.)

WASHINGTON AND CALIFORNIA MINING ASSOCIATION. At a meeting of the Association, on the 17th instant, the following resolutions were adopted, viz: 1. *Resolved,* That all applicants for membership must give satisfactory references, or produce testimonials of character. 2. *Resolved,* That the full amount of subscription ($175) must be paid in by the 10th day of March next. 3. *Resolved,* That the regular meetings of the Association for completing its organization shall be held every Monday, Wednesday, and Saturday, at 7 o'clock P. M., at the residence of Mr. John M. Farrar, on the east side of 6th street, south of Pennsylvania avenue.

J. GOLDSBOROUGH BRUFF, President. (WNI, Feb. 21, 1849.)

WHAT I SAW IN CALIFORNIA, being the Journal of a Tour, by the Emigrant Route and South Pass of the Rocky Mountains, across the Continent of North America, the Great Desert Basin, and through California, in the years 1846 and 1847, by Edwin Bryant, late Alcalde of St. Francisco, just published; for sale at the Bookstore of R. FARNHAM, cor. of 11th street and Penn. av. (WNI, Feb. 28, 1849.)

The Gold Hunter's Farewell to his Wife

BY ONE OF 'EM.

Tune—*"Don't care."*

Farewell, dear wife, keep up good cheer,
  There's glittering scenes before me—
You soon with me the wealth shall share
  That lays in California.

I'll hunt the mountains, search the sand,
  Through weather clear and stormy,
With shovel, spade, and sieve in hand,
  Dig Gold in California.

The Sacramento's banks are lined,
  "They" credibly inform me,
With metals of the richest kind—
  I *must* see California.

What makes you think I won't return,
  With *lots* of Gold to adorn you?
Dry up your tears and do not mourn,
  There's wealth in California.

'Tis true, like others, I *may* die,
  Or you may not *live* to see me;
But Gold is sparking in my eye,
  I am bound for California.

In two years I'll return again—
  Then you may look out for me;
Do hush (don't grieve) I'm not to blame,
  For going to California.

So you must do the best you can!
  Fix my old pants for Johnny;

The children, too, will help you plan,
  While I am in California.

My oxen's all in first rate plight—
  Don't be uneasy 'bout me—
O! there's the waggon hove in sight!
  Huzza!! for California.

Come let me once more see you smile;
  No, I *can't* wait till morning—
My fever's rising all the while,
  To get to California.

Now I must start, the team is here,
  The b'hoys are waiting for me;
So here's my hand, good-by my dear!
  Ge-ho-haw for California.

Ho, husband! stop! before you go,
  And let me just inform you,
I'll find *one* that won't serve me so;
  Well—go to California!

Wo-o-ho, back, wo, (Jake take the team,)
  Why bless you! dear wife Mary,
Those horned fixens you have seen,
  I bought to break the Prairie.
(ISJ, Feb. 21, 1849.)

Emigrantesses to California

The ladies are going to California. We are glad of it, for nothing less than feminine influence will prevent the men who go there, however respectable they have been here, from degenerating into a lawless, savage, brutal mob. Without woman, man cannot be anything higher than a quadruped on two legs, like any other monkey or dancing bear. Adam till he was introduced to Eve, was not fit for any other society than lions and tigers, bears and wolves, hogs and woodchucks, and other horned cattle. And one of Eve's very first efforts was to wean him away from such society. We admit that she did it at some sacrifice. But anything was better than such company to a refined, elegant, affectionate young creature, the very incarnation of domestic felicity; and *she did it*. Let a woman alone to accomplish anything where skill, tact, address are necessary, she is sure to get it.

Mrs. Farnham, formerly matron of the New York State Prison at Sing Sing, who goes to California to settle the affairs of her husband, who lately died there, has advertised for one hundred and fifty young women, not under twenty-five years of age, each of whom can furnish a certificate of character from her clergyman, and a capital of two hundred and fifty dollars, to accompany her to the new El Dorado. We hope that she will receive five hundred applications for the voyage.

But what sort of woman is Mrs. Farnham? We are told that she succeeded in humbugging and twisting round her finger every one of the directors at Sing Sing, all very intelligent men, so far as to govern absolutely in her department of matron. That is enough. Mrs. Farnham is the woman for the Ledger! Ordinary men, vulgar thinkers, who are mortally afraid of petticoat government, because it impeaches their dignity in *their own* estimation, say that these directors were humbugged. Now they were the very men to comprehend and appreciate such a woman as Mrs. Farnham, and therefore exhibited their good sense in yielding to her suggestions for the government of the female prisoners. She humbugged them precisely as Columbus humbugged *his* disciples. He found disciples only in those who had

brains enough to comprehend him. Only blockheads revolt from petticoat government. Josephine exerted a powerful influence over Napoleon. And she would have done it over Alexander, and Cæsar, and Alfred, and Edward I, and Henry IV of France, and Cromwell. But all her talents, her aspiration, her refinement, her expansive benevolence, her faith in God's justice and man's perfectibility, would have been thrown away upon an ass.

The Right Woman for the Job

Such is Mrs. Farnham, the very woman to conceive and execute such a project; the very woman with sufficient intelligence, courage, benevolence, aspiration, to understand that where the sexes are separated, woman is sent to the desert of Sahara, and man to hell! that, while thousands of men are going to California, to plunge into that gulf of perdition that always awaits every community of men exempt from feminine restraint, hundreds of women are left behind, to a life of cheerless, hopeless toil; that, sending women to California will rescue them from a life of both positive and negative gloom here, and the men from a life of disorder and crime there.

The women for whom she advertises may be found in large numbers in the sewing garrets of New York. Most of them are from the country, and have been educated in country schools, and to a much higher point of intellectual and moral development than is reached by very many children of fashion, bred in those seminaries of *humbug* that may be found in some of the great cities. They are not only well qualified for woman's appropriate province, the domestic fireside, but many of them might outshine the most fortunate in any department of American society. Here their chances of marriage, or of anything more than excessive toil for a subsistence in poverty, are few. Here they must "stitch, stitch, stitch" for the grovelling sharks who rapidly make fortunes out of bank credits and their miserably paid labor. In California, where men are numerous and women few, they will be well paid in every department of feminine labor, and will be eagerly sought in marriage by men who must marry them or none, and would be very fortunate in marrying them anywhere. We are told that 100,000 active and energetic men will reach California from the States, within the ensuing year. If so, nothing can save that region from becoming Pandemonium but a large emigration of women. Therefore we hope that Mrs. Farnham's *invoice* is only the beginning, and that not less than 20,000 young women will leave the States for California in the ensuing year.

Vulgar Taunts

Some of the newspapers are indulging in ribald ridicule of Mrs. Farnham's project. Of course she must expect this from all vulgar minds, in and out of the press; for no woman ever yet attempted anything beyond the *drudgery* of the household, without incurring the taunts, the jibes, the sneers of all those coarsely selfish animals who regard her merely as their own domestic convenience, and with no higher sentiment than those of a quadruped. But where is the ground for ridicule? "O they are going in pursuit of husbands!" Indeed! For the sake of argument we admit it, and then ask if the relation of marriage is so disgraceful that women cannot seek it without deserving ridicule and contempt? The Bible, as well as nature, tell us otherwise. Low-minded men ridicule women for being "old maids," a term and a taunt never yet uttered by a gentleman. Then truly their lot is hard, if they are to be ridiculed for celibacy, and also for decent and proper efforts to avoid it. But we will admit that these poor working women, with their ample store of personal, intellectual, and moral attractions, go all the way to

California in pursuit of marriage. Is "husband hunting" unknown among their more fortunate sisters? Do we never witness or hear of manœuvres among mothers and misses in what is called "fashionable life," to catch desirable matches? Let a young candidate for matrimony show his head in the pulpit of a fashionable church, and we are greatly mistaken if he have not his hands full of bible classes from daughters, and civilities from mothers. And if a rich broker from London, or Paris, or Vienna, or Frankfort, should come over and appear at an opera-house or theatre, and another broker, perhaps one of the firm, should lead scores of ladies out of their boxes into the new lion's box for an introduction, and the ladies should absolutely struggle for the first chance, would they exhibit any "husband-hunting?"

O no! They are too "respectable" for such imputation. And if all these civilities should suddenly die away, upon a report that that lion was not rich, would the "husband hunting" seem to flow from any mercenary motive? Would it show that the candidates for a "splendid alliance" were willing to sell themselves, if the bid were high enough? Certainly not. But if a poor sewing girl, perhaps with beauty, intellect, and cultivation that even the majority of wealth's favorites might envy, should leave her severe toil and scanty bread at home, and seek better wages and a better prospect of marriage in California, O the indelicacy! O the outrage! O the enormity! And who make the outcry? Among men, those whose estimate of woman is the Turk's of the old school. Among women, the fashionable wives and daughters of the very men who have made fortunes rapidly, by employing large numbers of women at starving prices. (PPL, Feb. 28, 1849.)

Buy Now!

FOR SAN FRANCISCO, CALIFORNIA, DIRECT, VIA THE STRAITS OF Magellan, the new and substantial steamship HURON, of 240 tons burthen, 3 years old, built in this city of the best material, copper fastened, and newly coppered, boilers entirely new, and is now undergoing thorough repairs for sea service, and will positively sail on or about the 20th of March. Her saloon and cabins will be handsomely furnished for ease and comfort, and a more profitable opportunity cannot be offered to those desirous of going to California. She will be disposed of by 100 shares of stock, at $500 each. The owner of each share will be entitled to his passage to San Francisco, and his equal undivided share of the ship, and all appurtenances thereto belonging, and of the profits and earnings of said ship, after her arrival at San Francisco. Each share of stock will be made transferable. Application should be made soon, as already over one half the stock is taken. For particulars, apply to AUSTIN & WATKINS, No. 8 South street, up stairs.   (March 2, 1849.)

FOR SAN FRANCISCO—RARE OPPORTUNITY.—THE RISING SUN is nearly full, and will sail in a day or two. This is a new and very fast sailing clipper built bark, and is likely to overhaul and pass most of the heavy freighted ships which have preceded her. The Rising Sun Company consists of 60 members. Five shares may yet be had if applied for immediately. Three airy and commodious staterooms, for families and single passengers, may also be secured. Competent geologists and mineralologists, under the instructions and advice of Prof. Silliman[1] and of Prof. J. D. Dana,[2] of the United States Exploring Expedition, are connected with the company, and will precede it overland. For further particulars apply to Isaac T. Smith, 101 Wall street, corner of Front street.   (NYH, March 2, 1849.)

News for the Million

That diamond which rolled down a hill in California and killed five men, was so heavy that it required two ships to carry it away.

FLYING.—A model flying machine is being constructed somewhere in New York, for a party of speculators who want to fly to California in 'five days!' They are not the only ones who are trying to GAS themselves to the Land of Promise.

LUCKY DARKEY.—A letter from a young officer in the navy, now in California, published in the Cincinnati Dispatch, tells the following tough 'un:—

"There was a most horribly ugly negro who went and married the daughter of an Indian Chief, and got the whole tribe to dig for him. He came down to San Francisco with as much gold as a mule could carry. This is a well attested fact."

EXPORTING WOMEN TO CALIFORNIA—A lady well known as an author and an enthusiastic phrenologist, has made proposals to take out a given number of females

---

1. Benjamin Silliman, Sr. (1779–1864), a noted chemist and geologist, professor of most scientific subjects at Yale, and the founding editor of the *American Journal of Science*—often called *Silliman's Journal.*
2. James Dwight Dana (1813–1895), geologist with the Wilkes expedition, professor of geology at Yale from 1850 to 1894. Mount Dana in Yosemite National Park is named for him.

as a bona fide commercial enterprise. Readers will draw their own conclusions.

A WRETCH in a town near Springfield removed his wife and two children to a boarding house, and then sold his house and furniture, took what money his wife had, and then deserted her. He is gone to California. (CPD, March 5, 1849.)

From the New York Sun

PANAMA, FEBRUARY 16, 1849.

I send you by the very last means of conveyance a few items of interest from California. They were received here this morning from a Spaniard who came passenger in the Peruvian barque from San Francisco.

Emigrants of all kinds and colors are pouring in in multitudes. Every language, race, color, and shade is represented. Lawyers, ministers, women in male attire, robbers, aristocrats, and outcasts from civilized life, all are flocking to the gold regions. All are frantic with hopes of finding chunks of gold as large as mill stones; but a few days' experience of California life changes their views of gold hunting.

Living is excessively high and mining for the precious minerals is one of the worst kinds of lottery; for each person that is so fortunate as to find a mass sufficient to enrich him for life, there are dozens who can scarcely make a living.

Many robberies have taken place, but they are chiefly confined to food and clothing. These things, at times, when there is a scarcity in the market, bring excessive prices. One day flour may at retail bring $200 a barrel, although a few days before it was sold for $15.

The necessities of many of the emi-grants and these varieties in prices lead to numerous thefts. Robberies for gold are rare. One or two murders have, however, occurred for this cause.

The new-comers and greenhorns are frequently swindled in the most shameful manner, and redress is out of the question. Perhaps great social crimes might be punished, but every thing is as yet too new, and thieving is too common to be punished in the absence of regular law.

For instance, a green one who has goods for sale often takes large quantities of glittering ore, supposing it to be gold, but too late finds it nothing but copper and iron ore—but he can do nothing to recover his property.

Spurious silver ore is common. On the first landing many are willing to sell the coats off their backs for this sort of pay.

The emigrants who have guns, powder, and ball to protect themselves, are frequently driven by hunger to leave their all and seek for provisions.

Gangs of desperadoes in the mountains steal the mules of the miners and kill them for food.

A company is about to be formed of those who can raise mules or means to travel overland, to the States. It would, in their opinion, be a terrible expedition; but they prefer doing so to living as at present.

The only thing that can give prosperity to California is its establishment into an independent State.

This is agitated, and, if carried out, the agricultural and mineral wealth might be developed, and California made to rival any country in the world.

(WNI, March 7, 1849.)

PROTECTIVE OVERLAND COMPANY TO CALIFORNIA, VIA CORPUS Christi, Camarro, Monterey, and Mazatlan, in 45 days.—A company is now forming to proceed to the gold regions, as above, escorted by a gentleman well acquainted with the route, and conversant with the language, manners, and customs of the people. This party will sail from New York on the 20th inst., in a fine new first class picket ship. Entire cost of passage through, including passports from Department of State and Mexican Consul, escort interpreter, medical attendant, tents, and camp equipage, provisions from New York to San Francisco, cooking utensils, &c., $150. Persons wishing to join this party should make immediate application at the company's office, 101 Wall street, corner of Front, between 10 o'clock A.M. and 5 P.M.

FOR CALIFORNIA VIA CHAGRES—THE SUBSCRIBER WILL despatch for Chagres, without delay, the superior very fast sailing Baltimore-built brig Col. Howard, Durkee, master. She is 332 tons burthen, newly coppered, refitted and put in perfect order. Her accommodations for passengers are of the first class, having just been completed at great expense. First cabin, $50; second ditto, $40. The bulk of 10 barrels freight allowed to each passenger, free of charge. For freight or passage apply on board, foot of Dover street, or to Fernando Wood, 161 South street, corner of Dover. Passengers by the Col. Howard will have the preference of passage from Panama to San Francisco, in a vessel expected to sail thence in April next.
(NYH, March 2, 1849.)

(From the WNI, March 6, 1849.)

A MAP OF THE EMIGRANT ROAD FROM INDEPENDENCE, (MO.) TO San Francisco, California, by T. H. Jefferson. This great and original Map is drawn upon a large scale, (in four parts,) from the regular survey of the author, who travelled over the entire route, in company with a party of emigrants, with wagons drawn by oxen. All the streams of water and springs are delineated, as well as the daily courses, distances, and camps made by the party. With this Map for his guide, the emigrant or traveller can set out upon the journey and pilot himself through. It is accompanied by a brief but practical description of the different modes of outfit, their cost, and other useful information. It conducts the traveller into the midst of the gold region. Price $3. Just published and for sale by   R. FARNHAM.

MAP OF THE GOLD REGION.—LAWSON'S MAP, FROM ACTUAL survey, of the Gold, Silver, and Quicksilver Regions of Upper California, exhibiting the mines, diggings, roads, paths, houses, mills, stores, missions, &c., by J. T. Lawson, Esq., California, together with a miniature map of the United States, Mexico, and South America, showing the different routes to California, &c. Just published and for sale by   R. FARNHAM.

A TOUR OF DUTY IN CALIFORNIA, INCLUDING A DESCRIPTION OF the
Gold Region, and an account of the voyage around Cape Horn, &c., with map
and plates, by Jos. Warren Revere, U. S. Navy. For sale by
TAYLOR & MAURY, Bookstore, near 9th street.   (WNI, March 6, 1849.)

CORRESPONDENCE OF THE
BUFFALO ADVERTISER
ACAPULCO, FEBRUARY 11, 1849.

We arrived at this place on the 8th instant, being eight days from our watering
place near Panama. We have on board
three hundred and eighty passengers. The
health of the passengers varies with the
day. We have at times twenty or more on
the sick list, sometimes not more than ten.
No deaths have occurred since leaving
Panama, yet it would not be at all surprising if some were to occur before reaching
San Francisco, so many of us being
crowded into such small space.

The stories of the immense amount of
gold in California grow larger as we near
this great deposit of the wealth of the
world. Many of the natives have left this
place months since for California, and perhaps an hundred are now waiting for passage hence to San Francisco; and it is said
that many more are waiting at every port
on the coast. We (the favored ones) will be
among the first, if not the first, arrivals
from the States.

Many who left New Orleans months
since in the Falcon and other vessels are
yet at Panama, but few having been able to
procure passage on board our steamer.
About a hundred might have procured a
passage with us if preference had not been
given to the same number of Peruvians,
who were taken on board at Callao—a fact
which ought to be condemned by every
citizen of the United States.

This is a small and lovely place. I think
its harbor cannot be equalled in the world;
there are many larger, but for depth of
water and safety from winds it cannot be
equalled. A vessel drawing twelve feet
water can anchor within fifteen rods of the
shore in any part of the harbor with perfect
safety.

I presume but few of our countrymen
will attempt the passage across the
Isthmus for several months to come; the
fact of the prevalence of the cholera, together with the many other usual and
natural disadvantages of crossing will deter them from it. That the cholera does exist is a positive fact, and that numbers of
the natives are dying with it is another
positive fact, if the statements of Doctors
Haley, Jones, and Clemons (who are with
us) can be relied upon, who state that very
many of the soldiers and citizens of Cruces
and Panama were daily dying of this fearful epidemic. Add to this my own knowledge of the symptoms of this disease, and I
am entirely satisfied that it does prevail,
even to a fearful extent, although but few
of our countrymen have as yet fallen victims to it.

I would advise all persons who intend
coming to California before January next
to come across land. The voyage around
the Cape is so tedious (unless made in a
steamer) that it amounts almost to an ab-
surdity to attempt it; besides which you
have not that variety of scenery and excitement of travelling through prairies and
forests, over mountains and across valleys,
that one would have in crossing from Fort
Leavenworth to Fort Hall and the Sacramento. The trip could be performed in seventy days, at an expense far below that of
any other route. The route across the Isthmus has the advantage of being made
much more speedily, but with much more
risk. Individually, with my experience, I
would come via the Isthmus, but at the
same time would advise my friends to take
the land route.   (WNI, March 24, 1849.)

An English View of California Emigration

[From the Liverpool Mail, Jan. 27]

We have been favored with an extract of a letter from New York, written by a correspondent on whose veracity we can rely, and who has, commercially, the best means of information in reference to California. It is as follows:—

"New York, 10th January, 1849.—It is supposed at least one hundred and fifty thousand people have emigrated to San Francisco and the banks of the Sacramento river, the last and present month, hence the great demand for articles of provisions and breadstuffs. I am much inclined to think the superabundance of gold there is a monstrous exaggeration, got up under the connivance of the government, to induce emigration on a large scale to their newly acquired territories on the Pacific. Time will show."

A Fraud Upon the People

It would be consistent with plain truth if the term "exaggeration" in the above extract were transformed into "swindling," for we are of opinion that a greater swindle has not been perpetrated even in America, so fertile of these things, for many years. That gold, silver, and copper are found in that part of the savage world we can easily believe, but that it is so plentiful as described we believe to be a gross fraud upon public credulity. What is most reprehensible in the matter is that the government of the United States, acting upon the authority of official servants, have encouraged the imposture.

The Californian Trap

That it is desirable that a flood of population should be induced to emigrate to the golden region, in order, eventually, to settle in the Oregon territory, we are not prepared to dispute. But when public policy is not based upon truth it becomes a criminal act. It is premeditated manslaughter. Two-thirds at least of the people who go to California will perish of starvation, disease, or the bowie knife, within the first years of their rash enterprise. But what does Mr. President Polk care for this? He has already put to death nearly one hundred thousand men, women, and children, (including his own fellow citizens,) in Mexico; and if ten or twenty thousand die in California it will, to a grand extent, be conducive to his policy. Impressed with these convictions, we most earnestly advise our readers, if they have an occasion, to persuade any friends they know not to fall into the inevitable wreck and miserable reverses of the Californian trap.

Rogues and Cannibals

It is well known that about 40,000 Mormons—fools and rogues, of course, with a very large preponderance of the latter—after being persecuted, as they said, by the United States government, left their city of Nauvoo, *en route* for this very California. But how many reached the golden paradise? Not quite 4,000, who had in their travels eaten their companions. It is no republican joke. The survivors, now the lords of California, were cannibals, perhaps from dire necessity, but they were cannibals, nevertheless. These men- and women-eaters are at present the republican aristocracy of the gold lumps; and there is every probability that when these minerals fail in procuring provisions and rum, which they are sure to do, this Nauvoon aristocracy will become cannibals again. Any fat Englishman who goes there will, consequently, have no chance. (NYH, March 13, 1849.)

The Trade to California

The following is a list of principal goods, entered (in considerable quantities) at the Liverpool Custom House, for export to California, up to the present time:—155 bales and 79 other packages of cottons; 133 bales and 27 other packages of woollens; 149 bales of blankets; 40 tons of bar, hoop, and sheet iron, and 50 boxes of tin plates;

419 packages of spades, hardware, shovels, nails, &c.; 15,000 bricks, and 38 boxes of glass; 160 tierces and 70 barrels of beer, and 165 ditto bottled; 71 packages of wearing apparel; a quantity of plain spirits, French brandy, and gin; castings, pickles and sauces, soap, medicine, shirts, umbrellas, parasols, thread and silk, 19 cases of cutlery, 69 barrels of vinegar, 28 packages of shoes, tool chests, &c., 200 iron pots, two ploughs, six cases of patent felt, stationary, one box of Seidlitz powders, one iron warehouse, a quantity of agricultural implements, 100 tons of coals, anvils, grates, 45 packages of galvanized tin, white lead, grindstones, biscuits, wove wire, and a variety of miscellaneous articles, of which the respective quantities were so small that we did not particularise them.—*Liverpool (Willmer) Mail, Feb. 24.*

(NYH, March 13, 1849.)

Letter from Jem Grant

PANAMA, NEW GRANADA, Jan. 26, 1849.

Jem Grant's Arrival at Chagres—His troubles in Crossing the Isthmus—His Impressions and Opinions—The Herald in New Granada, &c. &c.

I thought that it would be interesting to some of your numerous readers to know the truth as regards travelling over the Isthmus. I will endeavor to give it to you.

We arrived at Chagres after a pleasant passage of eighteen days from New York, and landed on the 31st December. Chagres is a most miserable place, with a population of about eight hundred; you can scarce get anything to eat, and as for a place to sleep in, that is next to an impossibility. It is a complete swamp; we only remained one night in it. We hired a canoe for 35 dollars, to take us to Cruces, which is at the head of the river, and started on new year's day for that place, amidst the most terrible rain you ever saw. One does not know what rain is till he comes here. I thought a Croton pipe had burst.[3] It seems to rain all the time.

We drank your health, with the compliments of the season, on the Chagres river, in good Scotch whiskey, to begin with. We were four days on the river, and it was raining all the time. The scenery is most beautiful all the way up; birds of beautiful plumage are abundant, and so very tame that those who had fowling pieces with them had capital sport, shooting all the way up. How astonished the birds seemed when one of them was shot! It was something new to them; had they been commanded by Queen Vic. to appear and be shot in a royal manner, they could not have obeyed her better than when they appeared before us.

At last we made Cruces; it is on a small hill, with a population of about eighteen hundred, who are very little better than those at Chagres. They are a miserable set of beings. They have very little to eat, and no bed to repose on. We reclined on our trunks for want of anything better, and I remained ten days trying to get my things across to Panama; but transportation is difficult to be had for love or money; you can scarce get your things across, there are so many going. Mules used to be hired for $3, and now it costs from $15 to $20 per load, and one hundred pounds is considered a load.

The cholera has been raging since my arrival here, and the people are getting frightened, for there are no doctors, and whoever is attacked with it lives from eight to ten hours only. I thought it best to move, leaving a great many of my things behind. I undertook to walk across, but it is the worst road—if you can call it a road—I ever saw or dreamed of. You go right up a very steep mountain, with mud and water

---

3. Water from the Croton watershed, some 30 miles north of New York City, was first delivered to the city through the Croton aqueduct in 1842.

up to your knees at every step, and often when you raise your foot you leave your boot behind, and have to turn round and pull it out, empty the water, and go on again, as there is no stopping by the way. This was too much for some poor fellows, who were obliged to lie down, and that was the last of them. Several died on the way. I gave out, but was fortunate enough to hire a mule just in time; I could not have gone much farther. The path is just wide enough for a mule to pass, and no more, and the care with which they climb the mountain would astonish you.

On the river, the men that paddle the canoes have no clothing, and have only a small piece of cloth, about a foot square. This constitutes their wardrobe; and in crossing the mountain, females have to ride in the same way as the men do. It is horrid; and you can do them a great service by letting them know what they have to encounter in crossing here. I saw several cross in this way, and they felt bad enough.

The living here is very poor; board at the hotels is two dollars per day, and only two meals per day—breakfast at 10 o'clock, and dinner at 6, and not over good at that. I went to market, and could purchase beef or pork, by the yard or pound, at from four to five cents per pound; eggs at three cents each, plenty of yams, and good rice, some tomatoes, a few onions; but plantain is the principal vegetable. The currency is in a miserable condition; Mexican dollars and five franc pieces are worth ten shillings; pistareens go for two shillings; one franc pieces go for two shillings. All kinds of money pass here; you must try and regulate the currency.

The weather is most delightful at present—about as warm as it is in New York in the month of August. The steamer California is here, and sails on Sunday. She made this port in the short sailing time of fifty-five days. She was detained so long on account of there being no coal at the different places where she expected to have got it. The Captain says that she is the best boat ever built, and he will sail her against any steamer afloat. So much for American enterprise. God speed them on! I go up in her, and will send you another scroll from the gold diggings.

I remain, dear sir, your most ob't serv't,

JAMES GRANT.

N. B.—A word to those coming this way. Take as few things as possible; get a bag, instead of a trunk; a few shirts, underclothing, two pair of boots, and things just sufficient for the passage; send the balance round the Horn; do not let the weight of your baggage be over 125 pounds. The reason that a bag is better than a trunk is because it is better to pack on the mule, and you will get it cheaper across. J. G. (NYH, March 21,1849.)

MORE CALIFORNIA NEWS.

We find the following under the head of "the latest from California," in the Boston *Traveller* of the 19th inst. We give it because it may be interesting to those who are fond of the marvellous. The *Traveller* is particular to find fault with anything that may be published in any other paper that looks the least like Mung news.[4] We advise the editors of that print to go and share the "ledge"[5] with the new millionaire in San Francisco. But here is its California news:—

We stated in Friday's *Traveller* that we had seen a private letter from San Francisco, dated January 20th, which contained statements in respect to the gold mines, exceeding, if anything, the marvellousness of former accounts. It having been very

4. False news. 'Mung' is a variation of 'mong': confused or jumbled.
5. In the sense of a lode or vein of ore.

courteously suggested by one of our contemporaries that the whole thing was a deception, we now publish the letter entire—with a single exception—and with the name of the writer attached. It was written to a relative in this city, and there is no room to doubt its authenticity. The original letter is in our possession. It is postmarked at St. Louis, and came overland, no doubt.

San Francisco, Jan. 20, 1849.

Dear Uncle—I set myself down to write a few lines, to let you know that I am in the land of the living, and that I am now enjoying tolerably good health. While I was in the gold diggings, my health was bad for a month or so; for there we had no houses, and had for the most part to sleep on the ground or under rocks where we could get a place. Talk of the army—I never saw half the hardships while I was in the service that I have seen in the gold diggings. . . .

As for gold, I have got plenty of it. I have got about 793 pounds. It sells here for from 12 to 16 dollars the ounce. I was in the diggings three months and a half, and if I had something to wash out the dirt clean, I should have got out as much again; for we can get nothing near all of it out. I have a number of pretty large pieces.—one piece weighing five pounds.

I want you to come out here; you can get just as much gold as you want. I know where there is a ledge that is almost solid gold—but I shall not tell any body, nor work at it, till my friends come out. I found it out by one of the Indian chiefs, whose life I saved, when he was about to be murdered. A great many are killed, and nothing is said about it.

The gold country is immense. I have been five hundred miles up the country; and the further we go, the thicker the gold is. I think on the river where I was, the fountain head is in the mountains; but it is awful travelling to get up to my ledge. I know where there is plenty of silver in the mountains. We found that when I was

with the Indians. They took me prisoner, and I was with them nine months. At last I discovered that one of the chiefs was a Free Mason, and he at once set me free. I find that a great many of the Indian chiefs are Free Masons. I was made a Mason by the recommendation of an aged friend, before I left Michigan. I left there when the war first began, and went and joined Col. Fremont's regiment. We crossed the mountains, and I got taken by the Indians. I was released in consequence of being a Mason; and I would advise that all who intend to come out to this wild country, to be Masons, for they will find true friends among the Indians. The Indians hold Masonry to be sacred—which it is. . . .

You never saw such a set as there is in this place. There are people of all nations and of all colors. . . The population here are getting to be awful bad; and it is caused by that curse of the earth, rum. If that had been kept out, there would have been no trouble here. . . .

There is gold enough for all the young men of the whole New England States; and I wish they were all here. But it is time enough yet, and there is gold and silver enough. . . .

I can go along with the Indians first rate. Only be kind to them and you can do anything with them. I could tell you ten times as much more, but I have filled my sheet. Yours, GEORGE W. MORRILL.

(NYH, March 21, 1849.)

The Emigration to California

Vessels Sailed Direct for California

Total in 198 vessels via Cape Horn	12,323
Total in 45 vessels via Chagres	3,229
Total in 8 vessels via Vera Cruz	594
Total in 11 vessels via Brazos	765
Total in 3 vessels via Corpus Christi	103
Total in 2 vessels via San Juan river	118
Total in 2 vessels via Tampico	87
Total in 1 vessel via Lavaca	122
Total in 270 vessels	17,341

(NYH, March 23, 1849.)

PORTABLE IRON HOUSES FOR CALIFORNIA. THE GALVANIZED IRON Houses constructed by me for California, having met with so much approval, I am thus induced to call the attention of those going to California to an examination of them. The iron is grooved in such a manner that all parts of the house, roof and sides, glide together, and a house 20 x 15 can be put up in less than a day. They are far cheaper than wood, are fire-proof, and much more comfortable than tents. A house of the above size can be shipped in two boxes, 12 feet long and two feet wide, and 8 inches deep, the freight on which would be about $14 to San Francisco. There will also be no trouble in removing from one part of the country to another, as the house can, in a few hours, be taken down and put up. By calling upon the subscriber, a house of the above size can be seen.

PETER NAYLOR, 13 Stone street.   (NYH, March 20, 1849.)

Interesting Letter from the Gold Diggings

CALIFORNIA, IN THE WOODS A PIECE, Jan. 2.

EDITORS [New Orleans] PICAYUNE: Every newspaper I see from the states, (and they are mighty few) contains one or more letters from out here somewhere giving the most awful description of things here imaginable—horrible murders, outrageous thefts, hanging people by scores on trees, lynch law, &c. Now as one of our company has made as much as he thinks will do him, and is going home, they have all agreed and requested that I should give you by his hands a little history of how we do things in our "diggins."

In the first place, we assemble every Sunday morning, numbering generally from 110 to 130, our whole number who have signed the by laws being 153. Our place of rendezvous is a large oak tree, on a beautiful hill, out of which gushes as pure a stream of water as was ever drunk by man.—You ought to see that tree. It looks as though it had been topped about two hundred years ago, and had never stopped spreading.

At 10 o'clock the secretary reads the by laws, after which the president rises and says, "Does any member know of any violation of the laws just read?" to which, three times out of five, there is no response; and since I have been a member,

which is about eight months, there has been no offence committed (with one exception), that required a higher punishment than a small fine, or a reprimand from the president.

The exception alluded to was a poor devil who was detected hiding a portion of the day's labor of his company. The members thereof, consisting of nine, immediately held a meeting among themselves, gave him his part of their joint earnings, which was about $3,000, and told him to go, as he knew what would be his fate next Sabbath. He accordingly went and has not been heard of since.

The penalty for theft is expatriation. What we mean by this is to leave our borders, and if found in them, the first time, nine-and-twenty; the second, he pulls hemp. One of our laws is, "There is to be no gambling of any description." Another is, "No profane or obscene language shall be used in the assembly on the Sabbath," neither of which has been violated in the first instance since I have been a member.

Now where would you go to find 153 more orderly men? and all this, too, without any law except common consent to do right. Not to the St. Charles, I am sure. I mention the St. Charles from a circumstance that took place there during a few day's stay on my way here. I walked into the billiard room with a friend, and looked on a game until played through. Upon leaving the room, I observed to my comrade that the game-keeper was a very careless scorer, or else he designed to cheat one of the parties. "Why, certainly," replied he, "one of the players is a gambler and the other a countryman. That fat-faced, sulky looking fellow was cheating for the gambler." "Why," said I, "did not some of those gentlemen tell him he was cheated." "Because," said he, "they are all gamblers, and all concerned in robbing the country fellow." Said I, "That polite, fine-looking old gentleman with gloves cannot be a gambler." "No," said he, "he has got rather old. His eye-sight ain't sharp enough for the new tricks now; he's what they call a faro broker, that means roping young men into the bank, and his commission is half the winnings." "But," said I, "suppose the bank loses." "Ah," said he, "that is not a supposable case. They don't play those kind of games." "Well, is that little doctor one of 'em?" "What? that sly, sheepish-looking fellow? Yes. He pretends to be a dentist—got a sign up across the way, but I expect never drew a tooth in his life—but can take 'em from any part of the deck."

Now, I would advise all such "brokers" and "tooth-pullers," if they have any idea of coming to El Dorado, not to come about the "big oak" unless they have made up their minds to abandon their old tricks, and are disposed to make an honest living; and I would advise all, any where who are doing well, to stay where they are; though fortunes can and will be made here, not by

picking gold out with a jack knife in four or five pound lumps, but with much toil and hard labor.

From the best information I can get, the average of our whole number per day, for the last eight months, has been $10.50. So you see fortunes ain't to be made in a day, nor a season. If you ever saw men at work on a canal or mill race or digging the foundation for a large house in your city, you have a very good idea of the labor in getting gold here. I would not have troubled you with this ill-digested epistle had it not been for the accounts I have read about this country. How it may be in other portions I know not; but what I have told you about our "diggins" is true. I feel much more safe here from every kind of harm than I would in your well organized city, or any other city. But I think there are more villains congregated in New Orleans than in any other place in the world. Go to some of your billiard rooms, and out of the multitudes usually there, nineteen out of twenty are gamblers. What drones upon a community! What a multitude living off of honest men! I have no doubt many expect to make their jack out of the gold "diggins" here, but if they should squat down about the "big oak" with any such view, they had better think of Vicksburg.[6]

Yours, &c., JNO. H. WALTON.

(CPD, March 27, 1849.)

[Possibly written from the community of Big Oak Flat.]

---

6. In the spring of 1835 a scarifying rumor spread throughout the South that the slaves were going to unite in a vast rebellion—a revolt that would encompass the entire slave region from Maryland to Louisiana. The object was purported to be the total destruction of the white population. The various white social and economic classes reacted in different ways to this dire news, and when there was no slave revolt whatsoever, elements of those classes gave vent to their fear, rage, and paranoia on the nearest targets. Some of the resulting incidents and clashes consisted of whites against whites. In Vicksburg, groups of "responsible citizens" attacked professional gamblers who worked on the river boats. One citizen was killed; five gamblers were captured, and quickly hanged. *Better think of Vicksburg.*

The Wife's Commandments

1. Thou shalt have no other wife but me.
2. Thou shalt not take into thy house any beautiful brazen image of a servant girl, to bow down to her, to serve her, for I am a jealous wife, visiting, &c.
3. Thou shalt not take the name of thy wife in vain.
4. Remember thy wife to keep her respectably.
5. Honor thy wife's father and mother.
6. Thou shalt not fret.
7. Thou shalt not find fault with thy dinner.
8. Thou shalt not chew tobacco.
9. Thou shalt not be behind thy neighbor.
10. Thou shalt not visit the rum tavern; thou shalt not covet the tavern keeper's rum, nor his brandy, nor his gin, nor his whisky, nor his wine, nor any thing that's behind the bar of the rum-seller.
11. Thou shalt not visit billiard saloons neither for worshipping on the dance, nor the heaps of money that lie on the tables.
And the twelfth commandment is, thou shalt not stay out later than nine o'clock at night.   (CPD, March 27, 1849.)

California Emigrants Moving West

The extracts from western papers will give some idea of the horde of California emigrants now making for the different rendezvous on the western frontier, to go overland from thence.—The St. Louis Republican of the 13th says:

"The steamer Niagara, from Pittsburg, yesterday brought around one hundred and eight passengers for California. Eighty of them are from Cincinnati, the balance from Pittsburg and Louisville. They come armed with rifles, and well supplied with clothing, but the most important and almost indispensable article they seem to have forgotten—mules—with which no traveler in the mountains can well do without, have become scarce in this quarter, and are enormously high; and it may be well to apprise emigrants at a distance of this fact. In the possession of the one hundred and eight persons on board the Niagara, there were not above a dozen animals.—Mules, horses, &c., they expect to purchase here; if so, they may expect to pay a round price for them."

Ho! for California

Four mining companies arrived this morning on the steamer Bay State from Cincinnati *en route* for California. The California Mining and Trading Company of Cincinnati consists of sixty members, who carry with them fifteen tons of merchandise and ten wagons. The California Miners and Traders of Cincinnati number four members, and they have with them three tons of goods, one wagon, and five mules. The California Traders of Lockland, Ohio, number eight members, and have with them four tons of goods and two wagons. The Honey Creek and White County Miners number eleven members. They intend leaving shortly for Independence, designing to cross the Plains.

Capt. Swift's company of miners, consisting of forty-seven members and possessing eighty-eight head of cattle and horses, arrived last evening on the steamer Belle Creole, from a place in Tennessee. This company will proceed shortly to California by way of the South Pass.
—*St. Louis Union.* (CPD, March 28, 1849.)

NEWS FOR THE MILLION

A Would-be Californian

According to Galignani's Messenger, an ex-convict recently broke the terms upon which he was set at liberty, by leaving the place where he was ordered to live and coming up to Paris. On being arrested, he said that the object of his visit was simply to ask the Prefect of Police to send him to California! He prayed the tribunal before which he was brought, earnestly to despatch him to the region of gold, but instead of granting this modest request, he was sent to prison for eight months. "Eight months!" ejaculated the fellow when he heard the sentence—"Eight months! There'll be no gold left in California by the time I get out!"

The Mexican Route to California.

A California engineer writes that the city of Mexico is a hard old place. To walk the streets in safety you must carry a revolver in each hand, and "keep your eyes skinned." Why, the first night we arrived here, two or three of our company went and took a bath. One of them was robbed of $150. The Alcalde was sent for, but he was found to be the owner of the establishment. I called on Mr. Clifford, our minister, this morning. He informed me that a few evenings since he saw a man lassoed and robbed before his own door. There is no safety here for Americans from assassination.   (PPL, March 28, 1849.)

From the Sandwich Islands

The Boston Traveller acknowledges the reception of Sandwich Island papers to the 10th November. The Polynesian of the 4th of November gives the following summary of the news of the previous week:

As we predicted in our last number, some of the gold diggers have come, and another 'rush' has taken place. On Monday morning the Mary Frances arrived from San Francisco, bringing a large quantity of the glittering treasure.

Several of our residents who left here a few months since have returned. Three or four gentlemen—not so greedy as the rest—came in the Mary Frances, and are shortly to sail for the United States, having, during their stay in California, acquired a little fortune by digging. The news has caused an increase of the fever.

Our harbor is crowded with ships. Forty-four whale ships and six merchant vessels are in the inner harbor, and quite a fleet lying off and on outside.

Letters from Tahiti, Society Islands, to the 8th of December, say that trade was exceedingly dull at the Islands. The news from California had just reached there, and the islanders are reported to be preparing to rush, almost *en masse,* for the gold diggings.   (WNI, March 30, 1849.)

California Emigration Overland

The Western papers abound in notices of the progress of large emigrating parties from all parts of the country towards the Plains, en route to the gold regions. The Baltimore Sun groups many of these particulars:

The Lafayette California Mercantile and Mining Company left Lafayette (Indiana) on Wednesday last, for California, on the steamer Genesee. They proceed to New Orleans, and take either the Vera Cruz, Mazatlan, or Rio Grande routes. They are all members of the Masonic fraternity, and before starting formed themselves into the "Sierra Nevada Lodge."

Two companies of New Yorkers, and one composed entirely of Germans, were in Pittsburg on the 23d instant. They will start as soon as the wagons, for which they have contracted with our manufacturers, can be made.

A telegraphic despatch from St. Louis advises emigrants to California to procure their mules at home. They were very scarce and high in Missouri. The lowest quotation was $90.

The Little Rock Gazette notices the arrival of several companies at that place, bound to California. Among them were the Knickerbocker company, from New York, numbering some 80 men, under command of Captain Ebberts; a company from Mississippi and Alabama, under command of Captain Smith; and a third numbering 30 or 40 men. A company was organizing at Little Rock, under Captain McVicar, and another at Memphis. They all go by way of Fort Smith, from which post a detachment of troops, under Major Bonneville, starts for the same destination.

The Louisville Journal of the 22d instant says that on the previous day seventy men, bound to California, came down the Kentucky on the Blue Wing. They left for St. Louis on the Pennsylvania and Melodeon.

The Lexington Atlas notices the departure of twelve men from that city for California.

A company of twenty-two left Lafayette, Indiana, on the 13th, for California.

The Louisville Courier of the 24th instant says that Capt. Aukrim's company of Californians, numbering two hundred and fifty men, from Pittsburg, crossed the falls early on Monday morning on the steamer Consignee. The boat was chartered at Pittsburg to convey them to Independence.

The new steamer San Francisco, and the Jewess, left Louisville for St. Louis on the 23d crowded with passengers, the majority of whom are going to California. The hurricane decks of both boats were covered with wagons and trappings.

A party of some fifty or sixty active and enterprising persons has been made up to leave the District of Columbia for California in a few days, by the western route.

Sixteen persons left Beaver, Pennsylvania, on last Tuesday week, for the gold diggings in California.

The Charlestown Mining Company of Virginia departed from Charlestown on Tuesday last. They number in all about seventy-five—embracing some of the best and worthiest citizens of the town.

The California company organized in Shepherdstown, in the same county, took their departure on last Wednesday week. The entire company number 31. The company take the land route, and expect to leave Fort Independence about the 1st of May.

MRS. FARNHAM'S CALIFORNIA EXPEDITION.—The New York Tribune of Monday says:

"We are informed by Mrs. Farnham that she has engaged passage for her company in the ship Angelique, a fine vessel of 500 tons, fitted up with convenient staterooms, and all appliances of comfort possible for a sea voyage. Mrs. Farnham leaves to-morrow for Boston to complete her arrangements. She has had many applications from all parts of the country, and there is every prospect that her band of female missionaries will be numerous enough to accomplish much in the way of refining and improving the rough California community."[7]

The barque Emma Isadora cleared at Boston on Tuesday for San Francisco with the "Mutual Protection Mining and Trading Company"—fifty-two in number. There are three or four other vessels at the same port which expect to get away during the week.

The barque Santee sailed from New York on the 22d instant for San Francisco, with fifty-seven passengers. Barque Samoset sailed the same day with the Otsego Mining Company, numbering eighteen individuals. (WNI, March 30, 1849.)

---

7. Eliza W. Farnham's (1815–1864) plan to take a sizable group of refined women to California fell through. After her husband died in San Francisco, she sailed for California with just her two young sons.

Hurrah for the Gold!

Hurrah for California

Hurrah for California! the greatest place
  in all creation,
Where gold is dug as 'taters are in
  this 'ere Yankee nation.
Where the "pewter" is so very thick
  'tis used in shoeing hosses,
And where there ain't no 'prentices,
  cos all on 'em are bosses.

O! won't it be a glorious time when gold
  runs down like water,
And nobody won't have to work,
  and nobody had oughter.
For who would plough, or sow, or reap,
  or endure labor's knocks,
When he can slap with either hand
  a "pocket full of rocks."
          (CPD, April 5, 1849.)

FOR SAN FRANCISCO—Via Lake Nicaragua—through in 60 days.—The second vessel of this line will leave New York on the 5th of April, for San Juan, Nicaragua. Passengers are conveyed up the river and across the Lake to Granada by steamboat, thence by a good road to Realejo on the Pacific, where a vessel is expected for San Francisco, despatched by an agent of the line.

The harbors of San Juan and Realejo are safe and easy of access, the route healthy and interesting.

Passage through, including provisions, camp equipments, &c., &c., $225.

For passage, or information, apply to

WM. GOODRICH & CO., 116 Market street, Philada., or to

WM. G. UHLHORN, 106 Front street, New York. (PPL, April 1, 1849.)

CALIFORNIA GOODS.—Just received by the subscribers a small assortment of the following goods, which are particularly recommended to gentlemen about starting for California:

    Colt's and Allen's Revolving Pistols
    Allen's Self-cocking Pistols
    Fine English belts, in great variety
    German belts   do
    Canteens, Powder Flasks, Pistol Belts, &c.
    Walker's fine English Caps
    Bowie Knives, assorted qualities and prices
    Belt Hatchets and Axes
    Fine English double-barrelled Fowling Pieces
    Day's patent Gun Canes
    Jenk's patent Carbines and Rifles

Together with an endless variety of articles too tedious to enumerate, all of which will be sold at prices which cannot fail to give satisfaction.
    JOHN W. BADEN & BRO.
    Pennsylvania avenue, south side, 3 doors from 6th st. (WNI, April 1, 1849.)

The Trip of the Gold Seekers

A correspondent of the Picayune, "Falcon," on board the Steamer California, writes from Mazatlan, Feb. 15th, as follows:

"A great deal of dissatisfaction has prevailed among the passengers, not only the steerage, but after cabin, in regard to our treatment on board. We, the steerage, are looked upon by the commander, Capt. Marshall, as entirely beneath his dignity and notice—so much so, I assure you, that not till our grievances had been represented to him several times did he deign to come forward to see us. The first and second officers, Capt. Brooks and Mr. Copland, have done all in their power to relieve our wants; and were Capt. Brooks placed in command of the steamer, it would be advantageous, not only to the owners, but also to Americans who come by Panama to take passage to California. We arrived at Acapulco, on the 10th inst., distance fifteen hundred miles from Panama. It has a delightful harbor, the water is very cold; we anchored in nine fathoms water, some one hundred yards from the Fort. From the sea it is impossible to see the town. We ran into a pass about two hundred yards wide, with mountains on each side; we turned an angle, when the broad Pacific was entirely hid from our view, and the city of Acapulco was immediately before us. We landed about 4 P. M., and found a very cleanly town.

"On the 13th we arrived at San Blas, distance from Acapulco three hundred and fifty miles. We laid here four or five hours, landed two Peruvian passengers, and then proceeded to sea. But one or two of the passengers went on shore; they reported that the most flattering accounts had been received from the gold region. They state that the region is now covered with snow from six to sixteen feet deep, and that there are now at San Francisco some fifteen thousand persons who have returned from the mines, waiting until the snow disappears, which will be about June. One ship and two brigs are lying at San Blas, chartered by Mexicans to take them to California. Some twenty-five Americans are there, who left New Orleans on the 3d January via Tampico, waiting for transportation. The Mexicans will not allow any American to go in any vessel they have chartered. Six of the Americans have purchased a long-boat, with which they leave for San Francisco in a few days. We left San Blas at 2 P. M. on the 14th, and arrived at the fort this morning at ten. I am writing this with a pencil, lying my length on the deck."

Another letter from another passenger on board the same steamer, dated San Blas, the 14th, and published in the New York Journal of Commerce, says:

"The California cannot comfortably accommodate more than 150 passengers; but the captain has received near 400 on board, and two or three more were added at this place. The reports they bring relative to California are astounding, but, probably, exaggerated. Among them it is said that gold is found in solid masses of several pounds weight; that the Mexicans are exasperated on account of having lost so valuable a country, and are meditating a plan of reconquering it; and that several thousand foreigners (Chinese, Sandwich Islanders, Mexicans, Peruvians, Chilians, and Europeans,) are in the country, and ready to combine in resisting the enforcement of American laws by our officers.

We Are at the Ready

"Now, as to Mexican intentions to reconquer the country, I receive it for just what it is worth—nothing at all; but there are some things which I know to be facts, and are worth thinking of. I know the Hispano-American race, from Cape St. Lucas to Cape Horn, being naturally greedy of gold, have been thrown into the intensest excitement—a perfect ferment—by the discoveries of that article in California; that this excitement has already started thousands of them toward the "placers" of the yellow god, armed to the teeth for war, and laden with implements for mining, and that three vessels are now at San Blas nearly ready to sail, full of men determined to share in the "spoils" of the gold region. I know also that we have on board this ship a military chief, who has the reputation of being one of the most cool, determined, and unwavering of the militant race, who is fully resolved that no foreigner shall work those "gold diggings" after his arrival; that we have near 400 men on board this ship, and twice that number are close astern of us, each of us whose arms are equal to a musket or rifle, a "revolver" and a Bowie knife; every one of whom would rally at the call of the hero of Contreras, and sacrifice his life rather than yield to such invaders.[1]

"Now, with such facts before us, what must be our prospects when in California? You can judge." (PPL, April 2, 1849.)

From the Upper Missouri

The cold in the Upper Missouri has been excessive. At Kanesville, the winter quarters of the Mormons who were not able to proceed with the others to the Great Salt Lake Valley, the winter has been very severe, and nearly four feet of snow has fallen. Up to February 18th there had been *thirty-one* days on which the mercury had fallen to or below zero. On the 11th of December it fell to *twenty* degrees below zero. Good sleighing lasted for three months. Late last month the snow was two feet deep on a level. Some hunters from Fort Vermillion, 150 miles further up, say that the Indians in that region are in a state of starvation on account of the deep snow preventing them from getting out to hunt and kill game. Many farmers of Missouri

---

1. The "hero of Contreras" (a battle in the Mexican War), was General Persifor F. Smith (1798–1858). He arrived at San Francisco on board the *California* on February 26, 1849, and replaced Col. Mason as the military governor of California.

have lost the greater part of their stock. Hogs and cattle are dying for want of food. It is apprehended that the weather at the Salt Lake, from the superior elevation of its site, has been hard upon the settlers in that vicinity, and compelled them to consume

their surplus stock of grain. The *Guardian* advises all Mormons who are going thither to carry a supply of provision to last them some time after they arrive there, and to take out milch cows. (PPL, April 3, 1849.)

FIRST VESSEL FOR SAN FRANCISCO, CALIFORNIA.—THE NEW AND substantial coppered and copper fastened Barque RALPH CROSS, HENRY F. DAVIS Master, having most of her cargo charged and going on board, will sail about the 5th of April. There are handsome accommodations for a few more passengers, and persons going to California are requested to call on board and examine this vessel before engaging elsewhere. As the number of passengers will be limited to forty, there will positively none be taken after that number is completed. DR. J. B. GROVES, of Virginia, will go out in this vessel as Surgeon.

(PPL, April 1, 1849.)

Interesting from San Francisco

[From the Boston Transcript, April 3]

The following letter was received by one of our most esteemed fellow citizens from his brother, formerly American Consul at the Sandwich Islands, but now of San Francisco, and attached to one of the very first commercial houses of that place.

SAN FRANCISCO, Jan. 20, 1849.

I avail myself of the opportunity to write you this Saturday evening a random letter about this wonderful land of gold, California. I suppose that ere this reaches you the excitement in the United States about California will run as high as it now does throughout the Pacific.

My partner arrived here on the 10th and I on the 21st November; and our sales already go above a half million of dollars. The great excitement which prevails in Chili and Peru relative to this gold country is fast depopulating those countries of their European population. Every vessel that arrives brings many passengers and reports of every body else winding up their affairs to join in the rush.

The quantity of goods that is pouring into the country is reducing the price materially; still every thing is, compared to the original cost, very high. I paid a bill to-day,

for our table; it ran thuswise: butter, $1; sausages, $1 per pound; pork, 25 cents; eggs, $2 a dozen; milk, $1 per bottle; a box of fine salt, $2; sperm candles, $2 a pound; raisins, $1 a pound; common lamp oil, $2 a gallon; bottle of mustard, (half a pound,) $2, &c. &c.

For the little unfurnished one-story building in which we stay—dining and sleeping in the same room—we pay $100 per month. Our cook receives $100 per month. My washwoman has condescended to do my washing for $6 per dozen. The carpenters employed on our warehouse threaten to leave unless we increase their wages above $8 per day. I paid a cartman this evening $72 for two days' work. You can judge by these quotations the quantity of money that a laboring man can obtain by a little work.

Riches from the Earth

In regard to the gold, every day only adds to the surprise created by previous reports of the quantity to be had. Yesterday morning an Indian showed me a specimen of ore intermixed with a stone, weighing five pounds. He sold it for five hundred dollars! To-day, some Oregon farmers, who came down to obtain gold, and remained a month at the mines, offered to sell me one hundred and fifty pounds of gold, which they had collected. Mr. Brannan, who has the establishments for storing and selling goods at the mines, told me to-day that seven men took from the earth, within one hundred yards of his upper store, thirty-three thousand dollars' worth of gold in four days; and the gold was weighed by a man in his employment.

At the dry diggings, one hundred dollars per day is paid to cooks. The general impression is that from ten to twenty millions will be taken from the mines the coming summer. It would not surprise me at all were it to be ten times that amount. The fact is, that it comes down from the mines by the peck—pure gold!

Land throughout California has gone up to enormous prices. The present week Mr. Cross purchased of Capt. Paty a building lot, say 100 feet square, on which there was an unfinished building, and paid $15,000 for it. Two years since, Capt. Paty gave a barrel of rum for it, or rather took it for a debt due for a barrel of rum. There is no lot of 150 feet square in San Francisco that can be bought for less than three to ten thousand dollars. Towns are being laid out in many ports or points on the Bay, and lots are selling at fifty to two hundred dollars.

The climate, to persons who have resided in the tropics, is not agreeable, because it occasionally rains, and is at times quite cold; but it is infinitely superior to New England. It has had an astonishing effect on me, and from a sallow looking skeleton (but not ill) I am getting fat, and am running out of my clothes fast. I suppose that in a week or more I shall have to throw them all aside. One thing remarkable in this climate is that every body, at all times, has a great appetite.

Let me know the balance, if any, pecuniarily, I owe you, and I will remit it in one solid piece of gold, let it be never so large. W. H. (NYH, April 5, 1849.)

FOR SAN FRANCISCO, CALIFORNIA.—The new and superior man-of-war built brig METEOR, J. Henry Smith, master, is bound for California, and will stop at intermediate ports for refreshments, &c.

The Meteor is built of live oak, is thoroughly coppered and copper fastened, and as regards speed, strength, and safety, is unequalled. The Meteor will carry no freight, her whole capacity being intended for the comfort and convenience of her passengers, and in this respect strict attention has been paid to the act of Congress of 3d March, 1849. Parties wishing to make a speedy and comfortable trip to California will find the Meteor a superior vessel, well calculated for any weather, and warranted to make a shorter passage than any vessel now in port. For further particulars apply on board, at 3d wharf below MARKET Street, to Capt. Smith, or to GRANT & STONE, 12 South Wharves. (PPL, April 1, 1849.)

CALIFORNIA, VIA VERA CRUZ, THE CITY OF MEXICO AND Mazatlan.—This company having made arrangements to sail on the 20th inst., in the fast sailing packet EUGENIA, which conveyed Capt. Hutton's company of 130 in fourteen days to Vera Cruz, we desire to inform those bound for California, that a few vacancies in the company remain. Further information given by Capt. BATTERSBY, from 1 to 4 P.M., at 100 Front street, up stairs.

(NYH, April 11, 1849.)

FIRST VESSEL FOR CALIFORNIA.—THE SPLENDID NEW Liverpool packet ship SUSAN G. OWENS now has all her freight on board, and will sail on the 14th instant for San Francisco. The news by the Crescent City shows that this is the only safe route, and this vessel offers the best accommodations of any yet up for that port. She is 730 tons burthen, but 5 months old, has a library of 500 volumes, bath rooms, patent ventilators, and every arrangement for the health, comfort, and safety of passengers. For passage only, apply to
BUFFUM & HANDY, 112 Broadway. (NYH, April 11, 1849.)

FOR CALIFORNIA, THROUGH TEXAS AND VALLEY OF THE GILA, in 90 days, with wagons, starting before or by the 1st of May. The fourth Mutual Protection Company, organized by D. Hough, Jr., is now filling up. Full particulars given at 40 Broad street, up stairs, from 9 A.M. to 1 P.M.
(NYH, April 11, 1849.)

An Overland Expedition to the Gila—The Gold Mines

NEW YORK, April 9th.

An expedition is being organized in this city, which, if successful, may open an unexpected source of wealth to our citizens, surpassing the golden promises of California, or the sparkling treasures of Golconda. An opinion has long been held at the "*Mineria*" of Mexico that somewhere in the mineral regions of the great basin of California was the land of precious stones, from whence Montezuma and his princely race drew those immensely valuable emeralds which Cortez sent to Spain. Many traditions, Spanish as well as Indian, point to the country north of the Gila and east of the Sierra Nevada, as the seat of inexhaustible mines of gold, quicksilver, and precious stones; but until the results of the late war left this vast country under our flag, there was no stable power to uphold those who had the courage and enterprise to lift the veil and learn the value of its mysteries.

Centralia, as they begin to term the territory this side of California proper and beyond Texas, has long been a fruitful theme with the hunters and Indians on its borders, who relate marvellous stories of ancient temples and palaces, of a fair-complexioned and half-civilized people, who till fields of Arcadian beauty, of plains glittering with diamonds, and precipices veined with pure gold. Allowing for all exaggerations, there is abundant evidence for the existence of the "gold mines of the Gila," and, for a long time, a bold and accomplished man, who, from a pure love of hardy adventure, had tasted deeply of the charms and perils of a ranger's life, has been waiting the hour to strike for them. This is Webber, the author of "Old Hicks, the Guide," and he has now published another work, full of romantic narrative yet embodying also the most authentic reasons, and inviting a plan for attaining the new land of gold.

The most facile and direct line of connection between sea and sea, on United States ground, is, as the maps prove, the new path to California via Corpus Christi, about to be opened by General Worth, from the Paso del Norte in Texas to the river Gila, and from those points to Corpus Christi, on one side, and to the bay of San Francisco on the other. This movement covers all the difficult and dangerous portion of the route, with military protection; and from the low price of mules at Corpus Christi, and the general abundance of grass, water, and game the principal part of the way, it is estimated that $150 will take the emigrant from New York to the gold regions of California.

Capt. Webber, in the work I just alluded to, the "Gold Mines of the Gila," proposes to take the tradition-renowned mines of Centralia, on the way to California; and if its storied temples of the Montezuman age really contain richer treasures than California, those of the party that choose may pause on the way, and found the new State of Centralia—and if not, no time is lost.

You can see by this that the *Centralia Exploring Expedition* has a higher object in view than merely to dig gold. It will march directly through the extensive and hitherto almost fabulous region of gold half-way this side of California, and mark out distinctly, in all its lights and shades, the shortest route to the Pacific that can be found on our own soil. That the probabilities are strongly in favor of interesting and valuable discoveries is generally admitted by all thinking and well read persons; and now that official reports and military action have put their sanction to Webber's long cherished plan of exploring the gold mines of the Gila, no American can fail to wish him a hearty and hopeful God-speed in the work. C. M.
(PPL, April 11, 1849.)

Authentic Letter from California

[Correspondence of the Cincinnati Commercial]
Gold Placer, (Upper California,)
November 6, 1848.

Dear Brother—I have not heard from home since I left. Many persons have arrived here from the States. Almost all persons in this country have received letters, but I, alas! have none. Many persons have sent letters by government express, and received answers, since my arrival here. I have sent letters by the same express, but no answer. I have sent by public and private conveyance—by land and sea, but no returning sheet has gladdened my eyes.—

Have you not heard that I left Oregon a year ago, and that I have been in this glorious country (California) since my last birth day? or do you think that I am in that detestable country, Oregon? And do you direct my letters there? I do not know why it is that I have not received letters from the States; one thing I do know, and that is that I am not already forgotten by my distant family and friends. No, I am remembered at home, but I think my relatives do not know of my yearnings that I continually have, for news from home. If to pay $1,000 for a letter fresh from home would give me one, I would pay it without a thought.

I am now at a ranch (farm) near the gold diggings. I was 75 miles from here in the mountains trading clothing to the Indians for gold, but was sent for to attend the owner of this ranch who has had a rifle ball discharged through his hand; he was attended three or four days before my arrival by a physician who lives at the ranch, but the patient saw fit to discharge his doctor—the case is a bad one—in great danger of mortification—he has had rapid pulse and irregular low delirium, &c., threatening a bad result; but I have made deep incisions, &c. &c., and the result is entirely satisfactory. My patient is quite smart this morning; he says that I shall not leave him till all danger is over. "Charge what you please, doctor," he says, "and it shall be paid; here is my ranch, with its horses, cattle, &c. &c., and I have a good large bag of gold."

Tending to the Sick

I am very sorry, dear brother, that I ever had doctor stuck to my name; it is more trouble than profit; I am vexed to death. I tell people that I can get more gold in the mountains by digging and trading than my conscience will permit me to charge my patients. I tell them that I have quit the practice of medicine, and am occupied with other pursuits more congenial to my feelings; but it will do no good when a man *begs* of me to go and see his friend, I cannot but go.

At first, here in the mountains, I charged $8 a visit if the patient was near, and very high mileage if he was at a distance; but you know how it is every where—people do not like to pay a doctor's bill, and I am a poor collector; three-fourths went away to other gold diggings without calling on me, although everybody said that my charges were not high in proportion to the amount of gold which every one had, and in proportion to other expenses of the mines—neither were they. I have bought flour in the mountains at $2 per pound, tea $4, sugar $4, candles $1 a piece; a pair of pantaloons, worth in the States $1.50, $24, but I cannot quit practicing. I tried another plan—I practiced without charging a cent; I showed every applicant that I went with extreme reluctance; I attended with negligence—told the friends of the patient that I was no longer a physician, that I shouldered no responsibility, &c. &c. But this would not do. I was pestered more than ever. I have now determined on another plan. I shall always have a quantity of medicine with me, shall attend patients when I have time, and charge abundantly. I will visit no patient for less than an ounce of gold—will ride no where to see the sick for less than ½ oz., unless it is a rare case, a case of poverty.

Maning, this is the richest gold country on the face of the globe; gold almost looks to me like a worthless toy, I have seen such vast quantities of it. A man here in the mountains who has about 10 or 20 lbs. of it is looked upon as a poverty-stricken man. I think the gold here is quite pure; it must be worth at the mint some $18 or $19 per ounce; the lowest value of washed gold is $16 an ounce, but gold here on account of the scarcity of coin, and the rifeness of speculation, is selling at from $5 to $10 per ounce. If I had $10,000 of coin I could convert it to $30,000 in two months.

The first month I was in the mines, myself and partner dug out three thousand dollars a piece, calling each ounce $16. The digging then became poor. A man had to work hard all day for only an ounce or two, so hundreds of people left and went to exploring, and I among the rest; I spent about two months exploring the mountains. We found gold everywhere, but did not stop to work—we wanted to find places where we could pick up, without much labor, two or three hundred dollars per day, but we were not fortunate enough to find such a place; but such places have been found, and are still to be found.

Everything to the Maximum

Several men got into a ravine where they got from $15,000 to $20,000 in two or three weeks. I have seen several pieces weighing 2, 3, and 8 pounds. The gold in the rivers is very fine like small fish scales. I have never worked on a river. I like to see the gold as I dig, and have worked in dry gullies or ravines. The first month I worked, my partner and myself hauled our dirt three miles to water, where we washed it in a trough made of boards. We could wash out five wagon loads in a day. The dirt, of course, varies much in richness. We washed one load in which we got 5½ pounds, and in other loads we would only get 5 or 6 ounces, but it was quite common to get a pound in a wagon load. If we had dug and hauled dirt the month we dug, we would have had much more gold, but we did not load our wagon half of the time, on account of our oxen straying, &c.; as it is, I have only cleared in the mines about 260 oz. of gold. My expenses have been great; horses from $100 to $200 each, and every thing else up to the maximum. I think in two or three days I shall load two or three horses with provisions and a few goods and go into the mountains, and spend the winter. It will be very unpleasant doubtless when the rain comes in the mountains, but gold is abundant, and there will be no lack of water to wash the dirt. There is a wholesale store about 10 miles from here where I can make an outfit. I think I know of a place where a few men more are, in which I can make five or ten thousand dollars more by spring.

Wages are of course high in this country.—You cannot get a man to haul your trunk across the street for less than five dollars. Laborers are paid from 10 to 20 dollars per day. You cannot get your dinner at a public house for less than from 2 to three dollars. You cannot get your handkerchief washed for less than one dollar—a dollar is the same here as 12½ cents in Ohio. This is fact, but every man is able to pay his bill, there is no credit—every one has a sack of gold.

Eternal Dissatisfaction

For the time I have been in the mines I have been more fortunate than the mass of the people, yet many have been more fortunate than I. One man found a piece of pure gold that has 20 pounds weight by the steelyards, and as many have done better than I have, I am not satisfied. I feel as poor with four or five thousand dollars in my trunk as I used to feel when I had but a hundred; why thus changed I know not. I am not at all miserly, if I ever was generous I still am the same, it gives me more real pleasure to confer a favor than to receive one. I know that a man can live in Ohio quite comfortably on ten thousand dollars, judiciously managed, all his lifetime; but that amount looks to me now-a-days quite paltry. I shall not leave the country with less than $100,000, and before 3 years I shall have that amount if my health is spared. I feel quite *sure* of it, and then, Maning, I shall spend my days in comfort and in dispensing blessings upon those poor mortals whom I have often wished to assist, but could not for want of means.

Gold has been discovered for 300 miles in extent of country, and it certainly extends still further, but beyond that has not been explored. Tell my relatives that they must not be angry with me when I urge you to come to this country. You are quite young, I know, but you have a good education and can thrive in this country; there is no country on the face of the earth where a fortune can be made so easy as in California. I believe that $10,000,000 of gold have been taken out of these hills since last May, and the population has not been large. Every mineral is here in abundance; there is enough of Quicksilver to supply the world. Silver is abundant, &c. &c. I sent father a specimen of silver and quicksilver ore; he doubtless received them long ago. The population is rapidly increasing, the news of the gold has extended like wildfire, every ship from the Sandwich Islands, Oregon, and the Southern coast is loaded with passengers; Oregon is *dead*. I saw 8 or 10 men from there the other day, they say that at least 1,000 men will be from there by the first opportunity.

Joseph Wadleigh is in San Francisco, came in by water, is well, and making from $20 to $50 per day at his trade (Tinner) so I am told, and am quite sure it is true; I have seen repeatedly a common tin pan (which is used to wash gold) sell in the hills for $16.[2] James Smith was a volunteer in the Oregon Indian war. He, the last I heard of him, got through the war without a wound, and was preparing to come here as soon as possible; he will be here by the next vessel I presume. Worstell is in these mines; the last time I saw him (two months ago) he had dug out $1,500.

Rough Living

I presume I will not have another opportunity of writing home again before spring, as I am going into the mountains to

---

2. "Joseph Wadleigh, maker of pans at Sutter's Fort 1848–49, went east with a fortune in '49." (Bancroft, v. 2, 765.)

live. I will not likely be able to get out when the rain and snow comes; there is never any snow in the valleys in the winter, but plenty of it in the mountains. I will at all events get out of the mountains by the first of May. I have lived somewhat rough here in the mountains; I have slept upon the ground in the open air every night for five months. I have frequently had to cook my bread and meat on a stick or in the ashes. We have lived as much as 4 or 5 days together on dried meat and coffee, without sugar or cream. I have got so that whenever night overtakes me, I feel as if I was in my house. I sleep as well on the hard ground with perhaps a root or stone under my ribs as if I was in the softest bed, and I am quite well also. I had quite a severe spell of bilious fever in August, but I had a good friend to nurse me, and I got well in two weeks.

I have a good deal more to say, but my ink is pretty nearly expended and I must stop. Come to California, Maning, immediately; come in the steamers by way of Panama, you can get here in thirty or forty days, and what is that. Come and I will be a good brother to you. You need not have a cent of money when you land, for I will divide generously with you, and take you as full partner in my business. Most of the merchants in San Francisco can tell you where I am; if you have not money sufficient to buy a horse and rigging to come to me, stop at a hotel and send me a letter, and I will come to you at the rate of 200 miles per day; come, Maning, for I want you as a partner in business. I have had two partners all along for the last two months, and one of them in whom I put the most confidence has cheated me out of

$700 or $800, and he has done it in such a way that to appeal to court would do no good. I trusted to his word without paper, or any other witness. I did not hear of it until last night, and to-day I have withdrawn from the concern, so that I am alone again. I will hereafter trust no man to any extent but a brother or a long tried friend.

I have written to each member of my family two or three times, and to father much oftener; give them all my best love, tell them I long for letters; give my best respects to all my old friends, tell Wm. T. Smith he had better quit hunting money in the States, and come to this part of Uncle Sam's vineyard, here he will find any kind that he fancies most. Write me, write to San Francisco, Upper California. I enclose a small sample of California gold. Get it made into two rings, give one to our stepmother and the other to Adeline. I remain your most affectionate brother, &c., &c.

BENJ. CORY[3] (CPD, April 11, 1849.)

Letters from Panama

[From the Georgetown Advocate]

Letters from Dr. Craigin, of Georgetown, who is on his way to California, describing the route over the Isthmus, and scenes in Panama.

PANAMA, FEBRUARY 19, 1849.

I am very comfortably quartered at No. 8, United States Hotel, where, after the experiences of the past week, every thing is a luxury. When I closed my letters we had not made land, and did not till Wednesday about 10 A. M., when we first saw high mountains before us on the horizon like dim clouds; as we approached we had a very picturesque view of mountain range behind mountain range, and ever

---

3. Benjamin Cory, a physician from Ohio, went to Oregon in 1847 and to California in November of that year. He settled in San Jose; went to the mines in 1848. Member of the first State Legislature, 1849–50; member of the San Jose City Council 1850–54; married Sarah Ann Braly in 1853; county physician in 1881; was still living in San Jose in 1882, with eight children. (Bancroft, v. 2, 768.)

and anon we came so near that with my glass I could even distinguish the forests that clothed them thickly to their tops. The rest of that day was a specimen of the Isthmus weather as I had pictured it to myself. We had some dozen showers, which was the first bad weather we had had since we left New York. We did not come to anchor till near 4 A. M. Thursday morning.

After breakfast, we were surrounded by large canoes with negroes in a state of perfect nudity, (except their straw hats,) to take us off to shore.

A committee of our passengers had landed the night before and engaged canoes to take our baggage to Gorgona from Chagres, and another committee landed at daylight on Thursday to engage canoes for passengers to the same place. We were landed at Chagres at the Captain's expense; eight of us engaged a canoe for $64 to take us to Gorgona. I wish I could describe to you our trip. We left the ship in a heavy sea, and some twelve of us got into a large canoe, made as all canoes here are, by hollowing out an enormous trunk of a tree some thirty feet long, five wide, and three deep. We sat down in the bottom of the boat, and came near being swamped several times by the large waves, some of which broke right upon our heads and drenched us through and through. We had about a mile to row to shore. Commanding the harbor was a very large fort built by Pizarro, all in ruins; it reminded me of Fort Washington, in its situation.

After rounding it we came in sight of the town of Chagres; a collection of thatched bamboo huts, containing some three hundred persons of the color of the yellow boys we see in town, many of them dressed neatly, with white pants, polished boots, white clean shirts, with plaited bosoms, and Panama hats; and the women with white dresses, shoulders bare, hats like the men, and *all* smoking cigars.

Up the Chagres River

The street is about ten feet wide, fit only for mules to hobble over. All the houses there and along the Chagres river to this city are built of bamboos fastened together and thatched with palm leaves, looking like hay stacks on poles; they are very airy, however, and in earthquakes (which were formerly frequent here) can receive no injury. The town lies nearly on a level with the water, but behind it are

Landing at Chagres.

grassy hills, which looked very inviting to our sea eyes. Here we bought biscuit, champagne, cider, and cocoanut cakes, took a large canoe, leaving our baggage in the hands of the committee to be forwarded to Gorgona, and started up the river about 2 P. M. The fore part of the canoe was occupied by one of us, the middle by our two naked Indian boatmen, and between the middle and the stern was a place some seven feet long, which was arched over with bent poles, and thickly thatched, to keep us seven squatted down in the bottom of the boat from the hot sun or rain; and the stern was occupied by the third Indian as steersman.

We left with the steamboat Orus, and I was never more disappointed in my life than in this river voyage—agreeably I mean. For some twenty miles the river is as wide as the Potomac from Georgetown across to the island; on each bank was a thick jungle of most beautiful tropical plants, the palm, cocoanut, mahogany, India-rubber, and other trees; lemons and oranges glittered like golden apples among the green foliage; palms with leaves twenty feet long and one or two wide; flowers of most gorgeous beauty and all sizes; birds with splendid plumage but harsh dissonant cries, from the eagle to the humming bird in size. Occasionally we would stop at a negro's hut to get coffee and buy a cocoanut to drink its milk. By 10 o'clock that night we had proceeded some sixteen miles to where the Orus lay, and spent the night at an Indian village of two hundred huts, where we had coffee, (always without milk,) and slept on a mat thrown upon the floor of the chamber, which was composed of bamboos; and with my India-rubber coat on, and my head on a block, I got some two hours sleep, when the moon rose and we started on our way again.

We passed the Orus, and by sunrise came to a level sandy beach, where we got out and washed, took our scanty breakfast, drank heartily of the pure river water,

fired off our rifles and pistols, and, as we were starting again, the Orus came up. Here she was obliged to stop, as the river became more rapid, shallow, and full of snags; and, as they were unprovided with sufficient canoes to convey all their passengers and baggage, the most of them had to stop there several days. We who had the canoes from Chagres got ahead of them, and most of them have not come through yet. That day was clear and warm, and the progress slow and laborious from the rapid current and snags. By nightfall, however, we had reached within seven miles of Gorgona, when some sixteen canoes were drawn up on shore, and we landed.

Fine Living

We built a fire, ate some preserved sausages one of us had, drank some brandy and water, smoked a cigar, and then some laid down on the sand with a blanket under and over them, but I, with A. and another, wrapped ourselves in our India rubber clothes, and lay in the wet canoe under the thatch, and soon fell soundly asleep. I woke about three o'clock, when the moon rose. Some were putting out their camp-fires, and we now got under way, much refreshed by one sound long sleep. At ten o'clock Saturday we reached Gorgona, some forty-seven miles from Chagres, without rain or accident; yet we had been so long cramped up in our little canoe that we were right glad to touch land and be at the end of our water journey.

As we passed along we saw several monkeys chattering on the trees and some small alligators, of which the Indians are very fond, and make fine soup of the young ones. We saw no snakes or insects except a few mosquitoes; and had we only four instead of ten in our canoe, our trip up the famous Chagres river would have been one of unadulterated pleasure. Gorgona is built up as Chagres is; and here we found our committee had not been able to forward our baggage, so we left A. to hire two canoes for $120 to go down again to Chagres and bring it on and whatever else they would hold. These two canoes at Chagres would have cost $200. We dined, looked through the town, hired two saddle-mules for $10 a piece, gave a guide $2, bought some biscuit and jerked beef, and five of us started for Panama, a distance of some twenty-five miles. We each rode and walked by turns, and in that way made the passage much pleasanter and cheaper, and with much less fatigue than if we had rode or walked all the way.

The Road to Panama

But such a road! It was a mere path, down steep hills, with gullies and mud-holes, and up stairs, and over trees, and sometimes plunging down two or three feet into gullies, but neither of our mules stumbled, and, by riding and walking, we got on very pleasantly. The first night we were overtaken by the darkness and were obliged to halt. The last of four matches I had in my pocket happened to catch fire, when we kindled some leaves, and then some small dry branches, and finally had a large fire blazing away in the dark woods. We stripped the mules, got together all the dry wood we could, gave our guide $2 to keep the fire going till daylight broke, and then some laid down on blankets and I wrapped myself in my India rubber leggings, coat, and cap, and, with the saddle for a pillow, tried to sleep. We had no water and could not hire the guide to get us any, though we would have given a good deal for a cool drink; so we took a mouthful or two of brandy, ate our dry biscuit, and by turns watching and sleeping we at last saw the day break, when we gladly got ready again to start. The ground was perfectly dry and the forest very thick, so we took no cold, but, on the contrary, felt in fine spirits and health. We had been disturbed by no evils, animals, snakes, or insects; and, as I lay and saw the stars gleaming through the trees, I thought of you.

In the morning (Sunday) we had not gone ten rods before we came to a fine clear running-brook, where we drank most heartily and washed, and felt again all right. About nine o'clock, as we were climbing a long hill, we saw two large panthers or cougars leaping from tree to tree, not more than five rods from our road, one on either side of us. Soon we leaped across, and just as we were about to fire at them with our rifles, they gave a leap and disappeared.

At ten o'clock we reached a rancho where some of the surveying party were encamped. We had some coffee with crackers and rice for breakfast, after which we pushed on, and reached Panama by one o'clock Sunday. On our way we saw several mules that had died of exhaustion or broken their necks. Most of those we met here said they were pitched off several times, but we were not once. The scenery, the fine tropical forests, the constant differences from every thing my eye has been accustomed to, made the ride very agreeable. On the route I picked several little flowers for you, but you will hardly recognize their beauty when they reach you. The thermometer has been almost constantly day and night from 75° to 83°, with a fine land breeze, so that we are as comfortable as in Georgetown in May or June.

A Sight for My Eyes

Tuesday.—This morning two ladies that came out in the Falcon arrived at our hotel; one brought a little boy, and both got through very well. It had been so long since I had seen an American lady, indeed any lady, that you cannot imagine how much good it did my worried eyes; I have learned another lesson of the worth of woman. Not one half of the passengers have come across yet, and we shall not get our baggage before Sunday or Monday at least. Looking back upon our trip, it has been very pleasant; we had no rain; every thing was interesting from its perpetual novelty; and when the *railroad* is completed, and steamers run *every week* between here and San Francisco, this route will be the best; as it is, there are some eight hundred people here waiting now for a passage. There is in port the "Belfast," that sails Saturday, and takes about one hundred persons; the Oregon steamer will take two hundred more; then there are two schooners which will be bought, and take off fifty or sixty each. But unless other vessels come here, all ready to take passengers, we may some of us be obliged to stay two months; we have long faces, but I shall employ myself in taking care of the sick who may send for me.

There is little sickness now, I believe. Two died last week, I understand. Over here I take care of myself in food, drink, and exposure. I rise at six in the morning, eat an orange, and stroll about town and on the beach for an hour; have coffee at seven, lounge and talk and think till breakfast, at nine, when we sit down to a table loaded with all kind of new and old dishes: fine fish, mutton, pork, steak of beef, chicken, omelets, yams, bananas, raw and cooked, and other vegetables whose names I have not learned. During the forenoon I read all old newspapers, advertisements and all, write, eat oranges, (of which you can get six very large and fresh ones for five cents,) call at various places, and then dine at four; soup first, then meats, yams, bananas, cucumbers, cimlios, rice, oranges, &c., and coffee and cigars, which are very good indeed, and cost a cent apiece. After dinner a siesta of an hour or so, coffee or tea without milk, and the evening devoted to thinking of home, filled with longings, hopes, fears, till in my weariness I sleep.

Wednesday.—Another clear, bright, warm day; but the atmosphere is filled with laziness and weariness. People are daily and hourly pouring in here, and flour is now $28 a barrel. Soon there will be one thousand persons to be fed and shipped off. There are no salt provisions here to victual a ship with; so, unless they come all fitted and ready to sail, it would take two months nearly to fit them out here. We are still without our baggage. When that comes, I shall feel easier and can look neater than I do now. Well, I shall have a fine opportunity to learn the great lesson of life, "to suffer and to wait."[4]

This is a city full of ruins. The Cathedral, right before my window, has its glass broken, and moss and ivy are growing from its towers; and most of the churches are absolute ruins. Water is carried about the streets in kegs, (one on each side of a mule,) and sold as milk is at home, dipped with a can or large mug. The streets are kept very clean by convicts, whom you see in gangs, chained together, and guarded by soldiers. They wear a uniform, bare feet, dirty white pants, blouses of some kind, and a kind of nightcap upon their woolly heads. They are all colored. One Yankee would frighten an army of them.

Our Own Celebration

Another clear, bright day, this Thursday morning. We were roused at 5 o'clock to celebrate Washington's birthday. The band of music belonging to the city guards was hired, and we all turned out in procession, with rifles, guns, pistols, &c. to march through the streets with the American flag, which we hoisted, fired salutes, cheered, and marched back again. We looked very formidable, compared with the diminutive natives, who flocked round to see us with some astonishment, lest, I suppose, we should storm the town. But every thing passed off pleasantly. Peachy came in yesterday, and we hardly recognized each

---

4. "Let us, then, be up and doing, / With a heart for any fate; / Still achieving, still pursuing, / Learn to labor and to wait." (Longfellow, *The Reaper and the Flowers*.)

Grand Cathedral, Panama.

other in our unshorn faces, our checked shirts, and rough *tout ensemble.*

Since yesterday nothing of any interest has occurred. We do not know what to do to kill time. Every body seems inclined to sleep; for it is too hot to go out in the sun, and we have no books or papers to read, and no news to discuss. We care for nothing but how we are to escape from this out of the way place. The town still continues healthy. I have a case of measles in the house, but he is doing well. If I only had something to read I would feel a little more content; but I hear you say, "Keep up a confiding, trusting heart, and all will yet be well." Many talk of returning, and, sometimes, when I see no chance of getting off from here for a month, may be, my heart is inclined to sing—

"Oh! carry me back to Old Virginny!"

A Heartfelt Response

Friday, 23d. Yesterday we had some hundred fresh arrivals, a good champagne dinner at our landlord's expense, and in the evening a concert by eight negroes, who gave us Washington's March, Yankee Doodle, and Hail Columbia, which drew forth repeated cheers from every heart.

The portrait of Washington was suspended upon the wall, with five wax candles burning before it, and opposite it the portraits of the Presidents of the United States. They performed sacred overtures to operas, native madres, &c., and with much taste and beauty of execution. One played as well as any violinist I ever heard except Ole Bull. He was possessed with the very demon of harmony, and with every limb and feature in rapid motion, now laying his ear upon his violin, now bending this way and that, rolling his eyes about, and bringing out the most brilliant movements with the greatest taste. To-day the British steamer is due from Callao, and before night we shall learn whether any ships may be expected here soon. I learned this morning that nine went back to Chagres from Gorgona, upon hearing the state of affairs here. Several say they shall sail to Vera Cruz and take the overland route if the steamer brings bad tidings. We learned also that our baggage lay at Chagres in the rain, when it was seen by acquaintances and housed. It will cost me $65 to get myself and baggage here from Chagres.

Saturday, 24th.—Hot, dry, and clear.

The steamer Oregon came in this morning, but nothing has transpired as to ships or any thing else. Passengers are still pouring in, and in a week's time there will be twelve hundred persons here. We have plenty to eat, and can live as we are at the hotel at $1.25 per day, or, by taking a room out, at seventy cents per day. We learned yesterday that A—— had reached Gorgona with our baggage, and will be here in a day or two. I wish I had secured a passage from here before I left; this great detention is heart sickening. I have seen a few sick persons, but none in dangerous positions. I would urge upon persons not to come this way unless they have secured a ticket on this side in a steamer. Some are buying tickets of others in the steamer, which cost $100, for $300, and cabin tickets, which cost $200, for $500.

Our Fortunes Decline

Tuesday night.—Once more I sit down to write. I have secured a passage on board the Equator, a whaler from New Bedford, which put in here on Sunday. Yesterday morning the captain came on shore, and was immediately surrounded and his vessel filled with passengers, one hundred and seventy in number, at $200 each. We are to live upon salt pork, hard crackers, and find our bedding, &c.; but still I am thankful to go away from here in any way. We shall not sail for twelve or fourteen days yet. People are constantly pouring in here from Chagres, so that a vacuum is filled again directly. Our baggage is yet at Gorgona, and I have been wearing one pair of stockings and linen until I am ashamed. Nobody wears any thing but pants and linen through the day, and in the evening put on neckcloth and their coat. There is considerable sickness among us now. Many eat fruits and drink rum and such liquids, and expose themselves to the sun, and worry and fret about having to stay here, and such are almost sure to get sick; some too are destitute of money, and have to work to get along. I saw a poor fellow last Sunday by the name of J. T. Wiley, or Riley, from Pennsylvania; he had been sick nine or ten days, and nothing had been done for him, and when I saw him he was dying. He lay in his dirty clothes in a hammock, and two others were sick in the same room, and one of them lying upon two trunks, with no mother or sister near to comfort them. The first one I mentioned died half an hour after I saw him, and was buried this evening. I have just heard of another death at Gorgona, and am writing this in the sick-room of an old friend of A——'s from Baltimore, a worthy gentleman by the name of Morrison, who, by imprudence in eating, has yesterday and to-day had considerable fever. He has been lying all this time in a cot bed, in his clothes, with a cloak over him and saddlebags for a pillow, till to-night, when I procured a sheet, so that he might undress and have it spread over him, a good pillow for his head, and a blanket. He is a good deal frightened, poor fellow, and we console ourselves with talking about our wives to each other, and the *dear sweet* homes we owe to them. I thank God for keeping me in such excellent health.

Facing the Pacific

I sat to-night on the top of the wall or rampart that surrounds Panama, with the waves of the Pacific dashing against the base of the wall at my feet, and looked to the south and saw nought but the water and beautiful islands—hills covered with forests dotting the bay; to the west the bright moon and evening star, perhaps even now watched by you from *our home.* These shone over the top of a high mountain, about a mile from here, north of the city, and further on are the hills we have crossed and the ocean we have sailed over; and further still lies the dear home, the sacred treasury of all our happiness——. Ah, poor wanderer, long does thy eye and long do thy thoughts dwell on the home thou has left and the new strange home thou goest toward! Will he be repaid for all this sacrifice? Will God bless his efforts to find means to give a happy home to those he loves, and to enjoy their society without interruption after a little?

Wednesday.—I have been with Morrison all day; I am nurse as well as doctor. To-morrow I hope to be able to give him quinine, and he will no doubt then begin to mend. Several are quite sick, but no more deaths. I learnt to-day that a person from Indiana coming up the Chagres river, being obliged to get out of the boat which had run upon a sand bar, was seized by a large alligator and instantly drawn under water and killed. Every day I have more reason to bless the good God for his kindness to me.

None of our baggage has come in yet. How glad I shall be to see you once again in your miniature, and read your writing in the little Bible. Here we see no ladies: the Spanish ladies are invisible, and all the rest are more or less colored, and far from pretty; they all wear hats of Panama grass, like the men. In every room you see one or two hammocks swung, which they use as sofas to lounge and sew in. The houses have no windows or fireplaces, and are as much open as possible; for windows they have a wooden shutter, which, when closed, makes the room perfectly dark; carpets are unknown, and they have none of the comforts of home that we have; board walls whitewashed and no ceiling. The houses look like white stone jails. At our hotel we fare well: the bar room is in the third story, and all the floors are paved with square bricks. All the water used by this population of between five and six hundred natives is brought from two large wells, where they have not even a pump to draw it up; they use a large gourd, fastened by a chord, with which they draw it up by hand.

Some Sail, Some Die

Another vessel was brought here to-day, which is already filled, and will take off about forty more; but another vessel

has arrived at Chagres with more than one hundred persons. Many who have to be here six or eight weeks from this time, and remain here more than a day or so, will no doubt be ill, and many die. How is it possible, in the midst of this tropical weather—amid cocoa trees, the golden orange, the long-leaved odorous pine-apple—these hot days and nights, to conceive of your February snow storms, anthracite fires in snug parlors, and soft carpets for the foot—no green leaves, no golden fruits! The bare branches of the apricot tree that two years ago this month I used to watch as I lay so sick, show no green buds, while here it is spring, summer, and autumn all at once—flowers, green fruit and ripe, all at the same time. About this hour you are all in the parlor, and are playing some new duet; or little —— sits with her little mouth screwed up with so much determination, and her tiny hands performing some wonder upon the piano. * * * * All this absence has grown out of that buggy ride by the President's, (do you remember it?) when we first spoke of California.

Sunday night.—Since my last, Morrison has got well. Several are still sick, but are recovering by proper treatment. The fevers and other diseases here are like our own in Washington and around Georgetown. Two parcels of my baggage have come in, and this morning all the rest, except my large trunk, which I need most of all. I must send for it to-morrow at Gorgona. We expect to sail in about a week or two. No other vessels have come into port, and many persons are about to return home.   C. H. C. (WNI, April 18, 1849.)

NEWS FOR THE MILLION

Sophistry is like a window curtain; it pleases as an ornament, but its true use is to keep out the light.

In 1835, only fourteen years ago, there were not 5,000 white inhabitants between Lake Michigan and the Pacific Ocean. Now there are nearly a million!

(CPD, April 12, 1849.)

Hi, ho, for California

[From the St. Louis Republican]

I say, stranger, whither bound? To California. Not with your family! Yes. Do you expect to get there with that old mare and colt, those poor weak oxen, and that old rickety wagon? Why, I reckon so. Where did you come from? Hiwasse District, Tennessee; I was fetched up in Bunkum, North Carolina, but when I grew up I moved to Hiwasse and married, but never could get ahead there, and when I heard tell of the California country, and gold to be picked up there, I sold out my improvements and took this wagon and team in payment, packed up our duds and are on our way there.—You know that fortune's blind; there's no telling the luck of a lousy calf, so I thought it might be my good fortune to get some of the gold as well as the others. But, sir, your team cannot get there. You will neither find grass, grain, or food for them or yourselves on the plains. It is a long, dreary road; no houses, no wood; and it will be two months yet before there will be grass enough to fill those oxen and beasts on the whole route; and further, when the grass is up near the settlements, it is a long time afterwards before any of account will be up beyond, and the further you go, the worse.

Well, I'll stop awhile—turn in and work till it grows. But where will you work? There is nobody to hire, or work to do—what then? You are too far advanced to return, you cannot go ahead, and you are in a dreary desert country, without wood, water, or anything to eat, with a wife and children looking up to you for relief and support; your team exhausted and become food for wolves, and before long yourself and family will follow your team. Thus ends the mad career of an Hiwasse pioneer and family.

In a Bad Fix

Next comes a company of young men from some eastern city, with fine appearance, strength, and talent, yet unacquainted with the life of an old campaigner, unused to lie on the ground cooking, and a thousand other little incidents at tending a long, monotonous, dreary march. In a few nights, pain seizes hold of you in every bone, muscle, and part, and you feel scarcely able to move; yet the time has come to be up and moving ahead, *another day's journey*—hunt up your oxen, yoke them, pack in your fixins, and gee-woo-haw, Buck, Bright, get along you Brindle—what are you about, old Bawley? Zip, you dogs, hie up—lend a hand here, John, Jake, Josh, for these darned horned horses can't budge an inch. While others are rolling on in the distance, you are stalled in the mud hole—broke an axle, tongue—something out of fix—away you tug, sweat, fret, and tear up the ground, but all to no effect; your steers won't pull—one has a sore neck, another lame; one gives out and none to put in his place, and you are in a bad fix.

Methinks I see, about the 20th of April, 1849, a thousand wagons spreading out from St. Joseph on the road towards Fort Laramie, with some three or four thousand emigrants—men, women, and children—all wending their way to the gold regions of the Sacramento, straining every nerve and urging on their teams to their greatest speed in order to be the first to arrive; the grass thinly scattered here and there, and in spots and places few and far between; the ground yet cold, the waters high, and, still further ahead, the snows of the past winter unthawed.

In yonder creek, some dozen wagons, horses, mules, and oxen, all tangled up in the harness; wagons broken, lame and crippled animals—all in a perfect jam—old men frisking about, children squalling, men raving, roaring, cursing, and sweating about their bad luck. A little ahead appears a portentous black cloud, the lightning flashing, thunders roaring, peal after peal; the rain begins to descend, the wind blows, thicker and faster falls the watery element; the whole canopy of Heaven becomes blackened and darker grows; the creeks swell, the water rolls and pours down; rivers run where, a few hours before, all was seemingly dry. Your goods are wet, your wagon covers shivered, tattered, and torn to shreds; your clothes all wet, and without tent, house, or shelter, stand up and sleep, and let it rain. Your cattle, horses, and mules, discontented, snort and snuff the breeze, fly the piquet, and away they go—horses and mules without a rider, oxen without a wagon, pell mell, over hill and dale, far away.

Gone to the Devil

The wolf, with his hideous growl, breaks in upon your ears, and he sings you a nightingale song, hoping to share the tit bits you will leave. The flavor arising from the fried bacon sharpens his appetite, until his notes become shrill and near. When darkness hovers o'er, his snuffing and growling becomes nearer. The guns being wet, priming out, and no sentinel shot to be heard, then comes reflection. O! what a fool was I to leave home and suffer here—nothing to shelter me from the north-western blast of an April's shivering rain, sleet, and hail, and all the imps of the evil one came to sing psalm tunes over my distress and misery. I wish I had stayed at home, as dad and mama said—ploughed the old fields, learned a good trade, and been contented when I was well off, instead of coming on this "wild goose chase."

However, a fellow may as well be "hung for an old sheep as a lamb;" "my fist is in," and this is only a beginning, and it is said that "a bad beginning makes a good ending."—So here goes, through thick or thin, thunder, lightning, or rain. But stop; where in the name of sense have those infernal brutes run to in this storm? They've got started back, and all creation can't get that thunder storm out of them until they reach the settlements; and just here, among these wild varmints—snakes, lizards,

wolves, and the Lord only knows what—those women, children, and wagons must stay until they are brought back. Gewhillikins, how they run! Old Zurababel couldn't catch them.

Hell's Afloat

How are you, stranger! Whose company is this?

Captain Pushafter's.

I see you are in a bad fix there—your wagons in that gully half buried in water! Where's your stock?

All run off last night in that storm like the devil was after them. I never see horned horses run so before in my born days, and the mules took after them—and it was raining so awful hard we could not see. But such a stampede and clattering of hoofs of four-legged animals! It fairly shook the yearth, it did!

Don't you know what started them?

No! I thought it was the thunder and lightnin', or the cursed wolves, that kept up such an infernal barking—it scared the children into fits.

Fudge! man. It's no wolves; but some roving bands of Lipans and Camanche Indians, who are all over the plain—for our boys saw them in the distance just before the storm, and they have run off our best horses and mules; but our cattle were so tied they couldn't run. We lost at least fifty horses and mules last night, and I'm out in search for them, while others have gone in different directions on the same errand. Did you see any come this way after night?

See hell! I couldn't see my shadow, it was so dark. How far ahead is your company?

About ten miles, on a small branch.

How many do you number?

Fifty.

Who commands?

Captain Knowsall. Good bye! I'm O P H.

"Hell's afloat, and the river's risin'."

Nancy! O! Nancy! tell your dad to come here. This child is mighty powerful sick, and I'm afeard it will die.

What's the matter, old woman?

Matter enough. This baby's goin' to die, I railly believe.

O, jest hush up! give it a drop o' whisky, and it'll get well.

And there's Molly, what picked up a lizard, thinking it was a bird—and it bit her hand so orful hard that it has swelled clean to the shoulder. And Jim says there's snakes all round here, for he seen them crawlin' under the blanket jest a bit ago. I'll tell you, old man, we'll all die here, or be eat up by the varmints. I wish we had stayed back, and let this gold go to old scratch. Hadn't we better turn back before we all die?

Well, I believe I can do well enough anywhere in "Elenoys" or "Misery;" but how's a feller to get back? Here we're three hundred miles from St. Joseph, all the oxen gone, wagon broke down, and no one to lend us a team—and too poor to buy, if we could.

Old Woman—I believe I can walk, if you'll only try to get back. We can pack all that's worth takin' on the old lame steer, and let the wolves have the rest, for to go ahead—we can't.

Old man—Agreed! by hokey, 'nough said.—Hurra for the settlements! You don't catch this child agin with your humbug. (CPD, April 12, 1849.)

TO CALIFORNIA GOLD DIGGERS, EXPLORING PARTIES, AND others.—The subscriber has constantly on hand and for sale, from the Union India-rubber Company, who have the exclusive right to use Goodyear's Patent Metallic Rubber, the following articles:

  Tents and Tent Carpets, Knapsacks, Camp Blankets
  Haversacks, Canteens, Leggins, Clothing Bags
  Water Bottles, Tarpaulins, Caps, and Capes
  Sou'westers, Texas Wallets, Gun Cases
  Coats, Cloaks, and Capes, Mexican Pouches
  Overalls and Pantaloons, Gold Pouches
  Air Beds and Pillows, Life Preservers
  Drinking Cups, Buckets, and Basins, Travelling Bags
  Portable Boats, Provision Bags, Saddle Bags
  Gold Washers, Baby Jumpers, Breast Pumps

And a variety of other articles, at the sign of the Star, between 4th and 6th streets, Pennsylvania avenue, Washington. S. EDDY. (WNI, April 13, 1849.)

Still at Panama

[FROM THE GEORGETOWN ADVOCATE]

We have been favored with the following extract, for publication, from another letter from our fellow-townsman, Dr. Craigin, to his friends in this place:

PANAMA, MARCH 11, 1849.

Days have dragged their heavy length along since I sent off my last letters by a gentleman returning home via New Orleans. My health is good, though a great many are sick here. Morrison had been sick again, but I have nursed and attended him, and he has recovered rapidly; others whom I have been attending are now all well. I expect to get passage in the "Equator," with a dreary prospect of from five to seven weeks' voyage to San Francisco; still this is better than being cooped in a vessel for six months. My baggage has come all safely through at last. My large trunk was brought in by two large negroes upon poles, for which I paid $14; it has cost me $65 to cross from Chagres here, with 450 lbs. of baggage, and my board will amount, with necessary expenses, to $35 more.

The Cathedral clock is just striking; mass has been said in the churches, and all the shops and billiard-rooms are open, and the cockpit is crowded with all classes. Nothing reminds you of the Sabbath, save memory which recurs to the holy Sabbath of home.

A Strange Country

I wish I could sketch for you upon paper the thousand curious novel views of ruins, scenery, &c., that you might form some idea of this strange country. I attended two funerals of natives a few days ago. One was in a church where the body lay in a coffin upon a kind of hand-barrow; masses were said for her, and, after a variety of ceremonies, they proceeded on to the cemetery; wax candles, lighted, were carried before and by the side of the body, which was preceded by priests singing masses or chants, and accompanied by a band of music; when they reached the gate the coffin was laid upon the ground, and after a few more chants the ceremony was over. The priests put on their enormous hats, lighted their cigars by the wax candles, and proceeded homeward. They do not bury ladies here in coffins, but at the grave take them out of the common open coffin, and bury them in their winding sheets. She was rich, and was buried thus with some ceremony. Passing a hovel the other day I saw a band of violins, guitars, and tambourines come out escorting a little bier upon which was carried the body of a small child; no priests accompanied it, but they moved off to a lively dancing tune. I looked in at the door and saw the table where the little body had lain, all strewed with fragrant flowers.

There have been no further deaths here among the Americans, though some have been very ill. In five weeks the rainy season will commence again, and yellow fever will make it dangerous for foreigners to delay here more than a day or so. I bless God for preserving me thus far; how desolate must be the sick bed in this land of strangers! I have done what I could to make all whom I have visited as comfortable as possible. How fondly many of them spoke of their absent wives, and longed once more for their homes.

Monday, 12th.—Hot bright day, but with a delightful land breeze through our room tempering the heat. Mr. Buckey, the gentleman who was shot in the leg in a canoe on the Chagres river . . . has been in my room, and is doing very well; the wound is almost entirely closed, and he goes on board the steamer to-day. Every body is busy now writing home; some seven hundred are going this week, but more than seven hundred are coming in from new arrivals in Chagres. I do not know how they are to get away. No more vessels have come in, and none are known to be coming here with certainty. The fare cannot be less than two hundred dollars, and many have not one hundred dollars. Soon the hot, rainy, sick season will commence, and their position will be full of danger. A good many have lost all their money by gambling, and such deserve to stay and suffer.

Tuesday.—I accompanied Mr. Buckey yesterday afternoon in a small sail canoe to the "Oregon." He got on board without any accident, and I returned alone. How I wished I had been fortunate enough to hold a ticket for a passage in her; it would be so much more pleasant running up along the coast, independent of fickle or contrary winds, with mountains and volcanoes ever in sight, than our anticipated voyage of thirty or fifty days in our whaler. The "steamer" left this morning at daybreak, and took off about two hundred and sixty persons. I hope to be off by Thursday or Friday at least. It is time for the return of the "California," but many doubt whether she will be able to do so from the desertion of her men and want of coal.

Wednesday.—The brig "Felix" sails to-morrow with fifty passengers, and the "Constellation," with about forty, at the same time. The "Equator" and "Calloony" will also leave this week; but the Equator will get far ahead of them all, as she is the best vessel and the fastest sailer here; well manned and officered and provisioned. Some of these vessels are going up along the coast, and will not reach San Francisco for three or four months; we shall get there, the captain says, within forty-five days. Another death occurred last night among the Americans from congestion of the head. I did not see him, but have found all my own cases to yield magically to large doses of quinine. A—— and I are exceedingly temperate and in fine health; we avoid all excesses, and *keep cool.* I feel in very good spirits to-day at the idea of leaving here soon, and going up more comfortably than I had anticipated. We are studying Spanish, and every day make some progress, and when at sea shall have abundance of leisure to devote to it.

"Friday, 16th.—Not yet gone. The Equator came up from the island, where she had been to get water, fresh provisions, fruits, &c. last evening, and we shall sail Monday at 6 P.M. Yesterday afternoon three of us ascended a high mountain that overlooks the city. We started about one hour before sunset, by a path much more practicable for mules than many parts of the Gorgona road, winding through thick jungles higher than our heads, and through patches of pine-apples, which looked a great deal like our meadow flag— through groves of young cocoa trees, bread fruit, and other strange tropical trees. We reached the summit just in time to see the sun set behind the clouds far in the west. Away to the west, north, and east rose thousands of sharp mountain peaks, of no great height, but beautiful in their sharp outline, the purple light that bathed them, and the little rivulets winding through them. Below us at our feet lay Panama, jutting out into the bay like a horse-shoe, with the tide, which was high, dashing against its walls and several vessels floating on its bosom. The "Constellation" was just getting under weigh, and, as its white sails filled and it slowly moved along, it bore some of our friends away on their long journey. They will be most miserably crowded and probably three months on the way. The "Felix" was stopped from sailing, as more were found on board than could by any possibility go. Some seventy-two persons crowded together on board a very doubtful vessel, of not more than seventy tons, so that they could hardly all stand upon her decks; so they have finally sent a goodly number ashore, agreed to give them one dollar per day to pay their board here, and to send them up to San Francisco by the first opportunity, at the owners' expense. I shall have an opportunity to send this letter to New York by a gentleman who returns in disgust, and who sold out at auction yesterday what he brought on for California, and at a good profit. I know of several who will return. We hear of more arrivals at Chagres, and I suppose, when all the vessels in port sail, there will be at least a thousand persons here who have secured no passage, and may have to wait a month or three months more.

Saturday night.—I have just returned from visiting a sick man who sent for me, and now am in the sitting room of the hotel enjoying the cool sea breeze which steals through. In this country the bars, &c. are in the third story. Doors, windows, and all are open. Some sit talking on the balconies, while others seem musing and dreaming of absent friends in the window-places. God give me an escape from this unhealthy place! And while yet another wife in New York offers up a prayer for her loved one, the dear husband, the father, lies dying. She, poor wife, knows nothing of it; rude coarse hands only soothe his dying pains; he moans for the loved ones, but his hand is cold, is not warmed by her warm clasp. You cannot imagine how sorrowful this poor man's fall has made my heart to-day. He will not live through the night. He is about my age, and has a wife and child, as I have, but I can do nothing, and this great agony must reach their hearts. What a blow it must be! C. H. C. (WNI, April 13, 1849.)

CORRESPONDENCE OF THE NEW YORK
JOURNAL OF COMMERCE
SAN FRANCISCO, NOVEMBER 13, 1848.

I am on duty for the present with the first dragoons, stationed at this place. They have *nearly all* deserted; consequently I have nothing to do in the way of earning my salary, and I am consequently up to my eyes in medical practice and speculations. This is the El Dorado of Medicos. I received $150 for one visit last night. To be sure, I had to cross the bay, and came near swamping in the boat; but what of that? "Nothing venture nothing have," my good old mother used to say. On landing this morning, on my way up to the hotel, I stopped at a house where a child was sick, and received an ounce for my visit. But there is one drawback to all this—one's expenses are enormous. I am living rather economically, and expend near ten dollars per day. So tell your medical friends to fill their pockets full of rocks before they come out here, for they will get rid of a small fortune before they can get a place to hang out their shingle. By the way, advise them also to join the temperance and anti-gambling, and all the other anti-societies. If they do not, and are not men of fixed and decided principles, they will go to destruction about as rapidly as you can conceive of the process taking place.

So much for *the* profession. Mechanics are in great demand. Clergymen are at a discount. Lawyers are not thought of, I believe. The little nest of them that were busy entangling the affairs of the town six months since have all left and gone into the more profitable business of buying the Indians' gold for such little gaudy things as they fancy. Dentists would do well. There are two or three in the country, but they are up at the mines digging. Merchants are the greatest men here, and will surprise some of our Eastern capitalists when they come in competition with them. The most profitable speculation I can conceive of is to make shipments to this port of *every thing* and *any thing*. For the next two years the demand will exceed the supply. People are already pouring in here from all the Pacific countries, and fifty thousand persons can be expected by next July from the United States and Europe. Provisions, clothing, furniture, wagons, gigs, carriages, harness, saddles, jewelry, watches, &c. will all sell at one, two, and three hundred per cent. advance now, and I believe will next August. Every thing must be of the best quality. People here spend their money freely, and there is no two-penny shaving going on. If you are cheated, it is on a grand scale. Drugs are in great demand and exorbitantly high, and as yet there is but one druggist here, and he has a very small stock. This will be a grand place to establish a large house. When the steamers commence running, every place on the American coast will look to San Francisco for their medicines.

The Rev. Mr. Leavenworth, who came out here as chaplain and acting surgeon on board the Brutus, has been elected alcalde, made a fortune, and gives universal satisfaction to the people of this happy little town.[5] (WNI, April 13, 1849.)

---

5. Thaddeus M. Leavenworth, native of Connecticut, physician and episcopal clergyman, came to California in 1847 as chaplain of the New York Volunteers. He was Alcalde of San Francisco, 1847–49; Leavenworth Street in that city was named for him.

The Overland Routes

In the "Alta Californian" (published in San Francisco) of February 1st, an interesting account is given of the city of San Francisco.

In June, 1847, it contained four hundred and fifty-nine souls. In the previous year thirty houses were built, and laborers received from two to three dollars per day. In July and August following, thirty-eight houses were erected. In March, 1848, the population had increased to eight hundred and twelve, (whites,) being an increase of one hundred per cent. in eight months.

In April, 1848, the people were gold struck, and the whole population rushed to the mines. Sickness having broken out in the mines they were nearly deserted in August and September, and the people crowded to San Francisco, and business began to revive. In November, when the fruits of the miner's labor began to be reaped, San Francisco began to lengthen her strides to prosperity and greatness.

Other advantages are claimed for the town. It is said to possess the safest, largest, and most accessible harbor on the whole coast. The situation of the town is picturesque and only four miles from the sea. The climate is healthy. The population has increased since March last to about two thousand souls. Real estate has risen in value from one hundred to one thousand per cent. The export of gold dust since May last is supposed to exceed two millions. The importation of coin for the purchase of gold dust in 1848 amounted probably to one million of dollars. The imports of merchandise for the same period were equal in value to one million of dollars. The duties collected in 1848 amounted to $196,074.66. The number of buildings erected in the year 1848 were more than fifty. Passengers arriving by sea, one thousand.—

Delta. (WNI, April 18, 1849.)

Our Isthmus Correspondence

PANAMA NEW GRANADA, March 28, 1849.

I have now been on the Isthmus more than a month, and the chance of a passage up the coast to San Francisco seems no better than when I first arrived. There is not one vessel here now to receive passengers. The commerce of this place is nothing, and a passing vessel seldom touches here. One whale ship, one British bark, and a few small schooners are the only sailing vessels that have taken emigrants hence, on their way to California. The steamer California and the Oregon have each taken one load of passengers, and the former has been expected back here for a fortnight, but as yet we have no tidings of her, and fear that some accident has befallen her, and kept her back. There must be now, at least, fifteen hundred persons on the Isthmus, waiting a passage, and more are coming every day. Most of us are sorry enough that we came this way, as our expenses are much more than we expected, and our chances of proceeding much less. It is reported here, this morning, that more than a hundred persons, in discouragement, are about setting out to return to the States, most of whom may be expected in the Northerner and Crescent City, now at Chagres.

This is the dullest place I was ever in. No business, no enterprise, no improvement is apparent. The city is gone to decay, and the inhabitants are too lazy and unintelligent to do anything. Though the climate is excellent, and vegetation luxuriant, no rich cultivated fields meet the eye. The people are too slack even to have a garden. All the necessaries of life are quite expensive, though a trifling amount of labor is all that is necsssary to produce them. This land waits for Yankee enterprise to take and improve it, and then it will be equal to any in the world. There is not even a grist mill in the city—not a steam engine—no machinery of any kind, driven by water or steam power. In fact, Panama is a hundred years behind the age; and will be, till the railroad is built, and the trains of cars come thundering along to wake up the sleepy inhabitants.

We advise no person to take this route at present. For some time it will be attended with much expense, delay, and fatigue. The survey for the railroad proceeds slowly. Nothing can be done this dry season except to explore the route. Next season, we hope they will begin in earnest to construct the road. (NYH, April 14, 1849.)

The Western Overland Route

[Correspondence of the St. Louis Republican]
ST. JOSEPH, MO., April 2, 1849.

The immense emigration to California by this route has given an impetus to business in the towns of Independence, Westport, Weston, and St. Joseph, unprecedented by that of any past season. The taverns and boarding houses are crowded to their utmost capacity, and it is with the greatest difficulty that the new comer is enabled to obtain quarters—many, for the want of other lodgings, being obliged to accommodate themselves in uncovered wagons and unoccupied out-houses. As near as can be ascertained, 2,500 persons are already at these points—by far the greater number being at Independence and St. Joseph—while every boat that arrives from below adds largely to this number. In addition to those who have arrived from via St. Louis, several companies from Northern Illinois, Ohio, and Missouri, and from Michigan and Iowa, have made their journey to these points overland.

Several companies, among whom is one of 271 gentlemen from Pittsburgh, come completely outfitted for the expedition, while others contemplate making their outfits at their places of rendezvous.

The principal and most important item of consideration is that of stock. At St.

Joseph, common to good American mules are selling at from $55 to $70, and choice from $75 to $100 per head, according to size and age. The supply, as also the demand, is limited, most of the emigrants providing themselves with stock before reaching this point. Oxen are selling at $45 to $60 per yoke, according to condition and quality, very few being offered for sale. The facilities for manufacturing wagons are very limited, the market being bare of any that are completed or ready for sale.

In this section of our State are a number of persons whose lives have been spent in mountain service and upon the plains. From them I shall inform myself of such matters as will prove of service to the emigrant in making his outfit, and in my subsequent communications give the benefit of their experience. They remark, without any conflicting opinion, that two and three year old American mules are unable to stand the service of an expedition to California, and most especially when put into harness. A number of emigrants are supplying themselves with such animals, under an impression that they will be more serviceable. This is a mistake; they have not the bone, nor are they sufficiently developed in their limbs to enable them to stand the trip. Mules from four to eight years old are greatly preferable.

Another remark is that young men, arriving at these points of rendezvous, instead of immediately forming a camp and enuring themselves to the hardships of a duty with which they are unacquainted, go into boarding houses, determining to lead an easy life until the time for their departure arrives. By performing camp duty in a vicinity where the necessary accoutrements for such duty can readily be obtained, they ascertain more correctly what they may desire, and are enabled to obtain it before being beyond the bounds of civilization or the facility for procuring such necessaries as may be deemed important; and further, they gradually become accustomed to the hardships of a camp life, while in the vicinity of a comfortable respite from the duty, should it be found too irksome.

Some weeks will yet elapse before any company will be enabled to leave the settlements. At present, and for several weeks to come, the grass will be too young and insufficient to justify them in starting. To attempt to carry food sufficient for their stock to last them up to a time when there will be range and pasture enough, would not only be an unnecessary expense, but in the end not in the least facilitate or expedite them in their journey. It is conceded, therefore, that the first of May is as soon as any company should leave.

A young man from Lancaster, Pa., named Cyrus Jacobs, attached to a company from Pittsburgh, fell overboard from the steamer Kansas, on her trip up, and was drowned. Last evening, at the Presbyterian church, an eloquent and appropriate funeral sermon was delivered by the pastor of the church.

A young man by the name of John B. Deitz, formerly of Washington City, suddenly died at Weston, a few days since, under circumstances painful in the extreme. A wager was laid with a friend, that he could drink the most liquor, to test which he filled a pint glass with brandy and drank it down; scarcely had the last mouthful been swallowed before he fell senseless, and in a few minutes he was a corpse. The deceased is of highly respectable connexion, to whom his untimely end will cause much sorrowing. (NYH, April 19, 1849.)

Movements for California

NEW YORK

The bark Galindo, Captain Macy, sailed on the 7th instant, for San Francisco, with 76 passengers.

MASSACHUSETTS

The ship Frances Ann, Capt. Proctor, cleared at Boston, on the 17th inst., for San Francisco, with 20 passengers.

The Boston and Newton Joint Stock Association started yesterday morning for California, overland, by way of St. Louis and Fort Independence.
(NYH, April 19, 1849, from the *Boston Evening Traveller,* April 17.)

NEW HAMPSHIRE

The Granite State Company, comprising thirty young men from the State of New Hampshire, eleven of them from the town of Pelham, arrived in this city yesterday, and will depart at ten o'clock this morning for California, taking the overland route, via St. Louis and Independence. The South Boston Company, also numbering about thirty men, will depart at the same time and take the same route. The two companies will travel together. Success to them. (NYH, April 19, 1849, from *Boston paper,* April 16.)

MISSOURI

Hundreds of adventurers, on their route to California overland, arrive here every day. Our hotels, boarding houses, and steamboats are filled with them, and camps are formed in the neighbourhood. The rush is tremendous. In our exchanges, not only in this state but throughout Indiana, Illinois, and Iowa, we are advised of the formation of companies in every town and county, and their departure for the land of promise. The early arrival of many of the companies on the frontier is a source of serious inconvenience to them, as the backwardness of the season prevents them from moving forward. The grass has scarcely commenced springing up, and it will be the last of April, unless there is a very great change in the weather, before they ought to take up the line of travel. When they do commence going forward, the train will exhibit a most extraordinary appearance, and at no time will the emigrants be beyond the reach of succor from each other. If fairly set upon the route, the cavalcade might be made to extend the whole distance from our western frontier to the gold region. It is not an extravagant calculation to say that thirty thousand persons will leave for California, by this route, in the next three months. (NYH, April 19, 1849, from *St. Louis Republican*, April 9.)

[From the New Orleans Picayune, April 10.]

A letter from California, name of the place not given, was received in Guadalajara in the early part of March, giving an account of a horrid outrage committed by five American deserters at the mission house of San Miguel. These ruffians broke into the premises, and murdered Donna Anita Linares, her husband, (an English-man,) Donna Guadelupe Vallejo, four children, a negro cook, two female Indians, and an Indian guide. The letter states that these crimes passed not only unpunished, but almost unnoticed. We have, however, received accounts of their having been pursued by an armed party, and all put to death. The Mexican papers publish these and a variety of other similar revolting details, to stay the progress of the emigration. It is, however, stated that the arrival of General Smith will probably have the effect of rendering life and property secure. (NYH, April 20, 1849.)

The Romance of the Emigration.

How the Gold was Discovered in California

The following is Capt. Sutter's account of the first discovery of the gold in California:

"I was sitting one afternoon," said the Captain, "just after my siesta, engaged, by the by, in writing a letter to a relation of mine at Lucerne, when I was interrupted by Mr. Marshall—a gentleman with whom I had frequent business transactions—bursting hurriedly into the room. From the unusual agitation in his manner, I imagined that something serious had occurred, and as we involuntarily do in this part of the world, I at once glanced to see if my rifle was in proper place. You should know that the mere appearance of Mr. Marshall, at that moment in the fort, was quite enough to surprise me, as he had but two days before left the place to make some alterations in a mill for sawing pine planks, which he had just run up for me some miles higher up the Americanos.

"When he had recovered himself a little, he told me that however great my surprise might be at his unexpected appearance, it would be much greater when I heard the intelligence he had come to bring me. 'Intelligence,' he added, 'which if properly profited by would put both of us in possession of unheard of wealth—millions and millions and millions of dollars in fact.' I frankly own when I heard this that I thought something had touched Marshall's brain, when suddenly all my misgivings were put to an end by his flinging on the table a handful of scales of pure virgin gold.

"I was fairly thunderstruck, and asked him to explain what all this meant, when he went on to say that according to my instructions he had thrown the mill wheel out of gear, to let the whole body of water in the dam find a passage through the tail-race, which was previously too narrow to allow the water to run off in sufficient quantity; whereby the wheel was prevented from efficiently performing its work. By this alteration the narrow channel was considerably enlarged, and a mass of sand and gravel carried off by the force of the torrent. Early in the morning after this took place, he (Mr. Marshall) was walking along the left bank of the stream, when he perceived something, which he at first took for a piece of opal—a clear, transparent stone, very common here—glittering on one of the spots laid bare by the sudden crumbling away of the bank.

"He paid no attention to this; but while he was giving directions to the workmen, having observed several similar glittering fragments, his curiosity was so far excited that he stooped down and picked one of them up.—'Do you know,' said Mr. Marshall, 'I positively debated within myself two or three times whether I should take the trouble to bend my back to pick up one of the pieces, and decided on not doing so, when, further on, another glittering morsel caught my eye—the largest of the pieces now before you. I condescended to pick it up, and to my astonishment found that it was a thin scale of what appears to be pure gold.'

"He then gathered some twenty or thirty similar pieces which, on examination, convinced him that his first suppositions were right. His first impression was that this gold had been lost or buried there by some early Indian tribe—perhaps some of those mysterious inhabitants of the west of whom we have no account, but who dwelt on this continent centuries ago, and built those cities and temples the ruins of which are scattered about these solitary wilds. On proceeding, however, to examine the neighboring soil, he discovered that it was more auriferous. This at once decided him. He mounted his horse, and rode down to me as fast as it would carry him with the news." (CPD, April 20, 1849.)

The Emigration to California

[FROM THE NEW YORK
COMMERCIAL ADVERTISER]

Since the gold excitement commenced, up to the 17th instant, there have left the different ports in the United States for San Francisco, &c. *three hundred and nine vessels,* two hundred and twenty-six of which intended proceeding round the Horn and through the Straits of Magellan; about fifty for Chagres, and the remainder to Vera Cruz, Brasos, &c. *These vessels took out nearly twenty thousand passengers.*

As the spring advances the overland expeditions are leaving the Northern and Eastern States in large numbers. Every steamer or railroad train brings to our city more or less of this class of emigrants. Their grand starting point is to be St. Louis, via Fort Independence.

(WNI, April 21, 1849.)

Government Expeditions to California

FROM THE NEW ORLEANS DELTA.

The Government has organized three expeditions, which will shortly proceed towards the Pacific, opening the way for and extending a full protection to all emigrants.

During all of the present month the column for Oregon, consisting of the rifles and two companies of artillery, will be organizing at Jefferson Barracks, Missouri, with a view to an early summer departure for Oregon. Those who desire to settle in that new and prosperous country may proceed thither under the escort of this large and efficient force. Those, too, who desire to proceed to California by a northern route, will find that many of the difficulties of the journey are overcome when they have arrived at Oregon—the ship communication between that colony and California being very easy and regularly established.

In addition to this expedition from a northern point another force of our army, consisting chiefly of dragoons, is preparing in the course of the present month to march from Fort Smith, on the Arkansas, towards New Mexico, with a view of discovering some practical route to our new territory. This command will be accompanied by officers of the Topographical and Engineering corps, and will be fully equipped to open roads and establish posts on that route.

The third and last expedition so wisely ordered by our Government, is that which will be under the direction of that gallant and experienced officer, Major General Worth. The General is now in our city, waiting for his family. On their arrival he will proceed to Lavaca, thence to San Antonio, where his column, consisting of a fully equipped corps of one thousand men, will be organized. Gen. Worth will carry a long train of wagons, and will proceed to El Paso, thence to the river Gila, where he will establish a strong post; thence the journey to the "gold diggings" will be found quite easy and practicable. Emigrants desiring to avail themselves of the protection of Gen. Worth's column, and to secure a safe and certain overland journey to California, should proceed with their wagons, stores, and equipments to San Antonio, Texas, and fall in the rear of Gen. Worth's column. The General will leave San Antonio about the first of May, and will be fully provided with all the necessary means of opening a good road as far as the Gila, where the pioneer will find that most of the difficulties of the road have been overcome. The route of Gen. Worth's column will be through a new, interesting, and healthy country. A continual variety of scenery, strange aboriginal tribes, rare botanical and mineral specimens, curious vestiges of antiquity, with all the excitements and pleasures of one of the most adventurous expeditions of modern times, will render Gen. Worth's march one of thrilling and romantic interest.

(WNI, April 21, 1849.)

The Mexican Route to California

FROM THE BUFFALO EXPRESS

We take pleasure in laying before the public the following letter from Seth C. Grosvenor, Esq., who went out to California in command of a company of adventurers, taking the Mexican land route.

GUADALAJARA, MEXICO, Feb. 27, 1849.

We are approaching the Pacific coast. Five days more and we are at San Blas, and, if we can get a vessel there, fifteen or less days will take us to San Francisco; if not, twenty days more on horseback is our fate, and that after a journey of nine hundred miles through the hot sands and dust

of Mexico, sleeping every night on the ground or on a brick floor, with a single blanket for a bed and a saddle for a pillow, after which we have frequently ridden ten leagues before breakfast.

These Mexican towns are queer things, and all look alike—every house being a castle and every church an immense pile of stone and mortar, with numerous spires and bells, and every thing looking ancient. The people, a mixed race of Spanish crosses and Indians, are the most polite to your face and the most treacherous behind your back that the sun ever shone upon, ready to shake hands one moment and assassinate you the next. It is no disgrace to steal here, and notorious highwaymen walk the streets unpunished. We have been over the whole of Scott's line of march, from Vera Cruz, where he landed, to Queretaro, where the treaty was signed, and are now two hundred miles nearer the Pacific than our army approached.

A Certain Dislike

This is a city of one hundred and fifty thousand inhabitants. At Queretaro and from that to this place the country is agitated with one of those petty revolutions for which Mexico is so famous. They are dissatisfied with the present Government, and desire Santa Anna's return from exile. He has many strong partisans in the north, and a general fight must yet take place. Who comes out best I care not; but they annoy us considerably, taking us first as partisans of this and then of that party. We are formally taken before the dignitaries and made to give an account of our military aspect and intentions. They treat us very politely, and hate us cordially. They are continually robbing the stage and any small parties they can find, but refuse to honor us with a trial. There are not more than two or three in our party but would be glad of an attack. While at Queretaro the stage came in, the driver shot, and the passengers all robbed. The next morning it was robbed again. That morning, when we went along, we saw the gentlemen on their splendid horses, a mile and a half distant, on an eminence, and as some of our party wanted better horses, we started for them; but, before we got to them, they cried out "Los Yankees," "Americanos," and, putting spurs to their horses, were off in a twinkling. They hate us most cordially, and hate to fight us as bad as they hate us.

We sold our wagons and mules at the city of Mexico; it cost me thirty dollars to get my baggage here by stage. We receive very flattering accounts from the mines, and also have information to-day that our Government had prohibited all foreigners from digging gold in California. The Mexicans are printing and throwing into our quarters inflammatory appeals against the Americans—saying they have taken their mines, will not let them dig, and now, with an impudence unparalleled, are passing through their country. They say our army did not come here, and if it had it would have been used up. And yet, with all their swaggering, I last night sent three men to clear our courtyard of one hundred and fifty clamorous Mexicans, and it was done as quick as if they had been sheep.

It has not rained since we have been in Mexico, and sometimes clouds of dust so completely envelop us that we cannot see each other. We pass over splendid bridges, under which is the bed of a river, and not a drop of water in it. It is the dry season here, and will be the dry season in California before we arrive, so that we expect to pass nearly a year without seeing a drop of rain. (WNI, April 21, 1849.)

From the Journal of Commerce

GUADALAJARA, MARCH 14, 1849.

We arrived in this city on Monday, 12th, making the trip from Mexico in fourteen days. Mr. Bidwell and myself enjoy excellent health, and, although this mode of travelling is slow and fatiguing, yet we have become accustomed to it, and enjoy it much. We expect to be on our way to Tepic to-morrow, expecting to reach that place in

four days, and San Blas in one more, if we decide to embark at that point. If we go on to Mazatlan it will require three or four more. We are informed that ships are waiting at both places for passengers. If so, we shall soon be at our journey's end. A fair wind will enable us to make the voyage in eight or ten days.

An unfortunate occurrence took place with us, a few days since, resulting in the death of Mr. Charles Dunham, of Warehouse Point, near Hartford, Connecticut. As the affair will be brought to the notice of the Government, I will relate the circumstances attending it in some detail. On the morning of the 7th instant, our party entered the city of Irapuato, one of the finest in Mexico, situated in a beautiful valley, midway between this city and Mexico, and containing 8,000 inhabitants. As our custom is, we separated into small parties, and entered several eating-houses to obtain our breakfast, the deceased with some others making one party. After eating, a dispute arose between him and the person keeping the house, the latter alleging that one shilling was due him, while Dunham averred that nine cents of it was paid. The Alcalde was then called by the Mexican to prevent Dunham leaving.

Upon this, Mr. Charles Carrell (one of our party) was called to act as interpreter, who stated the case to the Alcalde, the Mexican all the while denying that any thing was paid. Mr. D. directed Carrell to offer the Alcalde the remaining three cents, which was refused. At the same time Carrell was ordered to dismount. This he refused. The Guard, which was called by the Alcalde, then pointed their guns at him, our own men at the same time urging him to obey. Carrell then began to dismount, and at the same time took hold of his pistol. The guard, observing this, instantly struck him with their guns, and felled him to the ground. On this Dunham put spurs to his horse to escape, and had advanced a short distance when one of the soldiers shot him through the heart with two balls, making one opening in his back where they entered, and two in his breast where they escaped. He exclaimed they have killed me, and fell a lifeless corpse to the ground. The soldiers then fell upon our men indiscriminately, beating and firing at them; the result was that they were badly injured by blows only, the guns either snapping or missing. Mr. Bidwell, myself, and some twenty others were at some distance from this scene, and escaped unmolested through the kindness of two priests, who opened the gate of the Cathedral yard, and thus enabled us to escape from the mob. After several interviews with the Alcalde outside the city, in which he expressed much sorrow and regret that the affair had taken place, declaring it impossible for him to have prevented it, he brought out the wounded men, having first dressed all their wounds. He also promised a christian burial for the deceased. We parted with them, and resumed our march.

The deceased was an interesting and worthy young gentleman, who leaves a father and mother to mourn his loss.

The wounded have mostly recovered. During the affray, one of our men, being hotly pursued by a Mexican, turned suddeny upon him, and with a blow from the breech of his gun felled him to the ground, sinking the lock in his head just under the ear.   (WNI, April 21, 1849.)

Movements on the Overland Route

[Correspondence of the St. Louis Republican]
INDEPENDENCE, April 6, 1849.

At this time every State in the Union, excepting Delaware and Texas, is represented at this place, by a delegation of emigrants to California; and by reports from those who have arrived, the number will be greatly increased from each quarter. The various companies, as fast as they can complete their outfits, are going into camp, and accustoming themselves to the duty pertaining thereto, previous to leaving the set-

tlements. Could the wives and sweethearts of many of them see the awkwardness displayed in their new avocations, both in the culinary and laundry departments—for the late rains and muddy condition of the roads have caused considerable briskness in the latter—they would almost be induced to forsake the luxuries of a life at home, and accompany them on their far distant journey to the land of promise. However, practice will make perfect, and by the time they return, should such be their providence, much domestic handiwork, heretofore irksome, can be performed with greater avidity.

The character of the emigrants, generally, excites remarks from all. The greater portion are intelligent, sober, and industrious men of families; while even the single and younger portion, unusual to be found in such expeditions, possess traits of character for morality and virtue, promising in the extreme. Joy beams from the face of all, as they meet their fellow travellers at this great starting point; and, as a reverend old gentleman remarked to me to-day, "a great load had been taken from his heart, since he had seen the various companies; he could now travel in peace and security among any of them, without being compelled to hear blasphemous language, or witness scenes of debauchery, for," said he, "I expected to find the great majority composed of a different class." This is the general expression, and all are agreeably disappointed. Of course, there are exceptions, but they are very few.

In camp, about two miles west, is a company of gentlemen from Cincinnati, Ohio, numbering in all fifty-one men. They are organized into messes of five, are provided with ten wagons, twenty tents, and five marquees,[1] and calculate to start with eleven mules to the wagon. Two of the wagon bodies are made of sheet iron, and capable of being used as boats; as such they have been tested, and found to bear twenty men, or 2,500 pounds of freight, and only draw four inches water. They are completely outfitted, have the star-spangled banner waving over their camp, and, independent of their civil, are under military, regulations, for their better protection in making the journey, and provisions for twelve months after their arrival have been shipped by way of Cape Horn.

On the Santa Fe road, about four miles from town, a fine company of men, fifteen in number, from Summit county, Ohio, are in camp, and ready to march with the first body. They are provided with three wagons and one large tent, and intend driving mules. Each man is well armed, but for better protection they intend making the journey with some larger company.

In the same vicinity a company of thirty-five men, of fine appearance and bearing, from Wayne county, Indiana, are in camp, and ready to move. They are provided with seven wagons, six tents, nine months' provisions, and mules and cattle sufficient to make the trip. They are organized and governed by a constitution and by-laws. The result of their labors is to be divided mutually, share and share alike; and in case any of the company shall die, then his widow or other lawful heir is to receive the share he would have received had he lived. The company is composed of mechanics and farmers, who will turn their attention to the most profitable employment. Their prime object, however, is to dig for gold.

There are more persons from Ohio preparing to emigrate than from any other State. From what I can learn, large numbers are *en route*, overland, from the southern portion of this State and from Illinois. The number at present in this town has been variously estimated, but I should judge it will not exceed one thousand.

(NYH, April 22, 1849.)

Interesting from the Pacific

[Correspondence of the New Orleans Delta]
ACAPULCO, March 20, 1849.

The steamship California, Captain Marshall (Captain Forbes being sick on board), entered this harbor on the 9th of last month (February), and left on the 11th, having Governor Smith, family, and suite on board. The California was crowded to inconvenience. The number of passengers was three hundred and seventy-five. Considerable dissatisfaction prevailed on board, and it appears that the crowd, though select, was a very hard one. The captain had no control even over his own crew, who are all expected to desert him as soon as he arrives at San Francisco.

There are about twenty emigrants here, who anxiously await her return; so, indeed, does the whole population of this miserable town, as she left here some $3,000 in the purchase of eggs, chickens, frijoles, and other little articles. The report had reached here, in advance of the arrival of the California, that the emigrants had expended $60,000 on the Isthmus of Panama—a fact which filled the minds of this poor people with the most extravagant ideas of the wealth and liberality of the Americans.

A letter was received here yesterday, by a respectable German from a friend of his in California, dated about the 1st of February, giving a frightful account of the confusion, anarchy, and scarcity of provisions at San Francisco and the gold regions. To such an extent does the lawlessness prevail, that no one ventures out in the evening without being armed.

The Triumphant Loafer

A loafer passed here on the California, who managed to get from New York to Chagres without paying a cent, then walked across the Isthmus without paying

---

1. Large field tents of the type used by army officers.

a cent, and by connivance of a fireman on the California, stowed himself away among the machinery, and when the steamer was three days out made his appearance on the deck. This skillful loafer, attracting the notice of Captain Marshall, he instituted an inquiry into the matter, and caused the fireman who had connived at the loafer's scheme, to be put in irons; whereupon, all hands struck and refused to work, being seconded in part by the passengers, who threatened to throw the captain overboard if he resorted to such extreme measures. So the ingenious loafer triumphed, and on his way through this place made no secret of his exultation over the unfortunate captain. That chap will do. I would rather take his chance for a big pile of the dust than that of any other gold-seeker.

All accounts concur that thousands of persons in the vicinity of the placer have perished from cold and hunger during the past winter. It is feared that the mortality will not end here. Many more must perish from the want of food, for which the impatient gold-seekers have made no provision.—What perils and hardships will not men incur in pursuit of the root of all evil!

Last night four men set out from this port in a small whale-boat, on their way to California, intending to coast it all the way through, and on their arrival, to run their boat between San Francisco and the gold regions, for the use of passengers.—The crew consists of two yankees, a Spaniard, and an English sailor! I wish them a successful trip, but I fear they will have to return in distress. (NYH, April 22, 1849.)

From Chagres and the Pacific

The U. S. Mail steamship Isthmus, Capt. Baker, arrived at New Orleans on the 14th from Havana, after a fine passage of seventy-five hours. She brings news from Panama down to the 31st of March. A whale ship arrived on the 30th, and would take away 150 passengers for San Francisco. People were daily flocking to Chagres from all parts of the world. It is estimated that there were at Panama at the end of March 1,500 people *en route* to California; at Gorgona and Cruces 700 more. Much distress and some sickness are said to prevail upon the Isthmus.

[From the Panama Star, March 21.]

Let any one walk around Panama, and he cannot fail to notice the marks of the Anglo-Saxon. American signboards, in the regular catchline style, "Cheap Goods"—"Broker's Office"—"Licensed Auctioneer," &c. &c., meet the eye here and there. "Going, going, gone!" in a style that would do credit to Peter Funk,[2] in his palmiest days, echoes from different places along the street; the horse jockey and the pedlar are not behind the others, and yesterday we heard uttered, with an earnestness that would have honored Sam Slick, "You don't want to buy no dried apples, nor about half a biled ham, already cooked, nor a little less nor half a barrel of pickled pork, real, genuine, Boston harbor, nor nothing, do you?" Even Cave Johnson, the immortal Cave, would here find some one with whom to divide his honors and share his misfortunes.[3] The bulletin board of Messrs. Leech & Co., now bears the familiar words of "mail failed to-day," and then adds, "Nothing from beyond Gorgona." Tailors and rum sellers have become ship owners

---

2.   A shill or decoy who runs up the price at an auction.
3.   Cave Johnson (1793–1866) a seven-term congressman from Tennessee, was postmaster general in the Polk administration. It was during his term in office that postage stamps were first used in the United States—five-cent and ten-cent stamps issued in July 1847.

and ship brokers, and thus the once dull and quiet town of Panama, under the influence of American energy and industry, becomes the scene of activity and business.

(PPL, April 24, 1849.)

Our Central American Correspondence

SAN JUAN DE NICARAGUA, March 18, 1849.

Your correspondent arrived on the Mosquito shore, at the port of San Juan, on Sunday, the 11th of March, in company with the members of Gordon's California association, in the brig Mary, after a fair run of nineteen days from New York.[4]

Our run down the coast during the day had been exceedingly beautiful. Instead of finding a low, sandy, swampy coast, we found a bold and picturesque shore; sometimes swelling into hills, jutting out in promontories, or sweeping away in easy hollows. Tropical vegetation clothed the entire range of land as far as the eye could reach. . . . The harbor of San Juan is extremely picturesque. It is a beautiful sheet of water, about two miles across, clear and pellucid, and almost fresh enough to drink. It was strange to us, coming from the wintry ice-bound scenery of New York, to find ourselves, in a few days, in the very midst of green and verdant summer, and amongst a vegetation bending under the weight of its own luxuriance, and dipping its dark green foliage into the clear waters of the harbor and its branching lagoons.

We found San Juan a place of about 200 inhabitants, the major part of whom are Spanish Indians, deriving subsistence from the employment furnished to them by the merchants of the place, who are principally French and Spanish.

Living and provisions are exceedingly dear. Fortunately we have with us provisions, cooks, &c., in abundance; but those who missed their meals through the hurry and confusion of landing the cargo, paid about a dollar per meal at the houses of the merchants, who for the occasion turned hotel-keepers. On our landing, everything eatable advanced from 100 to 200 per cent at San Juan. The articles of fowls rose from

San Juan de Nicaragua.

---

4. Gordon advertised that his association would make the journey from New York to San Francisco, via Nicaragua, in sixty days. The first leg went well, but the rest of the trip was a disaster: they did not reach San Francisco until early October, seven and a half months after leaving New York.

18 cents to $1 each; eggs from 1 cent each to 3 cents; the loaf of bread sold for 25 cents—weight about 1½ pounds. French wines and spirits can be had here very good, and as cheap or cheaper than in New York.

The climate of San Juan is superb; the weather has been positively delicious. The thermometer never ranges above 90 or below 65 the year round, and a fresh and delightful sea-breeze sweeps over the town continually. Our people, 120 in number, have been hard at work all the week, some landing cargo, and often up to their middle in water—some building the steamboat—some hunting or fishing—and, I regret to say, a goodly number getting drunk and lying about exposed the night through, undergoing exposures in eating and drinking which would be fatal in a New York July, but all, so far, with perfect impunity.

Mr. Gordon contemplates establishing a permanent line through to the Pacific, from this point, and has brought out a steamboat in sections. It will be completed in about eight days, and we shall then start forward on our inland expedition. The boat only draws about 18 inches water, and we find native bungeys, drawing 3 or 4 feet, ascending and descending the San Juan river all the time, so that we anticipate no difficulty in getting across to San Juan on the Pacific, where our vessel awaits us that is to convey us to San Francisco.

The passage of the river, though practicable for light draft steamboats, is extremely difficult to make in the native boats; they are frequently 14 days in going up from San Juan to Granada, during which time passengers have to sit cooped up on a narrow seat, and sleep at nights in the same position. We hope to make the passage through in the steamboat in three days, and afterwards, when the river is known, the future passages are not expected to occupy more than two days.

Thus far our expedition has proved a very pleasant one; many of our boys, who had been living for some weeks in hotels in New York, found it rather hard to live on salt beef, pork, ham, and such like, and to drink their tea and coffee without milk on the voyage; and some others, who had never been away from home, found it marvelously awkward to turn to and help out with cargo, cook an extempore dinner on the beach, or sleep on the soft side of a plank now and then; but with these exceptions, we get along bravely, and are, in point of health and spirits, emphatically, "all well." (NYH, April 26, 1849.)

Our Saltillo Correspondence

SALTILLO, March 20, 1849.

I have been so much occupied since we left the Rio Grande that I had not time to write to you. Well, here we are, at this beautiful city (so called). This is a most miserable country.

We have not seen so much good land since we have been in Mexico as would cover the Washington parade ground. With the exception of a few acres here and at Monterey, all the land that is cultivated in this part of the country is watered by letting the rivers and springs run over them every day or two, so hot and dry is the climate.

We have lost one of our party; he died at Seralvo, of dysentery—some thought of cholera—his name was Searls; he was from East Granville, Mass., and has left a wife and three children. A party of men for California has just arrived at our camp, and they bring us the melancholy news of the loss of Dr. Wilks, of Madison county, New York. The circumstances are these: the Doctor was a member of that party that joined us in New York for the purpose of crossing the country together. They became rather jealous of our party, and separated from us at the Rio Grande. They also thought that they could travel much faster than we could on the road, on account of their party being smaller than ours, but we have kept ahead of them so far, and expect to keep ahead. Another misfortune they are subject to is, they refused to have any officers, or any organization among themselves; the consequence was that every man did just as he pleased, he rode a mile ahead or behind, just as it suited him. Well, yesterday afternoon, the Doctor took it into his head, at the pass of Rinconarda, to go a hunting while the party were halting, and he has not yet returned. He is undoubtedly murdered, by either Camanches or robbers, as the party kept a fire all night, and fired minute guns. I regret the loss of the Doctor very much. He was an excellent man. The cholera has been all round us, from our landing until we left Monterey. It was raging at Monterey with great violence—but, thank God, we seem to have out-travelled it. With the exception of one man, who is rather bad with dysentery, our party are in excellent health. We have got over most of our troubles, and we are getting along nicely. We have changed our route, and are going by Chihuahua and the Gila river. F. H. L.

(NYH, April 26, 1849.)

Ho for California!
"The Land Route"
Interesting Letter by a Clevelander

Col. Everettson's, opposite Presidio de Rio Grande, Texas, March 15th, 1849.

DEAR SIR:—When I left New Orleans I did not intend to write again until I reached the "Land of Promise;" but under existing circumstances, duty compels me to send you a few lines.

It is not necessary to mention what a sea-sick set of fellows we were crossing the gulf, or what a merry time we had beating up Aransas Bay to Corpus Christi in a little old fore and after against a norther. I will give you the particulars another time; suffice it to say we reached Corpus Christi on the 19th of January, in spite of wind and weather. Here we concluded to change our route from Mazatlan to Presidio El Passo, thence by Cook's trail, the river Gila, &c.

Left Corpus the 1st February, with wagons, had no road but traveled with a guide. On the 5th one of our party got lost, halted two days for him, we then resumed our march. On the 7th he arrived on foot, (the horse having broke down,) with a guide, having had nothing except water for nearly three days. This day we camped at a Cavy yard or Koral, where they catch wild horses. Game here is very abundant, consisting of deer, antelope, panther, a species of leopard, wolves, wild horses, &c. On account of our slow progress the company became dissatisfied, and on the 7th dissolved, being within two days' travel of the Lorado road.

Here we formed into parties of seven, each party taking a wagon and a share of the provisions; such things as could not be divided were sold at auction, a hand saw bringing six dollars, a coffee mill five and a quarter, &c. This novel scene undoubtedly astonished the natives if there were any lurking in the vicinity to witness it.

On the 21st, arrived at the Lorado and San Antonio road. 22d: Here a part of the company took the road for Lorado, the rest—some twenty-five of us, including Col. Abbot, Col. Everettson, Capt. Peoples, &c.—started for Presidio, through the wilds of Western Texas. We took some water with us, not expecting to find any the first night; we however found none the first nor the second night, and on the morning of the third two of our party turned back. We moved on this day until the teams broke down, then left the wagons with a man to each, and started with our horses in search of water. The Neuces lay in a N. E. course, and we expected to reach it in six or seven miles, we therefore took no provisions. Started at two in the afternoon, traveled until dark—no water—camped. Left next morning at day light—an anxious looking party, I assure you, in search of something more valuable than gold. About 9 A. M. came to a ravine, found some mud. Here the party became very much separated. We finally got started again, myself considerably in the advance. I went on this way some time when I discovered that the party had left me—they probably taking another course. I climbed a tree, but could not see or make them hear me. After waiting a short time to see if they would come up, I concluded to move ahead in search of the river—my horse being nearly used up it was folly for me to hunt the party.

The chaparal and prickly pear was almost impenetrable, and I was obliged to walk most of the way to save my horse. I arrived at the river at 2 P. M., very much exhausted. Here I was, some thirty miles from the wagons, without a compass, (having loaned mine the morning before to a friend,) and something more from the Lorado road. This I could find by following the Nueces down, and so I concluded to do, but found it impossible on account of the chaparal and prickly pear; but by keeping off the river I could get along.

The 27th I arrived at the Lorado road— need I say how, or in what condition? From here to Lorado it was fifty-two miles, and one watering place on the route, and no inhabitants. But ten miles from the Nueces I had the good fortune to meet four Texians guarding a couple of Mexicans who had killed a man on the road—they gave me a piece of bread. From here I reached Lorado without any difficulty. They told me here they had had no rain for seven months. The rainy season commences the first of April.

I remained here a few days, then crossed the river, procured a passport from the alcalde, and made my way up to Presidio, some forty leagues, where I found my companions—all well, but they had seen the "elephant." C. O. R.
(CPD, April 25, 1849.)

An Englishman's Views of the Gold Mines of California

By John George Harding, Esq., B.A.,
of Trinity Hall, Cambridge.

*Quid non mortalia pectora cogis
Auri sacra fames?—Virgil.*[5]

The accounts of travellers have been from time immemorial subject to the imputation of being a little exaggerated, or, to say the least, highly colored. The man who has visited barbarian countries, has associated with savage tribes, has seen the wild denizens of the forest in all the pride of liberty and independence; who has contemplated "nature's stores unrivalled," cannot well transfer his impressions to paper without a degree of imagery and enthusiasm which, with a great class of read-

ers, impeaches his general character for veracity.

The reader, in the centre of home attractions and domestic civilization, in the full enjoyment of his "languid hours of listless ease," conceives much that is recorded to be impossible, simply because it is "contrary to his experience," in the most narrow signification of the phrase. True it is that not a few authors have magnified their own adventures and embellished their works with fictions to gratify their own egotism and exhibit themselves, in grandiloquous language, "heroes of their own story." It becomes, then, difficult to draw a line of demarcation, to discriminate

5. "To what do you not drive the human heart, / O cursed lust for gold?" (Virgil, *Aeneid, Book 3,* lines 56–57.)

with any accuracy between skepticism and credulity, to determine where truth ends and romance begins.

When we first heard of the gold mines of California, and of the facility with which the precious ore was gathered by the fortunate occupants of the district, we might well be pardoned for requiring no ordinary authority to give so wondrous a narrative the authentic impress of veracity. It required, in the case of former El Dorados, the exertion of an indefatigable patience to arrive at the source of these "golden showers." The vicissitudes of climate; the toilsome march through a hostile country; the constant proximity of an active and enterprising enemy; the daily loss arising from pestilence, famine, and the sword, were the lot of Cortes and Pizarro. The bones of too many of their followers were bleaching in the desert ere the surviving pilgrims to the shrine of Plutus uttered the joyful "Eureka" of success, and received the golden crown of their labors. Their march was of incredible difficulty, a triumph of indomitable perseverance. It is not our province to dilate on the exploits of these well known leaders; it is enough that they have been immortalized in the vivid pages of Prescott, of European as well as American celebrity. Satisfied, from unquestionable documents and official statistics, of the existence of the precious metal, it will be our object to consider in the present article what effect the superabundance of the "universal idol" will have on the fortunes of the immediate occupants, and more or less on the destinies of the western hemisphere.

As might be expected, there appears to be an incredible anxiety to arrive at this golden Canaan; the *"amor innatus habendi"*[6]

seems to pervade all classes of men, from the wealthy capitalist to the hard working artisan. New York alone sends forth her twenty thousand in pursuit of wealth to be realized without toil and with the rapidity of a dream. Reality outstrips the inventions of fable, and the "Arabian Nights," "Tales of the Genii," &c. "pale their ineffectual fires"[7] before the gorgeous and golden zone of California. We read of vessels floating before their port, their crews deserted, their owners in the condition of Robinson Crusoe when he had completed his canoe and wanted leverage to render it of service to him. In short, California would seem to be a "Happy Valley," with no jealous barriers or guardian Cerberus to protect its sacred portals; all are at liberty to come and go and to garner the precious metals. Soldiers arrive at the frontiers of the country and find a new and material Calypso in the Californian and continental Circe. The iron bonds of discipline are relaxed, and the outraged authority of military *regimes* are (at present) violated with impunity.

In many cases where Nature has been most prodigal of her bounties it has been found that man cannot exist in a country so exuberant in vegetable and other productions. Yellow fevers and noxious *miasmata* too frequently hang on the populations of these seemingly favored districts. For instance, the shores of the Pacific are embellished with all the attributes which could enliven the eye and make glad the heart of those who contemplate that modern Eden of spontaneous fertility. The historian, however, after detailing on this beautiful exterior, goes on to tell us *"mais la mort était cachée sans ce manteau brillant, &c."*[8] (See De Tocqueville, *de la Democratie en Amerique.*) It would seem in this, as in others

---

6. The innate love for possession.
7. "The glowworm shows the matin to be near, / And 'gins to pale his uneffectual fire." (Shakespeare, *Hamlet, I, v, 89.*)
8. "... but Death was hidden within this splendid cloak. ..."

affairs of life, there is a grand system of compensations or balancings of good and evil, that man in his state of probation should, under some form or another, be subject to mortal vicissitudes, and that the *"surgit amari aliquid"*[9] should be the unfailing attendant on the "utile" [the useful] and the "dulce" [the pleasant].

A Well-Favored Land

At present California, so fertile in local attractions, seems to be favored also in point of climate. We read of no indigenous *malaria* to blight with death the pilgrims to a country situated within the limits of the temperate zone. Our fear, notwithstanding all these advantages, is that this superabundant wealth will not benefit the *great mass* of emigrants, who fondly hope that by a lucky stroke secured the fortunes of themselves and families. We think California will not be an exception to that seemingly invariable, though selfish rule, "The many still shall labor for the few."[10]

It would appear that the country in the immediate vicinity of the mines is fertile and in the highest degree adapted for agricultural development; yet it would seem that only one occupant is cultivating the ground. This gentleman, possessed of more than ordinary judgment, is aware that bread is the "staff of life," and that, in the long run, the holder of the food will be the possessor of the gold—with this exception, the Californians (to class them all under a local patronymic) have forgotten that man must earn his bread by the "sweat of his brow"—forgetting that they must subsist in the meantime, they are to a man intent in digging for gold; they realize the injunction of the poet, *"Quid sit futurum cras, fuge quærere."*[11]

It must be remembered, moreover, that when we read these glowing descriptions of California, there were about four thousand persons engaged in this occupation. Now supposing—and there can be no reasonable doubt on the subject—that the other great cities of the United States should be actuated by the same zeal as New York. There will shortly be, instead of four thousand, a human mass of more than a quarter of a million on the scene of action. How are they to be fed? What discipline can be brought into action to control this gigantic cohort of men in the prime of life, and under the powerful influence of avarice? Living, too, beneath the unguarded canopy of tents, or bivouacking in the open air—with no guaranty for safety but a reliance on their own personal courage—with no form or apology for law—no semblance of discipline—at a distance from the humanizing influence of female society—utterly segregated from the common usages of civilized life, it is fearful to contemplate the aspect of the panorama. Added to all these influences, the great scarcity and extravagant value of the bare necessaries of life; the lavish squanderings of the ore, at present so readily obtained; above all, the impending calamity of famine—the inordinate love of gaming, furious with the Mexicans as with the Germans of old—the swarming hordes of Mormons, who appear to claim the golden district as their peculiar property—the unbridled passions of an almost exclusively *male* population; all these considerations lead one to reflect on what must inevitably be the fate of California.

No Governing Power

At present, from the accounts we read,

---

9. "All in vain: since from the fountain of enchantments *there rises a drop of bitterness* that torments us in the very flowers." (Lucretius, *De Natura Rerum, book 4, lines 1133–1134.)
10. "Such hath it been—shall be—beneath the sun / The many still must labour for the one." (Byron, *The Corsair, canto I, st. 8.*)
11. "What will happen tomorrow? Avoid even asking!" (Horace, *Odes, book I, ode 9, line 13.*)

there is no governing power of any description; there is no Cortes, or Pizarro, or Columbus, who is looked up to as the chief of the enterprise; no one whose superior prowess or mental acquirements dazzle the eye of the "many-headed"—all appear to be "equal," in the most democratic interpretation of the term; all are (at present) in possession of that golden standard which exerts an adventitious but all powerful influence over the human family; all are *now* independent; there is no mutual reliance on the good offices of society; each man is exclusive and selfish, avaricious and ungrateful. When, however, the steady toil of industry, or superior craft, shall have enriched one man at the expense of many; when those rendered savage from long self-indulgence, and uncoerced by any bonds of discipline, shall hang as marauders on the outskirts of society, then will come indeed the "tug of war," and the absence of law and moral obligation will be too severely felt.

It is an old adage, "all is not gold that glitters;" we do not think California will be an exception to the general verity of the rule. Our impression is, that this "glut of gold," this modern incarnation of Pactolus, will not be beneficial except to the few; we repeat again, it will not alleviate the condition of the mass. These "golden showers" will find their way to the accumulated stores of the colossal capitalists; furnished with ready means, and the *opsonia*[12] which ready money can invariably command, he will buy up the labor of others—the costly aid of machinery and science will, ere long, be called in, and mining operations on an extensive scale will be put in requisition.

Government will sell allotted portions at high prices to individual proprietors, who will readily pay a large premium for the monopoly. California will no longer be an exception to the rest of the world, "the poor shall inhabit the land." We shall, doubtless, hear of some leviathan fortunes; the great cities of the West will each possess their California Crœsus—their overgrown proprietor, *"Attalicis conditionibus."*[13]

To argue from analogy, a great satiety of gold has never been productive of universal good. Spain, so glorious in El Dorados, would probably have maintained a more steady position among nations had she never been dazzled and corrupted by the gold of the western hemisphere. When were her days of glory, her palmy triumphs? Were they *before* or *after* the expedition of Pizarro?

The discovery was not only not beneficial to the mother country, but it proved a snare and a stumbling block to many of the partners of his expedition. A few indeed, it is true, when the plundered spoils of the Incas had been divided, had the wisdom to return (see Prescott) to their respective homes, *"post tot naufragia tuli"*[14]—the many sojourned to that land of promise, eager for more, and fell victims either to intestine quarrels, the vicissitudes of servile and civil wars, or the baleful effects of climate. Pizarro himself, in extreme old age, came to a violent death; so true is it

Sine cæde et vulnere pauci
Descendunt reges![15]

A Fearful Outcome

From the foregoing considerations it may be gathered that we entertain many

---

12. Provisions; anything eaten as a relish with bread.
13. "By such terms as an Attalus could offer." (Horace, Odes, book I, ode 1, line 12.) The wealth of the Attalids, kings of Pergamon in Asia Minor, was proverbial; the terms of payment (conditionibus) an Attalid king could offer would be very impressive.
14. "After so many shipwrecks I have endured."
15. "Without murder and wounds few kings come down!"

fears for the local condition of California; when we reflect on the fact of a small colony, tenanted by a few hardy settlers, surrounded by a wild country, a few months since only recognized on the map as the hunting-ground of the wild Indian, who are gradually ceasing to exist on the face of the earth; when we behold this neglected and isolated district becoming so suddenly a swarming hive of human population, deluged, as it were, by the influx of thousands in so short a space of time, actuated to a man by such engrossing passions, gathering with such rapidity the "*irritamenta malorum*,"[16] we cannot but tremble for the result.

Our friends on the other side of the Atlantic must not allow their judgment to be dazzled by the enthusiasm of their friends, or the gorgeous programmes of California intelligence. Before they abandon their industrious pursuits, their homely but honest competence, let them remember that they form individually but a solitary unit of the mass. The name of gold is, after all, but *relative*. Let not the artisan, who gains, in the *land of plenty*, his ten dollars per week, be beguiled by the promise of eighty dollars in California. If bread (not to mention the other necessaries of life) is eight times as dear at San Francisco as at New York, in what respect is he a gainer?

No man in his calm judgment can suppose that *every* pilgrim to California will return laden with gold; in this expedition the many will fail, the few succeed. So it was with the *railway mania*, which will long be remembered in the annals of this country. The extent of the *furor* can scarcely be comprehended by those who were not on the immediate sphere of action. No one was above or below the attractions of the siren: the butler and the banker, the clerk and the collegian, the soldier and the sailor, in short, every division of the social ladder furnished greedy candidates for *scrip*, and employed emissaries to negotiate affairs in the railway California of *Capel Court*. The lawyers were in a delirium of delight. There was only one drawback to their felicity, viz, a painful consciousness that the "golden eggs" must soon be exhausted, and the parent goose annihilated by such repeated incubations. We heard of "lucky hits" on 'Change. A few, a select few, made and kept fortunes. We heard little of the converse of the picture. Where was the clerk who had lost the thrifty savings of years, his situation and his character? Where was the wealthy firm who had employed their one hundred subordinates? Fortune, partial to the few, had frowned on the great mass of speculators; they were virtually erased from the page of life, and left alone to poverty and desolation.

We have adduced this parallel, and we think Californian candidates may draw from its momentous commentary.

(WNI, April 27, 1849.)

---

16. The "excitations of evil."

The Emigrants

Their Progress towards El Dorado

Our Flying Correspondence

RIO DE JANEIRO, March 13, 1849.

When, on the 13th of January last, the good ship Tarolinta left our wharf, two doves lit out upon our mainmast—omens which were hailed by many of us as an earnest of our *bon fortune*, in the future, and as the shores died away in the light of evening, many an eye was tears-wet, and many a heart saddened, in thinking of those whose hands he may never more grasp in the social circle, and whose familiar voices he may never hear again. The next morning, and the sky and sea were around us, and a favorable breeze, that continued without variation for some ten days. During this time a little blue bird came to us in a gale, and clung to the rigging, but soon was swept off, kindling the liveliest sympathy in our hearts for the poor lost one.

The Sabbath has been observed, and the service of the Episcopal Church read twice a day by your humble servant, at the united request of our passengers. There are some eighty-five in the cabin and some forty in the steerage—all of them above mediocrity in enterprise and intellect, and the most of them sanguine gold hunters. Capt. Cane is a Virginian, and a man well qualified to inspire confidence, being a thorough seaman and a kind-hearted man, and more than realized the opinion I had formed of him previous to leaving New York. When some thirteen hundred miles out, a strong head wind overtook us, and it was as much as we could do to maintain our position by drifting to and fro for a

fortnight; and during this time an entertainment called "Shaksperian Evening" was organized, in which Richard III, Hamlet, Macbeth, Lear, and Othello re-lived and re-died on board the Tarolinta. Another evening was also organized, in which Chrystie's African melodies floated o'er a moonlit sea, off the coast of Africa some two hundred miles, probably for the first time. There are several good vocalists, and they contribute largely to the pleasantness and variety of our re-unions on the quarter-deck.

At last, in our third week, we struck the longed-for trade winds, commonly called the northern trades, and they bore us nobly across the Equator, where, after a perfect flood of rain, we were becalmed three days. It was here that we lost the glorious old North Star, and in its stead the brilliant Southern Cross, never seen in our northern hemisphere, glowed in its magnificent radiance upon us, a fitting emblem of the faith of those who believe in His glory and worship His name. During these days the wonders of the deep began to display themselves, and although we had been surrounded by a school of whales when off the Cape de Verde Islands, and a few of Mother Carey's chickens,[1] and several sails each week had been descried, and the bark Croton spoken, yet the "luminosity of the sea" was the great marvel in our present latitude. The sea was lit up with phosphorescent light, and glowed like drifting new fallen snow.

After being forty-nine days out, Cape Frio loomed above the waters, a beacon

---

1. One of numerous types of sea birds; especially the stormy petrel.

hailed with joy by every one of us. Of the famed harbor of Rio de Janeiro, whose magnificent mountains and glittering emeralds of islands—pen can but feebly paint it. We were hailed at Fort Santa Cruz previous to our entering the harbor, and after we entered, a boat from the brig Perry, with Lieut. Russell and Purser Eldridge, came alongside and brought us news, and waited till the custom-house officer's examination was over. I then left the vessel, and took tea on board the Perry, where every thing was in the finest order.

The next day I went to see Bolufogo Bay, which is one of those spots well fitted to dream away existence in. The whitewashed cottages, with lovely gardens, and red tiles, with a back-ground of lofty and splendid mountains, and the bay sleeping at their feet, is enough to awake enthusiasm in the bosom of a mummy; for myself, I am quite in dreamland. The Jardan du Plants is another place where all the worldwide plants of the tropics flourish in their glory. And the city, with its environs and its fountains, and its churches, its beautiful *Senoritas,* and its cool shades, has made it to me to look more like a fairy vision of radiance and loveliness, such as I may not again behold.

The Portugese wonder very much at this sudden influx of *"los Americanos;"* yet they spend their money so freely that they cannot refuse to admit them with as little delay as possible. I had a very interesting interview with the bishop of this city. He is quite aged, and lives in a plain style at his palace. He possesses great acquirements and piety; I would that the clergy here followed his example.

The Portugese place no confidence in the gold stories, and think it will end as their diamond mines a few years since; viz.: *vamose.* Good bye,   CALEB LYON, of Lyondale.

(NYH, May 3, 1849.)

The Overland Emigrants

ST. JOSEPH, MO., April 11, 1849.

Arrivals at St. Joseph—Appearance and Size of the Place—The Emigration to California

I arrived at this place on Saturday, March 31st, whither I came with the Pittsburgh and California Enterprise Company, whom I intend accompanying to the modern Ophir overland, and of whom I proceed to give you some account, and also such other information of the California emigration from this point and Independence.

Harbor of Rio de Janeiro.

St. Joseph is situated upon the left bank of the Missouri river, one hundred miles above Independence, and, although it is a town of only four or five years growth, it contains a population of over two thousand—is rapidly advancing, and is destined to out-rival Independence in a few years, and become the great Western outfitting depot and general rendezvous of the Oregon, California, and New Mexico emigration and trade.

The Pittsburgh company, with whom I am associated, are now encamped in the suburbs of the town, undergoing military exercise, camp drill, breaking in mules, &c., to be in readiness to take up their line of march as soon as the grass is sufficiently grown to afford forage for the teams in crossing the plains. The company numbers 300, most of them from Pennsylvania.

There are encamped in and around St. Joseph, and boarding at the hotels, about thirteen hundred emigrants of all ages; from the smooth chinned youth of sixteen, up to the silver headed venerable of sixty —all buoyant with the expectancy of soon being to realize their bright anticipations and golden dreams of securing to themselves a competency by a few months' life upon the banks of the Sacramento.

Every day brings, by overland and steamboat, additional companies from all parts of the Union. I have, within one week, conversed with emigrants from all the New England, Middle, Western, and some of the Southern states.

With respect to those who intend going to California via the overland route, every article necessary for the trip, with the exception of rifles and sidearms, can be obtained at this place as cheap—and provisions cheaper—as at Cincinnati or at St. Louis. At all events, bring no mules, bacon, or flour. Wagons should not weigh over eleven hundred.

Although oxen are preferable, the Pittsburgh Company go with mules, having purchased them before they arrived here. Mules are sold here from $45 to $65; oxen, per yoke, $40 to $55; bacon, per lb., 5c.; flour, per hundred, $2.

The provisions for a mess of five are, generally, 1,000 lbs. sea biscuit, 200 lbs. flour, 100 lbs. corn meal, 600 lbs. meat (variously cured, generally smoked), 100 lbs. coffee, 100 lbs. sugar, 20 lbs. tea; and other articles, not necessary to mention.

This new study of muleism and oxism is, to nine-tenths of them, a novel business; and although they may become thoroughly initiated in the science, yet inexperience in crossing the plains will, I fear, prove the cause of great troubles, delays, and, perhaps to many, severe disappointments.

All the companies are making preparations to start within two or three weeks.

(NYH, May 3, 1849.)

[From the Norfolk Herald]

The brig John Petty, Capt. Flavel, hence for San Francisco, arrived at Rio Janeiro previous to the 12th of March, having put into that port to obtain a supply of water. A number of letters from the passengers were received in this city, sent home by the bark R. H. Douglass. One of them, from Mr. James W. Barry, of this city, dated March 12, has been politely handed to us, from which we make the following extract:—

There are upward of 40 vessels now here loaded for California. There are some which have been waiting here for six or eight days for water. We are fortunate to have ours already on board, as an old acquaintance of the captain's had a large supply, and not as many California customers as some. We hope to be off in two or three days at the farthest.

There must be upwards of 2,000 Americans (Yankees) now in Rio, and the Emperor has issued an edict to the guard to molest none, or interfere with them, unless under circumstances of great provocation. One was arrested, but he was released the next morning; and those who took him up were themselves imprisoned. If any are distrusted, the cry is "Californians to the rescue." None are, however, permitted to bring arms ashore with them. It is said the Brazilians were very much alarmed, asserting that the Americans (or Yankees) were pouring in under false pretences, that they were soldiers in disguise, &c. The report is that the Emperor is not altogether free from alarm. He has recently been more in the city than usual, and, what would tend still stronger to awaken their fears, there is a rebellion in the northern part of the empire. But they need not fear us; the only object now is California, and our visit must certainly make a good impression on the minds of the citizens, for although there has been a good deal of frolicking, the inhabitants are treated with the greatest respect, and as much order and decorum observed as an American citizen could desire—more than could be expected from what might be termed adventurers. The majority of those I have seen are young men of intelligence and respectability. (NYH, May 3, 1849.)

Interesting Letter from the West

CAMP, 10 miles from Independence,
Friday, April 15th, 1849.

DEAR FRIENDS:—We are all well and have arranged to start to-morrow for the "dust!"—We travel in connection with Mr. Paul's company, from Pittsburgh, making about 30 in all; we will still be the first out. Mr. Pye's company, that designed going with us, are not ready—they will leave next week. We have our six mules to a team purchased, all in good order—three ponies and a horse for saddle animals. The Lower Sandusky company were anxious to go with us, but they could not complete their outfit until three days after our date. We have our baggage all weighed—22

hundred to a wagon. There will undoubtedly be a number of companies follow immediately after us, as there are great numbers encamped, waiting for grass or the start of the first company. The road is literally lined with tents between this and Independence. The Independence people received some glittering news from their friends who went out last year—they are men of truth and say that they have made their fortunes. This news produces a great deal of excitement in Independence. They were five months and ten days in crossing the plains.—There are companies here from all parts of the Northern and Western States, and none further South than Kentucky and Virginia. There is a company of the Galena Lead Mines, Wisconsin. I see some of the Findlay company every time I go to town.

I have to congratulate myself that this is the last letter I shall write on the east side of civilization, as I am surely tired of these delays. I have my clothes all packed in three bags all weighing one hundred pounds. I have a very fair pony, and a good saddle. I shall pack him with a bushel and a half of corn, and lead him the first two weeks and feed it to him. Your next letter you will please to write to San Francisco, California, as the nearest place to our destination I know of. I shall try and keep a journal after I leave this place; but it will be very difficult as conveniences are small. I am now writing on my roll of blankets, with my comforter rolled up as a seat. Some of my little fixins I find very convenient.

Give my best respects to all friends. The boys are going to town for the last time, so good bye. B. B. B.

(CPD, May 2, 1849.)

THE CALIFORNIA EMIGRANTS
Their Movements by Sea and Land

Our Flying Correspondence

BRIG OSCEOLA, RIO JANEIRO, March 13, 1849.

The Perils of the Voyage—Throwing Over the Deck Load—Sad Fate of the Emigrants' Treasures—Incidents—Dinner Party on the Equator—Arrivals at Rio, &c., &c., &c.

The Osceola, James Fairfowl, commander, bound for El Dorado of the nineteenth century, California, dropped anchor in this port, on the 6th inst., after a passage of 47 days from the Capes of the Delaware. During the first eleven days of the passage we encountered a succession of northerly gales, which continued to rage with increased violence until the 29th of January, when the Captain ordered the principal part of the deck load to be thrown overboard, to ease the vessel, as she was straining very much, and, some imagined, in danger of going "down below." With the exception of a few ship's stores, the deck load belonged to the passengers, and consisted of provisions, brandy, and house frames, together with sundry gold washers. Several of the passengers, unfortunately, had their entire freights on deck, consisting of provisions for their subsistence during their stay in California. Poor fellows! they will be in a sad plight on landing in that far-distant country, without provisions, friendless, and almost penniless.

The throwing overboard a deck load at sea, for the purpose of saving the ship, is any thing but pleasant, when nothing but a plank separates one's self from eternity; but during the gale of the 29th January rather an amusing incident occurred, which I shall take the liberty of recording.

While all hands were busily engaged staving in the heads, and throwing overboard brandy, molasses, and vinegar casks, a fellow passenger who had "done the state some service" during the late war with Mexico, and being withal a great lover of the *crather*,[2] caught up from off the deck both hands full of a mixture of brandy, molasses, vinegar, and salt water; and, after taking a draught, exclaimed, at the top of his voice, "Jimmeny, boys, this is first-rate swankey!"[3] The same individual, during the wreck of brandy casks, labored very hard to preserve one from the general wreck, which, on being broached, turned out to be, to his great chagrin, a brandy cask filled with pilot bread!

While the casks composing the deck load were waltzing to one of the airs of that blustering roller, old boteas, two ship's boys and a passenger had their propellers slightly injured. The former are convalescent, but the latter is still hobbling about the deck.

Owing to the crowded state of the vessel, the accommodations both in cabin and steerage are most miserable. When the steerage berths were taken, a table was fitted up for the use of the passengers, at which thirty persons could be comfortably seated, and the steerage was tolerably well lighted by sky-lights. As the Osceola was on the eve of leaving the port of Philadelphia, the steerage table and seats were torn up by order of the owners, and the space occupied by them stowed with cases,

---

2. Any kind of liquor, but Irish whiskey in particular.
3. A fishermen's mixture of water, molasses, and vinegar. An ironic word, apparently derived from 'swank,' meaning luxurious or pretentiously stylish. Swankey is low-grade, no matter how you cut it.

chests, and trunks, a large portion of which belonged to cabin passengers; consequently, during the passage to this port, the steerage passengers have been compelled to mess alternately on chicken coops, pig pens, water casks, and trunks, subjected to almost every inconvenience imaginable; in fact, the vessel has been a perfect *Hades* since she sailed from Philadelphia. The steerage of this vessel contains less than six hundred and fifty superficial feet, and there are forty-four persons, including mates, stewards, cooks, and ship's boys, who sleep in it, being some twelve persons more than is allowed by the laws of the United States to passenger vessels passing through the tropics.

In consequence of the smallness of our camboose,[4] and the limited nature of the other cooking arrangements, our meals have been badly cooked and irregularly served the entire passage to this port. In addition to this, we are cursed with one of the most crabbed and disobliging specimens of human nature (if the term human may be allowed to apply to him) that ever presided over a camboose. I believe there is not one drop of the milk of human kindness in his entire composition. The old adage—"God sends provisions and the devil sends cooks!"—has been fully confirmed, so far as it regards the presiding genius of the camboose of this vessel.[5]

On the 18th February, in latitude 40° 11' south, and 25° 40' west longitude, we discovered a bark to the windward, steering a southerly course. Early on the following morning we exchanged colors with her, and about ten o'clock, A.M., our stern boat was lowered and manned by passengers for the purpose of visiting her. About one o'clock, P.M., our boat returned, bringing some ten or twelve passengers from the stranger—which proved to be the bark Croton, Captain D. V. Souillard, which sailed from New York on the 16th January, bound for San Francisco, California, with 54 passengers on board, destined for the "gold diggings" of that country. The boats were busily engaged during the afternoon conveying passengers to and fro between the two vessels. Some fifteen or twenty of the Croton's passengers dined on board of us, and about the same number of our passengers partook of a collation on board the Croton. Being the first dinner ever partaken by a majority of us so near the domicile of old Neptune, we concluded to drink the old Salt's health; consequently the wine bottle passed merrily around, and wit, sentiment, and song imparted a zest to the scene. Towards night the passengers returned on board their respective vessels, to all appearances well pleased with their first dinner on the Equator.

(NYH, May 4, 1849.)

California Success

The Independence (Missouri) Expositor contains a letter from Mr. T. McClellen, a gentleman of intelligence and veracity, who, with his family, went to California about a year ago. He made the trip out overland, in five months and five days, with the loss of only one animal. He says:

"I brought every species of property I started with, which is worth more here in gold than all I ever was worth put together in my life. I sold, when I landed in the mines, the wagon I bought of Oldham, and three yoke of oxen, for $1,000 in gold, and was offered $1,200 for the other wagon and oxen, but I would not sell it; it is worth as much to me as a steamboat is to its owner

---

4. A cooking shack on the deck of a ship; a substitute galley. Also spelled 'caboose' and 'canboose.' 'Caboose' was applied to the last car of a freight train in the U.S., probably because the two structures looked alike.
5. "God sends meat, and the Devil sends cooks." (John Taylor, *Works*, [1630].)

on the Missouri river. I have given it to young Nottingham, who drove it out, on the halves; he hauls from the Embarcadero, a town laid out at Sutter's Fort, forty miles from the mines, and the head of navigation at this time; the road is better than the road from Lexington to Independence; he hauls from thirty to forty hundred, and the price varies from $20 to $30 per 100 pounds, so that he clears for himself over $50 per day; time in making a trip from four to six days.

"I sold off all my horses—three at $100 a piece. The common prices for horses and mules vary from $100 to $400 per head; a great many sold at the latter price; the great demand is for transporting provisions and tools. I sold the pistols I bought of Henry Childs for $200, and the belt for $75, in gold. I have been in the country some three weeks, and have raised the rise of $3,000 in gold. My little girls can make from $5 to $25 per day washing gold in pans. So soon as we get ready I expect to ship at this port for Jackson county, Missouri, where I expect to spend the remainder of my days in peace and quietness. My average income this winter will be about $150 per day, and if I should strike a good lead, it will be a great deal more. The large majority of persons who have done well here in the mines (and all have done so that have tried) are going back to the States to live, at least nine out of ten.

"You know James M. Harlin; he has just bought a Mexican rancho, for which he has paid in gold $12,000 for the stock and land, averaging the stock at $50 per head, and it is thought that he has made at least $12,000 in the operation, which makes him stand monarch of $24,000; but this is nothing. Jesse Beasley is said to be worth at least $40,000. Governor Boggs has made an independent fortune for all his children. You know Bryant, a carpenter, who used to work for Ebenezer Dixon; he has dug out more gold the last six months than a mule can pack." (WNI, May 4, 1849.)

Ho for California!

St. Josephs, Mo., April 22, 1849.

DEAR PARENTS:—On our arrival in St. Louis we soon found out that there was nothing to be done there—oxen could not be had at all, mules were from $70 to $120—and therefore concluded to start as soon as possible up the Missouri, having heard, too, that everything was at least as cheap, if not cheaper, there than in St. Louis. I believe I wrote in my last letter that we intended to go to Council Bluff; but before we reached this point we changed our minds, and concluded to stop at St. Josephs. It took us 12 days to reach St. Josephs, and would have taken 3 or 4 weeks to arrive at Council Bluff—a terrible long time to be cooped up in an old boat, as our *Mustang* was—and therefore our determination to leave the old critter as soon as possible.

Nevertheless we endeavored to spend our time as pleasantly as we could with shooting, playing, reading, &c. Thousands of swans and geese were daily seen, but comparatively few shot.—The boat was crowded to suffocation with Californians—they could easily be distinguished, as they all have something singular and strange in their appearance, either a monstrous strong beard or eccentric dress. The greatest part were obliged to sleep upon the floor; we were among the number. Every evening the cabin was laid from one end to the other with straw-ticketts, and each company received their place. At precisely 4 o'clock in the morning they were pulled out from under us, and consequently our sweet dreams of the coming El Dorado were most ungraciously interrupted. We have not slept in a bed since our departure from Cincinnati. Fuhrtop thinks he can stand it very well—he was always the first at the table and the first in bed. Curfuerst speaks but little and is growing fat. He says if there is no gold in California, he will return to Cleveland again. Hoeper is living in good hopes and bright anticipations, practices shooting, smokes tobacco, and eats and drinks heartily. But the poor fellow has had severe misfortunes, which for the time being marred and overshadowed his brilliant illusion. His valuable day-book was found minus one morning; another morning his violin, of which we had made him a present, and with which he was to cheer our lonely wandering through the wilderness, was discovered in a sad and deplorable condition, the strings all torn off and the bottom out; the next morning his demijohn of first proof brandy, which had cost him $4.50 in St. Louis, was found emptied, the contents had gone, no one knew whither. Certainly this was enough to make any one desperate; but I suppose these will not be the only losses before we reach the gold regions.

Camp Life

Having arrived at St. Josephs, our duds were thrown head over heels on shore. It commenced raining—the taverns were crowded—consequently nothing remained for us to do but to pitch our tent, and cook our own dinner. We immediately bought us a small sheet-iron stove, with the necessary cooking utensils, and ham, eggs, and bread—made the Professor of Music head-cook, Fuhrtop assistant—and in less than no time had a glorious dinner. We have lived over a week in this way. If it rains hard we get a little wet, to be sure, and feel somewhat chilly, too, these cold nights, but nevertheless this camp-life agrees quite well with us all, and we are as healthy as fish in water.

Mr. Chapman (a Wolverene, and one of our company) and Mr. Curfuerst were in the country a few days ago, and bought us three noble yoke of oxen at $55 per yoke, chains and yoke included. They are a little higher than commonly, but so much better, too. Then we bought a pretty good wagon for $58, when new it cost $65. In fact, nearly every thing is very cheap here, and we did well not to buy our necessaries in St. Louis.

I have bought me a fine pony—the best that could be found—for $25 cash and my trunk; I can sell it again for $45. Bread we brought along, but it can be had just as cheap here. Should I start from Cleveland now, I would buy nothing until I reached this place, and then purchase two mules, and about 100 pounds bread, with some meat, and in this way make the journey.

We are now ready for the start, and only waiting for the grass, which will soon come up if the weather continues as favorable as it has been.

Our squad consists of five; we intend to go with the New York company, being well acquainted with them. There will be about 50 of us in all. I am glad that I do not belong to one of these large stock companies. There is not one that gets along very smoothly—there are too many minds that will not work together,—and many a man wishes himself home, many are going home. There are also whole companies broken up entirely, discouraged and out of means. Others have gambled their few dimes away, and some few breathed their last several days ago—so that probably one fifth will be going back, or at least not going to the gold regions. Our little squad, however, keep up courage, and are determined on going ahead.

You would probably like to know about the number of emigrants collected here. I should think that about 3,000 are encamped in the vicinity of this place. Every day hundreds are leaving with their teams farther north, while every steamer brings two or three hundred, and about four per day arrive. How many are in Independence, I could not say—no doubt as many again—and so they are all scattered along the river. I have no doubt but what there will be 30,000 going in all; how they are going to get forage is as yet a mystery to me. I have prepared myself to foot it should our oxen fail, and put the provisions on our ponies, of which we will get one or two more.

I am writing this letter in my tent,

about half a mile from the village. There is considerable noise about here—every one preparing to start in the morning up the river, on account of the corn being very high here—from $1.50 to $2.00 per barrel.

Do not write to me short of two months, as we may be five or six months on the way, and the letter would lay too long in San Francisco. My best respects to all my friends.   A. ALLARDT.

(CPD, May 7, 1849.)

Late from Chagres—Row between the American Emigrants and the Natives

The Baltimore American has a letter from a passenger on board the Orus, dated Chagres, April 9th, which gives the following account of a serious row which occurred the day previous:

Yesterday, about 1 P. M., several Americans were on shore, opposite the town where all the shipping lies, amusing themselves as best suited their inclinations, and many of the inhabitants of Chagres being idle, (it being Easter Monday,) and both parties indulging pretty freely of ardent spirits, a difficulty occurred between them, which resulted in the Americans being driven from the town and into the river. The natives were armed with knives and cutlasses. Several of the Americans were injured, and as is usual in such a case, those who were injured had nothing to do with commencing the fracas. This difficulty being perceived by the Americans on board the shipping, a call was immediately made to arms, for the purpose of protecting those who were so rudely driven from the town.

The call was immediately responded to, and a descent made on the town. Upon landing, the natives having become quieted, the whole force marched to the residence of the Alcalde and the Commandant, who, as soon as they had learned the cause of the trouble, assured us that they had endeavored in vain to quell the tumult

in the onset. Order was eventually restored by the arrest of several of the principal malefactors, who will be prosecuted and punished according to New Granadian law. Together with the Commandant and Alcalde appeared the Priest of the village. All three of them used every effort in their power to maintain order and tranquillity, and much credit is due these functionaries for their prompt and successful efforts. The American party then retired to their respective vessels and tents.

During the evening several shots were fired from the town, and it was feared some indiscreet Americans had attempted to seek revenge. Three gentlemen were despatched from the steamer "Orus" to the town, which on their arrival they found perfectly tranquil. . . .

We are happy to state that all hostile feelings on both sides have subsided, and every appearance of a mutually friendly feeling now prevails.

We heard from Panama this morning, by a party who had returned from there, that there were at least 3,000 persons at that place, some of whom are encamped about two miles from the city, (not being allowed to pitch tents nearer,) and others at the different hotels, paying $2 per day.

The U. S. mail steamer California had not arrived at Panama three days ago, nor had any other vessel arrived there recently from up the Coast, and how the 3,000 persons now waiting and others almost daily arriving are ever to get away, time will only tell. (PPL, May 8, 1849.)

Movements for California

[From the Louisville Courier, May 3.]

A small flat boat went over the falls yesterday, having on board forty-four New Yorkers. Their destination is California. The boat was built for them at Cincinnati, and has paddle wheels attached. The party take the broad horn conveyance as far as the Arkansas river. From thence they go through Arkansas and Texas.

[Correspondence of the St. Louis Republican.]
INDEPENDENCE, April 20, 1849.

During the last week, more emigrants have arrived at this point *en route* for California than at any previous time for the same period. They generally arrive completely outfitted, except in stock, and this being a principal and indispensable ingredient for an expedition, I will again give you a report of the market at this point, leaving those who are yet behind to avail themselves of any advantage that may be afforded in your city.

The supply of oxen and mules at this place exceeds the demand, and prices range at about my previous quotations—say, for ordinary and good mules, forty to sixty dollars, and choice at seventy to one hundred dollars per head, as in quality and condition.

Many emigrants, in purchasing their stock, are compelled to accommodate themselves to their purses, and in a market where the supply is so large, of course, many inferior lots are offered. Sales of oxen have been made as low as $22 the yoke, and mules at $30 per head, but are not the marketable rates; stock sold at these prices will last just long enough to carry their owners to a point where it will be impossible to replenish; and from the number of such that have been purchased, I fear there will be immense suffering on the Plains and in the mountains during this season. What men are thinking about, or calculating upon, when they provide themselves with such teams for a journey of nearly two thousand miles, is a mystery; yet hundreds are doing so, and even then confining themselves to barely a sufficient team to move their wagon. In my rounds I have met with companies, and not a few, who are provided with large heavy wagons, to which they allow but four mules, or two or three yoke of oxen; the empty wagon itself being a sufficient load for the team allowed, not including the weight of the provisions, &c., which must necessarily be transported for the subsistence of the

party. With such teams, and such a load, they move to the Plains, and if they have good luck and sufficient grass for their miserable stock, they may succeed in reaching a point where it may be impossible to remedy any oversight they have made in their purchase. They here meet with an accident, or their team fails them entirely. What is to be done? They have no remedy, new trains are not to be obtained, and it is impossible for them to proceed.

Dissensions have sprung up in many companies ready to move, resulting, in one or two instances, in a complete dissolution. One of these dissolutions, or winding up of affairs, came near proving fatal to an innocent party. In a recontre between two of the members of the company, Thos. S. Sawyer and Mr. Waters, of Illinois, respecting a balance claimed by Sawyer as due him, shots were exchanged, and a Mr. Alexander H. Baldwin, of Elmira, New York, who chanced to be passing the belligerents at the time, received the contents of a gun, fired by Sawyer, into his loins. Baldwin will recover. Sawyer was arrested; pleaded guilty to an assault, and was fined $1 and costs.

Family Men

Among the number emigrating are many men of families. I have had occasion to converse with many of them, and can assure the wives and families of at least one fourth that they will again return to enjoy the happiness thereby afforded, previous to visiting California. Many have positively determined on such a course; others are wavering, endeavoring to dispose of their outfits. After getting this far on their journey, they find out that at home they have a responsibility—some a wife and "three interesting children," and ranging from that number of responsibilities to "nine;" they discover that, while it is their duty to endeavor by all honorable exertions to provide for, and accumulate "something" to start these "dear ones" in life, they are reckless in the discharge of that duty, and hazarding much, when they run the risks and uncertainties pertaining to a trip to California, in order to accomplish such an end. Hence, they deem it "sensible" to return.

How to outfit—whether to start with mules or oxen—has occasioned much discussion among many companies, and a finely organized company from Massachusetts, fully equipped, excepting in stock, is about to divide upon this very point, both being unyielding for their favorite teams. What young men (the greater portion of whom never saw an ox or mule team before) know of the peculiar advantage of either, and are so well acquainted with them as to threaten eruption, in case their favorite is not selected, is surprising.

Several companies, in addition to those previously forwarded, have gone into camp, and ready to move. Among them is a company from New York, under the style of "German California Mining Company."

While several members of this company were engaged shooting at a mark, a gun in the hands of Dr. F. Wallace was prematurely discharged, by which a young man named Werner Hill was instantly killed—the ball passing through the upper lobe of the left lung. (NYH, May 9, 1849.)

The great Cavalcade for California!

Correspondence of the Missouri Republican
INDEPENDENCE, April 21.

Since my last, nothing worthy of note has transpired in this vicinity. Considering the large number of strangers that are congregated together, the contentions pervading and quarrels arising, and the reckless manner in which fire-arms of all descriptions are used, this is remarkable. To pass among the throng and witness the excitement existing at times among different parties, and hear the deadly threats exchanged, a person would be inclined to call the same way again to ascertain the extent of injury, or who was killed in the affray.

Happily, however, the great majority of such broils end in 'gassing.'

During my sojourn here, curiosity, heightened by the many reports I have heard of the doings of the 'tiger,' induced me, a day or two since, to make my debut into *one* of the gambling houses afforded in this town. In a room thirty by twenty feet, I found about sixty of the curious, congregated around six different tables, some just commencing to pay for a sight of the animal; others endeavoring, by paying more largely, to recover the amounts already contributed for that object, and evidently dissatisfied with the show. I found with some it was a matter of 'make or break'— that they had invested their funds in the concern to such an extent as to render what remained in their pockets of little benefit to them in accomplishing their original purpose—procuring an outfit in order to reach the gold diggins. Several were in this situation, and I left them 'bucking' away, desiring *only* once more to get even, and then they 'would quit.' How they made out I am unable to say. Many that I know and have heard of succeeded so far, in the end, as to lose their all, and were compelled to borrow from their more prudent associates sufficient funds to take them home.

One of these establishments is located on the public square, within a stone's throw of the Court House. So large is the company congregated in this small room, both day and night, that it is necessary for ventilation to keep the windows hoisted. This enables the passer-by and stranger readily to see where his fortune is to be made, while the music of jingling coin attracts his ear, and inclines him to venture in to see the doings. To make the thing more attractive and seducing, at each table will be found some honest looking 'bettor,' who wins heavily—that is, he wins where his bet is the only one made upon a card— and daily and hourly you can hear reports on the street of such a one 'beating the bank out of six hundred or a thousand dollars.' This heavy winner is a 'quiet partner,' and his success is a bait to others. It takes well; and men who never saw a game of 'monte' or 'faro' try their fortunes upon his success. They generally come out minus their all. There is no secrecy about this show—it is boldly opened to all; whether licensed by the corporation or not, I am unable to say.

Ohio has more emigrants in the field, at this time, than any other State in the Union.

In seeking information respecting the outfit of different companies, I have found that provisions for the trip, basing the time at from 100 to 125 days, have been provided by many companies. But few, very few, of the parties going by this route will be able to accomplish the journey in that period, let their calculations at present be what they may. Prudence, if not the necessity of the case, should suggest the propriety of a more ample supply being provided.

Nearly all the companies that have been forwarded you, both from this point and St. Joseph, 'intend to be the first to move to the plains.' This is their calculation, and I have no doubt each will make every exertion in their power to carry it into execution. To be sure of 'being first,' several have already moved as far as Kaw river, are there in camp, and ready to proceed when others appear. This desire to be in the lead will, I fear, cause many to urge their teams beyond their capacity at the start.

Much apprehension is manifested, owing to the immense emigration, that the grass in the vicinity of such places as must necessarily be selected for camping, will prove inadequate, even at the most favorable part of the season, to subsist the stock. Those best acquainted with the country, however, deem it ample for the number that will move this season, yet consider that companies hazard much by a too early start, unless provender is provided. The great majority that move first make no such provision.

The companies you have already published as in camp ready to move, including those given in this communication, comprise 2,500 persons, who will carry at least 3,000 head of stock, in oxen and mules. This body of men, with this amount of stock, intend moving the coming week. Allowing that all succeed in starting, each anxious to out travel the other, it is feared that the young grass they will find near their camping places will prove wholly insufficient, and, aided by tiring marches, tend to reduce their stock. This being done at the start, will retard them greatly in reaching their destination.

The past few days the weather has been pleasant and warm, and vegetation is advancing finely. CALIFORNIA.

(CPD, May 10, 1849.)

Our California Express

PANAMA, Central America
April 1st, 1849.

DEAR FATHER:—I am well, and still waiting for the steamer California. She is now looked for every hour. We expect she has had difficulty in obtaining coal, and if such is the case she is probably coming down under sail. I wrote you that Mr. H and myself had purchased tickets to take passage on her to San Francisco. We were obliged to purchase them from second hands, as no tickets for a steamer can be bought here in any other way. We took them before Mr. Nelson, the American Consul, and he pronounced them genuine—so you will see we are sure of a passage to San Francisco by the California, or any other of the company's steamers that may first arrive. I have now been in this place two weeks, so you will see my patience is being tried a little; but I stand it like a book, and feel first rate. It is very healthy here, and scarce any sickness at all, although there are at least 1,500 persons here from the States waiting to get off for the gold region. A great many who have no tickets for the steamer are getting the *blues,* and are returning home.

There are now no vessels in this harbor, nor has any person any positive assurance that there will be for some time to come. So you can see the chance of getting away soon, except by steam, is very slim. A party of seventy men have gone down to Calin, on the coast of Chili, by the English steamer, in hopes to charter a vessel from that port to take them up to San Francisco. Besides this a party of twelve men are fitting out a large canoe, or dug out, as they here call them, in which they soon intend to embark for California. This canoe is about fifty feet long and very narrow, and in my opinion they cannot carry either provisions or water enough to get one-third of the distance, and if such is the case, they must suffer greatly unless they make some port, which they may not be able to do. Such is the rage to be off and going.

Our board costs seventy-five cents per day, and very good living too. I take a good walk every day round among the ruins of the city and down to the battery. From this place a person gets a most magnificent view of the Bay and many beautiful Islands in it. The whole scenery is very mountainous and volcanic in its appearance. I shall write again before I leave this place.

H. C. SMITH

P. S.—April 4.—No steamer yet.

(CPD, May 14, 1849.)

Late From Panama

Doings of Panama—Interesting letter from Smith—Vessels in Port—Catholics, their Churches and bells—Speech of Col. Weller, &c., &c.

PANAMA, April 15, 1849.

Since my last letter to you bearing date April 4th, several of the Cleveland boys have arrived here, and all are in fine health.—I have now been here three weeks, and no steamer yet; but there are several sail vessels in port and now up for San Francisco. The steamer "California" has now been due five weeks and we hear nothing from her, and it is supposed that the crew have all deserted. I have looked matters all over, and have decided not to wait here any longer for a steamer, so I will tell you what I have done. I have sold my ticket for the steamer at about first cost, and have taken passage on an English brig. Her name is the "Two Friends," she is a fast sailer, and will probably make the passage in 30 or 35 days to San Francisco. The price of passage is $250. This is much better than to wait here any longer upon uncertainties. The brig will sail day-after-tomorrow if the wind shall be favorable. Capt. Wood of Akron, and three other gentlemen from the same place, go on this vessel. I know you will say that I have done right in taking the course I have. I will write you again after I arrive in California. I have made up my mind to take things easy, and put up with what I can't help.

I have seen a great many curious things here, and have passed off my time very pleasantly. The Catholics have great times here, and the bells of the cathedrals are ringing nearly all the time. They had a great time a few nights since, and the Americans were invited to join the procession. Long wax candles were distributed freely to all who wished to participate in the grand come off. The figures of Christ and some of the Apostles, together with the Virgin Mary as large as life, were paraded through the streets, each borne upon the backs of natives, and decked out in the most gorgeous manner, and surrounded by thousands of lights. This scene looked very novel and imposing, and was attended with loud blasts of singing and music, many of the Americans joined in, each carrying a lighted candle. I have made up my mind that if the D—— reigns anywhere, it must be in Panama. Some of the cathedrals have twenty or more large bells in them, and on Sunday they ring them like fury. The noise is perfectly deafening. There is about one church to every three or four houses, and the priests are as thick as grasshoppers.

The natives are the most disgusting set of beings I ever saw. The women as well as the men have cigars in their mouths from morning till night except when they eat. The children here go mostly naked; I have seen more cripples than I ever saw before in my life. I want to see home and all the members of the family, but I formed a resolution to go to California, and if my life shall be spared I shall see the gold region before I return to the States.

H. C. SMITH. (CPD, May 16, 1849.)

Later from California

The New Orleans Picayune has received by way of Mexico advices from San Francisco to the 7th March, as contained in the annexed private letters, written to his partner by Mr. Andrew Garr, of the house of Clifford & Garr, of New Orleans. Mr. Garr was a passenger in the steamer *California* to San Francisco, whence his letters were brought to Mazatlan by Mr. Parrott, who lately went to California as bearer of despatches:

SAN FRANCISCO, MARCH 2, 1849.

I have the pleasure to advise our safe arrival at this place on the 28th ultimo, after a tedious passage of twenty-eight days from Panama. We were detained nearly a week at Monterey, about ninety miles below this, in consequence of being short of fuel; after taking on board twenty cords of wood we arrived here with about two hours' supply of fuel on hand.

I have been on shore but a short time, and am heartily surprised with every thing that I see. Speculation of all kinds is rife, and exceeds any thing I ever witnessed in Mississippi in the palmy days of '36 and '7. Town lots are held at the most exorbitant prices, and every lot-holder is worth from fifty to two hundred and fifty thousand dollars. I have yet had no means of ascertaining the state of affairs generally, as I was prevented from going on shore yesterday in consequence of a severe cold, but cannot but believe that there is an unnatural and fictitious value placed on every thing, which will soon be corrected. Merchandise and labor are extraordinarily high.

There are two or three firms who monopolize the business of the place, whose original employment was selling their goods by retail to the natives and taking their pay in tallow and hides—the former shipped to the United States and the latter to Valparaiso. Since the fever broke out they have used their money in speculation and buying goods from vessels, which arrive in abundance from Mexico, Chili, Peru, the Sandwich Islands, &c.

The steamer will be detained here a month, and perhaps six weeks, for a supply of coal.

There are not houses enough to contain us in the town, and I shall camp out in the neighborhood with some friends who came out in the steamer. Some few buildings are going up, but very few, as carpenters' wages are eight to ten dollars a day. I am writing this in the cold, and my fingers fairly ache. The rainy season, accompanied with cold damp weather, will continue some weeks. This has been the severest winter, however, for years in this country. The rains have been heavy, and the communication with some parts of the mining region cut off. It will yet be a month before parties can leave this place with safety, owing to the snow and mud.

I have some doubts whether the present town of San Francisco will continue to be the place of business. It is situated a few miles from the entrance of the harbor, on the side of a hill; but the great objection to it, as a place of business, is that vessels cannot approach under a quarter to half a mile of the city, owing to a flat which makes off directly in front of it. Vessels are consequently obliged to be lightened, and the goods are again to be shipped up the bay into the interior. There are other sites up the bay more suitable, and I should not be surprised to see an attempt made to change the port.

SAN FRANCISCO, MARCH 7, 1849.

I wrote you a few days since on our arrival, and avail of the detention of the vessel for Mazatlan to give you some items of matters and things in this delectable country. In the first place, so far as one can learn, *the gold stories are all true.* The consequence is, that labor, rents, provisions, &c. are enormously high. Town property for cash is beyond any thing ever heard of in a new country, and lots are selling in this place from five to twenty thousand dollars; rents from five hundred to one thousand dollars per month. Carpenter's wages from eight to ten dollars per day.

The steamer *California* is deserted by every soul except the captain and chief mate, and there is no probability of her leaving under two or three months. This is speculation on my part, for there is no saying when she will get either fuel or a crew.

Fifty to one hundred dollars per day is nothing extraordinary for miners to make. There is, however, some danger from Indians and our own countrymen, prowling about the country committing murder and theft. Gold is very abundant and goods extravagantly high, and an immense population coming forward, who all resort to the mines and return merely to throw away the proceeds of their labor. In fact, I can hardly give you an idea of the state of the country. Those who have been here a year, with common industry and prudence, are worth from twenty thousand to two hundred thousand dollars. I have not been able to procure board in the place, and in company with Mr. Fraser and young Ducros have pitched our tent a quarter of a mile from town. Wages of servants $150 to $200 per month, and in the course of two or three weeks, when it will be seasonable weather to go to the mines, none will be had at any price. You may judge what a state of things exists when common laborers can go to the mines and return in a month or six weeks with from one to three thousand dollars in gold.

(WNI, May 16, 1849.)

The Pacific Mail Steamship *California,*
the first steam vessel to enter San Francisco Bay.

Westward Ho!

Westward Ho!—Letter from the Prairies—The Great Cavalcade in Motion—Oxen, Ponies, Children—Corn Bread and Ham

[Translated from the German
for the Plain Dealer]
ON THE PRAIRIES, 25 miles from St. Jo's.
Across the Missouri, April 30, 1849.

DEAR . . . . . :—This is probably the last letter you will receive from me in a long time. We are now on our winding way, and beyond the boundary of the United States. And I assure that I am glad we have got thus far. It is no small matter to prepare one's self for so long a journey. I have worked every day from 4 in the morning till late in the evening. For in the first place the corn was very scarce, so scarce that I had to go three miles into the country after it, and pay $2 per barrel at that. This I had to carry in on my pony. Then we had to lug in all the necessary articles from town—tend to the oxen—and at last Mr. Chapman got sick, (but is well again now,) and I had to wake with him several nights. You will see that we had not much time to spare.

But our small company, too, is destined to have some difficulty. The best manner to drive the oxen is the great exciting question, and this seemingly insignificant question may yet lead to *terrible* results. Mr. Chapman wants to drive them with kindness and little noise—Curfuerst wants to bring them ahead with much noise and lashes—and Fuhrrop wants to feed them to death—and each one is convinced that his own method is the best, and determined to carry it through; would I not at times intervene, I believe they would get each other by the ears. But I hope that this agitating question will soon be amicably settled. I will make a motion that we elect Mr. Chapman captain of the oxen, as he is the oldest and most experienced ox-tamer—as soon as he gets a little stronger.

I am the huntsman for the company, and must chase the Buffaloes. Prof. Hooper is still head-cook, which post he most admirably fills. He can fix up dumplings to a "T." To-day we had corn-bread and ham, to-morrow we have ham and corn-bread—evenings we have corn-bread and ham—and in this way we intend to have a change each day.

Yesterday we crossed the River, and arrived at beautiful prairies surrounded by woods. Towards evening we pitched our tent on a beautiful spot—in our rear steep hills and small hillocks—before us the green ocean-like prairie, lined in at a distance with the majestic woods—and on our side a stream of the purest water imaginable. The whole area before us is covered with teams, tents, and about 200 oxen, horses, and mules, having nearly the appearance of so many farms.

We have prepared ourselves for every emergency and accident. Should our wagon break, we can make a two-wheeled cart of it, and should this break also, we pack our things on the oxen—and if these too give out—why, then we will have to foot it, and pack as much as we can on our ponies—so that there is no returning back again, at least not for me. And I feel as well as ever I did in my life. I hope you will not be concerned about me—if small children can stand the journey, I think I can.

The only thing I am afraid of is that there will be a scarcity of food for the 30,000 head of cattle, and I believe that two-thirds will have to starve.

Many have taken too heavy wagons, and will never reach their destination. A company of Germans from Cincinnati got home-sick, and returned, selling their things for half price. But, nevertheless, it is a most interesting journey, and I intend to enjoy it as much as possible.

A. ALLARDT. (CPD, May 16, 1849.)

The Californians on the Frontier

The St. Louis "Union" has a letter dated at St. Joseph on the 25th ultimo, which thus speaks of some of the California emigrants from this part of the country:

"There cannot be less than four to five thousand encamped about the neighborhood of St. Joseph. Yesterday morning, per courtesy of Captain WASHINGTON, I visited the Virginia encampment. This company was organized in the neighborhood of Harper's Ferry, under the style of the 'Charlestown (Va.) Mining Company', and numbers seventy-eight members, embracing some of the 'choice spirits of the Old Dominion'. They have twelve tents, sixteen wagons, with a carriage for the sick, two sheet-iron portable boats, a portable forge for blacksmithing, a brass cannon, mounted, and all the necessary implements for mining and smelting, arms, ammunition, &c.

"I repaired to the "Washington Encampment," Captain BRUFF. The metropolitan "boys" do the honors with grace and dignity. Dinner was about ready, and ample justice was done the substantial viands. This company numbers about fifty, and is highly efficient and effective for any emergency. They take up their line of march in about a week.

"I regret to learn, by passengers who returned last evening, of the loss of the steamer Dacotah, on her way to Council Bluffs. I understand she struck a snag and sunk fifteen miles below Fort Kearny. She had on board a large number of passengers, many of them Mormon emigrants, most of whom lost their "little all." I also learn from a gentleman attached to the Fredericksburg (Virginia) Company that they lost all their outfit, provisions, &c., except their wagons and two tents. They appeared, however, nothing daunted, and

are back at St. Joseph beginning over again." (WNI, May 21, 1849.)

Overland Emigration to California

FROM THE ST. JOSEPH GAZETTE OF MAY 4.

Every boat that arrives at the wharf is crowded with emigrants for the gold regions. Within the last few days several hundred wagons have come through by land from Iowa, Illinois, Indiana, Michigan, and Wisconsin. Up to twelve o'clock yesterday there had been eight thousand three hundred and eighteen persons who had made this a point of departure for the Plains; and, from what we can learn, we should not be surprised if five thousand more landed here in twenty days. We also learn that a large number have crossed the upper part of the State, intending to cross the river at the Bluffs—say four thousand persons.

We do not think it extravagant to say that least EIGHTEEN THOUSAND PERSONS will leave the frontier between this place and the Bluffs; and many sestimate the number far above this. We have no means of knowing what number will leave Independence, but should suppose that six or eight thousand will depart from that point. This will make some twenty-five thousand on the Plains in a few weeks. A number of these are destined to perish upon the way, and we fear a large number who have undertaken the trip have not thought properly upon it. Some who have been accustomed to hardships may get along without much difficulty, while others who have never undergone any privations must suffer considerably on the Plains.

Mortality on the Missouri River

FROM THE ST. LOUIS REPUBLICAN OF MAY 12.

From Mr. PAPIN, clerk of the steamer *Highland Mary*, which arrived last evening, we have the following accounts in relation to the cholera on the Missouri. The Highland Mary left St. Joseph on the 8th instant.

Large numbers of emigrants were endeavoring to cross the river, preparatory to their final start for the Plains, and so great was the rush that the two ferry boats, though running all day and most of the night, were inadequate to supply the demand. Five dollars, and even as high as ten, had been paid for the transportation of a single wagon and team.

St. Joseph and the surrounding country is represented as being literally lined with wagons, teams, and emigrants. The health of the place continued good, and but few cases of cholera had appeared. A general move had commenced among the mass; all were anxious to be the foremost.

The cholera was still prevailing to some extent at Kansas [City] and Independence, and both places were nearly deserted. Six or seven deaths from the disease took place at the former place on Wednesday. The steamer Mary was met above Kansas; *thirty-five* deaths had taken place on board since she left this city. The steamer Kansas was met at Independence, and she had lost seven or eight. At nearly every town and village from there down cases were reported, and much excitement prevailed. At several points at which the boat landed no one came on board, and it was rumored that large numbers of the inhabitants were leaving the river for the interior settlements.

At Jefferson City the steamer *Monroe* was laid up, and nearly, if not quite, deserted by her passengers, officers, and crew. A number of deaths had occurred on board. The M. started from this city a few days since with between 150 and 200 Mormon emigrants. Several other boats, bound up, are reported as having had the disease on board.

The weather was pleasant at St. Joseph on the 8th instant, and vegetation was beginning to put forth.

(WNI, May 22, 1849.)

Sutter's Fort

[From the Liberty (Mo.) Tribune—Extra.]

We are under obligations to Col. Doniphan for the following extract from a letter addressed to him by Peter H. Burnett, Esq.:—

SUTTER'S FORT, UPPER CALIFORNIA,
February 2, 1849.

Col. A. W. Doniphan,—I am here at this point, having been attracted hither by the unlimited gold region of California.

Men are here nearly crazy with the riches forced suddenly into their pockets. I have had some opportunity in the course of my life to study human nature, but the school here is upon a grander scale than you or I ever saw before. Perhaps a few anecdotes may illustrate the state of things, and afford you some amusement. An honest, close fisted shoemaker, by the name of Spee, came from Oregon to California about a year ago. After the gold was discovered he went into the mines, and was soon making his hundred dollars a day. A quizzical fellow from Philadelphia met him one day:—

"Well, Mr. Spee, how do you get along?"

"First rate, sir. I would not be a member of Congress with his eight dollars a day, nor the President of the United States. I can make more money than they."

"Well, Mr. Spee, I suppose you will make no more shoes?" Our shoemaker thought himself insulted, and indignantly replied, "No, not I. Let those make shoes who will, I make no more." He is now a merchant, and deals in goods, wares, and merchandise.

I was here during the Christmas holidays, and saw great numbers of young men who had never worn a cloth coat before, with at least one thousand dollars of finery upon them. They were almost loaded down with trinkets. I saw one fellow dressed in a splendid suit of black, over which he wore a superb black cloth cloak; and instead of drawing his cloak around him to shelter him from the cold wind then blowing, he was careful to let it be unfurled, like a flag to the passing breeze, that he might catch the admiring gaze of the passers by. Another gay fellow

Sutter's Fort, 1849.

dressed equally as well, save the cloak, was strutting up and down before the door of a large tavern. In his right hand he held a large bell, and at short intervals he would stop and tingle his bell; as much as to say, "look here! this is me." Another dandy went into a store, took out a fine silk handkerchief, and commenced wiping the mud off his boots. The merchant said "you will spoil your handkerchief, sir." "Oh that's no difference, I have another. I wipe my boots with one and my nose with the other."

Some time during the last autumn a young man was at work in the mines, who had his heart set upon marriage. Whether he had courted the fair one and she had refused his offer, or whether he had always considered himself too poor to take upon himself the support of a family I do not know. At all events he had one day rolled aside, by means of levers and props, a large stone, under which there was a deposit of several hundred dollars of pure gold, in small pieces, the size of flax seed. The moment he cast his eye upon the shin-

ing treasure he threw himself flat upon his back, in an ecstasy, among the rocks, clapped his hands, kicked up his heels, and exclaimed "A married man by gosh!"

Col. you have been through Mexico and elsewhere, but you never saw any thing like the state of affairs here. The accounts you have seen of the gold region are not over colored. About $25 per day is the amount of the produce of one hand. I was in the mines forty days, and was careful to make an accurate estimate. The gold is positively inexhaustible. One hundred millions will be taken out annually in the course of two years. Town lots at San Francisco are worth $10,000 for the best, and no title at that.

Yours, &c. PETER H. BURNETT[1]
   (NYH, May 27, 1849.)

Disturbances on the Isthmus

CORRESPONDENCE OF THE WORCESTER ÆGIS
PANAMA, APRIL, 1849.

The number of Americans has largely increased in this city, and still they come. As might be expected, this tide of adventurers has brought with it a large and constantly accumulating throng of desperadoes, including gamblers and men capable and ready in the perpetration of any outrage. The extent to which gambling and all its attendant vices and crimes are carried on on the Isthmus is beyond all estimate enormous and frightful. At Chagres, at Gorgona, and, above all, at Panama, it is really startling to witness the enormity of these vices. The Governor of this Province has recently issued his public protest against gambling, and in vain has proclaimed the penalty of legal enactments against its indulgence, but the large number of Americans in Panama, and the want of sufficient means to enforce the laws, has completely intimidated the authorities, and rendered their power of no avail. At the present time there is but half a regiment of soldiers in the city, the main force of the army having been withdrawn to mingle in celebrating the election of the new President of the Republic, and the failure of the Governor to enforce the laws against gambling, although the order-loving portion of the American residents signified their willingness to sustain him, has had the effect to embolden reckless and desperate Americans into the commission of new outrages and fresh acts of insubordination.

Shocking Outrages

Along the whole route from Chagres to this city the dangers are rapidly increasing, and outrage and robbery of the boldest character are of daily and nightly commission. These acts are in most cases justly attributed to the blacklegs and those whom losses at the gaming table have rendered reckless and desperate. The number of these is fearfully increasing, and the outrages of the last few days are regarded as indications of a state of things which is rapidly usurping the reign of justice, and a regard for life and property.

Last night, about 12 o'clock, this city was the scene of a gross and shocking outrage committed by Americans, and instigated by two or three of the prominent gamblers. Sunday in Panama is always a holyday among the natives of the country, and a party of respectable ladies and gentlemen of the city were enjoying a cotillion dance, when a gang of half-intoxicated Americans rushed in to break up the amusement. The ball-room was in the main plaza, and but a few doors from our quarters. After the row had fairly commenced, it being about midnight, I went over to the hall to ascertain the cause of the disturbance, and found that the Americans had provoked a regular fight, and that pistols, bowie-knives, chairs, and other weapons were in free use. I should never wish to witness another such scene. Females were fainting, and men were lying upon the floors of the different rooms in almost every direction, some slightly and others badly wounded, and both the hall and the balconies outside were literally smeared with blood. The military were soon on the ground, and had not the disturbance nearly subsided as they were marched up, they would probably have killed every American who participated in the outrage.

I think some fifteen men were stabbed, some of them very badly. One of the natives died this morning, and another is but just alive. Some of the Americans were severely wounded, and one of them, a leading blackleg, was followed home by a Spaniard whose brother he had stabbed, and when upon the very steps of his own quarters, the Spaniard rushed upon him and made three or four shocking gashes on

---

1. Peter Hardeman Burnett (1807–1895), California's first civilian governor, serving from December 1849 to January 1851. At the time of this letter he was acting as business agent for Sutter's son.

his head and neck, one of which cut off nearly the whole of his nose! The night's outrage was also attended by several other scenes of violence in the streets, in which natives and Americans were engaged in bloody strife. I have just learned from the Government interpreter that a special messenger has been dispatched to Bogota for two regiments of soldiers, and that means will be taken to bring the perpetrators of this outrage to justice, and to enforce the laws of the country so soon as the soldiery shall arrive. Thus stands the matter to-day.

It is but fair to state that all reasonable Americans in Panama are unsparing in their condemnation of such violence towards those who have, on every occasion, manifested the utmost courtesy and forbearance, and especially towards a Government which has extended every civility and privilege to us foreigners, while passing through or residing within its territory. On the other hand, I have heard the most desperate threats made by Americans in the streets of Panama to-day, that the first arrest of one of their countrymen should be the signal for burning the city! Such foolhardy threats, however, are worthy of little regard, though the Americans here are armed to the teeth, and should an outbreak actually occur, there would undoubtedly be witnessed some scenes of brutal and bloody violence.

The last two weeks have witnessed an increase of sickness among the American residents in Panama, owing mostly to imprudence, exposure, and excesses of various kinds. Two Americans have died during the past week, both of whom were members of a company from the State of New York, and both were married men, one leaving a family at home consisting of a wife and six children, and the other a wife and three children. The funeral services of these two individuals, whose deaths were the result of exposure to the heat of the climate, were attended on two successive days, and were solemn and affecting scenes to every American in Panama. It is now the midst of the sickly season in this country, yet while a considerable number of Americans are down with fevers and other diseases, the natives are the greatest sufferers and are dying in much greater numbers. The city, however, is not more sickly than Worcester usually is in July. The rainy season is already commencing in the neighboring mountains, where showers are to be seen at almost every hour in the day. Only one has yet reached Panama, but the rain is beginning to be constant on the other side of the Isthmus, and the Chagres river has risen two feet in the last eight or ten days.

P. S.—A detachment of soldiers has just arrived in the city from Toboga, in answer to a summons from the Governor this morning. The Spaniard referred to in the foregoing account of last night's outrage is under arrest, but no Americans have yet been arrested. A very similar outrage took place on Sunday week at Chagres, an account of which will probably reach you before the receipt of this letter.

PANAMA, APRIL 26, 1849.

Sickness and death are rapidly increasing among the Americans in Panama. Five have died during the last three days. Yesterday evening a funeral procession of Americans passed our quarters bearing two coffins, containing the remains of two of their comrades who had died during the previous night. While I write this morning another procession is passing my window with the body of a physician from New York. Behind the cortege are walking two of his party with shovels to dig the grave and bury the dead. These are melancholy scenes, which we cannot look upon without the most thrilling and vivid remembrances of home and its loved ones. Such scenes, however, are to be expected among so large a number of Americans, most of whom have been so suddenly transferred from a cold winter at the North to the hot and oppressive atmosphere of this climate, and who, as a body, pay little regard to the means best adapted to preserve health during the process of acclimation in a country where a disease is so easily engendered and so difficult to arrest. It is a singular fact that a large proportion of the recent deaths among Americans in Panama has occurred in companies hailing from the State of New York. The last six deaths have been those of New Yorkers, and two more Americans from the same State are now lying at the point of death.

The month of May will most probably witness a great increase of sickness among Americans who may unfortunately be detained here, as the dry season is closing on this side of the Isthmus, and the rainy season, whose commencement is said to be most fatal to foreigners, is rapidly hastening on. It should be remembered by all who take the Isthmus route that a very large proportion of the mortality among foreigners here is the result of exposure or of eating too freely of fruits, both of which causes are almost sure to produce fevers, which, if not immediately checked, are either fatal or of long duration.

The disturbances between the Americans and the natives, of which I wrote you on Tuesday, have had the effect to produce a feeling of mutual hostility, from which more serious consequences are apprehended. Since the bloody outrage of last Sabbath night, in which the Americans were the aggressors, scarcely a man is seen in the streets unless armed with some weapon of defence. At night nearly every native carries a heavy bludgeon, one end of which contains a pound or more of lead. It is a savage instrument, but will hardly stand a brush with revolvers and bowie knives, which I am sorry to say are most provokingly displayed upon the persons of reckless and unprincipled Americans. The natives, if well treated, are the most harmless and civil people I have ever seen; and, though no American here mingles more freely with them than myself, I have never carried a single weapon, and have always found kind treatment a sure pro-

tection. The city is now under the surveillance of a military patrol at night, and it is creditable to a large body of the American residents that they manifest a determination to sustain the authorities, and to discountenance every appearance of insubordination and outrage on the part of their countrymen.

The Editor of the "Panama Star" chronicles the recent departure of a vessel from Panama for San Francisco, and on the margin of the paragraph writes "so with all:"

"The *Two Friends* left port for San Francisco on Wednesday night, having some one hundred and fifty-six passengers aboard, exclusive of crew. She was put up to carry one hundred and twenty. The wonder is, where such a mass of men can lie, stand, or be hung up in the concern! The wonder will be greater, however, if half the passengers ever see land again, unless it is down

"Full forty thousand fathoms deep," among coral caves and shelving rocks. For, cribbed and jammed together, as they were, like cattle in a railroad car, or slaves in a pirate ship, if pestilence and fevers do not make many of them food for sea-monsters, long ere they reach their destination, they may thank nothing less than Providential interference."

(WNI, May 28, 1849.)

A Sick Californian

A young printer, who, with a number of friends, left Rochester (N. Y.) for California, embarking in ship Tahmaroo at New York, writes from the island of St. Catherine's to the Rochester American, under date of March 9, as follows:

"I am glad to be once more permitted to cast an eye on terra firma. Our passage has been one of hardship. Here we are, two hundred and ten persons, cooped up in a ship of 340 tons burden. There is hardly room to lay one's self out straight; in fact, it is impossible to describe to you the miseries of a ship bound to California. The passengers are crowded and jammed together in a small compass, with all sorts of people, such as compose a great city like New York. Every one is compelled to keep his clothing, and every thing he has, under lock and key constantly, or else you may look for it in vain. To sum up the whole matter, I would rather suffer three years' imprisonment in the State prison, at hard labor, than a voyage to El Dorado. Advise all who are bound to the gold regions to cut their wind-pipes rather than undertake a voyage to California.

"Others have found to their hearts' content that a voyage to the gold regions is far different from what they anticipated. Never did I think I should have an opportunity to see those who led off the fashions in the gay city of Rochester crying at the pantry door of a ship for something that they could eat. Salt meat and hard bread make hard living for those who are not used to such fare." (WNI, May 18, 1849.)

Immense Lumps of the Precious Metal
The Excitement in Wall Street

The steamship Southerner, Capt. Berry, arrived yesterday morning from Charleston, whence she sailed on Saturday last.

Among her passengers is Lieut. Edw. F. Beale, of the United States Navy. He left San Francisco on the 14th April, in the steamer Oregon, and arrived at San Blas on the 22d, where he remained five days, coaling. He left San Blas on the 27th, and arrived at Panama on the 6th May, at 9 P.M., after touching at Acapulco for water.

On the 7th, he arrived at and left Chagres in the bark Florida, and arrived at New Orleans on the 21st.

Thence he took the mail route to Charleston, and thence came to this city in the Southerner, *thus performing the passage from San Francisco to New York in forty-four days, the quickest trip on record. He crossed the Isthmus in seventeen hours.*

The arrival of Lieut. Beale, in the Southerner, with this late news from California, *with a lump of gold weighing eight pounds,* threw Wall street into a state of the greatest excitement and delight. Mr. Aspinwall, of the house of Howland & Aspinwall, was surrounded with crowds of eager brokers and merchants, all curious to catch a glimpse of the eight pound lump. There was no mistake about it. Here was the pure gold fresh from *El Dorado.*

We learn that Lieut. Beale has in his possession a watch, encased in a big lump of pure California gold, $23\frac{1}{2}$ carats fine, with a brass cable chain, with large lumps of gold attached to every other link, hammered in in the roughest and richest profusion. Big lumps of gold were hammered together around the watch, till the whole, excepting the face, was encased in the precious metal. The key was a "chunk" of gold, with the pipe inserted in it for use. Altogether, it was one of the ugliest looking, and richest, and most valuable watches in existence.

Poor Beale was pestered to death, with the crowds anxious to hear from California, and to see his lump of gold, &c., &c. He was glad to get out of the city, and left in the train at half-past four o'clock yesterday afternoon, for Washington.

(NYH, May 30, 1849.)

[Correspondence of the Albany Atlas]
SAN FRANCISCO, March 4, 1849.

The Bay of San Francisco is very large and very beautiful. I am much disappointed in the situation of San Francisco. The land about it consists of sand hills, very rough and irregular, and covered with thick scrubby brush. It will require a vast deal of digging and levelling before any kind of a city can be made out of it.

This place contains some 200 houses, many of them unfinished, and a very few of them quite respectable buildings. There are also about one hundred tents, and about the place here there are now probably three or four thousand people. Some have remained in the mines all winter, and many are going out continually. A new hotel, known as Parker's Hotel, kept by R. A. Parker, formerly of Boston, fronting the plaza or public square, is the finest building in town. The City Hotel is an old building, which has been much enlarged in the rear by adding on a great number of rooms above and below. The rooms, like most of the new houses in town, are not plastered inside, and the wind whistles through, seeming only to gather wrath from the slight opposition.

The cold here is very excessive. The oldest inhabitants say that they have never known a winter like it. We have had considerable rain since we have been here,

and probably will have more. Day before yesterday it rained and snowed, and the next morning the hills all around the place were covered with snow, a sight which the residents here have never before witnessed, except upon the distant mountains. I eat now with Mr. T. and his party, who have a room and who cook for themselves. I am partially connected with them, but shall not remain with them. Some of them are professed gamblers, who live by gambling, and I wish no fellowship with them. Apropos to gambling: It is about the only business done here. The hotels are filled with gambling tables of every description, and hundreds of dollars are being won and lost continually.

Those who have returned from the mines do nothing but wander about, or gamble. They will not work at all. I can obtain a situation immediately that will insure me $1,200 a year, but am looking about for something better. Law business in a short time will be very plenty. I can of course say nothing now about returning, as to when or how. Lots here, which a year ago were bought for $10 and $15, are now

Parker House and Dennison's Exchange, 1849.

worth as many thousands. The lowest even among the sand hills sell for $500. Drugs and medicines sell most enormously high. Eggs are worth $6 a dozen.

If my health and life are spared, I shall bring home a few thousands, if not more.
(NYH, May 30, 1849.)

[From the Philadelphia Bulletin]
SAN FRANCISCO DE ALTA CALIFORNIA,
March 4, 1849.

Here I am in the golden country, and really a golden country it is; for I never, in my life, saw as much gold as I have seen in the five days since my arrival. At Valparaiso we were attacked so strongly with the gold fever that we left in a mass; that is, about 1,200 of the best and most active men of Chili, native and foreign, left the country and are now all here. A proportionate number from each other port has arrived, and about 25,000 over land.

I would like, if I had time, to give you some of the forty thousand accounts of persons who have been to the mines. The poorest man in this place can show from $500 to $1,500 in gold dust, that he has gathered by his own hand in a month or so. Some have found, in three months time, as much as $15,000 to $20,000; but they have been fortunate. No one, with the least labor, finds less than $15 to $20 per day; and by persevering and the least good luck, one may find from $50 to $100! This is truth. I could tell you the names of persons innumerable who, eight months ago, were not worth $100, who are now worth $100,000. Some, by good speculation, have amassed from one to two millions in that space of time.

Money has been made to an immense amount by purchasing at the mines gold dust at $3 to $8 the ounce, which sells here at $15 to $16. The consequence is that everybody goes to the mines—carried away by the excitement.

A common servant in a private house gets from $100 to $150 per month, and they are very independent at that. You go into a hotel and ask for breakfast; if the cook is gone (for he stays only one hour at each meal time) you get a slice of cold meat, bread, probably no coffee or tea, certainly no milk—and you pay $1; also $1.50 for a dinner of rice soup, a piece of very poor roast beef, and potatoes—all these eaten off a table of bare boards. Bottled ale is $2, brandy $3, wine $5, tolerably good; segars (very poor) three for 25 cents. Loaves of bread, worth at home 5 cents, sell here for 25 cents. A house which cost $70 in Valparaiso ready to put up, sold here for $2,300.

I am sleeping in a garret, two in a bed, and consider myself quite lucky, as people are living in all kinds of things—tents, empty hogsheads, &c.
(NYH, May 30, 1849.)

[From the Salem Register, May 28]
SAN FRANCISCO, March 6, 1849.

All you can possibly have heard is a bagatelle to the reality! Any report, I had almost said, is hardly possible to exaggerate. The tributaries of the Sacramento, particularly the American fork, the Feather river, the Mukelemnes, and Stanislaus, as far south as the San Joaquin and its tributaries, are full of gold diggings or washings—embracing, as far as is explored, an area of from five to six hundred miles in length and two hundred in breadth. Every one who goes up, comes back with a little competency. The gold, however, is the least part of the affair; the country is immensely rich in silver and quicksilver mines, and its capabilities for agriculture magnificent. In the interior it is very mild, and the soil is exceedingly rich and productive. It abounds with deer, elk, antelopes, wild horses, geese, canvass back ducks,—in fact, game of all descriptions.

But I wish particularly to call your attention to the great field for speculation. Furniture is a good article, as you may judge from the fact that lumber is only worth $600 a thousand, and carpenters earn from $15 to $30 a day. A pine table is worth from $12 to $20. This will be the case for a long time to come. Probably the gold is inexhaustible; at all events, it cannot give out in a hundred years; and while this state of things exists, labor will be very dear. A common servant earns $40 to $100 a month. No salary, hardly any profession, pays so well as digging, except it may be trading at the mines. Seamen run away, and are hard to get at $75 per month. Freights on the Sacramento, &c. are enormous—from $9 to $15 the cwt. Barges running between this port and different points vary from $1,000 to $1,200 net profits monthly. Of eatables and drinkables, too much cannot be brought. Frame houses are an excellent article for speculation. Thousands upon thousands to occupy them are arriving, and will arrive. Provisions of all kinds are enormously dear, and houses will be in demand for years, for the reasons I have given about labor—not for San Francisco alone, (for I do not think this will be the spot—Beneficio [Benicia] is considered the place,) but for different places on the coast and bay. Of provisions, I would recommend hams, cheese, pickled mackerel, halibuts' fins, salt codfish, (it sells enormously,) and preserved meats of all kinds. Salt pork is selling now for $60 a barrel. I do not think you can fail in making, on these articles, 100 per cent. People here are making 300 to 500 per cent on Valparaiso prices. Champagne here flows like water, to the tune of $4 per bottle.

Dried and preserved fruits of all kinds will always command an immense price, from the fact that none are raised, and they are much esteemed for the miners. Walnuts a dollar a pound, here in the town—at the mines $3. Figs are a splendid article, if they could be got here in good order.
(NYH, May 30, 1849.)

[From the Nantucket Inquirer]
SAN FRANCISCO, March 6, 1849.

Here I am in California, where gold is so plentiful that the veriest loafers go about with pockets full. I arrived here from Callao on Saturday, February 24, and the next day I came on shore to see if I could find any one I knew, and also to get a place to board. In cruising about, I naturally went into a building where I saw many persons congregated. It was the —— hotel, and there were not less than five tables where gambling was going on in every variety; gold ounces and silver dollars in abundance. I stopped but a few moments, and the next hour and a half was passed in a place perhaps more to your satisfaction. Passing by a small building about twenty feet by thirty, I heard the voice of prayer, and entering, found a congregation worshipping, consisting of about sixty persons. An orthodox minister is stationed here, with a salary of twenty-four hundred dollars a year.

I found houses very scarce, and board fourteen dollars per week. I did not succeed in finding a place to live in, and so returned to the ship. On Monday I came on shore again, and having fallen in with Mr. Peter F. Ewer, he introduced me to his landlord, who wished immediately to engage me to work for eight dollars per day, and to board me for fourteen dollars per week. As I was desirous to procure a place to lodge, I agreed to work for him till the first day of April, and make a commencement to-day.

There have arrived here, within a few days, by the steamer California and other vessels, nearly six hundred passengers, and the Lord only knows where they will find shelter, although parties are daily going to the mines. To give you some idea how much small craft are in demand to go up the river, I assure you that whale boats will sell here for from five hundred to one thousand dollars a piece. This is a fact. I know two men who bought a whale boat for $500, and in six weeks made, by carrying passengers from vessels to the shore, upwards of $2,500.

Tell Charles, if he can raise the money, to have a plain cottage house framed, and all the work done for it, inside finish and all, and send it out, and come himself across the Isthmus. A plain story and a half house, with a porch, such as would cost at home seven or eight hundred dollars, will bring here at least four thousand dollars. At the present time it would sell for eight thousand dollars cash, landed on the beach, without putting up. The best things to be sent out here for the present, and for a long time to come, will be small frame houses. Lumber, to-day, is six hundred dollars per thousand. Bricks there are none. Accordingly, in sending out houses, bricks must be sent with them for chimneys. Tell Charles to take no thin clothes with him, but good thick ones; also thick boots and shoes, and plenty of rubbers. If he should bring or send several cases of rubbers, he could get from four to six dollars a pair for them. It will be of no use for him to bring out his daguerreotype apparatus, as people here have other business to think of.

(NYH, May 30, 1849.)

Interesting Descriptions of Central America—Customs and Manners of the People —Incidents of Travel, &c.

PANAMA, April 12, 1849.

J. W. GRAY, Esq.—

DEAR SIR:—As information in regard to the Isthmus route to California may not be uninteresting to your readers, I improve the present opportunity of placing at your disposal my fortnights' experience on this portion of my journey. Myself, with one hundred and twenty others, sailed from New Orleans on the 12th day of March, on the brig Major Eastland, and after a tedious voyage of nineteen days anchored off Chagres. Three days after sailing, Thomas Lynch, of Toledo, O., an Irishman, died of Cholera, after six hours sickness, and was consigned to the deep. Within twenty minutes after death the body was sinking in the blue waters of the Gulf. The ceremony

was one of deep solemnity, and for a time cast a gloom over all.

On Friday the 18th, at sunrise, we saw the island of Cuba, and ran down the coast all day, and at dark Cape San Antonio was still on our larboard bow. For five or six hours we were in the midst of extensive reefs of coral, and at one time were in imminent danger of shipwreck. The vessel struck about amidships and went grating over a huge rugged rock within six feet of the surface, doing no other damage, luckily, than awfully frightening all on board. Had a heavy sea been running, our destruction would have been certain. The land, so far as we could see, was one unbroken forest, but two houses being in view, and the remains of an old Spanish fortification.

On Saturday morning, March 31, we came to anchor off Chagres, and two hours later were towed into harbor by the steamship Orus.

The appearance of the country is very different from what I had been led to suppose. Instead of being flat and low it is high and somewhat broken, but covered with a dense coating of vegetation, green and beautiful almost to the water's edge. The shores for many miles run nearly north and south, bending a little inward towards the mouth of the river. To the south they are rocky and in many places perpendicular to a considerable height, but to the north with the exception of some sharp bluffs running out, they are sand beach. On the south side of the river, at its mouth, on a high promontory of solid rock, stands an old Spanish fortification of considerable dimensions. The position is a commanding one, the approaches to it apparently difficult, and in the hands of Yankees I should think would be impregnable. On the opposite shore lie the wrecks of three vessels. The town is entirely hidden by the fort, and there is little indication of its existence from the anchorage.

Saturday and a part of Sunday I spent in visiting all that could be found interesting. The city of Chagres lies immediately behind the old fort. It contains about one hundred and twenty-five houses, and presents a very novel appearance. The houses are built in uniform rows, each dwelling standing detached and alone; they are composed of cane, generally without floors. Posts are set in the ground for a superstructure, and the spaces between are filled with bamboos standing upright, fastened to their places by thongs of the same material. The roofs are formed in the same way, and are covered with the long and narrow leaves of a species of cabbage tree, which are impervious to rain. At a distance they resemble very closely stacks of cornstalks.

The natives are composed of all shades of color, and are a mixture of Spaniards, Negroes, and Indians. From indications, the next generation will be a different kind of mixture. Their clothing is of a rather more airy character than very refined people at home would consider proper. The men wear a shirt and pantaloons—the women a chemise and petticoat, generally of linen, neat and clean, and the children are in the garb of Adam before Eve was tempted. The women very often dispense

with the chemise, and the men while engaged in labor wear nothing but the breech-cloth. Los Americanos are welcome in every house, and all keep something to sell, but generally nothing more than brandy, cigars, and coffee. Their diet is very simple, and they must live from hand to mouth, as they raise little or no fruit, and keep very few domestic animals.

The Work of Old Spain

The old fort is well worth a visit. As its dilapidated situation permitted I visited every part of it. It is a colossal structure, and one day was a magnificent work. The space it covers is, probably, an acre and a half, and is approachable only on the land side by a narrow way, which is again protected by a smaller work standing a short distance off, on a more elevated plateau of ground. The masonry work is nearly entire, the only symptoms of decay being in the brick work which forms the coping of the walls, the sentry boxes, and some portion of the buildings.

The wooden trucks of the cannon have gone almost entirely to decay, and the huge guns lie scattered around, the iron ones deeply corroded, and those of brass yet smooth and complete. They are large

Chagres, from the old fort.

beautiful pieces, splendidly ornamented with various devices, and bear date A. D. 1743. Pyramids of balls and shells are piled around, and the magazine is filled with very old and worthless powder. In one of the vaults there was a heap of ancient and clumsy wagon axles—another was filled with tiles. The prison rooms, though considerable in dimensions, looked very gloomy; they were lighted by a single grated window each, high up, looking out upon the ocean, from which there could be no escape with life. This fortification is, of course, the work of old Spain, and is one of the many monuments of her ancient greatness, and a standing and melancholy memorial of her present fallen condition.

The grave yard is situated near by, where lie the remains of Americans who have perished in a strange and distant land. The only memorial of the dead to be found is erected to the memory of Dr. Horace Smith, of Newark, Ohio, who died March 25, 1849, aged 23 years. It is a planed board, painted white, and rudely lettered in black. Simple as is the monument of our deceased countryman, it addresses a silent but eloquent appeal to those who have left friends in their distant homes. But I shall tire you by spinning so long a yarn. In my next I will give you an account of our trip to this city.

Yours, &c. DEACON.

Incidents Across the Isthmus

PANAMA, April 14, 1849.
J. W. GRAY, Esq.,

DEAR SIR:—In my letter under date of 12th inst., I gave you a short account of the town of Chagres, and I will now endeavor to give you a description of our journey to this city. We were greatly disappointed in learning that the steamboat Orus did not, nor never had, run either to Cruces or Gorgona. She is perfectly useless on the river, running up only fourteen miles, and I doubt whether she will ever be able to reach a higher point even during high water. It is a very crooked and, above fif-

teen miles, rapid stream, and can only be navigated with canoes, plied by vigorous arms. The Orus charges ten dollars passage and three dollars a barrel bulk for freight through to Gorgona. The natives are from two to five dollars cheaper, perform the trip in a little more time, and receive our money at a higher rate. In Chagres, American, Mexican, Spanish, and other coins of like value, as also five franc pieces, pass for one dollar and a quarter—dimes for reals, and francs for two reals, but I would recommend to all who deign to cross the Isthmus to procure dimes, half dimes, francs, or half francs only. In Gorgona and Panama neither gold nor silver coin are worth more than eight dimes for the dollar; doubloons are worth seventeen dollars, also eight dimes to the dollar.

On Sunday morning, April 1, we succeeded in hiring three canoes for forty-eight dollars, which contained our company, six persons, with all the baggage. The contract was written by the Alcalde, one half the money paid to him, and the balance was to be paid to *Seignor le Capataine* on the completion of the journey. The possession of so much money overcame his reason, and he imitated many of his white brethren by getting gloriously drunk, leaving us for three hours to broil in the hot sun on a mud bank where we could not reach shore.

Buzzards and Cockroaches

About 12 o'clock we pushed off and left Chagres, with its thousands of buzzards, its miserably lean pigs and leaner dogs behind. The river is about fifty yards wide, very deep, and maintains a uniformity of depth and width, with a quiet current, up to our stopping place for the night. The banks are high and steep, and every where covered with a perfect mat of vegetation. We made about twelve miles and stopped at a small native village—Brown and myself paid three reals each to sleep under shelter. Our host invited us to climb a pole to the loft where we lay down on our blankets and tried to sleep. Brown's fears were that we should break through the bamboo floor, and in a half waking state I thought only of scorpions. After a running fight with cockroaches, I went off into the land of dreams, and slept soundly till morning.

The two following days we made but about twenty-six miles. Paddles were entirely dispensed with, and poles only used. The whole distance was a succession of rapids, and it is with great labor the natives are enabled to force the canoes along. The river gradually becomes contracted, and in fact dwindles down to a mere creek, resembling much the streams of northern Pennsylvania. Its banks are generally high and steep, sometimes running up into peaks of five or six hundred feet in height, everywhere covered by a dense and almost impenetrable thicket of vegetation.

In the early morning we saw many species of the feathered tribe, with gay and beautiful plumage—parrots were plenty—monkies were playing on the trees, and very often the howl of the tiger could be heard; alligators are said to be plenty, although we saw none. During the afternoon of Tuesday we footed it in a cattle path up the left bank of the river, crossed over, and

put up for the night at a small village. Although the country presents a more settled aspect, still we passed not more than four or five houses during our walk. Cattle were plenty, of a handsome size, fat, and almost all of a dun color. One native told us he owned fifty cows, and yet we could not get any milk; they scarcely ever use it. We bought two yards of pork, cooked it by the light of a full and brilliant moon, ate it with our hard bread, with uncommon relish, bartered our English with a *Senora* for a limited amount of Spanish, talked till a late hour of our homes, wives, children, and friends, and turned in and took two reals worth of sound sleep on the ground floor of our hospitable host.

To Gorgona, a distance of six miles, we walked along a pretty fair trail, up the right bank of the river, and reached the town at nine o'clock. It is a larger place than Chagres, and contains a few old Spanish stone buildings with tile roofs. The situation is very pleasant, and the elevated table of land on which it stands is pretty extensive, and the ten or fifteen acres of cleared commons form a fine camping ground. The whole space was white with tents, the inmates of which were engaged in a variety of occupations, some cooking,

Passing a rapid on the Chagres River.

others eating, washing dishes, cleaning guns, pistols, and bowie-knives. The whole formed a striking and novel scene, and no one could regret becoming a portion of this mass of oddity. We pitched our tent, and for the first time slept under our own roof—our blankets were spread down on the ground, and the whole six of us turned into one bed. I got crowded into an inequality of the ground, slept badly, and next morning got up with a terrible backache.

Here I made my first real essay at cooking: my eyes sympathized with the smoke, I sweat terribly—but the boys pronounced the bean-soup superb, the coffee delicious, and our two yards of beef well cooked, but rather tough. Yours,

DEACON.   (CPD, May 31, 1849.)

From California

The following copy of a letter has been placed in our hands by Col. GRIFFIN. The writer is well known in this city and vicinity, and what he says *he has seen* can be relied on.—*N. Y. Express.*

CITY OF MEXICO, APRIL 15, 1849.

Here we are safe and sound, after a travel of fifteen days from Vera Cruz, the road being very bad and our wagons very heavy. After arriving here, finding that we could sell our wagons for a good price, and buy horses, we have done so, and have shifted the most of our baggage to Acapulco, to go from thence up the coast to San Francisco. We expect now to get along faster and more comfortably, and of course cheaper. We have had no trouble of any kind in coming, except that a party of robbers blocked up the road on the left of Rio Frio mountain one day, and waited for us, but when they saw what a savage looking party we were they started off, and we saw no more of them.

There are *three men* here on *their way home from California* with THREE HUNDRED THOUSAND DOLLARS WORTH OF GOLD with them, which they have made in *one year*, and

which THEY SHOWED US. The news they bring is better than ever, and our spirits are first-rate, and our courage equal to any thing that may come. Two or three of our party have had the fever and ague, and I have been doctoring them with the Tonic Mixture, which cures them right off.

Yours, F. C. WHITEHEAD.

(WNI, May 28, 1849.)

A New Play

The gold-diggers of California furnish the argument for a capital hippodramatic performance at Astley's. It is called "The White Maiden of California; or, the Horse of the Ocean." Some of the scenes and grouping are well presented, picturesquely managed, that their tendency may be mischievous. Especially that where the Indian or Yankeian maidens dig for ore, wash it, display it, and smile and caper at their success, their "gold for the gathering." The fear is that London at large may be thereby tempted to emigrate to California.

The plot turns upon the adventures of a *White Maiden*, who was saved from wreck by the "horse of the ocean" swimming ashore with her when a barque was foundering; the way in which the animal is seen breasting the surge is one of the triumphs of the piece; the maiden is in trouble, indeed in many troubles, among the Indians, but remains true to her love, Lieut. Waller, and is united to him at last, when the gold-seekers triumph over the savages, and virtue is rewarded amidst many colored fires—an exquisite tableau, which drew forth long and loud applause. Equally admirable is the gathering of the white warriors and their steeds in a gold cavern; gloomy and shadowy contrasting with the occasional sparkle of gold. The way, moreover, in which the horses of the Indians are shown to carry bags of the gold dust from the diggins could be given nowhere but at Astley's. (ISJ, May 30, 1849.)

Ever Onward

The Fleet at Panama—Joyous Times—Clevelanders in Luck— They Sail! They Sail!

PANAMA, April 18, 1849.

J. W. GRAY, Esq.,——We left Gorgona, after a stay of two days, on the 6th inst., at daylight, on our way here. About two miles from town the road winds around the base of a hill, on the top of which a flag is flying, indicating, as we were told, a position from which both oceans can be seen. I desired much to visit the spot, but climbing up the rugged ascent would have been a severe task, and without any deviation we knew there lay before us a long and weary day's travel.

The road, although one of the oldest in the country, is nothing more than a mere path only wide enough for a single animal, and is quite impassable in any other than the dry season. It runs generally along the base of the hills, although considerable elevations are occasionally attained, where huge loose stones cover the ground, and every two or three miles it crosses a small stream of cool water, which, during the rainy season, appear to be torrents.

No country was ever more libeled abroad than this. Instead of presenting the miserable aspect represented, the landscape is everywhere one of extreme beauty—high, broken, the hills steep, and sometimes rugged, and occasionally glimpses can be had of a dozen peaks at a glance, their tall, cone-shaped forms standing in full relief against the blue sky, and everywhere covered with an almost impenetrable growth of deep green vegetation. It has been represented as impossible to foot it over this road, that it ran over rocks, declivities, deeply indented by the mule travel of two hundred years, and that to attempt the journey on foot would be a desperate undertaking. We adopted this method from choice, and performed the distance, twenty-six miles, in about nine hours, including stoppages—a Scotch lady, the day previous, had the courage to do the same thing. These exaggerated accounts must have been written by weakly young men, both mentally and physically, who ought to have been kept tied to their mothers' apron strings; a few of them are now loose around Panama.

Beasts of Burden

Very few houses are seen on the road, but in the neighborhood of water a good many tents are pitched, where Yankees furnish refreshments to travelers, generally in the way of something to drink. The skeletons of horses are strewn along the whole distance: the number is very great, and they have been left to die just where they gave out. Those living are wretched, jaded beasts, very small, and nothing but skin and bones; they are kept constantly on the road till worn out, which is but a very short time. They carry but about one hundred and fifty pounds, and most of them are overburdened with that weight, although they are generally two days in going through. I saw very few mules, probably because they cannot be got. The natives transport, on their backs, a large amount of freight, and they can carry nearly as much as the horses—their largest loads are half barrels of pork, whiskey, or beef. The cost of transportation is heavy: ours cost us four dollars and thirty-one cents per hundred, but this is lower by two dollars than many pay. Confidence can generally be reposed in the natives—after seeing your baggage packed and started, it can be left to be bro't at their leisure. I have heard of but two or three instances where property has been lost, and only one of thieving; the laws punish for the crime of stealing very severely.

Five or six miles before reaching this city, the Cruces and Gorgona roads intersect. The former is paved its whole length, with large round stone, is about four feet in width, and one of the worst highways to foot it over imaginable. This solitary work of internal improvement is of a very ancient date, probably near two centuries old, but I am told it is yet perfect except such parts as have been washed out by high water.

At this interesting point we began to see cleared ground, and as we approached the city the quantity increased, but it all lies open and is no where cultivated.

At about two miles distant we had our first view of Panama. Although it presented a very novel appearance, the novelty was no balm to our wearied legs; enthusiasm was dead as we dragged slowly forward, and at four o'clock entered the walls of the town. Within ten minutes after our arrival we were cordially greeted by all the Cleveland boys. We were the last of the party, and more than one month behind the first who came.

There are a great number of people here, some of whom have been on the Isthmus three months, and their chances of getting away do not improve. It is estimated there are two thousand Americans in Panama, and there are rumors of five hundred more having landed at Chagres.

Ten vessels of all sizes are anchored in the harbor, but they will not be able to take off over nine hundred passengers, and the balance must wait for other opportunities. The California has been a long time due, and the idea has become so prevalent that she will not come, that the premium on her tickets have fallen from six hundred down to from two hundred and fifty to three hundred dollars. Unless a fleet comes in, large enough to take off all waiting, the price of tickets will not decrease, and those only will be able to get away who have plenty of money. There are six hundred people here who are not able to pay over one hundred and fifty dollars, and several hundred more have little or no means, some from the length of time they have been waiting, and others from too frequent visits to the gambling table.

The Panama will take all of the California's tickets possible; but a good many of a late date will necessarily be excluded; she is expected about the last of this month. Every vessel that has arrived, except one, has been bought up on speculation, and, of course, the tickets have been sold at enormous prices. The vessels will be clear, notwithstanding bought at three times their value, and, in some cases, a handsome sum realized in addition. The ship Humboldt, about five hundred and fifty tons burthen, sold for sixty thousand dollars—her tickets for steerage sold for two hundred dollars. A Peruvian brig, fourteen years old, of two hundred tons, for twenty thousand dollars—her tickets sold for one hundred and ninety dollars. Provisions are also dear, but water casks bear the highest premium. Whiskey barrels are worth twelve dollars each.

Smith has just come in to bid us good-bye—he sails this day on the brig Two Friends; Ellis sails to-morrow on the schooner St. John; Scovill, Brown, and Beardsley go in the brig Capioto in about eight days; Holladay in the ship Humboldt, in three weeks; and House will wait for the Panama. Yours, DEACON.

(CPD, June 1, 1849.)

Latest Intelligence from St. Joseph—Dissension among the Emigrants—Shooting Affair, &c.

Mr. Alding, a member of the Ottawa (Illinois) company of emigrants, returned to this city from St. Joseph yesterday.

He states that there exists the greatest dissatisfaction among the emigrants who have not yet left St. Joseph. Difficulties and quarrelling growing out of the general discontent were occurring daily. Many companies have disbanded and are selling out their outfits at any cost to raise the means to return home. The perfect sacrifice of property is an evidence of the dissatisfaction which exists.

Auctions are had daily where a person might procure himself a complete outfit, including clothing, saddles, &c., at a less price than they could be procured here, or in any Eastern city. Many emigrants also, whom extravagancies have plunged into pecuniary difficulties, have their equipments seized by the sheriff and sacrificed at auction. It was at one of these sheriff's sales that young De Camp, a citizen of Carondelet, engaged in a difficulty, which it is believed will result in his death. The outfit of one of his friends had been seized and put up at auction. Seeing that they would be sold at much less than their actual value, he endeavored to persuade the sheriff to stop the sale. Angry words were exchanged, when Smith, the sheriff, drew a pistol and shot him in the shoulder. Smith was arrested, and is under examination.

The general impression at St. Joseph seems to be that the emigrants will not only experience a great many difficulties and troubles in the journey, but that many heavy laden wagons will have to be left behind. The majority of wagons, it seems, have started out overloaded. The following incident seems to bear them out in their opinion. A teamster was engaged with his wagon to accompany one party with a load of corn to a distance of about 100 miles back of St. Joseph. He fulfilled his contract, and in returning literally filled his wagon with bacon and provisions of every description, which had been cast on the road-side from overloaded wagons.

Many emigrants are endeavoring to change their arrangements so as to go out with pack-mules. Some have already made exchanges of this character, and others are ready to avail themselves of the first opportunity to imitate the example. —*St. Louis Reveille, 22d inst.*

(PPL, June 2, 1849.)

NEWS FROM THE PLAINS
Cholera Among the Emigrants

St. Louis (Mo.) Union, May 25.

Major Armour left this city on the steamer Mary Blane; during the passage between here and Fort Leavenworth, a number of persons on board died of cholera, and several who were attacked were restored to health. . . . Maj. Armour confirms the report which we received and published a short time since, from Mr. Wm. Bent. He says that water and grass are abundant on the plains. The cholera was sweeping the emigrants off in great numbers, and had made its appearance in the regiment of mounted riflemen, which, when the major passed it, had been encamped for two days, forty miles beyond St. Joseph. Out of one company of New York emigrants, consisting of thirteen members, twelve had died of cholera; and twelve of another company from the same State had shared a like fate.

Many misfortunes had attended the emigrants on their journey, owing to their inexperience and the indifferent materials and construction of their wagons. He mentions that two of the wagons belonging to Dr. White's party, of this city, broke down within two miles of St. Joseph, and three belonging to Dr. Brown's party, also of this city, shared the same fate, some twenty miles beyond. Persons are crossing the plains under every variety of circumstances; sick and well, in wagons and carts, on horses and mules, and even afoot; not only men, but women and children, and women, too, with infants at the breast, are to be seen trudging along on foot. The major says he has realized all that he has ever heard said relative to the change that takes place in the manners of men while travelling on the plains is true. He says he saw but one company that appeared to have retained anything like the manners of civilized men, and that was a company of Kentuckians. It is a well known fact that men who are courteous and agreeable in their manners while surrounded with the comforts of civilized society, become little short of savages when crossing the plains. The major says that he saw those whose teams were unable to draw their wagons from a rut into which the wheels were suffered to run, apply to men around them for assistance in getting out, and so far from rendering aid, the persons thus applied to would only laugh and trifle with the unfortunate applicant, and the greater the trouble, the more it was enjoyed by the spectators. Between St. Joseph and the "Station," thirty miles distant, a place at which there is an Indian agency, a store, and a blacksmith's shop, the Major saw fifteen broken down wagons. There was a delegation of four chiefs from the Sioux and Fox at the station, with an explanatory letter from the agent, asking a small remuneration from the emigrants for the wood they would use while passing through their country, and expressing some fears of difficulty, in case the demand was not complied with, as wood is comparatively scarce, and the quantity used by the emigrants will be great. (NYH, June 4, 1849.)

Latest from the Isthmus—Trouble with the Consul—Arrival of Steamers

PANAMA, April 30, 1849.

J. W. GRAY, Esq.:—

DEAR SIR:—After a stop of nearly three weeks here, I am unable to give you as full as a description of the city and surrounding country as I wish. Owing to the constant and oppressive heat I have been unable to perform some expeditions I had projected, and I shall leave without visiting much of interest beyond the walls. The old city of Panama, seven miles distant to the north, presents the ruins of one of the oldest of the Spanish towns of America. It was settled early after the discovery of the continent, and flourished until destroyed by Morgan the buccaneer, I think, something over two hundred years ago. Little more than a mass of crumbling walls remain, although one tower yet rears its summit high above the dense forest which everywhere covers this once busy abode of man. It is totally uninhabited, no human being living in or around it, and the stillness remains unbroken except when curiosity calls thither some of our countrymen.

The modern city was commenced by the inhabitants of the old one, and is about two hundred years old. It stands on a tongue of land of no great elevation, and is surrounded by massive walls built in angles proper for planting cannon. The work is tolerably perfect except where, in a few places, the sea has undermined it, and the walls have fallen in. Not more than half a dozen cannon remain, and they lie dismantled and useless with the exception of two pieces which have recently been elevated on wooden trucks. They are brass thirty-two pounders, beautiful pieces, wearing the crown of Spain, and bear date 1777. Ruins meet the eye everywhere, many of them massive, and were once splendid and imposing edifices. It was once a city of churches, more than half of which are roof-less and in ruins, the walls overgrown with clambering vines, and the interiors filled with shrubbery. Some of the statues still standing in their niches, and the well preserved carving beneath the doorways indicate the beauty of the workmanship. The remains of an old Jesuit College are the most extensive, and are something over two hundred feet in length. All the buildings are stone, the roofs tile, and the ground floor brick; the floors, partitions, and doors are of hewn mahogany boards, and the whole inside work is of the rudest workmanship. Not a building has been erected in half a century, and a native told me that not one had been destroyed by fire in the same length of time.

In the churches are a great number of bells which are kept ringing nearly the twenty-four hours through. Some religious exercise is continually going forward, and, I suppose, every saint in the calendar receives due attention. Night processions are frequent, and that on Good Friday was quite brilliant. The lead was taken by a good number of priests carrying wax candles, and at intervals were elevated on the shoulders of men, pyramids of lights, in glass globes, surmounted by richly dressed figures of Christ, the Virgin Mary, &c.

Remains of the beauty of the churches yet exist, but little of the old riches is left. In one the grand altar is of silver, and much of the regalia is of the same material. The ceremonies seem a mere mummery, and the priests are perfect drones. One nunnery is in existence, but I reckon there would not be a great deal of romance, in rescuing, for love's sake, any of its inmates. A drink of good water can always be had there by asking, and it comes to you in a revolving cupboard, but no one can be seen. While partaking of a draught, I caught a glimpse of an eye fixed upon me through a small hole; it was large, dark, and handsome, but the skin around it was black as midnight.

Last Resting Place

The town outside the walls contains two-thirds as many inhabitants as the city. It is properly all one, being divided only by the walls and a deep ditch. The whole presents much the same appearance, except within the walls the buildings were originally of a better description. The road this way leads to the old Spanish cemetery, about half a mile distant; and near by, unenclosed, is the last resting place of Americans who have died here. A considerable number are lying side by side, and many are weekly added to the list. It is in the forest, and not a single memorial of the departed has been erected. The walls of the old cemetery are lined with skulls, and inside heaps of bones of the dead lie scattered rudely around. Groves of cocoanut line the road, and the spot is picturesque.

The rainy season has now set in, and the sky is constantly clouded over, and considerable rain is falling. Much sickness

prevails and mortality is greatly on the increase. Amongst New Yorkers, the fever has been most destructive, and New England people have suffered greatly. Ohio is largely represented, and yet I do not know of a single death and little sickness. All our party are in excellent health, and I never was better in my life.

No steamer has arrived, and all hopes are given up of either the *California* or *Oregon*. The *Panama* is daily looked for, this being her seventy-fourth day out. Several large vessels have arrived within a few days, enough to take away all the passengers now here, and all to arrive by the Falcon. Every vessel that leaves the port goes crowded, far too much so, and it will be no wonder to learn that much sickness and death has been the consequence. Yours &c.,   DEACON.

May 7.

P.S. Steamers California and Oregon have both arrived at this place. Great rejoicing and a general clearing out.

(CPD, June 5, 1849.)

GREAT OVERLAND ONSET
Fort Kearny, Nebraska Territory

[From the St. Louis Republican]
May 18th, 1849.

GENTLEMEN: The Mormon Mail from the happy valley of the Salt Lake has just dropped in upon us on its way to the frontiers, and I avail myself of the opportunity to send you a line—and a line it will almost literally be, as I have but a moment in which to write.

The ice is at last broken, and the inundation of gold diggers is upon us. The first specimen, with a large pick axe over his shoulder, a long rifle in his hand, and two revolvers and a bowie knife stuck in his belt, made his appearance here a week ago last Sunday. He only had time to ask for a drink of buttermilk, a piece of gingerbread, and how "fur" it was to "Caleforny," and then hallooing to his long-legged, slab-sided cattle, drawing a diminutive, yellow-top Yankee wagon, he disappeared on the trail towards the gold "diggins." Since then wagons have been constantly passing. Up to this morning four hundred and seventy-six wagons have gone past this point; and this is but the advance guard. Persons who have come through hurriedly from the frontiers say that every road is lined. This is an excellent point from which to see all that is desirable to be seen, as all the roads unite before reaching here. I have not the time, nor the power, to describe the queer outfits and the queerer people that are at the present to be found on the western prairies. Some other time I may attempt it.

All of Us

Every State, and I presume almost every town and county in the United States, is now represented in this part of the world. Wagons of all patterns, sizes, and descriptions, drawn by bulls, cows, oxen, jackasses, mules, and horses, are daily seen rolling along towards the Pacific, guarded by walking arsenals. Arms of all kinds must certainly be scarce in the States, after such a drain as the emigrants must have made upon them. Not a man but what has a gun and a revolver or two, and one fellow I saw actually had three Bowie knives stuck in his belt. Many of the parties as originally formed in the States have had dissensions, and are broken up, and each fellow is striking out for himself. This mode of life soon brings out a man in his true colors. No one knows a man, and he does not know himself, until he is brought out in his true character in the tented field or on some such expedition as is now occupying so many of our citizens.

However, all are jogging on their way, with the determination, apparently, of finding the end of the road—and in truth it matters but little whether a man is in an organized company or by himself, for it is impossible to get out of sight of wagons. Composed, as it mostly is, of the best material of our land, the country that receives it

must necessarily assume a commanding position. Many rascals, however, are along with the crowd, to give it a little wholesome seasoning. Several horses and mules have changed hands; but as it is an Indian country, the poor Indian must bear the blame.

Down East

The last arrival from the frontiers is a solitary foot traveler, who says he has come all the way from Maine, without the assistance of either railroad, steamboat, or telegraph wires. He is accompanied by a savage-looking bull-dog, has a long rifle over his shoulder, on the end of which he carries his baggage—a small bundle, about the size of your hat. He has no provisions, but gets along pretty well by sponging on his fellow travelers. He says he wants but a hundred meals to carry him through, and he guesses he'll find Christians enough to supply him with that number.

Our old friends, the Pawnees, have had a hard time of it during the winter. When they returned from their hunting grounds, their trail could be followed by the dead bodies of those who had starved to death. Children, young men, and women have shared this fate. Now that spring has arrived, their condition will be improved. They have abandoned their old village 75 miles below us, on the Platte, and have commenced a new one at the mouth of the Saline, some 80 miles nearer the frontiers of Missouri. Their old enemies, the Sioux, are pressing them hard, which is probably the cause of this step.— Several war parties of both nations are on the warpath, and several scalps have already changed owners. A large party of Sioux, a few days since came upon some half dozen Pawnees, and took three scalps and a small boy prisoner. This occurred some twenty miles from the post, and in the immediate vicinity of a party of emigrants, who if report be true, played any thing but an honorable part in the affair. The Pawnees, upon observing the overwhelming force of their enemies, who numbered about two hundred, took shelter with a train, but the gallant men composing it drove them forth without mercy. There was one squaw in the party, and the warriors finding they had to fight, told her to run for the river while they threw themselves between her and the Sioux, and died fighting bravely. The squaw reached the river and escaped. As soon as it was known here, Capt. Walker took twenty men, pursued and overtook the Sioux, rescued the prisoner and restored him to his mother. These little Indian fights, and the arrival of the emigrants, have broken in pretty effectually upon the monotony of our prairie life.

One of our men with the Mormon mail is just from the "diggings" in California, and he is certainly a happy fellow, for he says that he has as much gold as he wants. He showed me a stocking full as a specimen, and as you may well suppose, the emigrants opened wide their eyes at the sight of the glittering mass. Yours, &c.

PAWNEE.   (ISJ, June 6, 1849.)

Troubles of the California Emigrants

Every week brings reports from the vessels which have been leaving our shores for some months past, for San Francisco. The reports of many of them are what might have been anticipated, from the character of the vessels and the haste with which they were fitted out. A correspondent of the *Boston Traveller* gives the following pleasant account of things on board the bark Lanark, of that port:

RIO JANEIRO, April 25, 1849.

"We have arrived here after a long passage of 78 days, having been obliged to put in for water. Of the ten sail now in this port, our passage has been the longest but one. When six days out from Boston, we experienced a terrible gale. Our little barque, you may depend, trembled in every joint, and many on board had made

up their minds that Davy Jones Locker would fetch them up speedily. At half past 10 A. M. we were startled by the mate, who put his head down the hatch and in a harsh voice called on all the passengers who had been sailors to come on deck, or we should be lost. In an instant, some half dozen of us rushed on deck to render what little aid we could. The mate had just given orders to cut away the masts, but fortunately the captain countermanded it, or we should have assuredly gone to the bottom.

"Our deck load, including the framed house belonging to the Point Company; two boats and the long boat, was lost. We stayed on deck until everything was made snug; then we went below, and such a scene I never saw nor wish to see again. Some of the passengers had on life preservers, some had their bibles clasped to their bosoms, some were throwing their arms around their heads, bidding all goodbye, and others were getting signatures to a petition requesting the captain to put back, as they were already tired of the gold chase, and would sell out or give their all to be put any where on dry land.

"The ship Duxbury's provisions have been condemned and thrown overboard. The ship that Belcher Kay sailed in has been the scene of any quantity of *rows*. It is said that Belcher and three or four passengers made a line fast to the Captain and towed him quite a distance."

The *Traveller* has also extracts from a letter written on board the ship Pharsalia, between the 1st and 25th of March, in which the writer complains loudly of that ship, and her outfit for such a voyage, and of the state of things on board. About the 16th of March, in lat. 44° south, about 600 miles from Cape Horn, the ship encountered a severe gale, which continued three days. The writer says:

"The first hour, the jib, staysail, fore and main topsails went flying; in another, the main top gallant mast went by the board; everything was flying, all was uproar and confusion. The Captain tried to heave her to, but could not; she drifted in the trough of the sea, shipping seas every moment."

At a subsequent date the Pharsalia encountered another gale, in which she was blown off the coast 300 miles; all the bulwarks were stove and the rudder considerably damaged. On the 26th of March, however, the storm was abated, and the ship was on her course again. She was then in lat. 47° 01′, long. 46° 53′.

(PPL, June 13, 1849.)

News Extraordinary from California

We find the following letter in a New York paper. It must be read to be appreciated. Whatever doubts may be entertained of the other accounts we have had from Sacramento, it will hardly do for any one to doubt this. Some may laugh at it, but their laughing cannot but be good.

"A Letter from the Diggins"

VALLEY OF THE SACRYMENTO, April 20, 1849.

Eddyturs of the Sundy Times:—When I wrote before, spades was trumps—now it's dimunds. These preshus stuns is found in brilyant perfusion on the brow of the Sarah Nevady, and several as large as fenix eggs has been seen in a mountain of gold, diskivered last week, near the Sam Joking, and when the snow melts, it is supposed that many of the first water will come down with the current. Seed dimunds is remarkabul plenty, but a law has been made agen gatherin em, because it spoils the futur crop. None is aloud to be gathered under the size of a piece of chaulk. Emrulds abounds, but nobody is green enough to pick em up when they can get dimunds. Other jooils is a drug. Beyond the plains, on what they call a plato of the mountains, bushels of little peaces of silver has been dug up, which is very convenyent for small change.

A small stream runnin into Feather River, and partikarly rich in gold, has recently been diskivered by a German kumpany, and they have skewered the joint onership by the threatening to knife any one they catch poaching on their fork. In honor of some outlandish Dutch water privilege, they call it the River Rhine-o. Some of the xplorin sociation which has gone far into the intereyur, sends word that the sile there is all solid gold sot with roobees, but nobody bleves these out lying parties.

The depth of the odiferous sands on the Sacrymento is forty-eight feet eleven inches and three quarters. Wherever we find traces of gold, we sink shafts and draw it up with horses. The sand is so tarnation heavy it puts the mustangs to their metal, I tell you; but thers no help for em: they must hang on with all their might and mane, or down they go, and then its all up with em.

Imense quantities of gold, at the very least, has been sent to San Francisco for some time back, and as fast as it is got in it is turned into ingots. Thieves cannot egzist at the diggins—being hung on the slightest suspishun. Grub is moderate; floods of a spiritus natur very dear. All kinds of salt provisions is sold for a song; the tavern keepers most given em away on order to permote thirst. Salt pork is $5 a hogshead, and brandy $10 a half pint. Howsever, as gold is plenty, every Jack has his gill.

It is All Vanity

This puts me in mind of the noose by the steamer Californy, that a ship load of young wimmen was a coming out on a marryin spekelashun, with one Mrs. Farnham as shoopercargo. We look for the same anxshusly. What is gold—what is preshus stuns without wimmen? Nuthin but vanity and vexsashun of spirit. Solomon says—I red it tother day on a page of Proverbs I was agoin to use for waddin—Solomon says a vurtshus woman is more preshus than roobies, and in a kuntry without pettycoats one feels the force of the remark. When a man has wealth he wants hares to leave it to; and in course— no wives no hares. You couldn't send me out one, could you? I mean a wife, not a hare. If she's sum pitted with the small-pox even, I woodent care. The ordinariest goods are valuable when there is none in the market. There's duzzens I woodent a looked at in the States, that ud now be thankfully received and no questions axed. You can say, and truly, that I'm worth more than my weight in gold, for I've got a quarter of a tun of it in store at San Francisco, besides a sprinkling of dimunds.

We have a sort of make shift government here, (no allusion to the paragraff above,) got up extraperry as one may say, that ansers purty wel for a nu kuntry. Gen. Smith aint nobody. He is a clever chap and a spunky, no doubt o that; but he hainst got no more athority than a child in arms, if thar was sich a thing in the settlement. He ishoos genral orders and procla-mashuns and sich truck, and the people read em, perlite literatoor being scarce; but wen they've red em, they larf, and shet one eye, and go and do just as they d—n pleese. It's allus so in nu kuntries.

Agriculture in Californy is purty much left to natur. It sticks in folks' crops to be soeing corn when they can dig gold, and so they all go to the placers to make hay while the sun shines. This is the monster deposit bank of the unoversal world, and we're all casheres and directors. Bring yer taters here if you want em dug, we can't take the trouble to raise em. The only wegetable we cultyvate is the root of all evil, and if you'll send us the frutes of the earth, you can have that exchange.

The rainy season being over, the weather is settled. I bleeve the heat hasn't been below 99 for a week, which, with bad rum, has proved fatal to some consti-tooshuns. Emigrants of all kinds and kuntries keeps pourin in by land and water,

and the popalashun is very promiscous. We Mericans keep the upper hand of fur-riners so far; but it takes considerable powder and ball. Colt's pills is fine for munity.—The *bottle* causes a good many musses, but the *barrel* allus stops em. I shall probably ship my pile by the Californy, and if I escape the cholera, the injuns, and the yallar fever going through Mexico, you may spect to see me before very long, and perhaps sooner.   A DISBANDED VOLUNTEER.

(PPL, June 14, 1849.)

From the Californians—280 Miles from Independence, Mo., on the Plains

CAMP PAWNEE RIVER, within two days' drive of Big Platte River, May 20 '49.

FRIEND KING:—I have but a few moments to drop you a line, and must improve them, as a Frenchman on his way from Fort Laramie has just come into camp, and will take any letters we may hand him. Our train is composed of 27 wagons, 110 yoke of oxen, 116 men, and a small sprinkling of women. We have men from all of the states in the Union—Badgers messing with live Yankees from Maine, and Wolverines with suckers and buckeyes.[1] We are a mixed multitude.

We left Independence on the 1st of May, and have made about 16 miles per day. Yesterday, coming up the river (Pawnee,) over 150 wagons were in sight. About 500 wagons are ahead of us, but the main or larger body of the emigrants are in our rear. Generally all the trains lie still on Sunday. We have a sermon this afternoon, from a Rev. gentleman from Maine, a Universalist—preaching at 1 o'clock. Dirty duds are now being scoured for future wear: so you see Sunday is a work-day, if we do lie over to respect the sabbath. Some are fishing. A few nights since we had a

---

1.   Badgers, Wolverines, suckers, buckeyes—men from Wisconsin, Michigan, Illinois, and Ohio.

stampede with our teams, and the way they *"highsted"* their tails and put out from camp was not slow. All hands were roused for the chase, and about 8 o'clock A. M. we had them in yoke and on our way.

Take our train, men, teams—we are as well prepared for casualties as any train on the route. We are composed of men from all parts of the Union; most of them are men of good principles and morals, possessing energy and stability of character not surpassed by many—and if individuals left behind us term such the *fag ends of society*, they are bigoted, and only talk because there are those who will listen to them.

A few casualties have occurred on the road—a team ran away, (not in our train,) which passed over the body of the teamster and killed him. Another person was accidentally shot dead by the discharge of a rifle; several have been wounded by carelessness with revolvers, and some two or three have died from sickness. One grave I saw when about 200 miles on the plains, where an old lady, 72 years of age, was buried in 1846. To-morrow morning we put out again on our way, and shall be at the Platte, or Nebraska River, by Tuesday night, May 22d. Give my respects to all inquiring friends, and believe me to be

Your obedient friend and serv't.,

A. W. WRIGHT. (CPD, June 16, 1849.)

From the California Emigrants— Good News—Extraordinary Haste to Get to California

The St. Louis *Republican*, of the 7th instant, says:—

Letters were received in this city yesterday from emigrating parties to California, dated as late as the 18th of May. On that day they were 240 miles from St. Joseph, and all going on prosperously. These letters do not allude to the prevalence of the Cholera. They represent the health and spirit of the emigrants as excellent—the grass was fine, and, where it was thought the mules would fail, they were fattening. Not an Indian had been seen since the party left the Mission, 25 miles from St. Joseph. The party were greatly elated by meeting an express direct from California—the Mormon express—sent back, it seems, for the purpose of urging forward a part of a company which had been left behind. They were urged, it is said, to abandon their wagons and hurry on, on pack mules, as they had found richer diggins than ever, and wanted their assistance in securing the golden treasure. The whole country glittered with the wagons, carriages, tents, and animals by thousands, men, women, and children; young and old, who have engaged in this gold searching pilgrimage, and whose route leads over a distance of more than 2,200 miles.

These letters also speak of the reckless conduct of some of the emigrants in throwing away their double and single trees, and other necessary conveniences for all traveling. Some have left large wagons on the road-side, with cards on them intimating that those who came after may take them, if they wanted them. So eager are they to get along, that all surplus weight—stoves, pots, boxes, tobacco, bacon, &c., may be found scattered along the road, in the general rush towards the end of their journey. Poor fellows! they may want the provisions before they reach California.

(CPD, June 18, 1849.)

Interesting Intelligence from the Pacific

Voyage of the Steamer Panama—A Trip Around the Horn—Straits of Magellan— Passage of Sail Vessels

A correspondent of the New York Tribune, who went out in the U. S. Mail Steamer Panama, gives the following account of the voyage around the Horn, and the stopping places on the Pacific:

PANAMA, April, 1849.

We left Rio Janeiro on Sunday, March 25, with the wind ahead, and except for a few hours, kept it ahead until after we entered the Straits of Magellan, twelve days in all. We made Cape Virginia, the northern point of the Straits, at 9:30 A. M. on Friday, April 5. This cape is a high barren bluff, with lofty snow capped mountains in the distance. At 5:30 we came to anchor near the northern shore in Possession Bay, in 17½ fathoms water, where we laid until 6:30 on Saturday. When we entered the Straits we saw three vessels, two of which we took to be the Anthony and the A. Emery, both from New York, for San Francisco. They were both at anchor, but got under way as soon as we passed. The other was the fast-sailing pilot boat W. G. Hackstaff, from New York, 21 days from Rio for the Gold Diggings. She spoke us about midnight and reported all well.

At 10 A. M. on Saturday, spoke schr. Roe, from New York for San Francisco, all well and going at a fine rate. She came close to us and exchanged cheers, but owing to the strong breeze was unable to speak with us. She fell astern, not being able, like ourselves, to make a straight course in spite of wind and tide, which, at that place, runs very strong, say 8½ or 9 miles per hour, with 30 feet rise and fall of the tide.

The land along the shore is high clayey soil, covered with a kind of faded vegetation, but no trees or shrubbery. In passing along the shore we could see innumerable herds of animals resembling our deer and elk grazing. Both shores are bold, and the channel looks easy to navigate. The entrance of the Straits, between Cape Virgin and Cape Espirito de Santo, is 15 miles wide, though the narrowest place is not over two miles wide.

In the afternoon we passed three islands, called Elizabeth, Martha, and Magdalene Islands, from the northernmost and southernmost points of one of them reefs of rocks extend about a mile. Still I think there is no more danger or difficulty in working through the Straits than is found in all other narrow channels,—arising mostly from strong winds and stronger currents. The land on these is also of a clayey appearance, with a high bluff shore and intervals of low beach.

Port Famine

About 8 P. M., Saturday night, April 6, passed close to Port Famine, so called by the Spaniards who made a settlement there, all the members of which starved to death but four, before assistance was rendered, after which the place was wholly abandoned. We kept under way all night, with our captain on deck at his post. We had high rocky mountains close aboard on both sides, and the wind blowing violently, with rain. About midnight passed a schooner at anchor at Fortescue Bay.

At 8 A. M. of the 7th, saw a brig at anchor in York Roads, with the stars and stripes in her main rigging. A small boat, with five men, left her and pulled for our ship. Capt. Porter stopped for them. She proved to be the brig Saltillo, 104 days from Boston, for San Francisco. She had been 23 days getting thus far through the Straits, and still had more than a hundred miles to go before she could enter the broad Pacific. We gave them a file of papers. The captain offered us $500 to tow him through the rest of the passage.

We learned from him that the schr. Anthon, from New York, was two days ahead of him. They also told us there were great numbers of Indians near by. From our vessel we could perceive hordes of wild dogs, but no other animals.

At 9½ of the 7th we passed and exchanged signals with the schooner Iowa. About 12 we passed Glacier Bay, where both the mountain and the valleys were covered with a clear glacier of ice, having a most beautiful appearance, like blue waters with countless ripples. I had almost forgot to tell you of the lofty peak of Mount Sacramento, which we saw on Saturday from Elizabeth Island. It is 6,800 feet high, covered with perpetual snow, and can be seen at a distance of 90 miles.

The farther we advanced in the Straits the stronger became my opinion that square-rigged vessels would find great difficulty in getting through, owing to the great strength of the tide and the narrowness of the passage, which in some places does not exceed 1½ miles in width. When the wind blows in violent squalls from the gullies in the mountains, sailing is almost impossible. Fore and aft schooners may do well enough when they have the tide with them, but cannot make any headway against the tide. The schooners Iowa and Roe were doing well under short sail when we passed them, but as I have already mentioned, the brig Saltillo had been 23 days getting as far as York Harbor, and the Captain told us unless he had a more favorable chance it would take him 30 days longer to get to the other part of the passage, which is a little over 100 miles. This makes it certain that many of the square-rigged vessels which left New York for California via Magellan, will have a hard time in getting through. These remarks of course apply to the passage from the Atlantic to the Pacific. The shore on both sides is bold, having from 30 to 60 fathoms water, and in fact in some places there is no bottom to be found.

At 5 o'clock we passed St. Ann's Island which brought us into the sea reach, and at last we felt the swell of the Pacific. At 8 o'clock we passed Cape Tamour; we had a heavy swell on, with rain and squalls from the West; the wind was dead ahead. Our ship made the quickest time through on record—making the run from Cape Virgin to Cape Tamour in 37 hours running time: distance about 351 miles.

Our engine and machinery did nobly through this trial, and has done so all the way, not having to stop once for repairs since we left New York.

Frightful Seas

We passed Cape Pillow on Monday April 9, 2 A. M., with a heavy gale of wind and an awful sea, the ship pitching very much; the passengers generally, fore-and-aft, were much frightened. At 4 A. M. she pitched her head clear under, when the bolt which holds the bobstay was drawn and the bowsprit carried short off by the head. I have been at sea, off-and-on, twenty years, and I assure you I never saw it blow harder, nor a worse cross sea on. Of all the ships I have ever seen, there is none to be compared to the Panama as a safe and staunch sea vessel.

In all these trying scenes the Captain walked the decks with evident anxiety, for we were on a lee shore with a heavy gale and a tremendous sea, still he kept up the drooping spirits of many of our heartsick passengers, who would have given all in California to be ashore. But no accident happened to us except the breaking of the bowsprit, and the loss of the third mate from the top-gallant forecastle on the main deck. A monstrous wave carried him off, and we saw him no more. You may imagine how hard it blew when I tell you that some of our best seamen were afraid to go aloft. I never saw a vessel more easy in a sea. Both builders and engineers may be proud of their work. We had the same violent gale for two days, and the wind ahead, until we arrived in Valparaiso, April 17, after 22 days passage. Valparaiso is a neat, clean place, and is under good police regulations, far surpassing those of New York. The people here are very kind and civil, the ladies handsome, and the houses clean and neat. Yours, B. S. M.

(PPL, June 19, 1849.)

From the Plains

The St. Louis Republican of the 9th inst. has two letters from Fort Kearney, which contain matter of interest to those who are watching the stream of emigration over the Plains towards California.

The South Pass is now the favorite route. A letter of the 21st of May states that the number of emigrant wagons is increasing daily. On that day 214 passed Fort Kearney, making altogether 1,203

On the way to the Platte.

Bryant, with a train of this description, encamped within a mile of the Fort last night. He is pushing ahead rapidly. A large Mormon emigration is passing along on the opposite side of the river, and also several trains of Californians, but the water is so high that it is exceedingly difficult to cross, and I cannot therefore obtain the number of wagons on that side of the river."

The St. Joseph Adventure says that a mountaineer arrived there on the 27th ult., in twenty days from Fort Laramie. The first company for California, commanded by Capt. Paul of St. Louis, was five hundred miles west of St. Joseph, and all well.

wagons that have gone in that direction already this spring—without including a Government train of 50 wagons, belonging to the advance guard of the Rifles under Major Simonson, destined for Bear River, somewhere in the Happy Valley of the Mormons.

The writer says that 5,090 emigrants have passed Fort Kearney for California, and estimates that not less than 20,000 to 25,000 men, or 50,000 animals, will cross the Plains this season on that route. A letter of May 22d, from the same writer, says:—"Two hundred and thirty-two wagons reached here yesterday, making 1,435 that have gone past up to this morning. Besides these wagons, several parties with pack animals have also passed this place.

The road after the junction with the Independence road was much crowded—several teams abreast. There was sickness in every company, and some dying. Beyond Fort Laramie the grass is sparse.

(PPL, June 19, 1849.)

From the Land of Promise

SAN FRANCISCO, April 7, 1849.

Highly Important News from California—Discovery of New Gold Mines—Arrival of the Steamship Oregon at San Francisco—$7,000,000 of Gold Dust Shipped—The "Placers"—Astonishing Success of Gold Seekers—$12,480 Dug by One Man in Ten Days—What an Emigrant Should Carry to California—How to Reach the Gold Mines—A word of Caution and Advice

Hurrah! Here we are at last! The Land of Promise—*El Dorado* of the West! Our own bright, beautiful, bountiful California lies before us and around us—her lap full of riches. The blood and treasure of a great nation has been expended in the acquisition of this territory, and the strong arm and powerful mind of the Anglo-Saxon will soon make its rich streams and valleys—its fertile plains, and even its barren hills, to "bud and blossom as the rose."

I arrived in the steamship Oregon, Captain Pearson, on Thursday morning, April 1. We left Panama with 250 passengers, (77 in the cabin and 173 in the steerage,) making the trip in 19 days; running time, 16½ days. . . . After entering the Bay of San Francisco, which is unquestionably the finest in the world, the Oregon cast anchor in Saucilita Bay, six miles distant from San Francisco, and where we found at anchor the United States ship of the line Ohio, Com. Jones, the sloops of war St. Mary and Warren, and the U. S. store ship Southampton. Salutes were here fired, and the officers of the Ohio came on board. From them we learned that the steamship California was still at San Francisco. Most of her men had deserted, and she could not leave for want of coal. During the morning of our arrival, the sailors of the Oregon were ordered to hoist the baggage of the passengers out of the hold. They all refused, however, to do duty, and declared their intention of going to the placers. Capt. Pearson consulted with the Commodore, and in about ten minutes a body of marines marched our jack tars on board the Ohio, where they were informed they must remain until the Oregon was ready to sail. This was rather a summary process, and not exactly according to law, but under the circumstances there seemed to be no other course. Everybody is interested in the success of these steamships; they afford the only means of obtaining speedy advices from the States, and everybody, of course, seemed to think the arrest was right—particularly as the sailors had

signed a contract to remain three years on the ship. The result of the business will be, however, that the company will be compelled to increase their pay—probably to $100 per month.

We remained at Saucilita Bay until Monday morning, when we got up steam and proceeded to San Francisco, and dropped anchor alongside of the California. During Sunday night, the third mate and two firemen took a boat, in which Capt. Forbes had come on board the Oregon, and cut their stick for the placers. In the harbor we found about fifty merchant vessels, most of whom are without crews. On shore we ascertained that almost every nook and corner was full to overflowing, and that our only chance for sleeping was the soft side of a very narrow plank, or a blanket under a tent. But our greedy ears were mightily tickled with marvellous accounts of the rich placers, and our eyes dazzled with the sight of bushels of gold dust, and large lumps, some of them weighing five and six pounds. Everybody seemed to have plenty of "rocks," and a more stirring, active, and intelligent population than that of San Francisco, I have never seen.

Gold is found from Sutter's Fort to the head of the Sacramento, a distance of several hundred miles, and in great abundance on the San Joaquin, (Mem.—pronounced "walk in;" very inviting name, isn't it?) and on all the forks and tributaries of the two rivers. . . .

Any strong, able bodied man who is willing to labor five or six hours a day in a broiling sun, can make from $10 to $20 per day for three or four months in the year. The miner must expect to undergo all kinds of hardships, privations, and fatigue. He must be willing to sleep in a blanket on the ground—for tents, I am told, are found too confined for so hot a climate—eat little or nothing, and work like a slave. The country where gold abounds is very unhealthy, and but few have constitutions to bear the wear and tear of a campaign.

"Fitting Out" for the "Placers"

While I am on the subject of mining, I may as well state a few facts in relation to "fitting out," and getting to the "placers," which will prove of great benefit to those who intend coming. In the first place, those who come here for the purpose of "digging," had better bring no more personal baggage than they absolutely need for three or four months after arriving. The price of a passage to Sutter's Fort is $30, and the charge for baggage $5 a hundred pounds. From Sutter's Mill to the mines the charge for transporting goods and baggage to the placer is $1 per pound. This is owing to the fact that there are few tame horses and mules in that country. The price of a "mustang" is from $250 to $400, and those who buy them run a great risk of having them stolen. So that the idea of carrying much plunder to the placer is ridiculous.

As for bringing provisions, it is equally absurd. They can be purchased here and at Sutter's for about the same price it would cost to bring them out. The famous gold washing machines, which are so much puffed in the newspapers, will also be found valueless in this country. In the first place, they cannot be transported to the placers, except at enormous expense, and experienced miners who have examined those brought out by some of the Oregon passengers, declare they are good for nothing. All a man needs, who comes here to dig, is half a dozen coarse shirts, two suits of woollen clothes, and a pair of heavy woollen blankets. So, friends at home, don't spend your money in buying trash.

The merchants here in San Francisco are all making large fortunes just now, and the prices of most kinds of goods are enormous. Want of lumber prevents many stores and houses going up immediately, and business is done by few persons. There are a good many of the elements of civilization here in this region, however.

A large and commodious hotel has been recently erected, fronting on the plaza, by Robert A. Parker, Esq., formerly of Boston, Mass. The house is now open, under the superintendence of J. H. Brown, Esq., an excellent host, but it is not yet completed.

Mr. Parker is one of the most enterprising men in the place, and is said to be worth $300,000 to $400,000, most of which he has acquired here in two years. Connected with the hotel is a large slaughterhouse, a stable, and candle manufactory. The celebrated Saucilita, otherwise known as Whaler's Harbor, the famous watering place for ships, was recently purchased by Mr. Parker, who intends building up a town there. It has many natural advantages which San Francisco does not possess. Saucilita is eight miles nearer the entrance to the harbor than San Francisco, from which it is six miles distant. Here resides Captain Richardson, one of the oldest settlers in California, who is said to have a magnificent farm, well stocked with horses and cattle. It seems to be the opinion of the officers of the United States survey, that the government will erect a navy yard and dry dock at Saucilita. In fact, it is about the only place on the bay where they could be built with safety. A steam-saw and gristmill are now being erected there, which will doubtless prove very profitable.

P.S. To give you some idea of what the price of living in San Francisco is just now, I subjoin a list of a few articles, with the prices attached:—Eggs, $4 per dozen; butter, 50¢ per pound; champagne, $60 per dozen; egg nog, $1 per drink; smashers, $1 do.; blankets, $50 and $100 per pair; lumber, $600 per 1,000 ft.; porter, $2.50 per bottle, ale, do. do.   W. A. B.

(NYH, June 20, 1849.)

SAN FRANCISCO, April 9, 1849.

As the attention of the whole world seems now directed towards California, and as the people of the United States, whose territory it is, are particularly interested in knowing the resources of the country, I have been at some trouble in getting what I deem to be correct information, concerning a variety of matters, and beg leave to lay it before your readers. . . .

The site of the present town of San Francisco, or "Yerba Buena," as it was formerly called, was not the selection of a deliberate examination of the surrounding bay and coast, but almost purely the result of accident. Many years ago the Hudson's Bay Company applied to the Mexican government for permission to locate a trading post on the Bay of San Francisco. Although the request was granted, the Mexican authorities, with their characteristic jealousy of foreigners, restricted them to a point as near as possible to the entrance to the Bay, on the very threshold, as it were, of their territory, and under the guns of their presidio, which overlooks the narrow passage to the sea.

As the trade of this company declined here, the trade of the United States, through our enterprising Boston house, increased, and at length the old Hudson's Bay Fort was given up to the Bostonians. The house is still standing. Whalers also occasionally put in here, being an anchorage convenient to the sea, and on the outbreak of the war with Mexico, our squadron anchored off the site of the present town, which was then almost a solitude, there being not more than ten or twelve rough houses, and temporary buildings for hides, to relieve the view. The Mormons, who arrived in the Brooklyn and other ships, about this time, located themselves, desirous of the protection of the squadron and of the land forces stationed here in the old Mexican presidio. They built temporary habitations; and then came other emigrants, and thus was formed the nucleus, and so was born the child of accident—San Francisco.

There is another point on the Bay of San Francisco, called Saucilita Bay, which is said to possess much greater advantages for a town than those offered by the site of San Francisco. But it is probable that all these places will do well. American industry and skill will subdue natural defects, and make many blemishes disappear. But what the result of this great emigration will be, can only be answered by the eternal reply of the Californians—*Quien sabe?*[2] CARQUINES. (NYH, June 20, 1849.)

Springtime in California

SAN FRANCISCO, April 29, 1849.

Opening of the Spring—Arrivals of Emigrants—The Best Time to Work in the Mines— Town of Benicia—The Future to the Emigrant— Shocking Murders—Lynch Law—Gold Digging—The Crop of the Precious Metals—Hint to Emigrants, &c. &c. &c.

Spring has come upon us, and nature has spread her green carpets, and strewed her flowers over our own California; and one might think we could live here, at present, by feasting upon the beauteous scenes that are spread around us. But no; gold! gold! gold! we are knee deep in gold (and sand) on the San Joaquin and in the Sacramento Valley. Already the work has begun, and now drives bravely on; our roads are crowded with horsemen, wagons, carts, and pedestrians all bound to the great California bank, check (i.e., pan, pick, and shovel) in hand.

Sometime since I advised those of my friends who desired visiting the United States, to have patience, and the United States would visit us. Our emigration is coming by vessel loads. In June, when the Atlantic vessels that left in January arrive, we shall perhaps see some people. Great country this! everybody comes to this country! One would suppose that folks became quite aristocratic by living in this El Dorado—not at all. I asked a friend of mine how he contrived to keep a cook and stew-

---

2. Who knows?

ard—both healthy men; he said, by paying them over $100 per month each, and making them presents, and with his hat under his arm each morning, making most earnest inquiries with regard to their health, and proffering any service that they might need during the day.

It would be well for parties of six or eight persons each emigrating to this country, to bring out a frame house, or brick or iron one; the country has plenty of clay for bricks, and shell and stone for lime, but no brick or lime makers. Each company should have a boat, launch, or small craft, under fifty tons, to convey themselves and provisions from their vessel to the upper landing. Sutter's fort on the Sacramento, or some landing higher up on Feather river, or the town of Stockton on the San Joaquin. This town, laid off by Mr. Weber, is to be a place of much importance. Passage from San Francisco to Sutter's is over $20 in a launch, the passenger feeding himself; freight of a barrel of flour, $12; from Benicia the price is not much less.

Benicia—A new formed town up five miles on the Straits of Carquines, forty miles from the entrance of the bay, from the sea, has now received visits from several large vessels—steamer Propeller and the United States ship Southampton, among others. The passage having been thus proved to be safe and quick, is now causing many vessels to go there. Nine-tenths of all the passengers by sea, bound to the placer, will prefer being landed at the Straits of Carquines, where is the only ferry in that part of the country. Once there, the emigrant has a carriage road to the Sacramento or the San Joaquin. A horse will carry him to either in two days; on foot he can reach the different placers in four to eight days; by water he is a day higher than San Francisco, and the most dangerous bay passed.

The Wages of Crime

By July, I presume the Bay of San Francisco will have over 200 vessels without men. By October, many will be willing to ship. Thousands of people are to arrive this year; tens of thousands next year. Some to meet a fortune—many, very many, a disappointment. Pockets will be filled, and pockets emptied; morals corrupted, health lost, while death will make fearful havoc among its victims. There will be more deaths than burials. Gambling, over-trading, robbery, and murder will be

Between Sacramento and the mines.

rife among the multitude; yet every person is almost surprised at the continued good order, with few exceptions, that yet prevails. Since July, eleven men have, for murder or other crimes, been shot or hung. In a letter published by you in January, mention is made of a mate of a vessel, who was purchasing goods at a store in California, and said all his gold was in rough cowhide bags, containing one hundred ounces each. He reached his family, 100 miles south of Monterey, who, with his wife, children, and servants, eleven in number, including a child at its mother's breast, were all murdered by a party of five Englishmen and Americans. Thanks to the love of justice, and the activity of the inhabitants of Santa Barbara, two of the murderers were shot in chasing them and the other three caught, tried, and shot. One Californian lost his life in pursuing the murderers. Thus those few bags of gold dust have sent seventeen people out of the world.

All this amounts to nought in the great and earnest desire to dig gold in the grand placer of California, where some twenty to thirty thousand men will this summer be at work. Men are constantly passing to and from the diggings, some "prospecting"— looking out better places—others retiring to the towns to rest. I have to-day two carpenters at work at their trade, who refused $15.50 per ounce for the gold they dug during the winter. On inquiring of them why they left the diggings, they said they had worked hard four or five months, done middling, were tired, wished to recruit their health and rest a while, therefore proposed working at their trade in Monterey for two months; besides all that, one of them said that his diggings were reduced down to one ounce a day, and he felt too tired to go 'prospecting' for a better location. Strange country, as I said before; a workman knocks off and strikes, not for higher wages, but that he could rest himself by working as a carpenter for a month or so.

To conclude, although we are in the midst of gold, prudent men in the Atlantic States, who are making a good living and saving up something, should pause before they break up at home and start off for California. Many men now here, who are poor, will surely be rich, and the reverse will as surely take place. The shippers of dry goods from your port and N. E., will in many cases be disappointed. Those who have shipped provisions may obtain a profit, perhaps; pork, beef, hams, dried fruits, preserved meats, sperm candles, flour, etc., may continue to pay, should they have warehouse or ship room to retain them. An immense quantity of goods may be lost by the rains from November to March. We have had no rain since some time in February; in January it rained twenty-five days, and we had snow in the towns for the first time since 1826. It is safe to calculate on dry weather from the first of April to first of November. In November and March we have but small quantities of rain.

I learn that our first placer letters were not believed—Col. Mason's doubted—first in the States, since in England, and now in ports more remote. Excitement and so called delusions, founded and based on a gold region, 500 miles by 100, 5 feet to 30 feet deep, will not pass away from either the memory or the fingers of the present generation, whatever may be the future result to California, be it for weal or for woe. Nature here, for the present, is reversed; but nature will have its own regular way— water finds its level, and so will our placer. PAISANO.

(NYH, June 20, 1849.)

Gold Digging in California

A San Francisco correspondent of the New York Courier ventures the following advice to such persons as, being still at home, have the premonitory symptoms of the Gold Fever:

"To such as contemplate coming out here in companies and employing persons to dig for them, I will relate a short anecdote. Ten men belonging to a company established for this purpose, arrived one day upon the banks of Feather river, in the very midst of the gold region, where they met ten Indians, who were lolling listlessly about under the shade of a large tree. 'These are the very men for us,' thought and said the whites, and an offer was immediately made the Indians of two dollars a day for every man who would dig. This being the amount that the same people worked for *per month* in the settlement, was, at the time, thought a sufficient inducement certainly; but the Indians shook their heads. Five dollars were then offered; again the Indians shook their heads. Ten dollars was the next offer, when one of the Indians rose and said, 'Here are ten of you and ten of us; we make you the same offer. You, white men, dig for us, and we will give each of you ten dollars a day!'

"So, you will observe that none but hale, hearty, stout, well-knit, and healthy men need come out here for gold. And two-thirds of these (let me warn them in time) will lay their bones where they go with the hope of accumulating fortunes. My reasons for thinking thus must be obvious enough to persons at all acquainted with the country. When the unhealthy season sets in at the placer, the temptation for augmenting one's *heap* is too strong to be resisted. As each individual imagines that he will escape, or, at any rate, that the chances are somewhat in his favor, none leave until a raging fever has taken a strong hold, when, in most cases, it is too late to depart. But this is useless. No warning from me or any body else will turn a tide; and I fancy that every person coming to California intends to take this at the flood, feeling confident that it must 'lead on to fortune.'[3] But I know, from actual

observation, that the tide runs both ways out here. There is an ebb as well as a flood. *If any suppose that gold can be procured without labor, and that of the severest kind, they are, I assure you, very much mistaken.* Why, laying water or gas-pipes in the streets of New York is not half as toilsome work. No man should come to this country with the expectation of making his fortune at the mines by getting out gold, but such a one as feels fully able to dig about half a dozen graves a day, taking a cold bath every fifteen or twenty minutes during his work, and whilst in a profuse perspiration, and that without injury to the constitution. It would not be a bad plan to practise this for a month or two on the banks of some river before leaving the United States."

(WNI, June 22, 1849.)

California; General Smith

The Washington "Union" publishes the following extracts from a letter, dated at San Francisco, written by Major General PERSIFOR F. SMITH, commanding the U. S. army in that region:

"You only think of California in connexion with gold; and, indeed, a most wonderful connexion it is. As to the extent of country holding the precious metal, and the comparative facility with which it is procured, there has been no exaggeration. The whole slope of the Sierra Nevada, on the western side, for a length of more than four hundred miles, and in a belt of at least forty, contains it in greater or smaller quantities; and it may extend still further, as further research is made. It is found simply by digging and washing the earth; no expensive machinery and no intricate chemical processes are necessary to develop the magic hoard.

"A pickaxe, shovel, or even a butcher's knife, to loosen the earth and stones, and

---

3. "There is a tide in the affairs of men, / Which, taken at the flood, leads on to fortune."
    (Shakespeare, *Julius Caesar, IV, iii, 217.*)

the most simple basin for washing, have been as richly rewarded as the most approved machines from other countries. Good luck in the laborer choosing his location has more than compensated for want of skill. The real difficulties lie in the hardships to be encountered in the remote uninhabited spots where the gold is found. Want of food, overworking excited by success, bad water, exposure and dissipation, all combine to exact a heavy tribute for the wealth when found. All are not successful, but every one works on, hoping that the next blow of his will disclose a treasure that will surpass all he has hitherto heard of. Many die unheeded, many come off sick; but there are ten arriving from each quarter of the globe to replace every one who goes. Chinese, Sandwich Islanders, Chilians, Peruvians, Prussians, Mexicans, French, English, Irish outnumber as yet the Americans; but the latter will soon have their share. Provisions, woollen clothing, liquors, kitchen and mining utensils, sell at enormous profits in the mines; other articles scarcely sell at all. Women's gear is altogether a drug.

"The amount of gold hitherto found is hard to determine. It is said about $4,000,000 have been exported. I shall be able in a few weeks, from facts I am collecting, to make some approximation to it.

"In the mean time all this is disastrous for us. No servants are to be had; $250 a month has been refused in my presence by a cook. All my servants have quit, and yesterday I engaged one at $100 a month because he is too sick to go to the mines; but I shall certainly lose him if he gets his health.

"The quartermaster pays $5,000 a year for the house I live in, and it would make but a poor toll-house for a *country* bridge. The climate is cold all the year round, and foggy in the summer. The hills are bare, and the country is all hills (forgive the bull.[4]) The beef is execrable, and vegetables—none; and nobody has time to catch fish, if there are any—*voila la carte.*[5]

"Any one who will come here to dig gold, or bring goods with him to sell to the diggers, will make money. No other business will succeed. Whoever comes must bring a house with him; there are but few here, and lumber is $600 per thousand."

(WNI, June 22, 1849.)

Men and Business in California

From a letter published in the Journal of Commerce, and which that paper avouches to be from an intelligent source, we extract the following paragraphs:

SAN FRANCISCO, MAY 1, 1849.

The emporium of the Western Coast presents a busy scene. There are about sixty vessels in the harbor, of all classes, all deserted by their crews—a fate that awaits every vessel here, as soon as her anchor is down. Men have to be hired in unloading them at $10 per day.

Goods of all descriptions are becoming very plenty, and prices are moderate, except at retail, and in places distant from San Francisco.

The number of passengers who have arrived here by sea during the last four months is very great. The actual population of the country at this time cannot accurately be estimated, but may be thirty thousand. It consists of Americans, English, French, Mexicans, Chilenos, Peruvians, and, indeed, of almost all nations and languages; but those named are the numerous classes. The Americans, at this time, comprise less than one-half.

Lodgings in San Francisco are very difficult to be obtained. The greater part of the floating population live in tents. There

---

4. "Bull" is used here in an older sense: meaning a ludicrous contradiction or a bad pun.
5. There's the menu.

are, perhaps, four hundred houses here, of the poorest description generally, but as many thousands would scarcely be sufficient even now to afford all a shelter.

There are in California men of all trades and professions, but the physicians are the most numerous. One may sit down in any place in San Francisco and he shall see a doctor pass by once a minute all day long. There are certainly twenty doctors to one patient. Mechanics are also numerous, but there are scarcely any engaged in their trades except a few carpenters, who get $16 a day for their labor. Agriculture is entirely abandoned.

The ordinary occupations here are gold digging, regular trading, speculating, and gambling. Farm lots in San Francisco are held at from $3,000 to $25,000. Several other towns have been laid out, as Benicia, Stockton, Sacramento City, &c., and the lots sold at very high prices. Titles are but little inquired into; there is no doubt that they are generally bad.

Here a man will do almost any thing to make money, because there is no power to call him to account. Even official and professional employments are assumed by those not having the least rightful pretensions to them, who in this way extort thousands of dollars per month from the multitudes of strangers who come here. Every man is devoted to one pursuit, the acquisition of gold, and is not scrupulous as to the means employed.

There is no society, no such thing as friendship, no pleasure of any kind; there is no religion recognized in practice, and no Divinity worshipped but gold, and to its shrine multitudes of pilgrims are daily flocking. Although the country is without government, it is not absolutely without order—even better than existed at any time before it was annexed to the United States, and better than exists now in Mex-

ico or any of the South American Republics. Every man goes well armed, and as great insults and injuries are pretty sure to be followed by instant revenge, without any chance of escape by "the law's delay,"[6] they are not very frequently committed. Murders, larcenies, and robberies, if the offender is caught, are punished with great severity, after a trial by jury in due form. At the mines, as they have no prisons, hanging is the only mode of punishment. Upon the whole, life is considered tolerably secure, and property, too, when properly watched and guarded by the owner. But the effects of absentees, though they might not be feloniously stolen "contrary to the form of the statute," would be plundered and lost to the owner to all intents and purposes.

In California there is an utter subversion of the order of society as it exists in the old States, and a confusion of all ranks and distinctions. But in the state of affairs there is one peculiarity that pleases me. Labor is unshackled and unoppressed; it receives its full recompense. The roughest looking "customers" and the most hardy and laborious are likely to have the most of the "dust" here, and, as this commands respect, they are the aristocracy of California. A cook or a house steward commands in this country a higher salary than the Governor of New York, and an industrious drayman, with his cart and mule, is better paid than the Secretary of the United States. The salary of the Postmaster at San Francisco is less than the laundress would exact for washing his linen, and a good carpenter gets a higher compensation for his labor than the commander-in-chief of the squadron.

The climate of San Francisco and other places on the coast is the most disagreeable that I know of. Cold winds prevail during all seasons, and the temperature varies

---

6. Shakespeare, *Hamlet*, *III, i, 56.*

sometimes forty degrees in a day. The summers are worse than the winters. Every body suffers greatly on first arriving here. One requires warm clothing at all times. Although the climate is severe and disagreeable, I think it may be considered generally healthy, excepting in the Sacramento valley. (WNI, June 23, 1849.)

From the Western Plains

The St. Louis Republican furnishes the following interesting items of intelligence, obtained from a gentleman of the Pay Department of the Army who left Fort Kearny on the 27th ultimo:

Col. Loring, with his command, would reach Fort Kearny on the 1st of June. He had had several cases of cholera among his troops, and a number of deaths, but with this exception he was getting on very well.

Major Bonneville expected to reach Fort Kearny on the 5th of June.

Major Sanderson reached the fort on the 25th of May, and left the next day for Bear river, where a new fort is to be established. Major Sanderson had under his command one company of rifles. Another was expected under the command of Captain Roberts. It was to leave Fort Leavenworth on the 13th, and formed, as far as the line permitted, the escort of Gen. Wilson, the Agent of the United States for the Indian tribes in the valley of the Sacramento.

The condition of the emigrants on the Plains and in the vicinity of Fort Kearny is represented to be really distressing, and their difficulties have not yet more than commenced. Along the whole line, more or less of cholera and other diseases prevailed, and at frequent intervals the fresh graves of deceased persons might be observed.

Along the route the water was good, and, until they reached the valley of the Platte, the road was generally all that could be desired. But for more than twenty miles before reaching Fort Kearny—which is about three hundred miles from Fort

Leavenworth—the ground is exceedingly heavy, and it is with difficulty that any teams or heavy wagons can get through it. Along the route, from the settlements to Fort Kearny, the emigrants had followed the same road, and it is now as distinctly marked as any road in the United States. The grass for a mile or more has been destroyed and eaten up. Many of the oxen, mules, and horses were giving out, and at the fort men were abandoning every thing in their zeal to press forward. Many even went so far as to abandon their wagons, clothes, trunks, &c., and attempted to convert their harness into pack-saddles, and in this way to prosecute their journey. Coffee, sugar, meat, flour, &c. were offered to the sutler and persons about the fort at any price, and often thrown away for the want of a purchaser.

One of the editors of the "Western Expositor," (published at Independence, Mo.) who made a trip as far as the Crossing of Kansas river, presents the following statement in his paper of the 9th instant:

The number of emigrants who have passed the Kansas river from the first of May to the first of June is 6,456, having 8,184 head of animals and 1,364 wagons, averaging 2,500 pounds to the wagon. This amount does not include those who took the Santa Fe route, and who went with pack-mules; nor does it include those from our own State who made their outfits at their own town or county. Those who made their outfit at home may be set down as follows: 1,273 men, 2,550 head of animals, 400 wagons, averaging 2,500 pounds to the wagon. From the best information that can be obtained, about 1,600 men have taken the Santa Fe route, having about 2,400 head of animals and 380 wagons, with 2,500 pounds to the wagon. It is also estimated that 800 men, having 1,200 animals, with 160 wagons carrying 2,500 pounds to the wagon, crossed the Kansas river before the first of May, the time we reached that point. We will also estimate those who will pass after the first of June, and those who go by Santa Fe, who have not yet been numbered, at 800 men, 1,200 animals, and 200 wagons. This will give us a grand aggregate as follows: 10,929 men, 13,134 animals, and 2,504 wagons!

(WNI, June 26, 1849.)

Massacre of California Emigrants

FROM THE VICTORIA (TEXAS) ADVOCATE, MAY 25.

We are indebted to the politeness of a gentleman of this place for the perusal of a letter from a California emigrant, dated at San Fernando, Mexico, April 25th. This letter contains information confirmatory of the rumors of the sad misfortune of a portion of Captain Veatch's party, which we published last week. Indeed, it corroborates the published statement, and further says that Captain Veatch's party consisted of thirty-four men, who were all killed except one. The party of Indians who made the attack were composed of Camanches, Lipans, and Apaches, and numbered five hundred in all. The Americans killed one hundred Indians in the fight.

The writer says that his party, numbering 130 men, all well armed, were considerably annoyed by the Indians on their route from Bexar to San Fernando, who would show themselves sometimes in their front and at other times in their rear, driving in detached portions of the company, but fortunately doing no injury.

Several cases of cholera had occurred among them, and two members of the company had died, and at the date of the letter they were waiting for the third one to die.

The Mexicans are said to have been kind to the party, and gave them passports readily; but the alcalde of San Fernando would not permit them to pass through the town on account of the cholera being in the company.

The misfortunes of Capt. Veatch's party may be attributed to their separation from the remainder of their company. If they had all been together, the probability is the Indians would not have attacked them.

What else can men expect when they divide off into small parties to go through a country inhabited by numerous tribes of wild and hostile Indians? A party of eight or ten men, we understand, left Fredericksburg (Texas) a short time since, on foot, carrying their provisions on their backs, expecting to reach California. What folly, what madness! (WNI, June 27, 1849.)

The Overland Travel to California

The correspondent of the St. Louis Republican, writing from Fort Kearny on the 2d of June, states that 4,403 wagons, accompanied by about 17,000 persons, had already passed that point on their way to California. He adds:

"Those who passed along amongst the first were in fine spirits, but quite a change is observable in the centre and rear. Doubts begin to assail many as to the practicability of crossing the mountains, owing to the scarcity of grass and other causes. The grass, even on the river Platte, already begins to feel and show the heavy demands made upon it; what, then, must be expected in the mountains? Such suffering as but few have ever dreamt of will be experienced this year. Would they but preserve their provisions, much of this might be prevented, but in the anxiety to reach the end of their journey, every thing except what is thought to be sufficient to carry them through is abandoned."

(WNI, June 30, 1849.)

The Throng Advances

LATE AND IMPORTANT FROM CALIFORNIA
News to the 1st of May

The steamship Crescent City left New York at 4 o'clock P. M. on the 23d ult., with fifty-one passengers for Chagres, where she arrived on the 2d June, having been detained twenty-four hours off the land by thick weather.

The advices from San Francisco are to the 1st of May inclusive. By the accounts from the passengers per steamer California, Capt. Forbes, the statements respecting the enormous quantities of gold are by no means exaggerated. The Crescent City brings nearly half a million in gold dust and specie on freight, and the passengers on board have nearly as much more, which they bring from the mines.

The United States ship Warren arrived on the 30th April, and fifteen men deserted within twenty-four hours after. It is almost impossible to retain men on board the government vessels.

The steamer California, after innumerable delays, through the untiring exertions of Capt. Forbes, succeeded in leaving San Francisco on the 1st May at midnight. From the 26th March to the day of sailing, Capt. F. was occupied in gathering a crew together, the former crew having deserted upon his arrival. The C. arrived at Panama on the 21st May, having been under canvass above forty-eight hours.

Panama was deserted. With the exception of a few persons waiting for the California (to sail on the 15th) *all* had gone up the coast, no doubt "on their way rejoicing." Panama was healthy.

The road from Cruces to Panama is the one now travelled, although the rainy season had not fairly set in—that is, it rained only occasionally.

The Crescent City brings (by special order) three mails, consisting of fifteen mail bags from California, some of them as far back as March last. The causes of their delay has been the detention of the steamer at San Francisco, from want of fuel and hands, and the want of regularity in the departure of the mail steamers from Chagres.

[From the Crescent City]

San Francisco is crowded with the immigrants, such vast numbers of whom are continually pouring into the place. Accommodations of any kind are scarcely to be obtained. The meanest hut or shed, such as here would be considered uninhabitable, commands an enormous rent. Good provisions are almost equally scarce. The coarsest kind of food must be used, as no other can be procured. No person stays any longer in San Francisco than he can help; but all who are lucky enough to procure transportation, immediately take their departure for the mining districts.

(PPL, June 20, 1849.)

Interesting from California

We have been favored with the following very interesting letter from Colonel Jonathan D. Stevenson, descriptive of the gold mines of California. . . . James H. Brady, Esq., of this city, a son-in-law of Colonel Stevenson, to whom we are indebted for this letter, sails in a few days for the land of promise:—

SAN FRANCISCO, April, 1849.

At the time the official letters of Colonel Mason were written and forwarded to the United States, I was still in service and stationed at Los Angeles, some seven hundred miles from the gold region, and was as ignorant of the truth of the reports that reached us on the subject as you were in the United States, and remained so until my command was disbanded, in September. My official duty called me to Monterey, where I remained until November, when I started for the gold region, with a party of the volunteers, from Los Angeles. We reached the "gold diggings" on the Mocallomy very late in November. I remained in the gold region some six weeks before I returned here, and fully satisfied myself, from personal observation, that none of the statements made by Col. Mason came up to the real facts as to the extent and richness of the gold region.

Toil and Privations

New discoveries of gold are daily made by the miners, and at this time the region from which gold is daily taken extends north and south a distance of five hundred miles; along this whole distance there is not a river, stream, valley, or region in which gold is not found, and that, too, in great abundance, and any sober, industrious, prudent man can, in my judgment, realize at least an ounce per day, besides his board; and this, I assure you, will not more than pay him for the toil and privation he is forced to endure, for if he labors upon the rivers and streams, he must stand with his feet in water every moment he is laboring. If he works at the dry diggings, picking and sifting, he is constantly in a cloud of dust and dirt, and no man can distinguish his best friend by the color of his skin.

This labor would be more endurable if, at the close of day, he could enjoy the comforts of good food and rest; but this is out of the question—he must cook his own food, or go without it. 'Tis true that in some places boarding tents are established; but they have more than they can accommodate, and the food is rarely such as will satisfy the appetite of a fatigued and hungry man. Most of these boarding tents are kept by highly respectable people, who do all they can to make their boarders comfortable; but 'tis out of their power—the means are not within their reach. I have

seen men living for days without any other food than flour mixed with water, formed into a kind of dough and baked in the ashes. This kind of living forces them to the tavern and drinking shop (and the diggings abound with them) where they pay from four to twelve shillings for a glass of liquor. A half box of sardines, or food of that kind, is purchased at from $5 to $10 per box, which many will eat for a supper. The result is that living in this way produces sickness and disease, and many who come into the town with heavy purses of the precious metal, are broken in health and constitution. I am advised that scurvy has broken out in some parts of the region, and is making fearful ravages. This, it is feared, will be the case in nearly all the diggings, as neither vegetables nor other preventives can be had at any price.

Terrible Vices

Let no man flatter himself that gold is to be gathered without toil and peril; toil the most severe must be endured and peril to life, health, good morals and habits, hourly surround them; and many who leave their homes pure and good, free from the terrible vices of gambling and drunkenness, may return (if indeed they ever do return) with gold, but without those possessions infinitely more valuable than gold or diamonds to the man, his family, or his country. No one but those who have witnessed it can form the least idea of the perils and temptations that surround all, and especially the young and inexperienced. When the day of toil is over, they have no house or social circle to enter. The tavern tent is the resort of all; here the cards are the only books that are to be found or looked into. At first they drink and play lightly; but if successful, the thirst increases, stakes are doubled, more liquor is drunk, and many seek their bed (mother earth and a blanket—few have any other) with aching heads—and empty purses. The latter is regarded as of little importance, when from $20 to $50 can be earned by the next day's toil. Many avoid gambling at the mines who fall into the vice when they come here and in other towns; they find themselves suddenly possessed with more wealth than they ever had before, as they have no home but the bar room, the gambling table is the resort for excitement and amusement, and a few days finds them, like the sailor returned from a long voyage and at the end of his frolic, "cleaned out," and ready to embark again for the golden ocean.

An immense number of emigrants, from all parts, have arrived, and are continually arriving here; the hills and valleys in the neighborhood of this town are covered with the tents of emigrants. 'Tis most fortunate for those who bring tents, else they would be without shelter; for $50 per month is paid for a shanty, for a part of a room not more than 12 by 16 feet. There are many houses that did not cost to exceed $1,000, which rent for $200 per month. Property has advanced in proportion, and at this time there is scarcely an approachable point in the neighborhood of this bay where new towns are not being laid out, mapped, and sold.

From all the accounts we receive from the States, large quantities of goods must be coming out here, and I apprehend the shippers will suffer severe losses. I hope not; but I do assure you there is great danger, large as the population will be in this country, that they cannot consume, for a long time, the quantity of goods said to be on the way; and although we are in the midst of the gold region, where men set as little value upon money as in any part of the world, yet at this time gold dust is valued at $16 the ounce, and can be loaned out to some of the best mercantile houses in San Francisco at from two to five per cent per month, and that, too, secured upon bond and mortgage of improved real estate, worth double the amount. This, you are well aware, no business will justify, especially when you add to it the enormous expense of transacting business of every kind.

Wages and Prices

At this time, laboring men in stores get $125 per month; negro cooks, $125, boys to clean boots and knives, $50, a woman servant, Indian or Chilian, from $40 to $60; washing, $6 per dozen; and every thing in proportion. I am paying $64 per month for my board, $40 for my bedroom, and every other necessary convenience in the same proportion. No man can live here as well as he can live at home, in a respectable mechanics' boardinghouse, for $150 per month. At the mines, the board is from three to five dollars per day; at Sutter's Fort and the other landings, two dollars per meal and one to two dollars for lodging if you sleep in a tent.

The two steamers that have arrived— the California and the Oregon—have brought out many who will be valuable citizens—men inured to toil, of sound and industrious habits, many of the mechanics who, during the sickly season at the mines (which is about four months in the year), can turn their attention to other pursuits, and earn from five to ten dollars per day at their trade, or by labor; these are the kind of men that should come—they can serve themselves, their families, and their country; but all who do come should make up their minds to fare hard if they intend to gain gold. Young men who have been delicately reared, and whose habits are not firmly fixed, should not come, except under the guidance and control of men of fixed and firm character; for, I repeat, no where upon the habitable globe do the same temptations to vice await the young and inexperienced, as in California.

About the time of the sailing of the regiment of volunteers under my command from New York, it was the fashion to abuse us all, and the only credit awarded me by a set of miserable scribblers, was for relieving the city of a thousand knaves and vagabonds; and this abuse continued, as I am advised, up to the close of the war. We are now out of service, officers and men, and I can therefore now speak of all as they deserve:—I do not believe the same number of men were ever so indiscriminately collected together and embarked, either as soldiers or emigrants, who combined so much character for honor and integrity, and who possessed more useful knowledge and intelligence, from the learned professions of the artisan, mechanic, and laborer; and as an evidence of this, I unhesitatingly declare that at this time the most respectable and prosperous lawyers, doctors, merchants, clerks, and mechanics in California are those who composed the first New York Regiment of volunteers under my command. . . . I wish you to understand that I speak of the regiment in mass. That there have been some bad fellows among us is true; but their conduct injured themselves more than others. . . . The abuse heaped upon all was as void of truth as the thousand rumors of our unbounded wealth are at this time; the slanders were put forth by those who knew them to be false, and the present rumors of our great wealth are carried from a too fertile imagination.

Thus you have my views of the gold digging and business of California. They are formed from actual observation, and not from the floating rumors of the day; and any man coming here, expecting to find things very different, will be greatly mistaken. As regards myself, as usual, the papers speak falsely of me as to wealth; yet I hope to return to my native city at no distant day—perhaps only as a visitor—with means amply sufficient to meet every legal or equitable claim against me, and have sufficient left for all the purposes of my after life. More I do not require; and beyond this, 'tis of little consequence to any one in New York to know whether I have pounds or tons of gold.

Yours, &c., J. D. STEVENSON.[1]
NYH, June 22, 1849.)

From Those Who are There

[From the Nantucket Enquirer]
SAN FRANCISCO, March 14.

I arrived here, a short time since, in 77 days from Tahiti, in command of a schooner, which I have since sold for $3,700; and am now waiting for the roads to become passable, to go to the mines.

I wish you were here, for money is as plenty as any one could wish. It is difficult to get people to work; every body has bags full of gold dust. I board in a shed, with ten mates of vessels, at ten dollars per week apiece. One of our boarders, a Fairhaven man, who owns part of the ship in which he came out, has bought a whale boat, and goes in her himself, as waterman. He makes from fifty to seventy-five dollars per day. Nothing sells here for less than twenty-five cents.

There is no aristocracy here—no poor men; the merchant has to do his own drudgery. You will see the rich man with a wheel-barrow, carrying his own goods. I heard, the other day, a passenger that had just landed, offer a poor-looking man two dollars to carry up his trunk for him; but

---

1. Col. Jonathan Drake Stevenson, a former New York City Democratic ward politician, was the commander of the First Regiment of New York Volunteers. The regiment was recruited to serve in California during the Mexican War, and was derided by the New York press as consisting mainly of street thugs and idlers. The regiment sailed from New York in July 1846 in three ships, and by the time it arrived in California in March and April 1847, the war was over. The various companies of the regiment settled down to garrison duty, and were disbanded in the latter part of 1848. Many of the men stayed in California and became prominent in the state's early history.

the man looked at him with scorn, and said, "I will give you five dollars to carry it up yourself." The only law here is pistol law—consequently, any thing in the shape of a gun fetches from fifty to two hundred and fifty dollars.

SAN FRANCISCO, April 16.

This country is filling up fast with people from all parts of the world, and many articles can now be purchased here at a less price than in the United States. Thousands and thousands who have shipped out goods, calculating upon large profits, will be disappointed, especially in dry goods; lumber, bricks, lime, house-frames, boots and shoes, coarse clothing, provisions, and such like articles will sell well, and pay a handsome profit. Bricks sell for $75 per thousand. I am happy to say that there is a far better state of society existing in this place at this time than when I landed here three months ago.

There is a great deal of sickness at the mines; thousands of poor fellows who leave here in fine spirits will never return. The first mate of the ship which I came up in from Valparaiso, Mr. Tatch, of Fairhaven, bid me good bye a few weeks since, on the beach, bound up the river for gold, but he died in about one week after we parted. A man's life here is worth about fifty cents on the dollar. While I am now writing, a poor fellow lies tied hand and foot, raving mad, with the brain fever, and very little attention is paid to him. He is a stranger to all in the house. His name is H.B. Williams, of New Orleans, and he arrived here from Mexico last week; twenty four hours or so will close his troubles.

SAN FRANCISCO, April 26th.

A great many people are rushing here with the idea that everybody is digging gold by shovels full, in the streets; but to their sorrow and miserable disappointment, they will, in many cases, find the real state of the case quite the reverse of that. When I first came here, last May, I found a town of about 400 people, most of them going up to the mines quietly, and a great proportion of them getting over 2,000 dollars in three months' time, though some got little or nothing, and many, more than four or five thousand dollars.

But one side of the story has not yet been told, except in a very few instances—or rather has not been explained. A great many are now lingering with diseases brought on by exposure in the different mines, and their coarse manner of living; and in cases even of slight sickness, an almost entire lack of proper nourishment and attendance too frequently harries the victims to their long home.

The town of San Francisco is now overrun with people of all nations, but a small part of whom are able to find shelter in a house or shed of any kind. The beach and hills are covered with sailors, merchants, Spaniards, &c., &c., camped out in tents, with their goods lying about in the greatest profusion.

[From the Lowell Courier]
SAN FRANCISCO, April 27, 1849.

To see how certain other articles are selling, look on the other side:—Fine shirts, $1; all kinds of sheetings and shirtings, a drug—cannot find purchasers. I saw silk shawls, which cost in New York $50, sold at auction for $6 or $7. The best of kid and buck gloves sold for 25c. per pair—cost $1.50 to make. Board for $5 per day.

There has been a new mine discovered here, called the Stanislaus, very rich indeed. We have secured our passage to Stockton, only a few hours' sail, paying $35 apiece. From thence we have to walk 39 miles with our baggage, crow-bar, washbowl and shovel, and blankets. The mine of Stanislaus is situated on the San Joaquin. The rivers are all very high now. The mines on the Sacramento are still sought for. The Indians attacked the Americans above Sutter's Fort, and many were killed. Many men also have been killed in the mines, and many bodies found in San Francisco, around the outskirts.

I only wish I could tell you all, but I cannot. I have not the first cent in the world. Hundreds are leaving daily, on account of the sickness at the mines. I have got along well, so far. I have been offered $400 per month, and my board, as Inspector at the Custom-house, which I refused. You can have no idea of the kind of persons who have the principal charge of the place, and are the business men here—the *ton* of the place. I am surprised—indeed, I never was so much so in all my life. There are men who came out here in Col. Stevenson's regiment, abandoned to vice and dissipation—many of them immensely rich. One, a young man from New York, is said to be worth more than a million. He is spending $500 per day, and don't know enough to take his money and go home. I was introduced to him the other day, and immediately upon our introduction he turned about to his clerk, and said—"Bring me some money." He brought him out a bag full of silver dollars. He took it, and threw it as far as he could, saying, "Here, God d—n you, I want some money." The clerk went and got a bag of gold doubloons. He filled his pockets and turned around to me and said, "Now let us go and drink." That is the man that is called the first man of the place—drunk half the time.

They are trying to establish laws here, but cannot succeed. Soon a different set of people will be here—Yankees, who will turn the tide of affairs. It is no use for any man to come out here unless he has plenty of money to speculate upon. If I only had $5,000, I could make $100,000—of that I am sure. There is a lack of energy here—all are gambling. They have begun a wharf, which they cannot finish. There is a beautiful harbor. Upon my word, lumber is selling for $400 and $500 per thousand. One of our party has engaged his frame house, boards and all, as it is framed, for $800 a thousand, which cost, freight and all, to here, $50.

If only I had a cargo here, I could make my fortune complete; but plenty is coming soon. Nine vessels arrived here the day we got in, and they are arriving daily. There are now in port 65 vessels. The Ohio is here; and imagine my feelings, after travel-

The Stanislaus Mine.

ling 1,500 miles on horseback, to see the American flag once more floating in the breeze. All the crews are deserting here, as soon as they arrive; our crew are all handcuffed. All I want is to go the mines and get a little, and then come to San Francisco and speculate, as I think I can; time will tell all. I advise no one to come out here to make money. There is plenty of gold; but to get it is like a lottery. Some work for one day and go home; others stay months. I have not seen a man who has been digging gold a year.

I have made up my mind not to drink a drop of liquor. Such men as manage San Francisco now are rascals, with few exceptions—generally drunk. I will tell you a positive fact—that land sold here the other day for $600 a foot. Why, money is not considered here of any value. Can such a state of things remain long? No, no. Who is to give such enormous prices for articles? Certainly a reaction is to come; quantities of the higher articles I mentioned are shipped continually from the Pacific coasts. Yesterday, gunpowder was worth $10 per lb.; to-day $5; to-morrow, probably $10 again.

Here you see all nations. The regiment of infantry sent from New York has just arrived, and many of the officers I know well. Some wagons shipped on board a vessel by which A—— sent some things around on the 2d of November, sold for $800 a piece; and the boxes they came packed in sold for more than the original price of wagons, freight, insurance, and all. No one knows what is coming, and therefore cannot send for anything, because he either makes his fortune in trying it, or loses all.

San Francisco, April 29, 1849.

Having a few leisure moments, I will improve them by writing another letter from this important city of San Francisco. The blue laws prevail, or rather, Lynch laws. If a man be caught stealing, he receives 150 lashes on the bare back, and let-

ters are sent to all the other mines stating his crime and appearance; and if he is caught again, at any other mines, he receives 200 more; if again, he is taken to a tree, and shot.

It is singular how some things that are sent, supposed to be wanted most, are cheapest, and as cheap as in the States. Furniture, there is none. A man with steam engines and saw mill attached might make his fortune; for across the bay is some of the finest timber you ever saw—and near San Francisco there is more. But you cannot make money here unless you have capital to start with, that is certain. The land of San Francisco is very uneven indeed—laid out with no regularity, and comparatively nothing done for it as a city. There is no lime here at all; and so cheap is cotton cloth that it is taken to answer the purpose of ceilings and walls; painted, after being tacked on to intermediate joists, placed to receive it. I understand, after the first of May, no foreigners will be allowed to enter the port or land.

(NYH, June 25, 1849.)

Our Missouri Correspondence

St. Joseph, Missouri, June 5, 1849.

*The Overland Emigration to California—
Anticipated Suffering and Distress*

To you, from this remote frontier point, I propose to communicate some items of intelligence which, at this extraordinary immigrating era, may be interesting to the innumerable readers of your *Herald*, though doubtless you have been constantly advised of the preparations and progress of the immense throng of eager adventurers who have set out to cross the seeming endless plains, for that delusive country called Golden Fornia; and, oh! what patient toil, privation, and suffering are to be endured by them, before that far distant region of mineral wealth will be reached! and oh, what intolerable anguish and agony will overcome many a stout heart, and cause them to fall a prey to the devouring monster in a desert country!

First night on the Plains.

Alas! how mournful to reflect that many hundreds of those gay and jovial spirits, who left the frontier with such buoyant hopes, will strew the long, lonely pathway with their bones.

Your readers will probably term this a horribly dark picture; but when the unfortunate truths of the great disaster to this season's overland immigration shall reach you, and be printed in the columns of your *Herald,* next spring, then indeed will your readers be startled by its tale of horrors. — For think lightly of it now as they may, such disastrous immigration never before on this continent has been heard of, as this present season will realize; and thousands have madly rushed to encounter the perils when the facts were so strongly evident of the dangers, for at other seasons, when large numbers have attempted to make the journey, immense losses and suffering have been the consequence, and the highest number, at any previous time, did not exceed 6,000.

What must now be the result in the mountain passes, when there is more than five times that number on their way; and yet so well as it is known that for the want

of subsistence in the mountains and on the great Basin desert, a large portion of their mules and cattle there perished, and left the immigrants to the mercy of chance. Still the hazardous adventurer, with his senses open to the facts, rashly persists in attempting the desperate chances of his getting through. Many who had advanced nearly 500 miles on the journey, having become sensible of their desperate chance, have already returned to this point, disposed of their effects here, by private and public sales, and have left for their respective homes. Numbers are now daily returning here who have been out only from five to ten days; some from causes of dissension in their party; others from causes of sickness and great mortality; and others from causes of great perplexities and discouragements, unaccustomed as they were to the exposed hardships of such a tedious journey; and great numbers will be returning during the season, even some who have gone beyond the South Pass.

Some five to eight thousand will in all probability get successfully through, of those who were first off and in the advance, but after they shall have gone through the mountain passes and the subsistence for cattle been exhausted by their stock, then disaster and calamity will be severe upon those to follow, who unfortunately will be compelled to make the best of their chances for wintering within the mountain snows.

The Mormon train, which is to leave Council Bluff about the 20th of June, will number about 3,000. They expect to reach their settlement in September, and have been commanded to take six months' stores of provisions extra, in order to meet such emergency as may arise from the apprehended inundation of their settlement by the thousands of unfortunate California immigrants.

CALIFORNIA EMIGRANTS RETURNING.—Yesterday morning, the steamer "Kansas" arrived from St. Joseph. She had on board some ten or twelve persons who are just in from the encampments of those now crossing the Plains for California. Some of these persons went as far as three hundred miles out, when, becoming discouraged from the fatigue and hardships of the journey, they gave up the trip, and are now on their way back. They all agree that the undertaking was more than they could conveniently stand. They gave anything but a flattering account of the health and harmony prevailing in the different companies, and seem to think that large numbers will be returning before the main body gets beyond Fort Laramie. These rumors are to be taken with some degree of allowance, as the dissatisfied ones now coming back may view matters in a worse condition than really exists. They all state that the sickness was not as bad as when they first started; but their accounts about the grass, water, &c., materially disagree. Some say the former was fine and the latter in great abundance; others that the horses and mules were starving for the want of both—
St. Louis, Mo., Republican, June 18.

(NYH, June 25, 1849.)

Scenes on the Plains

[From the St. Louis Reveille]
A predicament—The Prairie Alive—
General Twiggs—St. Louis Emigrants—
Military Spectacle—Deaths

FORD OF LITTLE BLUE RIVER,
May 26th, 1849.

DEAR REVEILLE:—A gentleman by the name of Jas. A. Robinson, of Columbus, Ohio, who has been compelled, very much against his will, to return to the States, starts this morning, and has kindly consented to wait a few moments for me to write you a few lines. I am lying on the ground, under the tent, scratching away on the top of an old tobacco box, with fingers cold and benumbed.

We have experienced all sorts of luck since I last wrote to you from Kansas. A week ago to-day I started ahead of our company on a pony, designing to overtake the Kentucky train with which we had intended to travel, and rode at full speed all day, making inquiries of all the Indians and emigrants that I came across, but learned nothing definite. At night I overtook Mr. Thrope, the Secretary of one of the Kentucky companies, who had been detained by illness at Independence, and whose horses had died there. He was proceeding on foot in company with four others who were journeying with pack mules. He had taken a violent cold, and he was unable to proceed further. One of the others had volunteered to go on with all possible speed, and try to overtake the train, and as Mr. Thrope could not walk further, I sent him back on the pony to my friends, and I remained with the pack mules—any thing but an enviable situation, I can assure you. I jogged on about forty-five miles, leading a pack mule, and was just giving out from fatigue when we were overtaken by Eletner. We have as yet heard nothing from our folks ahead, but will persevere on till we reach the Platte, and if we do not overhaul them there, we shall join in some other mule train.

We have been running great risk, in traveling as we do now, of having our mules stolen by the Indians, as we camp alone nearly every night. We, however, keep up a good watch during the night, two of us being on guard at a time, relieved every three hours. This standing guard comes very tough, much worse than waiting till a late hour on the levee at St. Louis for the arrival of a fast steamer from New Orleans, with "late and important" news from Mexico; but I am getting accustomed to it.

Since leaving the Kansas we have passed at least one thousand teams, and we are still behind more than two thousand others. We are scarcely ever out of sight of the Emigrants. A long white line, before and behind, points out the road, relieving very much the monotony of these, to me, very dreary plains. Horsemen are constantly passing and re-passing, galloping over hill and dale; and it is very difficult to drive from the mind the idea that we are still within the precincts of civilization. Every now and then, as we ford a creek or pass through a small strip of wood, I look inadvertently for the fences and habitation of the husbandman, but all that can be seen that indicates that man has been here are the stumps of trees felled by emigrants and a well beaten road.

Day before yesterday we broke the sand-board of our wagon, and while lying by, we were passed by several trains, among which was Capt. James White's of St. Louis. In this company are Dr. White and family, and two other females. The army of Gen. Twiggs also passed the same day. One thousand mounted riflemen and a train of two hundred wagons presented a most grand spectacle, stretching along the road as far as the eye could see—officers and wagon masters galloping at full speed up and down the line.

We learn that several privates have deserted since starting, taking with them their horses, and a good many horses and mules have been lost at the different places of encampments.

As this train will proceed on the California road as far as the South Pass, ample protection will be afforded to the emigrants, in its immediate vicinity, from the Indians. No open attacks are to be feared; but the strictest vigilance will be required to keep the animals from being stolen.

As near as I have been able to ascertain from the emigrants, from fifty to seventy-five deaths have occurred on the St. Joseph and Independence roads. I have been unable to learn the names of any except three or four, who have been buried this side of the juncture of those roads. We give the following: John Deguier, of St. Genevieve, Mo.; Sloan McMillan, of Louisville, Ky.; John Abbott, of New Albany, Ia.; and James A. Groot, a native of Essex County, Vt. Most of the deaths have been from cholera and dissentary. Mr. Abbott was aged seventy-eight years, and possibly died from old age and exposure.

Night before last was the most stormy I ever experienced. A cold rain fell all night, accompanied by the most violent wind. I was on watch when it commenced storming—it blew down the tent in which my two friends were sleeping. I went to their assistance—drove down the pins, in which act I received a very severe cut from a hatchet, having struck at a pin in the darkness with the sharp edge of the hatchet downward. But all my efforts proved abortive; the tent fell down again. Keyes made for the wagon, and Elsler remained all night, enveloped in the bed clothes, under the prostrate tent, on which a long heavy rain beat.

Yours, truly,   MIFFLIN.
(CPD, June 25, 1849.)

FORT KEARNY, Nebraska Territory,
May 26, 1849.

DEAR SIR: Since my last, the army of gold diggers has received mighty and powerful reinforcements. It now numbers over 10,000 men, and has a baggage and provision train of 2,527 wagons. The prairie is dotted with them as far as the eye can reach; not an instant, for the last two weeks, has there been, that emigrants and emigrant wagons have not been in sight from this post. For two or three days past our weather has been most disagreeable, and the effect has been somewhat to dampen the ardor of the emigrants, particularly so as the rain has been falling in torrents most of the time. I have heard hundreds wish themselves at home, and several have actually turned back at this point.

The great majority now crossing the plains were profoundly ignorant, when starting, of what was before them—had no idea of what an outfit consisted of, and, in short, looked upon crossing the prairies as nothing but a pleasure trip, where killing buffalo, wolf hunting, &c., formed the prominent features. The result of such want of experience was that almost every wagon that left the frontiers was overloaded, not with articles absolutely necessary, but with such things as each might fancy he would want while on the prairies, or after he reached the end of his journey. Saw-mills, pick-axes, shovels, anvils, blacksmith's tools, feather-beds, rocking-chairs, and a thousand other useless articles for such a trip, filled the wagons as they left the Missouri river. Soon it was found that the loading was too great for the teams, and now overboard goes everything. The road is lined with various articles—even gold vases and gold washers are abandoned by the roadside. Quantities of provisions share the same fate, which, it is to be feared, will be sadly wanted by those who threw them away, before they reach the Pacific.

Several serious accidents have occurred on the road from the careless use of fire arms. Three men have been shot dead, and yesterday a young man was brought to the hospital dangerously shot through the shoulder.   (NYH, June 26, 1849.)

An Artist at the Diggings

[From the N. Y. Tribune]

CULLOMA MILLS,
South Fork of Rio Americano, April 18, 1849.

Messrs. Greeley & McElrath:—

This place, called by the Indians Curluma, and by Capt. Sutter Culloma Mills, is the spot where the gold was first discovered by a Mr. Marshall, who is now part owner of the saw-mill, which is still in operation, and kept so night and day to get out lumber at $40 the thousand feet, from fine trees which grow in abundance on the banks of the stream. The wood is not so easy to work as our pine, being somewhat harder, but not so full of pitch as the Southern pine. This village, consisting of about nineteen small frame and log houses and about as many tents at the present time, is situated on a plain nearly a mile square, surrounded by very high and steep hills. It is 47 or 50 miles from Sutter's Fort, from which we came on foot and paid for transportation of our baggage $20 per cwt. on ox-teams.

The first part of the road for about twenty-five miles is extremely level and hard, resembling the Macadamized road, but the latter part of the road is up and down high and steep hills, and in some places very rough. The first day we travelled twenty-one miles. There were several of our party and three teams. A merrier and happier set of fellows I do not believe was ever seen on the same road. Our path was literally strewn with flowers of all forms and hues; as far as the eye could see they stretched away, filling the air with delicious fragrance, and charming the eye with their beauty and color. It was no wonder that we were intoxicated with delight, and went on gathering handful after handful and wreathing them around our Panama hats.

Captain Sutter

We stopped at a rancho 12 miles from the Fort, where we were so fortunate as to meet Captain Sutter, accompanied by Mr.

Schoolcraft, the Alcalde of the Sacramento district. The Captain had been up to have a talk with the Indians, and was returning to the Fort with his friend and several Indians. When I learned who he was, I presented a letter of introduction, for which I am indebted to Capt. Folsom, and was received and entertained, as far as the circumstances would permit, with great hospitality and kindness. Capt. Sutter is a remarkably handsome man, about 45 or 50 years of age, 5 feet 8 inches high, wears a large moustache, and imperial, his countenance remarkably intelligent, and his air gentlemanly in the extreme. I do not remember to have met with any one on my whole route who has left a more pleasing impression than Capt. Sutter, and I have promised to accept his invitation to go and pass any leisure time with him at his country residence about 40 miles up the Sacramento. I shall make an effort to procure a portrait of him to take back with me when I return to the United States.

From him I learned that two Oregon men had been murdered near the Mormon Islands, and that a party from that part of the country had gone out in search of the murderers. At night we encamped 21 miles on our way. . . . The second day we advanced only 12 miles, and on the third day about 2 o'clock, after descending some very steep hills, we came to our long journey's end, and pitched our tent close by the hill on the golden sands of the south fork of the Rio Americano. Our first operations were not to gather gold for our pockets, but to get food for our craving stomachs. We dined in a log hut upon roast mutton, boiled rice, apple pie, good bread and coffee—nothing else—for $2.50 each, and were assured that that was a moderate price. One can board and lodge in a room where every inch is covered with human flesh at the moderate price of $7 per day, but we find it much cheaper to live on our provisions which we have brought with us. Salt pork and jerked beef is $1.50 the pound; flour 50 cts. At the Middle Fork, 15 miles from here, it is double that price, and for a meal you pay $4. Most persons buy a few pounds of flour and some beef, and with their tin pan, gun, blankets, and pistols packed up on their back, walk over; or else pack to the amount of 150 lbs. of provisions on a horse and lead him over the mountains between here and the Middle Fork, which seems to me the point of most attraction. These mountains are very high and steep, and he who travels them finds that he must labor hard if he would reap a golden harvest.

I shall remain here some time to dispose of some goods which I have to sell, and then try my skill at washing my own clothes, as well as sand; by washing the former I shall save $24 a dozen. But for washing sand you can make much more; the average now is very low, on account of the water being very high; most of the bars on which the richest washings are found being covered with water, and the estimate now is $24, with a tin pan. Many more can be made by machines. There are many ways by which one can make as much as at digging, and I am employing my leisure time here—when I cannot sell—in making scales for weighing gold, pocket scales being in great demand. I can earn at that, 2 oz. per day, if I did nothing else. I have sold several pounds of Hazard's powder since my arrival here, at $15 the pound;[2] powder flasks at $8; old papers, before the first of February, 50 cts. each; after that date, $1. Pistols and guns are not in so great a demand as I at first supposed, and the prices vary according to the want of the individual; percussion caps are $4 and $5 for 250

---

2. Gunpowder manufactured by the Hazard Powder Co. of Hazardville, Connecticut. The firm was bought by the Du Pont Company in 1876.

in the box. Red flannel shirts sell to the Indians for $16. Champaigne, $10 per bottle. Cheese, $3 and $4 per pound. I sold a gourd yesterday, for which I paid 5 cts. at Panama, for $1. Beads are not in so great a demand here as they were last year; they are bought at moderate prices, to be carried away by the traders who go out to trade with the Indians.

Killing Indians

At present the Indians do not visit here, owing to some difficulties existing between them and the Oregon men, five of the latter having been murdered, supposed by the Indians, although it is not known positively. Blood was found by their companions who had gone off a "prospecting," on their return to camp, found their machines broken, their flour scattered about, and other things thrown into the river. Upon digging under the sand, a bag of gold-dust was found, which was weighed in our scales and amounted to $312. Two of their party, who came here to buy powder, which they desired me to keep for them till they returned, said they were going out to hunt Indians, and I, not dreaming that they were in earnest, told them, jestingly, to bring me a scalp. The next day they drove up to the tent and presented, much to my horror, the scalp of one of four that they had killed that night. They represented the style in which they had shot them in the coolest manner. One of them killed three. He is the son of Old Greenwood, mentioned in Bryant's book— a very handsome half-breed, about six feet high, of splendid proportions, and brave as a lion. His father has led a very remarkable life—having lived among the Indians most of the time. The son has applied to me to write a life of his father, and says he will pay me well. Some of the incidents he has already related are of a thrilling nature.

One of those that were shot yesterday was a young warrior who had fled. Forgetting his arrows, he turned to get them— but, fearing the whites, fled again, and

again turned to see if he was pursued. Young Greenwood—who, it is said, never misses his aim—put a rifle ball through his heart at the distance of 150 yards. Another was shot by the same man, just as he raised his arms to dive into the water, between his shoulder-blades. When he rose again, with another pistol he put a ball into the back of his head, and he sank. There were six white men against 25 Indians. In their camp was found 400 lbs. of flour, with some other provisions and some pans with the names of the murdered white men on them; also, other articles known to have been in the possession of the whites.

The night after the Oregon boys went out, the Indian fires were seen on all the surrounding hills, which has created considerable alarm among the new comers, and has frightened some of them so much that they are about to return. For my own part I consider myself as safe here as I should be at home. If any are attacked, it will be Greenwood and his party. Greenwood has just rode by here, and he tells me that the Indians have threatened him. He says he is sorry for them, as he shall be obliged to kill them all; that he shall call the boys, as he terms them, together, and go out, and if they do not lay down their arrows, he will shoot them all. He is what might be termed a hard case to deal with. Another of his party has just gone by here in his hunting-shirt and deer-skin leggings, whittling away as unconcerned as though they had no care or fighting to do. In truth, I suppose that they do not fear the Indians, who are awfully afraid of fire-arms of any kind.

April 17.—Since the above was written, the Oregon boys have formed and gone out in search of Indians, and there has been a meeting called by those friendly to the Indians, and an express sent for Capt. Sutter to come up and make them come to a talk. Some of them represent that the bad Indians live far from here, up by the North Fork. We shall have peace now with the poor creatures, and it may be so for their sakes.

Rough Living

There are arrivals daily of Americans in parties of 20 and 30. They come in, pitch their tents, and many who had the fiercest fever on board the steamer have turned their steps homeward, frightened at a steep hill that presents a bold front just across the river. At this time there is little prospect of their realizing their extravagant anticipations. They hear the accounts of the new-comers who have not "got the hang of it," as the old washers term it, and consequently get but a trifle out of each panful of dirt, who no doubt with practice will do better, and they are disappointed. Many again find the sun a little too warm, and the nights too cold, and complain of hardships before they begin to experience them. Let one go from here to the Middle Fork, without tent, without bed, with only his blankets to wrap round him, as he lays himself down on the hard rock, or the most level place that he can find on the side of a ravine, as he is obliged to where the water is so high, he may then fancy that he had poor fare. Or when the water is low in July and August, working under the burning heat of the sun—when the thermometer is at 112 in the shade, which they say is the case. It is at this moment, while I am writing, at 90 in the shade here at the mill, at 10 o'clock, and a good breeze blowing at the same time.

Everybody came here with tents, beds, and everything that one can desire, but very few of these things go beyond these hills. Tents have been thrown away, cooking utensils left behind, and when thus arrived at the "diggings," they have learned to mix their flour with water on a rock, and rolling it round a stick, place it near the fire to bake, while their meat was broiling on the coals. I have seen several just in from the mines, who say that they won't stay there and work for nothing. You ask them what they mean by "nothing"—they answer 2 to 3 ounces. What they generally expect is $80 to $100 per day. Certain it is that they bring in a great quantity of gold in lumps and dust, which many of them

Sutter's sawmill at Coloma.

spend as freely as they get it, in drinking and eating. What they do not get rid of that way they lose at the gambling table. One young man told me that his Christmas treat cost him $1,000. His name is Caryck, formerly of Philadelphia. He boasts of having a hand in burning one of the churches during the Catholic riots.

Many represent the mines as being very unhealthy in the hot weather, but others say that it is not so if a man takes good care of himself and will keep himself clean. But it is too common for men to wear the same shirt unwashed from Spring to Fall, and never think of washing themselves. It is not to be expected that they should escape fevers and other evils incident to the want of cleanliness. We are here on the bank of a stream where the water is almost as cool as ice-water, and into which I plunge daily. It is delicious to drink in this warm weather, and while it lasts I have no fear of desiring anything else.

Ale is selling here at $4 the bottle, and is drunk in great quantities. There are several shops for the purpose of retailing liquor, where fortunes are made in a few weeks. Fish are said to be very abundant in the rivers, and in consequence of the cold from the melting snow on the mountains they are very hard and delicious. Deer may be found on every hill. We saw many coming up, and the dogs were chasing them all along the road. A teamster shot one and was cooking a part for his breakfast when we passed him.

It does not appear to me that a man can fail to do well here, if he is content to work hard. Gold cannot be had by any one who sits still, but he must labor hard—hard as the Irishman who carries the hod, or the paver who paves the street. This I had made up my mind to do before I left all the luxuries of home; but then I expected double pay; I expect gold, and I trust labor will give back my sight unimpaired, that I may pursue my profession once more. There must be something in gold digging when men can get $21 a day for their labor, and I know that Donald Grant, of New York, has been employed for several days at carpentering for the sum of $22 per day, and paid in gold. Books are in great demand, and bring a great price. Clothes are thrown away when once worn. No one thinks of washing them, or paying for having them washed.

Let those who are coming out here prepare for the worst kind of living and they will not be disappointed; but they may be sure of making $10 to $30 per day if they are industrious, and chance may give them a fortune in a very few months.

S. S. OSGOOD. (PPL, June 26, 1849.)

Who Discovered the Gold in California?

The first discovery of gold in California, it appears, was made by a Jerseyman, a native of Lambertville, in Hunterdon county, who has been in California some six years, long before the territory was ceded to the United States. Mr. Marshall went to Mexico about fourteen years since. In the following letter, which we find in the Lambertville *Diarist*, he gives an account of his discovery of the golden sand:—

COLLUMA SAW MILL, U.C., April 2, 1849.

In July, 1847, John A. Sutter and John W. Marshall entered into a copartnership for the purpose of building and running a saw mill on the American Fork river, about 40 miles from Sutter's. I had previously explored the mountains and found a suitable place, and a good route for a road to the same, for a mountainous country, notwithstanding the assertions of some four or five small parties sent out before I started, by Capt. Sutter, that on or near the waters of said river it was impossible to get a wagon road for pine timber. Some of these companies were composed of mountain men.

Upon my return, I told Capt. Sutter that there was a strong indication of mineral, and supposed it to be silver—the indications being strange to me. Since, I have found large and extensive silver, copper, iron, and gold beds. All this, mixed through a range of mountains, well might create an uncertainty as to what to expect, in a man who was but slightly acquainted with metals in their native state.

The articles of partnership made me the acting partner. In August or the first September I removed to the place of operation, having some five or six men with me, mostly Mormons—Peter L. Werner and family. I afterwards employed Charles Bennett and Wm. Scott, carpenters but not millwrights; myself being the only one capable of operating in that branch.

In January, 1849, I myself discovered the gold in the tail race of the mill. (The reason why I put so much stress on the "myself," is that I have seen publications making another the person, and giving me a companion.) Messrs. Scott, Bigler, Barger, Stephens, Smith, and Brown were in the mill yard at work, and Bennett at the house near half a mile off. So far, well. Being in debt, the country drained of money, except in the hands of a few sharpers, I had no other course left but to show the same, and finish the mill to pay the men as agreed to. Although it was good for only four to six dollars per day, yet rumor made ounces of dollars. Men soon came to the place where none but a fool or crazy man, they said, would go.

But alas, they left honesty and honor at home, with a few, very few exceptions. Then commenced a course of rascality, of which Sutter and myself were the principal subjects; at us it was aimed. That many-headed community plundered the persons who had given them wealth by their enterprise! Fourteen yoke of oxen were stolen and butchered, and from myself alone, six head of horses, plank, and tools were stolen. Indians were set against me who sought my life. My acquaintance with Indian character and habits prevented any evil befalling me, until Capt. Sutter and myself could get them together and hold a talk with them, when all became quiet again.

You will naturally suppose that I would bring the law to my protection. The rogue was

FROM A PHOTOGRAPH BY SIMAR.

James W. Marshall, late in life.

not to be found and caught. Cattle had a large enclosure—the whole mountains. So you see now the chance for justice. Judge, jury, testimony, were not disposed to skin the proprietors—nor had any been guilty; oh, no. Thus you see we were placed in the same situation as the United States, in forcing her frontier laws into effect. As for law, every body cried there was no law. I have seen men in many situations, that of want and gain, but it was only a few at a time. But now I have been and felt them without law, and the mass with a strong prospect of gain, and the principle displayed was a few swindling mean acts for wealth, and wealth will wipe it all out; and as Sutter's and Marshall's property was at first exposed, it became the prey.

Some newspaper accounts state that Marshall and Bennett discovered the gold. If Bennett is one of the discoverers, so is Werner Scott, [Bigler, Stephens, Smith, Barger, Brown.] Those enclosed in brackets are Mormons, and I found them men of honor—as most of the others employed at that time by me. But when I think of the past, and look over the list, God forgive me if I have but little or no confidence in man. Treachery, if gold is concerned against honor, but few, I find, can stand. JAMES W. MARSHALL. (NYH, June 27, 1849.)

The Number of Emigrants Across the Plains

The *St. Joseph Gazette* makes the following estimate in substance:—

The number of wagons which have crossed at St. Joseph is	1,200
At Duncan's Ferry	600
At Bontown	500
Savannah Landing	550
At Ferries from Savannah to the Bluffs	1,500
Total	4,350

These wagons will average about four yoke of oxen to the wagon, making in all about 38,000. The number of men to the wagon is about an average of four, making in all, 17,400.

Grand Total—4,350 wagons, 17,400 men, and 38,000 oxen.

About two hundred more men are gone with pack mules. Every eighty wagons will occupy one mile of the road, and the whole train will make up a grand column of fifty-five miles in length. It must be recollected that those who have started from points south of St. Joseph, Independence, Weston, Westport, &c., are not included in this estimate. The whole number upon the plains cannot fall much short of 36,000 men.—*St. Louis Reveille.*
(NYH, June 27, 1849.)

Cholera and Gold

From the Overland Emigrants

The Fort Kearney (Nebraska) correspondent of the St. Louis *Republican,* of the 21st ult., writing under date of the 2d ult., says:—The emigrants are still pressing forward in vast crowds towards the Pacific. Every day, every hour increases the number. Yesterday 381 wagons, the day before 400, rolled past us, making in all 3,739 west of this point, that are at this moment wending their way to the golden regions of California. Accompanying these wagons, and including a few trains of pack animals, are nearly 15,000 persons. Those who passed along amongst the first were in fine spirits; but quite a change is observable in the centre and rear. Doubts begin to assail many as to the practicability of crossing the mountains, owing to the scarcity of grass and other causes. The grass, even on the Platte, already begins to feel and show the heavy demands made upon it; what then must be expected in the mountains? Such suffering as but few have ever dreamed of will be experienced this year. Would they but preserve their provisions much of this might be prevented, but in the anxiety to reach the end of their journey, every thing except just sufficient to carry them through is abandoned. Thousands of pounds of the finest flour and bacon are offered for sale at one dollar per hundred, and if no purchasers be found, are left by the road side.

The weather continues to be exceedingly bad, raining almost every other day, and the consequence is, the roads are very heavy, and the progress of the emigrants slow. Thunder storms of the first magnitude can be got up along the valley of the Platte as frequently, and in as brief a period, as in any other quarter of the world. The other evening we were favored with one, when six and a half inches of water, as measured by the rain gauge, were precipitated upon us in a very brief space of time. Owing to the frequent rains, and the melting of the snow in the mountains, the Platte is much higher than it has been for a long time. Much difficulty must be experienced in crossing the South Fork.

The Rifle Regiment will be here tomorrow, *en route* to Oregon. Col. Bonneville, with one company of infantry, under the command of Lieut. Botts, arrived here yesterday, and is now in command of the post. Lieut. Davis, with another company of the 6th infantry, arrived on the 28th inst.

Many difficulties have occurred amongst the "pilgrims," many of the original companies have exploded; and not a few have already taken the back trail towards the settlements—more will follow anon.

Yesterday 194 wagons passed. In the last two days 470 more wagons have passed along, making in all 4,403. The Rifle Regiment is ten miles west of this place. (NYH, July 1, 1849.)

Cholera – Cholera

South and west of us the country is full of it.—It seems to pervade the great Mississippi valley, following its water courses, visiting the large towns, and traveling on its steamboats. Its ravages are terrible, as we shall see when we come to sum up the amount at some future day. New Orleans has averaged its 200 and 300 per day for weeks. It is estimated that one tenth of the slave population of Louisiana have been lost.—This is a property estimate. St. Louis with 65,000 inhabitants buries about 1,000 per week with no signs of abatement of the scourge. Her graveyards look like vast fallow fields just ploughed up. Cincinnati with about 80,000 population buries in all over 100 per day, mostly of cholera.

Funeral trains throng her streets from the rising to the setting sun.

The terror of this disease is in its mystery as well as its fatality. Pittsburgh with 40,000 people, and a city of the Ohio, has no cholera. A boat leaves Cincinnati loaded with passengers for Pittsburgh. Half are attacked with cholera and one-fourth die before they reach the latter city. This was the case with the Wyoming.—But Pittsburgh has no cholera, even though cholera boats land there every hour. Some attribute this peculiarity to the vast quantity of coal burned in that region. In the vain hope to arrest this plague the Cincinnatians have been burning coal in their streets for several days, but without effect. It must have been a solemn sight; these funeral piles burning at every corner; funeral processions constantly passing; the hearse rattling through the streets on its dismal errand; the bell incessantly tolling, and the people either following their friends to their graves, or standing in groups looking for the fatal plague to appear on themselves.

Perhaps it is a felicitous provision of nature that we can feel secure and enjoy our wonted spirits while this vast destruction of life is going on all around us. It is true, the earth itself is but one vast sepulcher. Every thing that animates the eye, springs from corruption. The very breeze that wafts music to our ear has been loaded with the groans of millions, and although, as yet, it brings health to us, we should recollect, in our joy, that we, too, are not exempt from the laws of mortality, and be careful how we fall into that gloomy forgetfulness, which often hovers over the realms of death.

> Our life is but a tale, a song, a dance,
> A little way that frets and ripples by,
> Our hopes the bubbles that it bears along,
> Born with a breath and broken with a sigh.

(CPD, July 2, 1849.)

Affairs in California

The late unfavorable reports from California give additional interest to the following information, which was recently communicated to the New York Courier and Enquirer, by Mr. JAMES L. LORING, who, after having spent some weeks in San Francisco, (whither he went on mercantile business,) left that place on the 1st of May on his return home:

"Mr. Loring represents the number of *foreigners*, chiefly from Peru, Chili, Mexico, and the Sandwich Islands, who are pouring into California as almost incredible. From three to four thousand, chiefly from South American ports, are supposed to arrive in California every week.. The proclamation of Gen. PERSIFOR F. SMITH, forbidding them to come, excites no attention whatever, and is not regarded in the least.

"Great peril to the whole country, he says, is to grow out of this great influx of foreigners. Not only do they seize upon the mines, from which they have been excluded by formal proclamation of the United States Government, but their deportment towards the Americans is said to be in the highest degree insulting and provoking. At the latest accounts the foreigners outnumbered the Americans *ten to one*, in the mining districts, and their demeanor was correspondingly overbearing and insufferable. This had created the deepest indignation among the Americans, especially as the Mexicans were foremost in insult and braggadocio. The Yankees had already taken steps towards organizing themselves into a *Native American Association*, and it is said that, upon the arrival of large bodies of Americans, who were understood to have sailed from various parts of the United States during the months of January and February, they were determined *to drive every foreigner out of the country at every hazard*. During the coming season Mr. Loring says there will inevitably occur the bloodiest and most terrible scenes, growing out of this feeling, that the imagination can conceive. The Americans are hardy, desperate, determined, and well armed; and they will not desist from their purpose till the whole country is cleared of foreigners, or they themselves are forced to yield.

"On the 18th of April news reached San Francisco that an attack had been made upon the Americans at the mines by the Indians. It proved that such an attack had been made, and that *five* Americans had been killed. It is supposed that the Indians were set on by the Mexicans. The miners immediately formed a strong party and started in pursuit. They soon overtook the Indians, attacked them, and *killed fifteen on the spot.* They also took *twenty-five* prisoners and brought them into camp. According to the usual forms of proceeding, steps were immediately taken to give them an *ex tempore* trial, which would, of course, have been followed by summary punishment. The Indian prisoners made an attempt to escape the first night after they were brought in. They were detected, however, *and twenty-four of them were killed on the spot.*

"It is said by Mr. Loring that Judge Lynch is the only advocate known throughout the mining region, and that his decrees are pronounced with all proper judicial forms and executed with relentless severity. There is no law, of course, for the district, except such as is created by the emergency of the case. No military force can be maintained there for a moment. Gen. Smith was applied to by an express from the mines for soldiers to chastise the Indians after their attack upon the American camp. The General smiled, and said that 'if he should send a *company* there would not be a *skeleton* to return.' Soldiers would desert of course instantly upon their arrival. There are none at the mines, and few in the territory—a small detachment being near San Francisco and the main body at Monterey.

"Whenever any offence is committed among the miners, the culprit is seized, a jury of twelve persons is empanelled, testimony is heard, the verdict rendered, and sentence promptly executed. All this is done, as we are informed, with perfect fairness and the greatest care. There is very little robbery or crime of any kind at the mines. Since the opening of the districts to emigrants, eight or ten executions have taken place for robbery and murder, and this has had a most salutary and restraining effect."

Some Mexican papers, (says the *New Orleans Bee*) contain a large amount of information respecting California, some of which, we imagine, is not entitled to much credit. First comes a letter signed JUAN REDDING, addressed to the editor of the *Trait d'Union,* and warning people not to go to California, as the dangers and difficulties to be encountered in obtaining the precious metal are incalculable. Mr. Redding says:

"The gold is not to be extracted with a knife, nor is it gathered by handfuls. To obtain it, excavations must be made from a yard to a yard and a half in depth, by the same width, with crowbars and pickaxes. These excavations, being made in the beds or on the borders of rivers, are consequently soon filled with water, an inconvenience not so much felt in the dry *placers.* The miners, who work in this water up to their knees, are exposed during the day to a heat as great as that of the *Tierra Calientés* of Mexico. They pass their nights, which are cold, either under a tent, if they have one, or in the open air if, as is more frequently the case, they have no tent. This is the true state of things. A few lucky persons gather gold; but, unfortunately, the majority do not find enough to defray their enormous expenses; and he who is enabled to return home in good health, with what he brought out with him, may be considered very lucky.

"The labor of the miners is that of a galley-slave. The most robust man cannot stand it a month. Upper California, the fertility of which of which has been so much vaunted, is, on the contrary, deplorably sterile, when compared with the Mexican Republic. It is a country where sufferings and privations are alone experienced."

(WNI, July 2, 1849.)

Progress of the Cholera

St. Louis, July 3d., P. M.

The interments yesterday were 160, of which 128 died of Cholera. The weather for several days past has been exceedingly hot and damp, but it is again pleasant. Quarantine law is rigidly enforced.

From Pittsburgh.
July 3rd, 8 P. M.

The river is falling with five feet three inches in the channel, Weather cool. There were four deaths by Cholera to-day.

BUFFALO, July 5—3 P. M.

Board of Health report 31 cases and 12 deaths by cholera in last 48 hours.

NEW YORK, July 5—3 P. M.

61 cases and 26 deaths to-day by cholera, and 84 cases and 26 deaths reported at noon yesterday.

CINCINNATI, July 5.

There were 180 deaths in 24 hours, ending noon yesterday.

(CPD, July 5, 1849.)

California

We gather the following geographical and statistical information from letters from San Francisco, running from March 6th to April 14th, forwarded from the Presbyterian Mission in California to the office of the Board in New York:

San Francisco is now a city of probably 5,000 inhabitants, of whom 1,000 have arrived in the last three weeks. There are a number of handsome houses and stores, but the majority of the people live either in shanties or tents. The difficulty of procuring lumber, and its high price, five or six hundred dollars per thousand feet, as well as the expense of employing carpenters, with wages from eight to twelve dollars per day, operate unfavorably for permanent improvements. Still the vast amount of capital continually augmenting here, from the immense production of the gold mines, causes the city to increase with unparalleled rapidity.

About forty miles to the north of this point, as ships sail, and at the head of ship navigation, has been laid out a city called Benicia. Many persons here are of the impression that this will be *the* city of California. 1st. Speculation threatens to injure San Francisco: no lot can be purchased near the centre of the city for less than twenty thousand dollars, and some sell for seventy thousand; lots two or three miles out sell for thousands of dollars. 2d. Difficulty of landing freight: ships anchor nearly half a mile from shore, and goods are landed in launches at immense expense; at Benicia vessels of the heaviest tonnage can lie so near the shore that a staging of planks can be laid across. 3d. Want of public spirit: no wharves are built, or lots allowed for churches, squares, or public institutions; one school house has been built, but it is expected that this will soon be converted into a court-house. 4th. San Francisco has no back country.

To the northwest the only roads to the fertile and already numerously settled valleys of Sonoma and Nappa river are by way of Benicia; and when the rivers are bridged the distance will be eight miles to the latter and fourteen to the former. To the northeast lies the vast valley of the Sacramento and New Helvetia, now called Sacramento city, at a distance of forty miles. The whole country between possesses an exceedingly fertile soil.

My own impression is that as San Francisco has now greatly the advance, it will probably continue to maintain it for the present. Benicia is unquestionably a better situation for a city, and may become a large place, but for many years inferior to its wealthy neighbor. The vast population flowing into California this summer will be centred at the mines; next winter will flood San Francisco, Benicia, and every city and village in the territory.

"The Flowery Land"

On Monday I rode from Benicia to the residence or rancho of George Yount, Esq.,[1] in the valley of Nappa river, a distance of thirty-two miles. The country through which I passed was generally exceedingly fertile and beautiful. The appellation the Chinese gave to the United States, "the flowery land," justly belongs to California; and as I rode over the green turf thickly strewed with wild flowers, and wound my way through broad lawns and lovely valleys, where every tree and shrub seemed vocal with the song of birds, I could not but look forward to the time when a dense population will cover the land. This country precisely answers to my idea of ancient Palestine.

On Wednesday I rode to Sonoma, distant seventeen miles. This is a pleasant village, in the centre of a lovely plain, and is considered one of the most desirable places for residence in all this country. Several Spanish families live here—one of them, the Vallejo family, being among the most extensive land-holders in California. Gov. Boggs's family, of Missouri, lives here, and Gen. Smith, Governor of the Territory, has selected it as his headquarters, although his family have not yet removed here.

On Thursday I rode to Nappa city, eight miles. This place will undoubtedly be a considerable village in a short space of time. Situated at the embarcadero, or head of navigation on Nappa creek, the people of the whole valley—a fine country, of about fifty miles in length by six in breadth—will mainly draw their supplies from thence. Several acres have been laid

Napa Valley.

---

1. George C. Yount (1794–1865) came to Los Angeles in 1831 via the Old Spanish Trail with the trapping party of William Wolfskill. In 1836 he became the first American settler in Napa Valley, where he built a cabin or blockhouse, and developed an extensive ranch. The town of Yountville is named for him.

out in dwelling lots, and find a ready sale; about a dozen houses have been built, and several more are speedily to be erected.

On Friday I returned to Benicia, twenty-two miles. At a distance of sixty miles, in a northeast direction, or one hundred and twenty miles by the bay and river Sacramento, is situated an important village, formerly called New Helvetia, but more commonly now Sacramento city. Various accounts represent the number of the inhabitants to be from two hundred and fifty to one thousand; probably the former number is not far different from the permanent and the latter from the floating population. The country about is considered quite unhealthy, chills and fever prevailing to a great extent; still the importance of the position will always collect a numerous population.

Sacramento city and Stockton owe their origin and growth, in a great measure, to the mines, and will probably treble their population this summer. If practicable, I design to visit them, though the rise in the price of horses, from $30 to $250, must greatly limit my operations.

(WNI, July 6, 1849.)

The Latest News from Panama— Excitement among the Gold Hunters—All off at Last

PANAMA, May 7, 1849.

J. W. GRAY, Esq.,

DEAR SIR:—We are now here, in the midst of excitement. Since my last letter we have had two arrivals from California. On Friday, the barque "Callao" came in from San Francisco, and on Saturday night, late, the booming of cannon announced that the steamer Oregon was in Port. The news has created great excitement, and all are anxious to be in El Dorado. The Oregon brought about fifteen passengers on their way to their homes in the United States, with what they say is for them *enough* of gold, and I have not heard that one of their number has been more than three and a half months in the mines. I saw several fine specimens, the largest one weighing nearly one ounce, and some of our boys saw pieces worth from eighty to ninety dollars, and it is said such specimens are not unfrequently dug up. All are sanguine of making their fortunes, and notwithstanding my habitual coolness, I must acknowledge my desire to be in the "diggins."

I conversed with one man who declared there was enough gold in California for an hundred thousand men to dig in one hundred years. It is reported the California will be here in a few days, as she was coaling when the Oregon left. Her entire crew had deserted, which had caused her long detention, and new hands were procured at the most extravagant prices only. The first engineer was sick, the first assistant, second, and third had sloped,[2] the latter was taken and put in irons on board the sloop of war Warren, for having threatened, it is reported, to blow up the steamer if he was kept on board.

The Panama arrived yesterday, after a passage of seventy-eight days from New York. It is said she had an unpleasant and stormy time, but rode the waves nobly and proved herself to be a staunch craft. A good deal of bitterness exists in consequence of her having taken on board a large number of Peruvian passengers. A good deal of quarreling is also likely to ensue, unless the California soon arrives, for precedence on board the steamers, as the holders of tickets for the California, second trip, claim a priority by date, over the holders of tickets for the Oregon. Should the California not arrive, there will be trouble.

A circular, under date of April 1,

---

2. Ran away or escaped; a hasty departure.

addressed by Gen. Smith to the American Consul here, gives notice that as soon as he shall have obtained sufficient force, he shall prevent all trespassing upon the public lands, and enforce the penalty for doing so of fine and imprisonment. If he means to include American citizens in his list, he will find it a hard regulation to impose, as most of those who have travelled so long a distance to better their fortunes, will not stop on the threshold of the land they have sought through difficulty and danger to reach.

We are now essentially broken up: our baggage is all packed preparatory to going on board, and at three o'clock, high tide, we are off, and sail this evening. Hersh and White also send off their baggage to-day and sail to-morrow—they go on the Sophia. We hope to reach our destination at about the same time and go in company into the "diggings." All are happy to get away, and deem themselves fortunate at escaping unharmed, this land of fevers. Many strangers already sleep their last sleep side by side: peaceful it may be here as anywhere, but it must be hard to die far from home, with no friend to console in the last hour, no loving heart to ease the bed of death.

Adios! Yours, &c. DEACON.
(CPD, July 9, 1849.)

Intelligence from California

Letter from Lewis Dent, Esq.

About the first of June, 1848, I wrote to you from Santa Barbara, where I had been called in my professional capacity as a lawyer. During my month's business engagements in the south, I was entirely ignorant of the change of affairs in Monterey. You may imagine my surprise on my return to find that place almost depopulated. To my anxious inquiries, the answer was returned that the inhabitants had gone "to

the mines." I knew that California abounded in mineral treasures, and I naturally supposed that a quick-silver mine, richer than any of the others, had been discovered; and that, when the curiosity of the good people was gratified, they would return to their homes. So without more ado I repaired to my office, and, shutting out the inquisitive sunshine, plunged into Blackstone's Commentaries.

Two days after, I was requested by my landlord to look out for another boarding house, as he intended in a few days to leave for "the mines."

My washerwoman returned my linen unwashed, with the information that she was off that day for "the mines."

My Indian servant took leave in the morning, without even saying *"con su licencia!"*[3]

More to divert my mind from these petty annoyances than because it was of pressing moment, I proceeded to the Alcalde's office, where I had a little legal matter pending; when, arriving there, lo! on the panel of the door flared these ominous words—"Left for the Gold Mines!"

I looked around—the streets were deserted; true, there was a solitary cur in sight, but even he appeared bent upon a journey. I returned to my office—secured the door and windows with an air of gloomy determination, and leaving a notice as to my whereabouts, departed the ensuing day—shall I say it?—for the "gold mines."

I started my wagons on the road, and proceeded myself to San Francisco. It presented the same desolate appearance as Monterey. The houses were tenantless—the busy throngs I had seen there a few months before were gone; the bay spread before my eye in undisturbed tranquillity, and

---

3. With your permission.

"Ships, sailorless, lay rotting on the sea."[4]

I first went to a river called the Yuba, flowing from the Sierra Nevada, and emptying into the Sacramento. My Sandwich Island servants, of whom I had employed fifteen, at forty dollars a month, deserted me at Sutter's Fort. I also had ten Indians and a colored man, a cook. The Indians remained faithful; his sable dignity condescended to remain on condition I would give him "Congressman's pay," i.e., eight dollars per diem. I was compelled to agree to his terms; one must eat, you know.

At the Yuba, we all set to work. The first pan-ful of earth I washed, which operation did not consume more than twenty minutes, yielded me fourteen and a half dollars. There were four of us in company. At the end of a month, after paying expenses, we divided nine thousand dollars.

The gold news had, by the middle of August, 1848, extended north to Oregon, and south through the northern provinces of Mexico. By the middle of September we had large contributions to our population. People are now flocking from all quarters—China, the Sandwich Islands, Mexico, the South American republics on the Pacific coast, are pouring a host upon our shores, and "the cry is still they come!"[5] San Francisco cannot entertain one-tenth of her present population.

I wonder if Missouri will be backward in sending us a portion of her enterprising citizens. The skies are very blue here, and albeit we have not many houses, surely they who are willing to encounter the hardships of the prairies, will not complain of a couch on the green earth, and a cloudless sky for a coverlid.

Perseverance

The Independence correspondent of the St. Louis *Republican,* writing under date of the 18th ult., says:—

I have an incident to relate. A man from Herkimer co., New York, about 35 years of age, as I should suppose, strong and athletic, withal one of the "Sons of Temperance," walked into the bar room of the Noland House, with this accost: "How d'ye do, mister? I want to stay all night with you, and something to eat, too; but I have not got the first red cent, by gosh! and if you do me this particular favor, I will pay you some time or other, I reckon." The worthy proprietor of that establishment told him he could stay, and welcome. The man then stated that he left his native village on foot, without a dime, had travelled thus far without money, but had followed trains and lent a helping hand in case of emergency, and had succeeded in getting his food by that means. He said his father had always impressed on his mind, "persevere," and it was constantly before his eyes—and by dint of that, he had succeeded in reaching here, and felt confident that he could cross "the mountains." Such a man is bound to get some of the "metal," if any is to be had. His "kit" consisted of two shirts, two pairs of pants, and a fine-tooth comb.

Small Town, Large Prices

SAN FRANCISCO, June 20, 1849.

From the point to which the eyes of all the world are gazing eagerly, I sit down to jot a few lines, showing you how we do things in this entrance to the cave of Aladdin.

---

4. Mr. Dent extracted a quotation from memory, and may perhaps have remembered incorrectly. The editor offers the following as a possibility of what he intended: "I looked upon the rotting sea, / And drew my eyes away; / I looked upon the rotting deck, / And there the dead men lay." (Samuel Taylor Coleridge, *The Ancient Mariner.*)
5. "Hang out our banners on the outward walls; / The cry is still, 'They come'; our castle' strength / Will laugh a siege to scorn." (Shakespeare, *Macbeth, V, v, 1.*)

When I landed on the pile of rocks which formed the apology for the wharf of San Francisco, twenty-seven months ago, this town boasted some ten houses. The turkey buzzards were gathering their prey about its streets, and an air of lifelessness pervaded them. Now and then a stray ship anchored in its noble bay, with the hope of fleecing the natives a little; and with even the enthusiastic ideas I then entertained of its growth, how little did I dream that it could be so rapid, so wonderful!

As if by magic, the ten houses have grown into between four and five hundred—the birds of prey have taken their departure to regions unknown—the streets exhibit all the busy eagerness of a large metropolis, and the harbor is filled with vessels from all parts of creation. Gold has done all this, and will yet, in time, I doubt not, make San Francisco the largest city on the Pacific coast.

Vessels are daily arriving from the States, bringing with them hosts of eager adventurers, all bent upon making their fortunes. The rush has been so great that it is impossible at present for a stranger to procure a lodging for love or money. Most of the new comers, therefore, pitch their tents upon the beach, and many remain here until their funds are all exhausted, when they make a push for the mines.

To one who has "seen the elephant," it is amusing to watch the movements of the new comers. Many of them appear to think that when they arrive at San Francisco they are "thar," and all they have to do is to take a pick and shovel and commence digging. Upon their arrival, learning their mistake, they immediately commence inquiries from everybody of where they shall go, and the contradictory statements they receive rather tend to perplex than satisfy them. Many become disgusted, and either return home, or accept situations as clerks, inspectors of customs, or, in fact, anything they can procure.

As a friend remarked to me a few days since, "this is a small town with very large prices." Board varies from 16 to 21 dollars per week; washing 8 dollars per dozen. A common lodging room—and none to be procured at that—rents for fifty dollars a month; stores and offices rent for from three hundred to a thousand dollars per month. A "clean shave" costs two dollars; a game of billiards a dollar; and last, though not least, the damage sustained to an individual's pocket in imbibing a gin cocktail is twenty-five cents!

The old hotel, which two years ago rented for a thousand dollars per year, now rents for sixteen thousand. A new and capacious hotel, called the "Parker House," built by Robert A. Parker, Esq., was opened a few weeks since with a splendid ball and supper. This house is a credit to California, being the largest in the country. As a specimen of the high rent here, two billiard rooms in this house, containing four tables, rent for twelve thousand dollars a year; two rooms appropriated to gaming rent for twelve thousand dollars per annum each; several smaller rooms for the same purpose, at six thousand each per annum; and the remainder of the building consists of dining rooms, lodging rooms, and offices, which rent at enormous prices. The Parker House is conducted in a style which will, I doubt not, meet the approbation of all strangers coming to San Francisco.

The market is overstocked with most kinds of goods, and they are generally selling very cheap. If this is so much the case now, heaven knows what will be done when those "hundred sail" which are daily expected reach here.

We had a very interesting gold fever on a small scale a few days since in our very midst. It seems that some keen-eyed genius, in travelling through one of the streets, saw lying on the ground a piece of gold. Stooping to pick it up he observed some more, and as he still continued at his occupation, all the greenhorns soon gathered around him. In half an hour the whole street was lined with gold seekers, and strange to say, all were finding some. Yes, there lay the "yellow mica" scattered in our very streets. The eager crowd soon attracted the attention of our citizens, and a variety of opinions were, as is usual in such cases, expressed. Many became quite enthusiastic; declared that San Francisco was resting on a gold mine, and threatened to bring pick-axe and shovel, and dig, to the great detriment of the public streets. One man did actually do so, but after wheeling his dirt and finding nothing in it, gave it up. The knowing ones soon solved the mystery. The fine particles of gold can be found in every street, and are the sweepings of the stores where gold is taken in exchange for goods. The excitement has died away, and the town has assumed its usual quiet, if there is any such thing as quiet in San Francisco.

E. GOULD BUFFUM.[6]

(NYH, July 10, 1849.)

A Scrimmage on the Plains— Ohio Boys Whipping Indians

PLATTE RIVER, Indian Ter.,
June 3d, 1849.

We have an unexpected chance of sending letters to the States, but have only a few moments to write. We are within about 50 miles of Ft. Kearny—will write from there. We have got along well the most of the time, until a few days ago. A party of Indians came to our camp; we gave them their dinner and some presents; they followed us and stole two oxen; we tracked four of them some eight miles into a ravine—the worst place I ever was in. Our party was small, there being but twelve of us. All at once we came upon

them—they had killed the oxen. They had stolen from other companies, but had never been followed, and so supposed themselves safe. It was not our intention to harm them; but we were on all sides of them before we or they knew it. A shower of arrows soon let us know what we had to deal with.

Capt. Pierce then ran forward and threw down his gun—called and motioned them to do the same—reached out his hand and cried, "throw down your arms!" A loud war-whoop that made our hair stand on end, and a dozen arrows, was their answer. The chief levelled his rifle at Pierce, but before he could fire, a ball from one of our boys laid him dead. They had every advantage of us, and were making good use of it—retreat was impossible—we must fight, or be every one of us cut off. The word "Charge" was given, and we soon routed them. Our horsemen were on the outside of the ravine, and met them as they came out—they shook their blankets and frightened the horses so that they could not control them.

When we came out of the ravine, about thirty yards to their left, they had three of our men in a corner—Mr. Fisher was one of them—we shouted, but they rushed on—one of the boys fell—another was down with two horses over him, and fourteen Indians were within thirty feet of them. Mr. Fisher turned his horse to charge with the bayonet, when we were almost deafened by the loudest report of a rifle I ever heard, and Mr. Fisher's horse fell dead under him, shot in the breast with an ounce ball. The one that was under the horses now raised his rifle, and their leader

6. Edward Gould Buffum came to California in 1847 as a lieutenant with Stevenson's First Regiment of New York Volunteers. He went to the gold mines in 1848, and was a reporter for the *Daily Alta California* in 1849 and '50. He went back east in 1850, and published his book *Six Months in the Gold Mines*. He returned to California in 1853, was a reporter and editor for the *Alta*, and a member of the legislature in 1855. In 1857 he went to Paris, where he wrote letters for the *Alta* and the *New York Herald*. He committed suicide in 1867 at about the age of 45.

fell dead. They then turned and fled, throwing away everything but their arms. One of our boys was shot through the leg—no one else was hurt.

SAMUEL T. KEESE.

(CPD, July 13, 1849.)

The Gila Route

The following is from one of the members of the military force which took the Gila route for California last fall. The troops arrived in California after much suffering.

East Bank of the Colorado River, 9 miles below the mouth of the Gila, State of Sonora, Mexico, Nov. 22, 1848.

My Dear Parent:—From the time we left Chihuahua until we arrived at the frontier settlement of Touson [Tucson], in the State of Sonora, (within some four days' travel of the Gila,) we got along quite pleasantly and smoothly, but as soon as we left Touson our troubles commenced. The whole country between where we are now encamped and Touson is a perfect desert of rock, mountains, and plains of sand. After we struck this river we came directly down its valley, encamping on its banks nearly every night, occupying nearly 25 days in traveling about 180 miles. It had been a rare sight to see a bunch of grass as large as a garden patch. We subsisted our mules on the little cane we found in the neighborhood of the river, and cottonwood brush. The consequences were that we were obliged to abandon much of our property. We arrived on this side of the mountains with 115 wagons and 5 traveling forges, being the whole number with which we left Chihuahua. Out of this number we have abandoned on the road between here and where we struck the river 31 wagons and 3 forges. We must have left behind us 200 mules and 100 horses. The rest of our animals are in a miserable condition, and the prospect is that we shall leave several wagons at this place. We arrived to-day, and the men are now at work making a raft to commence crossing the river to-morrow. Ahead there is no better prospect for us, for it is stated that for 60 miles the country is a sand desert, and, in addition to there being no grass, that we shall find but little water.

All our rations have run out excepting the flour, on which we are now wholly liv-

The Gila River.

ing. It is said to be something like 180 miles from here to San Diego; so you can see that, with our famished and worn-down animals, the prospects before us are not very flattering. Indeed we have got along slow from the first—the latter part of the time we were compelled to go slow—having left Camargo on the 15th of July and Chihuahua on the 1st of September. During the whole march we have been favored with pleasant weather.—The nights have become quite cold, making ice half an inch thick in a shallow vessel, but the days are just warm enough for journeying.

It is too cold to add much more, even if I had paper, for I make use of the last sheet I possess.   (ISJ, July 13, 1849.)

A California Farm

From the *Hartford Times*

Truth, it is sometimes said, is stranger than fiction. A fact connected with the California emigration—though not directly with its gold mining—has come to our knowledge, which, while it wears all the features of an invention of romance, is nevertheless strictly true in all its parts. It is the more interesting to our readers from the circumstance that the hero of the story went from this vicinity.

About a year ago, a young man in a neighboring town failed in his business, and after assigning his property, his assets fell short of his debts by about ninety thousand dollars. This was a pretty heavy load to carry, but he was not altogether discouraged, and said the time would come when he should be able to pay off his debts to the last cent. People, of course, were incredulous; but, strange to say, the probability now is that his promise will be fulfilled at a very early day.

He sailed for California to earn his living by labor, before any news had reached here of the wonderful gold discoveries of that region. He took out with him a small invoice of goods, and the machinery for one or two saw-mills. This cargo was wrecked before he reached his destination;

he lost all his goods and barely escaped with his life.

He sailed from the Sandwich Islands, where he had been carried after the ship-wreck, and found himself at San Francisco with $10 only left of all his property. He immediately opened a negotiation with an old settler for a fine tract of twenty-four square miles of the best timber land in that vicinity, with several saw-mills upon it. He finally bought it for $60,000, on credit of one and two years. He was able to obtain this credit by producing the invoices of the goods he had shipped, though he withheld the fact of their being wrecked. At the same time he secured the settler by mortgaging back the property to him for security. Soon after the purchase, the gold fever began—emigrants poured in from all quarters, and houses and shanties could not be supplied as fast as they were wanted by the new comers.

The consequence was that lumber rose to an enormous price—several hundred per cent., in fact, beyond its ordinary value, and the saw-mills of our penniless but enterprising adventurer soon began to coin gold for him much faster than the most favored of the gold diggers could find it. In three months' time he had cleared in solid cash $42,000 towards paying off his purchase of $60,000. With part of his earnings he bought the ship *Huntress,* and resold her a week afterwards at a clear profit of $15,000. With another portion of it he added to the number of his saw-mills and flour-mills—the latter paying nearly as round a profit as the former. Lumber still maintains its extravagant price—emigrants are flocking in thicker and faster than ever—every thing in the shape of a board or a shingle commands almost its weight in copper if not in gold—and our Yankee friend at the last advices, was confident that the profits of his business will largely increase for many months to come.

Nothing but some unforeseen contingency can prevent him from speedily becoming the richest man in California. He anticipates, with pleasure, returning home at an early day, paying off his creditors, principal and interest, and having a princely fortune to spare. Altogether, it constitutes a very rare and remarkable case of energy and enterprise, combined with good fortune.—The foregoing facts are fully confirmed by intelligent men who have been on the spot, as well as by letters from various and respectable sources. This man went out to work and carry on a regular business without thinking or knowing anything about gold digging; but of all the mines which have been thus far opened in California, it appears that he stumbled on by far the most productive.

(CPD, July 16, 1849.)

Progress of the Epidemic

The mortality of the past week has far exceeded that of the previous one. This result is singular, when we consider the opposite character of the weather of the two weeks. The one extremely warm and dry, and the one just passed cool and dry. A more salubrious air never was wafted over our devoted city than during the past week, coming from the north-west, north, and north-east, after a heavy rain from the north-west. If there was any *ozone* in the atmosphere before, the storm of last night week must have entirely driven it away. But the epidemic still rages—decreasing one day and then mounting still higher the next. Our weekly account is as follows:

Week ending June 30:
Cholera   525;
other deaths   236;
Total   860.

Week ending July 7:
Cholera   814;
other deaths   297;
Total   1,111.

Of the above interments, 802 were in the foreign cemeteries, and 78 in the Public ground. This shows a dreadful mortality among our foreign population. We should estimate that portion of our population at 40,000.

Acclimation is a great safe-guard in all epidemics; and those who are not "native to the manner born"[7] should be extremely careful and prudent. The change of water, from the East here, in nine cases out of ten, predisposes the subject to diarrhœa. Then how much more liable will those be who come from another continent and another climate. The German will find that the wine of this country is not the same he has been accustomed to drink; and the same with the beer. As for vegetables, while we would not recommend a total abstinence from what they have been accustomed to eat, it would be well to reject the most unwholesome and reduce the quantity of the others.

Such a course, with a radical, thorough cleansing of rooms and yards, and a thinning out of crowded localities, would soon work a wonderful change in the health of the city. Let influential men among them devote their time to impress the stern necessity of prudence, cleanliness, and room, in these times, and our lists will soon decrease to a healthy standard.

(CPD, July 16, 1849.)

Cholera Reports

Philadelphia, July 14.—In the course of the week ending yesterday there have been 393 cases of cholera and 142 deaths.

New York, July 14.—For the week ending this day there have been 678 cases of cholera and 274 deaths from that disease; of these, 123 cases and 51 deaths were reported to-day. The Board of Health has directed the starch, soap and bone-boiling

---

7. "But to my mind—though I am native here / And to the manner born—it is a custom / More honor'd in the breach than the observance." (Shakespeare, *Hamlet, I, iv, 14.*)

establishments, slaughter-houses, and other like nuisances within the city to be immediately shut up, and the business thereof discontinued during the prevalence of the epidemic.

Westchester, (N. Y.)—In the Westchester county Poor-house, located a few miles from Tarrytown, the cholera first made its appearance on Monday, the 2d instant, and on Wednesday thereafter there had occurred forty-three cases, of which twenty-one were fatal.

Cincinnati, July 13.—The Rev. Mr. Lord, of the Congregationalist Church, was taken last night with the cholera and died to-day. Mr. Moses, an exchange broker, was also taken at the same time and has since died. To-day 154 interments—112 from cholera.

Columbus, July 12.—The cholera rages dreadfully in the Penitentiary; 80 convicts have died. About 200 are now in the hospital, and they are dying at the rate of one per hour. Doctor Yard, one of our physicians, who volunteered his services, died of the epidemic last night. Dr. Lathrop, the resident physician, is not expected to live. The city is otherwise pretty healthy.

St. Louis, July 12.—The interments for the last twenty-four hours have been 186, of which 145 were from Cholera. This is an alarming increase of the disease, and has created renewed panic among us. The total deaths for the week ending 9th instant were 846, of which 642 were from cholera. The aggregate mortality for the past six weeks is 3,484, of which 2,529 were cholera cases.

St. Louis, July 13.—The cholera is on the increase in this city, and the interments yesterday reached 190. Several of our most eminent physicians have fallen victims to the disease.

At Belleville, (Ill.) there have been 92 deaths from cholera in a population of less than 4,000, and the epidemic still rages at Alton, Illinois. There were 10 deaths from cholera there yesterday.

Chicago.—The whole number of interments in Chicago for the month of June was 124, and of these 94 died of cholera. The Democrat of that place says that four-fifths of the cholera cases are among the foreign population, and quite one-half among the Irish.

Montreal, July 13.—Riots occurred at Quebec yesterday on account of the cholera, during which the hospitals in the populous districts were destroyed. Montreal continues quite healthy.

FROM THE NEW YORK EXPRESS OF SATURDAY.
CHOLERA UP TOWN.—Among the latest victims to the "prevailing epidemic," we are sorry to say, is the only son of Mr. GREELEY, Editor of the *Tribune*. It is a remarkable fact that the cholera prevails to a greater extent in the upper wards than it does down town, even in the filthy precincts of the Five Points.
(WNI, July 16, 1849.)

What the Ladies do in California

A gentleman who made the trip to California via the Isthmus, writes an interesting account of his travels to a relative in Salem, which is published in the Register. We give the closing part of his letter, dated Monterey, April 22:

"*Sabbath*—A bright and beautiful day. Distributed tracts this morning to soldiers.

"*Monday*—All very still now in Monterey. Men at the mines. There is good society here—Mr. Botts and family, brother of Hon. John M. Botts, of Virginia; Gen. Riley and family; Capt. Westcott and family; Major Canby and family; Mr. Larkin and family; Mr. Little and family; and others. There are several pianos in town, and next to nobody to play. We do not go to the mines to preach, because of the senormous expenses of living there—$8 or more a day—and because people are entirely scattered and moving. No service can be obtained of any sort, without the greatest difficulty. Ladies have the worst of it. Mrs. B. never did any work in Virginia, among troops of servants, but now she does all, and is obliged to do all her work, I think, including washing. Very good; when she saw she must do it, she doffed all ceremony, and does it nobly, and is none of the worse for it yet. So Mrs. C., a woman of complete education and refinement, she can do no other way, and she grows fat on it. Mrs. W. is a beautiful woman, and was brought up in luxury at home by an uncle. She brought out hired servants, and they had not done the first house cleaning, to move in, after they arrived, before they announced their intention to leave at once. Well, Mrs. W. cried awhile about it, and her husband offered $20 per month to the maid; but it was no inducement, and away she went, and Mrs. W. has cleaned her own house, and is 'well to do' yet." (WNI, July 16, 1849.)

From the Plains

We find the following interesting letter in the Upper Sandusky *Pioneer*, from Col. Andrew McElvain to his wife:

INDIAN TERRITORY, June 6th, 1849.

MY DEAR WIFE:—I once more have an opportunity of writing you a few lines by your nephew, R. J. Hunter, and others, who are now encamped with us on the Little fork of Big Blue. It becomes my duty to send you the melancholy news of the death of your brother, Major Joseph Hunter. He died about 13 miles west of Fort Kearney on the Big Platte. He died of the cholera, and upon mature reflection they thought best to return to the States, and in passing along this morning they were surrounded by 500 Indians, who robbed them of just such things as they wanted. The boys met us under such excitement, and you know when such men as Armitage and the Hunters become excited there is some danger.

I have another melancholy fact to communicate to you and the citizens of Upper Sandusky; that is the death of my old and highly esteemed friend, Judge Chaffee. We passed his grave last Thursday. He sleeps his last sleep three miles west of the junction of the Roads from Independence and St. Joseph; 180 miles from the former and 130 miles from the latter place, near the road on a bluff, left side of the road as you go west, with a neat head-board written thereon, "Joseph Chaffee of Wyandot county, Ohio, died May 25, 1849." I had not the pleasure of seeing my old friend's grave, being too sick at the time to look out of the wagon in which I was riding, having been attacked the day previous with the cholera, and at that time did not expect to ever leave our encampment, which was four miles west of that place; but it has pleased Him who rules and sways the destinies of man, to restore me once more to common health. But I am badly salivated, which causes me great pain here in the wind. Had it not been for the skill and gentlemanly attention of Dr. J. H. Drumm, of Little Sandusky, some three of my company must have gone the way of all livings, at the encampment I last spoke of.

This is a beautiful country, and the trip would be a pleasant one, had it not been for the cholera.

We have now with us Col. Lyle, Giles, Pordy, Swain, and Buck, from Upper Sandusky.

We are the finest and best set of men you ever saw.

Truly Yours,   A. McELVAIN.

(CPD, July 17, 1849.)

The Nicaragua Route to the Pacific

LAKE NICARAGUA, April 11, 1849.

On the 3d inst. we left the coast, *en route* for the Pacific, and were *only* seven days in reaching this point. Our company had arranged for three bungoes to convey us, with our baggage and effects, but were unable to get more than two, which left with five of the party early in the afternoon.

These bungoes are about fifty feet in

length and seven feet beam, having the stern part, for about eight feet, thatched over, making a sort of cabin to sleep in, and protect voyagers from the sun and rain. The cabin is barely sufficient for two persons. The bungoes generally have from eight to ten naked natives, commanded by a *patron* to manage the vessel, and they are individually and collectively bad specimens of human kind.

They are drunken, cowardly, and treacherous.

We had to leave with only six, as two of them were not to be found, being probably drunk in the woods. Some of the rest of the crew were also quite drunk, and behaved very ugly, and we had a great deal of trouble in getting them into the boat, as we had almost to shove them in by main strength, and it was 7 o'clock in the evening before we started. Five bungoes left before us, and although the last to leave of the advanced party, we soon overtook them. One good Yankee sailor is worth more than a whole crew of such fellows as we had with us. Our passage up the river was full of incident and adventure, affording great enjoyment for the time, and ample material for future reflection.

This is the dry season, and the river at this time is quite shallow; however, it is a very handsome river, and quite wide for the most of the way, and the rapids are not very dangerous, and could easily be overcome by Yankee enterprize. The river is about 90 miles long, and is navigable for steamboats of not more than two feet draught, *in any season,* and with some expense could be made navigable for boats of greater depth. On our trip up to this place we used our guns, when birds and animals incautiously tempted their fate, but being mostly confined to the bungo we could not follow the game. All the birds and monkeys that came within reach suffered some, and at night, for want of other music, we were grateful for the howlings of the cougars in the woods. One day, on our passage up, we saw an animal that throws all

accounts of Col. Fremont's woolly horse perfectly into the shade.

As I understand, the creature is called "Dante" [Manatee]. It lives in the water, and feeds on the grass growing on the margin of the river. It greatly resembles a mammoth hog, almost of the size of a cow, of a black color, with a proboscis similar to an elephant although not quite as long. It had a young one with it. . . . We tried our guns upon the creature, but, being at too great a distance, our buck-shot made no impression.

This is an insignificant place, as besides the public offices here, there are only a few miserable houses, occupied by the natives. When I arrive at Granada, I will give you an account of our voyage on the Lake, and some description of the city, and matters of interest; and as we are about to embark, I must hastily close.

Yours truly, "JORGE."
(ISJ, July 19, 1849.)

Dow, Jr. on California

MY HEARERS:—I know very well what you imagine will procure to you bliss by the hogshead: it is that wretched, filthy stuff called money. This it is keeps your souls in a flutter, and sets you jumping like a lot of chained monkeys at the sight of a string of fish. You think if you only possessed a certain heap of the lucre, you would lie off in lavender—make mouths at care—say, How are ye? to sorrow—laugh at time and feel as happy as an oyster in June. O, yes! if you only had enough of the trash, I admit you might feel satisfied, and of course contented; but in such cases, more requires more, the last more requires most, most wants more yet; and so on to the end of the everlasting. There is no such thing as enough in worldly riches. As well might the sow be supposed to get enough of wallowing in the mire, as for a mortal to be satisfied with rolling in the carrion of wealth. So false are your ideas of the means to obtain happiness that you would, if you could, coax angels from the skies to rob them of the jewels in their diadems. I haven't the least doubt of it.

My dear friends—I will tell you how to enjoy as much bliss as heaven can afford to humanity. Be contented with what you have, no matter how poor it is, till you have an opportunity to get something better. Be thankful for every crumb that falls from the table of Providence, and live in the constant expectation of having the luck to pinch upon a whole loaf. Have patience to put up with present troubles, and console yourself with the idea that your situations are paradises compared with some others. When you have enough to eat to satisfy hunger—enough to drink to quench thirst—enough to wear to keep you decent and comfortable—just enough of what is vulgarly called "tin" to procure you a few luxuries, when you owe no one, and no one owes you, not even a grudge—then if you are not happy all the gold in the universe can never make you so. A man much wiser than I once said: give me neither poverty nor riches; and I look upon him as the greatest philosopher that the world ever produced. All he wanted was a contented mind; sufficient bread and cheese, and a clean shirt. Take pattern after him, O ye discontented mortals who vainly imagine that bliss alone is to be found in the places of wealth and opulence.

My hearers—if you consider all creation too poor to afford you a penny worth of true blessedness, you must pray to become reconciled to its poverty. Grease your prayers with faith and send them up in earnestness, hot from the soul's oven. This manufacturing cold petitions with the lips, while heart continually cries gammon, is of no more use than talking Choctaw to a Chinese.—Heaven understands no gibberish; it knows only the pure simple language of the spirit—the soul's ver-

nacular. So when you pray, do it in as simple a manner as possible, but with red hot earnestness, and your souls will find rest wherever you are—whether nibbling at a crust in Poverty Hollow, or half starving in California while endeavoring to transmogrify a bag of gold dust into an Indian pudding. So mote it be.

Dow, Jr.[8] (CPD, July 20, 1849.)

Latest from California

No chance for Men of Moderate Means—
Dry Goods and Hardware below par—
What does sell well—Prices Current, &c.

The subjoined extract of a private letter, the Philadelphia North American states, is from a gentleman who sailed from New York with a large amount of means and merchandize, for the purpose of engaging in regular trade in San Francisco. His statements may be relied upon as those of a cool and calm observer:

SAN FRANCISCO, May 1, 1849.

We are quite lively in this new city of the West. Vessels are arriving daily—most of them from down the coast and the Sandwich Islands, with full loads of anxious gold diggers and goods.

Goods of some kinds sell well, and among them I may enumerate provisions, groceries, lumber, coal, wood, horses, and wagons. Dry goods can be purchased as cheap, or cheaper, than in Philadelphia, and crockery, iron, glassware, and many kinds of hardware will not pay expenses. The difficulties attending the landing of goods from vessels have not been overrated, and many of the lightering scows and boats in use have been sunk by the violence of the winds. The climate is very trying on the constitution, on account of the severe changes in the atmosphere. The comforts of life are few and far between. It is impossible to realize here what you

---

8. "Dow, Jr." was the pseudonym of the humorist Joseph F. Paige, a writer of burlesque sermons—or, as he called them, "Patent Sermons."

would call a good dinner—it cannot be had. The chief reliance is upon fresh beef, and provisions brought from the states, and there are no fish, oysters, or game. Add to this the fact that the labor to be done is exceedingly hard, and that to dig gold successfully one must have more than ordinary powers of endurance, and you have my experience of the gold region. Those who have made most money here are land speculators and merchants of Chili and the Islands.

There is no chance here for young men of moderate means, as it costs more to start in business than it does at home, and it must inevitably result in the disappointment of many young men coming with that purpose. Board is $16 per week, and house rent extravagant—as high as $100 to $200 per month being demanded and paid for a mere one story shed, 10 by 15 feet in dimensions. There is, besides, nothing of comfort or cleanliness, and everything is owned and controlled by a few speculators in the town. It has been with some difficulty that I have secured a lot on which to place my store.

Silver is plenty, and small change hard to pass, but gold coin is in active demand. The country back is much troubled by the Indians, and even among our own community there is scarcely a sign of law and order. In haste, yours,   B.

(CPD, July 24, 1849.)

EXCITING NEWS FROM THE GOLD REGION
Crowds of People and Crowds of Provisions

BOSTON, July 23.

Letters from San Francisco dated May 10 have been received here *via* Mazatlan. Market of San Francisco was overstocked with many descriptions of goods, which were selling at low rates. Many articles could be purchased at from 30 to 50 pct. discount on the invoice.—Provisions and clothing are abundant and cheap. Charge for landing goods and storing are enormously high; $3 to $4 per month, per ton, for storage.

The harbor was crowded with vessels, and others were arriving daily. Some hundreds of vessels were expected to arrive by the month of August. A dozen more from China were daily looked for.

San Francisco was full of people, and it is stated not to be uncommon for 20 or 30 individuals to occupy one small apartment. The tents about the town were crowded to excess. Rooms 20 ft. square were let for $600 to $800 per year. Building lots which two years ago were worth only $200, have been valued recently at $50,000.

A large portion of the inhabitants are speculating extravagantly in lands. New towns were being laid out in different spots around the Bay, and building lots in wilderness sites were selling at from $1,000 to $2,000.

Building materials, complete house frames, boats of good description, with everything complete, are in good demand, and sell well. Lumber was worth $400 per M. Flour is scarce.

The gold dust this season has not been dug very freely, owing to the swollen streams, but no doubts are entertained that as much will be gathered this year as last. The number of laborers this season much exceed those of the previous one.

At the mines matters yet remain quiet, but fears are entertained that ere long there would be serious disturbances between our countrymen and the Mexicans, as some 6,000 of the latter had arrived in the country, and evince a most turbulent disposition; but, says a letter writer, you may rest assured that should any important attack take place they would be shot down to a man.

News had been received at San Francisco that six men in 20 days procured $60,000 in gold dust. (CPD, July 24, 1849.)

Progress of the California Boys— Letter from a Clevelander

ACAPULCO, May 28th, 1849.

DEAR SIR:—Knowing how much pleasure it will be to the family to hear from me, I seize the present opportunity to let you know how I am getting along. I wrote you before I left Panama that I had engaged passage on the brig *Two Friends* to San Francisco. This vessel did not sail until eight days after the time I named to you in my letter; the reason of this was because she had so much difficulty in getting a supply of water at the Island of Taboga. From this place we put to sea on the 20th of April. The Island is a beautiful spot, being about fifteen miles in length, and covered over with high and lofty mountains. There is quite a town upon the Island, and the inhabitants are a much neater and finer set of people than those of Panama. I spent my time very pleasantly while there, and was well supplied with various kinds of fresh picked fruits, also sweet potatoes, &c.

Our trip to this place has indeed been a long one, having been becalmed several days off Panama, and the coast of Guatemala; but as we get further North the winds increase, and are more to be depended upon. You will perceive that we have had a passage of thirty-one days out, and not quite half way to San Francisco, though in point of time we consider we have made two-thirds of the distance, as twenty days is considered an average passage from this place to San Francisco. We are now taking in water, and will likely be off by the 30th inst. The steamers *Oregon* and *California* stopped here on their way down a few days ago, and you will have their news before you receive this.

I understand the family of GEN. SMITH will return to the States. Mrs. SMITH says she has sent her washing to the Sandwich Islands, as she could find no one to do such work in California.

Report says that those who are at the mines are collecting from sixty to one hundred dollars per day, in the poorest places. It is also said that there has been some difficulty at the mines between the Americans and foreigners; but this cannot last long, as the immense tide of the emigration now pouring in there from the States will soon restore order and quiet. We do not anticipate any trouble at all.

I am with Captain Wood's party, and will remain with them until my Cleveland friends shall arrive in California. I have been in excellent health ever since I left Cleveland—have not been sick a single day, not even sea-sick since leaving Panama, and we were out in a perfect hurricane a few days ago, such as I never before experienced—it was truly terrific and awful. I have not allowed myself to get home-sick for one moment, and have not once been sorry at my undertaking. You would be astonished to know what control I have over myself and my feelings, as compared with many others; I am in high spirits without being at all excited. I shall be prudent in every sense of the word, and have no doubt but that I shall be well remunerated, notwithstanding I am so long getting to California.

Now a little about Acapulco. It is a very difficult place to find from the sea, but our Captain had no difficulty in finding the harbor, and steered straight in, and was met by a pilot who took the brig into a beautiful bay, which was before hid from our view by high and lofty mountains. In coming into the bay the most beautiful scenery ever beheld was presented to view. The entrance of the harbor is through a very narrow place between two mountains, and is protected by a Fort, which stands upon a little eminence, and commands a fine view of the town situated in the valley below. I went on shore yesterday, and rambled about the town in company with Captain Wood and others, and

Acapulco.

was well pleased with the place. The town is cleanly, and the houses only one story high. We found the inhabitants very civil, and provisions plenty and cheap, and feel no disposition to find fault with anything.

I shall expect to hear from home after I arrive in California, and will keep you well advised of my whereabouts. I have written this in a great hurry so it could go immediately off; you will therefore excuse all mistakes, bad writing, &c.   H. C. SMITH.

(CPD, July 30, 1849.)

California—Incidents and Travel

MEXICAN OPINIONS OF CALIFORNIA.

The Mexican papers give most doleful accounts of California, the information being derived from disappointed gold hunters. The *Universal* has a letter which says—

I cannot describe to you how deceived we have been with regard to this country. There is an immense difference between the description and the reality, as between day and night. Many who came here for no other purpose than to dig gold have left, and every day numbers are leaving for San Francisco; and many remain here, because they have not the means to do so. It is really heart-rending to see so many young men, who have done well at home, perish here from want and misery. The company of S. Pauquenot, of Tepic, consisting of thirty-three men, have not found more than an ounce of gold on an average.

FURTHER OPINIONS OF THE MEXICANS
Another letter says—

When the last steamer arrived at San Francisco, it had 260 passengers—120 of them returned immediately, on seeing the true state of things. He met, on his return from California, on the road from Mazatlan to Mexico, large numbers of Americans, who were in the greatest misery, before getting to Mazatlan, as their money was exhausted before they got half way. Several Americans have joined Mexican robbers, and committed many outrages and even atrocities. . . . Most of the emigrants are compelled to sell their things on their arrival in San Francisco, as their means became exhausted. The *Gaviota* (a paper of Tepic,) is paid by merchants $60 to give glowing accounts. The accounts published in papers of Mexican ports are exaggerated, being in pay of speculators. He warns everybody who can earn $2 a day not to go to California. A merchant of Mexico bought in Guadalajara fourteen thousand *serapes*, (woollen cloaks for the natives,) at the average price of $15 a piece. He sold two thousand in San Francisco at $40—the remainder were bought by a house there at $5 a piece, and sold again in Guadalajara, from whence they came, at $10. Merchants in San Francisco have made immense profits—they know the articles which are most necessary, avail themselves of an overstock in the market, to buy them at a mere song, and wait for the best moment to sell.

WHAT YOU MUST NOT BELIEVE

A correspondent of the Tribune cautions people not to believe all they hear of California, a caution that a considerable number had a suspicion of before his gratuitous advice was given. He says:

I wish *The Tribune* to caution all persons coming here to think before they leap, and not to believe everything they hear about California, for I assure you not the sixteenth part of it is true. Emigrants starting from home want nothing but two or three suits of clothing, say one thin to wear on the way and two of woollen to wear here. This is one of the windiest places I ever saw, and cold withal. To let you know how cold it is here at this season, I will say that in order to be comfortable I am now wearing two flannel shirts, flannel drawers, thick trousers, and a heavy pea-jacket.

Neither gold-washers nor shovels are wanted by diggers. All they want is a round tin-pan, such as is used to wash dishes in, for a gold-washer; with that, and a hatchet to put up your fixins in the mines, you are provided for. All the gold-washers I have seen here prove a perfect failure, and are good for nothing. When the emigrants get their washers here, they leave them, owing to the expense of carrying them up to the mines.   E. G. Buffum.

(PPL, July 31, 1849.)

Money is the Root

California Items

EXPECTATIONS NOT REALIZED

A correspondent of the New York Post gives some capital sketches of things in California. We will make a few extracts:

"There were some long faces on the part of the passengers on the arrival of the Panama at San Francisco. The steamer had come to anchor near the U. S. sloop of war, the Warren. The passengers surrounded and eagerly questioned the young midshipman who boarded us; when they learned from him, in answer to their anxious inquiries, that the miners were averaging only ten dollars a day at the mines, and so hard was the work that most people preferred half that amount with hard labor at San Francisco, there was evidently a sad disappointment to their hopes. The wonders of Aladdin's lamp would not have satisfied the gold seekers; their expectations had been worked up to a height not easily defined, and were now let down to ten dollars a day—an amount within the limits of arithmetical calculation.

"It was interesting to observe the progress, for the first few days, of these adventurers. They clung to the steamer, till the good nature of the captain and the fresh provisions of the ship were exhausted together. They finally dispersed, most of them going to the mines, with their salt pork, tin kettles, tools, and India rubber contrivances. The parson, who had each Sunday during the voyage read to us the service, and preached against this world and its lusts, was off to the mines with tin pan and shovel. A sober, staid, and smooth-faced man, that had conducted himself like a saint on board ship, was to be seen, much to the surprise of all, dealing cards at a faro table at the Parker Hotel. The politicians, Hon. Messrs. T. Butler King of Georgia, and Gwynn of Louisiana, were playing their parts, and delivering themselves of vague generalities at the political gatherings in the public square of San Francisco. The speculators and financiers had announced themselves, in showy signs and on tin plates, as land agents, exchange brokers, and bankers, and were deep in the mysteries of gold dust, land sales, and bill brokerage. A youth, who had sported himself gaily on the voyage, might be seen peddling coffee-pots and drinking cups around the town.

SPECULATION IN LOTS

"Speculation in lots is rife at San Francisco. House lots and store lots are selling at from three to twenty thousand dollars each. The mate of the Panama, who some two years since, while on this coast, bought in a frolic a lot on the hill in the outskirts of the town for twenty-five dollars, refused the other day three thousand for it. Many of these prices are doubtless nominal, and although landed proprietors in the town are counting their fortunes by tens and hundreds of thousands, they could never realize a tithe of their supposed wealth. Beautifully colored and finally executed lithographic plans of extensive towns are to be seen, temptingly exposed in the offices of cunning lawyers and shrewd speculators. Benicia, Martinez, Sacramento City, New York of the Pacific, Sutterville, Webster, and Stanislaus sound largely in the mouths of greedy speculators, and extend their wide domains of streets, squares, and docks on paper and in the imaginations of the interested.[1]

THE CONDITION OF THE MINER

"Besides the moral and intellectual deprivations to which the miner has to submit, in abandoning home, friends, and society, there are physical sufferings and disease to which he is fated, the extent of which can hardly be overstated. There are to be seen in the private hospital, one of the most thriving and profitable enterprises of St. Francisco, men once sturdy, but doubled with rheumatism; youths whose blood once flowed rich and invigorating, and which now is impoverished and corrupted with the poison of scurvy. They may yet clutch their dirty leather bags of gold dust, but day by day, as they pay for the doctor's skill and nurse's care, the precious metal goes faster than it came. Comfort for the sick, which would be misery at home, is with difficulty got for ten dollars a day.

"There is a great deal of gold dust apparently in circulation in St. Francisco. At the shops you will see it turned out carelessly from dirty buckskin bags, and weighed as carelessly in rude scales, without any attempt to assay it or estimate with exactness its purity. Boys collect the sweepings of the stores and find it profitable, and men may be seen on all-fours, grubbing for gold in the dirt in the streets, thus doing away with the distinction of the Latin author, who distinguishes men from beasts by the fact of the former being erect and the latter prone on their bellies.

"You will think, from what I have written, that I take no very favorable view of St. Francisco. I believe that the gold resources of California have been overestimated, and that of course a false standard has been set up, by which mistaken opinions have been formed in regard to the progress of the territory. The natural effect of this error will be commercial embarrassment and much disappointment and misery. I am not, however, insensible to the imposing prospects of this Pacific me-

tropolis, nor I have any doubt of its future importance." (PPL, August 1, 1849.)

The Boston Traveller

announces the arrival of Mr. Jarvis, from California, and gives various items of intelligence derived from him, from which we select such as have any novelty:

The number of arrivals at San Francisco in June, by sea, was about 1,000 per week. By land, at the mines, from Lower California, Sonora, Durango, and Mexico generally, the immigration is computed at 15,000, with many thousand mule loads of merchandise, which has thus found its way into California duty free, to the great dissatisfaction of the sea-board merchants.

Coin was scarce at San Francisco, being absorbed by the custom house for duties. The average price of gold dust was $15.50 to $16 per ounce. It is computed that on the 20th of June $100,000 worth of flour was exposed in open air, and more than $500,000 worth of other merchandise, chiefly dry goods, for want of storage.

The average receipts of the French restaurant are $1 per minute. Mr. Jarvis informs us that his first dinner in San Francisco, ordered from a hotel for two gentlemen, two ladies, and four children, consisting only of meats and pastry, cost $90. Eggs $3 per dozen. Boat hire to go to steamer, 30 minutes' pull, $8.

Buildings were springing up very rapidly, mostly of the cheapest character. At present, one half of the population live in tents. The population increases slowly, as the departures for the mines about equal the arrivals. The risk to property at San Francisco from fire is very great. The buildings are all of the most frail and combustible description.

1. New York of the Pacific is the present city of Pittsburg; Sutterville, three miles south of the center of Sacramento, vanished; Webster, near Sacramento, likewise vanished; Stanislaus City was built on the site of the failed Mormon New Hope Colony on the Stanislaus River near the present town of Ripon, and lasted until about 1880.

Good order in general prevailed both at the bay and mines. As a general thing, property is respected, evil-doers being kept in check by fear of Lynch law.

Many shipments from the United States and Europe will prove a total loss, not paying expense of landing. Scow hire per day, taking but one load, is $150; men to discharge, $15; sailors receive $100 to $200 per month; mates and captains, from $300 to $600 per month.

Ship James Monroe, loaded at Honolulu at $20 per ton freight for San Francisco, took back a portion of her cargo at $10 per ton, without landing. Consignments of vessels and cargoes are daily refused.

Clerks at San Francisco get from $2,000 to $4,000 per annum and their board; 10 per cent. is charged on sales of merchandise, and one per cent. storage. A private mint has been established, which has issued thus far half eagles. Silver coin less than dollars is generally refused. Merchants will not take the trouble to count it.

(PPL, August 2, 1849.)

From our Correspondent

RIO DE JANEIRO, BRAZIL, S. A.
Monday, 28th May, 1849.

We left the city of New York on the 12th of March, a company of one hundred and sixty-three members, in the ship *Salem*, a very old vessel, but still considered good and strong, and ranking at the Insurance offices as A No. 2. We commenced operations about two months before this time, raised near thirty thousand dollars, furnished the vessel and re-coppered her, did sundry repairs, fitted up our berths, provisioned her for twelve months, and started out as her owners, with light hearts, lighter pockets, and still lighter exchequer for the vessel. But we did not think of this; we were on our way to the gold regions, and nothing but huge heaps of the yellow dross danced before our eyes.

A few days at sea dispelled the golden illusion, and nothing could be heard every day but wishes to return, many offering all their outfit to be put in N. Y. again. However, we had started for the promised land, and were *bound* to proceed. For a few days we had pleasant weather; we made an easterly course, but were gradually making some southing, although we did not care so to do,—our course properly was eastward. We at last found ourselves in the latitude of Bermudas, when contrary winds drove us up again as high as thirty-nine. The first Saturday night out we had a tremendous gale; the wind howled through the rigging, and sent forth a moaning sound; it rained hard, and looked dismal in the extreme; the sea looked like an ocean of fire, and our bows seemed to plough through liquid fire. Every ten or fifteen minutes the Capt. looked at his barometer; it kept falling, falling—and as it fell our spirits fell, for the lower the barometer gets the more fearful will be the tempest. In the highest of the gale we had to "lay to" for two or three hours—it abated shortly after midnight, and one by one we turned into our bunks, many not to sleep; nature had received too violent a shock to admit of instant repose. The following Sunday we had another storm, less severe than the first; those two are the only storms of consequence we have had. Other vessels, that have arrived here both before and after us, experienced hard weather. The ship Marianne, from Richmond, Va., arrived here five or six days since—in the "gulf" met with terrible weather, losing part of her deck load. One of the passengers offered the captain five thousand dollars to be put back.

We spoke a number of vessels—we put letters on board bark Seymour, for London, 90 days from Bombay, an East Indiaman— and a few days after, we spoke ship Anne, twenty days from London for New York; on board her we put another bag full, and two of our association left on her for home.

Finally we made port after a tedious passage of sixty-six days;—it has been made in thirty-five, and forty-five are common. This though does not militate against the sailing qualities of the *Salem*. She is a fine sailer, and very easy sea boat, riding over mountain waves with great ease. She leaked considerably, say four hundred strokes the hour, causing us to pump every two hours. Since being here we have re-caulked her, and found in her bows a "trunnel hole"[2] some three quarters of an inch in diameter, through which the water has been pouring ever since our leaving port. A few days before arriving here we sprung our main top gallant mast, and had to take it down; the same wind blew our jib into ribbons.

In this city, the chief city and capital of a mighty empire, I must confess that I am greatly disappointed. Although a great commercial city there is not a wharf for a vessel to load or discharge at, and the drayage of the city is mostly done on the negroes' heads—they toteing a sack of coffee of one hundred and fifty pounds without any apparent difficulty. A custom-house cart will contain a ton weight of goods, and it is propelled by eight negroes; this, of course, causes much work to go on slowly. A great number of vessels are in port, loading with the principal export—coffee. This now is, in consequence of a short crop, six and a quarter cents a pound.

The city contains many churches from one to two hundred years old, filled with carving and gilding from ceiling to dome—paintings, silver candlesticks, sculptured busts of Saints, Popes, and Priests. The more modern churches are plain like our own; all however being Roman Catholic, have their patron saints enshrined behind the altar with a profusion of garlands, blue and crimson damask, lace, embroidery, gold and silver tinsel, &c.

Rio is remarkably clean, far more so than any city I have ever been in, in the United States, and I have visited all the principal cities in the Union excepting two or three. No garbage or kitchen slops are allowed to be thrown in the streets. On the doors of public houses, since the Californians have been arriving here, you will see a slip of paper, having on it: "Gentlemen are requested not to throw orange peel, &c. about the door." Orange and banana peels are swept up every morning by the negroes.

The country around looks very beautiful, fresh and green, and every thing different from what we are used to in the States. The marma apple, large as a small child's head, and bright yellow; the pine apple, orange, banana with its light green leaves five feet long and twenty inches broad, the fig, Brazil nut, and various fruits that I know not the name of, all luscious and high flavored, strike the traveler with wonder and admiration. The birds, too, are all of the most brilliant plumage and song, and monkeys are occasionally seen chattering from the top of a tall cocoanut tree. Great varieties in size and plumage of birds can be bought in the market daily, and monkeys, too; plenty always for sale at from two to five dollars each.

Frio Grande lies opposite the city, about three miles across the bay. It is a place of about six thousand inhabitants, and stretches along the shore for two miles, the mountains behind hemming it in. The houses have all a very picturesque appearance, mostly of one story, all stuccoed with a white or yellow plaster, and having elegant gardens in front and around.

Botafojo is a small place three miles below town, and is inhabited by the aristocracy, foreign ministers, and other dignitaries. We sailed to this place on a small steamer, on our way to the "Botanic Gar-

---

2. A trunnel (also spelled 'treenail' and 'trenail') is a cylindrical hardwood pin for fastening timbers together in shipbuilding.

dens," which form one of the greatest objects of interest within the vicinity of the city, and I presume *any* city in America, for a sight of the kind. They cover upwards of two hundred acres, and were commenced by the late Emperor, Don Pedro I, and finished to their present state by the present Emperor, Don Pedro II. They lie about five miles below Botafojo, the road to them being the most delightful and picturesque imaginable. All the productions of the eastern continent in the torrid zone are here to be found in all their native luxuriousness, such as the nutmeg, clove, cinnamon, camphor, pimento, tea plant, &c. of the small tree and shrub kind; the coffee tree, lemon tree, orange groves, cocoanut, bread fruit, and other trees that I do not remember the names of, of a larger kind. Flowers in abundance, of course various from what we have in the States, of most brilliant colors, elegant form, and sweet perfume. These plants and trees are laid out in walks and groves, not single trees only—for instance, as you enter, a walk, level as a floor, and extending about as far as from Irwin's corner to the academy, fifty feet wide and planted at regular distances with the palmetto, with its elegant urn-shaped trunk, with its broad rings and elegant foliage, is presented to view—about mid-way of the walk is an elegant fountain, and from which diverge walks in various ways. Fountains, rivulets, cascades, and ponds abound throughout the grounds. The tea plant is cultivated on about ten acres of ground. I gathered a number of specimens of these plants, and seeds of fruit, and have sent them to New York, along with some Brazilian productions, artificial yet natural.

We are all anxious to leave port, as we consider every day we stay here a loss of a hundred dollars each. But we are poor and can hardly raise the tax necessary to pay expenses and get us off. We will probably not sail before Saturday next, 2d June. One hundred and eight California vessels have stopped here, and many more have gone right on—some stopping at Cape de

Verds,—some talk of making the voyage via Cape of Good Hope, to escape the dangers of the Horn. The bark Mazeppa returned here from the Falkland Islands with bowsprit knocked out. A report was current a day or two ago that 35 dead bodies were seen floating between here and St. Catharine. I remain truly yours,

S. RUCKEL WILEY.

(ISJ, Aug. 2, 1849.)

A Philadelphian in California

A letter from a gentleman formerly of this city, who is at present in California, is published in the North American:

If you have to pay high for what you get, you also *charge* high for what you do. Until my goods arrive and business offers to me, I am at work with my pen, translating Spanish invoices, making entries at the Custom House, &c., drawing maps, &c., and have received as high as $120 per day for my labor; $50, $60, and $80 are common, and if I don't make $30 to $40 I consider it a bad day's work, and *get low spirited.* I drew a bond, one page long, the other day, and the man gave me $30 of his own option. It cost me ten minutes to do it. I draw maps in a day, for which I get four ounces, and have more orders than I can fulfil for want of drawing paper. I would give an ounce a sheet for large size. Labor of every description is high. Mellus, Howard & Co.'s cartman gets $6,000 a year, *his board and lodging.* Jackknife carpenters receive $12 to $16, shipwrights $20. Sailors $100 to $200 per month; pilot on the river $500 a month; lumber sells for $350 *per M.;* drinks 25 cents (rot-gut) and if you can get a breakfast or dinner for less than $1.50, you have got a small stomach, for mine will contain three such meals very easily. Now as to the future.

Gold is plentiful, but no one can say how long it will last; appearances indicate many years; but appearances are deceitful, and it may be so far exhausted by the large numbers emigrating hither as to cease to be very profitable digging it.

So soon as this occurs, *heaps* of folks will vamos—many to Oregon, many home, and many to South America, Sandwich Islands, Mexico, &c., whence they came. It is *not* an agricultural country, though a good grazing one. Its mining wealth, exclusive of gold, is great. Quicksilver, silver, iron, coal, abound; but Oregon so far surpasses it—according to the numbers from there here, digging, who, so soon as they get a pile, go back—that it can't compete with it, should the gold stop short off, which the Lord forbid.

You would be amused, as *we old* settlers are, when a steamer or vessel with many passengers arrives, to see them come ashore, some dressed up fine, and expecting to do great things before night—but they conclude before sundown they HAVE *done great* things, if successful in their search of a bed. At present we are in the midst of political excitement—the people's party and the Governor's (old Riley.) As the old General has made a Notary Public and Commissioner of Elections of me, of course I am not one of the people, and expect to get licked yet—*but then it pays.*

Altogether we have lively times, and the place somewhat grows on acquaintance. If it were not for the horrid cold winds, it would be pleasant enough. One of our chief amusements is to go on board of newly arrived vessels and tell the passengers all about the country. They are generally willing to return by the time we have got through. (PPL, August 4, 1849.)

Pennsylvania Californians

The Reading Gazette has some letters from a company of Californians from that city who went overland by the Central American route. One is dated Chinendaigua [Chinandega] de Nicaragua, Central America, May 7, 1849, and says:

"We came through from Granada in five days, a distance of 140 miles, passing through the towns of Masaya, Managua, Nagarde [Nagarote], the city of Leon, &c. About six miles N. E. of Masaya we passed the volcanic mount. The cinder lays for miles round.

We were so long on the river that we run short of provisions, not having put food on board for more than ten days, which was the time we expected it would take us to go up. Monkeys were very plentiful along the shores of the river, and we had several fine messes of *monkey soup.* At another time we caught a very large shark, and made a chowder, which ate very well. Some of the boys cooked the hind part of an alligator. I tasted some of it; but the idea was too much—I could not go it.

"This route is by far the best for a small party that I know of. It is healthy, the living and travelling cheap, meals in the towns one real, and never more than two reals. A party of five or ten could stand a very good chance of getting on vessels at Realejo that touch there for water and provisions.

"Enclosed you will find a few seeds of the sensitive plant, which I gathered from among the ruins of an old Spanish fort, at the head of the San Juan river. It has been a tremendous building, but is all in ruins now. The whole was overgrown with these plants, which are very rare in the States."

The same correspondent writes from the city of Leon, C. A., June 4th:

"The natives through this country all treat us with great kindness and express themselves as very friendly to the North Americans passing through their country; but they are very bitter against the English, who, it appears, are trying to dispossess them of a part of their territory on the plea of extending protection to a tribe of Indians inhabiting the country around the port of San Juan and along the coast of the Caribbean Sea.

"Gen. Munoz, the head man of the country, gave a grand blow-out to our party the other day, at his house. Things were done up about right, after the custom of the country.

"The revolution that I spoke of as about brewing in my last, has broken out in some of the cities below. A number of

San Juan del Sur, Nicaragua.

persons were killed, and the cities besieged by the revolters. This city is the seat of government, and the citizens are nightly expecting to be attacked. Many of them are carrying their money, jewels, and other valuables to Dr. Livingston's house, the American Consul here, for protection."

The next is dated San Blas, June 29th, and is from the Reading Association, who went by the Mexican route, and shows some of the hardships to be encountered in such a journey:

"Capt. West has failed to carry us through, and we are now left on our own resources. We have come on our own means from Tepic, some 50 miles from here, and will have to get up the coast without aid from him. The extravagance of his partner, Mr. Diehl, and the insufficiency of the passage money, $200, are urged as excuses for the failure by his friends.

"At San Luis Potosi we were compelled to procure conveyance for the sick, as several of them were unable to ride. To hire would cost $175 to Guadalajara, 90 leagues. To purchase would be beyond our means, as a coach would cost some $1,500

or $2,000. An opportunity occurred for the purchase of two wagons with eight mules and harness complete, brought into the country by the army during the war.

"After encountering almost insurmountable difficulties, we succeeded in reaching Tepic with our wagons. Here the expedition failed, Captain West announcing that he had not funds for even another day's provisions. From that time we have been on our "own hook," as the saying is, and we succeeded in bringing our wagons, loaded with our baggage, this far over almost impassable roads, having been four days in travelling fifty miles. All but the sick, (or rather weak) walked. The last day we were often above our knees in water, the rainy season having set in several days before, forming lakes out of all the marshes, which often covered the road for half a mile. We are now lying here at an expense of $5 per day, tormented nearly to death by musquitoes and sand flies, waiting the arrival of the Panama steamer, which was due the day after we arrived, 24th inst. If the fare in the forward or second cabin is not more than $50 per man, we will take passage in her—if it is more,

we must look out for some other conveyance, as our means will not admit of it. Our
wagons and harness we will take with us if
we possibly can, as we understand there is
a good market for them. The eight mules
we will sell—they will help us to means."

(PPL, August 8, 1849.)

From the Plains

[From the Newark Advertiser, Aug. 11]

The following letter from a member of
the Buffalo California Company, a native
of this city, gives some further interesting
information concerning the ravages of the
epidemic.

NEAR FORT LARAMIE, June 25, 1849.

We reached this point about an hour
since, and having learned that an express
leaves for the States early to-morrow
morning, I take this opportunity to inform
you of our position and prospects. I wrote
last from near Grand Island; since then our
course has been near the Nebraska [Platte],
till we came to where it forked, and then
crossed the South Fork, and proceeded
along the North Fork, the band passing
Chimney Rock, Scott's Bluff, and other
places which you will find on the map.

We have been unfortunate in the extreme; the hand of Providence has afflicted
our little band in removing some of our
members. The cholera has been very severe along the route, and some days we
have passed 10 or 15 graves. On the 20th
instant, while encamped at Chimney Rock,
our doctor was the first attacked. He had
never entirely recovered from an illness
which he had at Cincinnati, and was pecu-
liarly fit for the disease. He died the next
day at 4 P. M. On the 23d, two others of our

company, Albert Hayden and Henry O.
Hayes, were seized at noon, and died before the next morning. They lie side by side
in the same grave. Scarcely had we moved
from the mournful spot, which was on the
bank of Horse Creek, when our Captain,
John J. Fay, was attacked, and we buried
him this morning.

Some few others of the company have
been ill, but are now rapidly recovering.
We have now found an excellent physician,
who is desirous of joining us if he can get
away from the train in which he now is.

The disease seems to frequent certain
low localities at which we have been
obliged to encamp, and all of our company
who died probably contracted it at the
same place. We have now come to higher
ground and purer air, and shall keep ascending. A refreshing rain has also fallen,
which has purified the air, the weather
having been intensely hot for two weeks
before. I think the danger from cholera is
now over, and hope to make the rest of the
journey safely; but we have many hardships and dangers still to overcome, and
the most tedious part of the journey is still
before us.

Mr. Hayes left behind him a family—
wife and six children; but the rest of those
who died were single men. I cannot but
feel gratified that there are none dependent upon me in case I should be taken
away. Some of our number have talked of
returning, but I think they will not. We can
stand fatigue and labor; but when death
comes in and cuts off one-third of our little
band of twelve, then indeed we feel melancholy in the extreme.   Yours, &c.

(PPL, August 13, 1849.)

The News from California

We yesterday had the pleasure of a long conversation with Mr. Henry D. Cooke,[3] a gentleman from San Francisco, who came hither on the Falcon. Mr. Cooke is a native of Philadelphia, and had for the last three years been trading on the coast of California. According to Mr. Cooke, the climate in the interior is delightful. The great valleys lying between the Sacramento and San Joaquin are fertile, as virgin lands must always be, and offer the finest prospects for agricultural labor. From the few water courses that exist, the hand of art will be required for purposes of irrigation.

Much of the dark coloring which the pictures of California, as drawn by the Mexicans, bore, is attributable to the general disappointment of operators at the mines, and which was occasioned by the rainy season and the consequent inundations that prevented the diggers from continuing on the placers, except at the loss of health, and with inadequate returns for their toil. . . . Mr. Cooke represents the country as offering the greatest inducements to all who are willing to work. Hundreds, however, unaccustomed to great bodily exertion—young men of tender rearing, with little natural energy—have tried the digging, and became disgusted with it, turning their attention to some other channel of industry. Hence there is at San Francisco at the present a great number of unemployed clerks, for whom situations cannot be readily obtained, in consequence of the comparative paucity of stores and counting-houses there. They have, however, a never-failing resource in manual labor, which is extraordinarily remunerated.

We learn from him also that most of the large companies that went out from the States, broke up on their arrival in California, from a very natural cause—it was easier for men to get along alone, or a few banded together, than in heavy parties. All the new machinery, large and small, that had been taken out by adventurers had been abandoned, and the new diggers resorted, after a trial or so, to the old wash pan, the cradle, pick and jack-knife, which were the most effective.

Immense sums, Mr. Cooke informs us, have been made in buying and selling town lots at San Francisco. Dr. Powell, U. S. N., is one among many examples. In 1847, during a period of impaired health, he obtained leave of absence, and took up his residence for a time at that port. Whilst there, he practised, and laid out a few hundred dollars in the purchase of land within the town. He died prematurely on his way back to the States, but his real estate at San Francisco has been lately sold, and an account of sales sent to his widow, exhibiting a sum of not less than $40,000 in his favor. Trade is also a means by which very large sums have been made in a short time. A gentleman who came hither on the Falcon started at San Francisco in June, 1848, on a small capital of $261. Mr. Cooke sold him his first venture of goods. That person is now in possession of from $17,000 to $18,000, the returns of his $261.

THE MINES

On my arrival at Stockton, I found a population of several hundred living in tents, there being but one frame building. For some time, this must inevitably be a place of immense importance. It is and will continue to be the depot for all the mines from the Macalemia [Mokelumne] river south. There is on average $10,000 of goods

---

3. Cooke went to California in 1847; he was a prominent businessman in San Francisco from 1849 to 1854.

disembarked there every day. From Stockton to the mines, seventy-five-miles south, there is a tri-weekly stage line running; the trip is made in a day, and the fare charged is two ounces of gold, ($32). The first of the mining is on Woods' Creek, south of the Stanislaus. The people from the State of Sonora, Mexico, and those from South America, settled at this point; but owing to some difficulties likely to occur between them and the Americans, they moved out and established a camp about four miles distant. The Mexicans and South Americans number about eight thousand; they keep up all the customs and habits of their country—bull fights, chicken fights, dancing, gambling, &c., on Sunday and Feast days. In all the other "diggings" Sundays are respected, though I have not heard of any preaching in them.

THE ADMINISTRATION OF JUSTICE
AT THE MINES

Notwithstanding the variety of population so suddenly thrown together, and coming from all parts of the habitable globe, there is the most perfect respect paid to law and justice—no man, high or low, escapes a merited punishment. As the people at present have no written code of laws, or system of government to enforce, they by common consent and mutual understanding adopted the following course of action: Whenever a camp is formed at which ten or more persons locate themselves, they meet and elect from among them by popular suffrage one person to act as alcalde, (civil magistrate,) before whom are brought all cases of a civil character, which are tried and decided according to sworn evidence—there is no appeal from his decision, and every person must conform to this system of government, or he is liable to be arraigned as a criminal, and then two to one he gets a flogging, or is driven out of camp in disgrace. In every camp a sound, sensible, practical man has been elected, and the dignity, form, and ceremony observed at the alcalde's office,

might be imitated to advantage in some of the inferior courts in the States. A fee is allowed the alcalde in all cases, so that he can without loss devote his exclusive time to the business of the public.

Criminal cases are decided differently. Whenever any man commits any act against the peace and order of the camp, he is at once arrested and brought before the alcalde with a specification and the evidence on both sides of the offence; the alcalde without delay summons a jury of twelve men to try the criminal, who selects whom he pleases to defend him, and the judge selects a prosecutor; after all the proceedings are terminated, the alcalde charges the jury to bring a true verdict according to the evidence. Some of the verdicts are a little singular in their character, and they may be laughed at, but no one can criticize their straight-forward justice.

I will give you a specimen, and then you can judge for yourself. A man was charged with killing another—the jury brought in a verdict "that the person committing the act was justifiable, as he had been attacked, but that he was always ready to quarrel and fight, and dangerous to the peace and good order of the camp, and therefore he must leave the country in thirty days; failing to do which, he should be shot down by the first person laying eyes on him." Another case was that of a merchant who caught a Spaniard stealing from him; he fell on the offender and commenced beating him with his fist, but after a few blows the fellow dead at the feet of the merchant. The jury brought in a verdict that the merchant was justifiable in whipping the Spaniard when he caught him stealing, and that the killing was accidental; therefore they acquitted him. A person charged with maltreating an aged man and destroying some of his property, the jury found him guilty and sentenced him to receive thirty-nine lashes on the bare back, to labor in the mines until he should reimburse the man for the destroyed property, and afterwards quit the country. Every part of the rigorous sentence was faithfully executed. A fellow had stolen some property and was convicted—it was in a mosquito region—he was sentenced to be stripped naked and tied so that the mosquitoes could peg him for an hour, unless he should sooner tell where all the property was secreted. After he had been exposed to the attack of the mosquitoes for fifteen minutes, he returned the property.

BOOK KEEPING AT THE MINES

Generally nearly all the articles command good prices in cash. There are few instances wherein credit is given, and I was not aware that there was any credit at all until the day I visited the Sonorian camp, when a gentleman handed me the account of a merchant who had just made an assignment for the benefit of his creditors. You will see that the style of book-keeping is quite primitive and original. The head commenced thus [Dt = Ditto]:

Accont Buk of John McGuire and
the people in thease diggins:

Remon Galpin, 4 lbs. of flour	$4 00
George Williams,	
the darkey white man	5 00
thomas millias the spaniard	
resons flower sugar	6 50
Manell Sanches groceries D C Dt	16 00
Red that lives with Dancing bill	30 50
Dancing bill needles, thred,	
shoes, stockins	18 00
the man thats in his tent	
pents and shoes	26 00
Martin that has the woman Dt	10 00
Inaca that has the woman with	
the big ring in her ear	53 00
the cozen to thomas bone Dt	70 00
hamilton for shoes Dt	5 00
The boy I left the tent with	47 00
Hoes Coleman Dt in all	25 00
Iasuz the Sonorian that stole the	
come flower bread	37 00
Chene in all up to this date	131 00
John that speaks English Dt	88 00
Polenary flowris that cut off the	
china man's hair, resons and	
pain killer medicine	48 00
Vicente and his two sons 8 ounces	
in gold dust lent	96 00
fecile the hoss jockey credit till	
morning pantaloons and shoes—	
red shirt	53 00
Le Spaniard that took the jacket	10 00
Loreuche the Spaniard that has	
the cattle	137 00
frank the man wats won that gambles	36 00
Manell Salyes, the Canaccer	
frenchman,	18 00
that has the white wife	24 00
and for two ounces in gold dust	
lent, in all	42 00
The man that fit about the woman over	
the dry creek frizzles for her head	32 00
The man that set up the store in the new	
diggins for what due on hatts, candles,	
serapys sorsagis sardenes coffee	
pantaloons pans red belts	300 00

(PPL, August 14, 1849.)

Massacre of Indians

Mr. S. S. Osgood, writing to the New York Tribune, gives the following account of the Indian difficulties at the California "Placers:"

CULLOMA MILLS, MAY, 1, 1849.

Since the date of my last, another party has been formed to revenge the death of Jack Doyle. They gathered about eighteen, and were gone two days in pursuit. Last evening they returned, and report that they took a squaw prisoner, and killed two out of a party that they met; that the squaw promised to guide them to the Indian ranchero, where they found from three hundred to five hundred warriors. Their numbers being too small to attack them to advantage, they passed the ranchero, and came upon a party of twenty-five who were engaged in digging gold. At the first fire seventeen dropped, but two of them rose up and made off; the others scampered, and they killed one more, making seventeen in all.

This morning they have formed a larger company, and are off again to attack one of the two rancheros that they found yesterday, each supposed to have nearly five hundred natives in them. Every horse or gun that could be had was mustered into service. One of those who escaped yesterday told them in Spanish that they meant to kill every white man that they could catch; but they will not be able to catch many unarmed, and they will not attack those that are. The whites are more prudent than they were; they have so great a contempt for these poor wretches that they have not had any fear of them. It is uncertain when the war party will return.

MAY 2.—The Indian hunters have returned, having killed thirty or forty, and brought in as far as Williams's ranche, about three miles from here, 70 women and children. I have seen several who went out, and all tell about the same story. The chief who escaped from here when the prisoners were shot, named Jesus, was the principal object of their search, as he is said to be the worst Indian in the neighborhood, and is the cause of all the murders. I am told by two gentlemen who went out to see the prisoners, that they were in tears, and did not wish to return to their chief Jesus, who had cut the throats of all their daughters that were from eight to twenty-three or twenty-four years of age, lest they should fall into the hands of the whites. Mr. Williams has promised the squaws that they shall not be molested, and that they shall have food, but I learn that he means that they shall pay for it by digging gold. Those of the fighting party relate the manner in which they shot these wretches as coolly as though they were speaking of having killed so many wolves. It is rumored that the chief Jesus has been to the Fort to see Capt. Sutter, and has said that if we want war we shall have it. I should suppose that he had already had proof that the white men here were ready for him. It is also rumored that the Indians are fast leaving for the South.

MAY 9.—To-day I have heard the manner in which the Indians were killed near Daly's ranche. They were emigrating, and were discovered on the plain just moving across it, when the war party overhauled them. A few ran and escaped; the others were surrounded by the whites, who were on horseback. When they discovered the whites on all sides, they gathered themselves closely, men, women, and children. The women and children were told to separate themselves from the men, that no one would be hurt save those who were guilty of murders. All their bows and arrows were taken from them, and while they were talking to them, and advising them to give up the guilty, a very tall, strong, well-made young Indian was seen tucking up his shirt, preparing to run. He was watched closely, and the moment he started was fired upon and fell; this alarmed the others, and they broke to run, and all were shot down. One squaw was shot by accident through the flesh of the shoulder, and a ball grazed the ankle of a young boy. They were both brought in with care and the wounds dressed, and are now doing well. This story is from Capt. Williams, who headed the whites, and at whose ranche the women and children are now. They have been told that they might depart when they choose, but they will not leave. Mr. Williams keeps them at work digging gold for him, and feeds them.

S. S. O.   (WNI, August 18, 1849.)

A correspondent of the New Orleans Bulletin, under date of June 5th, gives the following account of some of the hardships encountered in reaching the country:

A HARD PASSAGE

I took passage on the ship Philadelphia, which sailed on the 8th. We arrived here on the first day of May, making the long passage of 80 days. That you may know what I suffered, I will state that our Captain put to sea with only thirty days' provisions on board. After being out five days we were becalmed, and the Captain then stating this fact, put the passengers on short allowance. The current carried the ship down to latitude 4° 17′, and we had a continual calm of forty-two days' duration.

We drank water, to save life, from a cask caught during a shower, and running off the cook house on which hens had been kept, the hen dung at the bottom of the cask being a foot deep. We had a half biscuit of bread per day, half pint of molasses per week only, with salt beef and rice to match, allotted each passenger. Most of the passengers became sick in turn, but strange to say but one death. My finger nails became black, and for twenty days before the ship arrived I could hardly move, and it was two days after anchoring before I could be sent on shore. With as good attention as this place affords, I have been enabled to gain my usual health.

THE COUNTRY

In looking over the papers from the States, I find so many letters written, and so much said, that I hardly know that I can say anything new. A gentleman said just now that if Judge B[ryant] would tear the title page from the book he wrote, entitled What I saw in California, and insert instead thereof, "What I did not see in California," then his book would be nearer the truth than it is now. I have not been out of San Francisco, but I think the gentleman right in his remark. Instead of that eternal spring spoken of, the climate of this place (San Francisco) is the most objectionable that I ever was in. Early in the morning it is generally foggy and damp—at noon it is warm—at about 2 o'clock it begins to blow, and always at this season, (and for aught I can learn, at all other times) from the West a complete gale, and so cold and dusty that few venture out without being muffled up in great coats and mittens. Fires are necesary at all times. As you go about 40 miles into the interior the climate is agreeable— very pleasant at Pueblo de San Jose, Sonora, and other places I could name; but as much too hot at the "diggins" as it is too cold in this town.

VARIOUS ITEMS

A man by the name of H. B. Williams committed suicide at the house of Mr. Mer- rill, in San Francisco, on the morning of the 17th April, by severing the jugular vein with a piece of window glass.

The schooner Honolulu arrived at San Francisco from Hong Kong on the 10th June. She made her voyage from San Francisco to China and back in four months and sixteen days, via the Sandwich Islands, where she remained five days on her outward passage.

At a trial of a Californian before the second Alcalde of the Pueblo de San Jose for whipping his wife, he was found guilty, and sentenced to be banished to Benicia for three months.

A man named Antonio Valencia was tried on the 9th of May last at Pueblo de San Jose for the murder of one Edward Piles, who has been mining since May, 1848. Valencia confessed his guilt, and was executed on the 10th May. The reason he gave for having murdered Piles is because he was told to do so by one Anastacio Chobollo. This Chobollo, it appears, was present at the murder, and shot the body of the murdered man full of arrows, to lead to the impression, should the body be found, that Piles was murdered by Indians.

A correspondent of the New York Courier says:—The town is becoming Americanized by such signs as Centre Market, Washington Market, New York Store, &c., which, together with the numerous friends you meet from home, makes one forget that he is many thousand miles away from his fatherland. The shores of the harbor are heaped with merchandize, and there are not storehouses sufficient to hold a moiety of what has already arrived. As to the general appearance of the town, it may be likened to a resurrection of Jew shops, all kinds of old and new dunnage is being hawked at stands on the walk and in tents temporarily leased for the purpose, and without exciting the imagination, the passer by might fancy himself in Chatham street, where "every article on the board is only four cents;" auction shops are open day and night, and the goods of adventurers are sacrificed at most ruinous prices. Below I append a list of merchandize sold at auction, as also the general prices of produce and staple articles. There is no stability in the market even for a day, and the arrival of one vessel may depress prices 100 per cent.

There are no piers for shipping, and the numerous shipping in the bay presents a most imposing appearance. Sailors do not desert as much as formerly, owing to the discouraging reports from the mines, and I should judge that there would be but slight difficulty in obtaining crews to leave at $100 to $150 per month. Still there are very many vessels whose crews have abandoned them and gone to the mines or stopped on shore at lightering. The crew of the U. S. steamer Edith locked the captain and mate in the cabin, lowered the quarter boat, put in their dunnage, and deliberately went on shore. They left behind six months' wages, and their pay had been raised from $20 to $125 per month to induce them to remain. The newspaper mail brought by the Panama has proved a total failure. The immense mail, after some three days' delay, was assorted, but by some loose arrangement, owners of newspapers were allowed to search for themselves, and in a short time the whole mail was a confused medley, where each picked out such as suited him, until the whole mail was destroyed.

WHO OUGHT TO GO TO CALIFORNIA

A correspondent of the Mobile Advertiser says:—Any man capable of enduring hard labor realizes his ounce per day; but I see hundreds of poor, disappointed gold seekers daily in from the mines, who have not a dollar. Unable either to endure the labor, or unfortunate in the selection of placers, they have abandoned the project

of digging. Many resort to drink and dissipation for consolation; others are returning home. The average digging is about an ounce per day. There is destined to be more ruined fortunes, poor, heart-broken, and disappointed men here, than was ever collected together in one land before. There is gold here, and a plenty of it, but not one in ten that comes here is or will be any the better of it. If he digs, he must pay half he makes for a living in the mines, and if he loses his health he pays the other half for a little medical attendance. Let those come here who have no home, no occupation, no friends or families dependent upon them, and whose position is that of a cipher in society. All the world is the same to them; with such, fortune is an unlooked for triumph, and misfortune brings with it none of the stings of disappointment.

(PPL, Aug. 15, 1849.)

Scenes in the Far West

An Overland Journey to California—Tedious Traveling—Robbers—Deplorable Condition of an Unfortunate "Wight" Robbed of Everything— Difficulty of Mule Traveling—Beautiful Prairies— Col. Benton's California Railroad— Traveling Beds, &c., &c., &c.

Near Salt Creek, some 50 miles from
Old Fort Kearney, on the way to
Fort Childs, or New Fort Kearney,
19th June, 1849.

In my first I spoke only of getting up our teams and the loads in our wagons—a scene were it described by the pen of a "Pete Whetstone,"[4] would have taken the eyes of all lovers of graphic descriptions of real life,—as it is, I have only brought your mind to a very imperfect understanding of the true merits of the case.

There is no use in pretending to the contrary, in this prairie travelling (although every step we take we suppose ourselves a yard progressed towards the

---

4. A monumental liar; someone who takes the prize for distortion and falsehood.

real El Dorado of the ancients,) nearly all the ordinary etiquette and polite usages of better society are entirely left out of the catalogue of our civilities *en route* for California, however polished we may have been, or considered ourselves to have been, while in the societies we have so recently left. Our efforts now, and, indeed, our necessities, require us, as fast as we can, in practice at least, to go back to the better usages of primitive society:—patience, candor, truth, and friendship, amongst and towards each other; diligence and energy in going forward, with extreme caution, and even suspicion, of the red men of the forest, through whose nominal dominions we are passing,—not for fear of life or limb, but even a matter scarcely less important, the loss of our animals, which draw ourselves and our provisions. These gone, and we shall be exactly in the condition of an unlucky wight we met to-day, who, on his return from Salt Lake Valley (a merchant on his way to lay in a stock of goods), was robbed of everything, and set literally on foot. "Old Virginia never tires," nor does the American energy ever give way to any common mishaps, so he was pursuing his way as best he might—there were two of them. Only think of being so turned out on foot near the South Pass, and then think of the nerve, endurance, and energy necessary for two such wights to pursue with unabated energy the balance of their journey, about 900 miles, with the few clothes they happened when robbed to have on their backs, and without anything else, except that energy and determination known only to Americans. They had, when we met them, about 40 miles to go to reach the White Settlements.

On reaching Fort Kearney on the back of a mule (an animal I had never backed before, nor had I before I left Fort Leavenworth rode 50 miles in eight years, even on horseback), at the rate of 45 miles per day, I need hardly tell you I was greatly fatigued.

At Fort Kearney I learned, with almost dismay, that I had a ride of still 45 miles further before I could accomplish what the government had directed. I remounted my long eared friend, who was much less jaded than I, clapped spurs to her side (you know none ride a mule without spurs), and off we pushed still farther into the wilds of Iowa—a district of country scarcely equalled for fertility or beauty—but the melting snows of the mountains, towards which we were hastening at 20 miles per day, had filled to overflowing the Missouri, and the bottoms, up which lay my way, were almost covered with water, often to nearly swimming the animal, still more often to its belly, and almost always so deep as to impede its faithful and determined pace. Such a ride for such a distance few have been called upon to make.

I reached the point of my destination, and after two days' delay returned, but by a higher yet more circuitous road, to where my two wagons and teams, which had preceded me, lay, within five miles of the Missouri, where we were to cross, which cost us two days' and a half hard labor to accomplish, and which we completed the day before yesterday, entirely exhausted by the fatigue and labor it cost us—all bespattered with mud—where we met on this bank some persons on return from California, and, strange as it may appear, it would have taken nice discrimination to have told us from them, so fast had we fallen into the looks and manners of real California gold diggers. It is easy, not only in appearance but in fact, to make a savage out of a civilized man, but out of the former the latter can scarcely be made, even after the longest and most earnest efforts are made to effect it.

We have now been two days on the road and have 170 miles yet to travel to Fort Kearney, where I hope again to join my family; this will take us from 7 to 9 days, making, at that rate, my separation from my family about 19 days. For these two days our travel has been over one of the most lovely prairie countries I ever saw, every acre rich enough to raise 1,200 pounds of hemp, and more than half the miles over which we have traveled would not cost $100 to grade it ready for laying the rails of Colonel Benton's contemplated California railroad, and by the bye, say to all your friends—for they will all want to go to California next year—to back him up for the road, for while it would be the greatest national work ever accomplished by any modern nation, the whole face of the globe does not furnish any nation besides our own with a chance to make a work that would add such national glory as well as such national wealth; and since the creation, no nation has been so strongly called upon by the people to perform such a work, which could not fail to put money in "the purse" of every one of her citizens. To refuse to make it is to make riches for the people of other nations, when our people ought to pocket it themselves. Let all go for the California railroad.

It is getting late, and we have had a long day's travel, and I am quite fatigued, and must go to bed. Would you like to know what sort of a contrivance a bed is here? Well, I'll tell you: Immediately after I crossed the Missouri, the first wigwam I passed I selected a piece of bark which the Indians had peeled from an elm to cover their camp. It is about twenty inches wide and the proper length, that I put in one of our wagons, and at night I lay it in my tent smooth side up, spreading my saddle blanket on it, and down I lay, making a pillow of my saddle, and a nightcap of my hat, covering with the blanket I carry on the top of my saddle, and then I am what is considered here very comfortably bedded,

and, indeed, my Dutch wagoner, who carries it for me during the day in his wagon, laughs heartily when he gets it out for me, "smutters" his German, for he cannot speak English except only to swear at the mules, and very clearly insinuates that I am rather too much given to luxurious "doings." The point of excellence in the bark bedstead is that it keeps down the damp, which would easily ascend if only the blanket was under me. Good night. I turn in and expect to sleep equally as sound as I did when last so comfortably and so kindly lodged at your house.

Yours, J. W. (CPD, Aug. 15, 1849.)

From a California Missionary

The Rev. T. Dwight Hunt,[5] whose missionary labors at San Francisco are highly commended, writes to the Newark Advertiser on June 29 as follows:

Contracts are nothing in this land of liberty and gold. Companies bound together by the most solemn ties at home, have hitherto dissolved almost instantly on landing. Men of irreproachable character at home, and elsewhere, have often here violated their faith, and given themselves up to the guidance of personal interest. Mining *companies* have thus far proved a failure. A man who gets his six ounces a day is loath to share with an unsuccessful partner, who gets only his ounce or half ounce. Things are as they *are*—not as they should be, in this and almost every other important respect. We see here, if any where in the world, the rank growth of "the root of all evil,"[6] and the abundant

---

5. Timothy Dwight Hunt first came to San Francisco (then Yerba Buena) in 1841, from Honolulu. In 1848 he was invited back, and on November 1 was appointed Protestant chaplain to the citizens of San Francisco at an annual salary of $2,500. Worship took place in the public school on Portsmouth Square. In July 1849 Hunt organized the First Congregational Church, the third church in the city.
6. "The love of money is the root of all evil." (*I Timothy 6:10.*) "There are a thousand hacking at the branches of evil to one who is striking at the root." (Thoreau, *Walden.*)

and bitter fruit whose poison worketh death in so many souls.

HOUSEKEEPING

Mrs. H. arrived here from the Islands on the 4th instant. As I anticipated, the native servant whom she brought with her, under a written contract to remain, has gone to the mines. At Honolulu I paid him $10 per month, he finding himself. Here I paid him $50 per month and found him every thing. So we have no servant, and our experience is not *peculiar* in this particular. Our native man did our cooking and washing, and found our wood on the neighboring hills. This was a great saving, but now I must pay $100 per month for wood and washing alone. If we *eat*, or *drink*, or *wear* any thing, we must live beyond our income, for *rent, wood* and *washing* are equal to my whole salary—say $200 or more per month. Yet I have no fear that I shall suffer. I never have wanted any thing I *needed*, for me or mine; and I never expect to want while I am at work in the Lord's vineyard. *"Trust in the Lord and do good, so shalt thou dwell in the land, and verily thou shalt be fed."* And that promise includes wife and children, and mine among the rest. (PPL, August 16, 1849.)

Matters in San Francisco

SAN FRANCISCO, June 14th, 1849.

DEAR SIR:—Heaven's blessings on thee for thy kind remembrance. Your two letters greeted my longing eyes on my arrival here, with the first intelligence from *home* for seven long months. We left Milwaukee on the 11th January, and arrived here on the 12th June, five months and a day, and what a maze of strange scenes, incidents, and adventures go to fill up that gap! I am lost when I sit down with a sheet of paper before me, and allow my mind to turn back over them.

You received my letter from Corpus Christi. Well, we left that place and its hospitalities on the 19th February, twenty two of us, with two U. S. transportation wagons. Were 12 days to Laredo, on the Rio Grande, 140 miles. There we sold our wagons, and every man packed his own traps on his own mule, and rode his own horse. From Laredo our next point was Lampassas [Lampazos], the first watering place, being 70 miles. Our animals were 54 hours without water, and ourselves long enough to learn what it was to suffer for the want of it. This and another between Lampassas and Monclovey [Monclova] were the only occasions when our annoyances reached a point that amounted to absolute suffering; but they have left an impression on my mind that I shall only forget when my connection with this world and its busy scenes shall terminate. But *n'importe.* At Monclovey we changed our route, abandoning that by Chihuahua and the Gila, and made a strait wake for Mazatlan thro' Parras and Durango.

Arrived at Mazatlan on the 24th of April; found plenty of vessels, shipped on the 2nd of May on the French Barque *Olympe*, passage $75, sailed on the 4th and on the 12th inst. we were safely anchored in the best harbor in the world. There were 80 large vessels lying at anchor when we came in. Several have come in since, but I have heard of no vessel that left the Atlantic coast later than December. From the best information that I have been able to obtain respecting routes, my own opinion is that at present, one through Mexico is the surest, and the quickest: leaving the Rio Grande at Matamoras, carrying no baggage but a change of clothes, and buying your provisions on the road, as you need them, and having nothing to do with pack mules or low priced animals.

The Doctor and myself are in camp, living as comfortably as a couple of bachelors could desire; but will leave in a few days for the mines on the North Fork. My health has been perfectly good. I have been unwell but one day since I left home, slept in the open every night but two, from Corpus Christi to Mazatlan. Yours truly,

H. G. A. (CPD, August 18, 1849.)

From the California Placers: Account from a Gold Digger

CARSON CREEK, May 19, 1849.

I am happy to have the pleasure of letting you know my whereabouts. Our voyage from New York was more like a pleasure excursion than the reality of men emigrating to a new country, for the "root of all evil," viz: gold. Some amongst us did not relish either the discomfort they were forced to submit to, or the delay incurred by the various modes of travelling; but the younger and more energetic, regarding every trial with an air of confidence, consequently suffered but little from the many inconveniences natural to such an expedition. February 28, about 10 o'clock, we made the port of San Francisco, amid the loud huzzas of the citizens, and salutes from the man-of-war Ohio. In the evening an illumination came off in honor of the arrival of the first steamer up this portion of the Pacific coast. Next day we left the ship, and encamped some distance below town, on a hill side. The night proved stormy; in the morning the ground was covered with snow, but our canvass tent proved as comfortable to us as the more durable building at home.

From San Francisco there are two different routes of proceeding to the mines; the one by way of the Sacramento river, the other up the San Joaquin to Stockton, your ultimate destination being the "Steinish Loue River" [Stanislaus], situated some two hundred miles from San Francisco. The latter we took, after reaching Stockton, some one hundred and sixty miles from

the Bay. It is a small place, consisting of two frame houses, and some half dozen tents. From this point it is sixty miles to the nearest "placers." The modes of conveyance are by wagons and horses; freight is extremely high, commanding from forty to fifty cents per pound. For this reason many walk, with nothing but a sufficiency for their present use, as I did, and the others forming the company to which I belong. In travelling along, we spread our tents upon the ground, and slept in the open air, each man having his fire-arms at a moment's command, in case of need; but this appeared almost foolishness, for we met with nothing more formidable than a common hare.

After three days walking we reached this point, from which I now write you, viz: "Carson's Creek"—named after the person who discovered it last fall.[7] We immediately commenced operations, from which time we have averaged nine ounces a-piece per week; others have done better than this, while the mass have done much worse.

It requires from three to six in a company, and no more. The large companies, which I hear are now forming in the United States, will not remain united after reaching the mines, as we have quite a number of instances already, proving the fact.

While upon this subject, I beg the privilege of a word upon the "best man for the mines." It is the hard working, industrious, and persevering man who is best calculated to make money in the placers of

---

7. James H. Carson was a Second Sergeant in the 3rd Artillery regiment of the regular army, arriving in California in January 1847. He went prospecting for gold in August 1848, and made a good strike on the creek that still bears his name. In the spring of 1852 *The San Joaquin Republican* printed thirty-three articles, in three series, by Carson. The majority of these were published in book form later that year—the first book ever published in Stockton. This is generally considered to be the first memoir of an early California miner to get into print. The articles were published in their entirety in 1991: *Bright Gem of the Western Seas*, by Great West Books, the publisher of this volume.

California. Too many have come with the idea of picking up gold as they would stones upon the mountains. This class are already sick and tired of the phantom. Many have returned to San Francisco; some to their homes, where, I can assure you, they are much better off.s

Rather a melancholy circumstance happened here on the 25th of April, by which Lieut. R. M. Morrison, of the New York regiment of volunteers lost his life. If I am not mistaken, his father is an eminent member of the New York bar. The circumstances were these:—Lieut. Morrison had been visiting some of his friends that day, and towards evening met a German by the name of Friends, when some words passed between them, but they were separated. Each was on horseback, and armed— Lieut. Morrison with a bowie knife, and Friends with a revolver. Some more words passed, when Friends went past to go away, and Morrison's horse turned to follow the other, when Friends, supposing the other to be following him, turned and fired, the ball entering Morrison's right groin, which proved fatal in about six hours. The other was immediately arrested. Next day, Lieut. Morrison's body was sewed in a blanket, and buried under a large oak tree. We immediately elected (in less than an hour) a judge, assistant judge, and sheriff. The following day, Friends was tried under a neighboring tree, and in sight of the grave of his victim. The jury returned a verdict that Friends leave the mines within thirty days; if not, he forfeits his life.

Another instance—a man by the name of Ryan cut his own throat with a razor, three miles from this place; also, a man by the name of Tom Carnes lost his life while bathing among the *tulares* of the San Joaquin.

The Indians are perfectly wild, and have but little knowledge of the value of gold.

Many of the old miners are former residents of your city. On our arrival, they clustered around us like bees, every one inquiring for the *Herald*. Such was the demand that five dollars was offered for one, without success.

Your obedient servant,
JAMES GRANT. (NYH, August 19, 1849.)

Account From a Merchant

BARK WHITON, SACRAMENTO CITY,
(50 miles from San Francisco,)
June 23, 1849.

For a description of this city, I can only say that when we arrived, it had twelve to twenty shanties, stores, &c., not one of which was a real frame building, with a floor; and now several frame buildings are going up and, in all, I should judge that the town had doubled, both as to inhabitants and buildings, since our arrival. . . .

My business is wholly confined to the bark. It occupies me very closely, I can assure you; but I like it, as it is gratifying to be in a portion of the world where half cents, pennies, and sixpences are obsolete ideas, and where, when your property is sold, it is paid for without a credit of eighteen months upon book, then into a note, and then payment made in property actually harder to convert into cash than was the property originally sold.—Of the sales made, nine-tenths are for gold dust. Nothing else is expected, and after making a sale, we proceed to the scales to weigh the dust, of course.

The astonishing sacrifice that is made upon goods here is sufficient to alarm the natives. For instance, to speak of small matters, as you know many of the articles which were packed into my trunk for my own use, I will name some of the prices at which they were sacrificed, when I found that I did not need them. For instance, the woollen drawers, $5 per pair; red flannel shirts, $5 each; cotton socks, a few pairs, at $2; the rifle, which Fred brought on for me, from Woodstock, costing $10, I was obliged to sacrifice it, such was my distress for cash, for $100. But the best joke of all was that the man who bought it of me sold it

Sacramento City.

for $112.50, and that purchaser, taking it into the mountains, it seems got much more distressed for cash than I was, and sold it for $150. The revolver, which cost about $15, I sold for $75. Two pounds of powder, costing about 40 cents, I sold for $6.50 per lb. Ten boxes percussion caps (100 each), costing sixpence each, or near that, went at $1.50 or $2 per 100. The flask, costing 10s., went for $5 or $7, I forget which, as I kept no memorandum of any of them. The cheap novels, unbound (Harper's and others), costing 2s., go here for $1.50 to $2 each. Falling upon a small lot here of ten or twelve old ones, I bought them for $5, and sold them, in two lots, for $20. These things are given as they occur to my mind, as being a part of the history of the unprecedented state of affairs and prices here. Watches, of which I had three, I have sold none, not having had time to hardly show one, since getting here. But they will have all proper attention before the "harvest" is passed.

(NYH, August 19, 1849.)

The Picayune contains a letter from Mr. J. E. Durivage,[8] who arrived at San Diego on the 2d July, on his way to San Francisco. He gives a graphic description of crossing the desert before he reached the Gila, and one shudders at the recital of the sufferings of himself and party. He says:

"Without attempting in this place to give any elaborate reasons, let me state in so many words that the Gila route is unfit to be travelled, and that sufferings inevitably attend those who undertake it. To ensure a successful trip, the expenses would exceed that of any other route; and a strong constitution is moreover indispensable. *Gracias a dios*, I have arrived safe and sound, in excellent bodily health, saving the soles of my feet and the muscles of my legs, which are by no means 'unwrung.' The last 200 miles I have performed on foot, almost without food, and in six days—the road rough, mountainous, and stony, lying for miles in the wildest 'canonides' I ever beheld."

(PPL, August 20, 1849.)

---

8. John E. Durivage, who became an editorial writer for the *Daily Alta California* and other papers.

Society Upset in California

There appears to be what the French call a *bouleversement*—a complete over-turn—of the usual arrangements of society, at the gold region; for a specimen of which see the following extract from a San Francisco letter in the *Boston Courier:*

Since my arrival I have seen a lieuten-ant of the navy and a New York merchant dragging a handcart, at an ounce per load; a few days since I met a professor in one of your first colleges, driving his ox team, hauling emigrants' "traps" to the "dig-gings," at $20 for one hundred pounds. A Georgia planter cooks my salt pork, and does the flap-jacks brown; a printer from the Picayune office keeps my books, and two young gentlemen from jobbing houses in Pearl street take care of the mules, haul lumber, and act as porters in the store, each from $10 to $16 per day, with board. In California all labor, and one is daily fur-nished with innumerable sources of amusement by meeting old friends in such comical employment. Imagine our friend, the artist, with buckskin trousers, red flan-nel shirt, and California hat, peddling newspapers: "Sun, Herald, and Tribune, sir! latest dates from New York, *only two dollars each.*" (PPL, August 20, 1849.)

From a California Emigrant

Philadelphia Vessels in Rio Janeiro—
Difficulty among the Officers and Crews.
RIO JANEIRO, June 29, 1849.

Our brig, (the Meteor, of Philad'a,) had a pleasant passage of *forty-one* days from our Breakwater to Rio, the shortest passage by several days made from the States to this port. . . . Upon our arrival, we found some six or seven American vessels bound for California. Since our arrival, the ship Susan G. Owens, on the 26th instant, and the bark Ralph Cross, on the 28th instant, have arrived; both of these, you know, are from Philadelphia, and sailed from the Breakwater five hours before us.

On the 26th instant, the bark Othello, of Charleston, S. C., came out, in distress—*one hundred and forty-five days out*—having attempted to run through the Straits of Magellan, (Patagonia,) and lost both anchors, cables, windlass, and bitts. She sailed from Charleston, S. C. on the 31st of January, and makes a dismal report of the horrors of attempting to run through these straits. Nor is her case a solitary instance of the disasters attending these dangerous straits; *several vessels are reported by her as being ashore, entire wrecks, and all hands lost,* and her escape was a mere touch and go, as after they slipped her last cable they had to run to sea with only a close-reefed storm staysail, and even then she ran out at the rate of *fifteen* knots per hour, barely escap-ing the rocks. After she got out of the straits she had to scud under bare poles for three successive days. We have had about 20 or 30 vessels put back to this port out of some 200 which have been here bound to California, and out of these 15 or 16 have attempted to pass the Straits. Besides the danger, the delay consequent upon being obliged to return into port to refit is con-siderable, and when we consider that Rio de Janeiro is the nearest port where vessels can procure the articles necessary, it argues strongly against the propriety of attempt-ing this most dangerous passage. Our old-est and most experienced shipmasters, *all,* without exception, advise going around the *"Horn,"* (i.e., Cape Horn,) in preference to attempting the Straits of Magellan.

Rowdyism

The Brazilians have been extremely courteous to the Americans, and at first ex-tended to the Californians many privi-leges. For instance, upon the arrival of the first ships the Emperor threw open the public gardens and edifices to them, and gave strict orders to the police not to dis-turb them, unless violence actually took place. He was much pleased with the first few and expressed himself to that effect to our minister, Mr. Todd. But those who came afterwards were of a far different class, and he was obliged to repeal his orders. Rowdyism, extending almost to ruffianism, was of daily and hourly occurrence. Disgrace, of course, attached itself to all hailing to be California emigrants, and even now, although it is far better than when the rush was the strongest, the being known to be one is no recommendation. I am glad to be able to state that the class of California emigrants is now a considerable deal more respectable than they have been. It is true, indeed, you will always find among large bodies of men some of a more or less rowdy disposition. And indeed there is some excuse for men spreeing a little after a sea voyage. So far, since I have been here, there has nothing transpired of a serious character. One or two, I believe, have been arrested for being intoxicated and noisy in the streets, but nothing further.

Great difficulty has been experienced here between the officers of the different California vessels. The Osceola had both of her mates unshipped, and two others were shipped in their places. The U. S. Consul, Mr. Parks, has removed some four or five captains, and given their vessels to others. By what authority he does this is not known, but he certainly does not shrink from the responsibility. . . . Nor is this all—the crews of various vessels have had their share of the difficulties. The crew of the "Susan G. Owens" has, it appears, some difficulty with their officers, and have refused to do duty. The Consul, in consequence, has ordered them to be placed in irons, and has threatened to flog them. I heard the Captain (Barclay) ask him whether it would be necessary to take them on board of the frigate Brandywine to have them flogged. Mr. Parks answered "No; if the crew had anything against him, they could sue him."

The harbor of Rio is one of the finest in the world, and in the hands of Americans could be rendered impregnable, but under this miserable government I should think one frigate would be sufficient to capture the whole place. The soldiers are all negroes, and I am told not to be relied upon in action. . . . The Brazilians are expecting to be attacked by the Montevideans, and are preparing to meet them—almost every other man you meet is a soldier, and some of them look well, but a large number look anything but men who would be of any service in action.   THOS. R. STODDART.

(PPL, August 24, 1849.)

A California Incident

A digger at the mines, in his diary, records this incident.

"After dinner, prepared to go to the mill, and had promised there to-day. Took my India rubber blanket and bag, tin cup, double-barrelled gun and ammunition, and with my friend, with whom I had been working, set out for Collama after 3 o'clock P. M. On the way, passed a new made grave, with a cross over it, and a tin plate, such as we eat off of, attached to the cross, with the following inscription:—'God help starvation!' It proved to be the grave of a once respected young man, whose friends reside in Bond street, New York. He had associated himself with some young men of very bad habits—had become sick with scurvy, and they deserted him and left him to his fate. Some friends helped him, and gave him something to eat, and administered to his wants, more or less; but he continued to grow worse, and finally died. He refused to give his name, or the names of his friends, but looked as if he had seen better days."   (PPL, August 24, 1849.)

TALCAHUANA, May 16, 1849.
*The Fleet for California—Their Progress—
Disasters and Adventures—Appearance of
Talcahuana and Conception—Sport of the
Yankees—Solemnity of the Americans—
Murder of an American Sailor
by a Spanish Senorita*

Here I am, on board the good ship Albany, at the city of Talcahuana, on the southeast shore of the bay of Conception, longitude 73° west, latitude 36° 42' south, after having weathered the cape and paid all the penalties incident to its stormy shore.

The Albany sailed from New York on the 9th of January, and arrived here on the 10th of May. I need not say that we hailed "old mother Earth" with delight, as we had not touched at any port since our departure. The evening was delightful, as we came up the bay—a land-locked harbor, not unlike the centre of a circus—nine vessels were swinging at their anchors, and as twilight threw its mantle around us, the lights from the city became visible, calling up memories of home and friends, and anticipations of soon landing to enjoy the fruits, flowers, and a thousand other things for which this city is so famous in the records of our whaling voyagers.

The harbor is now gained, and the massive anchor flies through the green waters of the bay, to kiss old mother earth again. A boat is alongside—*el Grande Capitan del Puerto* ascends the ladder, and, with all the pomp and dignity of a true *Hidalgo,* demands our papers. (Let me inform our masters of vessels who may intend to call here, that it is necessary to have a list made out of their passengers, the number of boxes, bags, barrels, &c., on board, and a certificate from the health officer of the last place of departure.) The visit of inspection over, sixty passengers crowd around the gangway to go ashore. What faces, what dismay, when *el Grande Capitan* announces that no one can go ashore! Reader, were you ever 121 days on a crowded ship, and when within a hundred paces of shore learned you should not land? I almost hear you say no! Then you can form no idea of what we suffered. There, on the dim shore, could be seen "fairy figures" flitting to and fro. The bijuela, with its melancholy cadence, came over the sea like fairy music, and ever and anon was heard the welcoming song of the dark eyed Senoritas to *los Americanos.* You say it was too bad. So it was; but we determined to live on anticipation, (which, by the way, is half of all

pleasures,) and all hands mustered on deck to watch the lights and mark the smallest object that moved on shore, in the vain hope of bribing some adventurous boatman to land them.

Yankee Doodle

Among our invincible steerage is an old man who plays a little on a kind of nondescript bugle. When he learned the determination of the port officer not to permit the landing, he came on deck and struck up "Yankee Doodle." Scarce had the last note reverberated from the custom house, at which our gallant bugler blew so loud and fierce that it must have felt as if visited by an earthquake, when a cheer rang out from the nearest ship, a true Yankee cheer, followed cheer upon cheer from six other vessels, each vying to out cheer the other in honor of our national anthem. It is strange to witness the enthusiasm that can be created in a moment by a song, a tune, a shout, that speaks of home. Men shouted with joy and gladness who, a moment before, gnawed their own hearts with *ennui.* We thought no more of shore. What cared we for the shores of Chili; there we were, a little country of our own—a fair specimen of Yankeeism, shouting in ecstasies because we had heard a song of the "olden times," when the heralds of freedom first flung out the banners of our fathers. We thought no more of the dark eyed Senoritas; the wailing notes they sent echoing over the waters sank into insignificance, and served but to awaken memories of our own sweet Yankee girls. We were Yankees afloat on Yankee ships, and we made the city of Telcahuana know it.

Early next day we got on shore, at the city, as they call it. It is a kind of crescent, formed around an angle of the bay. The houses are all one story high, built for the most part of mud and covered with tiles. There is a grand plaza in the centre of the town, in which there is a barrack. The occupants of this den are more like the life guards of Pontius Pilate than soldiers of the nineteenth century. I could not learn their pay, but as it is very little, they are allowed to beg, or steal from everybody that comes on shore; in fact, they are a half-uniformed lazaroni. The dark eyed maids, yclept Senoritas, of the whole town, except, per chance, a dozen or so, are a curious mixture. Jack was, as usual, cruising in search of adventures, and to be met towing a Senorita along in every street at a kind of pace to which her feet seemed long a stranger. They wear none of those "long white veils" we read of in Spanish countries, but creep about on a sort of clogs, something, I should suppose, of the same pattern as those worn by Mrs. Noah, in the muddy days that must have followed the deluge.

Behind the Age

The adage "behind the age" should be the national motto on the shield of Chili. Their wagons, their axes, their furniture, nay, everything seems as if they were handed down from father to son since the days of the aforesaid deluge, with strict injunction not to change or alter them in the smallest particular. Cunning Yankees from the land of nutmegs were to be seen here and there disposing of their notions. Some paid court to Bacchus, while others worshipped at the shrine of Venus. The ten-pin alleys were in full blast, and the billiard rooms flourished, while the "boys" hired ox wagons and rode around the muddy streets, singing "negro melodies," to the great delight of the hosts of Senoritas that crowded the grated windows of the mud castles. Everything seemed redolent of life. I spent one day enjoying the richest scenes I ever witnessed, in this place, and started next morning for the city of Conception, three leagues off, where I was informed I would see the greatest city in Chili. The town was crammed with horses for hire. They were small cattle, covered with mud and dirt, with six or seven skins for a saddle. Some villanous looking ladroni had as many as four or five of these animals to

hire, for which they got a dollar and a half for the trip to Conception. They furnished huge spurs and pouches, a kind of square cloth, handsomely embroidered, with a hole in the centre, to each rider. The comicallity of the costume tickled the Yankees mightily, and in an hour sixty had reported as ready to march. They were principally composed of the passengers of the Albany. A Captain was chosen—a line formed, and in a way that would put to shame some of our New York troops, they deployed into the grand plaza amid the cheers of at least one thousand other Americans, who had assembled to witness the *Cabalgada a Concepcion*.

It was an exciting, amusing, comical scene in the plaza. The soldiers ensconced themselves in the court of the barrack, under arms—and, as I afterwards learned, feared we were about to take the city. The votaries of Bacchus hurled up their hats, the favorites of Venus, with her hand maids leaning on their arms, pointed out their friends in the cabalgada. An American at home is a kind of go-ahead business man, seldom, if ever, enlarged for fun or frolic; but if you only saw him enlarged in Talcahuana, you would swear he went ahead of anything in the comical line you ever did see.

Conception, like Talcahuana, is composed of mud edifices one story high, and contains about eight times the amount of inhabitants of the latter place—having 17,000 inhabitants.

Tragic Deaths

Amid these scenes of fun and frolic, a vessel (the Franklin, whale ship from Boston) hoisted her flag half-mast high. —— Foster, one of her crew, has fallen a victim to Spanish jealousy. He had become the *casaliero* of a beautiful Senorita. She grew jealous, and in a frenzy gave him poison— taking, at the same time, two doses herself. To be deserted she could have born, but she could not live after being rivalled. Pour creature! my blood ran chill as I looked upon her features, lovely even in death, and I heard her last prayer that she might moulder beside him. It will not be granted, as he lies in the consecrated earth—she is laid in the grave of the dishonored. On Tuesday, the 15th, at two o'clock, a funeral procession of at least eight hundred Americans received the body on the shore, and marched in solemn, decorous order to the burial ground, about a mile from the city. There they interred him, far from his kindred and his country, beneath a foreign flag. There were none to weep for him, but all desired to show him the respect due to him as their countryman. The silence that reigned throughout the city during the progress of the procession was very edifying, and showed that while our citizens lacked nothing of the powers of comicality, they also possessed, in the highest degree, the qualities of inspiring respect by their decorous demeanor when circumstances demanded its exercise.

While I write, two other California ships are coming up. The first vessel proves to be the Osceola, of Boston. Our skipper, Sherman, who, by the way, has been serving notice of a suit on his arrival at San Francisco, for his barbarity to the steerage passengers, will not permit a boat to come alongside. He is the most unpopular skipper that I ever sailed with, not only with the steerage but also with the crew and cabin passengers. But for the kind, gentleman-like conduct of Mr. George M. Bowen and Mr. Swain, our first and second mates, we would have had mutinies on board several times. While they continue in the ship we can get along; but if they were to leave her, half the cabin passengers would not proceed further, for fear of a mutiny among the crew. O'C.

(NYH, August 24, 1849.)

The Ship Susan G. Owens

By letters received from passengers in the Susan G. Owens, at Rio, on her way to California, it appears that great dissatisfaction prevails on board that vessel, and much disorder. Drunkenness, spreeing, quarrelling, and flogging of the seamen appear to have been frequent occurrences. A dead pig was one day thrown into the cabin. One letter we see published relates the particulars of a case of crim. con. on board, between one of the passengers and the wife of another. This person paints this picture, which is somewhat too strong, perhaps, in its coloring.

"To the other amusements which we have on board, I regret to add that gambling very generally prevails; and to complete the catalogue of dramatical performances we have only now to have a murder and mutiny. Profanity also prevails among the company to an alarming extent, and all these evils add grievously to the annoyances of the respectable and well disposed portion of the passengers. Even the 'Five Points' of New York, at midnight, could not present a more repulsive and melancholy spectacle than is often presented on board the "S. G. Owens," and this is the company so highly lauded when we started as "by far the most respectable set of gentlemen that have as yet embarked for California." Many have been made almost desperate by the deceptions practiced upon them, as they allege, before starting, and are now experiencing the bitterest misery and disappointment. And the officers of the ship contribute much to make the voyage an unpleasant one. We have sometimes witnessed the most barbarous manifestations of brutality, and on one occasion one of the men was tied to the mast, for no justifiable reason, as the whole company agree, and whipped on the bare back until the whipper actually sank to the deck from exhaustion."

(PPL, August 25, 1849.)

Rolling Out the "Bolders:" Streaks of Luck—Wealth, Wretchedness, and Rags

A letter dated San Francisco, June 30th, 1849, to the Picayune, says:

Since my letter of the 8th, I have made a visit to the southern mines—including those of Stanislaus, Tawalamia [Tuolumne], Mercedes [Merced], and Mariaposas [Mariposa] rivers and their tributaries. After all you have heard and read of the richness of the placers, you would be astonished to look over the country containing in its bosom so vast an amount of precious treasures—for miles and miles, between the Stanislaus and the Mercedes, the bowels of the earth had been upturned and ferreted, to the depth of six or eight feet, and still the gold appears as inexhaustible as when the miner first struck a spade into it. It would really appear as if the main body of the glittering metal had not been approached. Up to the present time, the only search has been made in the "dry diggins;" every one is anticipating a rich harvest as soon as the rivers fall sufficiently to enable them to work the beds.

From the Stanislaus to the Mariaposas, a distance of eighty or ninety miles, the gold region is of purely volcanic formation, and looks as if volcano after volcano had burst out from the earth, pouring over the face of the country layer after layer of pure gold. Many of the craters still exist as nature originally formed them; although little gold is found in the immediate vicinity of the eruptions, but in the drains and little creeks leading from them into the rivers it has been found in the greatest abundance. Wherever a hole is made in the ground, gold is to be found. There is a vein of white quartz rock, from ten to fifty feet wide, extending from the Stanislaus as far south as a small creek between the Mariaposas and King's river. I tried it at a great many places, and found it richly impregnated with gold at all points—the gold being locked up in the matrix, so as to require machinery to extract it.

There are now about 20,000 people at work in the south, including all ages, sexes, conditions, and colors. It may be safely estimated that they are taking out a thousand pounds of gold per day—whenever one of the miners gets less than an ounce a day, he thinks he is not paid for his labor, and seeks some better place. The insatiable thirst for gold keeps one fourth of the population continually going from one place to another, seeking more profitable "diggins."

(CPD, August 25, 1849.)

From the Plains

Terrible Battle between the Indians and California Emigrants!—Twenty Persons Killed and Wounded!!—Wagons Seized and Emigrants taken Prisoners!!

The following letter was received at Independence by a merchant of that place, from a California emigrant, which we believe is the only intelligence received giving any account of this horrible affair.

SOUTH PASS, June 15, 1849.

DEAR SIR: This morning at two o'clock we were aroused from our slumbers by an express rider, who states that the emigrants at Fort Hall (on Snake river,) were in a fierce strife with the Indians.

He states that when encamped at Fort Hall, a tribe of Indians (the name of which he did not know,) numbering about two hundred, attacked them about day break, on Sunday morning, and after turning all their mules and oxen loose, and making a general search of the wagons, they were put to flight by about a dozen of the emigrants, who fired upon them, killing one or two and wounding some half dozen. But while the emigrants were capturing their stray cattle, the Indians returned with a greatly increased force, and commenced a desperate attack upon those that were in search of their mules—killing three of them.

The emigrants at this time mustered all

their men together, numbered from 150 to 200, and under command of Capt. Cunningham, of St. Louis, were determined to protect their lives and property. They stationed themselves in and around their camp; and about 4 o'clock in the afternoon the Indians made their appearance, and after lurking around for half an hour, struck up a tremendous yell, which could have been heard a mile on the plains; and rushing into the camp, whereupon Capt. Cunningham ordered his men to fire upon them, which they did with great effect—killing four or five and wounding some 18 or 20. The Indians were prepared and fully determined upon their intent, they set up their war-whoop, and fought bravely and caused the emigrants to retreat.

In the course of a half hour after their retreat, the emigrants again rallied, and with renewed vigor and strength met the red skins face to face in open combat, but were again repulsed. Nothing daunted, they approached the Indians the third time, and commenced a deadly attack, and after a fierce struggle of forty minutes the red skins were obliged to retreat, and leave the field to the conquerors.

He further states that he does not believe there were more than 5 or 6 of the emigrants killed—three of them he says were teamsters.

When he left the camp, the dead and the dying Indians were still on the ground, and several were made prisoners.

He also states that while the express was coming, the wagons that were some few miles behind the main train were attacked by the Indians, and the emigrants completely stripped of their all, and at the mercy of the savages.

It might be here proper to say that Capt. Cunningham acted the part of a brave and daring officer—he never once flinched from his duty, but with the most encouraging and consoling words urged his men on, and like a true Christian as well as a soldier bade them be merciful if possible. He is as brave as he is daring, and as noble as he is patriotic. Messrs. Gray, Sloss, Hutchinson, and others are spoken of in the most flattering terms, and, in a word, the whole company fought bravely and patriotically. Too much praise cannot be bestowed upon this train for their gallant conduct at Fort Hall. It will teach the Indians a lesson, and will no doubt be the means of preventing similar depredations upon the California emigrants.

We will now push forward at as rapid a pace as possible, and hope that we may overtake those ahead of us, and be of some assistance to them—to those who are fighting the battles before us. We are but few in number, 118, and ready for a brush with the red men any time.

I must state that the information I have got of this terrible battle with the Indians did not come from a person who saw it, but from an express rider who brought the intelligence from where the other stopped off.

The express leaves in about half an hour. Grass is getting very scarce. We have had considerable wet weather; but to stake everything into consideration, we have got along much better than we expected when we first struck the plains; though it is a terrible thing to be where there is no town, house, nor anything that would cheer us up—here we are upon the broad plains, and at the mercy of the savages. I hope my next will give a full account of the fight with the Indians.

Yours, in haste, JAMES HARRIS.

(CPD, August 30, 1849.)

The Overland party attacked by Indians.

Having driven off the Indians, they continue their journey.

The Strait of Magellan

*A letter from a California adventurer
who made the passage in April last
in a vessel from New York*

FROM THE JOURNAL OF COMMERCE

Sixty days of pleasant sailing, the last three weeks of fighting pamperos and heavy gales excepted, found us in sight of the castellated heights of Cape Virgins, the eastern entrance to the far-famed Straits of Magalhaen.

These are classic waters. Through this narrow cut in the land, scarcely three hundred miles in all its tortuous course, bold Fernando de Magalhaen steered, and, despite of unfitness of vessels and treachery of officers, accomplished that wherein Columbus failed, and opened a new highway to the Indies. For many years afterwards this was supposed to be the only channel for ships, and many were the rich argosies that passed here with the fruits of sunnier climes; many, too,

> "Which struck where the white
>   and fleecy waves
>   Looked soft as carded wool,
> But the cruel rocks, they gored their sides,
> Like the horns of a hungry bull."[1]

Then Cape Horn was found to terminate the American continent, and few vessels, except those of simplest rig and smallest size, have since dared to attempt a passage from east to west through Magalhaen's Straits.

You will best understand the peculiar nature of this corner of the earth by following us from Cape Virgins to Cape Pilar.

The first day was spent in painfully beating up to the first anchorage in Possession Bay against violent gusts of wind, which lifted the tops from those deep green furrows, and drenched us with showers of inexpressible saltness. We anchored with the consort, the Seawitch of Mystic, the pilot-boat Anonyma, seventy-two days from Boston, and the clipper Eclipse, eighty days from Baltimore. Though thousands of miles from home, at a distance where the distinction between States should be less, and all viewed as a single nation, I was never more forcibly struck with sectional peculiarities than when contrasting the slow drawling reply of a Baltimorean with the hearty shout of the Bostonian, and the bluff independent hail of the Yankee smackman.[2] The little fleet which had thus gathered, in a single day determined to sail in company through the Straits, and it may safely be said four swifter vessels were never yet seen together on these waters.

At the second trial we succeeded in passing the first and second Narrows. These are each about ten miles in length and nearly two in width, the tide running through them a full ten or twelve miles an hour. By seizing it at the favorable time, no danger need be apprehended, except from the heavy ripplings, in which many vessels have been lost. In three days we had passed the first of the three great divisions which nature has marked in the Straits. The region of sand hills and granite cliffs yields to one which appears almost delightful in comparison with what precedes and follows it. Here the coast suddenly

---

1. "She struck where the white and fleecy waves/Looked soft as carded wool,/But the cruel rocks, they gored her side,/Like the horns of an angry bull." (Longfellow, *The Wreck of the Hesperus*.)
2. The owner or one of the crew of a fishing-smack.

tends southward, and the Strait expands into a broad sheet of water, thirty miles in width and three hundred fathoms in depth. The hills are thickly clothed with trees to the water's edge, and were it not for the humid climate and bogged soil, man could gain his livelihood from the earth. As it is, the Chilian colonies of convicts at Sandy Point and Port Famine are supported from home. Rain fell every day while we were there, and in a continual flood for a full third of the time. In this kind of experience we can fully equal even our brother hunters for gold who trudged across to Panama.

The Capital City

Port Famine, the capital of semi-civilization in this quarter of the globe, consists of a few houses, enclosing a wooden fort, in which lie unmounted two honeycombed twelve-pounders and a brass field-piece, tightly spiked! Buenos Ayres also claims this country, and Chili thus arms herself against her rival in imbecility. There is a rickety apology for a fence—a stout cat might paw it down—running around thirty or forty cells in four large styes, between which are gutters for streets, little stone islands for a sidewalk, and eighteen inches of mud for a pavement. I thought of New York! In each of these six-by-eight boxes, windowless and chimneyless, exists a family of convicts. About seventy from the fleet went ashore one evening, and saw a fandango. In Spain the dance may be graceful. Here, no wonder that the wretches pay one dollar a pound for soap, and make a good bargain at that!

Most vessels stop here needlessly for wood and water. Both can be procured as well, if not better, in most harbors further on, and time spent here is lost; for there is always a fair wind in this portion of the Straits, and many days must be spent at anchor before the Pacific is reached. Yet the water at Port Famine cannot be surpassed.

Men of experience say that months at sea do not alter its taste.

At San Nicholas Bay we saw a fair specimen of the Patagonians. This is that singular race of men which have so inexplicably lost half their stature in the last two hundred years! Magalhaen affirmed them to be nearly twelve feet high, Cordova and Sarmiento at least nine, Anson about eight, and our own school geography full seven. In truth, they measure about six feet, and are very strongly built. Whether time tears down tallness from men or from fables is a point for conjecture. These Horse Indians, as they are commonly called from their equestrian life, are friendly and very stupid. The Tierra del Fuegian, or Canoe Indians, are of the ordinary height, magpies in tongue, baboons in countenance, and imps in treachery. Many conflicts have taken place between them and sealing vessels. They are best seen at a distance.

At Cape Howard [Froward] the main channel turns sharply to the northwest. Here end the first two sections of the Straits, and all plain sailing. The whole body of water is here divided into a thousand little channels to the Pacific, of which the best known are the Cockburn, Barbara, Gabriel, and Main channels. The labyrinth of islands and sounds is so perfect that a good chart is indispensable. Unfortunate indeed is the vessel in Crooked Reach which has saved an unlucky sixpence in not providing several stout anchors and the best of cables at home or at the half-supplied depot in Port Famine.

"Woolliewaws"

Here the navigation assumes a new character. Nine days in ten, gales of westerly wind prevail, and beat fiercely upon the adventurous vessel which dares to struggle with their power. Rain falls several times each day, and, when that fails, showers of thick snow or stinging hail supply its place. There is a certain singular gust of wind very prevalent here, which the sailors have termed "woolliewaws" [williwaws]. When a vessel is caught at night out of the harbor by rain, snow, hail, gales, thick darkness, and woolliewaws, there will be little sleep on board. We were twice trapped in this manner, and always afterwards saved time and labor by seeking a harbor at three o'clock in the afternoon.

Strangely enough, the temperature of these high latitudes is equable, and not very cold. The thermometer ranges from 40 to 50 degrees Fahrenheit throughout the year. Decreased strength of winds alone marks the winter season.

In one day we sailed from San Nicholas Bay to Borja Bay; leaving the region of thick verdure, passing grim Mount Sarmiento, seven thousand feet above us, and struggling through a narrow island-spotted ribbon of water, with gigantic walls of granite overshadowing us from their immovable resting places. Cordova said that the mountain west of Cape Quod gave this portion of the Straits a "most horrible appearance." They do indeed seem very desolate and uninviting, almost all terminating in sharply serrated peaks, or slightly rounding knobs of bare granite, but there is a savage grandeur, a wild glory, upon their lofty summits, which far excels the smiles of the softest landscapes.

At Borja Bay we found the brig Saltillo, which had sailed from Boston some time last year, and had already spent five Sundays in the Straits. We also received New York papers to February 17th, from the steamer Panama. She reported several vessels at the entrance of the Straits, and among them the well known New York pilot boat Wm. G. Hackstaff, which sailed one day before us. At Swallow Harbor lay the Velasco, of Groton, and Iowa, of Sagharbor. Thus our fleet was increased to six schooners.

Both harbors are most secure and picturesque, locked in, as they are, by lofty mountains. Right at the bottom of each a magnificent cascade rustles down the sides of a broad, brown mountain,

"With the foamy sheaf of fountains falling through the painted air."

Furious Weather

Few things can be more lovely than these harbors, enclosed by bare cliffs, like gems set in granite. The weary sailor who looks for no beauty can never deny their comfort. The only objection to them is from the terrific woolliewaws that rush from the surrounding heights without a second's warning, and pounce upon the waters, gathering them into a narrow but boiling circle of foam, then skurry around, fan-shaped in every direction, and with resistless fury. "These woolies are queer things!" exclaimed our skipper. "See how they tie the water all up in a little heap, and then throw it every which way!" Even at anchor, the whole fleet rolls down in abject submission before them. Once, the Anonyma's clinker boat was torn from her stern, whirled over in the air, and sunk in a single second. It is fortunate that they last little longer.

It was only by very painful beating that we passed English Reach, Crooked Reach, Long Reach, and Sea Reach. The gale was diversified only with woolliewaws, the rain with snow and hail. Sometimes we are sailing along in rare sunshine, when a woolliewaw whirls a storm of sharp diamond hail into our faces, or a column of spray-beads to the very truck forces our little craft down into the water, till a rustling flood swashes along her decks, then moves leeward in a brown and distinct whirlwind, till it hides one end of a lustrous rainbow, whose other extremity is splendidly defined against some rough mountain. Meanwhile the glorious sunlight is over all. From Port Famine to the Harbor of Mercy, near Cape Pilar, they continually increased in fury. The day before we left this latter harbor there was a grand display of their impotent rage.

Our passage consumed twenty days, thirteen of which found us closely shut up in harbors. We overtook and passed square-rigged vessels which had been weeks in the Straits, unwilling to return and unable to proceed. Few square-riggers can hope for a short passage; the difficulties of managing them in a channel barely a mile wide in some places are too great.

The passage from the Atlantic is thus mostly confined to small vessels. From the Pacific, passages are often made by ships in two or three days, and the only wonder is why more do not save the distance around Cape Horn. There are scarcely any dangers which are not visible, so bold is the coast and deep the surroundings throughout the Straits.

Few portions of the earth can surpass this, so wonderful in the grandeur of its scenery. Here let the painter come, the poet too—all who love Nature in her wildest moods, and can discern a mystic loveliness behind her frowns. Only the mono-maniac gold-hunter views it with an indifferent eye.

We have left the Straits of Magalhean. Cape Pilar grows dim, Westminster Hall towers faintly afar, the sea-beaten Evangelists begin to loom in the evening sky, and Cape Victory, like a grim old warder, watches our departure in silence. On one side of us is the mighty group of Tierra del Fuego, on the other begins the immense continent whose other extremity is near the North Pole. Before us lies the great Pacific.   (WNI, Sept 5, 1849.)

The Overland Emigrants

FORT LARAMIE, June 23, 1849.

Since I wrote last from Fort Kearny, I have obtained further information as to the probable number of emigrants upon this route for California, and I find, from conversation with Maj. Rough, U. S. A., the Indian agent, the American Fur Company's agent, and emigrants who have reached this place via Council Bluffs, that instead of exaggerating in my list, that my calculations fall short of the true number.

There are now upon the road, between Forts Kearny and Hall, thirty thousand emigrants, with over fifty thousand head of stock, mostly oxen; and fearing that there will not be grass enough to supply them when they approach the mountains, they are all striving to get in advance. Hundreds of wagons have been cut up to make pack saddles, for five dollars is the most that can be obtained for the best. Mules and oxen can not be bought at any price— only exchanged, a mule for a yoke of oxen. Every man that can exchange his oxen for mules or ponies is abandoning his wagon and packing a few pounds of provisions; and those who go on with wagons are overhauling everything, making the nicest calculations of the amount of provision necessary to take him through, and throwing the remainder away.

The ground for two hundred miles is strewn with wagons, trunks, axes, picks, shovels, harness, bacon and lead in cords, flour, biscuit, beans, coats, pants, boots, shoes, chairs, &c., &c., &c. Such a destruction of property, and that so willingly and voluntarily, was probably never before witnessed by any one. Many of the cattle have now given out, and they are fast breaking down the rest by "pushing ahead," one to get in advance of the other.

The question is asked a thousand times a day—"Is there a sufficiency of grass in the mountains to feed fifty thousand head of cattle?" and as often unsatisfactorily answered.

If there is grazing sufficient immediately upon the road, so that emigrants will not be under the necessity of taking their teams far from the main route into the ravines, they will probably reach California as they anticipated when leaving the States; but if the opposite is the case, so much time will be consumed in finding grazing and going to and from the road, that they can make but a short distance each day, keeping them in the mountains until winter comes on, the only thing to be dreaded, for to those who are caught in the

Fort Laramie in 1849.

Sierra Nevada when snow falls, starvation is inevitable.

I do not wish to look upon the dark side of the picture, but the fate of the emigrants of '46 should at least be heeded, for the causes which produced so much misery then, are now not only in existence, but must operate a hundred fold greater. I do not intend to witness a scene of cannibalism such as was in the California mountains in '46, for to avoid it I have thrown away everything but a few pounds of clothing and provisions, and start to-morrow on pack mules, in company with Major Henly, ex-M. C. from Indiana.[3] We intend to go through in forty days.

There have been nearly or quite four hundred deaths among the emigrants, from cholera, since leaving the Missouri river. One company of fourteen lost nine. Some messes have all died except one.

(NYH, Sept. 11, 1849.)

Our Panama Correspondence

PANAMA, NEW GRANADA, Aug. 26, 1849.

The few Americans left here, awaiting the sailing of the "Oregon" and other vessels, have been amusing themselves by correcting the conduct and improving the manners of the agents of the Pacific steamers. There has been only an effort made, but I am afraid nature is too strong for any human device, and that however potent the voice of the people may be in political matters, it cannot effect the least reform in the point at issue. There are about four hundred Americans in this town, every one of whom signed the resolution offered at a public meeting held a few days since, in which the conduct of the American consul, the agents, and captains of the ships have been censured. No person can form any idea of the extent to which petty tyranny is practised, unless he is here an eye-witness.

You are already aware that this place

---

3. Thomas J. Henley, first elected to Congress from Indiana in 1840, and reelected twice. In California he went into banking, and was active politically but did not run for office.

has been well scourged by the cholera, and if there can be any idea formed from the number of funeral trains which daily parade the streets, I should say that it is still here, and by no means at rest. I regret to say that many Americans have been hurried to their last resting place by this disease, during the past month, and that nine out of every ten now in the town are ailing from effects of fever, caused by the humidity of the atmosphere and the effluvium which arises from the great quantities of decayed vegetation in and about the town. It is fortunate that there are not a greater number here at present; the weather is so wet and unpleasant, and the facilities for crossing the mountains so ineffectual and limited, that diseases could not be avoided, especially as proper medical aid cannot be had. There are a number of persons here claiming to be "Oxonians" and members of the faculty, from various parts of the world, most of whom would be puzzled to tell the difference between quinine and morphine.

There have been so many deaths from cholera and other diseases in the hotels, that they are completely deserted, all preferring private board.

The Board of Health of this town, after a sitting of about two months, finally came to the following conclusion, in regard to the existence of the cholera:—

It has been decided, that owing to a deficiency of electricity in the atmosphere, in the vicinity of Panama, the disease called the cholera is attracted and allowed to do its work of death, without let or hindrance, and it is now recommended that in order to banish it from our city, the air must be "stirred up," purified, and to do this, nine guns loaded with powder must be fired off from the ramparts, every afternoon, until the malady disappears.

In pursuance of this decision or order, we are saluted from the ramparts every day with that many guns. Here is a hint that the Sanitary Committee of New York might profit by, and rid Gotham of its worst enemy. I would recommend a free use of saltpetre, it is cheaper.

(NYH, Sept. 14, 1849.)

News from the Western Plains

Extract of a letter from a member of the Washington and California Mining Association, commanded by Captain BRUFF, *to his father at Washington*[4]

FORT LARAMIE, JULY 10, 1849.

Here we are, thus far on our way to California. Our prospects are brighter now than ever, and we expect to make the headwaters of the Sacramento in sixty days from this place.

On Sunday last, one of our men (Charles Bishop) was taken ill about six o'clock A. M. and died at about one P. M. Poor fellow, he was predisposed to the disease of which he died; and on his first attack, which was on board the boat, he was told by the doctor that he could not

---

4. The Washington City and California Gold Mining Association, with sixty-five members, was commanded by J[oseph] Goldsborough Bruff (1804–1889). In 1849, when he set off for California, Bruff was a draftsman to the United States Bureau of Topographical Engineers. While leading the association to California via the Overland Trail, Bruff also intended to write a guidebook for the trail. His journals, drawings, and other papers were finally published in 1944, in two volumes, under the title *Gold Rush*. A one-volume edition (794 pages) was published in 1949, omitting only "some earlier dairies and some other material" from the first edition. As the editors of the book wrote: "We know of no record of the route comparable to his for length and historical fact. . . ." This letter of Bruff's is not in *Gold Rush*, and probably has not been published since it appeared in the newspaper in 1849.

survive another. We buried him on Sunday evening on the summit of a high bluff overlooking the Platte river.

We are all well, and, with the exceptions of which you have been advised, have been since we left the States. We start to-morrow evening, after throwing aside some more of our provisions, &c., and *fixing* our wagons, with which we intend *trying* the mountains. Many teams—in fact nearly all the *mule* teams—have *packed* from this post, and wagons can now be bought at ten or even five dollars. As we have but seventy *available* mules, and have sixty-five men, we shall not think of *packing*.

The thermometer stands now in the tent of Lieutenant Duncan at 122°, and the air is actually *thick* with mosquitoes.

Guard tent, 11 at night.—The express starts in the morning. I would write more, but the mosquitoes not only cover my paper, but seem determined to put out my light. On arriving at the "dry diggings" we shall send a detachment for provisions to San Francisco. Address us at that place.

FORT LARAMIE, JULY 21, 1849.

At this post I have endeavored to get hold of all the items I could in relation to the emigration. As to the great train, there has been much sickness, many deaths, and a good deal of quarreling and fighting, but they are worrying on through it bravely, and will very likely nearly all get on to the gold region this fall.

Five thousand five hundred wagons have passed, averaging three and a half souls per wagon; and the number of deaths from the Missouri river to this point is about one and a half per mile, which is below the mark. The greatest fatality has been among the Missourians and the Western people generally, while among the people of the Eastern States it has been scarcely felt at all.

Since my last a gentleman in this train has furnished me a list of deaths on the road from St. Joseph to Fort Kearny; and to

this distance I have completed the schedule, so far as I have been able. It is not any approximation to the exact number, but only such as were along the road side, together with a few others which have been from time to time discovered in by-places. At the upper crossing of the South Platte I remained three days, and found four graves; but since I left I am informed that *eighteen* are buried together, at about a mile from the road, which the passers will never see, unless they go off to camp in that direction. During the time the cholera was at its worst along the route, the forward trains had swept all the pasturage from near the road, and the thousands of teams in the rear had to go off sometimes two or three miles to camp—and in hundreds of out of the way places graves and graveyards can be found, which, if the names of their tenants were arranged, would swell the fatal list to a melancholy size.

[Here the writer gives the names of sixty persons whose graves are marked.

Scores of graves have been passed which have no identity placed over their remains, and have not been enumerated in any catalogue. From this place west, the sickness did not follow the trains, so far as heard from.

At this point, and for some distance back, hundreds of wagons have been burnt, and tons of provisions thrown away, the owners *packing* the rest of the road. It is a fact of dear-bought experience that this is the only sensible way of going to California; and the next sensible idea is, that if men are so foolish as to bring wagons, be sure and haul them with oxen. Unless for families, there is no use for wagons. Only about one hundred families have crossed the plains this season. The road side is full of all sorts of patent gull-traps,[5] which caught Californians at almost every door in every city last spring—such as chafing boxes to cook with alcohol, &c.

At this fort there are four or five emigrants in the hospital from accidents with fire-arms.   (WNI, Sept. 8, 1849.)

Notes of a California Expedition

San Francisco, California, July 9, 1849.

Messrs. Editors:—After a passage of 49 days from Valparaiso and 174 days from New York, we are at length anchored in the Bay of San Francisco, where we arrived on the 6th inst. The Bay is a magnificent sheet of water, seventy miles in length, and varying in width from three to twelve miles, studded at intervals with beautiful islands, and is capable of affording an excellent harbor for as much shipping as ever can be sent to it. At the present time there are now here about one hundred vessels, (and among them the "Grey Eagle," of Philadelphia, which made the passage in 103 days, and was the *first* vessel from the United States,) the crews of all of which deserted shortly after their arrival, and they lay here dismantled of sails and upper spars, looking the picture of desolation. It will be some time before they can be got away, as sailors are offered and refuse $200 a month!

The *city* contains about one thousand houses, the greater portion of which are nothing more than muslin stretched over a light frame; and hundreds of tents belonging to those preparing to go to the mines are stuck along the shore. There is nothing like comfort to be found here. Every thing—houses, manners of the people, and the courtesies that render civilized life desirable—all, all are in the rudest possible state; added to which, the presence of persons of all nations, the Indian, Chinese, Mexican and Chilian, decked out in the gaudy variety of colors, and almost every man armed to the teeth, reminds one of some of the rude scenes in the dark ages, and inclines us to think it rather of the character of one of the romances of "Arabian Nights" than the sober reality. Common laborers receive $1 an hour, and car-

penters are in demand from $15 to $20 a day! Every thing else is in proportion, and the California value of money would not be believed if I were to write you the sober truth. Enormous schemes of land speculations, and the building of splendid cities—on paper—is carried on with a rivalry exceeding those in the United States several years since. As high as twenty thousand dollars have been paid for a lot here, and the prices are advancing every day.

So far as relates to the wonderful mineral wealth of California, the most exaggerated stories that have been told of it do not over-color the reality. The whole country is full of gold, which can be had for the digging of it. But those who come here, as many do, and imagine that it is easily to be picked up, will be wonderfully disappointed. The digging of gold, so far as regards labor, requires far more *excessive* work than the digging of canals. The ore is unequally distributed through the earth, of a very tough nature, which is compelled to be penetrated from the depth of one to eight feet before the stratum of alluvial is reached, that contains the gold. Then the trouble has but just commenced, for oftentimes the dirt has to be conveyed on the back in pails full, some distance to the water, to be washed. Machinery is of no use, and cannot be transported at present over the hard roads necessary to be travelled before the mines are reached; though those whose bodies are capable of enduring excessive fatigue, the rays of a burning sun 90 degrees in the shade, and who are willing to work steadily, may amass considerable though not the average immense fortunes so often related in the newspapers as having been obtained at one successful stroke.

Some difficulties between the Indians and whites have taken place, and several fights occurred in April and May, in which

---

5. Devices contrived to catch and dupe the credulous, the naive, the simpletons.

a number were killed on both sides, and a number of Indians taken prisoners. Everything is quiet now, except that the Americans have determined to drive from the mines every foreigner speaking the Spanish tongue. They are required to leave the mines in a certain time; failing in which, the "*Hounds*," a self-constituted tribunal of Judge Lynch, arrest, try, and hang them, or cut their throats! The consequence is that this gentle hint is generally taken, and hundreds of them are leaving the mines. One hundred Chilians sailed from here for Valparaiso on Monday last. We are preparing to go to the mines; so you must excuse the brevity of this.

Adieu,   D. N.

THE OVERLAND EMIGRANTS

A correspondent of the Tribune, writing from Sacramento city, July 28th, says:

I saw last week the first company of adventurers who have arrived by the overland route—Captain Goodyear's party,[6] which started from San Jose [St. Joseph] on the Missouri River, in May last. They report but 67 travelling days through, and all the party look hearty and rugged. Capt. Goodyear thinks that the first wagon train will enter the valley of the Sacramento by the 15th of July. Capt. G. expresses the belief that most of the wagon trains will suffer unaccountably from scarcity of grass for animals, although he represents the yield of grass as more than ordinarily good, and this is his third trip across the mountains. There has been another small

party arrived, both of which took the Salt Lake Valley route. They represent the Mormon settlements in the most flourishing condition, with the prospect of a glorious harvest in every branch of agriculture save corn, and the Mormons as universally kind to the emigrants who pass through their domain; in many instances they state that needy emigrants are furnished without reward with provisions and fresh cattle, accompanied with the hospitalities of good Samaritans. This speaks well for a persecuted people, whom malice has written down as thieves, and whom wrong has driven to this enchanted asylum beyond the desert—to this "lodge in the wilderness."[7]

MUSHROOM CITIES

The annals of '49, in California, says a correspondent of the Tribune, will so eclipse the records of the '36 land speculation in the States as to render the latter hardly worthy of note as an epoch. Gigantic schemes are being planned by scientific wire-workers[8] from the States, and immense paper cities adorn the counting-houses of most of the leading merchants at San Francisco and the various towns on the river. Certain interests are at work to make this or that locality of *immense* worth to those who may be so fortunate as to secure lots *before they are all taken up,* and men have that over-sanguine, half-deranged air about them that characterized the '36 victims. Some fourteen new cities have been laid out on paper and put into

---

6. Miles Morris Goodyear (1817–1849), born in Connecticut; became a trader and mountain man. He was first in California (Los Angeles) in January 1847. He returned to St. Joseph, and in the spring of 1849, following the call of gold, he led the party mentioned above back to California. His luck was good, and he made a rich gold strike on the Yuba River—but he caught a chill and died there on November 12, age 32.

7. "Oh for a lodge in some vast wilderness, / Some boundless contiguity of shade, / Where rumor of oppression and deceit, / Of unsuccessful or successful war, / Might never reach me more." (William Cowper, *The Task* [1785], Ib. II, *The Timepiece, l. 1.*)

8. Manipulators; perhaps derived from the word for those who pull the wires in a puppet show.

market. Few of them will ever be of any account, except for speculative purposes.

VOTE YOURSELF A LOT PARTY

Through the agency of some New York *Land Reformers* of the "Young America" school, (or Vote-yourself-a-Farm men) the inhabitants are setting Capt. Sutter's title aside, and *voting themselves any unoccupied town lots.*[9] Personally, Capt. Sutter has no interest in land speculations which are accredited to him, but is merely the tool of a set of speculators, who lay claim to a modest tract of 30 miles square, Government land, and many lots in Sacramento City have been actually sold for from $5,000 to $8,000, and stores are now erected upon them. This class complain loudly against the vote-yourself-a-lot men, but I think that when the *vote-yourself-a-lot* precedent is fully established, real estate must fall to the ground, as it has done at Coloma or Sutter's Mills, the fourth largest town above San Francisco in California. Here the mill men laid claim to miles square, but the claim was at nought, and each settler has voted himself a house and store lot.

THE LABOR AT THE MINES

A gold seeker at the Tuwallamy diggings, July 30th, says:—The labor of gold digging and washing is exhausting in the extreme. Thousands who come out here brimfull of hope and courage are bringing their exuberant stock to a poor market—

for, after divesting their white hands of their white kid gloves, and working *a la mode* for one week, your amateur dealers in gold dust find themselves bankrupt of mental "pluck" and physical strength, and leave in disgust, some (grown already way-wise) for home, but many to hunt down the *ignis fatuus.*[10] These unfortunate sportsmen will only be "in at the death" of their own unreasonable expectations. Any body can make from five dollars to an ounce per day, but he must work faithfully and intelligently, or he is as likely to make nothing as a buyer of lottery tickets is to purchase a blank.

THE CELEBRATION OF THE FOURTH OF JULY IN THE MINES

The 4th day of July was celebrated throughout the placers by an entire cessation of labor, and the usual discharge of fire-arms, squibs, crackers, and other patriotic combustifiers. Thousands of "Liberty poles"[11] arose, and mountains of blazing pines lent their rude fire-works to the occasion. All became drunken with enthusiasm, and I own I am sorry to say it, upon bad rum at $1 a glass.

THE CHARACTER OF THE COUNTRY

Gentlemen, do not advise a dog to come to California. Why have Col. Fremont, Farnham, and others so studiously misrepresented this parched, barren, mountainous country? The entire North-

---

9. This refers to the Anti-Rent War of the mid-1840s in New York State. The last remnants of feudalism in the United States existed on the huge holdings of the Van Rensselaers and Livingstons along the Hudson River between New York City and Albany. The tenants stopped paying rent, rebelled against the authorities, and people were killed when sheriffs tried to serve writs for overdue rent. "Young America" seems to refer to John Young, a candidate for governor in 1846, who was endorsed by the Anti-Renters because he promised to pardon their leaders. Young was elected; he was also supported by the "Native Americans," an anti-foreigner group that was the forerunner of the Know-Nothing Party of the 1850s. "Vote-yourself-a-Farm" is a sarcastic reference to the former downtrodden tenants, implying that they were simply appropriating land for themselves under the guise of instituting a democratic reform.

10. A will-of-the-wisp; a delusion.

11. A tall pole or flagstaff, topped by a liberty cap, flag, or any other symbol of liberty.

ern portion of Upper California is inferior to New England in every respect, while the Southern half of the same territory is baked and burned by a scathing, scorching sun for nine months of the year, without rain or dews, and deluged during the other three. The timber is sparse and almost valueless. It is so dry that a tree of one-and-a-half or two feet diameter will become thoroughly seasoned in forty-eight hours after cutting. Ought intelligent, fore-handed farmers to be induced to leave comfortable homes, and to bring their families to a land, however rich in mineral wealth, where Indians positively cannot live? The harvest of gold will be gathered in two years, and the gleanings will be poor indeed. After that, woe unto him whose cupidity or stupidity brings him hither.

PROSPERITY OF THE COUNTRY

I am happy to add that the country is prospering physically as well as morally, or rather commercially as well as politically. Prices of most articles are improving, particularly those of suitable clothing and of certain kinds of provisions. The absorbent capacities of the interior are so marvellous as to astonish every one. Many goods that were not worth landing when I wrote you six weeks since, are now in lively demand. Of this you will have some proof in the amount of specie carried out by this steamer, which is double that shipped in either of its predecessors.

POPULATION OF THE COUNTRY

The present population of the country is set down at 45,000. Some 12,000 more are yet to arrive from the States via Cape Horn, and I know not how many over the prairies and through Mexico and Texas. To this, which the American papers will furnish, add what you can learn of European emigration, and you will form a tolerably correct idea of the population six months hence. The emigration from this coast may be said to have ceased. Our countrymen are like pikes, who drive out all other fish from a pond. Encouraged by General Smith's Continental Proclamation from Panama, they have expelled most unjustly, and, as the picture will show, most injudiciously, all foreigners from the mines. Vessels bound down the coast are filled with Mexican, Peruvian, and Chilian emigrants, returning home. The country is thus deprived of the only available cheap labor within reach until the yield of the mines shall have fallen off 50 per cent. I am happy to hear that General Riley,[12] with equal good sense and humanity, has gone to the southern mines with a view to protect such foreigners still there as may decide to apply for letters of naturalization.

SICKNESS AT THE MINES

Sickness has already shown itself in the mines, and the next two months will, I fear, terminate the earthly hopes of many miners. A good many cases of diarrhœa had occurred in a form very like the Cholera. Unless checked within a day or two it proved fatal.

MISCELLANEOUS

A Yankee Trick — We were accidentally listeners, and not a little amused, at a colloquy held by a long, green Yankee with a machine similar to a common New England churn, which he was examining minutely: "I bought you for a gold washer, and you are *one* of the washers. Here I've lugged and backed and packed you all through Mexico, and now you ain't worth a continental darn—you've turned out only a churn; ain't I a sweet-scented darn fool, ain't I?" Here wrought into a passion and overcome by his feelings, he seized an

---

12. General Bennet Riley (1787–1853), miitary governor of California from April 12 to December 20, 1849.

axe and entirely demolished the churn, casting the cog-wheel and crank nearly into the middle of the Sacramento.—*Sacramento Times.*

A duel was fought on Friday morning last, in the west part of the town. Both parties are said to have behaved "handsomely," and one of them went off the ground with a severe graze on the side of his face and head. This was considered a sufficient salve for "wounded honor," and we believe the matter has since been amicably arranged. The quarrel is said to have grown out of some misunderstanding at a faro table.—*Alta California, July 26.*

(PPL, Sept. 15, 1849.)

Interesting Golden Intelligence

Our correspondence and papers from California, and from California emigrants *en route* to the gold region, are filled with interesting intelligence of all sorts. Among other documents, we have received plans of houses, diagrams of monster lumps of gold found in the placers, and bills of sale exhibiting the enormous prices paid for the necessaries of life in the early history of the golden excitement. With one of the diagrams of a lump of gold is the following description:—

Outline of a piece of gold found near the Stanislaus river in October, 1848, by Lorenzo Truxillo, weighing 12¼ lbs. avoirdupois, in parts about one and a half inches thick, but averaging about three-fourths of an inch, nearly entirely free from stone and dirt; there might possibly have been half an ounce, not more, of dirt upon it. It still remains in the possession of the finder.

FRANCIS MELLES.[13]

COLOMA, 47 miles above Sutter's Fort, CALIFORNIA, July 5th, 1849.

Letter to a Merchant in New York—
Experiences of an Emigrant—
Town of Coloma

For the want of a post office here, I had to pay to a merchant a dollar and a half postage on your letter from San Francisco. I am beginning to feel discouraged, the same as every one who comes out here. The long and the short is, the diggings are getting decidedly worse every day. Almost every foot of the gold regions, this side of the mountains, has been "prospected," and the richest taken. Opposition in merchandising continues to rage fierce as ever—every one, even here, is underselling his neighbor. My dreams of making a fortune quick are dispelled. I am doing about as well as any of my neighbors, and much better than a large majority, but I am not satisfied, for I was doing a fair business in New York (gun smith). It is true I am making a little more here, but none feel like making this their home, and therefore leave as soon as they are able. Laborers, at present, can make six or seven dollars per day; but persons who were in business, with only fair prospects at home, will ever regret coming to California.

I have built myself a house, 18 feet square, without a floor, and with brown sheeting roof, at a cost of $375; had I more means I would put up a house adjoining.

---

13. Francis Mellus, who came to California in 1839 at the age of fifteen. In 1849 he was a partner with his brother in the firm of Mellus, Howard, & Co. at San Francisco. Later he settled permanently in Los Angeles, and during the 1850s was variously county treasurer, councilman, and member of the state legislature. He died in 1863.

Dr. B. has hired a house near by—one room, window without glass, and looks, as he says, like a Yankee "hoss" stable, and pays $200 per month and pays $5 per day elsewhere. By living with extreme prudence, and the denial of every luxury and extravagance, I live at about $2 per day. The liquor bills of most of my neighbors would more than support me. I confess I am succeeding, but I am disappointed, because I expected to make four times as much.

I think your splendid "Bowery Patent Mudscow, Gold-digging Steam Machine" will be permitted to work, and get laughed at, too. Instead of sand in the bed of the streams, they will find nothing but rocks, and many of them tons weight, with a stream like a mill-race, and cascades every half mile. Some are engaged turning the course of some of the rivers, and have got a good deal of gold; but, as they have been at great expense, it is doubtful if it will repay.

The miners have driven the Mexicans, Chilians, and Sandwich Islanders from the mines, and declared that all foreigners must leave. English, Irish, German, and French are yet permitted to remain.

This town is an important point, and cannot long be without a post office. Our settled population is now 234 men, 15 women with their husbands, mostly from Oregon, 8 negroes, not remarkably beautiful, and 20 children, decidedly dirty. F. B.

(NYH, Sept. 17, 1849.)

SAN FRANCISCO, July 30, 1849.

My last letter, dated from Talcaguano [sic], I have no doubt reached your office, and has afforded some little pleasure to the friends of the various passengers whose arrival so far upon the golden road I reported. On the 12th we sailed out of that port in company with all the vessels reported, (as a fair wind is a rarity in that port, all the vessels took advantage of it,) and on the 10th of July we anchored off San Francisco. Yankee enterprise has placed pilot boats on this station now, and to the amazement of the captain of the Albany, they charge California prices. When the pilot boat came alongside it was blowing quite a gale, and as soon as the pilot reached the quarter deck the captain asked him how much he charged? "Only $12 a foot," was the reply. "It is too much," said the captain. "Never mind," said the pilot, "you will soon get used to California prices." The captain kept saying "$12 a foot" until the anchors were down, accompanied with a curse now and then at California and its pilot charges.

Men of All Nations

It would be folly to describe San Francisco in the *Herald*. So well has it been described, that any man who reads the *Herald* (and who does not?) knows all about it. We have here a kind of society such as probably the readers of the *Herald* never dreamt of. It would be well worth the trouble of coming by the Isthmus to get a glance at society here. We have men of all nations, creeds, colors, theories, and professions, from stern Puritanism down to Socialism and Mormonism. Philosopher Greeley, and a hundred or two other leaders of reform, could find here ample material ready to be moulded. Will they come? The Mormons have decidedly the advantage of all others here, having had a start, and secured all the property worth having around this city. They are now making great exertions to get possession of the political power of the territory; and having money, they will be likely to take hold for a time of the government, because the great mass of the emigrants take no interest in anything but the gold. Many readers may ask, what government do you mean? There has been no government established in California. Some documents, which I send you, will show you we have a government here—a rebellious government at that—for as Uncle Sam would not make a government for us, they have made a government that will govern the old gentleman himself, as far as California is concerned.

Among the Mormon leaders there are a number of men who may be set down as smart men. They do not like Uncle Sam, because he refused to protect them in their city of Nauvoo. These men have taken possession of large tracts of land about this city, and are very anxious to secure their titles by local legislation. They therefore constituted themselves into a "Legislative Assembly of the District of San Francisco."

The members of this assembly were elected by a kind of sham election, conducted somewhat after the fashion of a primary election in the Sixth ward. A body of men calling themselves the Hounds, and whose rendezvous is at a groggery rejoicing in the name of "Tammany Hall," officiated at the polls. The election over, these men were called upon to arm and aid the civil power, under the appointment of this new Assembly. Their first act was to enter the Alcalde's office and carry off the records of the town, and a catalogue of their subsequent acts would astonish anybody but a resident of California. One of their number having got shot by accident by a Chilian, the whole body marched to the Chilian's house, and proceeded to sell him out by auction. The man's goods soon found purchasers, and he was ordered to quit the town in two hours, a feat he was very happy to be permitted to accomplish. The Hounds carried off the money they received for the goods, and the walls of "Young Tammany" resounded with the shouts of revelry while a dollar lasted.

The Governor, however, was not idle while all these legislative and mobocratic assemblages were getting under way to govern the territory, and on the 4th of June issued a proclamation which, instead of at once disbanding the Hounds and dissolving the Legislature, had the effect of rendering them both more insolent and offensive.

At the same time the Governor issued another proclamation, pointing out the constitutional mode of proceeding to form a State government.

Blood and Plunder

This document has had a powerful effect, and since it was circulated, some ten or twelve days since, a powerful reaction has taken place in the public mind here. The Legislative Assembly hide their heads, the more knowing ones resigning their places and using their influence to get their names on the tickets for delegates to the convention under the Governor's proclamation. The election comes off on the first of August, and the Assembly, under the constitution prepared by the convention, will be elected in November. Whether there will be two rival Assemblies in the territory remains to be seen. If the government supply General Reilly [sic] with forces enough, he is just the man to put a stop to illegal assemblages. The Hounds are completely at bay. Imagining that, as they were the instruments of the government, they were charged with the regulation of the town and its environs, they had a parade on Sunday week, and headed by drum and fife they marched to the hill that overlooks the town, and on which a number of Chilians were encamped. Here they made a furious assault on the tents and persons of the Chilians, killing four and wounding thirteen of these unoffending people. They sacked the tents, and having satisfied themselves with blood and plunder, they marched back again to their rendezvous. This act of the Hounds was the signal for the friends of order to come forward. Hundreds who had suffered at their hands were willing to take up arms and expel the Hounds by force. Public meetings were held, speeches were made, the Alcalde offered rewards for their apprehension, and during Monday and Tuesday the gold fever ceased, to afford an opportunity for the law and order fever to burn. A police has been established, and before Thursday evening no less than twenty of the Hounds were running in couples, and kennelled on board the brig of war Warren.

Judge Lynch

That most potent lawgiver, Judge Lynch, never opened court with more solemnity than he did here, under the title of "Law and Order." The Alcalde, not wishing to sit as representative of his most potent and prompt judgeship Lynch, refused to try the prisoners in his court. Then there was a mighty clamor raised, and a meeting, called upon the spot, appointed two gentlemen, one named G. W. Gwyn and the other James Ward, both men of high standing, to sit with the Alcalde at the trial. Grand and petit juries were chosen to try these men. The whole trial was a complete farce, from beginning to end. Men were to be tried by a jury and judges all of whom were determined to find them guilty, and the result has been that four of the "hounds" are now on board the Warren, sentenced to be transported to the United States prison in the District of Columbia, for ten years. It remains to be seen whether the keeper of any United States prison will receive a committal from a "Lynch Law" Court. The prisoners were defended by Judge Barry, the only lawyer of eminence here. His analization of society here—its political texture—its desertion and betrayal of its own tools—the unblushing effrontery of men prosecuting those whom they themselves had led to believe that there was no law but that of might, was as keen almost as the *Herald's* editorials.

Having said so much of our political relations, we must wind up by a few words on our social condition, and the prospects of the gold harvest. The stories I read, before leaving New York, of the abundance of the gold, are all correct. The gold placer is inexhaustible. It does not follow that every emigrant that seeks will find it—or finding, will live to return with it. The climate, at this time, on the seaboard, is cool, rather so at night, but in the mines at midday, can find a comparison only in a baker's oven. The mines at present being worked are those on the San Joaquin and Stanislaus rivers to the south, or those on the Sacramento, North Fork, Mormon Island, and Feather rivers to the north.

You get from here to Stockton or Sacramento, about two hundred miles on the way to either river, for $16 on deck, or $30 in the cabin of small sloops; freight, $8 per 100 lbs. You are then about sixty miles from the mines, and will have to walk it; freight is carried for $75 the 100 lbs., and not one cent less. Thousands that have come cumbered with luggage leave it on the wharves here. A man could make a fortune by buying almost any kind of dry goods here and sending them back to New York for sale. Arms, boots, clothing, are for a song; bad liquor is not to be given away; best prime beef, N. Y. brand, is sold for $10 per bbl.; gold washers of every kind, sieves, dishes, and machines of all shapes, are strewn on the docks in hundreds, being too heavy to carry, and useless even if they were at the mines; shovels and pickaxes are much cheaper here than in New York; lodging is out of the question, you must have your tent (not an India rubber one—as they are too hot to sleep in, and too heavy to carry,) wagons sold well. I brought one which cost me fifty dollars, and harness about twenty; I could get eight hundred dollars for it. Horses and mules are very dear; instead of twenty dollars each, as I heard at New York, I had to pay two hundred and ten dollars each for two mules. With these I intend to travel to the mines, in September or October. There is nothing doing at the mines now; fever prevails there to an alarming extent. No person should come here under the impression that he can dig a fortune in a year. From the most authentic accounts, I have every reason to believe that the average of all who actually work does not amount to ten dollars per day. Every pound of bread he eats will cost from one to two dollars. There is no such thing as vegetables to be had, and game is few and far between. Those who keep store near the mines are the persons that make the large fortunes, not the digger; and young men should not leave home to undertake such a life without considering the chances.

House carpenters can obtain ten to sixteen dollars per day freely; laborers can get one dollar per hour, when working, or eight dollars per day. Every one that can aid in building up or decorating houses, or can do hard work, can find plenty of it at seven or eight times the ordinary wages of New York. Money is plenty; I have seen more coined money here than I have ever seen before. When there are lay courts established, and the laws of the United States are extended here, I doubt not it will be a good country to live in and enjoy life; but until then, society there will be none, and the people will have to tumble along unaided by the craft of lawyers, the benevolence of philosophers, the cant of sectaries, or the preachings of the millions of reformers that belabor the brains of all the world beside. O'C.

(NYH, Sept. 17, 1849.)

From our Epistolary Agent in California

[From the New York Sunday Times]

Talk of the ——, and he appears. We had just commenced writing the short article in another column referring to the "Alta California's" complimentary notice of our letters from the mines, when the following missive, bearing the San Francisco postmark of the 2d of July, and superscribed "per the Oregon," came to hand.

The old boy does not write with his usual alacrity of spirit. On the contrary, he seems to have been "quite chop-fallen." Not a word does he say about the wife he commissioned us to get for him, although we wrote him two months ago that we had filled the order, and would forward "with care, this side up," to any place he might designate. What is still worse, he is silent on the subject of that "pile of gold" mentioned in his former advices. Can the old fellow have been gambling?

SAN FRANCISCO, July 1, 1849.

Eddyturs of the Sundy Times:

I'm goin' hum—I am—by the next boat after the Orygon. Californy was a fust rate kuntry when I cum here; but its gettin too fashunable for me. The last four or five 'rivals has brought out sich a tarnal lot of dandies an lawyers an genteel loafers from New York, that I'm 'shamed to say I was raised among sich musherooms.—Why, sum of em went to diggin in gluvs—an darn my skin if one spider-waisted feller, as lisped like a babby, didn't have a fan to fan hisself when he got tired heving sand out of the canions. When I see *that,* I gin in, and started for the coste. Californy would be ruined darned soon if this Miss Nancy kinder cattle was to settle an breed here. A purty poppylashun they'd raise for a new kuntry—spindle shanked boys, an gals a dozzen to the armfull. Hows'ever, the sun an the moistoor soon wilts em down, and they die afore they've dug gold enough to pay a feller for berryin em. The principal bizziness besides gold diggin is makin cities.—Three tents an a shanty constitoots a city.—There's eighteen of em now in market, an 'cordin to the Alty Californy, every one of em "presens more advantages than any other in the territory." Most of em has enny number of streets an squars. The streets is so intarnal wide you can't see acrost em with a telescope, an all the squars is remarkably open, bein bounded on the north by Orygon, on the south by Lower Californy, on the east by the Sarah Nevady, an on the west by the Pacific Oshun.

Kurnel Stevenson, formally of your city, is consarned in one of these "commercial emporiums"—that's the name they give em.—The place is called the "New York of the Pacific," and is sitiwated at the jining of the Sackrymenty and the Sam Joking. It is laid out on the beautiful map. The streets is a hundred feet wide, and the lots fifty feet front, and all "fit for buildin purposes"—specially castles in the air. Vessels can lay rite longside the warfs and discharge into the warehouses—that is, when the vessels cum, and the warfs is made, and the warehouses is konstructed. At present its all as bare as the back o' yer hand. Fremont and Vernon, and Boston, is very fine cities on the Sacrymento an Merican Fork. They haint got no tents thar yet, but hope to soon. The grand plaiza at Fremont is ockypied at present by a very fine colony of prairie wolves. Indeed, these sasay anymils don't seem to have no respeck for map cities, for you find em more or less in all the "emporiums." I think the owners of the cities ought to advertise the live stock as well as the ground. They *do* say thar'll be a bust-up here afore long—the speckylators lay it on so all-fired thick. To hear em talk to new cummers, you'd think all the 'fore-said cities was settled and doin a thunderin bizness.

Politicks is all the go here now. They're agitatin the slave question, and the state question, and the tarnal improvement question, and the bankin question, and whether they shall submit to Guvernur Riley or give him a ride on a rail. I rayther think the majority is in favor of the last menshund line of policy. Furriners is gettin more an more onpop'lar with the boys—for as they get stronger they get sassyer. Don't be surprised if you hear of a gineral rumpus, and if it comes thar'll be a great many furriners funerals afore it's over. Some o' the boys say the poppylashun must be equalized. You can guess what that means. I shall be out of the kuntry afore the row begins, as I intend to sail in the Pannyma.

The feemale konsinement from New York have not arriv; but public ankziety does not run verry high, as it is understood there is no young wimmen on board, an old wimmen is not much account in the multiplyin and replenishin line.— Hows'ever, they will be purfeckly entertained, and requested to go back an state, from their own expeeriunce, the indoocements to feemale emmygration held out by the Calafornyens.—Young wimmens belongin to the manyfacturin and producin classes might drive a big bizness here. Yours,

A DISBANDED VOLUNTEER.
(CPD, September 18, 1849.)

A Journey through California

A correspondent of the Newark Advertiser, writing from San Francisco, gives the details of an overland journey to that place across the peninsula of Lower California, which presents a new phase of the California emigration. He says—

I left Mazatlan March 29th in the bark Mary Frances. We knocked about a week, without getting outside of Cape St. Lucas, and finally put in at San Josef, (35 miles from the Cape) for water. We were much crowded—having 130 in the steerage of a bark of 250 tons—our health suffering and little prospect of getting through. We had not room to spread our blankets below, and the weather was becoming too cold to sleep on deck. Under these circumstances four of us—Lieut. Miller, Smith, Van Buren, and myself decided to land, and try the route through the peninsula of Lower California. We were told that it was a fine country and that the journey could be performed in 30 to 35 days. Well, we found the country a perfect desert; our path lay over barren plains of sand, or mountains of bare rocks 3,000 feet or more in height. There was scarcely a sign of vegetation, except cactus, with which we would have willingly dispensed. We frequently lost our way, but always blundered into the right track again. At one time, owing to an error in our chart, we were very near going off to the coast, where we should have been four days without water.

One of the party, who was trying to lasso a wild horse, lost his way, and stumbled upon a rancho; that accident saved us. An Irishman, who left San Josef the day before us, lost his way here, and has not since been heard of. We suffered much from thirst, as we found water only at long intervals, and generally brackish. We lived very temperately on jerked beef, which we generally ate raw, as it excited less thirst. After leaving San Ignacio, (which is about half way up the peninsula,) the wolves came one night and stole part of our beef, so we were reduced to a half pound per diem each for several days. We then reached an Indian settlement of a few huts, when we procured a little meal, on which we lived for some days, having nothing else with the exception of a young eagle, which I killed with a pistol. We made soup of him, and called it chicken. We saw no buzzards, or we should certainly have cooked them, in spite of Achille Murat's malediction.[14]

About this time our horses gave out, and we were compelled to foot it, (shod with raw hide sandals,) for several days. After sixty days of this fun we reached San Diego, when Lieut. Miller found some brother officers, who received us with great courtesy. Here we procured some salt pork and hard bread, which, to us, was most luxurious fare. Bought some stout shoes, and fresh arrina, and started for San Francisco with renewed courage. The country above San Diego is well wooded and watered, and in some parts most beautiful; it seemed a paradise after the desert we had crossed. Well, here we are at last, having been 85 days in the saddle, during which time we passed but three nights under a roof, sleeping sometimes on the top of a mountain, sometimes in a marsh, and always well soaked with dew. In spite of this I enjoy vigorous health, having gained 10½ lbs. since leaving the vessel.

(PPL, Sept. 19, 1849.)

---

14. *"Je n'ai point de bon vin qui nous grise et nous damne."* I have no good wine that makes us drunk and damns us. (Achille Murat, *America and the Americans.*) Napoleon Achille Murat (1801–1847), eldest son of Joachim Murat, King of Naples, came to America about 1821 and settled in Florida. He was profoundly and favorably affected by the manners, morals, and democratic form of government in his chosen country. The book cited, and two others, are in the same vein as de Tocqueville's *Democracy in America.* Murat wrote: "I came to America, poor, friendless, and an exile, and have here found a home and country which Europe refused me."

Oh! California!

Suffering and Starvation on Board a California Vessel

The Boston Times publishes a long letter from Julius L. Clarke, Esq., formerly editor of the Worcester Transcript, who set out for California by way of Panama, at which place he took passage in the British barque Circassian. This letter describes the sufferings of the passengers and crew for want of food. The passengers numbered 110, and were composed of *eighteen* different nations. The passage from Panama occupied three months, and then they had not yet reached San Francisco. In a violent hurricane the ship was blown off, and in the calms that succeeded, their sufferings began. They started from Panama on the 6th of May, and had not reached San Francisco the middle of August, having experienced alternate hurricanes and calms. The letter was written on board the vessel, and came by the revenue cutter Ewing, which spoke the Circassian.

"We found our safety at the mercy of a drunken crew, who, from the deck boy upward, (the first mate excepted,) were frequently too intoxicated for duty, so that the passengers were sometimes compelled to interfere for the suppression of mutinous and brutal strife, in which, in one instance, a sailor came near being stabbed to death by the second mate, whom he had previously knocked down. The calms which detained us on the coast of Mexico, the continued spoiling of provisions, and our diminishing supply of water, rendered it necessary to put every man on half rations, a step that would have prevented much suffering had it been taken at an earlier period. Here, also, as if to add to our perplexities, the ship sprung a leak, in consequence, as was supposed, of a plank having been gnawed by a rat in pursuit of fresh water. This was some five weeks ago, and from that day to this the ship has made five feet of water every twenty-four hours, and as the leak could not be found, the pumps were our only resort, the working of which, once in every two hours, has thus far kept her clear. A sour wind rendering it impracticable to steer for Mazatlan, it was determined to make San Diego, some six hundred miles higher up the coast, in order to refit for the rest of the voyage, but this plan was also doomed to be frustrated.

At the Mercy of the Wind

"On the 23d of June, after an almost endless succession of calms and head winds, and almost destitute of water and food, we made the coast of California, and even approached within fifteen miles of the shore. This was twenty-seven days ago, and we have not seen land since, nor shall we enjoy that pleasure for some little time to come. We were driven off the coast by a heavy land breeze, and falling in with the trade winds, which at this season blow from the north and northeast, we were compelled to steer in a directly opposite course from that which we wished to pursue. Thus, at the mercy of a wind against which we could make no progress, we have been forced nearly two thousand miles from our direct course, and subjected for four weeks to various dangers and privations. Cold, thirst, and starvation have been our constant companions. During the latter part of June and the whole of July, up to the present time, we have found it extremely difficult to keep comfortable with overcoats and fires, the trade winds, which blow strong in these latitudes, gathering their chilling blasts from the snow-topped peaks of the Rocky Mountain range.

"To sustain life it became necessary, from time to time, to curtail our rations, so as to make the little water and food on board extend to the longest time which might be required to make our port. For the three weeks preceding the 12th of this month, the average allowance per man was one quart of water, two ounces of jerked beef, very much resembling the trimmings that might be taken from the hides at one of your tanneries in New England, and actually so wormy that it would literally crawl before being cooked, and also four ounces of bread which had become musty, and, like the beef, infested with worms, some of them large and fat. This was our daily allowance, although sometimes one *doughnut* would be substituted for the *jerkens,* which we usually threw overboard, while the bread was retained, as it could more easily be divested of its *live stock.* Our salt pork and beef had long since been thrown overboard, though some of it was cooked and eaten in its spoiled condition. Our water was also bad, and it was necessary to impregnate it with lime to render it in any degree palatable to the taste or smell. A passenger could draw all his ration of water, or relinquish a part for the same quantity of coffee. With all the serious consequences attached to such a state of things, there was, after all, much of comic and amusing incident growing out of the petty squabbles for the possession of a morsel of food which a dog would spurn, and in which lawyers, doctors, merchants, farmers, mechanics, and others, not forgetting even clergymen, were promiscuous actors. I could laugh a whole month over the recollection of some of these scenes.

"The Fourth of July came—the glorious Fourth—with all its multitude of pleasurable and endearing associations of home and country. Some effort was made by the Americans on board to celebrate the day, but like everything else around us, it partook of gloom and starvation. Those

The rush for dinner on a ship from Panama to San Francisco.

who could muster "a drop" from their private stores made merry in *their* way; but fortunately these were few, as nearly every one who tipped the bottle was *laid away* long before night. Others nibbled their wormy bread, and having tasted their scanty ration of water, passed the day in moody silence, or venting their chagrin, disappointment, and dismal forebodings at the prospect before us. For one, I tried to celebrate in the most rational style, and having soaked my hard biscuit in sea water, (I could not afford fresh,) and having picked out the worms and toasted them, I spread on a layer of pork fat, which I had salted and kept for *butter*, (it being the only specimen of that article I had seen for four months,) and thus I feasted on what, I assure you, was a rare luxury to a famishing man. Having drank off a whole pint of water, and taken a look at things on board, I turned in, to dream of brighter and happier scenes in the Old Bay State. At sunset, (it was a most beautiful one, too,) I went on deck to witness the lowering of the star-spangled banner, which, with the captain's consent, had floated from the ship's peak during the day. The event was announced by the firing of our swivel, and as hearty a three times three as our ghostly lungs would permit. Thus passed a Fourth of July celebration on board a British ship in the Pacific.

The Cheese Battle

"It was whispered among the passengers, a few days ago, that there were sundry provisions in the hold, which had been shipped as freight from Panama for a mercantile firm in San Francisco. A great excitement ensued, as might be expected among so many hungry men. A committee was immediately sent below to bring up everything of an eatable character; and although it was a piratical act, so long as there was flour and water on board, even in limited quantity, pork enough was found for three or four meals, and eagerly hoisted on deck, where it was broken open,

and junks of it snatched from the brine and swallowed raw with as much greediness as the most savory viands. A cheese next came up the hatchway, and instantly forty or fifty men made a headlong dive for the prize, which had been sent out to feast the palates of some emigrating family to California. Never did starved rats scramble with such rapacity as did these men, who by dozens were tumbling about the deck on all fours, to seize a crumb of the cheese which, in the melee of broken heads and bloody shins, had been torn and scattered in a thousand pieces. It was not only a wolfish affair, but a rare scene for a painter. The pork put us again "in town," and for a day or two it could be purchased at two dollars a pound from those who chose to sell their rations. At this time water was also in brisk demand, and fifty cents a pint was freely offered, with plenty of buyers but few sellers.

Water Water Everywhere

"This afternoon we commenced on our last tank of water, and the pints that are dealt out to each of us are very small, I assure you, so that if a man cooks half a meal of anything, he has but little over a gill of water for drinking purposes for twenty-four hours. This with two ounces of bread per day, and a *doughnut* of an ounce weight every other day, forms the whole sum and substance of our rations. A small quantity of rice, flour, and beans still remain, to which every man has free access, but as water cannot be spared to cook them, and as sea water renders food bitter and increases thirst, few will accept them—preferring either to eat them as they are, or go without. Thus, we get up in the morning and *loaf*, (we are all loafers now) without breakfast and without dinner—and at 4 P. M. we get our miserable rations and hasten to bed and to sleep, in order to keep, if possible, the imagination that we have feasted. This state of things had led to many privations which, to those who have never learned by experience that a man can subsist on an incredibly small quantity of nourishment, might be magnified into a hundred terrific scenes of misery and suffering.

"Several disturbances have already occurred among the passengers in consequence of petty thefts of water, so that no one can be sure that his pint will not be stolen unless he swallows it at once, locks it up, or carries it bottled in his pocket. I drink a gill and a half of my ration made into strong coffee in the morning, reserving half a gill for our *four o'clock windfall*, which I bake twice a week. In this way I can live like a *nabob,* and find others copying my plan. With three pints of sweet corn and a pint of molasses which I brought from New England, and which I have been reserving for the last extremity, I calculate that with half a pint of water per day I can subsist from three to four weeks quite well. And as to the ultimate prospect of reaching land in safety, I have not the least fear from what has yet occurred, although our position is one of danger and exposure."

(PPL, Sept. 21, 1849.)

A Strange State of Things

Extract of a letter dated San Francisco, July, 1849.

I am satisfied that we have made a great mistake in bringing out merchandise, for already, with not one-tenth of the vessels in that are known to have sailed, merchandise of almost every kind is selling much below cost—indeed, in many cases whole invoices were sold at 24 to 30 per cent. of cost. There is little or no accommodation as yet for storage of any kind, and labor of every character is very high. It costs more to land goods, store, and sell them than the freight from New York. Indeed, in many cases that I have heard of, nothing remained after paying freight and charges here, so that the entire original cost has been sunk. * * * I began to look about for a place of business, and finally hired a brick store, 40 by 60 feet, on a lot 127 feet deep, in the heart of the town, for $30,000

per annum. You can judge of our prospects from this transaction.

Mr. Albert Macy, who was one of the passengers in the Aurora, from Nantucket, writes: Time is worth in San Francisco from one to two dollars an hour. I have taken thirty dollars for two days' work, and thirty dollars for two and a half days' work this week. I have still two *adobe* chimneys to build this week.

You may tell the fathers and mothers of the Nantucket boys in this country that they are as sober a set of men as you will find from the United States; and thus far they are doing well.

We have sold off nearly all our things, and the following are some of the prices that we got:

For our house, which cost at home $100, we got $1,300; for the tent, which cost $50, we got $250; our wagon cost $100 and sold for $312; a cook stove, which cost $15, sold for $125; for 50 lbs. of saleratus $150 (three dollars per pound); for 1,500 lbs. of bread, $165; for 100 lbs. of butter, $100; six bbls. of flour, $48; two bbls. of pork, $30. We have sold nearly all our small stores, our whole sales amounting to about $2,500. For one thousand poor sawed cedar shingles we got $30.

If any of my townsmen are coming to California, tell them to bring only two suits of clothes, and those thick ones. I wish I had only what I have got on. I can get fine white shirts for $5 per dozen. Mechanics should bring their tools.

Dry goods and clothing are very low, as most of the emigrants bring clothes of their own. It costs fifty cents to have a shirt washed, when you can buy as good a one as I ever wore, at auction, for 25 cents. You can purchase calico at from three to six cents per yard, while it costs $25 to make a dress. So you see that labor is much the highest commodity in the market, and, wherever it attaches, it makes an exorbitant price. The best of beef can be bought for twelve cents per pound, but a dinner of roast beef costs about $1.50. An ordinary cook gets $12 per day and found; and a man gets $500 per month for driving a team. A strange state of things, is it not?

Gambling In California

Extract from a letter dated San Francisco, July 30th: "This is one of the strangest places in christendom. I know many men who were models of piety, morality, and all that sort of thing, when they first arrived here, and who are now the most desperate gamblers and drunkards."

(WNI, Sept. 21, 1849.)

Lecture on California

Mr. Stephen H. Branch, according to public announcement, delivered a lecture on California and gold digging last evening in the Chinese Assembly Rooms, to an audience numbering some five hundred persons or more. He gave a graphic description of his passage across the Isthmus of Panama, and of his trip from Panama to the city of San Francisco, and his trip thence to the diggings, as well as an account of his hair-breadth escapes by flood and field, and from Indians and Oregonians, those of the latter being, in his opinion, more formidable in the mountains of California than a dozen Indians.

After arriving at San Francisco in the midst of a gale, which was exceedingly dangerous, he proceeded, in company with one hundred and twenty others, in a sloop of sixty tons, up the bay towards his destination. The vessel was not capable of affording anything like comfort to so large a number; and in order to make the most of the little room they had, they ranged themselves, standing up in single file, in a series of circles on the deck. In order to cook their victuals, each man entered the galley in his turn, and used the fire to roast or boil his meat. By the time the last one had finished, the first would commence cooking his breakfast. Thus the time was passed during the trip, the passengers being obliged to stand all the time.

At length the mines were reached, and

the first place where Mr. Branch attempted to dig gold was John Murphy's encampment, situated among five hundred wild Indians, one-third at least of whom were drunk all the time. He did not reach this place without incurring great danger and trouble from Indians and Oregonians, his horse miring in the mud, and so forth. He commenced digging, but after going beyond his depth into the earth, with the thermometer at 120, he had nothing but his labor for his pains. He then picked up his traps, and after being fired at by the wild Indians aforesaid, who discharged arrows at him, he proceeded by a short cut towards the Stanislaus river, camping out at night, and sleeping in the fork of a tree, with one eye open, to escape the wild animals whom he heard around him. In due time, and after taking some short cuts, which proved in the end to be long ones, he reached the diggings, and there he met society of a very different character to what he left in New York.

The Cost of Justice

While there, a Jew from New York was tried by a jury for having light weights. He was found guilty, and fined two hundred dollars, which was taken out in liquor; but after that quantity was drank, the judge, jury, and all hands wished a horn or two more; so they clubbed together, raised a hundred dollars by subscription, which they finished the spree with—so that Mr. Branch, after making his contribution, paid as much as he would if there had been no verdict against the Jew. There was another jury trial. It seems that a merchant from Mazatlan thought he would take a lot of goods to the mines on speculation. The freight of one load from San Francisco to the mines cost $1,500, and he was willing to give it for the cost of transportation. This the teamster would not consent to. Before the journey was ended, the Mazatlan merchant had to expend on all his goods, consisting principally of pickaxes and other mining implements, the trifling sum of fifteen thousand dollars. This merchant had a man in his employ who broke the contract entered into between them; so he called for justice, and demanded a jury trial, according to gold mine law. His wish was gratified; the man was convicted and sentenced to pay a fine of $250. But the man was poor, and had nothing wherewith to pay. So the court took the case into consideration, and arrived at the conclusion that the plaintiff in the case, the Mazatlan merchant himself, must pay. The merchant having heard of a number of shooting cases, agreed to pay that sum; but the case was not then ended, for the convicted defendant was, in addition, compelled to work out $50 in cooking for the judge and jury who tried the case.

Mr. Branch's luck in digging gold was not good. With his patent machine and two negroes, whom he engaged to work on shares, they made only forty dollars between them the first day; and when they went to work the next week, they were warned to desist by some men overhead, who said they were undermining the bank on which they had pitched their camp. Mr. Branch immediately packed up his traps and cleared. However, the machine was not the thing exactly, so he concluded to sell it by auction, for he worked in another place with it, and in five days gathered only fourteen dollars worth of gold, while his expenses amounted to $5 per day. He concluded, therefore, upon selling the machine, and auctioned it away for $30. This he thought too great a sacrifice, especially as the expense of taking it from San Francisco amounted to one hundred and seven dollars, independent of the original price in New York, &c. He got it back again, and afterwards sold it at private sale for $107; a day or two afterwards it was offered to him for $15, but he declined to purchase it.

Mr. Branch gave several other incidents and anecdotes of California; but the most entertaining of all was the camp scene. This was rich. The man on watch during the night awakes those sleeping in the camp. "Halloo, there, wake up; it's eight o'clock, do you hear? wake up—hell! if you don't wake up I'll eat the breakfast myself." and forthwith he eats the trash in a washing pan. Soon the sleeping campers are awake and about. "Well Stiles, what will you take for your hole?" "$16." "No, I can't give that—how much did you dig there yesterday?" "An ounce, but I 'spect to make more to-day." "Well, I'll give $10." "It's a bargain." "Enough said." "Well, Jim, I'm darned if I stand this; here I've digged three ounces yesterday and you nothing—I can't help that but I'm not going to work any longer with you, and if you don't have better luck you must leave the camp." "It's not my fault if you have bad luck—I'll bet that I've dug more gold than any other man in the camp, during the week." "No, you have not." "I say I have." "I say you have not." "I say it's a lie." "Take that, (firing a pistol at and killing him—goes to work as usual.) Now take that, my fine fellow, and keep a civil tongue in your head."

Mr. Branch then acted the gold digger. "That's a good looking rock. I'll try it. (Strikes with the pickaxe.) Well, what a darned fool I was to leave my situation in New York of $1,500 a year, to come to this place. Well, I wish to see Coney Island again. (Strikes again.) I hope to eat some oysters once more. Here I am (strikes again), 18,000 miles from home by the natural route, and 6,000 by the unnatural route across the Isthmus, and I ain't earned my board yet. (Strikes harder, and the pickaxe breaks.) There goes fifteen dollars' worth; well, can't be helped; but here's gold, and no mistake." Mr. Branch then collected a lot of the earth, and after washing it in California style, until all the earth was removed, leaving only black sand in the bottom of the wash-pan, takes a large telescope to discover gold, but finds none. "Well, there is gold here, I know." Tries another panful, and finds a pound weight, which he pockets; and after debating in his mind whether he shall go to the groggery or not at night, he finally goes to sleep on the ground, but awakes with a snake in his

bosom. Another lecture on the same subject will be delivered soon by Mr. Branch.
(NYH, September 25, 1849.)

Oh, California! California, Oh!

In ancient times, old stories tell us,
There liv'd a host of jolly fellows,
Who rang'd the world, arm'd cap-a-pie,
To seek adventures. Land and sea
Alike proclaimed their search for riches,
Whereby they tore their coats and breeches;
By thirst and hunger no ways scared,
Magic itself was scarcely feared.
When golden ingots met their eyes,
Such booty was to them a prize
Not to be sneezed at; fair or foul,
Each seized upon it, cheek by jowl.
Amongst our heroes Jason bold
From Colchis sailed, a fleece of gold
To rob Admetus of—for which
He nearly fell into the clutch
Of a huge dragon—but he gave
Him a sad toothache—made him rave;
For out he jerked his teeth—in earth
He sowed them—and therefrom gave birth
To a whole crop of warriors bold,
To range and fight and hunt for gold.
Another chap, in magic bold,
Turn'd all he touched, we're told, to gold;
Even his food stuck in his throat,
To ingots turn'd, it there took root;
But he a pair of Uss' ears
Got for his pains, as it appears.
Why speak of Aladdin's old lamp?
Or why through Sinbad's valley tramp?
With hundreds more of the same stamp?
Cortez, Pizarro, and a host,
"Outside Barbarians," on our coast
Ravaged the "Halls of Montezu"
And Atabalipa of Peru.
They missed, however, Californ,
The true Dorado. Yankee born
Now dig up gold by pounds. But lo!
Fever and famine work them woe.

Stretched out full length, their arms
   and digits,
Nay, e'en their toes were in the fidgets
To circumscribe a given space,
Which each, in fee, proclaimed his place
That no one else should venture on
Who feared a Bowie knife or bludgeon.
"Placets"—non-placet—many cry,
Like Midas, now for food they sigh.
"Free Soil" has made them errant slaves,
As fools, they went to dig their graves
On Sacramento's banks—so rich,
But which to many proves a ditch
Wherein they wind up all their schemes,
And bury troubles, toil, and dreams!

Pray take a telescopic view
Of this poor, wandering, restless crew.
To beg 'tis true they are ashamed,
For which they will by none be blamed;
But dig, dig, dig, they all agree,
Whigs, Natives, and Democracy.
In ragged coats and rent-worn breeches,
They dig away in search of riches
Pent up in Californian rocks,
Or Sacramento streams, the stocks
Of glittering gold their eyesight tickle,
Albeit, in such a wond'rous pickle,
That lack of garments, food, and health
All go for nothing, if the wealth
Of Californian sands will bring
Them solid eagles on the wing,
To waft them home and live in folly;
But oh! alas! 'tis melancholy,
To think how many will return
With "flea in ear"—at home, to mourn
Their reckless, headlong, go-ahead,
Adventurous career—whilst, dead,
Hundreds of carcasses are spread,
Around the glittering, tempting soil,
The "Golgotha" of all their toil!
"Tarde sed tandem"—slow and sure,
Will fortunes make, that will endure
When all this ill-begotten prey
Shall take it wings—and fly away.
SCALES.   (PPL, Sept. 26, 1849.)

Views and Prospects of California

FROM THE BOSTON DAILY JOURNAL

The following carefully-prepared article, from the pen of T. O. LARKIN, Esq., United States Navy Agent at Monterey, we commend to the attention of our readers, as the best exposition of the present condition and future prospects of California which has ever been published. Mr. Larkin has resided in California for eighteen years, during the greater part of which time he has been officially connected with the Government. His statements, therefore, may be regarded as the result of matured observation and a thorough knowledge of every thing bearing upon the interests of the country. The opinions which have been expressed in relation to California, in the various letters which have been recently published, are necessarily crude and hastily formed, as the writers in most cases have been in the country but a short period. There is a great want of reliable information from that interesting region, which the letter of Mr. Larkin fully supplies.

MONTEREY, CALIFORNIA, JUNE 28, 1849.

1st. The population of California in July, 1846, was about 15,000, exclusive of Indians; in July, 1849, it is about 35,000 to 40,000. The Americans are the lesser half of the people. From July to January, 1850, probably 40,000 Americans, by land and water, will reach this country; and after September the Europeans will commence arriving here. By January, 1850, we shall number 80,000 to 100,000 people, and in 1851 from 175,000 to 200,000.

2d. The character of the natives prior to July, 1846, was proverbial for inactivity, indolence, and an unwillingness to learn or improve. They had no wish or desire to indulge or enjoy themselves in any new or foreign customs, and they were happy, and kind and hospitable to all strangers. Foreign residents, happily situated among the natives, improving their advantages, gradually became men of property, and many of them have married into some of the principal families in California. The American emigrants arriving here in future will be composed of our most restless, active, and ambitious countrymen. No faint heart will leave his home to essay a journey of ten thousand miles, when at the journey's end only the most active and bold will be able to hold their way. Very many of our emigrants are Mexicans and South Americans—laborers (*peons*) of the most abject class—mild and inoffensive in their general manners, who are guided with ease. They are, however, slothful, ignorant, and from early life addicted to gambling. They will sleep under the canopy of a tree, and enjoy themselves to the full if they have a blanket or a sheet with which to enwrap themselves; and they are content if they have only paper cigars to last them a week, and a montebank to resort to at will. This class of men are brought by their employers from Chili, Peru, and Mexico. The employers are men of ease and urbanity, who will in time take their departure from this country, most of their laborers or peons remaining behind to live and die here.

3d. The climate of the sea coast of California is healthy. At San Francisco, in the afternoons, during six months of the year, there is so much wind as to make the town a disagreeable one to reside in. At this great and rapidly-settling seaport, four-fifths of the imports of California arrive, which are mostly sent up the Sacramento and San Joaquin rivers. One of the novel features of San Francisco now is that *gold* is actually being picked up in the streets! Natives of the Sandwich Islands and Chili are seen daily engaged in this occupation. Whether it is dropped from people's pockets and rough leather purses, or is produced by the recent constant employ of carts, with iron tires, which have superseded those tireless, broad-wheeled affairs, previously in use, I am unable unadvisedly to say.

The town of Santa Cruz

is warm and extremely healthy; and, for timber and grain, it possesses advantages over any other town in California. Benicia is a newly-formed town on the straits of Carquines, thirty miles from San Francisco, and about the same from the sea. This place is more subject to cold and wind than Monterey, but not so much so as San Francisco. It is the chief point of passing from one end of California to the other. Its ferry will at some future day be of immense value, and the income constitutes an education fund for the school of Benicia. Before the resources of the Sacramento and San Joaquin valleys were known, the town of San Francisco was considered to be one of the greatest importance, the more so as it was said no large vessel could go any higher up. Many merchant ships and men-of-war have gone to and returned in safety from Benicia. The location and advantages of the place now promise that it will soon be of the first importance. It may be the meeting place of ships from the sea and of steamers from the river, which matter time and scientific men will soon determine.

The town of Sonoma, twenty miles from Benicia, with the valleys of the Napa and Suisun nearly adjacent, offers inducements of the highest order to the most lazy of our roaming emigrant families. In the Sonoma, Napa, and Suisun valleys the land is good, the country healthy, and the temperature is never very cold in winter, snow being seen only on the highest mountains. This part of the country contains the best of grazing land, many places being covered with clover and with wild oats. Cattle and horses lose flesh but a trifle in the winter; hogs perhaps not at all. In California, prior to 1846, not one horse or hog out of one hundred ever eat grain, and not one bullock out of one hundred thousand has yet done so; yet the horses and cattle are always serviceable. The proper

time for killing cattle is from May to September; June and July are the best months. Wheat produces well. It is sowed from October to January, and cut from June to August. The yield is large; say thirty to sixty fold. Beans, corn, and wheat keep four years or more; fruits and vegetables less time than they do in the Atlantic States.

Twenty miles above Benicia

some enterprising American gentlemen are laying out three towns, called Montezuma, Suisun, and New York. The banks of the river, as far up as these points, are without a doubt healthy. As California becomes populated, these new towns will contain their fair proportion of inhabitants, and there will be heard the busy hum of Yankee enterprise. On the San Joaquin there is a town laid off under the name of Stockton, which has now some hundreds of traders and wagoners living in tents. Lumber being landed in San Francisco and Benicia from Oregon and foreign ports, and held at two hundred and fifty to three hundred dollars per one thousand feet, and the price being much enhanced when it reaches the highest points of boating, there must for a time be a drawback to building within the limits of the placer locations. Higher up the San Joaquin, proposals are out to build two small towns, in which people are purchasing house lots at low prices. At Capt. Sutter's Fort, and extending to his embarcadero, there is a town called Sacramento City, with a thriving and numerous population of little less than a thousand people already. Several brigs and barques of light draught have reached this town, and also Stockton. On Feather river there are projections of a township. The people on the upper Sacramento river, Bute [sic] creek, Feather, Yerba, Americanos, Cosumnes, and Moquelemes (the last two members of the San Joaquin) rivers, and their vicinity, must depend at present on Sacramento City for supplies; the remainder of the rivers, lower branches of the San Joaquin, on Stockton; the upper branches on Monterey; Sacramento City and Stockton, by steamboats, will receive their supplies from Benicia and the town of San Francisco.

Monterey

may be considered at the present time the most pleasant place for a *residence* in California. The growth and prosperity of the town is slow, and there is but little business doing [in] it. The new emigration have not taken the prospects of the place in hand. By land it is nearer the placer than San Francisco. In Monterey the same wearing apparel and bed clothes are worn throughout the year. The Americans and English only use chimneys within their homes for comfort; the natives have no desire for them.

The pueblo of San Jose,

between Monterey and Benicia, and fifty miles from San Francisco, is situated in one of the most pleasant and healthy valleys in California. It is well watered, and for twenty miles north and south there is a perfect carriage road, with barely a mould of earth to lift a wheel. Its advantages for gardens, fruits, and grains are of the highest order. It only awaits those who are soon to be its owners, and it will flourish in all its destined beauty and luxuriance. From Monterey to San Diego every twenty to thirty miles there are large broken down missions, each so pleasantly located that they will entice people to settle near them.

The port of San Luis Obispo is half way from Monterey to Santa Barbara. It is an unsafe port in winter, and has an extensive farming country around it, but is not very well watered.

Santa Barbara is a small town, pleasantly located, surrounded by mountains, but affords little inducements to the present settler.

San Pedro

is the port of the Pueblo of the Angels, twenty-seven miles distant. The Pueblo is one of the better cities of California, equal to the upper Pueblo, and far preferable to it for grapes and wines. It is perhaps equal for vintage to any part of the world. The present stirring times and people have not yet reached this valley; land has therefore risen but little in value here. The rich placers urge every new comer to the north; but time will soon send thousands to this Pueblo, to Santa Barbara, and to Monterey. The heat and unhealthy climate of the San Joaquin valley and of part of the Sacramento, with the cold there prevalent in winter, must check the future settlement of those valleys.

Country lands, including those for planting and grazing, are selling at from 50 cents to $3 per acre. Many a square mile (of 640 acres) in the Sonoma and Napa valleys have been sold at $500 to $2,000. They are steadily on the rise in value. The old padres had each an orchard, which are now destroyed, and I know of but few instances of individuals who possess them.

The placer of the Sacramento

embraces almost the whole of the branches of the river on the east side. The most remarkable now worked is the upper part of the river known as Reading rancho, and on Feather river, above Larkin rancho, and Yerba, Bear, and Dry creek. Feather and Yerba are the richest. There are three branches of the American river which join the Sacramento near Sutter's Fort which have produced much gold. In the vicinity of the American there are many rich placers; in the ravines and valleys on every branch of the San Joaquin river gold has been found. These rivers irrigate slightly a large country of some three hundred miles to four hundred miles in length and breadth. Almost every spot that has been dug into has produced the precious metal in a greater or less quantity, and all over 20 carats fine.

The only well known quicksilver mine is ten miles from the Pueblo of San Jose, on the rancho of the Berezera family and Grove Cook's. The land which is now worked was, in January, 1846, taken from the owners by the Mexican law of denouncement, viz: A person gives information to the nearest alcalde that on such a place there is a valuable mine, and the informer files a memorial and deposites a piece of the ore. He has then some thirty days to excavate and to dig at least thirty feet deep in the mine. By the expiration of ninety days he must have performed certain conditions, and by survey, and the personal attendance at the land of the alcalde, obtain judicial possession. If this is all done within a certain limited time, he then as owner holds the right to work the mine. Should the denouncer quit the work a certain number of months, he is liable to lose his right.

In the winter of 1845

and '46 two California laborers offered to show Don Andres Castanoras, of Mexico, a silver mine; and on his examining it he pronounced it at once cinnabar. He proceeded immediately to denounce the spot, laid his plan off in twenty-four parts or shares—gave away twelve, and retained twelve. He then returned to Mexico. There he rented the mine for sixteen years to Alexander Forbes, Esq., of Tepic, who has now purchased many of the shares, some at $1,000 each, and is now working the mine, but not extensively. Mr. Forbes was a wealthy man, of no family, and of 70 years of age. His cares, great wealth, and the responsibility of his quicksilver mine, gave him much trouble. On Mr. Cook's land there are other locations containing rich deposits of cinnabar, that will produce a heavy per cent. of quicksilver. A pinch of pounded quicksilver ore dropped on a red hot iron will produce a vapor; by covering it with a teacup, the inside of the cup will be coated with a smoky substance, similar to that produced by the burning of a lamp. By tubbing this carefully over the inside of the cup with the finger, several globules of quicksilver will be brought into existence. There is, without a doubt, silver and lead in California in some quantities. I

have seen a little of each. Coal is known to exist, but I am inclined to think it is not of much account in quantity or quality.

I am of the opinion that the production of gold in the California placer will this year exceed that of 1848. The individual gains will not be so large, nor will so much be obtained in proportion to the number of people employed. Americans who had been some time on the Sacramento had every influence over the wild Indians, and each man to this day has from ten to thirty Indians at work on the upper streams. They protect, feed, clothe, and attend to the wants of these Indians.

On the lower rivers

the whites and Indians are destroying each other. It is said that the emigrants from Oregon commenced this bad business, and the loss will be severe. Less gold will be produced, and, through the disturbance, the sale of much clothing, &c. to the Indians on the rivers will be prevented.

The Whites, who are now or may be industriously employed this year in digging and washing the golden sands, will obtain from one to three ounces of gold per day; next year less, from the large number of laborers, and from the ground being so much worked over. Some who arrive here will never go far from the first port they land at, and many will return to the settlements after only two or three weeks passed in digging. The majority of these, if they seek for it, can obtain lucrative employ all over California as merchants, mechanics, clerks, storekeepers, farmers, hotel and innkeepers, &c., in towns and on the public roads, keeping coaches and stages, stables and boarding houses, running launches and wagons, cutting firewood for housekeepers, ships, and steamboats, and not be liable to the summer sickness in the placer.

Timber is plenty,

and much of it is softer than the white pine of Maine. Tools are very cheap. Live cattle for meat and for working are not high. One-inch boards bring $150 per M feet at the pit. This must, even this year, offer inducements for many laborers. Merchandise is very rapidly falling in value. Prior to the exchange of flags (July 7, 1846) in Monterey the maritime duties had averaged $85,000 a year, paid into the Mexican customs of Monterey. In April, 1849, the amount received by the American collectors for one month was over one hundred thousand dollars. The foreign goods received into the territory were chiefly from Boston; a proportion from Mazatlan, Valparaiso, and Oahu. The prices were stationary year after year. In 1846 and 1847 goods fell in value. In June, 1848, commerce began to feel the effects of the discovery of the placer, while from June to October, 1848, lands fell in price, foreign merchandise sold at unheard-of prices, and continued high until May, 1849.

Country lots have now risen in value, and town lots advanced thousands per cent., and this day are yet advancing, while merchandise is now suffering a rapid decline in prices. Bricks, ready-made frame houses, and lumber yet command the highest prices. The shippers of merchandise in our Atlantic States since January, 1849, while they saw one-tenth of their vessels chartered or purchased for California, and twenty millions of dollars invested in those vessels and their cargoes, were convinced that this department was to receive from 100,000 to 200,000 emigrants this year. These estimates were the minimum and maximum. At the same time they became participators in the supplies for two or three millions of people. They were far better judges of the number of emigrants, and the supplies sufficient, than residents of California could be.

The excitement

has gone throughout Great Britain, and is now agitating other parts of Europe. What is the result of all this? Large fleets of merchant vessels are laid up in the bays and rivers of San Francisco for want of seamen, and there is an immense sacrifice of mercantile property. There will not this year be sufficient warehouses to store the goods on the way for this country; nor can owners afford to pay the storage. Many of the owners will be present with their goods, depending on a prompt sale to satisfy their own wants, or to pay their debts. This itself will force the sale of much property, and without this the prospect for 1850 will not warrant owners or consignees to keep on hand goods for sale. A quantity will go to Oahu, San Blas, Mazatlan, Callao, and Valparaiso; some may even return to the Atlantic States. I do not believe that the goods landed here in September up to January (ensuing) from Europe will, in every instance, bring much more than sufficient to pay duties and other charges, leaving out any reference to first cost.

In this extraordinary position of affairs, the state of the emigrants is of primary importance, especially of that portion composed of women and children. Many will arrive destitute, and death will do his work among them. Houses cannot be obtained for one-half of this vast increase of people, nor will all provide themselves with a tent or even bush shed. The cold will not incommode the new comers, except those who may go to the mountainous parts of the Sacramento and Joaquin. In January and February, however, the rain will fall. As a general thing the climate is advantageous to the coming thousands, and in the course of time, with the immense and peculiar prospects before us, a large proportion, after some individual cases of suffering, will settle themselves, and subsequently obtain a gradual improvement of their state and situation. The want of schools must be felt for some time to come, at least within the vicinity of the placer. Monterey, Pueblo de San Jose, San Francisco, and Benicia have each a good school, paying the preceptor $1,800 to $2,000 a year. These towns have also each a Protestant clergyman settled among them. The towns of Monterey, San Jose, Santa Barbara, and Pueblo de los Angelos have each Catholic churches, with Mexican padres, and are well attended. The whole territory of California has scarcely a public building, exclusive of the town of Monterey, which contains two that were built prior to 1846. This town has also a wharf, built in 1845, and some buildings and a fortification, erected under the command of Colonel Mason in 1847 and 1848, and a fine stone building for a school and courthouse, and State Convention, built under the Alcaldeship of Walter Colton, Esq.

The prospects of California

are flattering in the prospective, more so than that of any other new State in our rapidly expanding Union. The climate of most parts of it is mild and congenial, yet changeable. The Sacramento and San Joaquin are prolific of ague and fever of the worst forms, and rheumatic complaints on the coast are prevalent. The mornings are invariably the most pleasant on the sea coast, especially at Monterey and San Francisco—the nights throughout the country are cool. At Santa Barbara and the lower Pueblo there is experienced little or no fog. The town of San Diego, now without trade, is of little consequence; at that place the climate is the mildest and most salubrious in all Alta California.

The rivers throughout this territory are low most of the year, and can be passed. Rains in November increase until February—they then decrease until April. During the summer, rain may fall once in the course of five or six years, but not sufficient to saturate the ground. In the months of December and January rain is the most copious. From the drought in the summer months, vegetation becomes much parched. On some ranchos (farms) the grass fails for the cattle at the driest season. The farmers are always desirous that some rain should fall in April to moisten their land just previous to their ploughing, before planting beans, corn, and potatoes. A person not acquainted with the soil and climate of California would doubt its ca-

pacity to produce any grain without summer showers; yet wheat produces abundantly. Gardens in towns require wells, excepting at the two Pueblos and Sonoma, where there are good streams of water, the country adjacent to which is best adapted for grazing. The Government have here horses and mules, kept up and fed on barley and wild oats, cut in May and June; individuals will also do the same. Oats and clover grow spontaneously over the country, and within the reach of every man. Formerly horses and bullocks were worked but a few days and then turned out to graze as many weeks, when these animals sold for ten to fifteen dollars each and breeding mares from two to three dollars. This plan to a Californian presented its advantages. The American farmer will do more work and to more advantage with four or five horses and twenty or thirty cows and steers than the natives do this day with hundreds or thousands of stock.

Eggs are from $1 to $2 a dozen; hens $2 to $4 each; turkeys $4 to $8 a piece; butter $1 to $1.50 a pound; potatoes, by the pound, 6 to 8 cents; turnips and cabbages, etc. still higher—opening other advantages to farmers than raising cattle. But few or none have engaged in supplying towns with the fruits of gardens, orchards, and the rich products of the dairy. This will all be done at less prices, but at very remunerating ones, even when the golden sands of California have been turned over and over again—washed and re-washed, and its soil delved deep into for the precious metal until nearly valueless. For some years, however, the labors of the hard-working and frugal gold-digger will yield him fair compensation, if he can avoid the chills and fever of July, August, and September.

The whites have,

in several instances, destroyed Indians in the placer, who, in their turn, have retaliated. This warfare will continue until the wild man and owner of the placer is exterminated. This may cause the people to have more tame Indian servants, as they will seek the towns where many get constant employ. The real cause of the shedding of blood is the too common enmity of the white man towards the aboriginals of our country; while too many, caring only to get a good share of the riches of the placer, as free laborers, look tamely on the atrocities they may see perpetrated. Before 1850 the two very distinct races will be separated into parties in the placer by the Spanish and Indian languages, being the vernacular of each other, and they will very likely be brought into fierce and deadly conflict. Those of Spanish extraction far outnumber the Americans, though this will not be considered worth a thought by the latter. Numbers opposed to them in battle array or in commerce are not counted, and when brought into collision with Yankee ingenuity are subverted or overthrown. However, the Americans in this country will in a short period outnumber the foreigners; and from the present time Mexican and South American emigration hitherward must decrease, and by 1851 the emigrants from Europe will not outnumber our own countrymen.

In all this astonishing influx of people we have a practical illustration of the fact that the absence of good laws cannot stagnate commerce or crush the energies of the people. Each alcalde of the different jurisdictions has some form, mode, and practice of administering law. There are Mexican laws in print, in theory, but in practice little is known of them by the judges or justices—of course less by the people. Yet peace and good order is fairly sustained, and murder and robbery is not of hourly occurrence. Where there is no known code of law, lawyers can have but little business. By the time there is business for them the present attorneys who are in this country will, by having other means of making a fortune, be able to live like the mass of the people.

A passage around Cape Horn,
from an Atlantic to a Pacific port, occupies from four to six months. The shortest trip on record is that of the "Grey Eagle," in one hundred and seventeen days to San Francisco; the "Col. Fremont" came in one hundred and twenty-seven days; one hundred and fifty is a fair calculation. This voyage is as safe and pleasant as those performed by sea and land; it occupies two, in some cases three, months more time. It has not the variety of a sea and land voyage, but a person has less risk of reaching his port of destination. The expense is $150 to $300, the passenger having to provide himself with bedding only. A trip via Chagres and Panama costs $250 to $600, the two steamers charging $175 and $200 to $400. The time occupied ought not to be more than forty days; in 1850 it will probably be less. At present but few reach here via Panama under sixty to seventy days from New York or New Orleans. Those who arrive here, as thousands have, in sail vessels from Panama, have been sixty to one hundred days in coming this distance. The passage to Vera Cruz is easy; and, if the Mexicans have mules and horses to sell at Vera Cruz, or in the vicinity, a traveller mounted may reach San Blas in twenty to forty days. At first he will be somewhat worn, perhaps nearly broken down, but in a week his spirits will be on the ascendant, and he will be able to pursue his way tolerably pleasantly. The travelling expenses on the road from Vera Cruz to San Blas or Mazatlan, will be about $1.50 to $2.50 per diem for man and mule. A laughing, happy, and contented traveller can get along with the Mexicans in his own way, and at his own prices—*if* he but please the people they will please him. At present, and I think hereafter, the supply of vessels for passengers from San Blas and Mazatlan to California will correspond to the demand. The charge for passage, $75 to $200; the time occupied, twenty-five to forty-five days.

The overland route

from the frontier of Missouri to the Sacramento valley is now so well known that a very correct estimate may be made of the time required, and the means necessary, to perform it with ease and safety. A family, carrying with them only such things as are necessary for the road, may calculate on making it in four and a half months. About the 1st to the 10th of May is a suitable time for leaving the Missouri frontier, and this would bring them into California from the middle to the end of September. Light but strong wagons, with mules, especially in the present condition of the road, are the most reliable and convenient means of travelling. Grass is at its best during the season which will be occupied by the journey, and the mules may always be kept picketed near the place of encampment, and consequently less risk will be incurred of their being stolen, and no time lost in hunting them up in the morning. The road being now well known the travelling may be regulated, and the animals never forced into extraordinary journeys, but make their average day's travel uniformly, and regularly have grass and water. The best way to travel is to start at sunrise and halt again, remaining at rest during the middle hours of the day, completing the day's march in the afternoon. This gives the animals abundant time to rest and eat, and in this way they will go through in good order.

Although there are many advantages in California over some of our other territories, and a wide field of enterprise for a new beginner, I would earnestly advise all those who are well situated at their places of nativity or adoption to remain as they are. To a young man, not yet in business, with little or uncertain prospects in our Atlantic or Middle States, I would say, try California; more especially if he is bold, active, restless, and ambitious, and not inclined to *dissipation*. Sickness he will be liable to here as elsewhere, even without exposure in the placers. *If he knew one card or one wine from another where he was educated, raised, or brought up, in California he will soon know the whole pack, and become a perfect connoisseur of liquors.* This will alter for the better as society becomes established. For a farmer, mechanic, or merchant, with ordinary prospects in any other State, to break up for the purpose of coming out, with the view of bettering his condition in California is, I think, if not utopian, at least hazardous.

My several official letters up to 1849, which have been published throughout the United States, were written for the use of the different Departments in Washington, to which I was at the time attached, and not for publication. When dispatched from California to Washington I had no expectation of their being published, and no one in this country could then have had any idea that our "placers" so soon, or even in any length of time, were to affect our whole Union and a part of Europe. In June and July, 1848, the American residents in California, especially the land owners, were apprehensive that the placers would prove of injury to them; the value of town lots, it was supposed, were more depreciated thereby than any thing else, but the contrary effect on real estate in town and country is now experienced, and in fact every class of property, and in every line of business throughout the Territory. The busy hum of incessant activity, and the enterprise of an industrious, go-ahead, Yankee population, now reverberates throughout the northern part of Alta California, and will soon extend from latitude 49 to 32 on the Pacific, and embrace the whole length and breadth of the country—of Oregon and California.

(WNI, Sept. 26, 1849.)

Letter from San Francisco

SAN FRANCISCO, July 30th, 1849.

MY DEAR BROTHER: After nine months of suffering, privation, and labor, I find myself in this unbuilt city, weighing 17 lbs. more than when I left Philadelphia, and richer by $15,000 than when I bid farewell to the city of brotherly love. Our company suffered much on the journey from sickness, and the early loss of our mules and wagons. At one time we were disposed unanimously to retrace our steps, but after sleeping upon it, we resolved to go ahead. Other companies lost many of their numbers, but we only lost two. The preservation of our lives and health on the route and at the mines was owing to the provident care of our Captain, in laying in a supply of Brandreth's Pills before we started. We found them so effectual in their operation, that upon the first symptoms of sickness they were taken, and in all cases and on all occasions they proved the most invaluable medicine. We sold to other companies at the mines many boxes of Brandreth's Pills for an ounce of gold for a box of pills, and we could have sold any quantity if we had had them to spare.[1]

(PPL, Sept. 28, 1849.)

News from the Cleveland Boys— Their Progress over the Plains— Indians, Buffaloes, and Cholera

INDIAN TERRITORY.
August 14th, 1849.

DEAR SIR:—We are now encamped 320 miles west from Council Bluffs, and 200 miles from Fort Laramie, in company with a party of Mormons, numbering about seventy wagons and five hundred head of cattle. There has been considerable alteration in the company since our start from Cleveland. On our arrival at Oskaloosa, some got so disheartened and mortified at the slow progress we made in wagons, and being the majority, of course ruled, so that the wagons were disposed of, and carts got in

their places. By the time we got to the Bluffs another change came upon them, and that was disunion, by which method three of the party were thrown out, not having means enough to proceed, leaving us the same number that we had when we first started.

At present, each man is for himself, and the probability is it will remain so. We each laid in provisions at Kanesville for one year, so that if we stop at the "Valley," as it is called by the Mormons, we shall have enough and to spare in order to prosecute our journey in the spring. If we continue on this winter, we in all probability will strike South by San Diego to the Pacific, going through that section of the country which in the latest maps is marked unexplored, but which we find out now to be far otherwise, containing six or seven large towns, but fertile only on the banks of the streams.

In many respects our journey so far has been very fortuitous. We saw at the ferry across the Missouri some four or five Indians; since then we have seen none, although we encamped right amongst them one night previous to our joining the Mormons, but knew nothing of it until the return of a Mr. Rockwood, who crossed over Grand Island to Fort Kearney. Besides those, none are known to be along the course of the Nebraska, as far up as Laramie. From what I can learn, all the Indian tribes with the exception of the Sioux are following the fate of their predecessors, but with much more rapid strides. At Belleville, on this side of the Missouri, the cholera broke out amongst the Pawnees, Omahaws, and Ottos, and carried them off so fast that they did not pretend even to bury the dead. Those who survived left the

1. Benjamin Brandreth's "Universal Vegetable Pills" purported only to treat constipation. But Brandreth concocted the theory that constipation caused vitiation of the blood, and thus was the underlying cause of all disease. He claimed that his pills were curative *and* preventive—the perfect panacea.

main roads and water courses for fear of the epidemic as soon as possible. This is thought to be the reason, by persons who have traveled this route many times, for our not seeing any Indians.

"Winter Quarters," on the west side of the Missouri, opposite the Ferry, the place where the Mormons laid through the winter after they were not allowed to live in the State of Iowa, is one of the most beautiful situations for a city that I have ever seen: from here you get a most magnificent view of the Bluffs, and can see some ten miles of the windings of the Missouri, and thousands of acres of the richest bottom land in the world.

While crossing the Missouri, some of the frontier men, who were probably much in want of some funds, endeavored to get us to hire them to ferry us across the Elk Horn, the first stream we met after leaving the Missouri, and one of the branches of the Nebraska, stating there were about three hundred Indians in camp there; but we found no Indians there, although we had much trouble in crossing, occupying almost one day and a half, and having the advantage, too, of a very poor raft left by the Mormons. In swimming our horses, Blackwell came near being drowned. No other accident has happened except the accidental discharge of a gun by a young man from Utica, by which he shot himself thro' the hand and killed his horse.

The roads are not as good as we anticipated, but the feed is much better than it ever was known before, on account of the great abundance of rain which has fallen all this season, making the streams very bad to ford. All the streams are very wide and shallow, and a little more of a yellow tinge than you have in the canal at Cleveland. The Pawnee villages, between the Elk Horn and Loup Fork, the principal tributaries to the Nebraska, are entirely deserted, and the Pawnees now number only about 200 souls, almost starved, and not

daring to hunt for fear of Sioux, who drive as far as in their power all the Buffaloes away from their hunting grounds.

The Mormon encampments, when we first got sight of them, presented one of the most splendid views I ever witnessed. They contained three hundred and fifty wagons—such as we started with, only better—and about four thousand head of cattle. They yoke cows and oxen together. One of the companies had lost four men: two from cholera, one in crossing the upper ford of the Loup, and one was shot by the Indians. We found the remains, such as the wolves would leave, of some eighteen Indians, where we first struck the Nebraska, and yesterday the remains of one man supposed to have been a white man.

Until we came into the Buffalo country, graves appeared staring at us on almost every rise of ground; amongst others I found one of Lambert Kellogg, but could not find out what place he was from. The majority of deaths are from cholera, but also women and children from other diseases. Our party enjoy first rate health, and as regards my own it was never better. Yesterday a young woman was run over by a wagon while watching a large herd of buffaloes.

A soldier from Fort Laramie, on his way to Fort Kearney, is just in and starts right off. He states the Indians are numerous and not peaceable, even killing the traders.

Buffalo meat is so plenty that it is spoiling, and one-half that are killed are not brought into camp. I ate breakfast this morning from the hump of one I killed yesterday, weighing about 1,200 lbs. dressed. In fact at present we are hardly ever out of sight of them. But I must close, as most of the camp have left. More particulars from the Fort.

Yours, in great haste,
EDWARD T. KELLOGG.
(CPD, September 28, 1849.)

The Increase of Everything

Letter from a Cleveland Gold Hunter—Affairs on the Pacific— Description of Acapulco

ACAPULCO, MEXICO, June 18, 1849.

DEAR SIR:—After a protracted passage of thirty-five days we dropped anchor here on Friday afternoon, having to come in for wood and water. Our progress has been exceedingly slow from constant calm weather, some portion of the time the sea being still as a pond and glassy as a mirror. From the position of this harbor, it is found with difficulty—we were knocking around on the coast three days before the search was successful. The bay is completely land-locked and the entrance to it narrow.—No part of the town can be seen from outside, and no improvements whatever indicate the abode of man. The bay is one of the most beautiful sheets of water I ever saw. It is from two to three miles long and from a half to three quarters of a mile wide and surrounded by rugged granite mountains whose peaks reach into the clouds. Every where huge masses of rock peep out from amidst the deep green vegetation, giving the distant landscape a wild and desolate aspect. The thunders roll from peak to peak with a grandeur I never heard equalled, and the flashes of lightning are dazzling in their brilliancy. One can look upon this war of the elements without fear, as the thunderbolts spend their strength in the distant peaks.

The town is built on the sloping sandy shores of the bay, which are about half a mile in width, and containing a population of from 2,000 to 3,000. The houses are composed of sun-dried bricks, plastered on the outside, one story high, with porticoes running all round and roofed with tiles. There are but two churches, both small and containing little wealth—these are constantly open. Ruins are not plenty—two only of any extent are to be seen, and they are the remains of churches destroyed long ago by an earthquake. The fort, originally a splendid work, has fallen a good deal to decay, and the few mounted guns look

Acapulco.

rusty and time worn; it is occupied by soldiers who present anything rather than a martial aspect. Altogether the town is exceedingly clean and neat, and hidden almost, as it is, in groves of cocoanut, it is the most picturesque place I ever saw.

The men appear lazy and indolent, and the women, *as ever,* vivacious and talkative. Our people are well treated and much respected.—They call us Americans, say they love us all, *but they hate the Yankees*—they think Americans and Yankees a different people, and when spoken to of the latter they draw their hands across their throats to signify they think them cutthroats.—All nearly are full-blooded natives, very few of Spanish descent or foreigners living here. As along the coast generally the English monopolize the trade—goods are high and not of good quality: coarse cotton shirting retails at twenty-five cents per yard. Some enterprising Yankee, I think, would do well to locate here.

The marketing is done in the plaza and attended to entirely by women and children, who sit upon the ground and spread out their wares at their feet. The supply of fruit and vegetables is fair, and beef, pork, chicken, eggs, &c., is abundant. I never saw a finer breed of hogs, a great many very fat and of a large size. Altho' they expect to get a much larger price for every thing from an American, yet we can all live well for seventy-five cents per day. No money less than six and a quarter cents circulates; the only currency in use less than that amount is small cakes of soap which are current at three cents. I imagine our nice young dry goods clerks would little fancy Acapulco small change.

We sail from here on Wednesday, and hope to reach San Francisco in from twenty to thirty days. The news from the land of gold makes us anxious to reach our destination. It is said provisions and goods of all kinds are plenty and cheap and gold very plenty, but there is a rumored difficulty with foreigners. There are about fifty Americans here who came overland waiting for passage to California; many of them, it is said, have no money left; what they will do it is hard to tell. My next letter will probably be dated at the "Diggings." Till then, adios! Yours, DEACON.
(CPD, October 3, 1849.)

A Breakfast in California

Mr. Freaner writes the following to the *Picayune.*

I was very much amused in a restaurant a few days since, at a stout, able-bodied fellow, who had just arrived from "the States," across the mountains. He was dressed in buckskin breeches, cloth pea-jacket, worn out fashionable vest, buttoned up to the chin, a slouched hat, and a red shirt, none the better for two months' wear. He walked into the room with an air of confidence, seated himself at one of the little tables in a style and manner that showed he was not an entire stranger to the good things of the world, which are sometimes found at a restaurant. Thus seated, he slapped his hand on the table and cried out to the waiter, "Bring me something to eat."

"Yes sah, yes sah," cried a little Frenchman, "vat you vill have for eat?"

"Eggs, got any eggs, mutton chop, beef steak? beef is good in this country; veal cutlets, eh?"

"Yes sah, yes sah, got him all. You vill have you eggs boil, fry, or de omelette?"

"Half a dozen boiled with all the fixings, and a bottle of wine," replied our friend in a stentorian voice that attracted the attention of all the persons present.

Away went the little Frenchman with "yes sah," thinking no doubt he had got a first-rate customer just from the mines, with his pockets filled with dust. In due time came a breakfast that would have served three men at least under ordinary circumstances. Ample justice was done to it, fully confirming our first opinion that the new visitor had wanted a breakfast more than once on his route. After he had finished he straightened himself up as if to make all possible room for crowding, and demanded what the bill was.

The Frenchman was in apparent ecstasies, looking over the table and repeating eggs, beef steak, mutton chop, veal cutlet—ah, yes, de vine, then summed as a sort of guess work, "thirteen dollars, sah!"

The stranger seemed quite astonished at this last announcement, and inquired, "What do you say, thirteen dollars?"

"Yes, *my friend*," said the Frenchman, "thirteen dollars."

"You don't call me your friend," replied the other, "do you?"

"Oh, yes sah, I call all de people my friend who eat de good breakfast and pay for him."

"But you're joking about charging thirteen dollars."

At this remark the man of the restaurant became somewhat indignant, looking all the characteristics of a man of his position, being proprietor of the principal restaurant, and said: "Yes, sah, $13. You no eat the egg fetch from Oregon, de beef from cross de bay, de good mutton Baron Steinberger butcher for my house, de veal cutlet, de best wine I have; G—d d—n! suppose something—you no eat de best breakfast—ah! de very best!"

At this announcement the stranger raised himself up quite coolly, and said, "Well, I have eaten a good breakfast, and that is a fact."—Running his hand into his buckskins, he pulled out $4.75, looking the Frenchman steadily in the face for a moment or two, nothing escaping the lips of either. He then leisurely pulled off his pea-jacket and laid it on the table—Frenchman still looking on without talking. The stranger then off with his seedy vest, and laid it across the coat. No reply being made to this, off came the red shirt, and followed the coat and vest, leaving him with a dirty, half-worn flannel one. Things now became exceedingly interesting.—The restaurant man, evidently a little frightened, looked first at one and then at another, as much as to say, "Is he going to shoot?" The only response to his looks from the lookers-on appeared to be, "Don't care much if he does." However, fortunately for the Frenchman, he broke the silence by saying, "Look here, stranger, I'll be darned if you mustn't trust me for the balance until I come down from the mines when I'll pay you."

And so saying, he stalked out of the room with the same confidential "fight or drink" air that he came in with. After our laugh, we followed him to inform him that if he would eat a dinner he should not be troubled about the pay; but the last we saw of him he was striding towards the bay, where the river boats lay at anchor. It is currently reported, since, that when a man from over the mountains stops at the restaurant, the Frenchman has not got any eggs.   (CPD, October 3, 1849.)

Sufferings of the Emigrants

Our Golden Correspondence

SAN FRANCISCO, August 8, 1849.

I arrived here last week, after a long and severe journey. A party of us, sixty in number, left Vera Cruz on the 24th of February; but that number did not continue together but for a week, as we found out that such a large party could not get accommodations very well on the road. Fif-teen and myself withdrew from the division, and we styled ourselves the "Independent Enterprise Division." We travelled through without being molested in any manner whatever.

Thirst

When we arrived at Mazatlan we took passage in the schooner Dolphin, Captain Winslow, for which we paid sixty-five dol-

Mazatlan.

lars a head. We sailed on the 23d of April; and when we were three days out we discovered that we were running up the Gulf of California, and soon after we were running down. We then put out to sea; and we run for ten days, when some of the passengers said that the water was getting short. We then appointed three persons to examine the water and make a report, which they did. They said there was twenty days' water, at one quart per day for each man, which we thought we could get along with. We then continued on our way for fifteen days, when we discovered that the provisions also were near out. We had a meeting called, the object being to mark out a course to pursue. Several proposals were made; and one to come down to a pint of water per day was adopted, and another, for the captain to make for the main land, was carried. We made the main land in three days, but could not make a

landing, as the breakers ran so high. We continued up the coast for four days longer. We then called a meeting in the cabin, and it was resolved that all the passengers who were able should go on shore, and walk up to San Diego, and leave the water for those who stopped on board to work the vessel to San Diego, where the captain was to wait until their arrival. A total of 48 gentlemen landed. Twenty-one stopped on board—making 69 in all.

A Dreadful Desert

In the afternoon of the 29th of May, in latitude 23° 6', we made a landing; and at six o'clock we were on the beach.[1] We moved over the sandhills that evening for about six miles. At 9 o'clock we halted, and each man unstrapped his blanket and lay down for repose, without fire, as travellers generally do. The next morning we were aroused by the howling of wolves. That morning we appointed Mr. Klein leader of

---

1.   This is about twenty miles north of Cabo San Lucas, the southern tip of Baja California.

the party, as he had some experience in the Rocky Mountains. We started pretty early, so that we might get out of the sandhills before the burning sun arose. We all started off in good spirits, hoping that we might soon strike a settlement. Some had a little rice, some a little hard bread, and others nothing at all to eat. At 10 o'clock we struck the bed of a river, and dug in some spots for water; but we could not find any. We continued up the ravine; and at noon we encamped, and one of the party went out to cut a cacti. In a short time he came running back crying out "water." We soon reached the spot, and by digging about three feet deep we found plenty of water. We then followed up the ravine, and we found more water, but it was a little brackish; and the further we went up it continued to get better. We continued on the same course for three days; we found a road. It appeared more like a cow-path than a public highway. Owing to this circumstance we felt somewhat pleased; and we had great hopes of soon coming to the settlements. That day and the day before, we had thrown away almost every thing we had, save our guns, and we should have cast them aside, too, had it not been for the fact that we did not know what kind of a country we were in, and whether the Indians were hostile or friendly.

We travelled on, finding some horse marks—we had some hopes of finding something to eat before long, for we were suffering severely for want of something for food. My supper was a rattlesnake, and there not being many of them, some of my companions ate some toads—also, on the evening of the first of June we met with a horse, the one that we tracked so far. He was not long in our possession until he fell a victim to our appetites. We ate heartily of him—I then thought of the comforts of a home which I had left to come to the land of promise. We continued our journey on the next day, and on the 4th of June, at nine o'clock, we were some miles ahead of the main body, for we were determined to keep on all night as it was cool for travelling, and, in short, we heard the toll of a bell. We rushed on with high hearts, hoping to find habitations of some kind. We soon came up, and we found that it was the deserted village of San Fernando. We found some travellers, (Mexicans,) who gave us some farina, which some parched and some boiled. In the morning we got an Indian to give us a little oat meal. He gave us all he had, and that only came to half a pint to each man, and then we had to walk forty miles to the town of Rosario [Rosarito] before we could get anything to eat. We reached there on the 6th, where we found sufficient food, which consisted of corn cakes, beef, and beans, and plenty of milk in the morning. The people treated us very kindly indeed, but any people that ever saw so poor, miserable a set of human beings as we were, could not help but pity—to see some have shoes and others none, some have blankets and some none, and others a gun and others a pistol, and what was worst of all, we had a wearied and pale countenance for American people, and our feet were all sore from the effects of the stones of the road, for the previous week had worn out our shoes and left our feet exposed to the ground.

After we left Rosario, about five miles, the road run along the beach of that great ocean on which we had spent thirty-nine days, and the greater part of that time in misery. We continued along up the coast, and that evening we espied two sails ahead, which we intended to reach that night; but night coming on, we encamped on the beach, and the next morning continued our journey. On reaching them we found one to be the schooner Dolphin and the other the brig Paradiso from San Blas, who had put in for water. Some of our companions went on board of the Dolphin. We again continued our journey and arrived at San Diego the 24th of June, where I took passage in the brig Paradiso, which had come in for provisions, and arrived here after a passage of twenty-one days from San Diego. I saw three of our companions who had sailed from San Diego in the schooner Dolphin, but had abandoned her about fifty miles below Monterey, and walked up here. They told me that they had to keep pumping her continually. She has not arrived here yet, and I fear she never will.

I leave for the diggings to-morrow—I shall write to you from there.

ONE OF THE MANHATTAN.
    (NYH, Oct. 15, 1849.)

From San Francisco

We extract the annexed paragraphs from a letter of Mr. Freaner, dated at San Francisco on the 31st of August:

"We have received news in this place that the emigrants crossing the Plains are suffering very much. On its being reported to Gen. Persifor F. Smith, from a reliable source, he ordered an expedition, with $100,000 in transportation and provisions, to set out immediately to their relief. This will enable many to reach their destination in this prosperous land who would have otherwise perished on the road.

"The news from the mines is of the most varied character. Hundreds of persons have come to this country who are not fit for the work, either by habits or by physical attributes; of course they give the most gloomy accounts and proclaim the scarcity of the precious metal; whilst others return well rewarded for their labors, happy and contented. One thing is certain, the gold is abundant, nay, inexhaustible, but it takes labor to procure it, whether a man operates in the mines, at the workbench, or in the counting-house. This is no country for idlers, and it is the first time, in the course of my observation, that labor, in all practical details, has had the advantage of capital. Machinery, with the use of quicksilver, in the mines continues to produce most extraordinary results, producing not less than four to five ounces per day to the hand.

"I understand that about two hundred

passengers are returning by the steamer which is to sail to-morrow—some of them loaded with treasure, while others are sick, disappointed, and disheartened.

"No pen can describe properly the progress of improvement in this country. The first we hear in the morning and the last we hear at night is the noise of the hammer and saw. It is utterly impossible for any person to keep pace with the onward march of general melioration in all things. Walk the town of San Francisco to-day and make a memorandum of all the new houses, and some one will follow right after and report the erection of a new building. I came hither about three months ago, and since that time the town has more than quadrupled in size. Commerce and trade of every kind keep pace with the increase of the buildings. The streets are filled with merchandise, while the beach is fairly covered with goods, arriving and shipping for the coast and rivers. Real estate is cash in hand and sixty days, but still it has continued steadily to advance. Within the last two months it has risen more than 100 per cent. There is nothing we feel the want of so much as a mint. Large amounts of gold dust are daily arriving from the mines, but it is with the greatest difficulty coin enough can be procured to pay duties, and this scarcity reduces the value of dust to $15 per ounce. The harbor presents a perfect forest of masts, affording a most beautiful and lively scene. Some of the finest ships in the world float on our waters, rivalling each other in beauty and speed."

The editor of the Boston Journal

has seen and conversed with a gentleman, formerly a resident of that city, who, leaving San Francisco on the steamer *Panama*, and coming from Chagres in the *Empire City*, reached Boston in the short passage of thirty-nine days. From the information which he furnishes the Journal we copy the following items:

Two gentlemen, who were among the

first who went out after the announcement of the gold discovery, were passengers aboard the Panama, on their return home. They had been in California but about four months, and had obtained about $19,000 each.

As to slavery, our informant says that it *cannot exist there.* Upon this point he thinks there cannot be the least doubt. The population individually and collectively are opposed to the system.

The feeling of hostility existing among the American miners in California against the foreigners is chiefly directed against the Spaniards, who have flocked there in large numbers from various parts of Mexico and the western shores of South America. This feeling has been in a good degree engendered by the action of these Spaniards, who have gone into the mines with a large number of *peons,* men whom they hold by virtue of some obligation, contracted before arriving there, and who labor under their direction and for their profit, receiving themselves but very trifling remuneration for their toil. It has often been the case that when a small party of Americans would strike upon a rich vein, before they could gather the golden harvest which awaited them, large numbers of these Spanish or Mexican laborers would crowd upon them and bear away a portion of the gold which the Americans considered as their exclusive property. Thinking this not hardly fair treatment, the Americans became exasperated, and have resolved that all foreigners must leave the mines, and this point they are determined to enforce at all hazards. A large number of foreigners had already left the diggings.

A letter in the Boston Traveller,

dated at San Francisco on the 30th of August, confirms the sad and alarming accounts of the sufferings of some of those who are on their way overland to California. The letter says:

"News came on Tuesday evening last that unless relief was immediately extended, the suffering of the women and children must be terrible indeed. Some of the party just in say that they were obliged to eat the flesh of their mules to keep them from starvation, and that those long in the rear must perish, in sight of the bones of those poor creatures who perished some time since, the accounts of which we read in the papers last winter, if I mistake not. The horses and mules are killed and eaten; but the chief amount of suffering will be for want of water, for as soon as the way-worn traveller enters the desert or plain, he has before him sixty long and tedious miles to travel, with only one spring, and that a hot sulphur one, to supply himself and the weary jaded beast on which he rides. It was stated that five hundred teams were on their way across this desert."

(WNI, October 16, 1849.)

California Items

VALUE OF PROPERTY
IN SAN FRANCISCO

The Parker House, a building 40 feet front by about 60 deep, rents for $110,000 yearly. At least $60,000 of this is paid by gamblers, who hold nearly all the second story. Adjoining it on the right is a canvas tent, 15 by 25 feet, called "El Dorado," and occupied by gamblers, which brings $40,000. On the opposite corner, a building called the "Miners' Bank," used by Wright & Co., brokers, brings $75,000. It is about half the size of our fire-engine houses at home. On the left of the Parker House, a small two-story frame building, which is just finished, has been taken at $80,000. The second story contains eight gaming tables, each of which pays $200 a night.

A friend of mine, who wished to find a place for a law office, was shown a cellar in the earth, about 12 feet square and 6 deep, which he could have at $250 a month. The owner came here about three months ago, without enough money to pay his passage; he is now worth $20,000. One of the common soldiers at the battle of San Pasquale is now among the millionaires of the place, with an income of $50,000 monthly. A noted firm has $110,000 loaned out at ten per cent. a month! A citizen of San Francisco died insolvent last fall, to the amount of $41,000. His administrators were delayed in settling his affairs, and his real estate advanced so rapidly in value meantime, that after his debts were paid his heirs have a yearly income of $40,000.

INCREASE OF THE TOWN

In April, there were only about 30 or 40 persons in San Francisco, and not more than 20 persons could be seen in the streets at any one time—now there are some 500 houses or tents, and a floating population of 6,000. It is calculated that the town is increased daily by from 15 to 30 houses.

MODE OF LIFE AMONG THE DIGGINS

The labor to be performed is no harder than the digging of canals or grading of railroads, but the hard-working 'Pat' that performs these labors at home has abundance of healthy food, a good bed, and a comfortable house to hide his head in. Here, however, the possession of the least of these would be considered most unpardonable effeminacy. Your bed is a blanket on the sand; your breakfast, pork and pancakes made of flour and fried in the pork; your dinner is of pancakes and pork, and your supper of both together, washed down perchance by a little tea or coffee; your house is the broad canopy of heaven. Of the two articles pork and flour, the prices are respectively $1.40 per lb., so that such living, when you do your own cooking, costs about $3 per day. Of course under such a mode of life the scurvy is by no means unfrequent, nor are the continual variations of the thermometer from 55 to 115 deg., nor the miasma arising from the beds of streams now 30 or 40 feet below high water mark, at all unfavorable to the spread of that meanest of all diseases, fever and ague. Dysentery is likewise alarmingly prevalent throughout the whole country and has caused the deaths of many promising young men.

GAMBLING AT SAN FRANCISCO

The number of gambling establishments, or rather gambling *tables,* in San Francisco cannot fail to surprise any visitant, however familiar he may have previously been in such establishments, more quietly conducted, in the United States. Almost every hotel, refectory, and drinking establishment, of which there are at least a hundred within the present limits of the city of San Francisco, contains from two to half a dozen, and some of them even a greater number than this, of these tables, comprising every game in the gambler's catalogue. All these are thrown entirely open to the whole public, and are nightly thronged by the promiscuous population here assembled—of every conceivable clime, sex, and color. One gambler, who *commenced business* on a large scale, has already been fleeced during the week he has been there, by those betting against his *"bank,"* to the tune of some $6,000, which was promptly paid. One of these betters, a passenger in the Panama also, has during the same time won $10,000. This species of gambling is scarcely less precarious now than the speculations in building lots, based, as these speculations are known to be, chiefly on credit. I am assured by one whose position gives him great facilities for obtaining correct information that there is not less than $7,000,000 of paper, issued upon real estate transactions, now afloat in San Francisco and vicinity.

(PPL, Oct. 17, 1849.)

Daguerreotype View of San Francisco

A correspondent, writing from San Francisco, calls this modern Dorado a homeless, houseless city—a straggling, ricketty town of pine board and ragged sail-cloth. Of the interior cities, which exist most flourishingly on paper plans, he says a great deal of money and a great deal of fever and ague are to be got by going there. (PPL, Oct. 19, 1849.)

View of Sacramento City—Its Rapid Growth—The toil and Fatigue of Gold Digging— Wealth and Sickness— Sufferings of the Emigrants

SACRAMENTO CITY, Aug. 20, 1849.

Our company have located in this place, put up the store, and are now opening and selling goods. This place is about 120 miles above San Francisco, and lies upon the left bank of the river of that name. It was, a year since, a perfect wilderness; it now contains about 2,000 inhabitants, all males. It is a very flourishing, lively place; houses are in plenty, some of rough wood, and others of canvass, mostly of the latter class. The dust is about as thick and plenty as mud used to be in Detroit. Goods are selling much cheaper than formerly. I have had some difficulty in selling butter at over one dollar per pound. Pork is selling at $40 a barrel here, and $1 per pound.

We are here in about the middle of the mining country—the diggins are scattered all about us at a distance of forty or fifty miles, and from that to a hundred. The gold is as plenty as ever, and new spots are found continually. The large lumps, which used to excite so much astonishment, are very rarely if ever found, but an ounce of gold per day is a common average; every one can make that, at least, but the labor of obtaining it is so very severe, that with all its glittering prospects, they often get tired of the toil, privation, and disease incident to obtaining it. There are many already here and gone away with gold indeed, but with a loss of health, and a ghastly countenance, which more than counterbalances for the gold they have gained.

Another year, I think, will put an end to mining in the present style—too many lives are lost, and too much health sacrificed at present. I have not as yet been to the mining regions proper, though I have washed out a little gold. When the store is properly organized, and things going on straight, I intend to go up to the farthest point and make an effort with some new-fashioned gold washers, highly recommended to me. The present style is to use an ordinary tin pan, worth here $6, fill it with the soil, and stand in the water and wash off the earth; the feet and legs being in cold water, and the head exposed to a vertical sun, soon produces disease, as you may suppose.

General Riley passed through Benesia [Benicia] a few days since, while I was there on board the ship, and spent the day and night with me. The general looks much thinner than when I saw him last, and in much poorer health. He is heartily tired of California, and so is almost every one else, and I am sure I would be glad enough to get out of it, although there is every prospect of my making money; for thus far we have succeeded as well as we hoped, and we expect to do much better hereafter.

There are a great many sick here during this excessive warm weather. Thus far I have enjoyed most excellent health, although I have been hard at work at all times, day and night, under a broiling sun, and under dews as heavy as rain. Of course you know that this is the dry season, and I have never seen in any country the land so parched up as it is here. The earth, in spite of the heavy dews, is seamed with large cracks, and except upon the low ground, immediately upon the river, the scanty herbage is completely burned up. At San Francisco and Benesia they have continual high winds and cold weather. Upon this river, enclosed as it is with high hills and thick trees, not a breath of air is to be had, but the sun shines as hot as at Vera Cruz.

Hundreds of emigrants are arriving by every possible mode of conveyance across the Isthmus, across Mexico, around Cape Horn, and across the mountains from Oregon and the Missouri. Those who have

On the desert.

come across the mountains have suffered terribly from disease, death, hunger, and fatigue. Those who do get through after all their toils and troubles have been obliged to throw away all their goods, and have arrived here, their first landing place, destitute of everything. Gen. Smith has just ordered (this evening) our company to supply trains, provisions, &c., to suffering emigrants. Col. Marsh, our President, has just set off on the charitable errand. It was a case that called loudly for the aid of Government, and General Smith has added to his reputation by attending to it. I suppose I shall be obliged to go upon the road for the same purpose.

Wages are high here; even to my teamsters I pay $300 per month. I bought a schooner the other day, and pay her captain $800 per month, and want a clerk for her. (CPD, October 19, 1849.)

Letter from Capt. Thomas S. Hart

SUTTER'S FORT, August 11th, 1849.

DEAR SIR:—I write to inform you that I am still in the land of the living. We arrived here yesterday—it being the 108th day since we left Independence. No person can imagine the hardships we had to un-

dergo. I would not undergo the same hardships again for all the gold in California.

From the time that we struck the Rocky mountains until we reached this place, which is a distance of about 1,500 miles (the whole of which distance I walked, which was a pretty hard walk I assure you,) we were hardly ever out of sight of snow. In crossing the Sierra Nevada, on the first day of August, we traveled over and passed through banks of snow from 50 to 60 feet deep. But the greatest place of suffering is along the St. Mary's or Humboldt river; there is at the present time between 200 and 300 miles of what may be called desert—as there is no vegetation at all. The water which we found for 150 miles along the river was so impregnated with alkali and other poisonous substances, that it was dangerous to use. In some places, it would kill the horses or cattle in a short time after drinking it. From the link of St. Mary's river across to Pilot river, a distance of about 50 miles, is the great place of suffering.[2] —The road is composed of heavy sand, which is almost impossible for animals to drag a wagon through.

---

2. The Forty-Mile Desert. Pilot river is now named South Fork of the Carson River.

Famished for Water

I do not think there can be a more gloomy or desolate region in the whole world. When we got within 9 or 10 miles of Pilot river, we had to leave our wagons and drive our stock on to the river. I stayed with the wagons, and that day was a day that never will be effaced from my memory, for that was a day that I saw human as well as animal suffering, in all its forms.— Men came walking along through the scorching sun, famished for water; they offered any amount for a drink of water; one man offered me $100 for a pint of water. I refused it, and told him that water was one of the free gifts of God, and as long as I had it would distribute it freely; but, unfortunately, I had but a couple of gallons, which soon run out. Then came the time that I duly appreciated the value of water, for I suffered for it myself. The last accounts that we received from there was afflicting indeed; a great many people had lost their stock, and were left in a terrible condition: destitute of water and provisions. I should not be surprised to hear of thousands of persons perishing on the route, as it is supposed that there is some 30 or 40,000 on the way here. The citizens here are raising subscriptions to purchase provisions to send on to their relief.

I am happy to inform you that the state of affairs here are in excellent condition. There is no stealing, murder, or other depredations committed since they have put lynch law in force. The law is to hang a fellow up as soon as he is caught in the act of stealing.

The best and principal gold washer that is used here is made just like a child's cradle, with rockers, and rocked in pretty much the same manner. I think there is many a young man here that will learn to rock the cradle before he is entitled to be called father.

I remain with the greatest respect, yours, &c.   THOMAS S. HART.

(CPD, October 22, 1849.)

Letter from the Diggings

A. G. Sawtell, formerly of this city, but lately of Southport, writes to his friends as follows:

SACRAMENTO CITY,
July 22, 1849.

MR. SAMUEL FRANCIS—DEAR SIR: Having a few leisure moments before starting for the Gold Mines, I thought I would improve them by informing some of my Southport friends of what is going on in this land of gold.

Myself and brother arrived at Sutter's Fort on the 19th of this month, after a hard journey of 70 days from old Fort Kearny on the Missouri River. We have traveled the distance, 2,100 miles, in 55 traveling days—the quickest trip ever made. We traveled with our wagons to Fort Hall, and there took pack mules. Left the rest of the Southport company behind. Killed three of our animals on the way—bought more and pushed through, and here we are in this Pandemonium of the world; and I want to take one more such trip and die.

The Southport boys I expect in about 10 days, if they ever get through the Sierra Nevada Mountains alive, who a great many believe never will. There will be more suffering on the mountains this fall than has ever yet been known. There are 2,000 teams between this place and the Missouri river that never will cross the mountains—there is not feed for their animals.

This is a great country, and no mistake—a great place to make money; but I would advise no man, who is well situated in the States, to come here; he had better stay at home. The man who thinks it a mere pleasure trip to go to California is most woefully mistaken. But I am here, and if I don't have my breeches lined with the "Yaller" within one year, you call me lazier than my old Spanish jackass. I can make my $25 a day, and work at anything I choose; and so can any man. We sold three mules to the Government the day after we arrived here for $450, and had to deliver them up the river ten miles. I thought I would see if I could get some fellow to drive them up, and I came across a half-breed Indian, and asked him what he would drive them up to the rancho for; he looked at me about five minutes—said he, "I will go for $100"—a half day's work! I broke and run. I have since done all my work. A man will not work here five minutes for less than a dollar.

There is only one thing but that they don't have here, and that is pretty women; there are none. I would give my right arm to cast my eyes upon a well-formed, lovely, and pretty damsel of eighteen.

ALBERT G. SAWTELL.

(CPD, October 24, 1849.)

Letter from California

SAN FRANCISCO, Aug. 26th, 1849.

Dear Father:—Here I am at last safely arrived in the Golden Land, and although I have now been here two weeks I can hardly realize the state of affairs existing in this place. At the present time, everything is bustle, noise, and confusion; men drive around as if their life depended on saving five minutes of time, and there is more business done here in one day than there would be in a place of ten times the size in the States.

But I must not get on so fast. My last letter to you was dated at Panama, April 29th. The next day I was attacked with diarrhœa, which gradually increased on me for a week, and ended in a violent dysentery. I became reduced to a mere skeleton, and at one time was out of my head. Dr. Smith left me in the house lying down in a hammock, and when he came back I had *vamosed*; he found me after three or four hours' search, walking at a furious rate round the city, and after some trouble succeeded in getting me home. From this time, thanks to his care and attention, I began slowly to recover.

On the 8th of May I weighed only 115 pounds; the next day I went on board the brig Copiapo, but we did not weigh anchor until the 11th, on account of the passengers demanding that some of their number should be set on shore, as we were very much crowded; the difficulty was finally settled by taking off twenty-five passengers, who were transferred to another brig, the Callao. We finally started with a fair wind on the 11th, but our wind did not last long. During the next two weeks we were either becalmed or had head winds. On account of the great number still on board, I (with about twenty others) was obliged to sleep on deck all the time, This was no great hardship, but very inconvenient, as in these latitudes we had violent rains five days out of six, and as for going below I greatly preferred being in the rain and fresh air than dry and almost suffocated with the smell of the between decks.

Sojourn in Acapulco

After beating about for a month, we concluded to put into Acapulco after fresh provisions and water. We arrived there on the 15th June, and staid until the 21st. This town has the appearance of all other Mexican towns, the houses are mostly of stone, one-story in height with porticoes in front. It is very prettily situated with a beautiful bay completely landlocked, and capable of containing a large fleet. The town is on rising ground, with high hills all around, at the back and on each side. Our arrival created a sensation, and as we found out afterwards, prices rose 100 per cent. We engaged lodgings ashore at 75 cents a day, which was considered very cheap. While we were there, bananas, plantains, and all other kinds of fruit were in great demand.

After leaving this place, we were again favored with an abundance of calms and head winds, and on the 4th of this month deemed it advisable to put into Monterey, as we had only about two days more of provision and water. We arrived there on the 6th; the harbor is merely an indentation of the coast; exposed to the north and winds from that direction, there must be a heavy roll of the sea coming in.

We found the place almost deserted; nearly every one had gone off to the mines. We were introduced to Mr. Willey, a clergyman attached to the mission here;[3] he had been in the place about two months; he took us up to the Capitol, a building of stone, two stories in height and about 60 feet long wide by 50 wide; his school room is in the second story. He has a class of about fifty young natives, and he says that the facility with which they master the English language is incredible. The building was almost finished when the Gold fever broke out, and the workmen immediately left it; the cost was $14,000; it could not now be built for $150,000. Mr. W. kindly proferred to us the use of his bedroom in the building; we accepted it as well as the reading of his late papers from home. In looking over a copy of the Alta Californian I saw the notice of the arrival in this port, S. F., of the ship Capitol, and as she had nearly all our goods aboard, and moreover, Justin had taken passage in her, I determined (as the brig would in probability be delayed in beating up) to walk over here.

Walking to San Francisco

After making the necessary preparations in the morning, I started at noon-time over a very sandy road, into which I was sinking nearly up to my knees at every footstep. I overtook and passed a number of Indians with their wooden bowls, &c. This sand ends at a river or rather creek, about 12 miles from town. I waded over this and then had most delightful walking before me over a level and very fertile plain. After leaving this, the road winds around the beautiful valley of Lomo, the hills rising abruptly from within a short distance of either side of the road. After leaving this I entered the valley of San Juan; after passing through this and over 8 or 10 miles of hilly ground, I came into the valley of Yarno; this varies from 10 to 30 miles in width, and is 50 or 60 miles long. On the road I frequently overtook and passed "garetas" [carretas]; these are the carriages of California, and are nothing more than rough carts mounted on two low wooden wheels about two feet in diameter and six inches wide. Families moving or on a visit to a neighboring town always use this conveyance; it is a very slow one, being drawn by oxen, and also very rough, as the wheels are made of a solid piece of wood, and get worn down more on the side parallel with the grain of the wood than they do on the other sides, and consequently are sometimes quite oval, and the way they jolt the poor damsels is a pity.

Kindness of the Ladies

Puebla,[4] 80 miles from Monterey and 70 from San Francisco, is quite a thriving town and full of bustle; there are two hotels in it, kept by Americans, as also Yankee stores, where they exchange all sorts of goods and provisions for the *dust*. Santa Clara is a small place, containing a church, a dozen stores, and some private dwellings; this is five miles beyond Puebla. It happened to be the "Feast Day" of Santa Clara, and the road was filled with caballeros on horseback, attending their fair senoritas in the *garotas*, also swarms of pedestrian Indians. I accepted the invitation of five or six fair young ladies in a garote, to take a ride with them, and jumped in, the gentlemen on horseback attending them, and dressed in the extreme of California fashion, looked rather disdainfully on my dusty apparel; but I had the ladies on my side and did not care much for him. I paid for my temerity,

---

3. The Reverend Samuel Hopkins Willey, born in New Hampshire in 1821; arrived in California on board the steamer *California,* the first steamer to reach the Pacific Coast.
4. Pueblo de San Jose.

however, in being nearly jolted to death, and also losing my bundle, consisting of a handkerchief, containing a shirt and some meat, which I had cooked at a rancho in the morning and intended for my day's provisions. When the girls found out what it contained, they made me accept a loaf of bread and half a pound of cheese, and it was with great difficulty I could dissuade them from replacing the other articles.

The road from here is again over a perfectly level plain for 20 miles, thinly studded with oak trees; then I first caught sight of the noble bay of San Francisco. The hilly and sandy country again commences 18 miles from San Francisco. At the mission of Dolores, three miles from town, I came in view of the forest of masts of the shipping lying in the bay opposite the town. I involuntarily took off my hat and gave three times three cheers. I was overjoyed to be at last in sight of it after six and a half months' travel.

The whole of the country I passed through is fertile in the highest degree, and with proper cultivation would produce enormous crops. It is now only used as grazing ground for the immense herds of cattle and horses which are to be seen in all directions over it. The time is not far distant when it will present a different appearance and be studded over with farms, richly repaying the enterprising occupants for the little labor necessary to be bestowed on them.

Hospitality of the People

I came over the high sand hills and into town at noon-time. My journey took five days for the 150 miles. This was a day longer than I had calculated on, but I unfortunately stumbled against a root a few hours after leaving Monterey and fell, severely straining my knee, so that I was obliged to limp all the way. In my pocket it cost me nothing; the people are very hospitable, and thinking that I must be *very poor*, having no horse or *serape,* (a blanket with a slit in the centre to allow the head to pass

through,) and would not take any money. I pocketed the affront with the best possible grace and gave them "muchas gracias" instead. The only difficulty I experienced was want of water, having on several occasions to walk 15 or 20 miles without it.

San Francisco is now the most bustling, busy place you can possibly conceive; buildings are going up in all directions with the rapidity of magic, and as soon as the sills and first floor are laid, are occupied. Carpenters make from $12 to $18 per day; day laborers from $6 to $8. House frames shipped here have been bringing large prices. A one-story building, 15 by 20, is worth from $1,400 to $1,700. I have seen a ship's caboose sell for $500. Lumber is worth 35 to 40 cents per foot. These prices are now falling, as great numbers of houses are constantly arriving from the States and China, and many vessels are bringing in lumber from Oregon. House rents are very high; small stores rent from $150 to $500 per month.

A bustling place, but . . .

The town is prettily situated on a small bay formed by two points of land jutting out on each side, and between which, about half a mile from the beach, lay the shipping; sand hills enclose the town on three sides. As a place of residence it is one of the most disagreeable places I ever was in. The nights are cool, mornings and evenings misty, days hot, and regularly at noon, the land breeze commences and blows strongly until night, bringing down clouds of sand and dust from the hills; everything is covered with it, and you cannot walk out without getting your eyes full, and as for keeping clean, it is out of the question. Goods of all kinds lie about the streets and on the beach, in the greatest profusion. They are perfectly safe; stealing is almost unknown here. In the first place there is but little motive, for any one who is inclined to work can find plenty to do and good pay for it; secondly, the risk is too great, for if caught, the unlucky offender receives his desserts at very short notice. Murder is very rarely heard of, either here or at the mines.

An Odd Circumstance

One case, however, happened a few days since, a Frenchman was murdered and robbed between this place and the Mission of Dolores; the murderer has not yet been arrested. Last week I was passing with Dr. Smith along the beach, when we heard a tremendous groaning noise, coming apparently from a small schooner lying at the end of a small pier. We hastened down, and as the unearthly noise still continued issuing from the hold of the schooner, I took off the hatch and jumped down. Some one from the crowd then handed me a match, and on lighting it what did I see but a great grizzly bear, just brought down from the mountains. As soon as he perceived me he made a dive at me, and as he had plenty of slack to his chain, I *vamosed* in a hurry.

At the lowest part of the town is quite a large encampment on a space of low marshy ground, about two or three acres in extent; this is "Happy Valley." There are probably two or three hundred tents pitched; the location is unfavorable for health—many are suffering with diarrhoea, supposed to be produced by the water found here; in other parts of the town very good water is obtained.

Gambling is carried on here extensively. I went this morning into several Saloons; they were all crowded, and betting ran high at "Monte," their favorite game. I saw one rough-looking customer lay down on the board ten Spanish Doubloons, and these kind of stakes were by no means uncommon. $5,000 to $10,000 frequently changed hands in one evening. There must be an intense fascination in gaming, judging from the glistening eyes and clutching fingers I saw in these places—the only safeguard is never to *commence* play.

A new paper, (tri-weekly,) called the "Pacific News," was started here last Sat-urday—it has a very neat, pretty appearance—price $16 per year. In going over some of the hills back of the town, I stumbled across a genuine Yankee washing establishment, close by a small pond. The operations were conducted by two men, one washing in a large machine and the other busy ironing—they told me it paid well at $6 per doz.

Growth of the Country

Towns are growing up rapidly on the various rivers between here and the various diggings. Benicia, on Suisun Bay, Sacramento City, and Stockton are the most flourishing. New York city and Boston are commenced, but not yet finished. In going through the town you meet men from every quarter of the globe. Yankees are predominant, but Englishmen, Frenchmen, and the phlegmatic Dutch are also quite numerous; besides there are plenty of Kanakas, from the Sandwich Islands, Chilians, Mexicans, Peruvians, Indians from the interior, and last though not least, numbers of Chinese direct from Hong Kong—these are busy in putting up houses just imported from the Celestial Empire. But to describe every thing new and novel here would require too much space, and I must therefore merely touch some of the main features. Labor is here the capital which is most in demand, and consequently mechanics of all kinds and laboring men reign supreme. Provisions of nearly all kinds are as cheap as in the States, but at the same time labor is so dear that boarding is charged for at very high rates; the cheapest here is $14 a week, and from that it goes up to $50, according to quality. Bread is 25 cents for a very small loaf; they sell at the Restaurants small pies for 50 to 75 cents. One dollar for a single meal is considered exceedingly cheap, but in Happy Valley we buy our own provisions at wholesale and do our own cooking. Those who do not wish to buy soft bread eat hard; butter I have not tasted since I left home—here it is $1.75 per pound.

Small schooners are continually going up and down the rivers, carrying passengers; they charge $16 to Stockton or Sacramento City; from there up to the mines, from 60 to 80 miles, 25 cts. per lb. for baggage, and you walk. Reports from the mines are various and not much to be depended on, unless you receive it from undoubted sources. Many placers which were considered rich a year ago are now deserted, and the miners have sloped to new diggings. Up the Sacramento it is considered unhealthy, but quite the reverse up the San Joaquin. The former river is better for slow and sure work, but on the latter all the large lumps have been found. I saw yesterday a solid lump, weighing 14 lbs., from there. A carpenter, with whom I am acquainted here, was yesterday making four boxes to send home gold dust in, $20,000 worth in each, for one merchant here. The impression prevalent in the States that the mines are uninhabitable in the rainy season, is all erroneous. I have seen many persons here who wintered in the mines last season, and although it rains a good deal and snows some, yet the country is by no means flooded. The best months for working are October, November, and December. I will start to go up about the middle of next month.

The ship Humboldt, which left Panama just before us, did not arrive here until yesterday; seven died on the passage up. The brig Two Friends also left before us; the last heard of her was at Cape St. Lucas; she is now about 125 days out; great fears are entertained of her safety.[5] The U. S. ship-of-the-line Ohio is lying here; also the Warren. Among the fleet here are 6 from China, 6 from France, 12 from England, and several from the Netherlands.

Information came into town night before last that there was great suffering among the overland emigrants. There are now many thousands of these unfortunate people the other side of the Sierra Nevada in a state of starvation. A meeting was called yesterday in town, and well attended, for the purpose of taking measures for their *immediate* relief. Your affectionate son,   THOMAS TENNENT.

(PPL, Oct. 25, 1849.)

The Rush for California

is still on the increase, and whole families, rather than individual members, are now making preparations to start for the gold region. At New York twenty-eight vessels are up for California; the brig Grecian, which was built by order of a young man, now in California, expressly for the comfort and convenience of his relatives, whom he wishes to join him in his new home. She has as passengers the father, two brothers, and a brother-in-law of the person who sent for them, with their wives and little ones.

A young lady of Boston has accepted an offer of $400 per month to act as bookkeeper in a mercantile house in San Francisco.

The frame of a building for a hotel has lately left Boston for San Francisco, accompanied by all the materials for an extensive bar-room, and a bar-tender has been engaged at $200 per month.

The brig Colorado, which sailed from Boston on the 23d instant, takes out a company (twenty in number) who are going to settle at the new city of Benicia, besides five females. They carry with them a large frame for a building, to be used as a hotel, with the furniture, &c.; also a number of wagons, carts, trucks, &c.

(WNI, October 29, 1849.)

---

5.   The *Two Friends* eventually arrived, taking more than five months to go from Panama to San Francisco.

Death and Dollars

Latest from the California Trains

The Lexington (Mo.) Express has the following extract from a letter received by Mr. Anderson, of Lexington, from his brother, dated:

COLORADO RIVER, CALIFORNIA,
July 24, 1849.

We are now lying on the east side of the Colorado river, intending to cross to-day. We are yet 700 miles from the gold mines, at which we expect to arrive in seven weeks from this day. We left Fort Kearney on the 9th of May, and have been traveling ever since.

For some time our train has been in great excitement, and much danger of being captured. In the mountains around us there are about 200 deserters from the Oregon battalions, well armed with rifles and swords. They have threatened, and no doubt intend, to attack us.

They are making their way to the mines, and are in great want of provisions. We are ready for the attack—we number 60 brave men, armed with 25 double-barreled shot guns, 25 rifles, 34 six-barreled pistols, 10 rifle pistols, and some brass-barreled pistols—we sleep on our arms—our *coral* is equal to any breastwork, and we are always ready for their attack.

The cholera has caused great distress on the plains. Mr. Slagle is the only man who has died in our train; the rest have had good health. Some days we have passed five or six graves, whose tenants had fallen victim to that destroyer of the human race.

(CPD, November 1, 1849.)

Vessels for California

The Baltimore American of yesterday contains a list of sixty-five vessels which have departed from the United States for California during October. . . . Besides these, during the month the steamships Empire City, Crescent City, and Ohio have sailed from New York for Chagres, and the steamships Falcon, Alabama, and New Orleans, from New Orleans, for the same port, carrying together at least one thousand passengers. So that it may be safely estimated that during the month of October at least twenty-three hundred persons have left the United States, by sea, bound to California.

The Boston Shipping List gives the total number of vessels that have left the United States for California since the beginning of the gold excitement at five hundred and seventy-three; of this number there had arrived at California at the latest date one hundred and sixty-seven.

There are now upwards of a hundred vessels up for California, viz. at Boston 30, New Bedford 6, Newburyport 6, Bangor 4, New York 27, Philadelphia 6, Baltimore 5, New Orleans 8, other ports 11—making a total of 104. (WNI, Nov. 3, 1849.)

From the Plains and Salt Lake

[From the St. Louis Republican, Oct. 26]
GREEN RIVER, CALIFORNIA TERRITORY,
August 19, 1849.

Since I addressed you from Laramie, little has presented itself of general interest to your readers; but to us pilgrims bringing up the rear, scenes and occurrences have been constantly coming to view, as far as this point, that had no parallel on the eastern part of our journey. From Laramie, the Rocky Mountains really start their foundation; and although it is three hundred miles from there to the summit, it is nothing but a succession of knolls and knobs until you turn over the culminating point to Pacific Spring, where the water runs westward. In reference to the adjacent country, there is nothing rising to the dignity of a mountain on this whole route.

Ruin and Death

From Laramie, grass began to fail for our stock, and the utmost diligence had to be used to sustain them. From thence, after the first fifty miles, dead cattle and fragments of wagons come in sight, and as far as here I have counted about one thousand wagons that have been burnt or otherwise disposed of on the road. Destruction seems to have been the prevailing emotion with everybody who had to leave anything on the trip. Wagons have been wantonly sacrificed, without occasion, by hundreds—being fired for the apparent purpose of preventing them from being serviceable to anybody else, while hundreds have been used by piecemeal, for fuel, at nearly every camping ground, by each successive train.

From Deer Creek to the summit, the greatest amount of property has been thrown away. Along the banks of the North Platte to where the Sweetwater Road turns off, the amount of valuable property thrown away is astonishing—iron, trunks, clothing, &c., lying strewed about, to the value of at least fifty thousand dollars, in about twenty miles. I have counted about five hundred dead oxen along the road, and only three mules.

The reason of so many wagons having been disposed of was the apparent necessity of packing, in order to insure a quick and certain transit to the mines; and people did not care for the loss of any personal goods, just so they reached there.

Let people who come out this way next season beware of crossing the Platte at Deer Creek. Keep up the south side as high as possible—at least up to the "Mormon Ford," and higher if possible—before they strike over to the Sweetwater. During this summer there was a ferry kept at Deer Creek, and the bulk of the emigration crossed at it, but the road is much worse,

and every one regrets having crossed so low.

The last train of the Pioneer line, day before yesterday, took Sublette's Cut Off, and left us at the junction of the Oregon and California roads. They were all well, and are bound to get through.

Many of the St. Louis boys have left their names and respects to any of their friends behind, on the smooth trees and rocks along the road, and it is sometimes cheering to see a well known name pencilled at a crossing or watering place.

Death seems to have followed the emigration out thus far, although in a mitigated degree as to numbers. Eight or ten of those below are buried in the Pass, and there are some others also who have no identity on their graves.

List of Graves on the Road
west of Fort Laramie

J. M. Hay; Dr. McDermett, of Fairfield, Iowa, died July 21—aged 28.

Mrs. Mildred Moss, late of Galena, wife of D. H. T. Moss, died 7th July—aged 25 years.

John Woodside, died June 19, 1849—buried at Warm Spring.

John B. Mastin, July 5, of Pontatoc, Miss., aged 15 years.

T. George, died June 18.

Jesse Clark, jr., died June 28, of Breeden, N. Y.

Thomas M. Rankin, June 25, aged 28 years, of Lewis county, Mo. (It might be St. Louis, defaced.)

David Hines, of Madison county, Ill., June 26, aged 25.

W. Drennen, drowned May 20, at Platte crossing, aged 35, late of Ohio.

N. Glenat, July 7, aged 45, from Dubuque, Iowa.

Nancy Tremble, June 25, 1849, aged 24, at Willow Spring.

Herr Saltzer, June 10, aged 22, from Indiana.

William Moore, July 20, aged 56, Oswago, Ind.

John McDowell, of St. Joseph, Mo.

Joseph Barnett, August 26, 1844.

Mrs. Bryan, July 25, 1845.

James Estell, June 20, of Lawrence county, Mo.

W. Rector, July 28; Geo. C. Pitcher, July 20, late of Henry county, Illinois, and formerly of New York—both at Pacific Spring.

J. R. Nelson, June 26, aged 39 years, of Adams county, Illinois—at Big Sandy.

The express rider states that he will pass four and five graves a day, all the way down Bear river, and so on further westward. (NYH, Nov. 4, 1849.)

From Fort Laramie

we have a private letter, from which we take the following extracts:—

FORT LARAMIE, (Ind. Ter.) Sept. 18, 1849.

I reached here, from Fort Kearney, towards the latter end of July, and had hardly got my tent pitched when I was ordered over to Fort Pierre on the Missouri, with ten rifles, to escort Col. Mackay to that point, and to keep the Sioux and other red gentlemen of the prairies from molesting his scalp. The trip was a most interesting one, as our trail ran through the celebrated "Mauvais Terre," where petrefactions of all kinds can be found by the cart load. The country is also well stocked with game, and many a fine buffalo fell beneath my rifle, and many a "side rib" and "fleece" were discussed around our evening camp fires. While in the "bad grounds," I picked up some bushel or so of petrefactions, which I will show you some of these days—that is, provided I ever again take the trail towards the frontiers.

All hands are driving away at our new buildings, and strong hopes are entertained that before the mercury is at zero we shall be around our new hearths.

We were visited, a few days since, by about two hundred Cheyennes and Sioux, who danced a little, stole a little, eat a great deal, and finally went on their way rejoicing. These Platte Sioux, by the way, are the best Indians on the prairies. Look at their conduct during the past summer. Of the vast emigration which rolled through their country this year, not a person was molested, not an article stolen. Such good conduct deserves reward.

News from the Salt Lake has just reached here, and the accounts from the emigrants are anything but flattering. You may recollect that early in the season I predicted great suffering amongst them. It is now about to be fulfilled. Between fifteen and twenty thousand emigrants, according to these accounts, will be obliged to pass the ensuing winter amongst our Mormon neighbors. Such a number of additional mouths, you will readily see, must play the deuce with the limited supplies of the Mormons. This detention was caused by the careless or wanton conduct of the leading portion of the emigration, in burning the country beyond the Salt Lake. All the grass is consumed for nearly two hundred miles, which, of course, renders the passage of animals impossible.

Those grand rascals of the Plains, the Pawnees, have again been imbruing their hands in the blood of the whites. Two men—Thomas and Picard—carrying the U. S. mail from Fort Hall to Fort Leavenworth, were attacked by them a few days since, about half way between this post and Fort Kearney, and it is feared that both were killed. Lt. Donaldson, on his way to this post, found the dead body of Thomas, and the hat of Picard stained with blood. Before he reached the spot he met a war party of Pawnees, who evinced by their actions that they were the perpetrators of the deed. Thomas' body had several arrows sticking in it. Lt. D. had but two or three teamsters with him, and he could only give the body a hasty burial, without searching very thoroughly for the other man. These Pawnees have recently plundered some government wagons below Fort Kearney, and it is high time they should be brought to their senses. The chiefs and head men are well disposed, but the young men of the tribe are the worst Indians in the West. The troops at Fort Kearney, I presume, will pay these gentlemen a visit at their village on the Platte, at the mouth of the Saline, and it is to be hoped that the commanding officer, Major Chilton, will overhaul them with a rough hand.

A sort of Indian war, it would appear, could now be got up. That is, three or four small Indian wars in different quarters, but entirely disconnected. The Seminoles, Comanches, and Pawnees all want a thrashing, and I hope will get it; and while our hand is in, the Yancton Sioux, over on the Missouri, might be included. They killed a white man last season, and performed other antics.

I have run this out to a much greater length than I at first anticipated, and will, therefore, throw down my pen, take a drink of brandy, smoke a segar, and delib-erate on the safest way of attacking a grizzly bear, which I intend to do in a few days. (NYH, Nov. 4, 1849.)

News from Col. Collier's party

LIGOUNA INDIAN VILLAGE,[1] Sept. 1, 1849.

DEAR FATHER:—We are encamped at the foot of a mountain, in a very pleasant valley. Our march yesterday was over high mountains in winding and narrow paths.—You will see in one of Emory's plates, mules descending high mountains, which fully pictures our road yesterday. At one of these turns away went one of our litters, with two mules. They fell about ten feet; any other animal but a mule would have been killed. The litter was broken in fine pieces, and they had to leave it. Some of our Mexican muleteers wanted to desert last night. Our captain put them under arrest, and will make six of them foot it a few days living on bread and water. This

Mules crossing a mountain—Emory's plate, referred to above.

1. Laguna Pueblo, New Mexico.

has detained us a day or so, to get other Indians to take their places.

We have in our train 250 mules and about 100 men. There are also about us about one hundred emigrants, who it seems have been waiting for the benefit of our guide. Our camp is surrounded by Indians. They are the friendly Pueblos; we are also in the vicinity of the Navahoos, but have not had sight of them yet. Our route crosses the mountains over to Salt river, and then down the Rio Gila. We are about 50 miles from Albugeree [Albuquerque].

This town [Laguna] is built on a solid foundation of rock, and the same as all others with mud, and is built in self-defence from hostile tribes. The walls are about twelve feet high. They enter with ladders, and at night draw them up after them—no doors outside. This is what I call living in suspense. Our mode of sleeping now and has been the open air, and heaven's canopy for a spread. We expect to reach San Diego in about thirty-five days. We are all well and in good spirits. In great haste, writing out in the open air on my pack.

WILLIAM SMYTH.

(CPD, November 5, 1849.)

Letter from "Solitaire"—Gold Digging and the Mining Region

WOOD'S DIGGINGS, SAN JOAQUIN, CALIFORNIA, Aug. 17th, 1849.

EDS. REVEILLE:—I consider this subject worth a chapter exclusively, and I shall attempt to make a description of the diggings—notwithstanding they have been described by other pens.—In the first place, the spot where I am now writing can be reached from San Francisco by payment of the sum of fifty-seven dollars—the fare by water, from Stockton to San Francisco and *vice versa*, is twenty-five dollars, by stage from Stockton to "Sonorian," the fare is thirty-two dollars.

The Cosumnes, Dry Creek, Mokelamies, Calaveras, Stanislaus, or, more properly, Tanislaus, Teuahimle, Mercedes, Meraposa, and King's River are the southern streams, or termed southern diggings; the South Fork, Middle Fork, and North Fork are tributaries of the Sacramento, and, with Bear Creek, Yuba, Feather, and Sacramento rivers, are called the northern diggings. Every ravine on these streams, with the exception perhaps of King's River and the Meraposa, have been thoroughly "prospected," and the location of gold thereon fully ascertained. All the beds of the streams mentioned, with the exception of the two last and the dry ravines leading in to them, have been partially dug, but they yet contain much more gold than has been taken out. A number of men have fairly commenced upon the Meraposa, and among them Col. Fremont has a party. Last spring the Indians were in such numbers in that neighborhood, and so hostile, that those who attempted to work there were driven out, but the whites are now too numerous to be moved by any force the Indians can muster. King's River, at the head of the Tule lake, is the grand camping ground of hostile Indians, and, as yet, miners have only been to "prospect" it, which, however, has fully satisfied them that its bed contains the precious ore.

Trade and digging, last winter, were immensely profitable. Many of the southern mines were then opened, and they yielded richly, and where gold was thus abundant among the diggers, the traders reaped a harvest. Provisions brought a high price, and were sold for the dust at a value of from seven to ten dollars per ounce. The Indians knew then very little about the value of gold; and if they saw in a trader's tent a sash, blanket, or suit that they fancied, they would give all the gold in their possession for it, sometimes to the amount of three or four pounds.—Freight from Stockton to the diggings was at the rate of one dollar per pound. When men took out pounds they squandered ounces freely, but now a change has come among many of them—the diggings require more

Miners at work in 1849.

labor and the miners have to dig deeper for ounces than they formerly did for pounds. It is true that the gold is scattered over a large district of country, but it is confined to the water courses, and the narrow *gulches* leading to them. The Indians have now learned the true value of the shining ore, and the competition among traders has taught them how much they can obtain for it at its full value.

All Up for Grabs

Digging is very like a *lottery*, with this difference however that all who labor industriously may draw prizes, but the number who obtain the large sums are few in comparison to those who obtain but half an ounce per day. One hundred men have been digging in the bed of the creek opposite here, and have not averaged more than half an ounce per day for the last two weeks. During that period there were two large prizes drawn, one by an Irishman and the other by four Americans. About a week since an Irishman dug out a round lump of stone, banded and interlaced with

about three hundred dollars' worth of gold; it was a very pretty specimen, and as the son of Erin held it up and wiped off the clay, he sagely remarked:

"Be J—s, thur's lots of the yellow stuff here yit, if yez only know where to dig for it——faith, I like to dig ditches where the gravil is mixed wid that same kind of *dust!*"

The other prize was drawn that evening, about two hundred yards above Dent's tent, by four men—they reached a pocket about evening and uncovered a very pretty nest of gold. A man looking at them when they uncovered the ore offered them the amount of eight pounds for it, but they believed it more, and refused; on taking it out, however, it only weighed four and a quarter pounds. The same four men had been digging for eight days previous, without realizing sufficient to pay their expenses. One man told me that he dug nine large holes at Sullivan's, without realizing enough to pay for his salt, and he moved from there, after expending nearly three months' useless labor, to Murphy's diggings, upon a tributary of the Toualimne, and in two weeks he dug out, at the latter place, two and a half pounds.

A spree generally follows a successful discovery, and whisky and monte then receive their half of the prize. Mercurial temperaments soon become dissatisfied, if the hole they are digging in yields but a small sum, and, ill-luck still following them, instead of striking deeper, they leave for other diggings reported to be richer, where they go through every other course of superficial exploration.

The falling off of the miner's receipts has caused trade to be very dull, and many of the store keepers are not realizing expenses. When the rains come, trade will revive, for then the dry gulches can be worked with profit. All kinds of goods are now selling at half the price they brought last spring. All provisions, such as meat, flour, sugar, coffee, &c., are selling at 50 cents per pound; but when the roads make transportation impossible, they will no doubt double their present rates. Clothing is cheap, and shovels, crowbars, and pans may be obtained at half an ounce each. Liquors are at from four to five dollars per bottle.

How the Foreigners Live

Upon these different streams there are now nearly 30,000 diggers, and at least 20,000 of that number are South Americans, Sandwich Islanders, and the English, Irish, and Scotch residents of South America. All the southern republics are represented here, but by far the largest number are from Chili and the department of Sonora. At least $10,000,000 of gold has been taken from these *placers* by the foreign emigration. English, Irish, and Scotch residents of Chili have brought up hosts of *peones,* bought from their masters, and with them swept the placers. Rich men from Mexico and Chili, who were there engaged in mining, have transported their *slaves* here, and these practiced laborers

have far outstripped Americans in the search for gold. The Chilian and Mexican *peones* will live upon a little dried beef, a few tortillas, and a pint of cooked beans per day; while the American, used to abundance, will spend more for one day's living than would furnish six South Americans; consequently the latter, when they leave the placers for home, carry off the largest quantity of the gold.

The Sonorians brought large droves of mules here by land, and soon reduced the rate of freight to the placers; but recently many of the timid ones have returned home with their animals, having obtained sufficient gold, and being, at the same time, fearful that a day was approaching when the Americans would drive them off without giving them a chance to carry off their plunder.

Yours, ever,   SOLITAIRE.
(CPD, November 5, 1849.)

One Day's Emigration from Boston for California

[FROM THE BOSTON TRAVELLER]
Yesterday four vessels sailed from this port for California, viz. the ships Argonaut, Richmond, Henry Ware, and brig Archelaus. These vessels carried a total of four hundred passengers, among whom were only three women, viz. the wife of Captain Winn, of Richmond, and his two daughters, of Salem. There are a very large number from Quincy, and indeed from many of the shoe towns. These passengers will reach their destination somewhere about 1st of May, 1850.

Ship Hamilton sailed to-day for California. This ship is owned and loaded by a mercantile firm of this city. She takes out lumber, frames for houses, and two steamboats. One is the fast steamer "Sarah," that formerly ran on the North river, New York, and lately on the Merrimack.

Brig Ark, for California, detained yesterday in consequence of the southeast gale of Monday night, was to sail from

Newburyport this morning for California. She has one hundred and seventeen passengers.

The Providence Journal says three vessels from Providence sailed for California on Tuesday. The barque Rio sailed from Newport, with sixty-five passengers; the barque Walter with sixty-three passengers. The schooner Curlew also went to sea. She was only 99 tons burden.

(WNI, Nov. 6, 1849.)

From California

The St. Louis Republican has a letter dated at "Stockton, August 27th."—The writer says he was one of the first that came through without leaving wagons. He describes the country above the sink, for two hundred miles, as a desert—and the last forty-five miles as horrible. He saw men suffering with thirst, whose throats were so swollen that they could not speak or shut their mouths. The stench from dead animals was intolerable. He describes the road over the mountains as worse than imagination could picture—six mules would hardly pull up an empty wagon. But he finally arrived at El Dorado. He thus concludes his letter:

"For a week after our arrival, we did some of the tallest sleeping and eating that you ever heard of; the first three or four days I never got up except to eat. After resting for awhile we commenced looking out for something to do. But there was so much confusion, so many conflicting statements in regard to everything, and so much gold, that we were perfectly bewildered. We found that there was money to be made at anything a man could go at; but that it was utterly impossible to attempt anything without more capital than most of us possessed. The only chance for one without money was to drive a team or cart, chop wood, or go up to the mines. I was not sufficiently recruited to do either of the first, though twelve dollars a day was exceedingly tempting, and it was thought by all too hot to work in the mines.—Hum-

phrey Marshall and myself have, therefore, started down to San Francisco to try our fortunes there.

"If I can get any employment I shall remain till November; if not I shall go back to the mines.—There are so many mining at present that the labor is greatly increased and the profits very much diminished. Half an ounce being considered a good average per day. Those placers from which such large amounts were dug last year have all been exhausted. The whole country is still full of it, but it requires an immense deal of labor to wash it out. Gold has been found in every other part of the country that has been tried, and is considered so inexhaustible by every one until at last all have been disappointed in California. It can never be an agricultural country." (ISJ, Nov. 8, 1849.)

A Repentant Californian

The Journal of Commerce has been favored with the following extract of a letter from a hardy, intelligent mechanic, well-known and much respected in that city. It was addressed to a returned emigrant from California:

SAN FRANCISCO, Sept. 1, 1849.

Dear Sir:—I still remain in this horrible place, and not any better satisfied than when you left. My health is not as good by ten per cent. as it was at that time. Nothing has transpired in this place that would make you regret leaving it. Your blue blankets are pleasant companions the warmest night in summer; in fact, I have not seen anything like summer as yet. The mines are about the same in the production of the precious ore as when you left. At present the mortality at the mines is great; in Sacramento City every third one is down sick—hospitals erected in abundance, and doing a smashing business. The passengers who go up and down the rivers are half eaten up by mosquitoes. You never saw such a sight as they present; they all declare there is not gold enough on earth to pay the damage done them. Mr. ——

has gone home in disgust, and so have a good many more of our fellow passengers. I think, if God spares my life, I shall cross the Isthmus before Christmas.

It blows the same old gale here every day, and the dust makes such clouds that you cannot see a foot from your nose. I am fairly worn out. The whole face of the earth is burned up, so that you would think it impossible that anything green would ever appear again. I think if I had a mouthful of green grass, I would be satisfied.

I wonder if you saw that letter that stated that Mr. —— returned from the mines worth $75,000. So did I. I wish I could caution the people against believing letters that are false in every sense of the word. I have just seen Mr. ——. He says he has been sick all the time he has been at the mines. D. G. (PPL, Nov. 10, 1849.)

Our California Correspondence

SAN FRANCISCO, Oct. 1—5 A. M.

When all the world—for this is a world, and a great one in itself—is wrapped snugly in the arms of Morpheus, dreaming of gold and greatness, your humble servant for one night abjures the influence of the presiding deity of Somnus, for one object—to keep you posted up to the latest moment with the affairs of the new country. It is an unusual thing, even here, where sleep is so much and so highly appreciated, to resist the tempting and natural enjoyment of the cot; but a promise is held here as binding as abroad, signed and countersigned at the courts of the kings or monarchs of Europe.

At present there is but one opinion held by all here, and that is certainly strengthened by events and circumstances, too palpable to be overlooked—this country must and will become the great commercial focus of the Pacific. Even at this early period, the operations in commerce give evidence of the fact, inasmuch as lines of sailing vessels are established, and in full operation, between this port, the Sandwich Islands, and various ports on both the upper and lower coasts. Steamers of various sizes and capacities navigate the adjacent rivers, bringing the numerous and thriving towns, which have sprung up as if by magic influence, in close proximity to the metropolis. Laws and civil institutions are in course of formation; and the attempts made by a few to organize religious bodies and circles are respected and encouraged by all.

Chaos and Confusion

The city of San Francisco, at present, contains a population of twenty-five thousand, not including the floating population, which must number at least ten thousand more. With this omnifarious community—the conflicting habits of the various nations represented, and the entire absence of any settled form of government—there is not in the world, nor has there ever been, a more quiet, peaceable, or orderly place. There appears to be an intuitive sense of what is right pervading all classes, and the feelings and personal property of every individual are protected from insult and harm. The energy, intelligence, and the respect for equity and civil laws brought from home by our people, exercises a beneficial influence over the more lawless spirits from other countries. It is impossible to give the readers of the *Herald* a correct view of the country. Everything is yet wanting system; all is chaos and confusion; no rule or usage is regarded, in trade, that does not agree with the peculiar views of the individual. Yet all such operations are strictly in accordance with the standard of mercantile honor—but no customs borrowed from the mother country are held in esteem, inasmuch as they do not suit the peculiar existing circumstances.

Emigration still continues, and large numbers, from all parts of the world, flow in daily; many remain, and try their fortunes in politics and speculations; others, less ambitious of fame, leave for the mines; the majority, however, take the latter course, and, although their work is hard and their privations great, manage, in a little time, to realize a portion of their anticipations. The traffic on the rivers, at present, is immense. Some ninety vessels, of all classes, including three steamers, are constantly employed transporting passengers and merchandise to the various points, villages, and towns that border the noble streams of the valley of Sacramento. The *embarcados* or landing places that girt the town exhibit, from morning till night, one continued scene of bustle and confusion; the levee at New Orleans or the wharves at New York will not, in the most hurried season, surpass the pebbly beach of San Francisco in the amount of business transacted—in a small way.

Every man has his little business to attend to, and may be seen through all hours hurrying to and fro, intent upon its consummation. Land speculators, lawyers, miners, tradesmen, and even the few loafers are, all alike, swallowed up in the enormity of their transactions. Naval officers, whose lawful pay would scarcely give meat to a dog, are forced, through necessity, to shift and follow the tide, for a decent or even a necessary subsistence. . . . This California climate will have a very desirable effect upon many of these young gentlemen, not only in a business point of view, but in giving them a just appreciation of the worth and value of labor.

The Electric Spirit

Hotels and houses spring up like mushrooms; every day brings a change in the appearance of the place, and a man who absents himself for a week is utterly lost on his return. To give you an idea of the despatch and the electric spirit of building and speculation, I will state a fact that occurred a few days since. Going to dinner, I met a young man of my acquaintance who seemed to be unusually hurried, and asked him the cause, or what it was that impelled him on at such a pace; he answered that he had just leased a house to a party of traders, and as they wished to take possession that night, he had as much as he could well do, to build and make it ready for their accommodation. He had actually rented and built the house in the space of six hours.

Whole towns go up in this way. The means of making money are as numerous and various as the characters that follow them. Physicians, instead of riding in their gig, make more profitable calls at digging cellars, carting dirt, and other respectable occupations. One I noticed sails his aquatic gig, visiting his floating patients. The bay is literally a city afloat, and although many of the habitations are deserted, there are yet enough left to give business to more than one disciple of Esculapius. The harbor presents for miles an unbroken forest of masts—ships from every nation and country lay here, idle and worthless, with no prospect of ever leaving—many must go down at their anchor, for there are not men enough unemployed to work the twentieth part of them. The men will leave; there is no way of detaining them for duty on board; the naval force has been weakened by desertion, and there is no human effort or possibility to prevent the "custom" of deserting. Com. Jones has barely force enough on board to form a crew, much less to tender assistance to merchantmen. There are yet scores of vessels in port that have been months endeavoring to discharge—some have no consignees, others too many—many have captains, while numbers are without them, and without use for the commodity. We have many converted into store houses, hotels, lodging houses, and hospitals.

People in the United States, where the appetite can be gratified, though the most fastidious, imagine that we have no good living here. Look at this bill of fare. Wouldn't some of the gents who pick their teeth on the Astor steps prick up their ears at an invitation to such a dinner. Prices high, true, but the people are rich.

(NYH, Nov. 12, 1849.)

Delmonico Restaurant – The Bill of Fare

SOUP

Mock turtle	1.00	Rice	25

FISH

Fried	50	Boiled, with sauce	75

BOILED

Leg mutton, caper sauce	75	Cold ham	50
Veal, galentine	50	Venison, galentine	75

ENTREES

Fried brains	75	Boeuf à la mode	75
Venison, English sauce	75	Mutton chops	50
Sausage, wine sauce	75		

VEGETABLES

Sweet potatoes	50	Tomatoes	50
Potatoes, fried	35	Rice, boiled	25
" boiled	25	Cabbage and sausage	75

ROAST

Beef	50	Mutton	50
Pork	50	Veal	50
Apple sauce	25		

GAME

PASTRY AND DESSERT

Apple Pie	—	Madeira nuts	25
Fruit and melons	—	Peach pie	—
Raisins	—	Mince pie	—
Almonds	25	Grapes	—
Tarts	25	Sweetmeats	—
Coffee	—		

LIST OF WINES AT THE DELMONICO RESTAURANT

CHAMPAGNE

MADEIRA

Clio Madeira; Binengen & Co.

SHERRY

Superior Old Pale Sherry	Romano
Superior Old Brown Sherry	

FRENCH AND GERMAN WINES

Table Claret	Chateau Margeaux
St. Julian Medoc	Superior Old Sauterne
Superior London	Muscat
Superior Sparkling Hock	

PORT

Best London Dock	Kotch's London, very old
Burgundy Port	Old Cabinet

CORDIALS

Anisette	Old Tom
Amaraschino	Orgeat

MALT LIQUORS

Robert Byass' best London Dock Ale	
Superior Old Scotch Ale	Superior Aloe Ale

The Emigrants

SACRAMENTO CITY, August 25, 1849.

Arrival of the Overland Expedition—Life on the Prairies—Sufferings on the Route— Crossing the Sierra Nevada

I arrived here on the 21st, thirty-one days from Salt Lake, with but comparatively little difficulty, when placed in the balance with that to be overcome by those emigrants with wagons. As regards those behind, numbering some twenty thousand, time can only tell whether or not they get through with, or without, their wagons.

On the desert, a distance of seventy miles, commencing about twenty-five miles above the sink of the Humboldt River, and extending on one route to Trackie's River, on the other to Salmon Trout River,[2] there were lying dead between six and seven hundred head of stock, and only five hundred wagons had entered it, and over seventy of these were abandoned and left deserted on the road. Those who do not get through with their wagons are compelled to take their team through to the river, there recruit two or three days, and return for them. Families can lie here that length of time without much suffering, if water is packed to them in season, on the backs of some fresh animals. For the last hundred miles on Humboldt River there is little else than willows to support stock, so that they are compelled to enter the desert with their stock nearly exhausted, with the absolute certainty staring them in the face of their teams soon giving out. This difficulty no longer exists; a large tract of grass (a Godsend and salvation to the emigrants) has been discovered about twenty miles above the sink, and some eight miles east of the road.[3] Here they all go before attempting to cross the desert, and recruit their animals, cut and make hay, which they take with them to cross the barrens. When first the news came back of the discovery of this grass, the dark forebodings which shrouded the countenances of all were dispelled, and cheerfulness once more held the sway. It is in fact the emigrant's salvation.

Across the Sierra Nevada

One more difficulty to overcome, and they are here. It is to cross the Sierra Nevada mountains; and if the northern or old route, via Johnson's Ranche,[4] is as rich in obstructions as the south or new route, (and I learn that it is,) there must be a great destruction of property, if not suffering and loss of life. About one-fourth of the wagons which had entered the mountains when I crossed, were left broken to pieces upon the rocks. If they do not cling too long to their wagons, they may yet all get safely over. If the rear trains get belated (as they must) their only resort, to avoid the snows, will be to leave their wagons, pack provisions upon their oxen, and make the best of their way to the nearest settlement.

I was in the mountains three days, the second of which, August 17th, was freezing cold, the night previous there having been a series of tremendous thunder showers, which terminated in hail and snow. If the snow does not come for six weeks, all may safely arrive in California.

This town, Sacramento City, is situated at the confluence of the Sacramento and American rivers, two miles below Sutter's Fort, of only three months' growth, and yet

---

2.   There were routes on both sides of the Humboldt River. Trackie's River is apparently the Carson route; Salmon Trout River is the Truckee River—the Donner route.
3.   Great or Lassen's Meadows, where Rye Patch Reservoir now is.
4.   William Johnson and Sebastian Kayser built an adobe house at this place in the middle 1840s—the place became known as Johnson's Rancho, site of the town of Wheatland.

contains a population of three thousand five hundred; houses mostly of muslin, about sixty only of wood.

As to prices: All mining tools are high, as are also all articles upon which labor has been performed here. Picks, $5; pans, $5; cradles for washing gold, three feet long, worth about two dollars in the States, sell here for $40; flour from $8 to $10 per hundred; pork, $50 per hundred; coffee, $18; board, $21 per week, or $1.50 per meal, with the privilege of sleeping under the nearest tree unoccupied. At the mines, 60 miles distant, prices are doubled, and of some things trebled. Brandy, $2 per bottle.

At the mines, they are making on an average an ounce of gold per day. One man who arrived here this month, made in two weeks twenty-five thousand dollars, and has gone to San Francisco to take passage to the States.

Labor is in proportion to the produce of the mines, ranging from eight to eighteen dollars per day.

The latest news from the States is contained in the *New York Herald,* June 30th, which were sold in the streets yesterday at 50 cents apiece, and quick at that.

I am going, in a day or two, to the mountains, on a prospecting tour, and on my way shall again visit the principal mines, when I shall again report to you.

S. Z. F. C.   (NYH, Nov. 12, 1849.)

Never Before Witnessed

RANCHO DEL CHENO, Aug. 24, 1849.

Since I last wrote you, from Mazatlan, I have experienced no small portion of the vicissitudes and trials that befell, more or less, every one who may attempt to visit California by an overland route.

I am now stopping at the hospitable

residence (above named) of Col. Isaac Williams,[5] situated 30 miles east of Los Angelos, and about 250 west from the Colorado, on the whole of which distance Col. Williams is the only American residing on the road. The colonel has a splendid property, comprising 63,000 acres of the best land in the universe. Almost everything is, or can be, raised here that you can name, and in such profusion, and at so little expense, that I forbear particulars, for fear of damaging my reputation. The climate is the most delightful that can be imagined. In the morning the weather is warm, but towards noon a delightful sea breeze springs up, and for the rest of the day there prevails a most exhilarating atmosphere. The colonel has, in his fields, about 20,000 head of horned cattle, 1,000 horses, several hundred mules, and sheep without limitation. But for the events of the war, this number would have been much increased. The Mexicans visited his ranche with a force of 600 men, and after having been fought for some twelve hours, his ammunition having become exhausted, the colonel was obliged to surrender. His property was then seized, his house plundered of everything it contained, and set fire to. His pastures were then robbed of thousands of his most valuable animals. From this attack, Col. W. lost upwards of $150,000 worth of property.

The Great Thoroughfare

This ranche is on the great thoroughfare over which all must pass who take the overland route from Texas, Santa Fe, or Mexico to California. The consequence is such an influx and efflux of suffering humanity as mortal man has never witnessed out of California. It is the opinion of candid observers that at least 20,000 persons have

5. Isaac Williams (1799–1856), a native of New York, was one of Ewing Young's trappers; he came to California in 1832. He was naturalized in 1839 and married the daughter of a prominent Californian. His father-in-law gave him the Rancho Santa Ana del Chino, in present Riverside County.

Junction of the Gila and Colorado rivers. Looking up the Gila.

passed here within the past twelve months, and the number that pass daily is now much increased. Indeed, I have heard it estimated that there are over 10,000 persons now on the road between the Colorado and the Rio Grande. And then, again, the number of Mexicans that are returning has got to be very numerous.

It may interest many of your city readers to know that the Knickerbocker company, commanded by Captain Ebbetts, which left New York early in February last, have passed here—at least a portion of them. Col. Golding, so well known in New York as a surgical instrument maker, was the first to arrive, and has been stopping with us for a week. The company formed by Major Webb and Mr. Audubon is daily expected. This company left New York the middle of February last.

I can advise no one to take either of the routes that lead by this place to the Placera. It is very good travelling to come from Matamoras to this place in three months, and from Santa Fe in two. Besides, there is

imminent danger of being robbed and murdered on the road. The Indians at the Colorado are in a state of open hostility with all that pass. Two young men, one from Charlestown, Mass., S. Kingsby by name, and another, P. Spalding, of Nashua, N. H., were killed by them a few days since. The company to which they belonged, who were all from Boston and its neighborhood, were also robbed of nearly every thing they had. I enclose a communication which Colonel Williams has sent on to Gov. Riley, which will give you some idea of the state of things here. I can assure you that the statements are not at all exaggerated. Since that was written, one party has arrived who lost twenty-seven mules and much baggage. Another, among whom were several of the Knickerbocker company from New York, lost nineteen mules, $600 in cash, and much baggage— in all, they estimate their loss at $3,500. The condition of some of the emigrants who arrive here is most distressing—on foot, nearly naked, and many of them without an ounce of provisions or a shilling of money. Even when they do not have their baggage stolen, if they lose their animals they are obliged to throw it away, and the road, in consequence, for many miles this side of the Colorado, is strewed with guns, clothes, &c., &c., A few days since, Emanuel Eells, whose father, I am told, is a merchant tailor in Broadway, died from fatigue and exposure upon the desert, and was there buried.

The robberies of the Mexicans, too, continue to be most extensive. According to the report of one party that arrived last night, they saw in one drove fourteen splendid horses and four mules with Col. Williams' brand upon them, and most of the other parties of Mexicans had more or less of Col. W.'s animals with them. Other proprietors of stock suffer equally severely. If Gov. Riley does not respond to this appeal of Col. Williams, there will be warm work at the river before long. There are men here who are determined to take the matter in their own hands. This you may not be surprised at, for independent of the desire for revenge there is large expectations of booty to be obtained, both from the Indians and the Mexicans.

A party that has just arrived via Fort Smith, Santa Fe, &c., report that between Fort Smith on the Arkansas and Santa Fe they passed nearly 300 wagons with emigrants for the diggings; between Santa Fe and the Colorado, at least 160 wagons; and that at the Placera, near Santa Fe, besides pack mules, companies innumerable. These wagons are mostly drawn by oxen. These parties are very generally accompanied by their women and children.

(NYH, Nov. 12, 1849.)

All Bucks Making Money

SAN FRANCISCO, Sept. 27, 1849.

I get my washing done at the Sandwich Islands $4.50 cheaper than here. The way we do it is this: Get all the clothes we can together, take a memorandum of them, and give them to the captain of the schooner, who has them done in fine style by the natives of the islands, and returns with them in less than sixty days. Washing coats, in this way, including everything, $1.50 per dozen, while here they are miserably done at $6 per dozen.

Jim Grant is building a little house, which he intends dedicating to Bacchus. He will not go to the mines. Fallon, who used to be keeper of the city prison, is chief of the police.

F. T.——, once clerk in the post-office, New York, is here a distinguished lawyer.

All bucks making money, and spending it equally fast. The weather is fine, resembling our own; but the heat and cold do not run to that extreme here. The people are doing but little at the mines. The work is too hard. One seldom, if ever, returns to the diggings who has been there once. You are compelled to work awfully hard, and risk sickness, for about $12 per day, which sum is computed to be the general average dug by each individual. Living is beyond conception. You cannot begin to exist here short of $4 per day. Dave and myself pay for a little room in the loft of a store, ten by twelve, without furniture, the sum of $150 per month, or $1,800 per annum. We then pay $1 a meal each at the restaurant. So, you see, one must make money fast to pay these enormous prices.

There must be a smash here in less than six months. Think of a wretched shanty, not two stories high, or as large as a common dwelling-house in New York, bringing $36,000 per annum; and some, a little larger, bringing $50,000, and even as high as $75,000.

The largest fleet of vessels I ever saw is now in the harbor, numbering over 300 sail. They are selling for one-third of their real value. Every day I see chances in this line. Vessels worth $20,000 in the United States go for $5,000. If you can, send me anything in my line—that is, from selling a needle up to a frigate. There is no limit to a man's business here.

Drinking is all the go here. New Orleans is no comparison. The water being very bad, every person deems it necessary to use liquor. (NYH, Nov. 13, 1849.)

From the California Mines

[Communicated for the N. Y. Tribune]
WOOD MINES, about 300 miles from
San Francisco, July 30, 1849.

I am at last in the gold region and will attempt a description of my tedious journey here. We arrived at Stockton after a fair passage, remained there a few days, and then started for this place. In coming here we crossed an arid plain of 32 miles—no navigation, no shade, no water, except what we carried with us, and one of the hottest days I ever experienced; after taking on each of our backs 60 or 70 pounds, and filling a little keg with water, some 15 of us started in company.

The first day we made about 13 miles and then laid down to rest our exhausted frames on the ground, with a single blanket each for covering. The second day we traveled but 5 miles in the morning and 5 or 6 in the evening. This day a man from Massachusetts gave out and could go no further. As he was out of water I let him wet his lips with mine, and some others did the same; but all we could do to revive him proved unavailing. He was determined to die, and we to save our own lives were obliged to leave him as our stock of water was getting very short. We had some 15 miles to travel before we came to the river. I never shall forget the scene of leaving that poor man to die on the barren plain; but that was nothing to what followed.

Death from Thirst

The next day our water was reduced to a few drops. At 11 o'clock the sun was pouring down with unheard-of-intensity, and not a breath of air stirring, when another very fine young man from New Hampshire, when we were within seven or eight miles of the river, wilted right down under the sun and could go no further. I gave the poor fellow a few drops of water, and such a scene as presented itself when we were about to leave him I hope never to witness again. He drew me down to the ground and, kissing me, said, "O! God! can you leave me here to die alone?" I told him to keep up courage, that we would go to the river where there was a tent, and that we would rig up something to carry him on, and would be back as soon as possible, so we bid him good by and started. Before we reached the river I felt myself as if I must surely fail, but I knew if I gave up at all it was to die, and when such thoughts as halting came over me I would arouse as from a sound sleep. I never experienced such feelings. I think death from heat or exhaustion would be an easy one. Before we got to the river two more dropped, but the survivors could do nothing for them, but were obliged to press forward toward the river in order to save their own lives. We at last came in sight of the long-looked for river, and such feelings of joy as we experienced I will not attempt to portray.

After replenishing a little we procured three mules and went back for our friends. I was in hopes to find the one who dropped first alive, but when I arrived and jumped off the mule I found a handkerchief over his face. I raised it; he lay as though asleep with his hands crossed on his breast; but he was quite dead. We put him on a mule; and one of the other two was so weak that he could not sit alone, and so we trudged back to the tent, found an Indian blanket, sewed him up in it and buried him. I staid at the river two days to recruit, than came on to this place. There is one other route to cross this plain where there is water in one place, but we got on the wrong road.

(ISJ, Nov. 14, 1849.)

Ship Susan G. Owens

VALPARAISO, Aug. 16, 1849.

MESSRS. EDITORS:—We have just cast anchor in 40 fathoms at this harborless port, which on shore resembles very much

Gibraltar, but exceeds it very far in beauty. The mountain ridges present continuous parapets of beautiful villas of one story, behind which are seen the broken peaks of the snowy Andes, far more beautiful and picturesque than any thing I have looked upon in Switzerland. With the exception of the winter prospect thus presented, all is green and greatly fertile with cattle upon a thousand hills,[6] and provisions of all kinds plentifully returned to the cultivator. The dewy irrigation takes the place of rain, which has not fallen for six months. We left the Breakwater in company with Meteor and Ralph Cross, the former arrived here the evening before us; the steamer Senator left New York 40 days before us is now coming in.

We had a fine run from Rio to lat. 37° south, when we had a severe gale and continuous bad weather for two weeks, when we took a bold south-easter carrying us to the latitude of the Cape, which we passed in fine weather, with top gallant and studding sails set, (a most extraordinary circumstance) on the 1st of August, at 6 P. M.

The third day on the Pacific we took a hurricane of fearful character. Our noble ship complained nowhere, although the last sail (the maintopsail) was finally furled. I have seen many storms at sea, but never witnessed anything so perfectly *furious*; the seas came in such *extraordinary shapes*. We did not venture upon deck, but from my state-room I saw that no ordinary ship could weather what we were enduring. They came in shape almost perpendicular, at a height not short of 40 feet above me, (the notion that seas never rise over 13 feet not being true.) During the night the storm abated some, and we in the morning made the land on our lee beam, the *Island of Desolation* covered with mountains of alternate rock and icy snow—under a heavy press of canvas making three

miles to leeward to one ahead; we finally left a dangerous lee shore and had, after that, a fine run to this port.

Our hottest day since we left was on the Delaware; our coldest in lat. 48° south, at 31 deg. F. Our shortest day 7 hours, and for myself I had no occasion to and did not put on a coat between Rio and this place, but went round Cape Horn in sleeves enjoying the exercises of the deck among those coated up to suffocation.

It is perfect nonsense, however, to talk lightly of the voyage round Cape Horn. Let no one attempt it not entirely prepared to meet a fearful destiny of suffering, if not of death. We have had a providentially good fortune, but enough to satisfy any man of sense that no ship but of the strongest make can withstand the storms of those latitudes in any season, and that the winter there is the best season, as the easterly winds only then prevail, excepting by tempest occasioned in summer by the meeting of counter temperatures. Many persons here have returned from California hopelessly disappointed; but the people here have no Yankee nerve about them—and surely California is no country for an idle man. From what I see of this country, I can imagine how California, of similar climate, may produce freely without rain. I have a word of advice to give to those emigrating to "our" country.

1st. Pay your own way, and don't give $200 for your passage to one who gets it from the ship for $125, and a share of your earnings beside.

2d. Go in a ship where there are neither ladies or women, unless of your own family, or with their families.

3d. Be sure your captain is not only respectable, but a good navigator. Had ours been anything short of *first-rate* seamanship, we might have been in very different circumstances.

---

6. "Every beast of the forest is mine, and the cattle upon a thousand hills." (*Psalms 50:10.*)

4th. *Go by land,* and not without plenty of means.

Your ob't servant, PAUL K. HOBBS
(PPL, Nov. 14, 1849.)

Houses for California

[*New York Tribune.*]

Messrs. Robbins & Treadwell, of New York, are having built for California 450 or 500 houses of a story and a half in height and 15 by 25 feet; about 120 houses are now in process of construction for Capt. Billings, who is also having 80 others built in Brooklyn—among them is a bowling alley 20 by 70 feet; also two hospitals. There have been shipped for various firms in New York 100 portable section houses, to be carried over the Isthmus on pack-mules; also, 175 houses, of sizes varying from 12 feet by 16 feet, to 90 feet by 65 feet, and from one to 3½ stories in height, for shipment around the Horn. There remain to be sent something over 100 houses, belonging to various parties, among which is a large hotel 3½ stories high, 180 feet front, and 90 feet deep, to be erected at San Francisco, under the name of the Astor House. It will have 100 rooms, 10 stores on the second floor, and a wide ornamental entrance. 120 houses have been constructed for Captain A. Miner, to be shipped to California by the ship Diadem.

Not far from 600 buildings have been sent out since 1848, including nine stores or warehouses for the United States Government; also, a hotel for Livingston & Wells, to be called "The Iron Hotel," which was taken across the Isthmus. An order for 30 or 40 more is being executed for Mr. John Parrott, United States Minister at Mazatlan. The ship Birmingham, which sailed from Bath, Maine, November 2, takes out a cargo of lumber, 21 house-frames, and all the materials for erecting and finishing the same, bricks, shingles, wagons, &c. One house in Cincinnati intends shipping 50 houses to California, properly prepared to be put up immediately on their arrival at California. Wm. H. Ranlett, of Augusta, Georgia, is about to start for San Francisco with 50 dwellings and stores, all complete and ready for setting up and use.

(WNI, Nov. 15, 1849.)

Letter from the Captain of the Osceola

ST. FRANCISCO, BRIG OSCEOLA, Aug. 30, 1849.

MR. D. J. J. E., DEAR SIR:—According to promise, I perform in part what I did, all along, intend should be a full and glowing account of this and the surrounding country, but in reality there is little to write about. You can form a partial idea from the many letters you see published in the different papers, making allowance for homesickness and the want of many a comfort, (which is in general little thought of at home) in this quarter of the globe, and which, however much they may be wanted, are not attainable here.

I conversed with a young man from the mines a short time since; he states distinctly that gold digging is not exactly what it is cracked up to be. He and three others dug and dug, for seven days; their expenses during that time were $110—moderate living at that—salt pork, and beef roasted on a bayonet, which they picked up, their bread was the pure flour and water; and the produce of their labor was five and a half ounces of gold, at $14 per ounce, would be $77. One of them got the shakes, more vulgarly called the ague, another got the cramp, the third got the rheumatism, and the fourth and last got the gold and ran off, and was seen shortly after daylight on the top of Mount Barro, going off to the east, and in the direction of the Great Salt Lake, it was supposed by his late comrades to join the Mormons or Latter-Day Saints.

He was also rigged as an angel, (not of mercy,) for on his right shoulder hung a bag containing the meat of swine, and on the left another bag, containing the flour; both of these articles gave him that angelic appearance that they almost wished they were in company. Still there was a spark of honor attached to his character, for he left them the demijohn of water, without which they would have had to travel seven miles to have got a drink. All three came limping into Stockton, and from thence took ship and landed here, just two weeks ago to-day. One was a graduate from Yale College, the other a Philadelphia lawyer, and the other, a farmer's son, a doctor; three very worthy men, as far as I have seen. Mr. H. was a servant to the others whom they had picked up, and then picked himself off.

Better Off at Home

I have made a grand mistake here, my dear sir. You wanted information about California, and here I am talking about Saints, Lawyers, and Angels. Other parties, I may say, are more fortunate at times, and get one and two ounces a day. Some hit a lucky spot, and do even better than this.

Those who have not been used to it cannot stand the fatigue of bending, digging, and shovelling, and sleeping frequently on the damp ground. Many give it up, come down to this place and go to work until they master up enough to pay their passage back; others return again, thinking to be more fortunate the next time. My candid opinion is that making even a precarious living where you are, at your business, you are a thousand times better off than in this country, where you may say everything is uncertain. The laboring man is well paid for his work, to be sure, but then the mode of living is as yet miserable in the extreme, and they pay twelve and fourteen dollars per week board.

I may also state that a great many, on arriving here, wish themselves immediately back again. This, of course, will always take place in all such enterprises; men are not all of one temperament or character. On arriving here, some of my

The *Osceola* in a gale off Cape Horn.

passengers handed me a slip cut from one of the papers, and headed, "Mutiny on board the Osceola;" and in the different letters that were sent here for them, surprise was expressed that nothing of this had been mentioned to their different families. How could it be, when none of us knew anything of it? The only mutiny that was on board was confined to the bosom of the writer of the letter or letters. Our passage to Rio was 47 days—not 49, as stated by the letter-writer—and during the passage we passed no vessel, with the exception of the Croton. Neither were the steerage passengers always wrangling with the commander of the vessel; on one occasion only one of the steerage passengers made use of language towards myself which was far from being agreeable. To have noticed or checked this tirade at that time might have been attended with serious consequences. That evening, a committee of two waited on me, and stated that the language that had been made use of to-day was not the sentiments of the steerage passengers, and that they were sorry that it had occurred. Next day the offending party called on me and made an apology, which was freely granted, and during the remainder of the passage, (170 days,) I had not a more steadfast or useful friend on board. I have frequently since felt inwardly gratified that I overlooked that momentary ebullition of ill-feeling. I had many good, gentlemanly men in the cabin; on the steerage, however, was my main dependence for aid, especially off Cape Horn, where the weather was most severe. All I had to do was to mention to my friend noticed above that five or six of the passengers were wanting for each watch during the night, and they were immediately on the spot. I have frequently been surprised to observe with what determination they would hold out during the many hard squalls of hail and rain, while taking in and setting sail, and they not having the usual appendage of oil clothes. I may state to you further that all of the passengers were landed in good order and condition; no sickness nor accident to any of them, and all appeared to be perfectly satisfied. There may have been one or two exceptions, and I presume they never were satisfied anywhere. How could I expect it on board the Osceola, where there was so little room, and all jammed up together? My kindest regards to all the brethren.

I remain, dear sir, yours with respect,
JAMES FAIRFOWL.
(PPL, Nov. 19, 1849.)

We Have Arrived

The arrival of emigrants

during the month of October at San Francisco was 4,069, of which 2,665 were Americans, and 1,414 foreigners—79 American and 49 foreign females. The total number of arrivals in August, September, and October was 13,677, generally of a good character.

The subjoined extract from the correspondence of the New York Tribune gives a view of the progress of business and other matters in California:

SAN FRANCISCO, NOVEMBER 1, 1849.

This is a stirring time for California. Since the last steamer sailed the population of the country has been increasing by about 15,000 emigrants, 4,000 of whom arrived at this port by sea. The excitement of politics has been added to that of gold digging and land speculation. San Francisco was something of a whirlpool before, but now it has widened its sweeps and seems to be drawing every thing into its vortex.

The morning after I reached here I went about the town to note the changes and improvements. I could scarcely believe my eyes. The northern point, where the bay pours its waters into the Golden Gate, was covered with houses nearly to the summit, many of them large three-story warehouses. The central and highest hill on which the town is built was shorn of its chaparral and studded with tents and houses; while to the eastward the streets had passed over the last of the three hills, and were beginning to encroach on the Happy Valley. The beautiful crescent of the harbor, sketching from the Rincon to Fort Montgomery, a distance of more than a mile, was lined with boats, tents, and warehouses, and near the latter point several piers jutted into the water. Montgomery street, fronting the bay, had undergone a marvellous change. All the open spaces were built up; the canvas houses replaced by ample three-story buildings; an exchange, with lofty skylight, fronted the water; and for the space of half a mile the throng of men of all classes, characters, and nations, with carts and animals, equalled Wall-street before three o'clock.

In other parts of the town the change was equally great. Tents and canvas-houses had given place to large and handsome edifices, blanks had been filled up, new hotels opened, market houses in operation, and all the characteristics of a great commercial city fairly established. Portsmouth Square was filled with lumber and house frames, and nearly every street in the lower part of the city was blocked up with goods. The change which had been wrought in all parts of the town during the past six weeks seemed little short of magic. At first I had difficulty in believing that what I looked upon was real, so utterly inadequate seemed the visible means for the accomplishment of such wonderful ends.

All Nations Rejoice

On my way to call upon Col. Fremont, whom I found located with his family in Happy Valley, I saw a company of Chinese carpenters putting up the frame of a Canton-made house. In Pacific street another Celestial restaurant has been opened, and every vessel from the Chinese ports brings a fresh importation. An olympic circus, on a very handsome scale, is in full operation, and a company of Ethiopian serenaders amuse the public nightly. "Delmonico's" is the fashionable eating house, where you get boiled eggs at 75 cents each, and dinner at $1.50 to $5, according to your appetite. A little muslin shed rejoices in the title of "Irving House." A number of fine billiard

San Francisco from the head of Clay Street, 1849.

rooms and bowling alleys have been opened, and all other devices for spending money brought into successful operation. The gamblers complain no longer of dull prospects. There are hundreds of monte, roulette, and faro tables, which are crowded nightly until a late hour, and where the most inveterate excesses of gaming may be witnessed.

The rents of houses have increased rather than fallen, since I last wrote. I might give hundreds of instances, but it would be only a repetition of a hundred others already mentioned. Money brings 14 per cent. monthly on loan. Mr. Marye, of Baltimore, who came out in the Panama, has sold a steam engine which cost him $2,000 for $15,000. Some drawing paper, which cost about $10 in New York, brought $164 here. Town lots are continually on the rise, fifty vara lots in the Happy Valley, half a mile from town, bring $2,500.

Growth of the City

I estimate the present population of San Francisco at 15,000. A year ago it was about five hundred. The increase since that time has been made in the face of the greatest disadvantages under which a city ever labored—an uncultivated country, an ungenial climate, exorbitant rates of labor, want of building materials, imperfect civil organization—lacking every thing, in

short, but gold dust and enterprise. The same expense on the Atlantic coast would have established a city of a hundred thousand inhabitants. The price of lumber is still $300 to $400 per M. Five saw-mills at Santa Cruz, belonging to the same owner, rent for $50 each *daily*. All the mills of Oregon are kept going, lumber even there bringing $100 per M. There is no end to the springs of labor and traffic which this vast emigration to California has set in motion, not only on the Pacific coast, but throughout all Polynesia and Australia.

The sickly season on the Sacramento, which was unusually severe and protracted this year, is nearly over. At least one third of the miners have more or less suffered from chills and fever, and large numbers have died.

The sufferings among emigrants on the overland routes increase as the season advances. Major Rucker, acting under the orders of Major Canby, has established posts of supplies at the distance of a day's march apart, across the passes of the Sierra Nevada. The emigrants are still pouring into Sacramento city, many of them in a destitute condition. Gen. Darcy, of Newark, New Jersey, was encamped with his party on the American Fork, himself dangerously ill. A man who recently came in by the same route states that at least 2,000 wagons are scattered along the trail as far as the sink of Humboldt's river. Many of the emigrants will be obliged to winter in the Great Basin. Rumors from the South state that the river which miraculously opened in the Great Desert is again disappearing.

The speculation in town lots has not in the least abated. Sacramento city, with its 7,000 inhabitants, and San Jose, newly made the capital, are next in demand after San Francisco property. Stockton is not far behind; while the towns of Sutterville, Vernon, and Fremont, in the Sacramento Valley, and Towalume and San Joaquin cities to the south, are rapidly springing into importance. Benicia improves slowly, but will never be a rival to San Francisco, and New-York-of-the-Pacific (abominable name!) looks quite lonely with its three houses and mosquito-burdened air.

(WNI, Dec. 10, 1849.)

From California

Extracts of a Letter from a Washingtonian in California to his father in this city, dated 16th September and 31st October, 1849.

CAMP ON ST. MARY'S RIVER, SEPT. 16.

We have arrived within two hundred miles of the Sacramento Valley, and are about to send a party of six men in advance for the purpose of getting letters at San Francisco, and to ascertain where provisions can be had most conveniently.

I wrote you from Fort Laramie; since then we have had some very severe times. We had one terrific hailstorm on the mountains, which had like to have battered us to pieces, and cold enough to freeze us. The storm detained us two days to repair damages and dry provisions.

We crossed the South Pass of the Rocky mountains on the 1st of August, and had ice as thick as a dollar in the morning, and in the middle of the day a scorching sun. It is the most desolate country I have ever seen, nothing but barren mountains and sand plains between, extending forty and fifty miles, and not a drop of water or

blade of grass to be seen. In such cases cattle suffer severely.

After leaving Fort Laramie we passed about thirty dead oxen on an average day for at least a month and a half. We have lost eight mules so far. We met a train of wagons returning to the States: the party are to winter at the Mormon settlements. They left on the 10th of July, gave us very encouraging accounts of the gold regions, and showed us some fine specimens of virgin gold, but evaded all our questions as to how much they had. We had every reason to believe, however, that their wagons had a pretty good store of the precious metal. We are lying by here two days to cut grass to carry us through a desert of fifty miles, and expect to reach the valley in fifteen days.

The disposition to separate into small parties still manifests itself. I have enjoyed very good health considering the rugged trip, and an awful rugged one it is. From my experience I would not advise no person to come to California by this route. Go by water, by all means.

SAN FRANCISCO, OCTOBER 31, 1849.

You will be surprised at the date of this letter. It is thus accounted for: Becoming dissatisfied at the slow and trifling movements of the company, which had only some ten or twelve days' provisions, myself and another, at a meeting of the company, asked for one mule and six days' provisions each, and abandoned all interest in the company. This was granted. We packed the mules with our clothing and provisions, after throwing away considerable clothing, and started on foot. We had besides twenty pounds of flour that we bought on the way. The distance to the mines was thought to be about two or three hundred miles, but turned out not less than five hundred; this caused us nearly to give out. We drove our mules before us from twenty to thirty miles a day at the first start. It took us twenty-two days to get to Feather river, and we had a terrible hard time; our provisions gave out, and we could not buy at any price for a day's march. The next day, however, we came up with a train, which accommodated us with bacon and flour at fifty cents per pound each. We had to buy several times at that price, and sometimes higher. At last my mule gave out. Throwing away some more of my clothing, and packing the rest on my partner's mule, we continued our course towards Feather river, where we arrived on the 20th October.

I soon began to think it was a golden humbug. Thousands were there, two-thirds of them sick. Those who were able to work made from fifty cents to half an ounce per day, and provisions selling very high; flour 50 cents per pound; pickled pork 75 cents; hard bread 75 cents; strong liquor $3 to $4 per pint; a pick and shovel $10 each; a tin pan to wash in $10; a gold washer from $40 to $70.

Shank's Mare

I concluded not to risk my health at that price; so I put my bundle on my back, and started for Sacramento city, (one hundred and twenty miles,) which I made in three days. Pretty good walking, you will say; but I am used to it now, and can out-walk most every thing on the road. There are hundreds walking to and from the mines. I then came to this place, expecting to get letters from you.

The mails have been very irregular. The steamship Panama has just come in this evening, and it is reported that she has three mails on board, but it will be some days before they are assorted. Therefore, as I am going up the river to-morrow, and as the mail closes this evening, I have concluded to send this to let you know of my whereabouts.

All kinds of wages are falling. Carpenters have been getting from $16 to $20 per day; they are now getting from $8 to $12. There is plenty of work, and I think it would be better than gold digging.

(WNI, Dec. 12, 1849.)

Latest from California

[From our regular Correspondent]
WOOD'S DRY DIGGINS, CALIFORNIA,
Sept. 29, 1849.

J. W. GRAY, Esq.:—After a most protracted silence, I have summoned strength to attempt to give you some account of California, obtained from personal knowledge, which, though scanty, you may depend upon as authentic. I should not have thus suffered my correspondence to flag, but Providence has seen fit to inflict me with a sickness, which has lasted since the 4th day of July. My sickness was a bilious fever, the elements of which were gathered in Panama, and for some twenty days all recollections vanished from my mind. That period forms but a *mackled* page in my existence; by the unremitting attention of my friends, however, my life was saved, and the living wreck is now out of danger.

No man can imagine the horrors of a passage from Panama to San Francisco by a sail vessel, especially at the period I came. The tonnage and accommodations of vessels were misrepresented, and the victuals and abuse bestowed upon passengers were such as we would not inflict upon our dumb animals. Our vessel, the "Copiapo," was advertised by Mr. Nelson, the then Consul of Panama, as a ship of 220 tons, and was sold to a Manchester (N. H.) Company for $20,500. She was represented as loaded with provisions of the best kind, and it was said she would be better provisioned than any craft that has left or would leave the harbor. John B. Clark, *Esq.*, the manager for this Company, a bigger rascal than ought to fill such a situation, received us at the moderate sum of $190 each. He told us they were to receive but 120 passengers, and praised largely the superior arrangements on board. The facts, however, were quite different. On going on board, we found a small vessel of 170 tons or less, on which were crowded 178 people, and baggage and freight piled higher than the bulwark, and all full below. From the temporary floor erected in the hold to the deck above was just five feet and three inches. In this space was erected the tiers of double berths, and in front of all those it was expected hammocks would be hung, and all this in a climate where the thermometer was never less than 90 deg. After three days of negotiations, we succeeded in removing twenty-five people, and sailed on the night of May 11. Our whole passage, a period of 95 days, was the most unpleasant imaginable, and all were glad when it terminated. Our food was all of the most wretched character, and full of worms, and for thirteen days we were on a very short allowance of this. They were obliged to put into Monterey for water, wood, and provisions, where we remained six days; but as I was confined below, I did not see the town, so I am unable to give any description of it. I only mention our wretched passage because it is, as near as I can learn, what nearly all who come by sail have to undergo, and to warn all your readers, who think of coming to California, from falling into a similar trap.

From Dark to Light

On Tuesday, August 14, the *Copiapo* dropped her anchor in the Bay of San Francisco. This darkest page in the history of our lives was finished, and all were happy. A new and glittering leaf was about to be turned, which would disclose its unknown richness to the vision. All were anxious—none were doubting; but subsequent events have changed every mind. I remained on board the vessel until Friday, the day we sailed for Sacramento City, and was then on shore only for a short time. My walk through the streets was with the assistance of two friends, and I have a recollection of being stared at as one who had taken too much strong drink.

The afternoons are very cold, the wind blowing strongly off land, and cold as our March winds. The town is located at the foot of high sand hills, and is completely enveloped in dust; and although money

A crowded vessel.

may be made here, it is the last place I should want to live. The business part of the city is crowded about equal to Wall street, and everywhere heaps of merchandize are piled wherever there is room. Most of the places of business are slight frames covered with cloth, which in the States would soon bear the knife cuts of the thief, but here are never or very rarely disturbed. During the rainy season, which comes on in December, such tenements must be replaced by something more substantial, or a ruinous loss of merchandize will be the consequences. The harbor, crowded with over two hundred sail of vessels, all riding at their anchor and most of them wearing the stripes and stars, looked novel and interesting, as we sailed away.

We left San Francisco on Friday afternoon, and arrived at Sacramento City on the following Monday morning. I had but a single view of the shores of the bay; they were very high and everywhere covered with a heavy growth of wild oats, on which it is said extensive herds of cattle luxuriate. While passing through the delta formed by the Sacramento and San Joaquin, (pronounced here *Waukien*) river, we were nearly eaten up by myriads of most savage mosquitoes. The cabin literally swarmed with them, and I was driven to the deck, where for two nights a constant fight was kept up, and I got little or no sleep. There was one *rancho* on the river, at which we lay waiting for the tide. Some of the passengers bought water and muskmelons at from $1 to three dollars each, and a few beets, onions, and potatoes were purchased by the vessel at the same high rates. The shores of the river are low, inundated, it is said, at high water, and cannot form eligible sites for a settlement. But I am spinning out a dull letter to an immoderate length, *Adios,* DEACON.

(CPD, December 13, 1849.)

Letter from San Francisco

Among the Mountains in the Gold Diggings, 260 miles from San Francisco, at Towalumares, Oct. 18th

We have arrived here from Stockton, having in all about 50 pack mules and 50 or 60 persons on foot. We went down to a place where no one thought of looking for gold. It was among the rocks, and had all been worked over. I said to Mr. P., "I am going to raise that rock," pointing to it. Said he to me, "I don't think you can do it." "Well," I said, "I'll do nothing else for I think I smell gold there." I left him, walked up the hill and borrowed an axe up the mountain. I went in search of a tree to make a lever. I cut down a white oak about five inches in diameter, cut it up some eight or ten feet long, went to the rock and fixed my pry, as we used to call it at the saw-mill, under the edge of the rock. I put my weight on it a little. "There," says P., "you shake it." I said, "I'll shake it worse than that when I get the air under it." Sure enough, I did turn it over; it weighed about a half ton. We went to work, and took that day four ounces of gold, which paid for our rocker twice over the first day. "Well," says P., "you are one of the b'hoys."

The next day we took out three ounces more; that made seven ounces under that one, and if it had not been for the water we could have got more. I tried some other rocks near by, and took out in six days 23 ounces of gold, which in Philadelphia will be worth more than $20 the ounce. The gold on this river is said to be worth $2 the ounce more than any that is found in California. It is very fine; the largest lump I found was fifty cents worth. I tried to keep persons from seeing me get it; they would come sneaking around, saying, "I guess you've got a pretty rich spot." "Not very hard work," I said; "I think I shall get two or three dollars to-day." P. would say to me, "I expected you would certainly see gold to-day." Not very much. That day we got out over five ounces. Thus far I beat any of the new beginners, and P. said to me, "You understand it." "Yes," I said, "I have quarried stone, but never quarried gold before." No one ever thought of raising the rocks until they saw me.

A Hard Life

If I keep my health and strength, there is gold in California for me. It is hard work. How it made my back-ache when I only got an ounce a day; but when one gets three or four ounces a day he don't feel any back-ache. Gold is here beyond a doubt; but to look for it you would think there was none. There was one poor fellow who came out in the same steamer that we did, came also to this place. When he saw what gold digging was, he sit down and cried. He has left; with many others that never take hold of the shovel and pick, they expect they can pick it up like gathering walnuts, but they are very much mistaken. It is hard work, hard fare, hard sleeping, and a hard road to travel to get at the gold. There is a company of one hundred engaged in digging a canal, six hundred feet long, in order to turn the channel of the river. We have been at it a little over a week. It will be completed to-morrow. I suppose we have near a pound out. We shall drain the river about a quarter of a mile. There will be digging for us all for at least six weeks, it is thought. In every instance where this has been done, it has always paid well. There were a party of thirteen that made a dam and turned the river only about thirty feet, which took about twelve days, and the first day's digging they got ten pounds. The rich deposit of gold is in the bed of the river. There was one yesterday who had dammed a small hole alongside of the river where we are now draining.

He hired four or five men to bail out the water for him, and he took out a little over 16 ounces in about a space, so one of the men told me, of not more than 20 inches square. The men that helped him he paid $10 a day, and out of that very hole there has at least been taken out some

three or four thousand dollars. There have been many instances, under my own eye, of over a pound taken in less than half a day. There are some very rich spots in the bed of the river. A miner told me to-day that he thought we would take at least fifty pounds out of one hole that he pointed out to me. I hope so.

There is one thing—if I had all the gold that will be taken out of where we are draining, I would have enough; I would soon start for the States. It will have to be divided amongst one hundred men. It could not be done unless many joined together. There are many that wish to join us, but we will not consent; and some want to buy others out. Very few have any desire to sell. One man told me he would not take ten thousand dollars for his chance. I would. I have no idea of making anything like that; if I get one thousand, I would be well paid. There are not less than ten or fifteen thousand dollars taken out daily on this river alone. I don't believe there is a mountain stream but what gold can be found on it, and it is the hardest kind of labor to obtain it, although some have made a fortune in a very short time. If every grain of gold could, in the space of one mile up and down the river, be got out, I believe there would be from one to two millions of dollars; the very rocks have it in them.

I am afraid, by giving you such a golden description, that others will be tempted to come out to California to gold digging. For my part, I will never persuade any of my friends to come. They have no idea what they have to go through. So far, I have never regretted coming to California. If I have my health and strength, I can make more than I could at home. I could send home 25 ounces of gold dust, if I were at San Francisco; but in the first place, it would not do to leave the diggings at this time; it is the best season to dig; the river is getting lower every day; and, in the second place, it would take me two weeks to go and come, and cost me about sixty dollars.

In a month from this time, if I have any luck, and I could find any person I could trust, I would send down, but not without. You must not be discouraged if none comes this winter. It will come, I hope, if I have my health.   D. T. J.

(PPL, Dec. 12, 1849.)

Sufferings in California

The suffering experienced by emigrants in going over the land route to California, though frequently alluded to, is not realized except in such pictures as are presented by actual eye witnesses. At one point of the road, a woman with two children were found feeding themselves upon the bark of a tree. They were not able to move on. The woman's husband had died, and she was not able to get any farther, and their provisions had been exhausted for some days. A physician in San Francisco, who crossed overland, says that he had been threatened with the severest treatment on account of having recommended the delay of the wagons for a few hours to relieve the very sick ones, who were almost dying with fatigue. A correspondent of the New York Courier saw an old gentleman driving an ox team into the city the other day, and I thought from the man's actions that he must be either crazy or under a great pressure from exhilaration. I asked him if he came across the plains. "Oh, yes, yes; I've got here—I've got here, and I wish I could express my gratitude, my delight." He would have said more, but his chest began to heave and tears began running down his dusty face, whilst with perfect intoxication he ran from one yoke of the poor oxen to another, applying the whip as though he were not safely out of the difficulties until he had reached the very spot where his wagon was to stop.   (PPL, Dec. 13, 1849.)

The California Emigration

Since the breaking out of the California fever, less than a year, seven hundred and thirty vessels have left the Atlantic ports for that country, by way of Cape Horn, containing fifty thousand persons as passengers. There have arrived, at as late as intelligence has been received, two hundred and sixty-five of the above number.

(PPL, Dec. 14, 1849.)

Without the Romance

The writer of the following letter, in the Boston Transcript, does not furnish a very alluring picture of the pleasures of the overland journey, or the profits of the gold diggers:

"All is not gold that glitters. Since I left Boston I have travelled seven hundred miles on foot without shoes—have crossed deserts, where we were ten days without water, and three without food. It took us fifty-seven days to travel fifteen hundred miles. Many have come out here expecting to get rich in a few days, and are now working for dear life to get enough to return home with, which is the height of their ambition.

"You want me to advise you about coming out here. My advice is, when a man is doing well enough, to let well enough alone. If you are determined to come, do not go through Mexico or Lower California. First try an experiment as follows: take a blanket and go to the top of the highest hill when the wind blows fresh; take a stone for your pillow, and pebbles for feathers; sleep here a few nights; then go, when it rains, where the ground is wet, and the weather cold. When you get used to this, try flour and water and jerked beef for food, *once a day*; then go without either until you get so hungry that you can eat mouldy bread and say that it is good. When you get used to this, work in the water up to your middle, and say gold will compensate you for it. If you can endure all this, I advise you to come—but not till then."

(WNI, Dec. 18, 1849.)

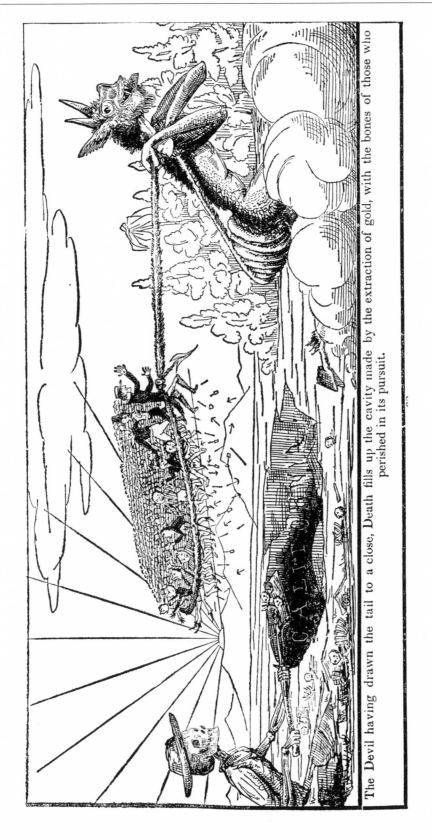

The Devil having drawn the tail to a close, Death fills up the cavity made by the extraction of gold, with the bones of those who perished in its pursuit.

The Golden Shore

Life in San Francisco

CORRESPONDENCE OF THE
NEW YORK EVENING POST
SAN FRANCISCO, NOVEMBER 15, 1849.

The people of San Francisco are mad, stark mad. In Bedlam you may have seen, perchance, an occasional madman—there are hundreds such in California—out at elbows, strutting with a lordly step, with head erect, and eyes staring wildly about, proclaiming himself, in his happy delusion, the lord and proprietor of untold wealth. He will tell you, with an air of happy contentment, as you look sadly upon the long dismal wards filled with madmen, grinning, raging, moaning, the great thick walls, the barred door, and the grated window, that he is the fortunate possessor of all you see, of the whole structure, which appears to his diseased fancy a palace, but which you know, as the keeper turns the lock and the iron bar upon him, is but a prison house for the mad.

A dozen times or more, during the last few weeks, I have been taken by the arm by some of the *millionaires*—so they call themselves, I call them madmen—of San Francisco, looking wondrously dirty and out at elbows for men of such magnificent pretensions. They have dragged me about, through the mud and filth almost up to my middle, from one pine box to another, called mansion, hotel, bank, or store, as it may please the imagination, and have told me with a sincerity that would have done credit to the Bedlamite, that these splendid (they had all the admiration and fine adjectives to themselves) structures were theirs, and that they, the fortunate proprietors were worth from two to three hundred thousand dollars each. Such wealth and such millionaires have existed before, as we read in the history of Law's Mississippi scheme, the South Sea bubble, and other bubbles.

There is a great deal of wild excitement, as you might suppose, engendered by the present state of things in San Francisco; there were no less than four suicides this last week. There is misery, too, and misery that is fully realized, for there is no illusion about sickness and staring want. There are no less than fifty paupers at this moment supported by the town of San Francisco, at an expense of five dollars each a day. There is comedy, too, as well as tragedy, in San Francisco; some odd contrasts and droll inconsistencies. Purple and fine linen are not the clothing of the rich here; and Dives has come to the level of Lazarus.[1]

Fortune Gone Awry

Society here is in a strangely dislocated state; all its members are out of place. Dame Fortune has chosen her favorites contrary to the usual laws of prudence. The scrub horse has gone in for the cup and won. The tail is where the head ought to be. Poverty is certainly the respectable thing in California. There is a Delmonico's restaurant in San Francisco, where, in the absence of the French cutlets and chateau margaux of the original, you may be sure of getting, at all seasons, the rare luxury of being waited upon by a score or more of gentlemen belonging to the learned profession or other genteel walks of life. You can

---

1. The parable of the rich man and the beggar. (*Luke 16:19–31.*)

see there respectable middle-aged, bald-headed gentlemen, just such as in New York on a Sunday pass up and down the middle aisles with a silver plate, collecting the offerings of the benevolent—vestry men, deacons, and such like, whose duty it is to collect alms—you can see just such passing up and down among the tables, waiting and tending upon the customers as common waiters.

It is rumored that, at the present time, there is in San Francisco a judge from Oregon, now waiter at Delmonico's; a professor of Yale College driving an ox team, and a Methodist parson tending a bar, and that the latter numbers more than one temperance lecturer among his regular customers. The ideas of the young children—for there are a few such here—must be strangely exalted in regard to money. I saw a group of them the other day about a fruit and candy stall in the chief square, the youngest of whom, a child of some three years old, grasped a big silver dollar in his hand—it would have been a penny in New York. There are some few cool-headed men in possession of capital, who, availing themselves of the fluctuations in prices, will succeed in making money; but, believe me, the present prosperity of San Francisco is apparent, not real, and that most here will be ruined.

From Dust to Mud

The daily deluges of rain remind us that the rainy season has set in, and as there is not a house in the whole town that does not leak, and since many people are houseless, and since the dust of summer has become the mud of winter, and the whole site of the town has been turned into a slough of half liquid mud, into which

you penetrate at every step to the height of your knees, it is likely that the inhabitants of San Francisco will become, as Mantalini threatened to make himself, "demnition cold moir bodies," and remain so till the return of summer.[2] Men go about plunging into the mud and puddles, for there are no pavements, and it is useless labor to attempt to pick their way, with their legs encased in enormous boots, like Prince Albert's, about which Punch has let off so many jokes. Boots and heavy brogans, as you will see by the price current, have risen into very considerable commercial importance, and are quoted at enormously high prices, and with an upward tendency—as the merchants say.

There is quite a range of buildings fronting the town, which are now, since the commencement of the rain, only connected with the main lands by means of narrow wooden bridges, and which bid fair, before the winter is over, to declare their independence, and establish a town of their own on the opposite side of the bay. A strong southeasterly gale has been blowing for some days, stirring up the harbor, causing the ships to drag their anchors and bring them together to their manifest disadvantage. All communication between ship and shore was cut off for several days in consequence of the storm, a frequent occurrence at this season, it is said.

Progress of the Town

There is a dock, called the Central wharf, a brick house or two, a nightly performance of some circus riders, new hotels, and new pine houses rising by the dozen, every day or so, and other evidences of development. There is the steamboat Senator, too, that reminds one of the North

---

2. The letter writer generally recalls the speech of Alfred Mantalini, "an idle profligate," who could not express himself without the incessant use of "demnition," "demmit," "demnebly," and "demd." Mantalini threatened to drown himself because his wife was going to reduce his allowance. "She calls me cruel—me—me—who for her sake will become a demd, damp, moist, unpleasant body!" exclaimed Mr. Mantalini. (Dickens, *Nicholas Nickleby*, II, 14.)

river, plying daily between San Francisco and Sacramento city! The town of San Francisco has certainly made much progress during the last two months, partly from the necessity of things, and partly under the stimulus of artificial prosperity.

There must be nearly two thousand houses, besides tents, which are still spread in numbers, giving the outskirts of the town the appearance of a military encampment. And what do you suppose to be the rental, the yearly value of this card-house city? No less, it is said, than twelve millions of dollars, and this with a population of about twelve thousand. New York, with its five hundred thousand inhabitants, does not give a rental of much more than this, if as much.

The rainy season is floating the population of the mines and of the interior towns into San Francisco. Stockton and Sacramento, (on the site of the latter, Gen. Vallejo told me he had frequently sailed in a boat,) as they are situated on sloughs generally overflown in the rainy season, and as man is not an amphibious animal, must of course be deserted by their inhabitants during the winter.

There are some forebodings of famine; there is in truth reason to fear that many of them in the mines, and the immigrants by land, may die of hunger, as all communication will probably be cut off between them and the towns where supplies are alone to be had.

All Are Gamblers

I have seen some of the miners, who have told me that it was with the utmost difficulty that they succeeded in reaching the river towns, as this is the beginning of the rainy season, such was the state of the rivers and the passes. Provisions, too, are said to be very scarce even in San Francisco; the prices of them are certainly very high. Pork sells at sixty-five dollars a barrel, and flour at forty, though it is doubtful how far these prices are owing to scarcity or to the juggling of the speculators. The loaf of bread, about the size of a breakfast roll, which was selling at twenty-five cents, rose in price in a single day to fifty cents, and beef from one shilling to two shillings. This looks as if the speculators had been at their tricks. The fact is, the whole town is converted into one mighty gambling hell; it is not only the card dealer, who is shuffling cards at the faro and monte tables, but the merchant and land speculator as well, that prey upon the community; they are gamblers all.

There is necessarily a great demand on the part of the newly-arrived immigrants for shelter for themselves and property. The dealers in houses and land, buying their wood and building their crazy wooden tenements by means of money borrowed at the rate of *ten per cent. a month*, avail themselves of the necessities of the newly-arrived, and demand enormous rents, from five hundred to five thousand dollars per month. These speculators calculate upon realizing fortunes in the space of a few months; and as they pay enormous rates of interest for borrowed money, they raise the rents accordingly. There are no permanent resources in the country sufficient to justify this state of things. The immigrants who come with more or less property, and the mines, are the principal sources of wealth; the former are squandering their means in store rent, house rent, and expenses of subsistence, and the yield of the latter has been very much overrated.

It is difficult to get any very correct statements in regard to the gold mines. I am told that there is plenty of gold there, but I know that the obstacles in getting it are so great that most are deterred, after a first attempt, from continuing their search. There are, indeed, some lucky diggers; I know one man who has dug himself twenty thousand dollars in value, of gold dust, in the course of six months; but he tells me that most about him were not paying their daily expenses. It is a lottery, where the prizes were few and the blanks many. When the average is spoken of as ten dollars a day, the fair expression of the fact would be, that one in a hundred makes his thousand dollars, while the ninety and nine make nothing at all. They are beginning to use more scientific means for gathering the gold; during the last month or so, the process by amalgamation with mercury has been very extensively employed, and quicksilver has been in consequence in great demand, and has brought in the market five and six dollars a pound.

From the Ends of the Earth

San Francisco is a rendezvous for people of all nations—the Chinese, Lascars, Sandwich Islanders, and others from all parts of the known world. There is a Chinese restaurant, where you can take your cup of souchong, outside barbarians though you may be, served by a veritable compatriot of the great Confucius and worshipper of Josh,[3] in flaming trousers, and illimitable pig-tail. You may have your linen done up for eight dollars a dozen by a woman from the Sandwich Islands, possibly a first cousin of Queen Pomaré. The bullock from which your beefsteak is cut is brought in from the interior by a true Spanish cavalier, as melodramatic, and with as fine brigand air and look as Fra Diavolo in the play,[4] and who is, doubtless, a lineal descendant of the great Cortes; and you may have, it is said, your pocket picked by a genuine "Sidney bird," fresh from New Holland.[5]

The commercial relations of San Francisco with foreign countries are certainly very extensive. Apart from the first arrivals from all parts of the world, attracted by the discovery of gold, there are vessels passing between San Francisco and the commercial ports on the American continent, the Sandwich Islands, Oregon, and Vancouver's Island, China, New Holland, and the East Indies.   (WNI, Jan. 2, 1850.)

From San Francisco

Arrival of the Meteor—Fees of the U. S. Consul at Rio de Janeiro—San Francisco by Daylight—Mud—Gambling—Gold— Advice to Gold Seekers—Prices—Natives Productions of California

San Francisco, California, Nov. 25, 1849.

Messrs. Editors—No doubt you wonder what has become of me since I last wrote you from Rio de Janeiro, but the truth is that when I arrived at Valparaiso I found that in order to secure the safe transmission of a letter to the United States, I should have to pay the U. S. Consul one dollar per sheet, in addition to the postage of 40 cents per single letter, which I thought an imposition. By what authority such a tariff or tax has to be paid I know not, nor do I believe it legal, and therefore forbore writing until I should arrive here and get a little settled. This, I hope, will be excuse enough for not writing sooner. I only saw to-day, by accident, a copy of your paper of August 24th, containing my last. I wish you would be kind enough to put me on your list of mailers to this port, as a paper from home is greatly prized here, your paper costing a cent at home, fetching readily *one dollar* here.

I left Rio on the 5th of July on board the "Meteor," and after a pleasant and quick passage to Valparaiso, arrived there on the

---

3. The writer has mistakenly substituted a diminutive name for the pidgin English 'joss,' a Chinese household idol or god.
4. Fra Diavolo (1771–1806) was the popular name of an infamous Italian brigand and military irregular. The name gained worldwide notoriety as the title of an 1830 opera by the French composer Auber.
5. Usually "Sydney Ducks" or "Sydney coves": English convicts who had been allowed to leave the penal colony in New South Wales (Australia).

13th of August, making our time from the Breakwater 93 days, including stoppages, and only 81 days sailing time, being far better than any vessel excepting the "Grey Eagle," which was about the same time, but then we lost ground in going into Rio, whilst she went straight on, so that I reckon we even beat her. At Valparaiso I left the "Meteor," as I understood she would probably proceed no further towards this port, and joined the bark "Montgomery," Captain A. G. Jones, of New Orleans. I was too short a time at this port (Valparaiso) to see much, and therefore only state that there were in the port a number of vessels bound to California, probably some 200 vessels, whose names I did not learn.

A Neophyte in the City

On the 21st of August we sailed, and arrived here on the 21st October, and now begins my description of California. On Monday morning, October 22d, I landed in San Francisco for the first time in my life. I took a hasty stroll through the city, if city it can be called, that boasted of two or three brick and about 30 or 40 frame and *adobe* houses, 160 or 200 *canvas* ditto, and the balance tents, ships' cabooses, and various other temporary contrivances, to see as much as I could.

The city of San Francisco is *built* upon rising ground, retreating back from one of the prettiest harbors in the world, situated about five miles southeast of the entrance of the Bay of San Francisco. This cove or harbor has been heretofore known as *Yerba Buena*. The prospect of this scene is considerably heightened by an island nearly opposite the harbor of the same name; the eastern shore of the Bay, distant from twelve to fifteen miles, making the back ground, the shipping the foreground, and the Bay of San Francisco forming to the north and south as far as you can see.

As to the number of ships in port, I can only approximate; they extend almost as thick as the shipping in New York, for

about two miles. This, I should imagine, would make the amount, at a rough guess, about 400 to 500. But this does not include the men-of-war and various other vessels, laying about seven miles north of this place, at another harbor on the Bay, called Sausalita, (pronounced *Sou-sal-ee-ta*,) nor sundry craft plying up the rivers which occasionally are here. These ships are composed of all nations—principally, however, American, English, Hamburgh, Russian, Chilian, and French. Upon landing, if at this season you might fancy that you had mistaken and landed *in* the harbor at low water—the mud is actually *knee-deep*. You may talk and burlesque New York for her mud, but New York is *clean* in comparison to San Francisco. The next thing that attracts your attention is every one busy; no idlers to be seen in the streets—and perhaps you meet a "Chestnut street" buck, shovel in hand, digging a cellar, up to his knees in the rich, tough clay; or you see a fashionable young man driving a team of mules, with as much *sang froid* as he used formerly to lounge along Broadway.

No Man an Idler

You enter a hotel and you are surprised to see gambling carried on to an unprecedented extent in the open barroom, and are still more astonished to learn that it is licensed by the authorities. You stroll up to the bar for a drink and a cigar, and suddenly find yourself mulcted in the sum of 37½ cents. You next wish dinner, and order what you conceive a decent moderate dinner, and have to pay (for such a dinner as would cost at a respectable hotel in Philadelphia, one dollar,) the small sum of five dollars. Disgusted, you determine to seek boarding, and discover that board is from $20 to $35 per week. In a few days you discover that you cannot lay idle here, you naturally desire to enter the business you have been used to, but after a fruitless search you are compelled to take up with such employment as you can obtain. In short, you find that although there is plenty of work, you cannot choose your employment. Here doctors may be seen driving teams; shoe-makers upon the roofs of houses painting or tarring them to render them water-proof; tailors, paper-hanging, and watchmakers working at the blacksmith's forge. Enough is to be seen here in one short hour, that would startle the castle-building youth who dreams that California is the place to pick up gold by the pound, merely by stooping down for it. Alas! the reality is as every where else, gold is not to be had except with the greatest and most toilsome labor imaginable. Even in the mines, although lumps are occasionally found varying from a penny weight to an indefinite number of pounds, yet the exertion to get it is so great that very few succeed.

Therefore, let no one come out here unless he has made up his mind to undergo privations of hunger and excessive toil, for without this resolution he cannot possibly succeed in California. Neither let him come out here unless he comes with as little baggage as possible, but not forgetting to have a few hundred dollars in his pocket after he arrives. Letters of recommendation are useless here; the best recommendation is never to refuse a job of work, no matter what it is. Let his personal baggage be composed of good, warm, and strong rough clothes. Cowhides or strong gum elastic boots, a water proof dress, a good tent, a good rifle and shot gun—if you please, no pistols, knives, gold washers, or the thousand other *etceteras* most emigrants bring. A few barrels of flour, hard bread, beef, pork, and beans may be advantageous, but not absolutely necessary to him. Let him come by the Isthmus, as, after all, it is not only the *quickest* but the *best* route he can come. If I were coming again I would come *no other* way, and out of all that I have conversed with, who have come round the Horn, overland, or through Mexico by other routes, I have *not* found one who *coincides* with me.

The next advice I have to give to emi-

grants is, when they arrive they must be particularly careful in their method of living; if not, they may be sure to get the diseases of the country, Dysentery and Ague. I do not mean that they *will* not catch them if they are careful, but simply that their chances of escaping their effects is considerably lessened. Drunkenness and careless exposure is almost certain to carry them off. Also, the free use of water, (which, by-the-by, is very bad and strongly impregnated with some mineral,) or fresh beef is very apt to give fresh comers dysentery, especially as vegetables are very scarce.

Riches Greater Than Gold

Of the native productions of California, there are two species of the potato that I have noticed; wild currants; gooseberries; sweet acorns, (nearly equal to chestnuts;) dewberries; strawberries, and a red berry, said to be eaten by the natives, growing in bunches; several kinds of oak; cypress; red wood, similar to our cedar, but heavier and always splitting straight, making beautiful timber; several species of pines, some of which the seeds are edible, and are equal to the finest shellbarks; hazel; gold; silver; iron; granite; limestone; copper; quicksilver; platina; diamonds; rubies; emeralds; excellent sea-fish; salmon of an enormous size, some as large as five and six feet long; ducks; geese; brant teal; curlew snipe; California quail; elk; deer; antelope; wild cattle; grizzly bear; California lion, a species of the panther; cayota; sea otter; and wild goats.

I now come to what many, no doubt, are itching to see—an account of the gold. If I were to say that there was gold, I would be giving but a faint statement of the truth. There is not only gold, but enough of it for *all*, for many years to come, who can stand the labor necessary to procure it. Few, very few, make large fortunes, owing to their want of energy, prodigality, want of foresight, and numberless other causes, disease among the rest in the category; yet, some do amass large fortunes. Many, after amassing enough to make themselves comfortable for the rest of their lives, gamble it all away, and begin again; this is perhaps done several times by the same individual, before he ultimately grows wise enough to return with a small amount. Foreigners, generally, are less liable to lose their all than Americans. It is astonishing to see with what *nonchalance* men who would, in the States, have hardly risked a dollar at any game of chance, gamble away thousands. As an instance, a gentleman lost in *one bet*, last night, the large sum of $56,000 as coolly as if he were only losing fifty cents. This occurred at the City Hotel, one of the most fashionable houses here. Neither does the evil stop here; men, who in the States never drank, are here irreclaimable *drunkards*. This is no fiction—it is too true.

Our population in the State of Alta California is rising 100,000 souls, and in San Francisco something upwards of 36,000, or more than one third of the entire population of the State.

On the 23d of October two brothers named John and Peter Black were executed, one on board the sloop-of-war St. Mary, and the other on board the schooner Ewing, for desertion and mutiny under aggravated circumstances. There were three other men sentenced to be hung at the same time, but who had their sentences commuted to 100 lashes each, for the same offence.

To-day, (Nov. 28) it is reported in town that a courier has arrived bringing the intelligence of the loss of the mail steamer "Oregon," on Cape Conception, and a number of passengers, said to be upwards of one hundred, drowned. I hope this may prove false, although she is now due 13 days.[6]

It is melancholy to go through the different burying grounds and see the numbers who have come out here and died. . . .

The rainy season has begun this year unusually soon, and will cause great suffering in the mines for want of provisions, as it is impossible to transport any thing after that occurs. The miners, such as are able, are hurrying down, and many disgusted with the country are returning to the United States. You must not put too much reliance in their reports of the country, as for the most part they have come out with too extravagant ideas of it, like many others, although no doubt there is much sickness here. As for my part I am not tired of the country, nor will I return until I give it a fair trial.

I am, Messrs. Editors, yours, truly,
THOMAS R. STODDART.
(PPL, Jan. 15, 1850.)

Description of San Francisco

SAN FRANCISCO, Nov. 30th, 1849.

MESSRS. EDITORS OF LEDGER:—Imagine yourself coming in from the broad Pacific through a strait of three to four miles by one, walled by mountains on either side, the right or south being low ranges, till you come to a bluff upon which lie some four or six cannon, giving the character and name of "fort." Then opens to your view to the right and left the long string of water of the Bay, with one or two islands and some desolate rock before you, and a shore verdant as woodless bounds the view of the waters, save the bush top hills back of the city. Then you descry tents, shanties, and about 2,500 frames of small and large

---

6. This news was indeed false.

houses, covered with carpenters, working them into fitness for occupation, ringing your ears with the rattle of the hammer. These extend in slopes by straight streets from the hill top, with intervening gorges, down to the Bay shore, where you find some 150 lighters, mostly busy between the shipping lying off in deep water and the beach, into which project long wharves from several points, as at Boston. *Landing at this season* (1st December) you find yourself in the midst of thousands of casks, bags, machinery, merchandise of value and of no value, strewed on the ends of the streets at the water line, some buried for months in mud; sugar washing away with rains; cartmen bawling, screaming, swearing, and slashing their poor horses, mules, and oxen, up to their bellies in mud, and splurging to haul about 3 cwt. up the street at an expense of six dollars the load to the owner or merchant.

Having landed with a jump from your boat, you proceed, climbing over casks, rails, &c., to keep yourself from wetting the bottom of your pants up to the waistcoat, by splurges through mud, and passing store after store, at all of which you find the same noise, jam, and bustle as I have described on the "wharf" all in great good humor—even ale and brandies in dozens, laying before the stores exposed in all ways night and day, and never touched; (people *can* live here without stealing.) Music, music, music; the rattle of the roulette, the monte, the faro bank, &c., salute you about twice in each square; jamming into restaurants, butchers' stalls, vegetable stores, and red flags before some going, going, gone auctioneer, who sells a cargo in just about three shakes of a sheep's tail, (at least *Wm. H. Jones* does.) Bang you go over an upset cart left in the mud, and patter, patter, patter runs the rain into some half covered warehouse of China silks, till you arrive at your hotel. These are the 'ventures from the ship. There you get into another; a room 8 by 4 to lodge in, at $1.25 per night, on shaving mattresses, one blanket, and sometimes a cotton sheet, sometimes not, but always with *lots of fleas.*

In the midst of this confusion and dirt, the most energetic measures of remedy are adopted, and in a very short time the streets will be planked at the side-walks, and drained and planked in the centres, at an expense of probably $250,000 to the Corporation, maybe a million. They have sold lots in two days belonging to the city to the extent of the latter sum, for purposes of improvement.

Property is as sacred from theft here as in true Turkey—the *quarrels*, however, between captains and passengers and sailors and landlords and landowners are immense, and lawyers are reaping a tremendous harvest, as $100 is the very lowest fee I have known taken, and thousands are given where we would give hundreds in the north.

Pleasure carriages are lying all round for sale, "cheap," with few buyers, as merchants, lawyers, &c. pay enough expense and have enough bother without bringing water and currying down a pair of mules or horses. Lots of horseback riding, mule riding, &c., and, my stars! I *did* see three milkmen, with cans, riding on horseback this week—one dollar the bottle.

Lots of farms can be had at $5 to $100 per acre, all very productive, and many are just going into this—the best sort of gold digging. One man I know made $15,000 this year off of three acres. Nearly every hardy vegetable produces *two crops* to three per annum, and now the weather here is about as the 1st of May, the rains being always from the southeast and warm, and the intervening clear days are beautiful indeed, whilst the summer gives hot mid-days and very cold nights. This town is rapidly concentrating all the commerce of the Pacific Ocean and of the great East and West combined.

Finally, California is in all respects the greatest go ahead country in all creation.

(PPL, Jan. 15, 1850.)

Index

Cover design by Larry Van Dyke
Text design by Peter Browning
Text Typeface: Palatino 10/12
Printed on 60-lb. Booktext Natural, acid-free
Printing and binding by BookCrafters,
Chelsea, Michigan